DORLING KINDERSLEY
ULTIMATE
VISUAL
DICTIONARY

**EXTERNAL FEATURES
OF A BUTTERFLY**

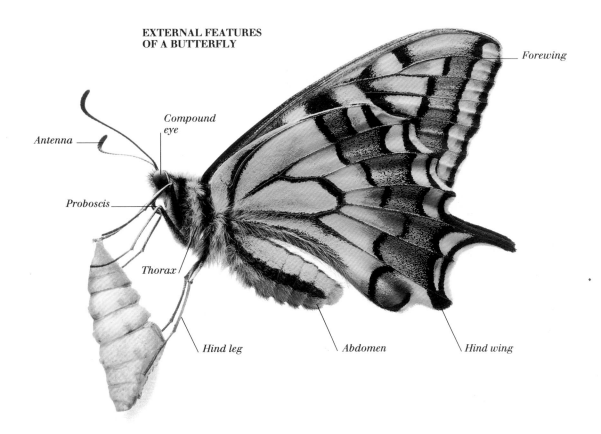

Forewing

*Compound
eye*

Antenna

Proboscis

Thorax

Hind leg

Abdomen

Hind wing

INTERNAL FEATURES OF BRACHIOSAURUS

First electron shell

Second electron shell

Nucleus

ANATOMY OF A FLUORINE–19 ATOM

Location of Solar System

Nucleus

OVERHEAD VIEW OF OUR GALAXY

Ovary

Bract

Pith

LONGITUDINAL SECTION THROUGH SUNFLOWER INFLORESCENCE

Cervical musculature

Lung

Fault plane

Dip of fault plane

Hade of fault plane

STRUCTURE OF A FAULT

Gizzard

Exhaust port

Floral design

VELOCETTE OHV ENGINE

MOSAIC DESIGN

Metacarpal

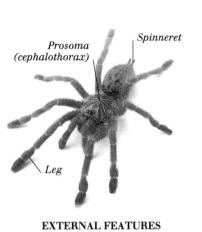

Prosoma (cephalothorax)

Spinneret

Leg

EXTERNAL FEATURES OF A SPIDER

Canopy

Fin

G-BNHB

Main landing gear

SIDE VIEW OF ARV SUPER 2 AIRPLANE

Frontalis

Brachialis

Deltoid

Rectus femoris

SUPERFICIAL SKELETAL MUSCLES

Barrel

Permanent black ink

FOUNTAIN PEN AND INK

Architrave

Podium

TEMPLE OF VESTA, TIVOLI, ITALY, c.80 bc

Sepal

Pedicel (flower stalk)

Swollen fleshy tissues of receptacle

LONGITUDINAL SECTION THROUGH A STRAWBERRY

CONTENTS

Low pressure gases

Central electrode

BALL CONTAINING HIGH TEMPERATURE GAS (PLASMA)

Nonbreakable plastic

Shock absorber

FOOTBALL HELMET

Introduction

THE ULTIMATE VISUAL DICTIONARY is a completely new kind of reference book. It provides a link between pictures and words in a way that no ordinary dictionary ever has. Most dictionaries simply tell you what a word means, but the *Ultimate Visual Dictionary* shows you —through a combination of detailed annotations, explicit photographs, and illustrations. In the *Ultimate Visual Dictionary*, pictures define the annotations around them. You do not read definitions of the annotated words, you see them. The highly accessible format of the *Ultimate Visual Dictionary*, the thoroughness of its annotations, and the range of its subject matter make it a unique and helpful reference tool.

How to use the Ultimate Visual Dictionary
You will find the *Ultimate Visual Dictionary* simple to use. It is divided by subject into 14 sections— The Universe, Prehistoric Earth, Plants, Animals, The Human Body, etc. Each section begins with a table of contents listing the major entries within that section. For example, The Visual Arts section contains entries on *Drawing, Tempera, Fresco, Oils, Watercolor, Pastels, Acrylics, Calligraphy, Printmaking, Mosaic,* and *Sculpture*. Every entry includes a short introduction explaining the purpose of the photographs and illustrations, and the significance of the annotations.

If you know what something looks like, but don't know its name, turn to the annotations surrounding the pictures; if you know a word, but don't know what it refers to, use the comprehensive index to direct you to the appropriate page.

Suppose you want to know what the bone at the end of your little finger is called. With a standard dictionary, you wouldn't know where to begin. But with the *Ultimate Visual Dictionary* you simply turn to the entry called *Hands*—within The Human Body section—and you will find four fully annotated color photographs showing the skin, muscles, and bones

of the human hand. In this entry you will quickly find that the bone you are searching for is called the distal phalanx. In addition, you will discover that it is attached to the middle phalanx by the distal interphalangeal joint.

Perhaps you want to know what a catalytic converter looks like. If you look up "catalytic converter" in an ordinary dictionary, you will be told what it is and possibly what it does—but you will not be able to tell what shape it is or what it is made of. However, if you look up "catalytic converter" in the index of the *Ultimate Visual Dictionary*, you will be directed to the *Modern engines* entry on page 344—where the introduction gives you basic information about what a catalytic converter is—and to page 350—where there is a spectacular exploded-view photograph of the mechanics of a Renault Clio. From these pages you will find out not only what a catalytic converter looks like, but also that it is attached at one end to an exhaust downpipe and at the other to a silencer.

Whatever it is that you want to find a name for, or whatever name you want to find a picture for, you will find it quickly and easily in the *Ultimate Visual Dictionary*. Perhaps you need to know where the vamp on a shoe is; or how to tell obovate and lanceolate leaves apart; or what a spiral galaxy looks like; or whether birds have nostrils. With the *Ultimate Visual Dictionary* close by, the answers to each of these questions, and thousands more, are readily available.

The *Ultimate Visual Dictionary* does not just tell you what the names of the different parts of an object are. The photographs, illustrations, and annotations are all specially arranged to help you understand which parts relate to one another and how objects function.

With the *Ultimate Visual Dictionary*, in seconds you can find the words or pictures that you are looking for; or you can simply browse. The *Ultimate Visual Dictionary* is not intended to replace a standard dictionary or encyclopedia, but is instead a stimulating and valuable companion to ordinary reference volumes. Giving you access to the language that is used by astronomers and architects, musicians and mechanics, pilots and professional athletes, it is the ideal reference book for experts and novices of all ages.

Sections of the ULTIMATE VISUAL DICTIONARY
The 14 sections of the *ULTIMATE VISUAL DICTIONARY* contain a total of more than 30,000 terms, encompassing a wide range of topics:

●In the first section, THE UNIVERSE, spectacular photographs and illustrations are used to show the names of the stars and planets and to explain the structure of solar systems, galaxies, nebulae, comets, and black holes.

●PREHISTORIC EARTH tells the story of how our own planet has evolved since its formation. It includes examples of prehistoric flora and fauna, and fascinating dinosaur models—some with parts of the body stripped away to show anatomical sections.

●PLANTS covers a huge range of species—from the familiar to the exotic. In addition to the color photographs of plants included in this section, there is a series of micrographic photographs illustrating plant details—such as pollen grains, spores, and cross-sections of stems and roots.

●In the ANIMALS section, skeletons, anatomical diagrams, and different parts of animals' bodies have been meticulously annotated. This section provides a comprehensive guide to the vocabulary of zoological classification and animal physiology.

●The structure of the human body, its parts, and its systems are presented in THE HUMAN BODY. The section includes lifelike, three-dimensional models and the latest false-color images. Clear and authoritative annotations indicate the correct anatomical terms.

●GEOLOGY, GEOGRAPHY, AND METEOROLOGY describes the structure of the Earth—from the inner core to the exosphere—and the physical phenomena, such as volcanoes, rivers, glaciers, and climate, that shape its surface.

●PHYSICS AND CHEMISTRY is a visual journey through the fundamental principles underlying the physical universe, that provides the essential vocabulary of these sciences.

●In RAIL AND ROAD, a wide range of trains, trolleys and buses, cars, bicycles, and motorcycles are described. Exploded-view photographs show mechanical details with striking clarity.

●SEA AND AIR illustrates hundreds of parts of ships and airplanes. The section includes civil and fighting craft, both historical and modern.

●THE VISUAL ARTS shows the equipment and materials used by painters, sculptors, printers, and other artists. Well-known compositions have been chosen to illustrate specific artistic techniques and effects.

●ARCHITECTURE includes photographs of exemplary architectural models and illustrates dozens of additional features such as columns, domes, and arches.

●MUSIC provides a visual introduction to the special language of music and musical instruments. It includes clearly annotated photographs of each of the major groups of traditional instruments—brass, woodwind, strings, and percussion—together with modern electronic instruments.

●The SPORTS section is a guide to the playing areas, formations, equipment, and techniques needed for many of today's most popular sports.

●In EVERYDAY THINGS, familiar objects, such as shoes, clocks, and toasters, are taken apart—down to the very last screw or length of thread—to show their inner workings and to give a special insight into the language that is used by their manufacturers.

THE UNIVERSE

Anatomy of the Universe

Fireball of rapidly expanding, extremely hot gas lasting about one million years

THE UNIVERSE CONTAINS EVERYTHING that exists, from the tiniest subatomic particles to galactic superclusters (the largest structures known). Nobody knows how big the Universe is, but astronomers estimate that it contains about 100 billion galaxies, each comprising an average of 100 billion stars. The most widely accepted theory about the origin of the Universe is the Big Bang theory, which states that the Universe came into being in a huge explosion—the Big Bang—that took place between 10 and 20 billion years ago. The Universe initially consisted of a very hot, dense fireball of expanding, cooling gas. After about one million years, the gas probably began to condense into localized clumps called protogalaxies. During the next five billion years, the protogalaxies continued condensing, forming galaxies in which stars were being born. Today, billions of years later, the Universe as a whole is still expanding, although there are localized areas in which objects are held together by gravity; for example, many galaxies are found in clusters. The Big Bang theory is supported by the discovery of faint, cool background radiation coming evenly from all directions. This radiation is believed to be the remnant of the radiation produced by the Big Bang. Small "ripples" in the temperature of the cosmic background radiation are thought to be evidence of slight fluctuations in the density of the early Universe, which resulted in the formation of galaxies. Astronomers do not yet know if the Universe is "closed," which means it will eventually stop expanding and begin to contract, or if it is "open," which means it will continue expanding forever.

COMPUTER-ENHANCED MICROWAVE MAP OF COSMIC BACKGROUND RADIATION

Pink indicates "warm ripples" in background radiation

Pale blue indicates "cool ripples" in background radiation

Deep blue indicates background radiation corresponding to -454.5°F (remnant of the Big Bang)

Red and pink band indicates radiation from our galaxy

Low-energy microwave radiation corresponding to about -454°F

High-energy gamma radiation corresponding to about 5,400°F

ORIGIN AND EXPANSION OF THE UNIVERSE

Quasar (probably the center of a galaxy containing a massive black hole)

Universe one to five billion years after Big Bang

Protogalaxy (condensing gas cloud)

Galaxy spinning and flattening to become spiral shaped

Dark cloud (dust and gas condensing to form a protogalaxy)

Elliptical galaxy in which stars form rapidly

Universe today (10–20 billion years after Big Bang)

Cluster of galaxies held together by gravity

Elliptical galaxy containing old stars and little gas and dust

Irregular galaxy

Spiral galaxy containing gas, dust, and young stars

OBJECTS IN THE UNIVERSE

CLUSTER OF GALAXIES IN VIRGO

COLOR-ENHANCED IMAGE OF 3C273 (QUASAR)

NGC 4406 (ELLIPTICAL GALAXY)

NGC 5236 (SPIRAL GALAXY)

NGC 6822 (IRREGULAR GALAXY)

THE ROSETTE NEBULA (EMISSION NEBULA)

THE JEWEL BOX (STAR CLUSTER)

THE SUN (MAIN SEQUENCE STAR)

EARTH

THE MOON

Galaxies

SOMBRERO,
A SPIRAL GALAXY

A GALAXY IS A HUGE MASS OF STARS, nebulae, and interstellar material. The smallest galaxies contain about 100,000 stars, while the largest contain up to 3,000 billion stars. There are three main types of galaxy, classified according to their shape: elliptical, which are oval shaped; spiral, which have arms spiraling outward from a central bulge; and irregular, which have no obvious shape. Sometimes, the shape of a galaxy is distorted by a collision with another galaxy. Quasars (quasi-stellar objects) are thought to be galactic nuclei but are so far away that their exact nature is still uncertain. They are compact, highly luminous objects in the outer reaches of the known Universe; while the farthest known "ordinary" galaxies are about 10 billion light-years away, the farthest known quasar is about 15 billion light-years away. Active galaxies, such as Seyfert galaxies and radio galaxies, emit intense radiation. In a Seyfert galaxy, this radiation comes from the galactic nucleus; in a radio galaxy, it also comes from huge lobes on either side of the galaxy. The radiation from active galaxies and quasars is thought to be caused by black holes (see pp. 28-29).

OPTICAL IMAGE OF NGC 4486 (ELLIPTICAL GALAXY)

Globular cluster containing very old red giants

Central region containing old red giants

Less densely populated region

Neighboring galaxy

OPTICAL IMAGE OF LARGE MAGELLANIC CLOUD (IRREGULAR GALAXY)

Tarantula Nebula

Dust cloud obscuring light from stars

Emission nebula

Light from stars

OPTICAL IMAGE OF NGC 2997 (SPIRAL GALAXY)

Glowing nebula in spiral arm

Spiral arm containing young stars

Galactic nucleus containing old stars

Dust in spiral arm reflecting blue light from hot young stars

Hot, ionized hydrogen gas emitting red light

Dust lane

OPTICAL IMAGE OF CENTAURUS A (RADIO GALAXY)

Dust lane crossing elliptical galaxy

Galactic nucleus containing powerful source of radiation

Light from old stars

COLOR-ENHANCED RADIO IMAGE OF CENTAURUS A

Red indicates high-intensity radio waves

Blue indicates low-intensity radio waves

Radiation from galactic nucleus

Outline of optical image of Centaurus A

Yellow indicates medium-intensity radio waves

Radio lobe

Radio lobe

COLOR-ENHANCED RADIO IMAGE OF 3C273 (QUASAR)

Radiation from jet of high-energy particles moving away from quasar

Blue indicates low-intensity radio waves

Quasar nucleus

White indicates high-intensity radio waves

OPTICAL IMAGE OF NGC 1566 (SEYFERT GALAXY)

Nebula in spiral arm

Compact nucleus emitting intense radiation

Spiral arm

COLOR-ENHANCED OPTICAL IMAGE OF NGC 5754 (TWO COLLIDING GALAXIES)

Blue indicates low-intensity radiation

Red indicates medium-intensity radiation

Spiral arm distorted by gravitational influence of smaller galaxy

Large spiral galaxy

Smaller galaxy colliding with larger galaxy

Yellow indicates high-intensity radiation

The Milky Way

**VIEW TOWARD
GALACTIC CENTER**

THE MILKY WAY IS THE NAME GIVEN TO THE FAINT BAND OF LIGHT that stretches across the night sky. This light comes from stars and nebulae in our galaxy, known as the Milky Way Galaxy or simply as "the Galaxy." The Galaxy is shaped like a spiral, with a dense central bulge that is encircled by four arms spiraling outward and surrounded by a less dense halo. We cannot see the spiral shape because our Solar System is in one of the spiral arms, the Orion Arm (also called the Local Arm). From our position, the center of the Galaxy is completely obscured by dust clouds; as a result, optical maps give only a limited view of the Galaxy. However, a more complete picture can be obtained by studying radio, infrared, and other radiation. The central bulge of the Galaxy is a relatively small, dense sphere that contains mainly older red and yellow stars. The halo is a less dense region in which the oldest stars are situated; some of these stars may be as old as the Galaxy itself (possibly 15 billion years). The spiral arms contain mainly hot, young, blue stars, as well as nebulae (clouds of dust and gas, inside which stars are born). The Galaxy is vast—about 100,000 light-years across (a light-year is about 5,879 billion miles); in comparison, the Solar System seems small, at about 12 light-hours across (about 8 billion miles). The entire Galaxy is rotating in space, although the inner stars travel faster than those further out. The Sun, which is about two-thirds out from the center, completes one lap of the Galaxy about every 220 million years.

**PANORAMIC OPTICAL MAP OF OUR
GALAXY AND NEARBY GALAXIES**

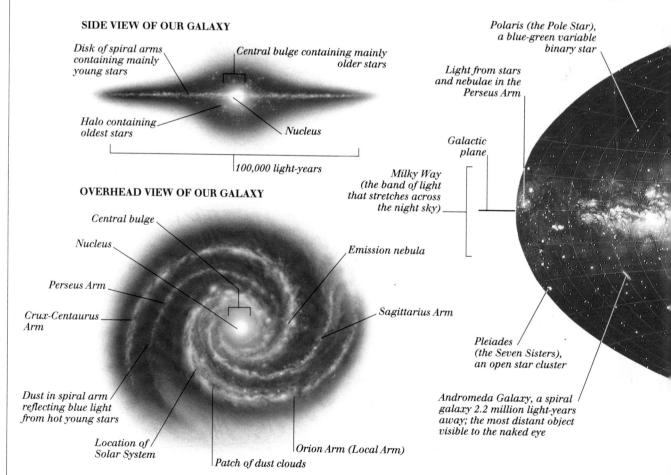

SIDE VIEW OF OUR GALAXY

Disk of spiral arms containing mainly young stars

Central bulge containing mainly older stars

Halo containing oldest stars

Nucleus

100,000 light-years

OVERHEAD VIEW OF OUR GALAXY

Central bulge

Nucleus

Perseus Arm

Crux-Centaurus Arm

Emission nebula

Sagittarius Arm

Dust in spiral arm reflecting blue light from hot young stars

Location of Solar System

Patch of dust clouds

Orion Arm (Local Arm)

Polaris (the Pole Star), a blue-green variable binary star

Light from stars and nebulae in the Perseus Arm

Galactic plane

Milky Way (the band of light that stretches across the night sky)

Pleiades (the Seven Sisters), an open star cluster

Andromeda Galaxy, a spiral galaxy 2.2 million light-years away; the most distant object visible to the naked eye

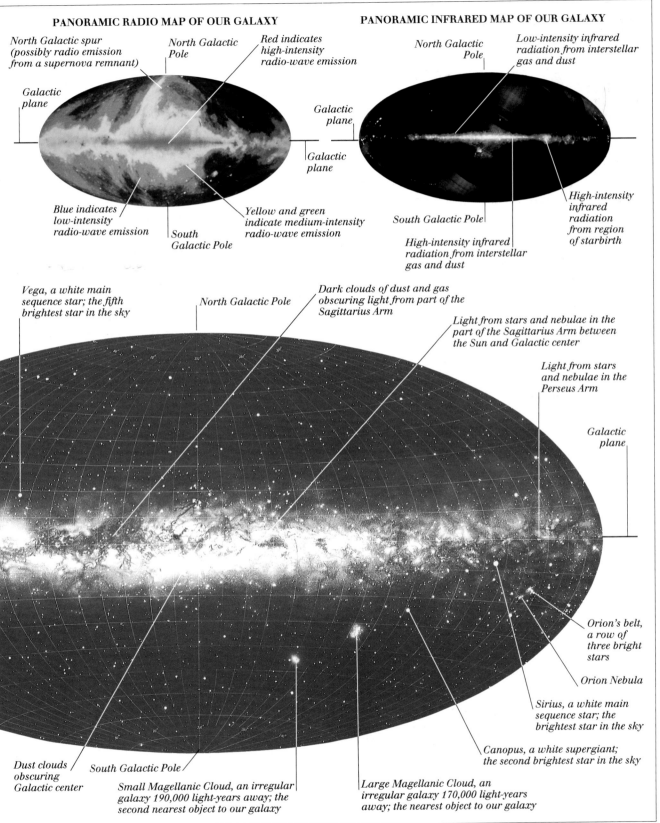

PANORAMIC RADIO MAP OF OUR GALAXY

North Galactic spur (possibly radio emission from a supernova remnant)

North Galactic Pole

Red indicates high-intensity radio-wave emission

Galactic plane

Blue indicates low-intensity radio-wave emission

South Galactic Pole

Yellow and green indicate medium-intensity radio-wave emission

PANORAMIC INFRARED MAP OF OUR GALAXY

North Galactic Pole

Low-intensity infrared radiation from interstellar gas and dust

Galactic plane

Galactic plane

South Galactic Pole

High-intensity infrared radiation from interstellar gas and dust

High-intensity infrared radiation from region of starbirth

Vega, a white main sequence star; the fifth brightest star in the sky

North Galactic Pole

Dark clouds of dust and gas obscuring light from part of the Sagittarius Arm

Light from stars and nebulae in the part of the Sagittarius Arm between the Sun and Galactic center

Light from stars and nebulae in the Perseus Arm

Galactic plane

Orion's belt, a row of three bright stars

Orion Nebula

Sirius, a white main sequence star; the brightest star in the sky

Canopus, a white supergiant; the second brightest star in the sky

Dust clouds obscuring Galactic center

South Galactic Pole

Small Magellanic Cloud, an irregular galaxy 190,000 light-years away; the second nearest object to our galaxy

Large Magellanic Cloud, an irregular galaxy 170,000 light-years away; the nearest object to our galaxy

Nebulae and star clusters

A NEBULA IS A CLOUD OF DUST AND GAS inside a galaxy. Nebulae become visible if the gas glows or if the cloud reflects starlight or obscures light from more distant objects. Emission nebulae shine because their gas emits light when it is stimulated by radiation from hot young stars. Reflection nebulae shine because their dust reflects light from stars in or around the nebula. Dark nebulae appear as silhouettes because they block light from shining nebulae or stars behind them. Two types of nebula are associated with dying stars: planetary nebulae and supernova remnants. Both consist of expanding shells of gas that were once the outer layers of a star. A planetary nebula is a gas shell drifting away from a dying stellar core. A supernova remnant is a gas shell moving away from a stellar core at great speed following a violent explosion called a supernova (see pp. 26-27). Stars are often found in groups known as clusters. Open clusters are loose groups of a few thousand young stars that were born in the same cloud and are drifting apart. Globular clusters are densely packed, roughly spherical groups of hundreds of thousands of older stars.

**HODGE 11, A
GLOBULAR CLUSTER**

TRIFID NEBULA (EMISSION NEBULA)

*Reflection
nebula*

*Emission
nebula*

Dust lane

*Starbirth region
(area in which
dust and gas
combine to
form stars)*

**PLEIADES (OPEN STAR CLUSTER)
WITH A REFLECTION NEBULA**

*Wisps of dust and
hydrogen gas
remaining from
cloud in which
stars formed*

*Young star in an
open cluster of
300–500 stars*

Reflection nebula

HORSEHEAD NEBULA (DARK NEBULA)

*Glowing filament
of hot, ionized
hydrogen gas*

*Alnitak (star in
Orion's belt)*

Dust lane

Emission nebula

*Star near southern
end of Orion's belt*

Emission nebula

Horsehead Nebula

Reflection nebula

*Dark nebula
obscuring light
from distant stars*

ORION NEBULA (DIFFUSE EMISSION NEBULA)

Glowing cloud of dust and hydrogen gas forming part of Orion Nebula

Dust cloud

Trapezium (group of four young stars)

Red light from hot, ionized hydrogen gas

Gas cloud emitting light because of ultraviolet radiation from the four young Trapezium stars

Green light from hot, ionized oxygen gas

Glowing filament of hot, ionized hydrogen gas

HELIX NEBULA (PLANETARY NEBULA)

Planetary nebula (gas shell expanding outward from dying stellar core)

Stellar core at a temperature of about 180,000°F

Red light from hot, ionized hydrogen gas

Blue-green light from hot, ionized oxygen and nitrogen gases

VELA SUPERNOVA REMNANT

Supernova remnant (gas shell consisting of outer layers of star thrown off in supernova explosion)

Hydrogen gas emitting red light due to being heated by supernova explosion

Glowing filament of hot, ionized hydrogen gas

Stars of northern skies

Wʜᴇɴ ʏᴏᴜ ʟᴏᴏᴋ ᴀᴛ ᴛʜᴇ ɴᴏʀᴛʜᴇʀɴ sᴋʏ, you look away from the densely populated Galactic center, so the northern sky generally appears less bright than the southern sky (see pp. 20-21). Among the best-known sights in the northern sky are the constellations Ursa Major (the Great Bear) and Orion. Some ancient civilizations believed that the stars were fixed to a celestial sphere surrounding the Earth, and modern maps of the sky are based on a similar idea. The North and South Poles of this imaginary celestial sphere are directly above the North and South Poles of the Earth, at the points where the Earth's axis of rotation intersects the sphere. The celestial North Pole is at the center of the map shown here, and Polaris (the Pole Star) lies very close to it. The celestial equator marks a projection of the Earth's equator on the sphere. The ecliptic marks the path of the Sun across the sky as the Earth orbits the Sun. The Moon and planets move against the background of the stars because the stars are much more distant; the nearest star outside the Solar System (Proxima Centauri) is more than 50,000 times farther away than the planet Jupiter.

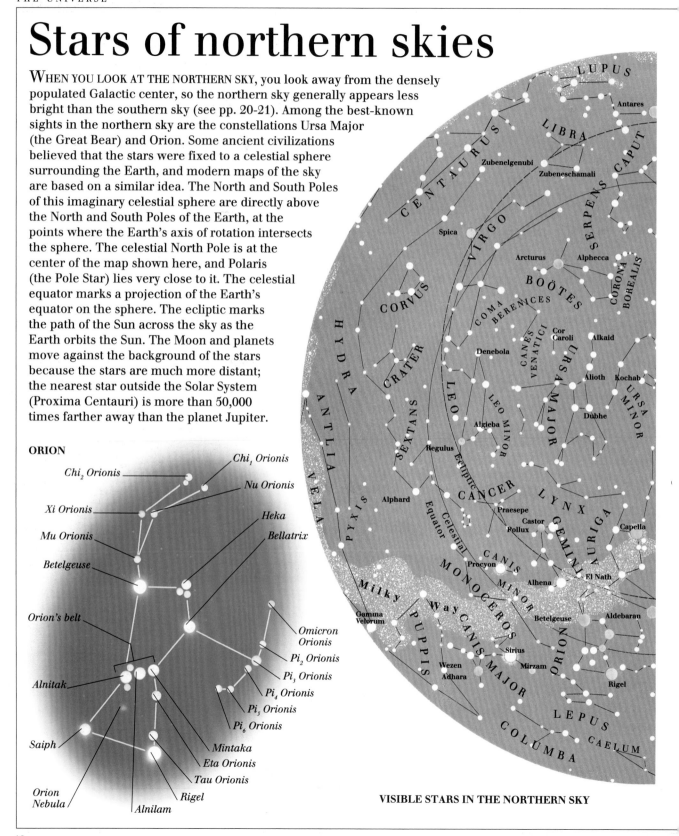

ORION

VISIBLE STARS IN THE NORTHERN SKY

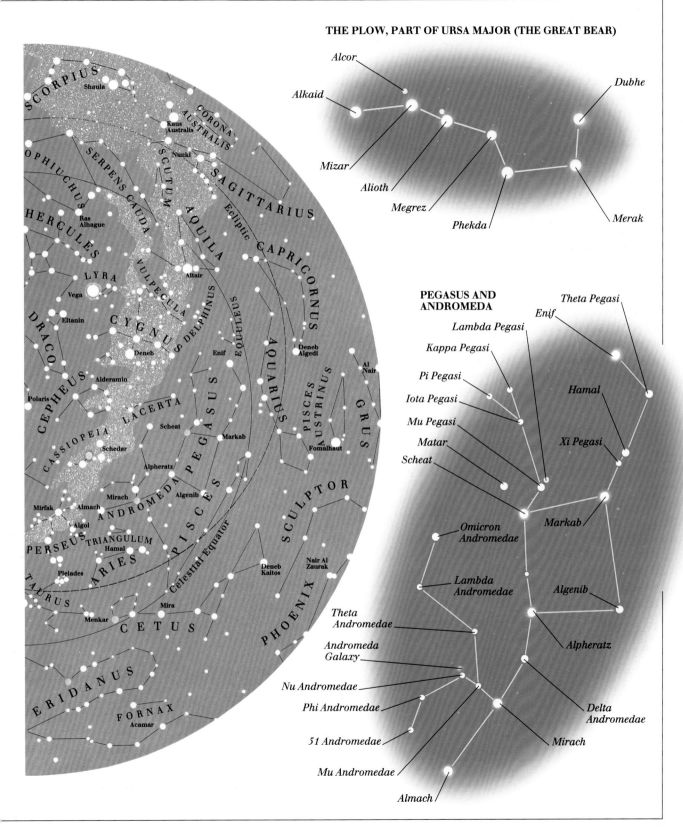

THE PLOW, PART OF URSA MAJOR (THE GREAT BEAR)

Alcor
Dubhe
Alkaid
Mizar
Alioth
Megrez
Phekda
Merak

PEGASUS AND ANDROMEDA

Theta Pegasi
Enif
Lambda Pegasi
Kappa Pegasi
Pi Pegasi
Hamal
Iota Pegasi
Mu Pegasi
Xi Pegasi
Matar
Scheat
Omicron Andromedae
Markab
Lambda Andromedae
Algenib
Theta Andromedae
Alpheratz
Andromeda Galaxy
Nu Andromedae
Delta Andromedae
Phi Andromedae
51 Andromedae
Mirach
Mu Andromedae
Almach

Star chart labels: SCORPIUS, Shaula, CORONA AUSTRALIS, Kaus Australis, OPHIUCHUS, SERPENS CAUDA, SCUTUM, Nunki, SAGITTARIUS, Ras Alhague, HERCULES, AQUILA, Ecliptic, CAPRICORNUS, Altair, LYRA, VULPECULA, Vega, Eltanin, CYGNUS, DELPHINUS, EQUULEUS, DRACO, Deneb, Enif, Deneb Algedi, AQUARIUS, Al Nair, CEPHEUS, Alderamin, LACERTA, PEGASUS, PISCES AUSTRINUS, GRUS, Polaris, Scheat, Markab, CASSIOPEIA, Schedar, Fomalhaut, Alpheratz, ANDROMEDA, Algenib, SCULPTOR, Mirach, PISCES, Mirfak, Almach, Algol, PERSEUS, TRIANGULUM, Hamal, Nair Al Zaurak, ARIES, Pleiades, Celestial Equator, Deneb Kaitos, TAURUS, Menkar, Mira, PHOENIX, CETUS, ERIDANUS, FORNAX, Acamar

Stars of southern skies

WHEN YOU LOOK AT THE SOUTHERN SKY, you look toward the Galactic center, which has a huge population of stars. As a result, the Milky Way appears brighter in the southern sky than in the northern sky (see pp. 18-19). The southern sky is rich in nebulae and star clusters. It contains the Large and Small Magellanic Clouds, which are the two nearest galaxies to our own. Stars make fixed patterns in the sky called constellations. The constellations, however, are only apparent groupings of stars, because the distances to the stars in a constellation may vary enormously. The shapes of constellations may change over many thousands of years because of the relative motions of stars. The apparent movement of entire constellations across the sky is due to the Earth's motion in space. The daily rotation of the Earth causes the constellations to move across the sky from east to west, and the orbit of the Earth around the Sun causes different areas of sky to be visible in different seasons. The visibility of areas of sky also depends on the location of the observer. For instance, stars near the celestial equator may be seen from either hemisphere at some time during the year, while stars close to the celestial poles (the celestial South Pole is at the center of the map shown here) can never be seen from the opposite hemisphere.

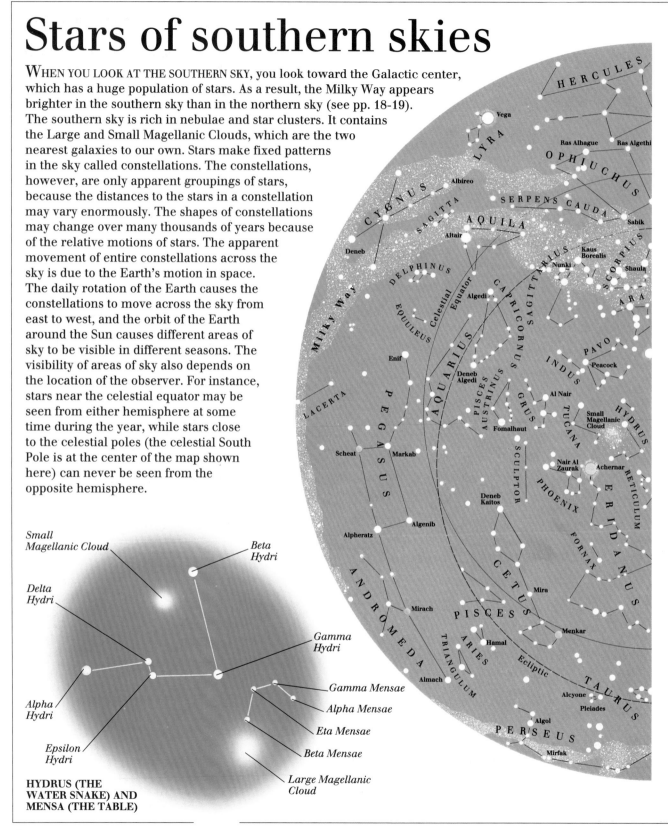

HYDRUS (THE WATER SNAKE) AND MENSA (THE TABLE)

Small Magellanic Cloud

Beta Hydri

Delta Hydri

Gamma Hydri

Gamma Mensae

Alpha Mensae

Alpha Hydri

Eta Mensae

Epsilon Hydri

Beta Mensae

Large Magellanic Cloud

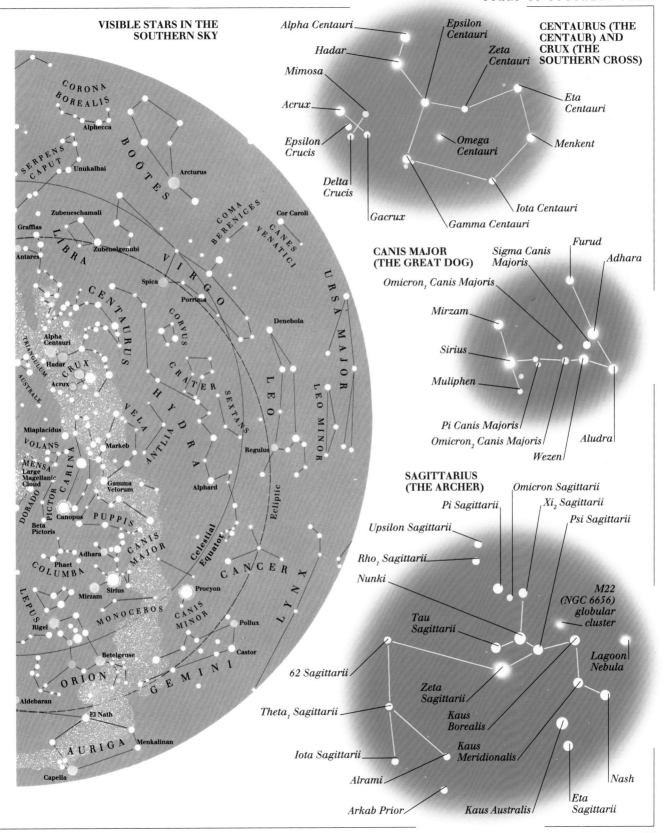

VISIBLE STARS IN THE SOUTHERN SKY

CENTAURUS (THE CENTAUR) AND CRUX (THE SOUTHERN CROSS)

Alpha Centauri
Epsilon Centauri
Hadar
Zeta Centauri
Mimosa
Eta Centauri
Acrux
Epsilon Crucis
Omega Centauri
Menkent
Delta Crucis
Gacrux
Gamma Centauri
Iota Centauri

CANIS MAJOR (THE GREAT DOG)

Sigma Canis Majoris
Furud
Adhara
Omicron₁ Canis Majoris
Mirzam
Sirius
Muliphen
Pi Canis Majoris
Omicron₂ Canis Majoris
Wezen
Aludra

SAGITTARIUS (THE ARCHER)

Omicron Sagittarii
Pi Sagittarii
Xi₂ Sagittarii
Psi Sagittarii
Upsilon Sagittarii
Rho₁ Sagittarii
Nunki
M22 (NGC 6656) globular cluster
Tau Sagittarii
Lagoon Nebula
62 Sagittarii
Zeta Sagittarii
Theta₁ Sagittarii
Kaus Borealis
Iota Sagittarii
Kaus Meridionalis
Alrami
Arkab Prior
Kaus Australis
Eta Sagittarii
Nash

Within the map of Visible Stars in the Southern Sky:
CORONA BOREALIS
Alphecca
SERPENS CAPUT
Unukalhai
BOÖTES
Arcturus
COMA BERENICES
CANES VENATICI
Cor Caroli
URSA MAJOR
Zubeneschamali
Graffias
LIBRA
Zubenelgenubi
VIRGO
Antares
Spica
Porrima
Denebola
CENTAURUS
Alpha Centauri
CORVUS
CRATER
LEO
Hadar
CRUX
HYDRA
SEXTANS
Acrux
TRIANGULUM AUSTRALE
VELA
ANTLIA
LEO MINOR
Miaplacidus
Markeb
VOLANS
CARINA
Regulus
MENSA
Large Magellanic Cloud
Gamma Velorum
Alphard
DORADO
PICTOR
PUPPIS
Ecliptic
Canopus
Beta Pictoris
Celestial Equator
Adhara
CANIS MAJOR
CANCER
LYNX
COLUMBA
Phaet
Mirzam
Sirius
Procyon
LEPUS
MONOCEROS
CANIS MINOR
Rigel
Pollux
Betelgeuse
Castor
ORION
GEMINI
Aldebaran
El Nath
Menkalinan
AURIGA
Capella

21

Stars

**OPEN STAR CLUSTER
AND DUST CLOUD**

STARS ARE BODIES of hot glowing gas that are born in nebulae (see pp. 24-27). They vary enormously in size, mass, and temperature: diameters range from about 450 times smaller to over 1,000 times bigger than that of the Sun; masses range from about a twentieth to over 50 solar masses; and surface temperatures range from about 5,500°F to over 90,000°F. The color of a star is determined by its temperature: the hottest stars are blue and the coolest are red. The Sun, with a surface temperature of 10,000°F, is between these extremes and appears yellow. The energy emitted by a shining star is produced by nuclear fusion in the star's core. The brightness of a star is measured in magnitudes—the brighter the star, the lower its magnitude. There are two types of magnitude: apparent magnitude, which is the brightness seen from Earth, and absolute magnitude, which is the brightness that would be seen from a standard distance of 10 parsecs (32.6 light-years). The light emitted by a star may be split to form a spectrum containing a series of dark lines (absorption lines). The patterns of lines indicate the presence of particular chemical elements, enabling astronomers to deduce the composition of the star's atmosphere. The magnitude and spectral type (color) of stars may be plotted on a graph called a Hertzsprung-Russell diagram, which shows that stars tend to fall into several well-defined groups. The principal groups are main sequence stars (those which are fusing hydrogen to form helium), giants, supergiants, and white dwarfs.

STAR SIZES

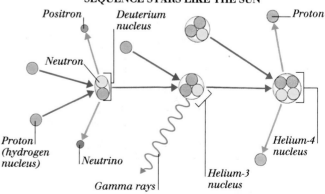

Red giant (diameters between about 10 million and 100 million miles)

The Sun (main sequence star with diameter about 870,000 miles)

White dwarf (diameters between about 2,000 and 30,000 miles)

ENERGY EMISSION FROM THE SUN

Nuclear fusion in core produces gamma rays and neutrinos

Neutrinos travel to Earth directly from Sun's core in about 8 minutes

Lower-energy radiation travels to Earth in about 8 minutes

Earth

Sun

High-energy radiation (gamma rays) loses energy while traveling to surface over 2 million years

Lower-energy radiation (mainly ultraviolet, infrared, and light rays) leaves surface

STAR MAGNITUDES

APPARENT MAGNITUDE

ABSOLUTE MAGNITUDE

Brighter stars

-9

0

+9

Fainter stars

Sirius: apparent magnitude of -1.46

Rigel: apparent magnitude of +0.12

Objects of magnitude higher than about +5.5 cannot be seen by the naked eye

Rigel: absolute magnitude of -7.1

Sirius: absolute magnitude of +1.4

NUCLEAR FUSION IN MAIN SEQUENCE STARS LIKE THE SUN

Positron

Deuterium nucleus

Proton

Neutron

Proton (hydrogen nucleus)

Neutrino

Gamma rays

Helium-3 nucleus

Helium-4 nucleus

HERTZSPRUNG-RUSSELL DIAGRAM

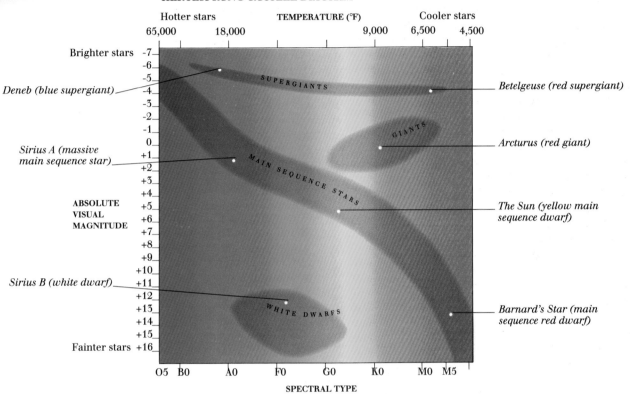

Hotter stars   **TEMPERATURE (°F)**   Cooler stars

65,000   18,000   9,000   6,500   4,500

Brighter stars -7
-6
-5
-4
Deneb (blue supergiant)
-3
-2
-1
0

Sirius A (massive
main sequence star)   +1
+2
+3
+4

**ABSOLUTE
VISUAL
MAGNITUDE**   +5
+6
+7
+8
+9
+10
+11
Sirius B (white dwarf)   +12
+13
+14
+15
Fainter stars +16

SUPERGIANTS

GIANTS   Betelgeuse (red supergiant)

Arcturus (red giant)

MAIN SEQUENCE STARS

The Sun (yellow main
sequence dwarf)

WHITE DWARFS   Barnard's Star (main
sequence red dwarf)

O5   B0   A0   F0   G0   K0   M0 M5

SPECTRAL TYPE

STELLAR SPECTRAL ABSORPTION LINES

Calcium line   Hydrogen
gamma line   Hydrogen
beta line   Helium line   Sodium
lines   Hydrogen
alpha line

**STAR OF SPECTRAL
TYPE A (e.g., SIRIUS)**

**STAR OF SPECTRAL
TYPE G (e.g., THE SUN)**

Hydrogen
beta line   Magnesium
lines   Sodium
lines   Hydrogen
alpha line

Small stars

**REGION OF
STAR FORMATION
IN ORION**

SMALL STARS HAVE A MASS of up to about one and a half times that of the Sun. They begin to form when a region of higher density in a nebula condenses into a huge globule of gas and dust that contracts under its own gravity. Within a globule, regions of condensing matter heat up and begin to glow, forming protostars. If a protostar contains enough matter, the central temperature reaches about 27 million °F. At this temperature, nuclear reactions in which hydrogen fuses to form helium can start. This process releases energy, which prevents the star from contracting further, and also causes it to shine; it is now a main sequence star. A star of about one solar mass remains in the main sequence for about 10 billion years, until the hydrogen in the star's core has been converted into helium. The helium core then contracts again, and nuclear reactions continue in a shell around the core. The core becomes hot enough for helium to fuse to form carbon, while the outer layers of the star expand, cool, and shine less brightly. The expanding star is known as a red giant. When the helium in the core runs out, the outer layers of the star may drift off as an expanding gas shell called a planetary nebula. The remaining core (about 80 percent of the original star) is now in its final stages. It becomes a white dwarf star that gradually cools and dims. When it finally stops shining altogether, the dead star will become a black dwarf.

STRUCTURE OF A MAIN SEQUENCE STAR

Core containing hydrogen fusing to form helium

Radiative zone

Convective zone

Surface temperature about 10,000°F

Core temperature about 27 million °F

STRUCTURE OF A NEBULA

Young main sequence star

Dense region of dust and gas (mainly hydrogen) condensing under gravity to form globules

Hot, ionized hydrogen gas emitting red light due to stimulation by radiation from hot young stars

Dark globule of dust and gas (mainly hydrogen) contracting to form protostars

LIFE OF A SMALL STAR OF ABOUT ONE SOLAR MASS

Cool cloud of gas (mainly hydrogen) and dust

Dense globule condensing to form protostars

NEBULA

Glowing ball of gas (mainly hydrogen)

Natal cocoon (shell of dust blown away by radiation from protostar)

PROTOSTAR
Duration: 50 million years

About 870,000 miles

Star producing energy by nuclear fusion in core

MAIN SEQUENCE STAR
Duration: 10 billion years

STRUCTURE OF A RED GIANT

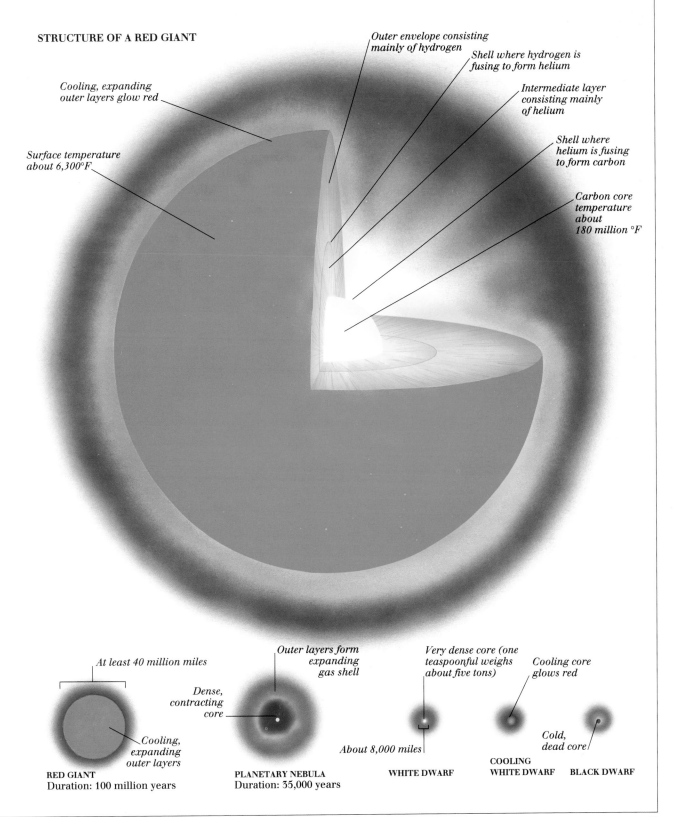

Cooling, expanding outer layers glow red

Surface temperature about 6,300°F

Outer envelope consisting mainly of hydrogen

Shell where hydrogen is fusing to form helium

Intermediate layer consisting mainly of helium

Shell where helium is fusing to form carbon

Carbon core temperature about 180 million °F

At least 40 million miles

Cooling, expanding outer layers

RED GIANT
Duration: 100 million years

Outer layers form expanding gas shell

Dense, contracting core

PLANETARY NEBULA
Duration: 35,000 years

Very dense core (one teaspoonful weighs about five tons)

About 8,000 miles

WHITE DWARF

Cooling core glows red

Cold, dead core

COOLING WHITE DWARF

BLACK DWARF

Massive stars

MASSIVE STARS HAVE A MASS AT LEAST THREE TIMES that of the Sun, and some stars are as massive as about 50 Suns. A massive star evolves in a similar way to a small star until it reaches the main sequence stage (see pp. 24-25). During the main sequence, a star shines steadily until the hydrogen in its core has fused to form helium. This process takes billions of years in a small star, but only millions of years in a massive star. A massive star then becomes a red supergiant, which initially consists of a helium core surrounded by outer layers of cooling, expanding gas. Over the next few million years, a series of nuclear reactions form different elements in shells around an iron core. The core eventually collapses in less than a second, causing a massive explosion called a supernova, in which a shock wave blows away the outer layers of the star. Supernovae shine brighter than an entire galaxy for a short time. Sometimes, the core survives the supernova explosion. If the surviving core is between about one and a half and three solar masses, it contracts to become a tiny, dense neutron star. If the core is considerably greater than three solar masses, it contracts to become a black hole (see pp. 28-29).

SUPERNOVA

TARANTULA NEBULA BEFORE SUPERNOVA

STRUCTURE OF A RED SUPERGIANT

Outer envelope consisting mainly of hydrogen

Layer consisting mainly of helium

Layer consisting mainly of carbon

Layer consisting mainly of oxygen

Layer consisting mainly of silicon

Shell of hydrogen fusing to form helium

Shell of helium fusing to form carbon

Shell of carbon fusing to form oxygen

Shell of oxygen fusing to form silicon

Shell of silicon fusing to form iron core

Surface temperature about 5,500°F

Cooling, expanding outer layers glow red

Core of mainly iron at a temperature of 5.4–9 billion °F

LIFE OF A MASSIVE STAR OF ABOUT 10 SOLAR MASSES

Dense globule condensing to form protostars

Cool cloud of gas (mainly hydrogen) and dust

NEBULA

Glowing ball of gas (mainly hydrogen)

Natal cocoon (shell of dust blown away by radiation from protostar)

PROTOSTAR
Duration: a few hundred thousand years

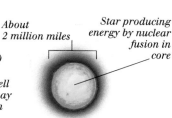

About 2 million miles

Star producing energy by nuclear fusion in core

MAIN SEQUENCE STAR
Duration: 10 million years

FEATURES OF A SUPERNOVA

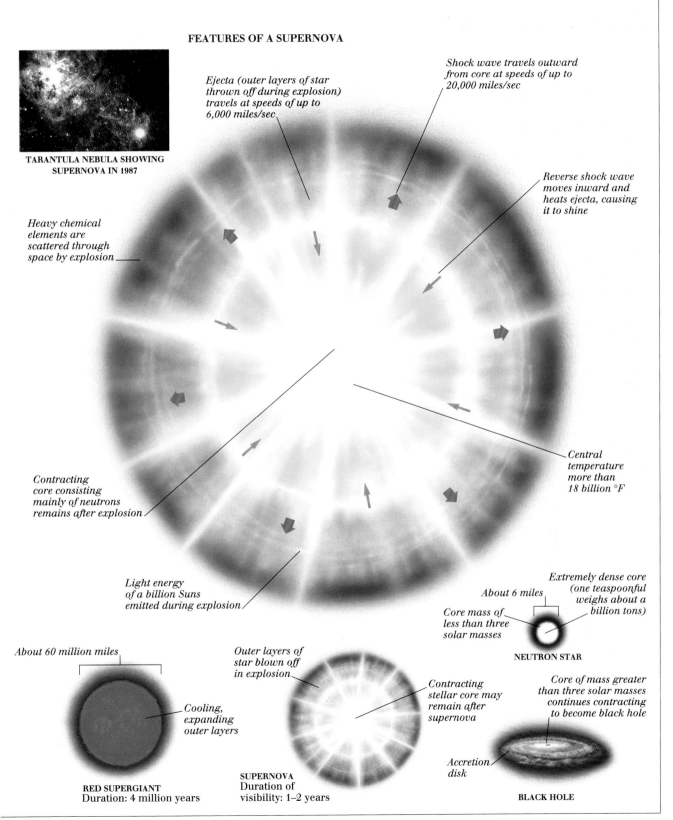

TARANTULA NEBULA SHOWING
SUPERNOVA IN 1987

*Ejecta (outer layers of star
thrown off during explosion)
travels at speeds of up to
6,000 miles/sec*

*Shock wave travels outward
from core at speeds of up to
20,000 miles/sec*

*Reverse shock wave
moves inward and
heats ejecta, causing
it to shine*

*Heavy chemical
elements are
scattered through
space by explosion*

*Contracting
core consisting
mainly of neutrons
remains after explosion*

*Central
temperature
more than
18 billion °F*

*Light energy
of a billion Suns
emitted during explosion*

*Extremely dense core
(one teaspoonful
weighs about a
billion tons)*

About 6 miles

*Core mass of
less than three
solar masses*

NEUTRON STAR

About 60 million miles

*Cooling,
expanding
outer layers*

RED SUPERGIANT
Duration: 4 million years

*Outer layers of
star blown off
in explosion*

*Contracting
stellar core may
remain after
supernova*

SUPERNOVA
Duration of
visibility: 1–2 years

*Core of mass greater
than three solar masses
continues contracting
to become black hole*

*Accretion
disk*

BLACK HOLE

27

Neutron stars and black holes

NEUTRON STARS AND BLACK HOLES form from the stellar cores that remain after stars have exploded as supernovae (see pp. 26-27). If the remaining core is between about one and a half and three solar masses, it contracts to form a neutron star. If the remaining core is considerably greater than about three solar masses, it contracts to form a black hole. Neutron stars are typically only about six miles in diameter and consist almost entirely of subatomic particles called neutrons. These stars are so dense that a teaspoonful would weigh about a billion tons. Neutron stars are observed as pulsars, so-called because they rotate rapidly and emit two beams of radio waves, which sweep across the sky and are detected as short pulses. Black holes are characterized by their extremely strong gravity, which is so powerful that not even light can escape; as a result, black holes are invisible. However, they may be detected if they have a close companion star. The gravity of the black hole pulls gas from the other star, forming an accretion disk that spirals around the black hole at high speed, heating up and emitting radiation. Eventually, the matter spirals in to cross the event horizon (the boundary of the black hole), finally disappearing from the visible Universe.

X-ray emission from pulsar (neutron star rotating 30 times each second)

X-ray emission from center of nebula

X-RAY IMAGE OF THE CRAB NEBULA (SUPERNOVA REMNANT)

PULSAR (ROTATING NEUTRON STAR)

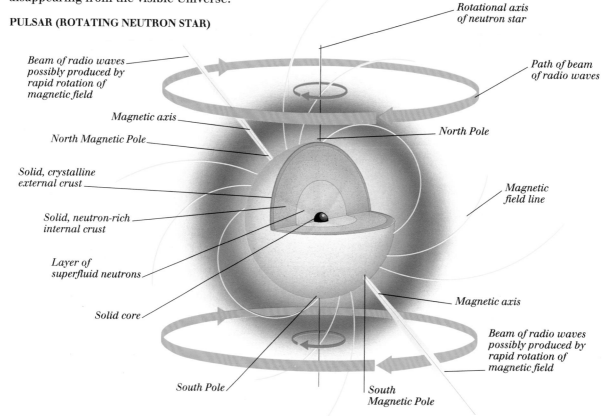

Rotational axis of neutron star

Beam of radio waves possibly produced by rapid rotation of magnetic field

Path of beam of radio waves

Magnetic axis

North Magnetic Pole

North Pole

Solid, crystalline external crust

Magnetic field line

Solid, neutron-rich internal crust

Layer of superfluid neutrons

Magnetic axis

Solid core

Beam of radio waves possibly produced by rapid rotation of magnetic field

South Pole

South Magnetic Pole

STELLAR BLACK HOLE

Blue supergiant star

Gas current (outer layers of nearby blue supergiant pulled toward black hole by gravity)

Singularity (theoretical region of infinite density, pressure, and temperature)

Hot spot (region of intense friction where gas current joins accretion disk)

Gas in outer part of accretion disk emitting low-energy radiation

Event horizon (boundary of black hole)

Hot gas in inner part of accretion disk emitting high-energy X-rays

Accretion disk (matter spiraling around black hole)

Black hole

Gas at temperatures of millions °F spiraling at close to the speed of light

FORMATION OF A BLACK HOLE

Stellar core remains after supernova explosion

Light rays increasingly bent by gravity as core collapses

Core shrinks beyond its event horizon to become a black hole

Light rays cannot escape because gravity is so strong

Core greater than three solar masses collapses under its own gravity

Density, pressure, and temperature of core increase as core collapses

Event horizon

Singularity (theoretical region of infinite density, pressure, and temperature)

Outer layers of massive star thrown off in explosion

SUPERNOVA

COLLAPSING STELLAR CORE

BLACK HOLE

The Solar System

THE SUN

THE SOLAR SYSTEM consists of a central star (the Sun) and the bodies that orbit it. These bodies include nine planets and their 61 known moons, asteroids, comets, and meteoroids. The Solar System also contains interplanetary gas and dust. Most of the planets fall into two groups: four small rocky planets near the Sun (Mercury, Venus, Earth, and Mars), and four planets farther out, the gas giants (Jupiter, Saturn, Uranus, and Neptune). Pluto belongs to neither group—it is very small, solid, and icy. Pluto is the outermost planet, except when it passes briefly inside Neptune's orbit. Between the rocky planets and gas giants is the asteroid belt, which contains thousands of chunks of rock orbiting the Sun. Most of the bodies in the Solar System move around the Sun in elliptical orbits located in a thin disk around the Sun's equator. All the planets orbit the Sun in the same direction (counterclockwise when viewed from above) and all but Venus, Uranus, and Pluto also spin around their axes in this direction. Moons also spin as they, in turn, orbit their planets. The entire Solar System orbits the center of our galaxy, the Milky Way (see pp. 14-15).

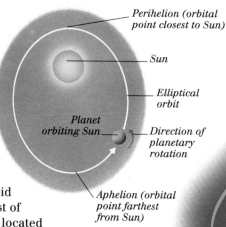

Perihelion (orbital point closest to Sun)

Sun

Elliptical orbit

Planet orbiting Sun

Direction of planetary rotation

Aphelion (orbital point farthest from Sun)

Aphelion of Neptune: 2,819 million miles

ORBITS OF INNER PLANETS

Mercury

Perihelion of Mercury: 28.5 million miles

Perihelion of Venus: 66.7 million miles

Perihelion of Earth: 91.4 million miles

Average orbital speed of Venus: 21.8 miles/sec

Average orbital speed of Mercury: 29.8 miles/sec

Average orbital speed of Earth: 18.5 miles/sec

Average orbital speed of Mars: 15 miles/sec

Mars

Perihelion of Mars: 128.4 million miles

Earth

Venus

Sun

Aphelion of Mercury: 43.3 million miles

Asteroid belt

Aphelion of Venus: 67.7 million miles

Aphelion of Earth: 94.5 million miles

Aphelion of Mars: 154.8 million miles

Aphelion of Pluto: 4,583 million miles

MERCURY
Year: 87.97 Earth days
Mass: 0.055 Earth masses
Diameter: 3,031 miles

VENUS
Year: 224.7 Earth days
Mass: 0.81 Earth masses
Diameter: 7,521 miles

EARTH
Year: 365.26 days
Mass: 1 Earth mass
Diameter: 7,926 miles

MARS
Year: 1.88 Earth years
Mass: 0.11 Earth masses
Diameter: 4,217 miles

JUPITER
Year: 11.86 Earth years
Mass: 318 Earth masses
Diameter: 88,850 miles

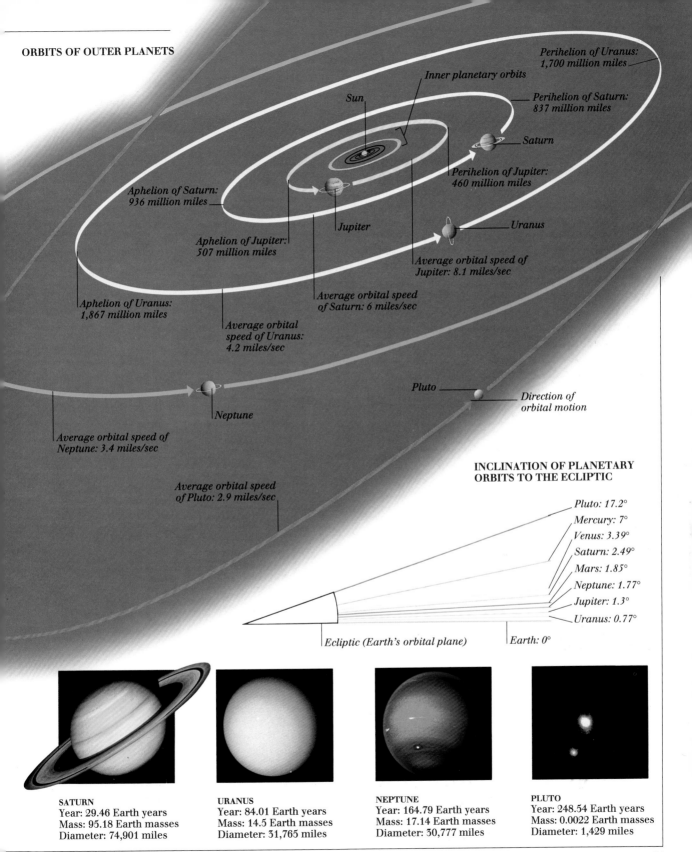

ORBITS OF OUTER PLANETS

Perihelion of Uranus:
1,700 million miles

Inner planetary orbits

Perihelion of Saturn:
837 million miles

Sun

Saturn

Perihelion of Jupiter:
460 million miles

Aphelion of Saturn:
936 million miles

Jupiter

Uranus

Aphelion of Jupiter:
507 million miles

Average orbital speed of
Jupiter: 8.1 miles/sec

Average orbital speed
of Saturn: 6 miles/sec

Aphelion of Uranus:
1,867 million miles

Average orbital
speed of Uranus:
4.2 miles/sec

Pluto

Direction of
orbital motion

Neptune

Average orbital speed of
Neptune: 3.4 miles/sec

Average orbital speed
of Pluto: 2.9 miles/sec

INCLINATION OF PLANETARY ORBITS TO THE ECLIPTIC

Pluto: 17.2°
Mercury: 7°
Venus: 3.39°
Saturn: 2.49°
Mars: 1.85°
Neptune: 1.77°
Jupiter: 1.3°
Uranus: 0.77°

Ecliptic (Earth's orbital plane)   *Earth: 0°*

SATURN
Year: 29.46 Earth years
Mass: 95.18 Earth masses
Diameter: 74,901 miles

URANUS
Year: 84.01 Earth years
Mass: 14.5 Earth masses
Diameter: 31,765 miles

NEPTUNE
Year: 164.79 Earth years
Mass: 17.14 Earth masses
Diameter: 30,777 miles

PLUTO
Year: 248.54 Earth years
Mass: 0.0022 Earth masses
Diameter: 1,429 miles

The Sun

SOLAR PHOTOSPHERE

THE SUN IS THE STAR AT THE CENTER of our Solar System. It is about five billion years old and will probably continue to shine as it does now for about another five billion years. The Sun is a yellow main sequence star (see pp. 22-23) about 870,000 miles in diameter. It consists almost entirely of hydrogen and helium. In the Sun's core, hydrogen is converted to helium by nuclear fusion, releasing energy in the process. The energy travels from the core through the radiative and convective zones to the photosphere (visible surface), where it leaves the Sun in the form of heat and light. On the photosphere there are often dark, relatively cool areas called sunspots. These usually appear in pairs or groups and are thought to be caused by magnetic fields. Other types of solar activity are flares, which are usually associated with sunspots, and prominences. Flares are sudden discharges of high-energy radiation and atomic particles. Prominences are huge loops or filaments of gas extending into the solar atmosphere; some last for hours, others for months. Beyond the photosphere is the chromosphere (inner atmosphere) and the extremely rarified corona (outer atmosphere), which extends millions of miles into space. Tiny particles that escape from the corona give rise to the solar wind, which streams through space at hundreds of miles per second. The chromosphere and corona can be seen from Earth when the Sun is totally eclipsed by the Moon.

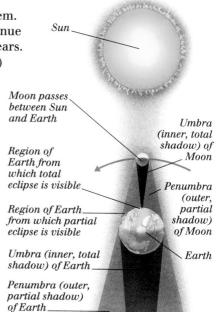

Sun

Moon passes between Sun and Earth

Umbra (inner, total shadow) of Moon

Region of Earth from which total eclipse is visible

Penumbra (outer, partial shadow) of Moon

Region of Earth from which partial eclipse is visible

Umbra (inner, total shadow) of Earth

Earth

Penumbra (outer, partial shadow) of Earth

SURFACE FEATURES

Gas loop (looped prominence)

Prominence (jet of gas at edge of Sun's disk up to hundreds of thousands of miles high)

Spicule (vertical jet of gas)

Photosphere (visible surface)

Chromosphere (inner atmosphere)

TOTAL SOLAR ECLIPSE

Corona (outer atmosphere of extremely hot diffuse gas)

Moon covers Sun's disk

SUNSPOTS

Granulated surface of Sun

Penumbra (lighter, outer region) containing radial fibrils

Umbra (darker, inner region) temperature about 7,200°F

Photosphere temperature about 9,900°F

**EXTERNAL FEATURES AND
INTERNAL STRUCTURE OF THE SUN**

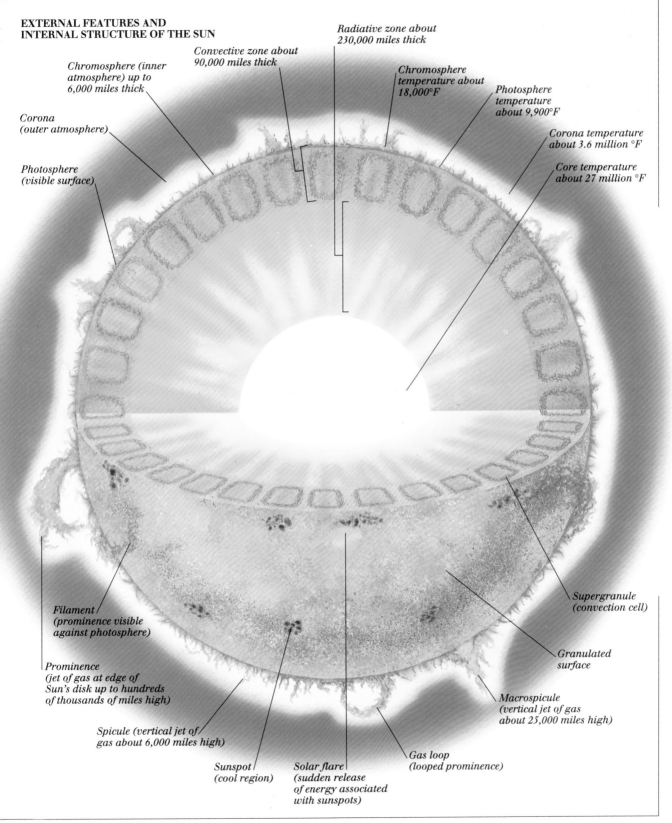

*Chromosphere (inner
atmosphere) up to
6,000 miles thick*

*Convective zone about
90,000 miles thick*

*Radiative zone about
230,000 miles thick*

*Chromosphere
temperature about
18,000°F*

*Photosphere
temperature
about 9,900°F*

*Corona
(outer atmosphere)*

*Corona temperature
about 3.6 million °F*

*Core temperature
about 27 million °F*

*Photosphere
(visible surface)*

*Supergranule
(convection cell)*

*Filament
(prominence visible
against photosphere)*

*Granulated
surface*

*Prominence
(jet of gas at edge of
Sun's disk up to hundreds
of thousands of miles high)*

*Macrospicule
(vertical jet of gas
about 25,000 miles high)*

*Spicule (vertical jet of
gas about 6,000 miles high)*

*Sunspot
(cool region)*

*Solar flare
(sudden release
of energy associated
with sunspots)*

*Gas loop
(looped prominence)*

Mercury

MERCURY

MERCURY IS THE NEAREST PLANET to the Sun, orbiting at an average distance of about 36 million miles. Because Mercury is the closest planet to the Sun, it moves faster than any other planet, traveling at an average speed of nearly 30 miles per second and completing an orbit in just under 88 days. Mercury is very small (only Pluto is smaller) and rocky. Most of the surface has been heavily cratered by the impact of meteorites, although there are also smooth, sparsely cratered plains. The Caloris Basin is the largest crater, measuring about 800 miles across. It is thought to have been formed when a rock the size of an asteroid hit the planet and is surrounded by concentric rings of mountains thrown up by the impact. The surface also has many ridges, called rupes, that are thought to have been formed when the hot core of the young planet cooled and shrank about four billion years ago, buckling the planet's surface in the process. The planet rotates about its axis very slowly, taking nearly 59 Earth days to complete one rotation. As a result, a solar day (sunrise to sunrise) on Mercury is about 176 Earth days—twice as long as the 88-day Mercurian year. Mercury has extreme surface temperatures, ranging from a maximum of 800°F on the sunlit side to -270°F on the dark side. At nightfall, the temperature drops very quickly because the planet's atmosphere is almost nonexistent. It consists only of minute amounts of helium and hydrogen captured from the solar wind, plus traces of other gases.

TILT AND ROTATION OF MERCURY

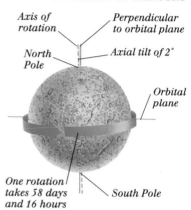

Axis of rotation
Perpendicular to orbital plane
North Pole
Axial tilt of 2°
Orbital plane
One rotation takes 58 days and 16 hours
South Pole

DEGAS AND BRONTË (RAY CRATERS)

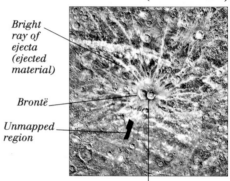

Bright ray of ejecta (ejected material)
Brontë
Unmapped region
Degas with central peak

FORMATION OF A RAY CRATER

Debris thrown out by impact
Path of meteorite colliding with planet
Wall of rock thrown up around crater
Impact forms saucer-shaped crater
Fractured rock

METEORITE IMPACT

Path of rocky ejecta (ejected material)
Ejecta forms secondary craters
Loose debris on crater floor

SECONDARY CRATERING

Wall of rock forms ring of mountains
Ray of ejecta (ejected material)
Small secondary crater
Loose ejected rock
Central mountain rings form if floor of large crater recoils from meteorite impact
Falling debris forms ridges on side of wall

RAY CRATER

Venus

RADAR IMAGE OF VENUS

VENUS IS A ROCKY PLANET and the second planet from the Sun. Venus spins slowly backward as it orbits the Sun, causing its rotational period to be the longest in the Solar System, at about 243 Earth days. It is slightly smaller than Earth and probably has a similar internal structure, consisting of a semisolid metal core surrounded by a rocky mantle and crust. Venus is the brightest object in the sky after the Sun and Moon because its atmosphere reflects sunlight strongly. The main component of the atmosphere is carbon dioxide, which traps heat in a greenhouse effect far stronger than that on Earth. As a result, Venus is the hottest planet, with a maximum surface temperature of about 900°F. The thick cloud layers contain droplets of sulfuric acid and are driven around the planet by winds at speeds of up to 220 miles per hour. Although the planet takes 243 Earth days to rotate once, the high-speed winds cause the clouds to circle the planet in only four Earth days. The high temperature, acidic clouds, and enormous atmospheric pressure (about 90 times greater at the surface than that on Earth) make the environment extremely hostile. However, orbiting satellites have managed to land on Venus and photograph its dry, dusty surface. The Venusian surface has also been mapped by probes with radar equipment that can "see" through the cloud layers. Such radar maps reveal a terrain with craters, mountains, volcanoes, and areas where craters have been covered by plains of solidified volcanic lava. There are two large highland regions called Aphrodite Terra and Ishtar Terra.

TILT AND ROTATION OF VENUS

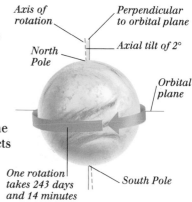

Axis of rotation

Perpendicular to orbital plane

North Pole

Axial tilt of 2°

Orbital plane

One rotation takes 243 days and 14 minutes

South Pole

CLOUD FEATURES

Polar hood

Dark, mid-latitude band

Cloud features swept around planet by winds of up to 220 mph

Dirty yellow hue due to sulfuric acid in atmosphere

Bright polar band

VENUSIAN CRATERS

Danilova

Ejecta (ejected material)

Central peak

Howe

COMPUTER-ENHANCED RADAR MAP OF THE SURFACE OF VENUS

Metis Regio

Maxwell Montes

Bell Regio

Tethus Regio

Sedna Planitia

Eisila Regio

Guinevere Planitia

Phoebe Regio

Alpha Regio

Themis Regio

Lavinia Planitia

Helen Planitia

ISHTAR TERRA

APHRODITE TERRA

Atalanta Planitia

Leda Planitia

Tellus Regio

Niobe Planitia

Ovda Regio

Thetis Regio

Aino Planitia

Lada Terra

**EXTERNAL FEATURES AND
INTERNAL STRUCTURE OF VENUS**

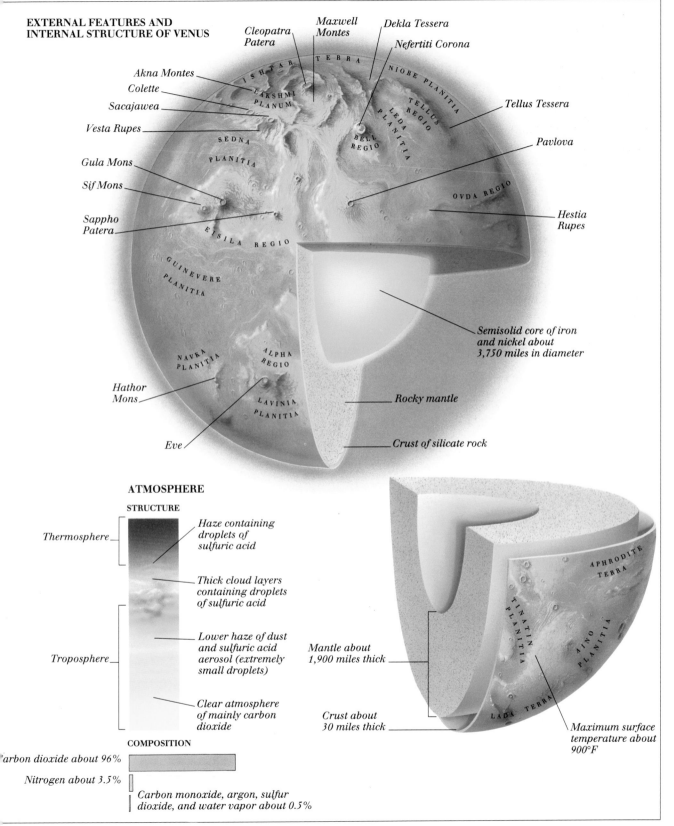

Cleopatra Patera

Maxwell Montes

Dekla Tessera

Nefertiti Corona

Akna Montes

Colette

Sacajawea

Vesta Rupes

Gula Mons

Sif Mons

Sappho Patera

Hathor Mons

Eve

ISHTAR TERRA

NIOBE PLANITIA

LAKSHMI PLANUM

TELLUS REGIO

LEDA PLANITIA

BELL REGIO

SEDNA PLANITIA

ETSILA REGIO

GUINEVERE PLANITIA

NAVKA PLANITIA

ALPHA REGIO

LAVINIA PLANITIA

OVDA REGIO

Tellus Tessera

Pavlova

Hestia Rupes

Semisolid core of iron
and nickel about
3,750 miles in diameter

Rocky mantle

Crust of silicate rock

ATMOSPHERE

STRUCTURE

Thermosphere

Troposphere

Haze containing
droplets of
sulfuric acid

Thick cloud layers
containing droplets
of sulfuric acid

Lower haze of dust
and sulfuric acid
aerosol (extremely
small droplets)

Clear atmosphere
of mainly carbon
dioxide

COMPOSITION

Carbon dioxide about 96%

Nitrogen about 3.5%

Carbon monoxide, argon, sulfur
dioxide, and water vapor about 0.5%

APHRODITE TERRA

TINATIN PLANITIA

AINO PLANITIA

LADA TERRA

Mantle about
1,900 miles thick

Crust about
30 miles thick

Maximum surface
temperature about
900°F

The Earth

THE EARTH

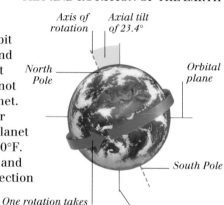

Axis of rotation

Axial tilt of 23.4°

North Pole

Orbital plane

South Pole

One rotation takes 23 hours and 56 minutes

Perpendicular to orbital plane

THE EARTH IS THE THIRD of the nine planets that orbit the Sun. It is the largest and densest rocky planet, and the only one known to support life. About 70 percent of the Earth's surface is covered by water, which is not found in liquid form on the surface of any other planet. There are four main layers: the inner core, the outer core, the mantle, and the crust. At the heart of the planet the solid inner core has a temperature of about 7,230°F. The heat from this inner core causes material in the molten outer core and mantle to circulate in convection currents. It is thought that these convection currents generate the Earth's magnetic field, which extends into space as the magnetosphere. The Earth's atmosphere helps screen out some of the harmful radiation from the Sun, stops meteorites from reaching the planet's surface, and traps enough heat to prevent extremes of cold. The Earth has one natural satellite, the Moon, which is large enough for both bodies to be considered a double-planet system.

THE FORMATION OF THE EARTH

The heat of the collisions caused the planet to glow red

The cloud broke up into particles of ice and rock, which stuck together to form planets

Microorganisms began to photosynthesize, creating a supply of oxygen

4,600 MILLION YEARS AGO, THE SOLAR SYSTEM FORMED FROM A CLOUD OF GAS AND DUST

THE EARTH WAS FORMED FROM COLLIDING ROCKS

4,500 MILLION YEARS AGO THE SURFACE COOLED TO FORM THE CRUST

THE CONTINENTS BROKE UP AND REFORMED, GRADUALLY TAKING THEIR PRESENT POSITIONS

Solar wind enters atmosphere and produces aurora

Magnetosphere (magnetic field)

Solar wind (stream of electrically charged particles)

THE EARTH'S MAGNETOSPHERE

Axis of geographic poles

Van Allen radiation belt

Earth

Axis of magnetic poles

EXTERNAL FEATURES AND INTERNAL STRUCTURE OF THE EARTH

Greenland

Atmosphere about 310 miles deep

Crust 4–25 miles thick

Mantle about 1,740 miles thick

NORTH ATLANTIC OCEAN

Outer core about 1,430 miles thick

Cyclonic storm

COMPOSITION OF THE EARTH

Other elements less than 1%

Aluminum 0.4%

Calcium 0.6%

Sulfur 2.7%

Nickel 2.7%

Silicon 13%

Magnesium 17%

Oxygen 28%

Iron 35%

Core temperature about 7,230°F

Surface temperature between about -126°F and 136°F

Molten core of iron and nickel

Solid inner core of iron and nickel about 1,490 miles in diameter

EUROPE

Gutenberg discontinuity (boundary between outer core and mantle)

Atlas Mountains

AFRICA

Sahara (desert region)

Mantle of mostly solid silicate material

Mohorovicic discontinuity (boundary between mantle and crust)

Congo Basin (tropical rain forest)

SOUTH PACIFIC OCEAN

SOUTH AMERICA

SOUTH ATLANTIC OCEAN

Crust of silicate rock

Land forms about 30% of surface

Amazon Basin (tropical rain forest region)

Cloud typically covers about 50% of surface

Andes (mountain range near crustal plate boundary)

Oceans cover about 70% of surface

Earthquake region along crustal plate boundary

39

The Moon

THE MOON FROM EARTH

THE MOON IS THE EARTH'S only natural satellite. It is relatively large for a moon, with a diameter of about 2,155 miles—just over a quarter that of the Earth. The Moon takes the same time to rotate on its axis as it takes to orbit the Earth (27.3 days), and so the same side (the near side) always faces us. However, the amount of the surface we can see—the phase of the Moon—depends on how much of the near side is in sunlight. The Moon is dry and barren, with no atmosphere or water. It consists mainly of solid rock, although its core may contain molten rock or iron. The surface is dusty, with highlands covered in craters caused by meteorite impacts, and lowlands in which large craters have been filled by solidified lava to form dark areas called maria or "seas." Maria occur mainly on the near side, which has a thinner crust than the far side. Many of the craters are rimmed by mountain ranges that form the crater walls and can be thousands of feet high.

TILT AND ROTATION OF THE MOON

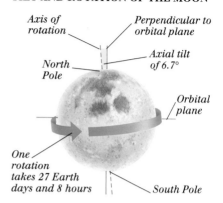

Axis of rotation

Perpendicular to orbital plane

North Pole

Axial tilt of 6.7°

Orbital plane

One rotation takes 27 Earth days and 8 hours

South Pole

CRATERS ON OCEANUS PROCELLARUM

Aristarchus

Cobra Head (head of Schröter's Valley)

Herodotus

NEAR SIDE OF THE MOON

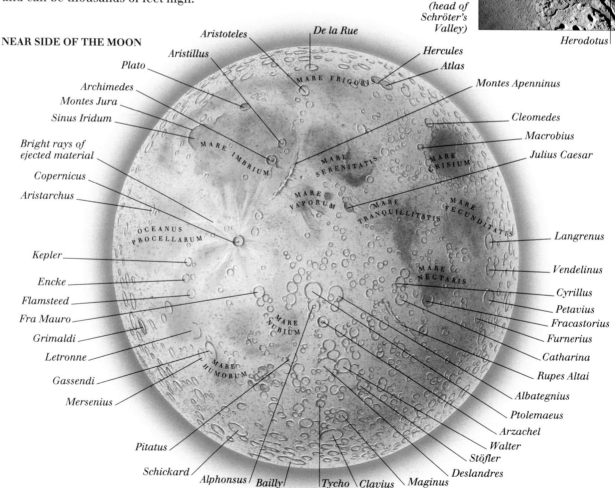

De la Rue
Aristoteles
Aristillus
Plato
Archimedes
Montes Jura
Sinus Iridum
Bright rays of ejected material
Copernicus
Aristarchus
Kepler
Encke
Flamsteed
Fra Mauro
Grimaldi
Letronne
Gassendi
Mersenius
Pitatus
Schickard
Alphonsus
Bailly
Tycho
Clavius
Maginus
Deslandres
Stöfler
Walter
Arzachel
Ptolemaeus
Albategnius
Rupes Altai
Catharina
Furnerius
Fracastorius
Petavius
Cyrillus
Vendelinus
Langrenus
Julius Caesar
Macrobius
Cleomedes
Montes Apenninus
Atlas
Hercules

Hercules

MARE FRIGORIS
MARE IMBRIUM
MARE SERENITATIS
MARE VAPORUM
MARE TRANQUILLITATIS
MARE CRISIUM
MARE FECUNDITATIS
MARE NECTARIS
OCEANUS PROCELLARUM
MARE NUBIUM
MARE HUMORUM

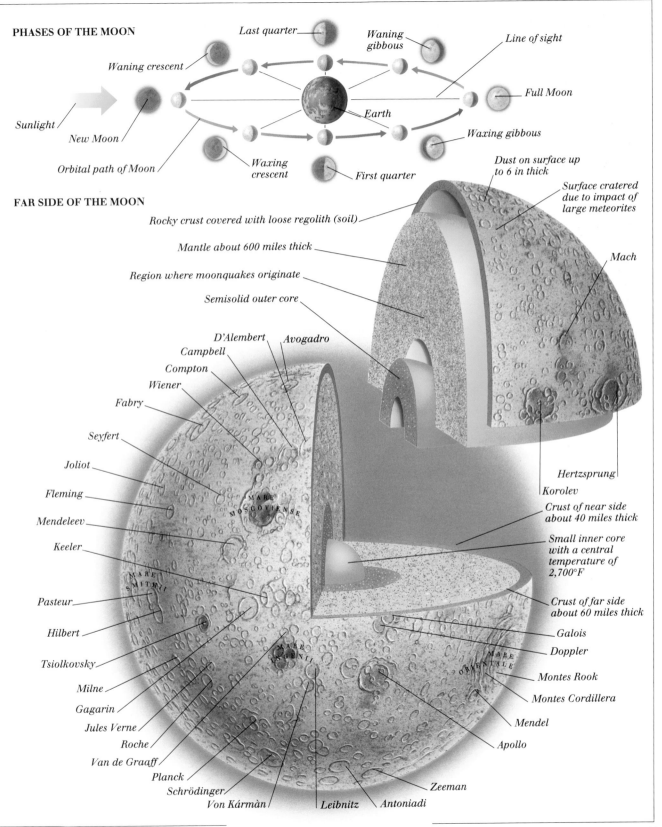

PHASES OF THE MOON

Last quarter

Waning crescent

Waning gibbous

Line of sight

Sunlight

New Moon

Full Moon

Earth

Orbital path of Moon

Waxing crescent

First quarter

Waxing gibbous

FAR SIDE OF THE MOON

Rocky crust covered with loose regolith (soil)

Mantle about 600 miles thick

Region where moonquakes originate

Semisolid outer core

Dust on surface up to 6 in thick

Surface cratered due to impact of large meteorites

Mach

D'Alembert

Avogadro

Campbell

Compton

Wiener

Fabry

Seyfert

Joliot

Fleming

Mendeleev

Keeler

Pasteur

Hilbert

Tsiolkovsky

Milne

Gagarin

Jules Verne

Roche

Van de Graaff

Planck

Schrödinger

Von Kármàn

Leibnitz

Antoniadi

Zeeman

Hertzsprung

Korolev

Crust of near side about 40 miles thick

Small inner core with a central temperature of 2,700°F

Crust of far side about 60 miles thick

Galois

Doppler

Montes Rook

Montes Cordillera

Mendel

Apollo

MARE MOSCOVIENSE

MARE SMITHII

MARE INGENII

MARE ORIENTALE

Mars

MARS

MARS, KNOWN AS THE RED PLANET, is the fourth planet from the Sun and the outermost rocky planet. In the 19th century, astronomers first observed what were thought to be signs of life on Mars. These signs included apparent canal-like markings on the surface, and dark patches that were thought to be vegetation. It is now known that the canals are an optical illusion and the dark patches are areas where the red dust that covers most of the planet has blown away. The fine dust particles are often whipped up by winds into dust storms that occasionally obscure almost all Mars's surface. Residual dust in the atmosphere gives the Martian sky a pinkish hue. The northern hemisphere of Mars has many large plains formed of solidified volcanic lava, while the southern hemisphere has many craters and large impact basins. There are also several huge, extinct volcanoes, including Olympus Mons, which at 370 miles wide and 15 miles high is the largest known volcano in the Solar System. The surface also has many canyons and branching channels. The canyons were formed by movements of the surface crust, but the channels are thought to have been formed by flowing water that has now vaporized almost completely and escaped from the atmosphere. The Martian atmosphere is much thinner than Earth's, with only a few clouds and morning mists. Mars has two tiny irregularly shaped moons, Phobos and Deimos. Their small size indicates that they may be asteroids that have been captured by the gravity of Mars.

TILT AND ROTATION OF MARS

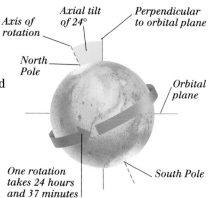

Axis of rotation

Axial tilt of 24°

Perpendicular to orbital plane

North Pole

Orbital plane

One rotation takes 24 hours and 37 minutes

South Pole

SURFACE FEATURES OF MARS

Bright water-ice fog

Fog in canyon about 12 miles wide at end of Valles Marineris

Syria Planum

NOCTIS LABYRINTHUS (CANYON SYSTEM)

Summit caldera consisting of overlapping collapsed volcanic craters

Crater

Gentle slope produced by lava flow

Cloud formation

OLYMPUS MONS (EXTINCT SHIELD VOLCANO)

THE SURFACE OF MARS

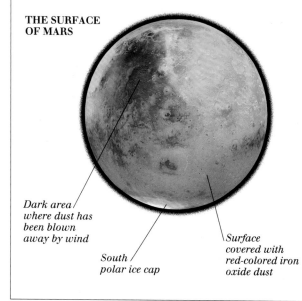

Dark area where dust has been blown away by wind

South polar ice cap

Surface covered with red-colored iron oxide dust

MOONS OF MARS

PHOBOS
Average diameter: 14 miles
Average distance from planet: 5,800 miles

DEIMOS
Average diameter: 8 miles
Average distance from planet: 14,600 miles

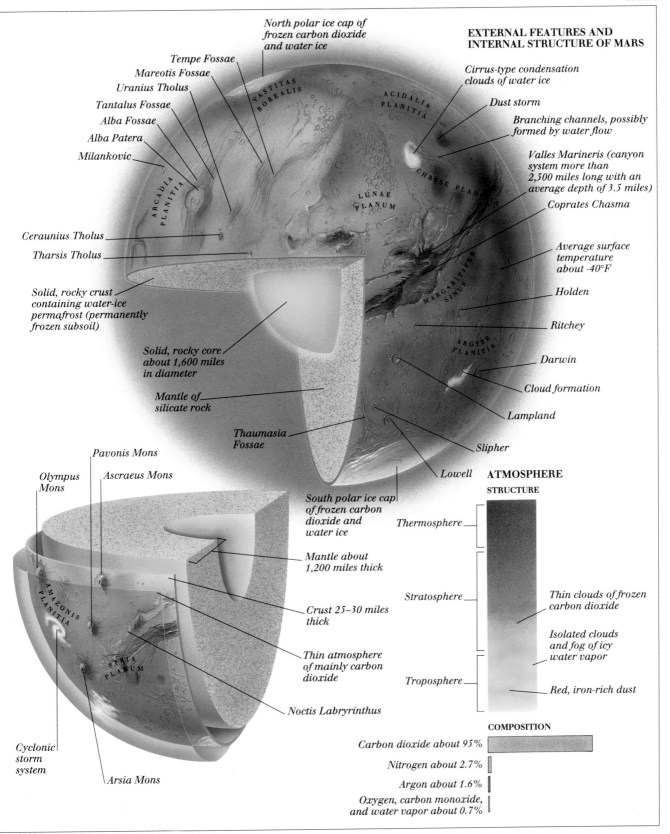

**EXTERNAL FEATURES AND
INTERNAL STRUCTURE OF MARS**

North polar ice cap of
frozen carbon dioxide
and water ice

Tempe Fossae

Mareotis Fossae

Uranius Tholus

Tantalus Fossae

Alba Fossae

Alba Patera

Milankovic

Ceraunius Tholus

Tharsis Tholus

Solid, rocky crust
containing water-ice
permafrost (permanently
frozen subsoil)

Solid, rocky core
about 1,600 miles
in diameter

Mantle of
silicate rock

Thaumasia
Fossae

Cirrus-type condensation
clouds of water ice

Dust storm

Branching channels, possibly
formed by water flow

Valles Marineris (canyon
system more than
2,500 miles long with an
average depth of 3.5 miles)

Coprates Chasma

Average surface
temperature
about -40°F

Holden

Ritchey

Darwin

Cloud formation

Lampland

Slipher

Lowell

VASTITAS BOREALIS

ACIDALIA PLANITIA

ARCADIA PLANITIA

LUNAE PLANUM

CHRYSE PLANITIA

MARGARITIFER SINUS

ARGYRE PLANITIA

Olympus
Mons

Pavonis Mons

Ascraeus Mons

Cyclonic
storm
system

Arsia Mons

AMAZONIS PLANITIA

SYRIA PLANUM

South polar ice cap
of frozen carbon
dioxide and
water ice

Mantle about
1,200 miles thick

Crust 25–30 miles
thick

Thin atmosphere
of mainly carbon
dioxide

Noctis Labryrinthus

ATMOSPHERE

STRUCTURE

Thermosphere

Stratosphere

Troposphere

Thin clouds of frozen
carbon dioxide

Isolated clouds
and fog of icy
water vapor

Red, iron-rich dust

COMPOSITION

Carbon dioxide about 95%

Nitrogen about 2.7%

Argon about 1.6%

Oxygen, carbon monoxide,
and water vapor about 0.7%

Jupiter

JUPITER

JUPITER IS THE FIFTH PLANET from the Sun and the first of the four gas giants. It is the largest and the most massive planet, with a diameter about 11 times that of the Earth and a mass about 2.5 times the combined mass of the eight other planets. Jupiter is thought to have a small rocky core surrounded by an inner mantle of metallic hydrogen (liquid hydrogen that acts like a metal). Outside the inner mantle is an outer mantle of liquid hydrogen and helium that merges into the gaseous atmosphere. Jupiter's rapid rate of rotation causes the clouds in its atmosphere to form belts and zones that encircle the planet parallel to the equator. Belts are dark, low-lying, relatively warm cloud layers. Zones are bright, high-altitude, cooler cloud layers. Within the belts and zones, turbulence causes the formation of cloud features such as white ovals and red spots, both of which are huge storm systems. The most prominent cloud feature is a storm called the Great Red Spot, which consists of a spiraling column of clouds three times wider than the Earth that rises about five miles above the upper cloud layer. Jupiter has one thin, faint, main ring, inside of which is a halo ring of tiny particles extending toward the planet. There are 16 known Jovian moons. The four largest moons (called the Galileans) are Ganymede, Callisto, Io, and Europa. Ganymede and Callisto are cratered and probably icy. Europa is smooth and icy and may contain water. Io is covered in bright red, orange, and yellow splotches. This coloring is caused by sulfurous material from active volcanoes that shoot plumes of lava hundreds of miles above the surface.

TILT AND ROTATION OF JUPITER

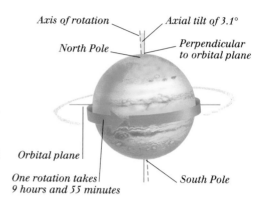

Axis of rotation
Axial tilt of 3.1°
North Pole
Perpendicular to orbital plane
Orbital plane
One rotation takes 9 hours and 55 minutes
South Pole

GREAT RED SPOT AND WHITE OVAL

Great Red Spot (anticyclonic storm system)

Red color probably due to phosphorus

White oval (temporary anticyclonic storm system)

GALILEAN MOONS OF JUPITER

EUROPA
Diameter: 1,950 miles
Average distance from planet: 416,900 miles

CALLISTO
Diameter: 2,983 miles
Average distance from planet: 1,168,200 miles

GANYMEDE
Diameter: 3,270 miles
Average distance from planet: 664,900 miles

IO
Diameter: 2,263 miles
Average distance from planet: 262,100 miles

RINGS OF JUPITER

Main ring

Halo ring

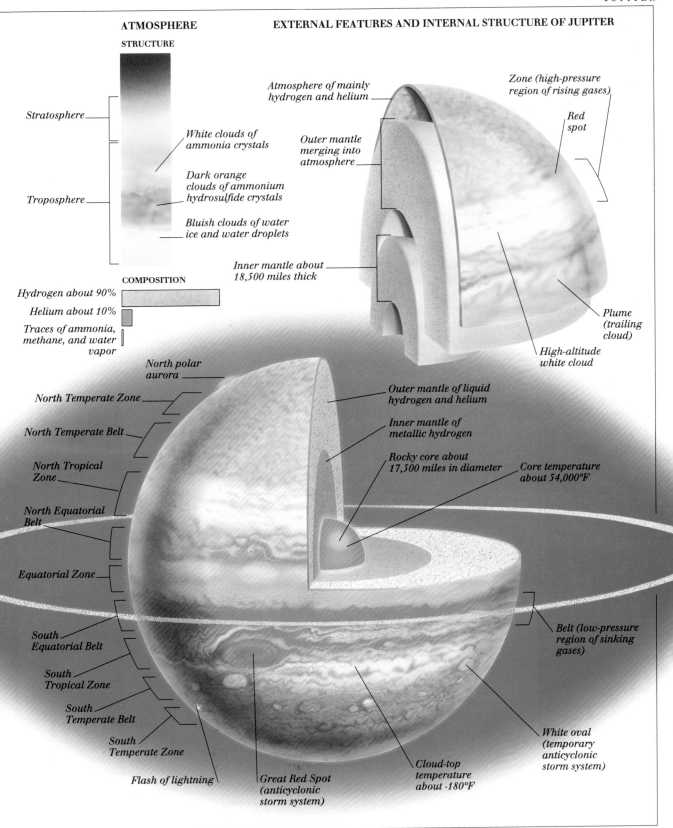

ATMOSPHERE

EXTERNAL FEATURES AND INTERNAL STRUCTURE OF JUPITER

STRUCTURE

Stratosphere

Troposphere

White clouds of ammonia crystals

Dark orange clouds of ammonium hydrosulfide crystals

Bluish clouds of water ice and water droplets

COMPOSITION

Hydrogen about 90%

Helium about 10%

Traces of ammonia, methane, and water vapor

Atmosphere of mainly hydrogen and helium

Outer mantle merging into atmosphere

Inner mantle about 18,500 miles thick

Zone (high-pressure region of rising gases)

Red spot

Plume (trailing cloud)

High-altitude white cloud

North polar aurora

North Temperate Zone

North Temperate Belt

North Tropical Zone

North Equatorial Belt

Equatorial Zone

South Equatorial Belt

South Tropical Zone

South Temperate Belt

South Temperate Zone

Flash of lightning

Great Red Spot (anticyclonic storm system)

Cloud-top temperature about -180°F

Outer mantle of liquid hydrogen and helium

Inner mantle of metallic hydrogen

Rocky core about 17,500 miles in diameter

Core temperature about 54,000°F

Belt (low-pressure region of sinking gases)

White oval (temporary anticyclonic storm system)

45

Saturn

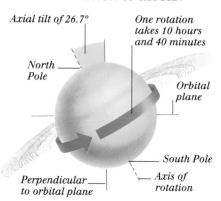

COLOR-ENHANCED
IMAGE OF SATURN

SATURN IS THE SIXTH PLANET from the Sun. It is a gas giant almost as big as Jupiter, with an equatorial diameter of about 74,900 miles. Saturn is thought to consist of a small core of rock and ice surrounded by an inner mantle of metallic hydrogen (liquid hydrogen that acts like a metal). Outside the inner mantle is an outer mantle of liquid hydrogen that merges into a gaseous atmosphere. Saturn's clouds form belts and zones similar to those on Jupiter, but obscured by overlying haze. Storms and eddies, seen as red or white ovals, occur in the clouds. Saturn has an extremely thin but wide system of rings that is less than one mile thick but extends outward to about 260,000 miles from the planet's surface. The main rings comprise thousands of narrow ringlets, each made of icy lumps that range in size from tiny particles to chunks several yards across. The D, E, and G rings are very faint, the F ring is brighter, and the A, B, and C rings are bright enough to be seen from Earth with binoculars. Saturn has 18 known moons, some of which orbit inside the rings and are thought to exert a gravitational influence on the shapes of the rings. Unusually, seven of the moons are co-orbital—they share an orbit with another moon. Astronomers believe that such co-orbital moons may have originated from a single satellite that broke up.

TILT AND ROTATION OF SATURN

Axial tilt of 26.7°

One rotation takes 10 hours and 40 minutes

North Pole

Orbital plane

South Pole

Perpendicular to orbital plane

Axis of rotation

COLOR-ENHANCED IMAGE OF SATURN'S CLOUD FEATURES

Ribbon-shaped striation caused by winds of up to 335 mph

Oval (rotating storm system)

INNER RINGS OF SATURN

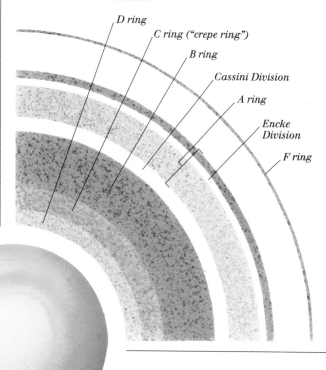

D ring

C ring ("crepe ring")

B ring

Cassini Division

A ring

Encke Division

F ring

MOONS OF SATURN

ENCELADUS
Diameter: 309 miles
Average distance from planet: 148,000 miles

TETHYS
Diameter: 652 miles
Average distance from planet: 183,000 miles

DIONE
Diameter: 695 miles
Average distance from planet: 234,000 miles

MIMAS
Diameter: 247 miles
Average distance from planet: 115,600 miles

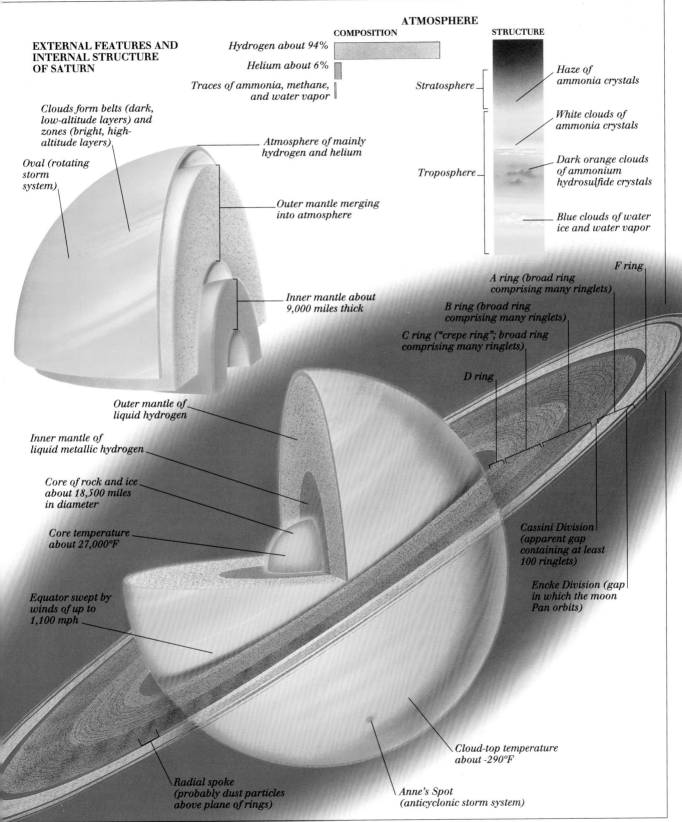

ATMOSPHERE

EXTERNAL FEATURES AND INTERNAL STRUCTURE OF SATURN

COMPOSITION

Hydrogen about 94%

Helium about 6%

Traces of ammonia, methane, and water vapor

STRUCTURE

Stratosphere

Troposphere

Haze of ammonia crystals

White clouds of ammonia crystals

Dark orange clouds of ammonium hydrosulfide crystals

Blue clouds of water ice and water vapor

Clouds form belts (dark, low-altitude layers) and zones (bright, high-altitude layers)

Oval (rotating storm system)

Atmosphere of mainly hydrogen and helium

Outer mantle merging into atmosphere

Inner mantle about 9,000 miles thick

F ring

A ring (broad ring comprising many ringlets)

B ring (broad ring comprising many ringlets)

C ring ("crepe ring"; broad ring comprising many ringlets)

D ring

Outer mantle of liquid hydrogen

Inner mantle of liquid metallic hydrogen

Core of rock and ice about 18,500 miles in diameter

Core temperature about 27,000°F

Cassini Division (apparent gap containing at least 100 ringlets)

Encke Division (gap in which the moon Pan orbits)

Equator swept by winds of up to 1,100 mph

Cloud-top temperature about -290°F

Radial spoke (probably dust particles above plane of rings)

Anne's Spot (anticyclonic storm system)

Uranus

COLOR-ENHANCED IMAGE OF URANUS

URANUS IS THE SEVENTH PLANET from the Sun and the third largest, with a diameter of about 32,000 miles. It is thought to consist of a dense mixture of different types of ice and gas around a solid core. Its atmosphere contains traces of methane, giving the planet a blue-green hue, and the temperature at the cloud tops is about -350°F. Uranus is the most featureless planet to have been closely observed: only a few icy clouds of methane have been seen so far. Uranus is unique among the planets in that its axis of rotation lies close to its orbital plane. As a result of its strongly tilted rotational axis, Uranus rolls on its side along its orbital path around the Sun, while other planets spin more or less upright. Uranus is encircled by 11 rings that consist of rocks interspersed with dust lanes. The rings contain some of the darkest matter in the Solar System. They are extremely narrow, making them difficult to detect: nine of them are less than six miles wide, whereas most of Saturn's rings are thousands of miles in width. There are 15 known Uranian moons, all of which are icy and most of which are farther out than the rings. The 10 inner moons are small and dark, with diameters of less than 100 miles, and the five outer moons are between about 290 and 1,000 miles in diameter. The outer moons have a wide variety of surface features. Miranda has the most varied surface, with cratered areas broken up by huge ridges and cliffs 12 miles high.

TILT AND ROTATION OF URANUS

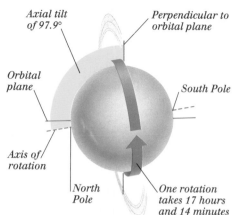

Axial tilt of 97.9°

Perpendicular to orbital plane

Orbital plane

South Pole

Axis of rotation

North Pole

One rotation takes 17 hours and 14 minutes

OUTER MOONS

MIRANDA
Diameter: 293 miles
Average distance from planet: 80,700 miles

RINGS OF URANUS

Epsilon ring

Ring 1986 U1R

Delta ring

Gamma ring

Eta ring

Beta ring

Alpha ring

Rings 4 and 5

Ring 6

Ring 1986 U2R

RINGS AND DUST LANES

ARIEL
Diameter: 720 miles
Average distance from planet: 118,800 miles

TITANIA
Diameter: 981 miles
Average distance from planet: 270,900 miles

UMBRIEL
Diameter: 726 miles
Average distance from planet: 165,300 miles

OBERON
Diameter: 946 miles
Average distance from planet: 362,000 miles

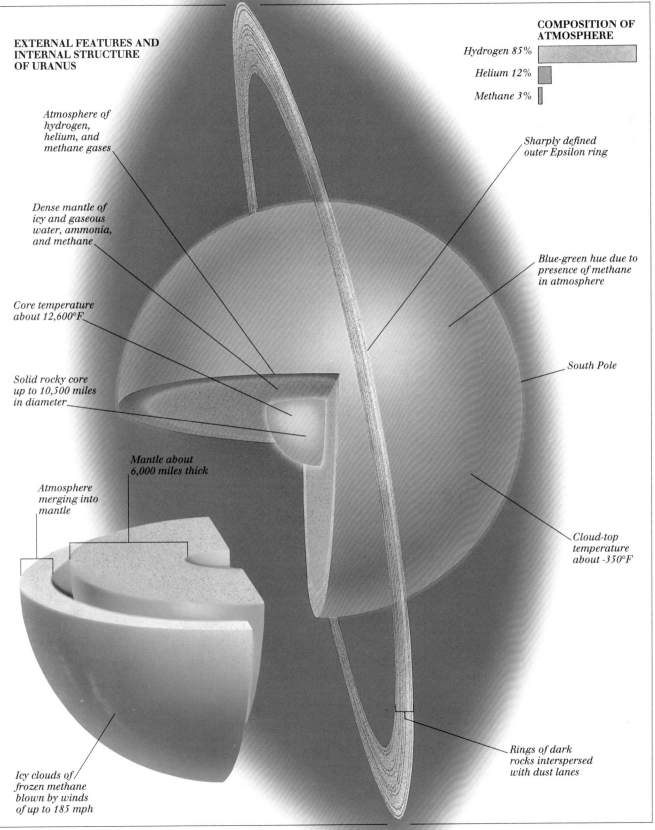

**EXTERNAL FEATURES AND
INTERNAL STRUCTURE
OF URANUS**

**COMPOSITION OF
ATMOSPHERE**

Hydrogen 85%

Helium 12%

Methane 3%

*Atmosphere of
hydrogen,
helium, and
methane gases*

*Dense mantle of
icy and gaseous
water, ammonia,
and methane*

*Core temperature
about 12,600°F*

*Solid rocky core
up to 10,500 miles
in diameter*

*Mantle about
6,000 miles thick*

*Atmosphere
merging into
mantle*

*Icy clouds of
frozen methane
blown by winds
of up to 185 mph*

*Sharply defined
outer Epsilon ring*

*Blue-green hue due to
presence of methane
in atmosphere*

South Pole

*Cloud-top
temperature
about -350°F*

*Rings of dark
rocks interspersed
with dust lanes*

Neptune and Pluto

COLOR-ENHANCED IMAGE OF NEPTUNE

NEPTUNE AND PLUTO are the two farthest planets from the Sun, at an average distance of about 2,800 million miles and 3,700 million miles, respectively. Neptune is a gas giant and is thought to consist of a small rocky core surrounded by a mixture of liquids and gases. The atmosphere contains several prominent cloud features. The largest of these are the Great Dark Spot, which is as wide as the Earth, the Small Dark Spot, and the Scooter. The Great and Small Dark Spots are huge storms that are swept around the planet by winds of about 1,200 miles per hour. The Scooter is a large area of cirrus cloud. Neptune has four tenuous rings and eight known moons. Triton is the largest Neptunian moon and the coldest object in the Solar System, with a temperature of -391°F. Unlike most moons in the Solar System, Triton orbits its mother planet in the opposite direction to the planet's rotation. Pluto is usually the outermost planet, but its elliptical orbit causes it to pass inside the orbit of Neptune for 20 years of its 248-year orbit. Pluto is so small and distant that little is known about it. It is a rocky planet, probably covered with ice and frozen methane. Pluto's only known moon, Charon, is large for a moon, at half the size of its parent planet. Because of the small difference in their sizes, Pluto and Charon are sometimes considered to be a double-planet system.

TILT AND ROTATION OF NEPTUNE

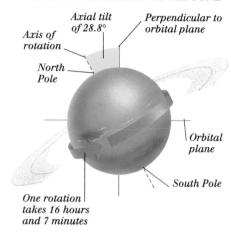

Axial tilt of 28.8°

Perpendicular to orbital plane

Axis of rotation

North Pole

Orbital plane

South Pole

One rotation takes 16 hours and 7 minutes

CLOUD FEATURES OF NEPTUNE

Great Dark Spot (anticyclonic wind storm)

Scooter (cirrus cloud)

Small Dark Spot (cyclonic wind storm)

RINGS OF NEPTUNE

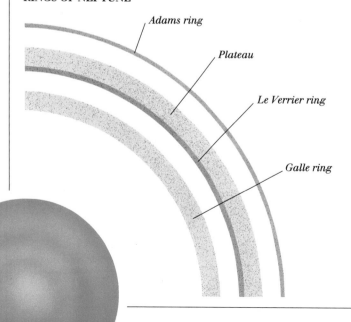

Adams ring

Plateau

Le Verrier ring

Galle ring

HIGH-ALTITUDE CLOUDS

Methane cirrus clouds 25 miles above main cloud deck

Cloud shadow

Main cloud deck blown by winds at speeds of about 1,200 mph

MOONS OF NEPTUNE

TRITON
Diameter: 1,681 miles
Average distance from planet: 220,500 miles

PROTEUS
Diameter: 259 miles
Average distance from planet: 73,100 miles

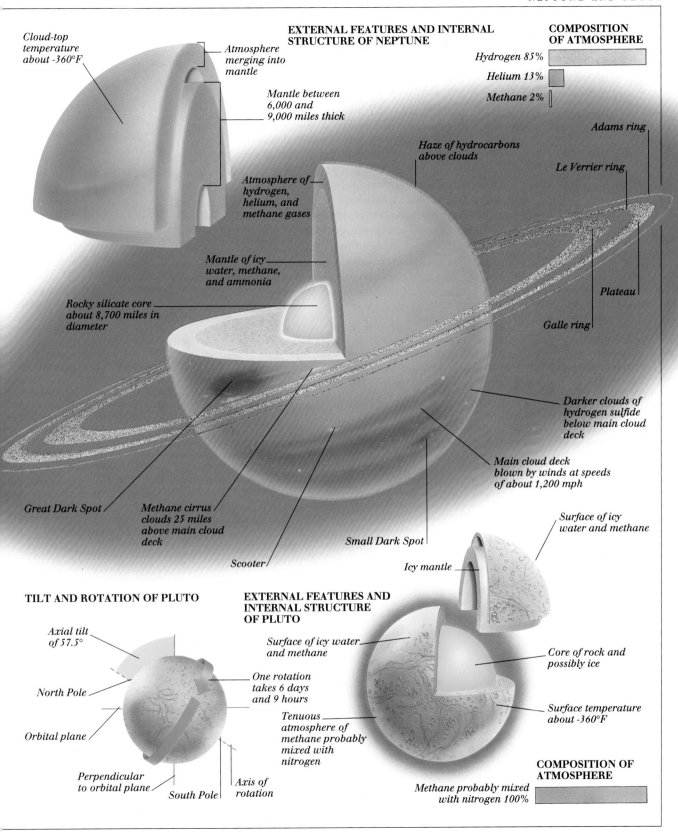

EXTERNAL FEATURES AND INTERNAL STRUCTURE OF NEPTUNE

COMPOSITION OF ATMOSPHERE

Hydrogen 85%

Helium 13%

Methane 2%

Cloud-top temperature about -360°F

Atmosphere merging into mantle

Mantle between 6,000 and 9,000 miles thick

Haze of hydrocarbons above clouds

Adams ring

Le Verrier ring

Atmosphere of hydrogen, helium, and methane gases

Mantle of icy water, methane, and ammonia

Plateau

Rocky silicate core about 8,700 miles in diameter

Galle ring

Darker clouds of hydrogen sulfide below main cloud deck

Main cloud deck blown by winds at speeds of about 1,200 mph

Surface of icy water and methane

Great Dark Spot

Methane cirrus clouds 25 miles above main cloud deck

Scooter

Small Dark Spot

Icy mantle

TILT AND ROTATION OF PLUTO

EXTERNAL FEATURES AND INTERNAL STRUCTURE OF PLUTO

Axial tilt of 57.5°

Surface of icy water and methane

Core of rock and possibly ice

North Pole

One rotation takes 6 days and 9 hours

Orbital plane

Tenuous atmosphere of methane probably mixed with nitrogen

Surface temperature about -360°F

Perpendicular to orbital plane

South Pole

Axis of rotation

COMPOSITION OF ATMOSPHERE

Methane probably mixed with nitrogen 100%

51

Asteroids, comets, and meteoroids

ASTEROID 951 GASPRA

ASTEROIDS, COMETS, AND METEOROIDS are all debris remaining from the nebula in which the Solar System formed 4.6 billion years ago. Asteroids are rocky bodies up to several hundred miles in diameter, although most are much smaller. Most of them orbit the Sun in the asteroid belt, which lies between the orbits of Mars and Jupiter. Comets may originate in a huge cloud, called the Oort Cloud, that is thought to surround the Solar System. They are made of frozen gases and dust, and are a few miles in diameter. Occasionally, a comet is deflected from the Oort Cloud to orbit the Sun in a long, elliptical path. As the comet approaches the Sun, the comet's surface starts to vaporize in the heat, producing a brightly shining coma (a huge sphere of gas and dust around the nucleus), a gas tail, and a dust tail. Meteoroids are small chunks of stone or stone and iron, some of which are fragments of asteroids or comets. Meteoroids range in size from tiny dust particles to objects tens of yards across. If a meteoroid enters the Earth's atmosphere, it is heated by friction and appears as a glowing streak of light called a meteor (also known as a shooting star). Meteor showers occur when the Earth passes through the trail of dust particles left by a comet. Most meteors burn up in the atmosphere. The few that are large enough to reach the Earth's surface are termed meteorites.

COLOR-ENHANCED IMAGE OF HALLEY'S COMET

High-intensity light emission

Nucleus

Medium-intensity light emission

Low-intensity light emission

COLOR-ENHANCED IMAGE OF A LEONID METEOR SHOWER

METEORITES

DEVELOPMENT OF COMET TAILS

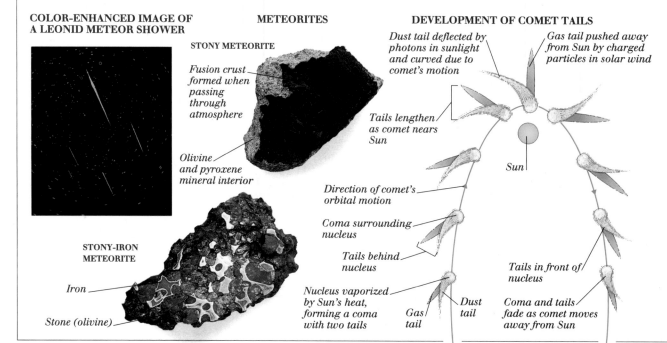

STONY METEORITE

Fusion crust formed when passing through atmosphere

Olivine and pyroxene mineral interior

STONY-IRON METEORITE

Iron

Stone (olivine)

Dust tail deflected by photons in sunlight and curved due to comet's motion

Gas tail pushed away from Sun by charged particles in solar wind

Tails lengthen as comet nears Sun

Direction of comet's orbital motion

Coma surrounding nucleus

Tails behind nucleus

Nucleus vaporized by Sun's heat, forming a coma with two tails

Gas tail

Dust tail

Sun

Tails in front of nucleus

Coma and tails fade as comet moves away from Sun

FEATURES OF A COMET

Thin, straight gas tail

Broad, curved dust tail

Gas molecules heated by Sun and emitting light

Comet tails up to 62 million miles long

Thin, straight gas tail blown by solar wind

Head (coma and nucleus)

Coma surrounding nucleus

Nucleus a few miles across

STRUCTURE OF A COMET

Glowing coma up to 600,000 miles across surrounding nucleus

Possible core of silicate dust

Crust with active areas emitting jets of gas and dust

Jet of gas and dust produced by vaporization on sunlit side of nucleus

Ices, including water ice, and frozen carbon dioxide, methane, and ammonia

Broad dust tail curved along comet's orbital path

Dust particles reflecting sunlight

53

PREHISTORIC EARTH

The changing Earth

THE EARTH FORMED FROM A CLOUD OF DUST and gas drifting through space about 4,600 million years ago. Dense minerals sank to the center while lighter ones formed a thin rocky crust. However, the first known life forms—bacteria and blue-green algae—did not appear until about 3,400 million years ago, and it was only about 700 million years ago that more complex plants and animals began to develop. Since then, thousands of animal and plant species have evolved. Some, such as the dinosaurs, survived for millions of years, while others died out quickly. The Earth itself is continually changing. Although continents neared their present locations about 50 million years ago, they are still drifting slowly over the planet's surface, and mountain ranges such as the Himalayas—which began to form 40 million years ago—are continually being built up and worn away. Climate is also subject to change: the Earth has undergone a series of ice ages interspersed with warmer periods (the most recent ice age was at its height about 20,000 years ago).

Small mammals appeared (e.g., Crusafontia)

Dinosaurs became extinct

Global mountain building occurred

Multicellular soft-bodied animals appeared (e.g., worms and jellyfish)

Shelled invertebrates appeared (e.g., trilobites)

Marine plants flourished

Land plants appeared (e.g., Cooksonia)

CRETACEO

ORDOVICIAN   CAMBRIAN   PRECAMBRIAN TIME

SILURIAN

DEVONIAN

Unicellular organisms appeared (e.g., blue-green algae)

Earth formed

Coral reefs appeared

Vertebrates appeared (e.g., Hemicyclaspis)

More complex types of algae appeared

Amphibians appeared (e.g., Ichthyostega)

GEOLOGICAL TIMESCALE

MILLIONS OF
YEARS AGO (MYA)

4,600	570	510	439	409	363	323	290

					MISSISSIPPIAN (NORTH AMERICA)	PENNSYLVANIAN (NORTH AMERICA)	
	CAMBRIAN	ORDOVICIAN	SILURIAN	DEVONIAN	CARBONIFEROUS		
PRECAMBRIAN TIME	PALEOZOIC						

EVOLUTION OF THE EARTH

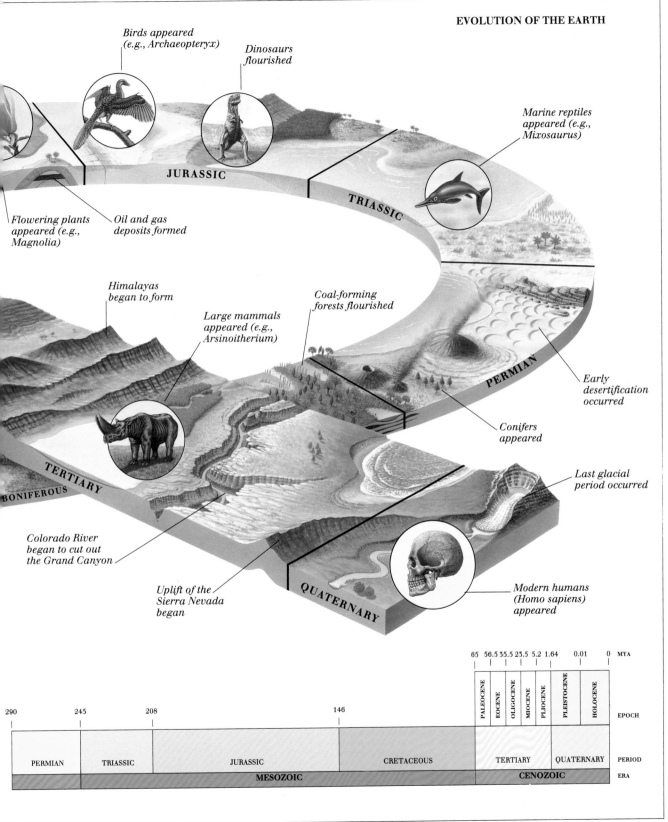

Birds appeared
(e.g., Archaeopteryx)

Dinosaurs
flourished

Marine reptiles
appeared (e.g.,
Mixosaurus)

JURASSIC

TRIASSIC

Flowering plants
appeared (e.g.,
Magnolia)

Oil and gas
deposits formed

Himalayas
began to form

Large mammals
appeared (e.g.,
Arsinoitherium)

Coal-forming
forests flourished

PERMIAN

Early
desertification
occurred

Conifers
appeared

TERTIARY

BONIFEROUS

Last glacial
period occurred

Colorado River
began to cut out
the Grand Canyon

Uplift of the
Sierra Nevada
began

QUATERNARY

Modern humans
(Homo sapiens)
appeared

		65	56.5	35.5	23.5	5.2	1.64		0.01	0	MYA
		PALEOCENE	EOCENE	OLIGOCENE	MIOCENE	PLIOCENE		PLEISTOCENE		HOLOCENE	

290	245	208		146					EPOCH

PERMIAN	TRIASSIC	JURASSIC	CRETACEOUS	TERTIARY	QUATERNARY	PERIOD
		MESOZOIC		CENOZOIC		ERA

57

The Earth's crust

THE EARTH'S CRUST IS THE SOLID outer shell of the Earth. It includes continental crust (about 25 miles thick) and oceanic crust (about four miles thick). The crust and the topmost layer of the mantle form the lithosphere. The lithosphere consists of semi-rigid plates that move relative to each other on the underlying asthenosphere (a partly molten layer of the mantle). This movement is known as plate tectonics and helps explain continental drift. Where two plates move apart, there are rifts in the crust. In mid-ocean, this movement results in seafloor spreading and the formation of ocean ridges; on continents, crustal spreading can form rift valleys. When plates move toward each other, one may be subducted beneath (forced under) the other. In mid-ocean, this causes ocean trenches, seismic activity, and arcs of volcanic islands. Where oceanic crust is subducted beneath continental crust or where continents collide, land may be uplifted and mountains formed (see pp. 62–63). Plates may also slide past each other—along the San Andreas fault, for example. Crustal movement on continents may result in earthquakes, while movement under the seabed can lead to tidal waves.

ELEMENTS IN THE EARTH'S CRUST

Other elements 2%

Potassium 2.6%

Calcium 3.6%

Aluminum 8%

Magnesium 2%

Sodium 2.8%

Iron 5%

Silicon 28%

Oxygen 46%

FEATURES OF PLATE MOVEMENTS

Ocean trench formed where oceanic crust is forced under continental crust

Subduction zone

Ridge where magma is rising to form new oceanic crust

Region of seafloor spreading

Rift formed where two plates are moving apart

Magma (molten rock) erupts at rift

Magma rises to form a hot spot

Volcano develops over hot spot and builds up to form an island

Volcanic island that originally formed over hot spot

Oceanic crust melts

Magma rises to form a volcano

58

MAJOR PLATES OF THE EARTH'S CRUST

Hellenic plate

Eurasian plate

North American plate

Plates sliding past each other

Pacific plate

Cocos plate

Philippine plate

Caribbean plate

Nazca plate

Plates converging

South American plate

African plate

Indo-Australian plate

Plates moving apart

Boundary along which two plates slide past each other

Mountain range uplifted where subducting oceanic crust compresses and deforms edge of continental crust

Lithosphere (crust and topmost layer of mantle)

Asthenosphere (upper part of mantle)

MOVEMENT OF LAND ALONG OCEANIC RIDGES

Land moves apart at a constant rate, perpendicular to ridge

STRAIGHT OCEANIC RIDGE

Land moves apart at a constant rate, perpendicular to curve

CURVED OCEANIC RIDGE

Staggered parallel ridge sections take shape of curve

Transform fault

STRESSES RESOLVE INTO SECTIONS

Faults and folds

THE CONTINUOUS MOVEMENT of the Earth's crustal plates (see pp. 58–59) can squeeze, stretch, or break rock strata, deforming them and producing faults and folds. A fault is a fracture in a rock along which there is movement of one side relative to the other. The movement can be vertical, horizontal, or oblique (vertical and horizontal). Faults develop when rocks are subjected to compression or tension. They tend to occur in hard, rigid rocks, which are more likely to break than bend. The smallest faults occur in single mineral crystals and are microscopically small, while the largest —the Great Rift Valley in Africa, which formed between 5 million and 100,000 years ago—is more than 6,000 miles long. A fold is a bend in a rock layer caused by compression. Folds occur in elastic rocks, which tend to bend rather than break. The two main types of fold are anticlines (upfolds) and synclines (downfolds). Folds vary in size from a few millimeters long to folded mountain ranges hundreds of miles long, such as the Himalayas (see pp. 62–63) and the Alps, which are repeatedly folding. In addition to faults and folds, other features associated with rock deformations include boudins, mullions, and *en échelon* fractures.

STRUCTURE OF A FOLD

Crest
Axial plane
Limb
Angle of plunge
Hingeline

STRUCTURE OF A FAULT

Fault plane
Dip of fault plane (angle from horizontal)
Upthrow
Throw (vertical displacement of fault)
Hade of fault plane (angle from vertical)
Downthrow

STRUCTURE OF A SLOPE

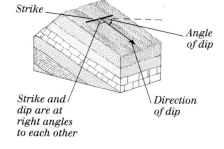

Strike
Angle of dip
Strike and dip are at right angles to each other
Direction of dip

FOLDED ROCK

Crest of anticline
Steeply dipping limbs
Plunge

SECTION THROUGH FOLDED ROCK STRATA THAT HAVE BEEN ERODED

Dipping bed
Anticlinal fold
Monoclinal fold
Mineral-filled fault

Upper Carboniferous Millstone Grit
Lower Carboniferous Limestone

EXAMPLES OF FOLDS

Anticlinorium

Monocline

Syncline

Overturned fold

Overthrust fold

Chevron fold

Synclinorium

Anticline

Isocline

Recumbent fold

Fan fold

Box fold

Cuspate fold

EXAMPLES OF FAULTS

Sinistral strike-slip (lateral) fault

Dextral strike-slip (lateral) fault

Horst

Tear fault

Normal dip-slip fault

Reverse dip-slip fault

Thrust fault

Oblique-slip fault

Graben

Cylindrical fault

SMALL-SCALE ROCK DEFORMATIONS

Competent bed (rocks that break)

Tension

Tension

Tension

Incompetent bed (rocks that bend)

Competent bed breaks into sections

Incompetent bed

Tension

Tension

Tension

Competent bed

Competent bed splits into prisms

Masses of rock shear past each other

Tension

En échelon fracture

Tension

Joint opened by stress

BOUDIN

MULLION

EN ECHELON FRACTURE

Mineral-filled fault

Dipping bed

Gently folded bed

Horizontal bed

Mineral-filled fault

Dipping bed

Upper Carboniferous Millstone Grit

Upper Carboniferous Coal Measures

61

Mountain building

**FORMATION OF
THE HIMALAYAS**

THE PROCESSES INVOLVED in mountain building—termed orogenesis—occur
as a result of the movement of the Earth's crustal plates (see pp. 58-59).
There are three main types of mountains: volcanic mountains, fold mountains,
and block mountains. Most volcanic mountains have been formed along plate
boundaries where plates have come together or moved apart and
lava and other debris have been ejected onto the Earth's surface.
The lava and debris may have built up to form a dome around the
vent of a volcano. Fold mountains are formed where plates push

Asia

*Himalayas
formed by
buckling of
sediment and
part of the
oceanic crust
between two
colliding
continents*

together and cause the rock to buckle
upward. Where oceanic crust meets
less dense continental crust, the oceanic
crust is forced under the continental
crust. The continental crust is buckled by the
impact. This is how folded mountain ranges,
such as the Appalachian Mountains in North
America, were formed. Fold mountains are also
formed where two areas of continental crust meet.
The Himalayas, for example, began to form when
India collided with Asia, buckling the sediments

**BHAGIRATHI PARBAT,
HIMALAYAS**

*India moves
north*

*India collides
with Asia about 40
million years ago*

and parts of the oceanic crust between them. Block mountains are formed
when a block of land is uplifted between two faults as a result of compression or tension
in the Earth's crust (see pp. 60-61). Often, the movement along faults has taken place
gradually over millions of years. However, two plates may cause an earthquake by
suddenly sliding past each other along a faultline.

EXAMPLES OF MOUNTAINS

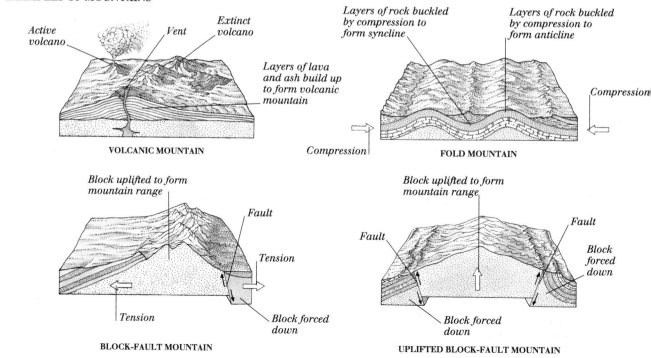

*Active
volcano*

Vent

*Extinct
volcano*

*Layers of lava
and ash build up
to form volcanic
mountain*

VOLCANIC MOUNTAIN

*Layers of rock buckled
by compression to
form syncline*

*Layers of rock buckled
by compression to
form anticline*

Compression

Compression

FOLD MOUNTAIN

*Block uplifted to form
mountain range*

Fault

Tension

Tension

*Block forced
down*

BLOCK-FAULT MOUNTAIN

*Block uplifted to form
mountain range*

Fault

Fault

*Block
forced
down*

*Block forced
down*

UPLIFTED BLOCK-FAULT MOUNTAIN

STAGES IN THE FORMATION OF THE HIMALAYAS

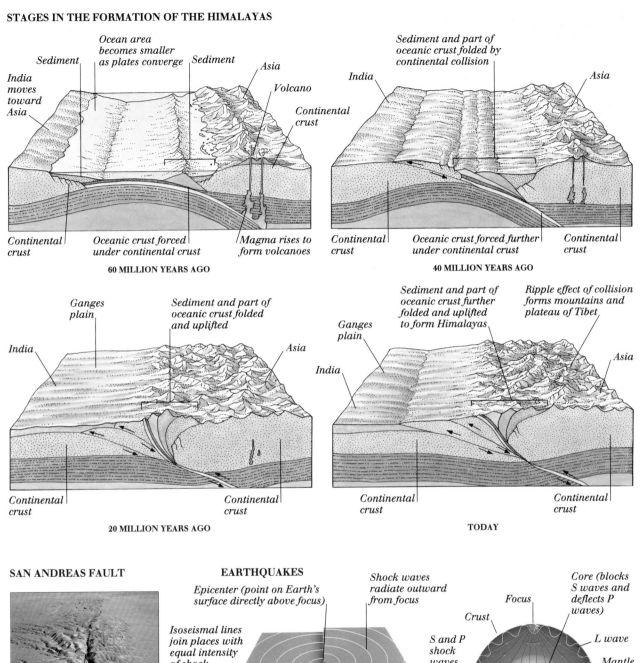

Sediment

Ocean area becomes smaller as plates converge

Sediment

Asia

India moves toward Asia

Volcano

Continental crust

Continental crust

Oceanic crust forced under continental crust

Magma rises to form volcanoes

60 MILLION YEARS AGO

Sediment and part of oceanic crust folded by continental collision

India

Asia

Continental crust

Oceanic crust forced further under continental crust

Continental crust

40 MILLION YEARS AGO

Ganges plain

Sediment and part of oceanic crust folded and uplifted

India

Asia

Continental crust

Continental crust

20 MILLION YEARS AGO

Sediment and part of oceanic crust further folded and uplifted to form Himalayas

Ripple effect of collision forms mountains and plateau of Tibet

Ganges plain

India

Asia

Continental crust

Continental crust

TODAY

SAN ANDREAS FAULT

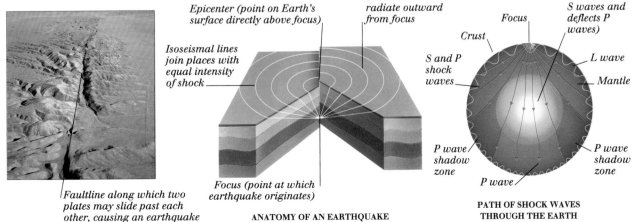

Faultline along which two plates may slide past each other, causing an earthquake

EARTHQUAKES

Epicenter (point on Earth's surface directly above focus)

Shock waves radiate outward from focus

Isoseismal lines join places with equal intensity of shock

Focus (point at which earthquake originates)

ANATOMY OF AN EARTHQUAKE

Core (blocks S waves and deflects P waves)

Focus

Crust

S and P shock waves

L wave

Mantle

P wave shadow zone

P wave shadow zone

P wave

PATH OF SHOCK WAVES THROUGH THE EARTH

Precambrian to Devonian periods

WHEN THE EARTH FORMED about 4,600 million years ago, its atmosphere consisted of volcanic gases with little oxygen, making it hostile to most forms of life. One large supercontinent, Gondwanaland, was situated over the southern polar region, while other smaller continents were spread over the rest of the world. Constant movement of the earth's crustal plates carried continents across the earth's surface. The first primitive life-forms emerged around 3,400 million years ago in shallow, warm seas. The build up of oxygen began to form a shield of ozone around the earth, protecting living organisms from the sun's harmful rays and helping to establish an atmosphere in which life could sustain itself. The first vertebrates appeared about 470 million years ago, during the Ordovician period (510–439 million years ago), the first land plants appeared around 400 million years ago during the Devonian period (409–363 million years ago), and the first land animals about 30 million years later.

MIDDLE ORDOVICIAN POSITIONS OF PRESENT-DAY LANDMASSES

North America
Greenland
China
South America
Australia
South Africa
Africa
Scandinavia
Europe
Siberia
India
North East Africa
Central Asia

EXAMPLES OF PRECAMBRIAN TO DEVONIAN PLANT GROUPS

A PRESENT-DAY CLUBMOSS
(*Lycopodium sp.*)

A PRESENT-DAY LAND PLANT
(*Asparagus setaceous*)

FOSSIL OF AN EXTINCT LAND PLANT
(*Cooksonia hemisphaerica*)

FOSSIL OF AN EXTINCT SWAMP PLANT
(*Zosterophyllum llanoveranum*)

EXAMPLES OF PRECAMBRIAN TO DEVONIAN TRILOBITES

ACADAGNOSTUS
Family: Agnostidae
Length: $^1/_3$ in (8 mm)

PHACOPS
Family: Phacopidae
Length: $1^3/_4$ in (4.5 cm)

OLENELLUS
Family: Olenellidae
Length: $2^1/_2$ in (6 cm)

ELRATHIA
Family: Ptychopariidae
Length: $^3/_4$ in (2 cm)

THE EARTH DURING THE MIDDLE ORDOVICIAN PERIOD

Siberia

Laurentia

China

Kazakstania

Gondwanaland

Baltica

FOSSIL NAUTILOID
(*Estonioceras
perforatum*)

FOSSIL BRACHIOPOD
(*Dicoelosia bilobata*)

TRACE FOSSIL
(*Mawsonites spriggi*)

FOSSIL GRAPTOLITE
(*Monograptus
convolutus*)

EXAMPLES OF DEVONIAN FISH

RHAMPHODOPSIS
Family: Ptyctodontidae
Length: 6 in (15 cm)

PTERASPIS
Family: Pteraspidae
Length: 10 in (25 cm)

COCCOSTEUS
Family: Coccosteidae
Length: 14 in (35 cm)

BOTHRIOLEPIS
Family: Bothriolepidae
Length: 16 in (40 cm)

CHEIRACANTHUS
Family: Acanthodidae
Length: 12 in (30 cm)

PTERICHTHYODES
Family: Asterolepidae
Length: 6 in (15 cm)

CHEIROLEPIS
Family: Cheirolepidae
Length: 6³⁄₄ in (17 cm)

CEPHALASPIS
Family: Cephalaspidae
Length: 8³⁄₄ in (22 cm)

Carboniferous to Permian periods

LATE CARBONIFEROUS POSITIONS OF PRESENT-DAY LANDMASSES

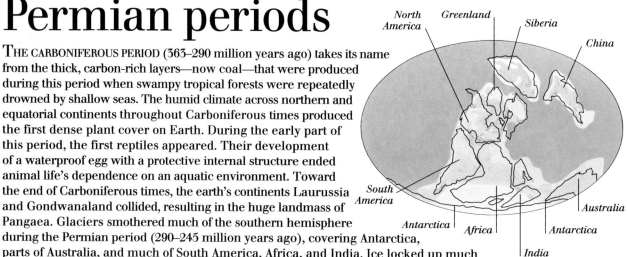

THE CARBONIFEROUS PERIOD (363–290 million years ago) takes its name from the thick, carbon-rich layers—now coal—that were produced during this period when swampy tropical forests were repeatedly drowned by shallow seas. The humid climate across northern and equatorial continents throughout Carboniferous times produced the first dense plant cover on Earth. During the early part of this period, the first reptiles appeared. Their development of a waterproof egg with a protective internal structure ended animal life's dependence on an aquatic environment. Toward the end of Carboniferous times, the earth's continents Laurussia and Gondwanaland collided, resulting in the huge landmass of Pangaea. Glaciers smothered much of the southern hemisphere during the Permian period (290–245 million years ago), covering Antarctica, parts of Australia, and much of South America, Africa, and India. Ice locked up much of the world's water and large areas of the northern hemisphere experienced a drop in sea-level. Away from the poles, deserts and a hot dry climate predominated. As a result of these conditions, the Permian period ended with the greatest mass extinction of life on earth ever.

EXAMPLES OF CARBONIFEROUS AND PERMIAN PLANT GROUPS

A PRESENT-DAY FIR
(Abies concolor)

FOSSIL OF AN EXTINCT FERN
(Zeilleria frenzlii)

FOSSIL OF AN EXTINCT HORSETAIL
(Equisetites sp.)

FOSSIL OF AN EXTINCT CLUBMOSS
(Lepidodendron sp.)

EXAMPLES OF CARBONIFEROUS AND PERMIAN TREES

PECOPTERIS
Family: Marattiaceae
Height: 13 ft (4 m)

PARIPTERIS
Family: Medullosaceae
Height: 16 ft 6 in (5 m)

MARIOPTERIS
Family: Unclassified
Height: 16 ft 6 in (5 m)

MEDULLOSA
Family: Medullosaceae
Height: 16 ft 6 in (5 m)

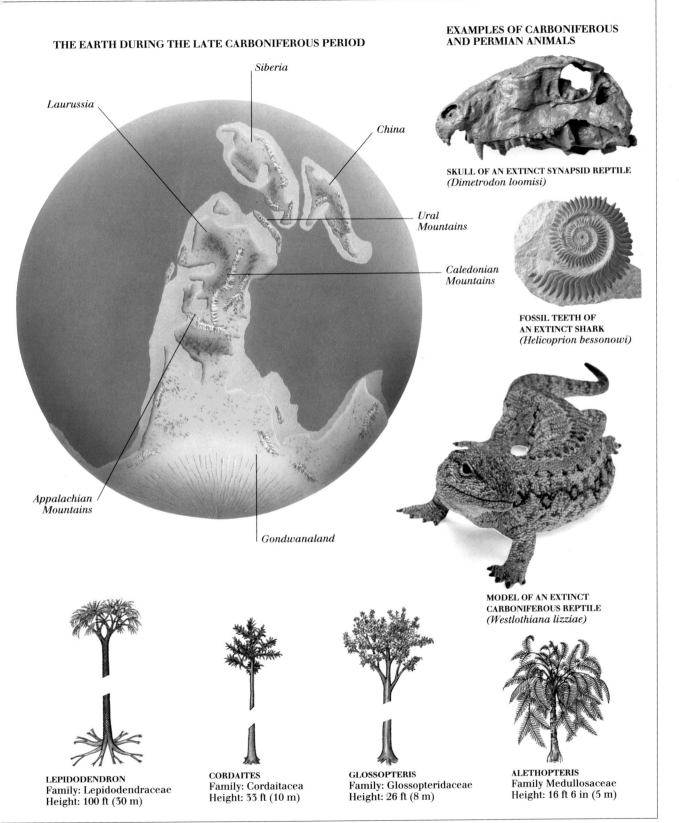

THE EARTH DURING THE LATE CARBONIFEROUS PERIOD

Siberia

Laurussia

China

Ural Mountains

Caledonian Mountains

Appalachian Mountains

Gondwanaland

EXAMPLES OF CARBONIFEROUS AND PERMIAN ANIMALS

SKULL OF AN EXTINCT SYNAPSID REPTILE
(Dimetrodon loomisi)

FOSSIL TEETH OF AN EXTINCT SHARK
(Helicoprion bessonowi)

MODEL OF AN EXTINCT CARBONIFEROUS REPTILE
(Westlothiana lizziae)

LEPIDODENDRON
Family: Lepidodendraceae
Height: 100 ft (30 m)

CORDAITES
Family: Cordaitacea
Height: 33 ft (10 m)

GLOSSOPTERIS
Family: Glossopteridaceae
Height: 26 ft (8 m)

ALETHOPTERIS
Family Medullosaceae
Height: 16 ft 6 in (5 m)

Triassic period

THE TRIASSIC PERIOD (245–208 million years ago) marked the beginning
of what is known as the Age of the Dinosaurs (the Mesozoic era).
During this period, the present-day continents were massed together,
forming one huge continent known as Pangaea. This landmass
experienced extremes of climate, with lush green areas around
the coast or by lakes and rivers, and arid deserts in the interior.
The only forms of plant life were nonflowering plants, such
as conifers, ferns, cycads, and ginkgos; flowering plants had
not yet evolved. The principal forms of animal life included
primitive amphibians, rhynchosaurs ("beaked lizards"),
and primitive crocodilians. Dinosaurs first appeared about
230 million years ago, at the beginning of the Late Triassic
period. The earliest known dinosaurs were the carnivorous
(flesh-eating) herrerasaurids and staurikosaurids, such as
Herrerasaurus and *Staurikosaurus*. Early herbivorous (plant-eating)
dinosaurs first appeared in Late Triassic times and included *Plateosaurus*
and *Technosaurus*. By the end of the Triassic period, dinosaurs dominated
Pangaea, possibly contributing to the extinction of many other reptiles.

**TRIASSIC POSITIONS OF
PRESENT-DAY LANDMASSES**

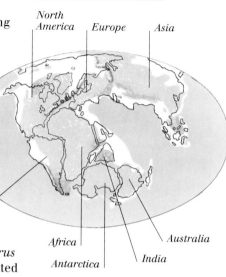

North
America
Europe
Asia
South
America
Africa
Antarctica
India
Australia

**EXAMPLES OF TRIASSIC
PLANT GROUPS**

A PRESENT-DAY
CYCAD
(*Cycas revoluta*)

A PRESENT-DAY GINKGO
(*Ginkgo biloba*)

A PRESENT-DAY CONIFER
(*Araucaria araucana*)

FOSSIL OF AN
EXTINCT FERN
(*Pachypteris* sp.)

FOSSIL LEAF OF AN
EXTINCT CYCAD
(*Cycas* sp.)

EXAMPLES OF TRIASSIC DINOSAURS

MELANOROSAURUS
A melanorosaurid
Length: 40 ft (12.2 m)

MUSSAURUS
A plateosaurid
Length: 6 ft 6 in–10 ft (2–3 m)

HERRERASAURUS
A herrerasaurid
Length: 10 ft (3 m)

PISANOSAURUS
A primitive ornithischian
Length: 3 ft (90 cm)

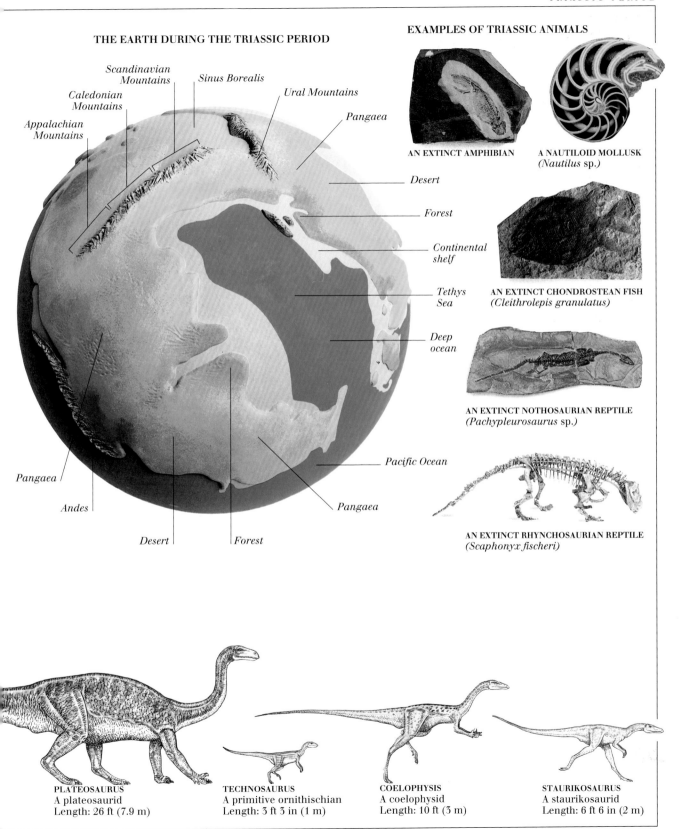

THE EARTH DURING THE TRIASSIC PERIOD

Scandinavian Mountains

Caledonian Mountains

Appalachian Mountains

Sinus Borealis

Ural Mountains

Pangaea

Desert

Forest

Continental shelf

Tethys Sea

Deep ocean

Pangaea

Andes

Desert

Forest

Pacific Ocean

Pangaea

EXAMPLES OF TRIASSIC ANIMALS

AN EXTINCT AMPHIBIAN

A NAUTILOID MOLLUSK
(*Nautilus* sp.)

AN EXTINCT CHONDROSTEAN FISH
(*Cleithrolepis granulatus*)

AN EXTINCT NOTHOSAURIAN REPTILE
(*Pachypleurosaurus* sp.)

AN EXTINCT RHYNCHOSAURIAN REPTILE
(*Scaphonyx fischeri*)

PLATEOSAURUS
A plateosaurid
Length: 26 ft (7.9 m)

TECHNOSAURUS
A primitive ornithischian
Length: 3 ft 3 in (1 m)

COELOPHYSIS
A coelophysid
Length: 10 ft (3 m)

STAURIKOSAURUS
A staurikosaurid
Length: 6 ft 6 in (2 m)

Jurassic period

THE JURASSIC PERIOD, the middle part of the Mesozoic era, lasted from 208 to 146 million years ago. During the Jurassic period, the landmass of Pangaea broke up into the continents of Gondwanaland and Laurasia, and sea-levels rose, flooding areas of lower land. The Jurassic climate was warm and moist. Plants such as ginkgos, horsetails, and conifers thrived, and giant redwood trees appeared, as did the first flowering plants. The abundance of plant food coincided with the proliferation of herbivorous (plant-eating) dinosaurs, such as the large sauropods (e.g., *Diplodocus*) and stegosaurs (e.g., *Stegosaurus*). Carnivorous (flesh-eating) dinosaurs, such as *Compsognathus* and *Allosaurus*, also flourished by hunting the many animals that existed—among them other dinosaurs. Further Jurassic animals included shrewlike mammals, and pterosaurs (flying reptiles), as well as plesiosaurs and ichthyosaurs (both marine reptiles).

JURASSIC POSITIONS OF PRESENT-DAY LANDMASSES

North America
Europe
Arabia
Asia
South America
Africa
Antarctica
India
Australia

EXAMPLES OF JURASSIC PLANT GROUPS

A PRESENT-DAY FERN
(*Dicksonia antarctica*)

A PRESENT-DAY HORSETAIL
(*Equisetum arvense*)

A PRESENT-DAY CONIFER
(*Taxus baccata*)

FOSSIL LEAF OF AN EXTINCT CONIFER
(*Taxus sp.*)

FOSSIL LEAF OF AN EXTINCT REDWOOD
(*Sequoiadendron affinis*)

EXAMPLES OF JURASSIC DINOSAURS

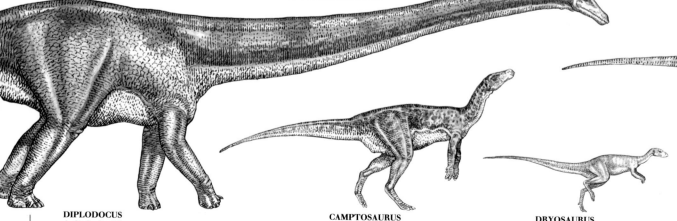

DIPLODOCUS
A diplodocid
Length: 88 ft (26.8 m)

CAMPTOSAURUS
A camptosaurid
Length: 16–23 ft (4.9–7 m)

DRYOSAURUS
A dryosaurid
Length: 10–13 ft (3–4 m)

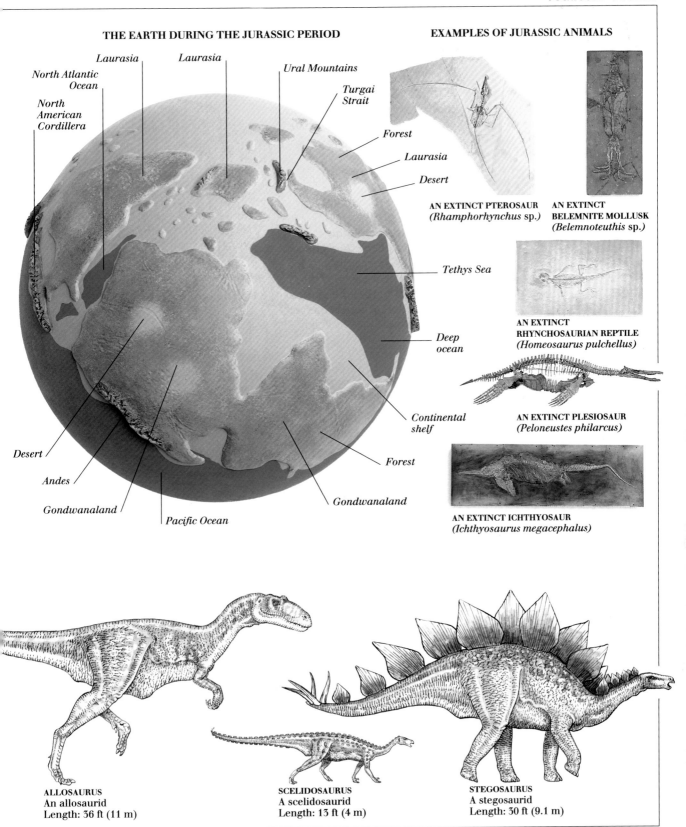

THE EARTH DURING THE JURASSIC PERIOD

Laurasia

Laurasia

North Atlantic Ocean

Ural Mountains

Turgai Strait

North American Cordillera

Forest

Laurasia

Desert

Tethys Sea

Deep ocean

Continental shelf

Desert

Forest

Andes

Gondwanaland

Gondwanaland

Pacific Ocean

EXAMPLES OF JURASSIC ANIMALS

AN EXTINCT PTEROSAUR
(*Rhamphorhynchus* sp.)

AN EXTINCT BELEMNITE MOLLUSK
(*Belemnoteuthis* sp.)

AN EXTINCT RHYNCHOSAURIAN REPTILE
(*Homeosaurus pulchellus*)

AN EXTINCT PLESIOSAUR
(*Peloneustes philarcus*)

AN EXTINCT ICHTHYOSAUR
(*Ichthyosaurus megacephalus*)

ALLOSAURUS
An allosaurid
Length: 36 ft (11 m)

SCELIDOSAURUS
A scelidosaurid
Length: 13 ft (4 m)

STEGOSAURUS
A stegosaurid
Length: 30 ft (9.1 m)

Cretaceous period

THE MESOZOIC ERA ENDED WITH the Cretaceous period, which lasted from 146 to 65 million years ago. During this period, Gondwanaland and Laurasia were breaking up into smaller landmasses that more closely resembled those of the modern continents. The climate remained mild and moist, but the seasons became more marked. Flowering plants, including deciduous trees, replaced many cycads, seed ferns, and conifers. Animal species became more varied, with the evolution of new mammals, insects, fish, crustaceans, and turtles. Dinosaurs evolved into a wide variety of species during Cretaceous times; more than half of all known dinosaurs—including *Iguanodon, Deinonychus, Tyrannosaurus,* and *Hypsilophodon* —lived during this period. At the end of the Cretaceous period, however, large dinosaurs became extinct. The reason for this mass extinction is unknown but it is thought to have been caused by climatic changes due to either a catastrophic meteor impact with the Earth or extensive volcanic eruptions.

CRETACEOUS POSITIONS OF PRESENT-DAY LANDMASSES

North America
Europe
Arabia
Asia
South America
Africa
India
Antarctica
Australia

EXAMPLES OF CRETACEOUS PLANT GROUPS

A PRESENT-DAY CONIFER
(*Pinus muricata*)

A PRESENT-DAY DECIDUOUS TREE
(*Magnolia* sp.)

FOSSIL OF AN EXTINCT FERN
(*Sphenopteris latiloba*)

FOSSIL OF AN EXTINCT GINKGO
(*Ginkgo pluripartita*)

FOSSIL LEAVES OF AN EXTINCT DECIDUOUS TREE
(*Cercidyphyllum* sp.)

EXAMPLES OF CRETACEOUS DINOSAURS

SALTASAURUS
A titanosaurid
Length: 40 ft (12.2 m)

TOROSAURUS
A ceratopsid
Length: 25 ft (7.6 m)

HYPSILOPHODON
A hypsilophodontid
Length: 4 ft 6 in–7 ft 6 in (1.4–2.3 m)

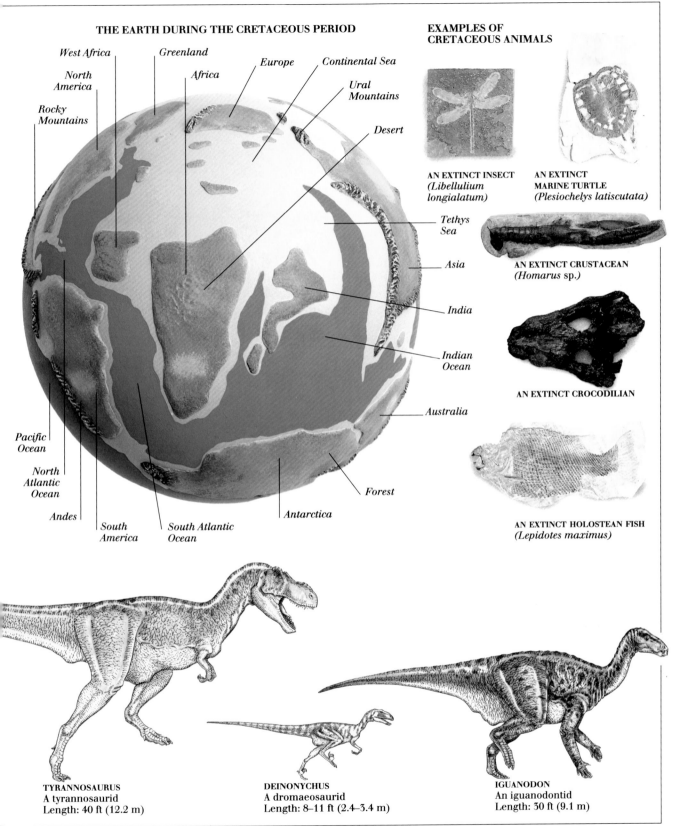

THE EARTH DURING THE CRETACEOUS PERIOD

West Africa

North America

Greenland

Africa

Europe

Continental Sea

Ural Mountains

Rocky Mountains

Desert

Tethys Sea

Asia

India

Indian Ocean

Australia

Pacific Ocean

North Atlantic Ocean

Andes

South America

South Atlantic Ocean

Antarctica

Forest

EXAMPLES OF CRETACEOUS ANIMALS

AN EXTINCT INSECT
(*Libellulium longialatum*)

AN EXTINCT MARINE TURTLE
(*Plesiochelys latiscutata*)

AN EXTINCT CRUSTACEAN
(*Homarus* sp.)

AN EXTINCT CROCODILIAN

AN EXTINCT HOLOSTEAN FISH
(*Lepidotes maximus*)

TYRANNOSAURUS
A tyrannosaurid
Length: 40 ft (12.2 m)

DEINONYCHUS
A dromaeosaurid
Length: 8–11 ft (2.4–3.4 m)

IGUANODON
An iguanodontid
Length: 30 ft (9.1 m)

73

Tertiary period

FOLLOWING THE DEMISE OF THE DINOSAURS at the end of the Cretaceous period, the Tertiary period (65–1.6 million years ago), which formed the first part of the Cenozoic era (65 million years ago–present), was characterized by a huge expansion of mammal life. Placental mammals nourish and maintain their young in the mother's uterus; only three orders of placental mammals existed during Cretaceous times, compared with 25 orders during the Tertiary period. One of these 25 included the first hominid (see pp.108–109), *Australopithecus*, which appeared in Africa. By the beginning of the Tertiary period, the continents had almost reached their present position. The Tethys Sea, which had separated the northern continents from Africa and India, began to close up, forming the Mediterranean Sea and allowing the migration of terrestrial animals between Africa and western Europe. India's collision with Asia led to the formation of the Himalayas. During the middle part of the Tertiary period, the forest-dwelling and browsing mammals were replaced by mammals such as the horse, better suited to grazing the open savannahs that began to dominate. Repeated cool periods throughout the Tertiary period established the Antarctic as an icy island continent.

TERTIARY POSITIONS OF PRESENT-DAY LANDMASSES

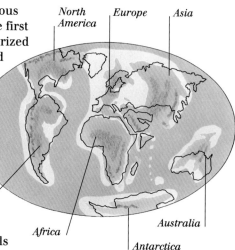

North America
Europe
Asia
South America
Africa
Australia
Antarctica

EXAMPLES OF TERTIARY PLANT GROUPS

A PRESENT-DAY OAK
(*Quercus palustris*)

A PRESENT-DAY BIRCH
(*Betula grossa*)

FOSSIL LEAF OF AN EXTINCT BIRCH
(*Betulites sp.*)

FOSSIL STEM OF AN EXTINCT PALM
(*Palmoxylon*)

EXAMPLES OF TERTIARY ANIMAL GROUPS

HYAENODON
An hyaenodontid
Length: 6 ft 6 in (2 m)

TITANOHYRAX
A pliohyracid
Length: 6 ft 6 in (2 m)

PHORUSRHACUS
A phorusrhacid
Length: 5 ft (1.5 m)

SAMOTHERIUM
A giraffid
Length: 10 ft (3 m)

THE EARTH DURING THE TERTIARY PERIOD

EXAMPLES OF TERTIARY ANIMALS

North America

Rocky Mountains

Sierra Nevada

Appalachian Mountains

Pyrenees

Europe

Alps

Asia

Continental sea

Zagros Mountains

Himalayas

Tethys Sea

Australia

India

Andes

South America

Atlantic Ocean

Atlas Mountains

Africa

Antarctica

Vegetation

Indian Ocean

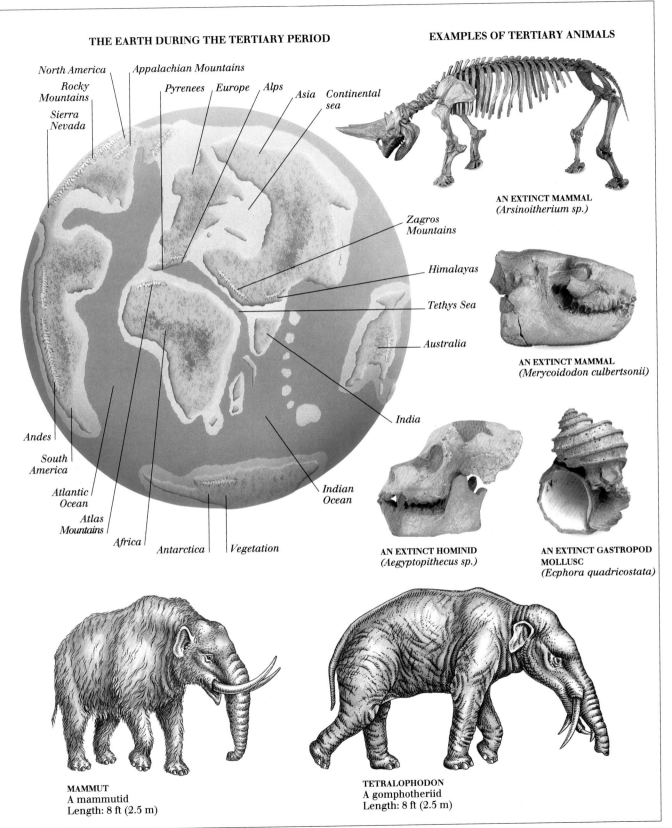

AN EXTINCT MAMMAL
(*Arsinoitherium sp.*)

AN EXTINCT MAMMAL
(*Merycoidodon culbertsonii*)

AN EXTINCT HOMINID
(*Aegyptopithecus sp.*)

AN EXTINCT GASTROPOD MOLLUSC
(*Ecphora quadricostata*)

MAMMUT
A mammutid
Length: 8 ft (2.5 m)

TETRALOPHODON
A gomphotheriid
Length: 8 ft (2.5 m)

Quaternary period

QUATERNARY POSITIONS OF PRESENT-DAY LANDMASSES

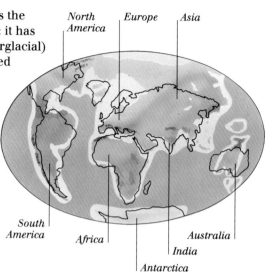

THE QUATERNARY PERIOD (1.6 million years ago–present) forms the second part of the Cenozoic era (65 million years ago–present): it has been characterized by alternating cold (glacial) and warm (interglacial) periods. During cold periods, ice sheets and glaciers have formed repeatedly on northern and southern continents. The cold environments in North America and Eurasia, and to a lesser extent in southern South America and parts of Australia, have caused the migration of many life forms toward the Equator. Only the specialized ice-age mammals such as *Mammuthus* and *Coelodonta*, with their thick wool and fat insulation, were suited to life in very cold climates. Humans developed throughout the Pleistocene period (1.6 million–10,000 years ago) in Africa and migrated northward into Europe and Asia. Modern humans, *Homo sapiens*, lived on the cold European continent 30,000 years ago and hunted mammals. The end of the last ice age and the climatic changes that occurred about 10,000 years ago brought extinction to many Pleistocene mammals, but enabled humans to flourish.

EXAMPLES OF QUATERNARY PLANT GROUPS

A PRESENT-DAY BIRCH
(*Betula lenta*)

A PRESENT-DAY SWEEETGUM
(*Liquidambar styraciflua*)

FOSSIL LEAF OF A SWEETGUM
(*Liquidambar europeanum*)

FOSSIL LEAF OF A BIRCH
(*Betula sp.*)

EXAMPLES OF QUATERNARY ANIMAL GROUPS

PROCOPTODON
A macropodid
Length: 10 ft (3 m)

DIPROTODON
A diprotodontid
Length: 10 ft (3 m)

TOXODON
A toxodontid
Length: 10 ft (3 m)

MAMMUTHUS
An elephantid
Length: 10 ft (3 m)

THE EARTH DURING THE QUATERNARY PERIOD

Pyrenees
Alps
Appalachian Mountains
Ice sheet
Rocky Mountains
Asia
North America
Vegetation
Carpathian Mountains
Taurus Mountains
Himalayas
India
Australia
Desert
Andes
South America
Indian Ocean
Atlantic Ocean
Ice cap
Atlas Mountains
Africa
Antarctica

EXAMPLES OF QUATERNARY ANIMALS

A MAMMAL SKELETON
(Hippopotamus amphibius)

SKULL OF AN EXTINCT CAVE BEAR
(Ursus spelaeus)

SKULL OF AN EXTINCT TORTOISE
(Meiolania platyceps)

A MAMMOTH TOOTH
(Mammuthus primigenius)

DEINOTHERIUM
A deinotheriid
Length: 13 ft (4 m)

COELODONTA
A rhinocerotid
Length: 13 ft (4 m)

AUSTRALOPITHECUS
A hominid
Length: 4 ft (1.2 m)

Early signs of life

FOR ALMOST A THOUSAND MILLION YEARS after its formation, there was no known life on Earth. The first simple, sea-dwelling organic structures appeared about 3,400 years ago; they may have formed when certain chemical molecules joined together. Prokaryotes, single-celled micro-organisms such as blue-green algae, were able to photosynthesize (see pp. 138–139), and thus produce oxygen. A thousand million years later, sufficient oxygen had built up in the earth's atmosphere to allow multicellular organisms to proliferate in the Precambrian seas (before 570 million years ago). Soft-bodied jellyfish, corals, and seaworms flourished about 700 million years ago. Trilobites, the first animals with hard body frames, developed during the Cambrian period (570–510 million years ago). However, it was not until the beginning of the Devonian period (409–363 million years ago) that early land plants, such as *Asteroxylon*, formed a water-retaining cuticle, which ended their dependence on an aquatic environment. About 363 million years ago, the first amphibians (see pp. 80–81) crawled onto the land, although they still returned to the water to lay their soft eggs. Not until the emergence of the first reptiles would animals appear that were not dependent on water in this way.

STROMATOLITIC LIMESTONE

Alternate layers of mud and sand

Layers bound by algae

Layered structure

Limestone

Long, beaklike snout

Growth line

Dorsal plate

Dorsal spine base

Fixed lateral plate

Bony dorsal shield

FOSSILIZED JAWLESS FISH

Glabella

Eye

Thoracic pleurae

Tail shield

Tail area

FOSSILIZED TRILOBITE

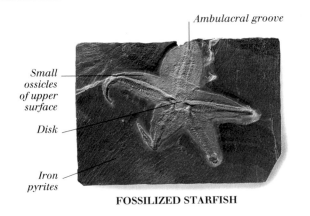

Ambulacral groove

Small
ossicles
of upper
surface

Disk

Iron
pyrites

FOSSILIZED STARFISH

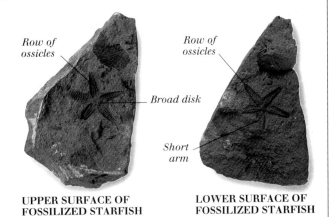

Row of
ossicles

Row of
ossicles

Broad disk

Short
arm

**UPPER SURFACE OF
FOSSILIZED STARFISH**

**LOWER SURFACE OF
FOSSILIZED STARFISH**

Jointed
leg

Chelicera
(jointed
pincer)

Jointed leg
with oar-
shaped
paddle

Segmented
abdomen

UNDERSIDE OF FOSSILIZED EURYPTERID

Growing tip

Disk-shaped
sporangium
(spore-case)

Leaflike scale

Telson (tail
spine)

Abdominal
segments

Shell contains eight
somites (thoracic
segments)

Hingeless,
bivalved
shell

FOSSIL OF AN EXTINCT SHRIMP

Stem

RECONSTRUCTION OF ASTEROXYLON

Amphibians and reptiles

THE EARLIEST KNOWN AMPHIBIANS, such as *Acanthostega*
and *Ichthyostega*, lived about 363 million years ago
at the end of the Devonian period (409–363 million
years ago). Their limbs may have evolved from the
muscular fins of lungfish. These fish can use their
fins to push themselves along the bottom of lakes
and some can breathe at the water's surface. While
amphibians (see pp. 182–183) can exist on land, they
are dependent on a wet environment because their
skin does not retain moisture and they must return to
the water to lay their eggs. Evolving from amphibians,
reptiles (see pp. 184–187) first appeared during the
Carboniferous period (363–290 million years ago):
Westlothiana, the earliest known reptile, lived on
land 338 million years ago. The development of the
amniotic egg, with an embryo enclosed in its own wet
environment (the amnion) and protected by a waterproof
shell, freed reptiles from the amphibian's dependence on
a wet habitat. A scaly skin protected the reptile from
desiccation on land and enabled it to exploit ways of life
closed to its amphibian ancestors. Reptiles include the
dinosaurs, which came to dominate life on land during
the Mesozoic era (245–65 million years ago).

FOSSIL SKULL OF ACANTHOSTEGA

MODEL OF ICHTHYOSTEGA

SKELETON OF ERYOPS

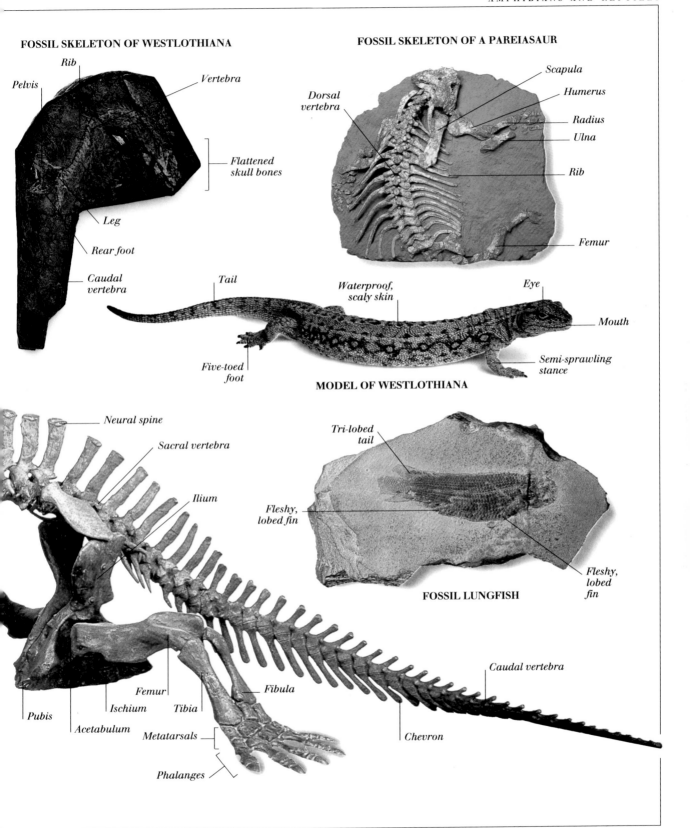

FOSSIL SKELETON OF WESTLOTHIANA

Rib

Pelvis

Vertebra

Flattened
skull bones

Leg

Rear foot

Caudal
vertebra

FOSSIL SKELETON OF A PAREIASAUR

Scapula

Humerus

Dorsal
vertebra

Radius

Ulna

Rib

Femur

Tail

Waterproof,
scaly skin

Eye

Mouth

Five-toed
foot

Semi-sprawling
stance

MODEL OF WESTLOTHIANA

Neural spine

Sacral vertebra

Ilium

Tri-lobed
tail

Fleshy,
lobed fin

Fleshy,
lobed
fin

FOSSIL LUNGFISH

Caudal vertebra

Pubis

Femur

Fibula

Ischium

Acetabulum

Tibia

Metatarsals

Chevron

Phalanges

The dinosaurs

THE DINOSAURS WERE A LARGE GROUP of reptiles that were the dominant land vertebrates (animals with backbones) for most of the Mesozoic era (245–65 million years ago). They appeared some 230 million years ago and were distinguished from other scaly, egg-laying reptiles by an important feature: dinosaurs had an erect limb stance. This enabled them to keep their bodies well above the ground, unlike the sprawling and semi-sprawling stance of other reptiles. The head of the dinosaur's femur (thighbone) fits into a socket in its pelvis (hipbone), producing efficient and mobile locomotion. Dinosaurs are categorized into two groups according to the structure of their pelvis: saurischian (lizard-hipped) and ornithischian (bird-hipped) dinosaurs. In the case of most saurischians, the pubis (part of the pelvis) jutted forward, while in ornithischians it slanted back, parallel to the ischium (another part of the pelvis). The enormous variety of dinosaur species equals that of mammals. The Dinosauria were the most successful land vertebrates ever, and survived for 165 million years, until their extinction 65 million years ago.

STRUCTURE OF SAURISCHIAN PELVIS

Ilium
Hook of preacetabular process
Postacetabular process
Ilio-pubic joint
Acetabulum
Ilio-ischial joint
Pubis
Ischium
Pubic foot

GALLIMIMUS
A saurischian dinosaur

POSITION OF PELVIS IN A SAURISCHIAN DINOSAUR

STRUCTURE OF ORNTHISCHIAN PELVIS

Ilium
Preacetabular process
Postacetabular process
Ilio-pubic joint
Ilio-ischial joint
Prepubis
Acetabulum
Pubis
Ischium

HYPSILOPHODON
An ornithischian dinosaur

POSITION OF PELVIS IN AN ORNITHISCHIAN DINOSAUR

BAROSAURUS
A saurischian dinosaur

COMPARISON OF ANIMAL STANCES

SPRAWLING STANCE
The thighs and upper arms project straight out from the body so that the knees and elbows are bent at right angles.

COMMON IGUANA
(*Iguana iguana*)
A present-day reptile

ERECT STANCE
The thighs and upper arms project straight down from the body so that the knees and elbows are straight.

SEMI-SPRAWLING STANCE
The thighs and upper arms project downward and outward so that the knees and elbows are slightly bent.

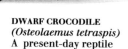

DWARF CROCODILE
(*Osteolaemus tetraspis*)
A present-day reptile

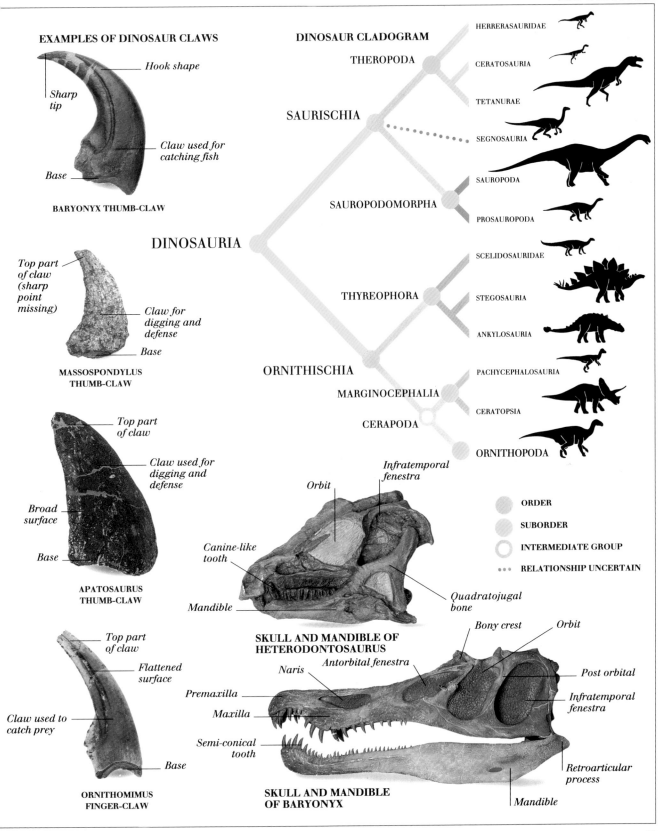

EXAMPLES OF DINOSAUR CLAWS

Hook shape

Sharp tip

Claw used for catching fish

Base

BARYONYX THUMB-CLAW

Top part of claw (sharp point missing)

Claw for digging and defense

Base

MASSOSPONDYLUS THUMB-CLAW

Top part of claw

Claw used for digging and defense

Broad surface

Base

APATOSAURUS THUMB-CLAW

Top part of claw

Flattened surface

Claw used to catch prey

Base

ORNITHOMIMUS FINGER-CLAW

DINOSAUR CLADOGRAM

HERRERASAURIDAE

THEROPODA

CERATOSAURIA

TETANURAE

SAURISCHIA

SEGNOSAURIA

SAUROPODA

SAUROPODOMORPHA

PROSAUROPODA

DINOSAURIA

SCELIDOSAURIDAE

THYREOPHORA

STEGOSAURIA

ANKYLOSAURIA

PACHYCEPHALOSAURIA

ORNITHISCHIA

MARGINOCEPHALIA

CERATOPSIA

CERAPODA

ORNITHOPODA

○ ORDER

○ SUBORDER

○ INTERMEDIATE GROUP

••• RELATIONSHIP UNCERTAIN

Infratemporal fenestra

Orbit

Canine-like tooth

Quadratojugal bone

Mandible

SKULL AND MANDIBLE OF HETERODONTOSAURUS

Bony crest

Orbit

Antorbital fenestra

Naris

Post orbital

Premaxilla

Infratemporal fenestra

Maxilla

Semi-conical tooth

Retroarticular process

Mandible

SKULL AND MANDIBLE OF BARYONYX

Theropods 1

AN ENORMOUSLY SUCCESSFUL SUBORDER of the Saurischia, the bipedal (two-footed) theropods ("beast feet") emerged 230 million years ago in Late Triassic times; the oldest known example comes from South America. Theropods spanned the whole of the Age of the Dinosaurs (230–65 million years ago) and included most known predatory dinosaurs. The typical theropod had small arms with sharp, clawed fingers; powerful jaws lined with sharp teeth; an S-shaped neck; long, muscular hind limbs; and clawed, usually four-toed feet. Many theropods may have been warm-blooded; most were exclusively carnivorous. Theropods ranged from animals no larger than a chicken to huge creatures, such as *Tyrannosaurus* and *Baryonyx*. The group also included ostrichlike omnivores and herbivores with toothless beaks, such as *Struthiomimus* and *Gallimimus*. Many scientists believe that birds are the closest living relatives to the dinosaurs, and share a common ancestor with the theropods. *Archaeopteryx*, small and feathered, was the first known bird and lived alongside its dinosaur relatives.

INTERNAL ANATOMY OF ALBERTOSAURUS LEG

Iliotibial muscle
Iliofemoral muscle
Femorotibial muscle
Internal tibial flexor muscle
Femur
Iliofibular muscle
Gastrocnemius muscle
Digital flexor muscle
Fibula
Tarsal
Metatarsal
Ambiens muscle
Femoro-tibial muscle
Anterior tibial muscle
Common digital extensor muscle
Toe
Claw

Cranium
Orbit
Supraoccipital crest
Cervical vertebrae
Naris
Dorsal vertebrae
Ilium
Cervical rib
Scapula
Shoulder joint
Ulna
Phalanges
Metacarpals
Wrist joint
Elbow joint
Coracoid
Rib
Humerus
Mandible
Serrated tooth
Femur
Ischium
Hip joint
Pubis
Knee joint

SKELETON OF TYRANNOSAURUS

Naris
Eye
Thigh
Scaly skin
Tail
Hand
Forelimb
Knee
Ankle
Foot
Hind limb
Toe
Claw
Tibia
Fibula
Metatarsals
Phalanges
Ankle joint
Hallux (first toe)

EXTERNAL FEATURES OF TYRANNOSAURUS

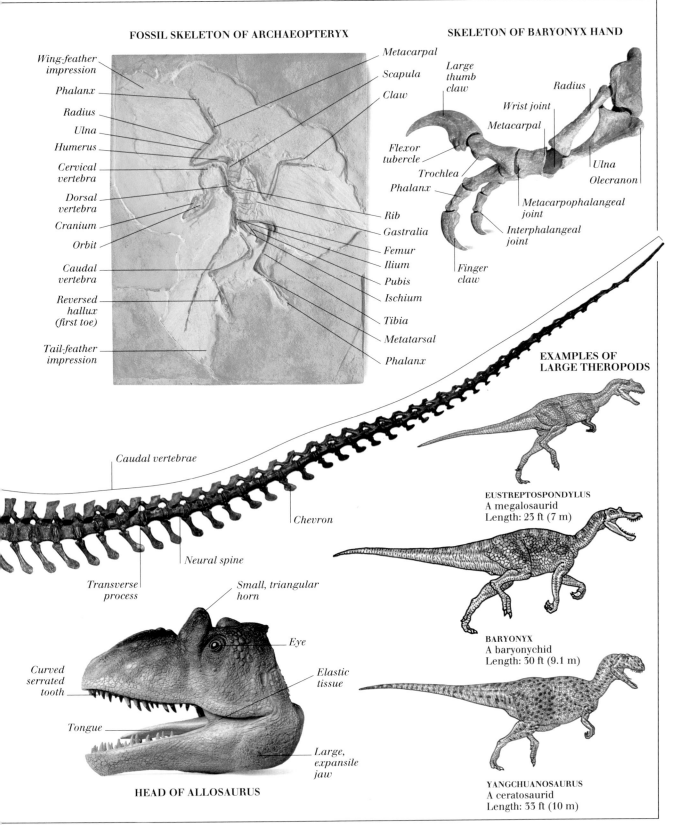

FOSSIL SKELETON OF ARCHAEOPTERYX

Wing-feather impression
Phalanx
Radius
Ulna
Humerus
Cervical vertebra
Dorsal vertebra
Cranium
Orbit
Caudal vertebra
Reversed hallux (first toe)
Tail-feather impression

Metacarpal
Scapula
Claw
Rib
Gastralia
Femur
Ilium
Pubis
Ischium
Tibia
Metatarsal
Phalanx

SKELETON OF BARYONYX HAND

Large thumb claw
Flexor tubercle
Trochlea
Phalanx
Finger claw
Wrist joint
Metacarpal
Radius
Ulna
Olecranon
Metacarpophalangeal joint
Interphalangeal joint

EXAMPLES OF LARGE THEROPODS

Caudal vertebrae
Chevron
Neural spine
Transverse process

EUSTREPTOSPONDYLUS
A megalosaurid
Length: 23 ft (7 m)

BARYONYX
A baryonychid
Length: 30 ft (9.1 m)

YANGCHUANOSAURUS
A ceratosaurid
Length: 33 ft (10 m)

Small, triangular horn
Eye
Curved serrated tooth
Elastic tissue
Tongue
Large, expansile jaw

HEAD OF ALLOSAURUS

Theropods 2

Eye

Toothless beak

EXAMPLES OF ORNITHOMIMOSAURS

DROMICEIOMIMUS
Length: 11 ft 6 in (3.5 m)

GARUDIMIMUS
Length: 11 ft 6 in (3.5 m)

Cervical musculature

Scapula

Trachea

Lung

Rib

Gizzard

Dorsal vertebra

Ovary

Kidney

Ilium

Hip joint

Femur

Shoulder joint

Coracoid

Heart

Posterior brachial muscle

Anterior brachial muscle

Humerus

Liver

Intestine

Pubis

Femoral musculature

Tibia

Anterior crural muscle

Eye

Claw

Anterior antebrachial muscle

Ulna

Posterior antebrachial muscle

Metacarpal

Snout

Short forelimb

Grasping claw

Long shin

Hallux (first toe)

Tail

Ankle

Foot

EXTERNAL FEATURES OF AN EARLY THEROPOD (HERRERASAURUS)

INTERNAL ANATOMY OF FEMALE GALLIMIMUS

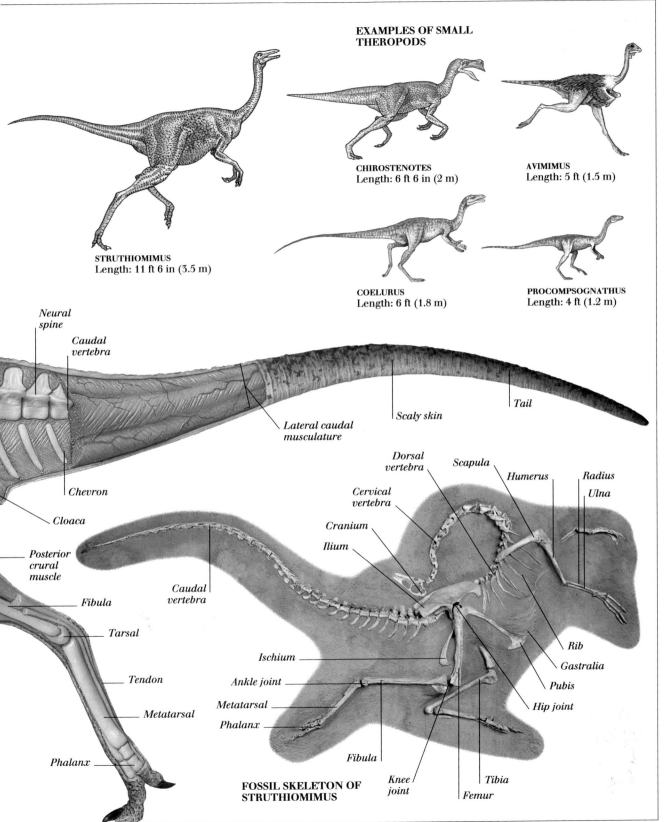

EXAMPLES OF SMALL THEROPODS

CHIROSTENOTES
Length: 6 ft 6 in (2 m)

AVIMIMUS
Length: 5 ft (1.5 m)

STRUTHIOMIMUS
Length: 11 ft 6 in (3.5 m)

COELURUS
Length: 6 ft (1.8 m)

PROCOMPSOGNATHUS
Length: 4 ft (1.2 m)

Neural spine

Caudal vertebra

Tail

Scaly skin

Lateral caudal musculature

Chevron

Cloaca

Dorsal vertebra

Scapula

Humerus

Radius

Ulna

Cervical vertebra

Cranium

Ilium

Posterior crural muscle

Caudal vertebra

Fibula

Tarsal

Rib

Gastralia

Tendon

Ischium

Pubis

Ankle joint

Hip joint

Metatarsal

Metatarsal

Phalanx

Phalanx

Fibula

Tibia

Phalanx

Knee joint

Femur

FOSSIL SKELETON OF STRUTHIOMIMUS

Sauropodomorphs 1

THE SAUROPODOMORPHA ("lizard-feet forms") were herbivorous, usually quadrupedal (four-footed) dinosaurs. A suborder of the Saurischia, they were characterized by small heads, bulky bodies, and long necks and tails. There were two infraorders: prosauropods and sauropods. Prosauropods lived from Late Triassic to Early Jurassic times (225–180 million years ago) and included beasts such as the small *Anchisaurus* and one of the first very large dinosaurs, *Melanosaurus*. By Middle Jurassic times (about 165 million years ago), sauropods had replaced prosauropods and spread worldwide. They included the heaviest and longest land animals ever, such as *Diplodocus* and *Brachiosaurus*. Sauropods persisted to the end of the Cretaceous period (65 million years ago). Many of these dinosaurs moved in herds, protected from predatory theropods by their huge bulk and powerful tails, which they could use to lash out at attackers. Sauropodomorphs were the most common large herbivores until Late Jurassic times (about 145 million years ago), and appear to have survived in southern continents long after they had disappeared from the north.

THECODONTOSAURUS

SKULL AND MANDIBLE OF PLATEOSAURUS

Naris
Antorbital fenestra
Orbit
Mandible
Serrated, leaf-shaped tooth
Infratemporal fenestra
Paroccipital process
Mandibular fenestra

SKELETON OF PLATEOSAURUS

Dorsal vertebrae
Sacral vertebrae
Ilium
Cervical vertebrae
Humerus
Scapula
Shoulder joint
Rib
Hip joint
Ischium
Pubis
Femur
Knee joint
Tail
Curved thumb claw
Elbow joint
Radius
Tibia
Wrist joint
Ulna
Fibula
Metacarpal
Ankle joint
Metatarsals
Cranium
Phalanx
Orbit
Mandible
Phalanges
Naris

THUMB CLAW OF MASSOSPONDYLUS

Top part of claw (sharp point missing)

Curved body of claw

Base of claw

Caudal vertebrae

Neural spine

Chevron

Transverse process

EXAMPLES OF PROSAUROPODS

MASSOSPONDYLUS
A massospondylid
Length: 13 ft (4 m)

LUFENGOSAURUS
A plateosaurid
Length: 20 ft (6.1 m)

RIOJASAURUS
A melanorosaurid
Length: 36 ft (11 m)

MELANOROSAURUS
A melanorosaurid
Length: 40 ft (12.2 m)

EXTERNAL FEATURES OF ANCHISAURUS

Naris

Eye

Leaf-shaped tooth

Long, flexible neck

Shoulder

Forelimb

Elbow

Hand

Large, curved thumb claw

Finger

Toe

Claw

Thigh

Toe

Claw

Forelimb

Hind limb

TOP VIEW OF ANCHISAURUS

Slender snout

Long body

Hip

Scaly skin

Thigh

Tail

Knee

Ankle

Hallux (first toe)

Hind limb

Foot

SIDE VIEW OF ANCHISAURUS

Sauropodomorphs 2

SKULL AND MANDIBLE OF DIPLODOCUS

Orbit
Antorbital fenestra
Cranium
Maxillary fenestra
Maxilla
Sclerotic ring
Peg-shaped tooth
Infratemporal fenestra
Mandible

FOREFOOT OF ELEPHANT

Wrist
Nail

FOREFOOT BONES OF ELEPHANT

Radius
Ulna
Carpals
Metacarpals
Phalanges

COMPARISON OF THE FOREFEET OF AN ELEPHANT AND DIPLODOCUS

FOREFOOT BONES OF DIPLODOCUS

Radius
Ulna
Carpals
Metacarpals
Phalanges

MIDDLE SECTION OF DIPLODOCUS SKELETON

Coracoid
Dorsal vertebra
Scapula
Sacral vertebra
Ilium
Caudal vertebra
Hip joint
Ischium
Femur
Humerus
Rib
Elbow joint
Knee joint
Ankle joint
Ulna
Tibia
Radius
Fibula
Wrist joint
Phalanges
Metacarpals
Caudal musculature

Neural spine
Small intestine
Dorsal vertebra
Ovary
Kidney
Rib
Large intestine
Hip joint
Cecum
Pubis
Femur
Oviduct
Cloaca
Thigh musculature
Posterior crural musculature
Fibula
Anterior crural muscle
Ankle joint
Metatarsal

FOSSIL EGG OF TITANOSAURID

Fossil eggshell fragment

Fossil egg

Fossil eggshell fragment

Outer ear

Naris

Eye

Mouth

Orbit

Antorbital fenestra

Naris

Maxilla

Cranium

Spoon-shaped tooth

Infratemporal fenestra

Mandible

SKULL AND MANDIBLE OF CAMARASAURUS

INTERNAL ANATOMY OF FEMALE BRACHIOSAURUS

Cervical vertebra

Scapula

Trachea

Esophagus

Intercostal muscle

Scapular muscle

Shoulder joint

Lung

Humerus

Gizzard

Anterior brachial muscle

Posterior brachial musculature

Elbow joint

Radius

Ulna

Posterior antebrachial musculature

Wrist joint

Metacarpal

CETIOSAURUS
A cetiosaurid
Length: 59 ft (18 m)

SHUNOSAURUS
A cetiosaurid
Length: 33 ft (10 m)

SALTASAURUS
A titanosaurid
Length: 40 ft (12.2 m)

DIPLODOCUS
A diplodocid
Length: 90 ft (27.4 m)

91

Thyreophorans 1

THYREOPHORANS ("SHIELD BEARERS") were a group of quadrupedal armored dinosaurs. A suborder of the Ornithischia (bird-hipped dinosaurs), they were characterized by rows of bony studs, plates, or spikes along the back, which protected some from predators and may have helped others regulate body temperature. Up to 30ft (9m) long, with a small head and small cheek teeth, Thyreophorans had shorter forelimbs than hind limbs and probably browsed on low-level vegetation. The earliest thyreophorans were small and lived in Early Jurassic times (about 200 million years ago) in Europe, North America, and China. Stegosaurs, such as *Stegosaurus* and *Kentrosaurus*, replaced these older forms. The earliest stegosaur remains come from England and China. Several genera of stegosaurs survived into the Early Cretaceous period (146–100 million years ago), but only in India did they persist into Late Cretaceous times (97–65 million years ago). Ankylosaurs, with their toothless beaks and cheek teeth adapted for cropping vegetation, appeared later than stegosaurs. They originated in the Late Jurassic period (155 million years ago) and in North America survived until the extinction of the dinosaurs, 65 million years ago.

TUOJIANGOSAURUS
A stegosaurid
Length: 23 ft (7 m)

Dorsal plate

Caudal plate

Caudal spike

Small head

Beak

Cervical plate

Scaly skin

Hind foot

TOP VIEW OF STEGOSAURUS

Dorsal plate

EXTERNAL FEATURES OF STEGOSAURUS

Scaly skin

Cervical plate

Outer ear

Eye

Naris

Beak

Cheek

Neck

Shoulder

Short forelimb

Elbow

Hip

Thigh

Knee

Long hind limb

Wrist

Nail

Forefoot

Ankle

Hind foot

Nail

SIDE VIEW OF STEGOSAURUS

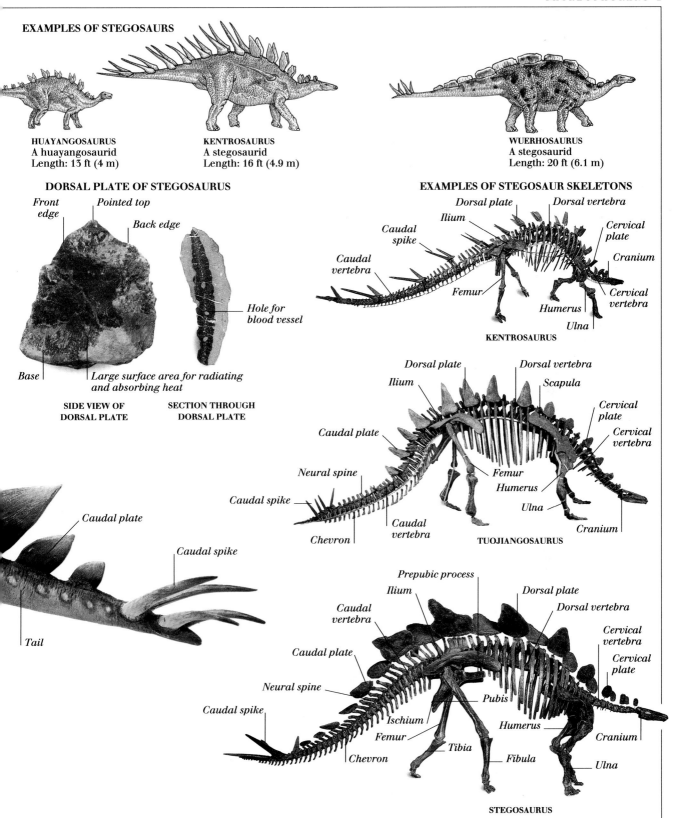

EXAMPLES OF STEGOSAURS

HUAYANGOSAURUS
A huayangosaurid
Length: 13 ft (4 m)

KENTROSAURUS
A stegosaurid
Length: 16 ft (4.9 m)

WUERHOSAURUS
A stegosaurid
Length: 20 ft (6.1 m)

DORSAL PLATE OF STEGOSAURUS

Front edge
Pointed top
Back edge
Hole for blood vessel
Base
Large surface area for radiating and absorbing heat

SIDE VIEW OF DORSAL PLATE

SECTION THROUGH DORSAL PLATE

EXAMPLES OF STEGOSAUR SKELETONS

Dorsal plate
Ilium
Dorsal vertebra
Caudal spike
Cervical plate
Caudal vertebra
Cranium
Femur
Cervical vertebra
Humerus
Ulna

KENTROSAURUS

Dorsal plate
Ilium
Dorsal vertebra
Scapula
Caudal plate
Cervical plate
Cervical vertebra
Neural spine
Femur
Humerus
Caudal spike
Ulna
Chevron
Caudal vertebra
Cranium

TUOJIANGOSAURUS

Caudal plate
Caudal spike
Tail

Prepubic process
Ilium
Dorsal plate
Caudal vertebra
Dorsal vertebra
Caudal plate
Cervical vertebra
Cervical plate
Neural spine
Pubis
Caudal spike
Ischium
Humerus
Femur
Cranium
Tibia
Fibula
Chevron
Ulna

STEGOSAURUS

93

Thyreophorans 2

EXAMPLES OF ANKYLOSAUR SKULLS

Maxilla

Orbit

Posterolateral horn

Naris

Cranium

Beak

Tooth

Mandible

Jugal plate

SKULL AND MANDIBLE OF EUOPLOCEPHALUS

Posterolateral horn

Nasal bone

Maxilla

Cranium

Orbit

Naris

Beak

Tooth

Mandible

SKULL AND MANDIBLE OF ANKYLOSAURUS

Orbit

Beak

Nasal bone

Naris

Cranium

Infratemporal fenestra

Mandible

SKULL AND MANDIBLE OF PANOPLOSAURUS

Dorsal vertebra

Rib

Small intestine

Gizzard

Iliotibial muscle

Ilium

Reproductive canal

Ischium

Scapula

Lung

Shoulder spike

Coracoid

Cervical musculature

Head horn

Humerus

Radius

Wrist joint

Heart

Liver

Iliotibial muscle

Femur

Knee joint

Metacarpal

Fibula

Gastrocnemius muscle

Toothless beak

Large intestine

Digital extensor muscle

Ankle joint

Ventral antebrachial muscle

Ulna

Elbow joint

Metatarsal

INTERNAL ANATOMY OF FEMALE EUOPLOCEPHALUS

94

EXTERNAL FEATURES OF EDMONTONIA

EXAMPLES OF ANKYLOSAURS

Hind limb

Flank spike

Dorsal scute

Dermal armor

Scaly skin

Nuchal ring

Shoulder spike

Broad, flat snout

Ankle

Elbow

Forelimb

Caudal vertebra

Neural spine

Ureter

Forefoot

Blunt nail

Naris

Terminal plate

Chevron

Cloaca

Lateral plate

Lateral caudal musculature

Ossified caudal vertebra

FOSSIL OF ANKYLOSAURUS TAIL CLUB

Tail club

PINACOSAURUS
An ankylosaurid
Length: 16 ft 6 in (5 m)

MINMI
A nodosaurid
Length: 8 ft (2.4 m)

POLACANTHUS
A nodosaurid
Length: 13 ft (4 m)

Ornithopods 1

ORNITHOPODS ("BIRD FEET") were a group of ornithischian ("bird-hipped") dinosaurs. These bipedal and quadrupedal herbivores had a horny beak, plant-cutting or grinding cheek teeth, and a pelvic and tail region stiffened by bony tendons. They evolved teeth and jaws adapted to pulping vegetation and flourished from the Middle Jurassic to the Late Cretaceous period (165–65 million years ago) in North America,

IGUANODON TOOTH

Europe, Africa, China, Australia, and Antarctica. Some ornithopods were no larger than a dog, while others were immense creatures up to 49 ft (15 m) long. Iguanodonts, an ornithopod group, had a broad, toothless beak at the end of a long snout, large jaws with long rows of ridged, closely packed teeth for grinding vegetation, a bulky body, and a heavy tail. *Iguanodon* and some other iguanodonts had large thumb-spikes that were strong enough to stab attackers. Another group, the hadrosaurs, such as *Gryposaurus* and *Hadrosaurus*, lived in Late Cretaceous times (97–65 million years ago) and with their broad beaks are sometimes known as "duckbills." They were characterized by their deep skulls and closely packed rows of teeth, while some, such as *Corythosaurus* and *Lambeosaurus*, had tall, hollow, bony head crests.

SKELETON OF IGUANODON

SKULL AND MANDIBLE OF YOUNG IGUANODON

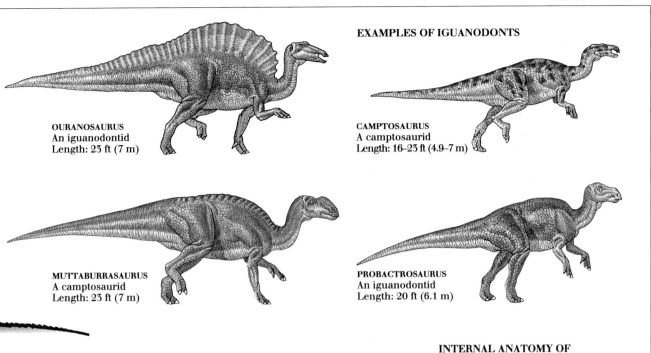

EXAMPLES OF IGUANODONTS

OURANOSAURUS
An iguanodontid
Length: 23 ft (7 m)

CAMPTOSAURUS
A camptosaurid
Length: 16–23 ft (4.9–7 m)

MUTTABURRASAURUS
A camptosaurid
Length: 23 ft (7 m)

PROBACTROSAURUS
An iguanodontid
Length: 20 ft (6.1 m)

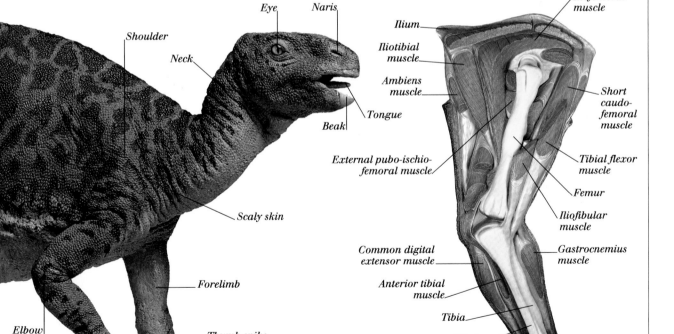

EXTERNAL FEATURES OF IGUANODON

Eye

Naris

Shoulder

Neck

Tongue

Beak

Scaly skin

Forelimb

Elbow

Wrist

Hand

Finger

Thumb-spike

Hooflike nail

INTERNAL ANATOMY OF HIND LEG OF IGUANODON

Iliofemoral muscle

Ilium

Iliotibial muscle

Ambiens muscle

Short caudofemoral muscle

External pubo-ischio-femoral muscle

Tibial flexor muscle

Femur

Iliofibular muscle

Common digital extensor muscle

Gastrocnemius muscle

Anterior tibial muscle

Tibia

Fibula

Tarsal

Metatarsal

Toe

Hooflike nail

Ornithopods 2

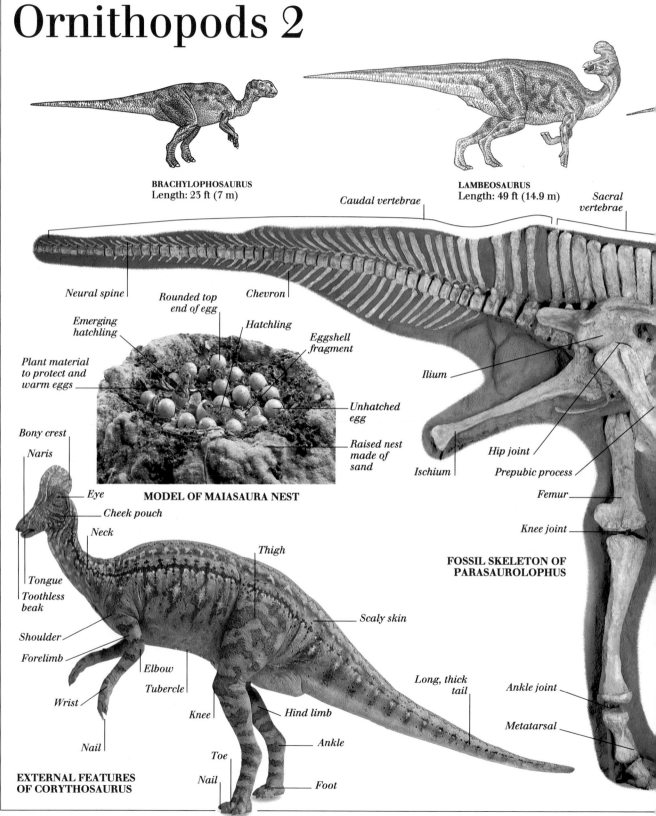

BRACHYLOPHOSAURUS
Length: 23 ft (7 m)

LAMBEOSAURUS
Length: 49 ft (14.9 m)

Caudal vertebrae

Sacral vertebrae

Neural spine

Chevron

Rounded top end of egg

Hatchling

Eggshell fragment

Emerging hatchling

Plant material to protect and warm eggs

Unhatched egg

Raised nest made of sand

Ilium

Hip joint

Ischium

Prepubic process

Femur

Knee joint

MODEL OF MAIASAURA NEST

Bony crest

Naris

Eye

Cheek pouch

Neck

Thigh

Tongue

Toothless beak

Scaly skin

FOSSIL SKELETON OF PARASAUROLOPHUS

Shoulder

Forelimb

Elbow

Tubercle

Knee

Hind limb

Long, thick tail

Ankle joint

Metatarsal

Wrist

Nail

Ankle

Toe

EXTERNAL FEATURES OF CORYTHOSAURUS

Nail

Foot

EXAMPLES OF HADROSAURS

HYPACROSAURUS
Length: 30 ft (9.1 m)

HADROSAURUS
Length: 26–33 ft (7.9–10 m)

GRYPOSAURUS
Length: 26–33 ft (7.9–10 m)

Dorsal vertebrae

Bony crest

Air passage

Cranium

Infratemporal fenestra

Orbit

Cervical vertebrae

Mandible

Naris

Orbit

Infratemporal fenestra

Air passage

Naris

Mandible

Tooth

SKULL AND MANDIBLE OF JUVENILE LAMBEOSAURUS

Scapula

Shoulder joint

Tibia

Rib

Fibula

Humerus

Elbow joint

Ulna

Radius

Wrist joint

Phalanges

Metacarpal

Phalanges

Sclerotic ring

Cranium

Bony crest

Orbit

Naris

Infratemporal fenestra

Mandible

Premaxilla

SKULL AND MANDIBLE OF ADULT LAMBEOSAURUS

Marginocephalians 1

Thick, high-domed cranium
Supraorbital ridge
Orbit
Naris
Mandible
Neural spine
Cervical rib
Humerus
Ulna
Radius
Wrist joint
Metacarpal
Phalanx
Prepubis
Ilium
Ischium
Metatarsals
Phalanges

HEAD-BUTTING PRENOCEPHALES

MARGINOCEPHALIA ("margined heads") were a group of bipedal and quadrupedal ornithischian dinosaurs with a narrow shelf or deep, bony frill at the back of the skull. Marginocephalians were probably descended from the same ancestor as the ornithopods and lived in what are now North America, Africa, Asia, and Europe during the Cretaceous period (146–65 million years ago). They were divided into two infraorders: Pachycephalosauria ("thick-headed lizards"), such as *Pachycephalosaurus* and *Stegoceras*, and Ceratopsia ("horned faces"), such as *Triceratops* and *Psittacosaurus*. The thick skulls of Pachycephalosauria protected their brains during head-butting contests fought to win territory and mates; their hips and spines were also strengthened to withstand the shock. The bony frill of Ceratopsia would have added to their frightening appearance when charging; the neck was strengthened for impact and to support the huge head, with its snipping beak and powerful slicing toothed jaws. A charging ceratops would have been a formidable opponent for even the largest predators. Ceratopsia were among the most abundant herbivorous dinosaurs of the Late Cretaceous period (97–65 million years ago).

EXAMPLES OF SKULLS OF PACHYCEPHALOSAURS

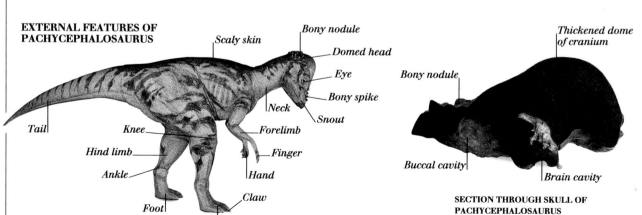

Orbit
Thickened dome of cranium
Maxilla
Bony ridge
Tooth
Mandible
SKULL AND MANDIBLE OF STEGOCERAS

Orbit
Thickened dome of cranium
Maxilla
Bony nodule
SKULL OF PRENOCEPHALE

Thickened dome of cranium
Bony spike
Maxilla
Orbit
Bony nodule
SKULL OF PACHYCEPHALOSAURUS

EXTERNAL FEATURES OF PACHYCEPHALOSAURUS

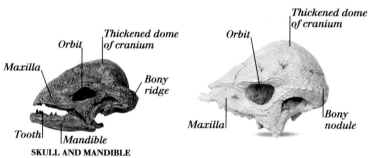

Bony nodule
Scaly skin
Domed head
Eye
Bony spike
Neck
Snout
Tail
Knee
Forelimb
Hind limb
Finger
Ankle
Hand
Claw
Foot
Toe

Thickened dome of cranium
Bony nodule
Buccal cavity
Brain cavity
SECTION THROUGH SKULL OF PACHYCEPHALOSAURUS

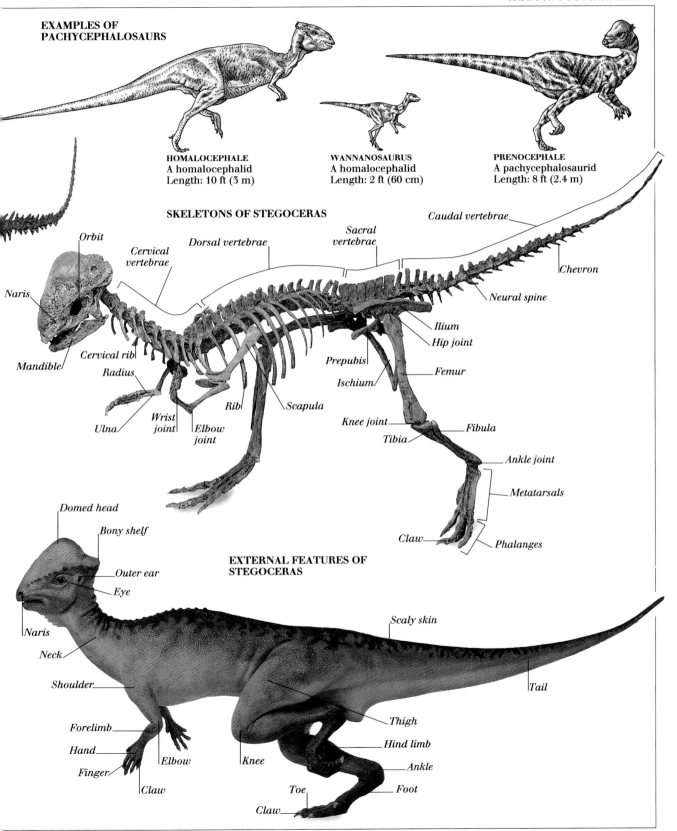

EXAMPLES OF PACHYCEPHALOSAURS

HOMALOCEPHALE
A homalocephalid
Length: 10 ft (3 m)

WANNANOSAURUS
A homalocephalid
Length: 2 ft (60 cm)

PRENOCEPHALE
A pachycephalosaurid
Length: 8 ft (2.4 m)

SKELETONS OF STEGOCERAS

Orbit

Cervical vertebrae

Dorsal vertebrae

Sacral vertebrae

Caudal vertebrae

Chevron

Neural spine

Naris

Ilium

Hip joint

Mandible

Cervical rib

Radius

Prepubis

Femur

Ischium

Ulna

Wrist joint

Elbow joint

Rib

Scapula

Knee joint

Fibula

Tibia

Ankle joint

Metatarsals

Claw

Phalanges

EXTERNAL FEATURES OF STEGOCERAS

Domed head

Bony shelf

Outer ear

Eye

Naris

Neck

Scaly skin

Tail

Shoulder

Forelimb

Hand

Finger

Elbow

Claw

Knee

Thigh

Hind limb

Ankle

Toe

Foot

Claw

Marginocephalians 2

SKULL AND MANDIBLE OF STYRACOSAURUS

Parietal fenestra

Epoccipital bone

Parietosquamosal frill

Nose-horn core

Supraorbital ridge

Naris

Orbit

Cranium

Mandible

EXTERNAL FEATURES OF TRICERATOPS

Brow horn

Parietosquamosal frill

Nose horn

Epoccipital bone

Thick, scaly skin

Thigh

Tail

Ankle

Hind limb

Nail

Elbow

Forelimb

Wrist

Eye

Naris

Toothless beak

SKULL AND MANDIBLE OF PROTOCERATOPS

Cranium

Postorbital bone

Nasal bone

Orbit

Lacrimal bone

Naris

Beak

Rostral bone

Predentary bone

Dentary bone

Tooth

Mandible

Parietosquamosal frill

Parietal fenestra

Infratemporal fenestra

Jugal bone

Surangular bone

Angular bone

SKELETON OF TRICERATOPS

Parietosquamosal frill

Ilium

Hip joint

Prepubis

Dorsal vertebrae

Caudal vertebra

Chevron

Neural spine

Ischium

Femur

Knee joint

Fibula

Tibia

Ankle joint

Metatarsals

Phalanges

Rib

Scapula

Humerus

Elbow joint

Ulna

Sternal bone

Coracoid

Shoulder joint

Radius

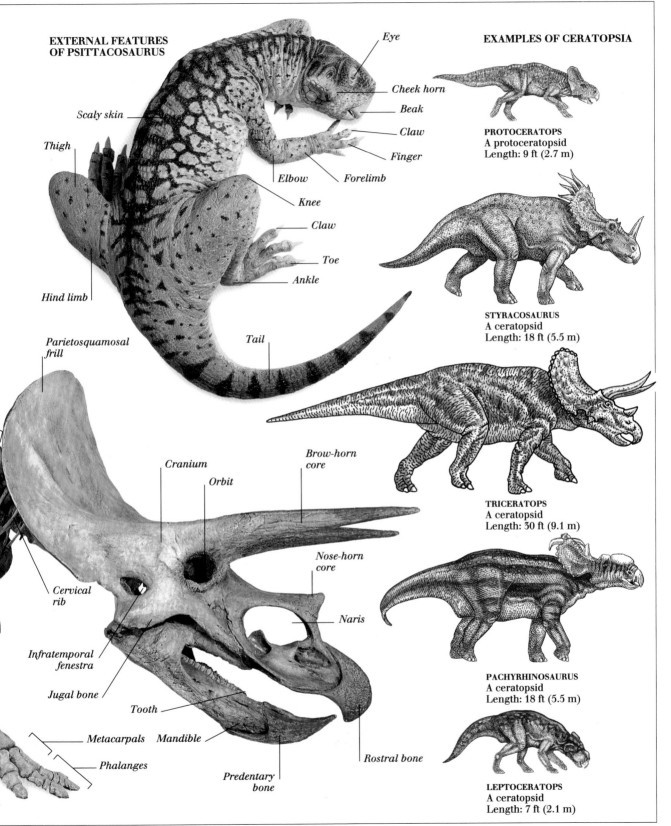

**EXTERNAL FEATURES
OF PSITTACOSAURUS**

Eye

Scaly skin

Cheek horn

Beak

Thigh

Claw

Finger

Elbow

Forelimb

Knee

Claw

Toe

Ankle

Hind limb

Parietosquamosal
frill

Tail

Cranium

Orbit

Brow-horn
core

Nose-horn
core

Cervical
rib

Naris

Infratemporal
fenestra

Jugal bone

Tooth

Metacarpals

Mandible

Phalanges

Predentary
bone

Rostral bone

EXAMPLES OF CERATOPSIA

PROTOCERATOPS
A protoceratopsid
Length: 9 ft (2.7 m)

STYRACOSAURUS
A ceratopsid
Length: 18 ft (5.5 m)

TRICERATOPS
A ceratopsid
Length: 30 ft (9.1 m)

PACHYRHINOSAURUS
A ceratopsid
Length: 18 ft (5.5 m)

LEPTOCERATOPS
A ceratopsid
Length: 7 ft (2.1 m)

Mammals 1

**TETRALOPHODON
CHEEK TEETH**

SINCE THE EXTINCTION of the dinosaurs 65 million years ago, mammals have been the dominant vertebrates on Earth and include terrestrial, aerial, and aquatic forms. Having developed from the reptilian Therapsids, the first true mammals—small, nocturnal, rodentlike creatures, such as *Megazostrodon*—appeared over 200 million years ago during the Triassic period (245–208 million years ago). Mammals had several features that improved on those of their reptilian ancestors: an efficient four-chambered heart allowed these warm-blooded animals to sustain high levels of activity; a covering of hair helped them maintain a constant body temperature; an improved limb structure gave them more efficient locomotion; and the birth of live young and the immediate supply of food from the mother's milk aided their rapid growth. Since the end of the Mesozoic era (65 million years ago), the number of different mammal orders and the abundance of species in each order have varied dramatically. For example, the Perissodactyla (the order that includes *Coelodonta* and modern horses) was the most common group during the Early Tertiary period (about 54 million years ago). Today, the mammalian orders with the most populous species are the Rodentia (rats and mice), the Carnivora (bears, cats, and dogs), and the Artiodactyla (cattle, deer, and pigs), while the Proboscidea order, which included many genera, such as *Phiomia, Moeritherium, Tetralophodon,* and *Mammuthus,* now has only one member: the modern elephant. In Australia and South America, millions of years of continental isolation led to the development of the marsupials, a group of mammals distinct from the placentals (see p. 74) that existed elsewhere.

Long tail aids
balance

Insulating
hair

Neural
spine

Scapula

Cervical
vertebra

Humerus

Nasal horn

Naris

Orbit

Predentary
bone

Mandible

Radius

Ulna

Chisel-edged
molar

Metacarpal

Phalanx

UPPER JAWBONE (MAXILLA) OF A HORSE

Molars

Premolars

HOOFBONE (THIRD PHALANX) OF A HORSE

Articular surface

Tendon insertion

Cranium

Naris

Predentary bone

Molar tooth

SKULL AND MANDIBLE OF A MOERITHERIUM

Nasal tusk

Molar tooth

Shovel-shaped tusk

SKULL AND MANDIBLE OF A PHIOMIA

Trunk

Thick hide

Short tusk used for rooting up plants

MODEL OF A PHIOMIA

Dorsal vertebra

Ilium

Ball and socket joint

Rib

Pubis

Caudal vertebra

Femur

Tibia

Fibula

Metatarsal

Phalanx

SKELETON OF AN ARSINOITHERIUM

Cranium

Teeth

Elongated digit

Mandible

Humerus

Hind limb bone

FOSSIL SKELETON OF A BAT

Mammals 2

LOWER JAW OF A BEAR

Articulation
with skull

Large
canine

Diastema

Low cusp

Molar

Premolar

SKELETON OF A TOXODON

Scapula

Neural
spine

Cervical
vertebra

Cranium

Zygomatic
arch

Orbit

Coronoid
process

Maxilla

Nasal bone

Incisor

Canine

Mandible

Molar

Humerus

Radius

Ulna

Large
breastbone

Metacarpals

SKULL OF AN OPOSSUM

Orbit

Cranium

Naris

Occipital
region

Canine

Infraorbital
foramen

Molar

**FOSSIL SKULL OF
AN HYAENODON**

Orbit

Sagittal crest

Cranium

Naris

Canine

Neck
insertion

Infraorbital
foramen

Mandible

Molar

**LOWER JAW OF AN
AUSTRALOPITHECUS**

Expanded
occlusal
surface

Premolar

Molar

SKULL OF A SMILODON

Orbit

Muscle scar

Naris

Sagittal crest

Infraorbital
foramen

Occipital
condyle

Canine

Dentary
bone

Slicing
tooth

Zygomatic
arch

Ilium

Femur

Rib

Knee
joint

Tibia

Fibula

Metatarsals

Phalanx

RECONSTRUCTION OF A MAMMOTH

Thick,
insulating
coat

Ivory tusk

Woolly
underhair

Hairy trunk

The first hominids

MODERN HUMANS BELONG TO THE MAMMALIAN order of primates (see pp. 202–203), which originated about 55 million years ago; they comprise the only extant hominid species. The earliest hominid was *Australopithecus* ("southern ape"), a small-brained intermediate between apes and humans that was capable of standing and walking upright. *Homo habilis*, the first known human appeared at least 2 million years ago. This larger-brained "handy man" began making tools for hunting. *Homo erectus* first appeared in Africa about 1.8 million years ago and spread into Asia about 800,000 years later. Smaller toothed than *Homo habilis*, it developed fire as a tool, which enabled it to cook food. Neanderthals, a near relative of modern humans, originated about 200,000 years ago, and *Homo sapiens* (modern humans) appeared in Africa about 100,000 years later. The two coexisted for thousands of years, but by 30,000 years ago, *Homo sapiens* had become dominant and the Neanderthals had died out. Classification of *Homo sapiens* in relation to its ancestors is enormously problematic: modern humans must be classified not only by bone structure, but also by specific behavior—the ability to plan future action; to follow traditions; and to use symbolic communication, including complex language and the ability to use and recognize symbols.

JAWBONE OF AUSTRALOPITHECUS (SOUTHERN APE)

Larger jawbone than modern human

Large back tooth

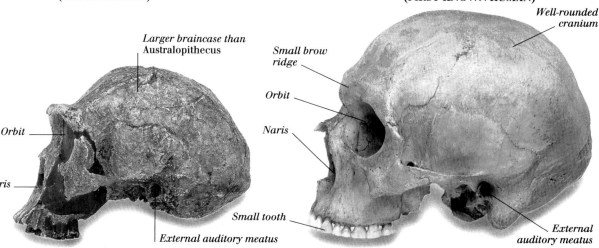

Jutting brow ridge

Cranium

Orbit

Naris

Jutting jawbone

SKULL OF AUSTRALOPITHECUS (SOUTHERN APE)

Orbit

Naris

SKULL OF HOMO HABILIS (FIRST KNOWN HUMAN)

Larger braincase than Australopithecus

Orbit

Naris

External auditory meatus

SKULL OF HOMO ERECTUS (UPRIGHT MAN)

Well-rounded cranium

Small brow ridge

Orbit

Naris

Small tooth

External auditory meatus

SKULL OF HOMO SAPIENS (MODERN HUMAN)

FLINT TOOL MADE ABOUT 250,000 YEARS AGO

Point

Sharp edge used to cut meat

Flint may have been carved by Homo erectus

FLINT HANDAXE

FLINT FLAKE

Hammer head used to detach chips of flint

Head used to mine flint

Handle

Handle

ANTLER HAMMER

RED DEER ANTLER HAMMER

Handle

FARMING AXE

EXAMPLES OF TOOLS USED BY HOMO SAPIENS

Axe used to clear land

Leather binding

FIRE-MAKING TOOLS

Wooden mouthpiece held drill securely

WOODEN MOUTHPIECE

Wooden drill turned in drill hole to create spark

Bone

Leather bow kept drill upright

BOW DRILL

DRY STRAW

Drill hole

WOODEN HEARTH

EXAMPLES OF PREHISTORIC FOODS

MINT

WHEAT GRAINS

SALMON

SPEAR AND ARROW HEADS

Antler

HARPOON POINT

Twine binding

FISHING TACKLE

Wooden point hardened by fire

WOODEN ARROW

Flint glued into groove cut in shaft

FLINT ARROW

PLANTS

Plant varieties

THE ARE MORE THAN 300,000 SPECIES of plants. They
show a wide diversity of forms, ranging from delicate liverworts, adapted for life
in a damp habitat, to cacti, capable of surviving in the desert. The plant kingdom includes
herbaceous plants, such as corn, which completes its life cycle in one year, to the giant redwood tree, which
can live for thousands of years. This diversity reflects the adaptations of plants to survive in a wide range of
habitats. This is seen most clearly in the flowering plants (phylum Angiospermophyta), which are the most
numerous, with over 250,000 species. They are also the most widespread, being found from the tropics to the
arctic. Despite their diversity, plants share certain characteristics. Typically, plants are green, and make their
food by photosynthesis. Most plants live in or on a substrate, such as soil, and do not actively move. Algae
(kingdom Protista) and fungi (kingdom Fungi) have some plantlike characteristics and are
often studied alongside plants, although they are not true plants.

FLOWERING PLANT
Bromeliad
(*Acanthostachys strobilacea*)

Leaf

GREEN ALGA
Micrograph of desmid
(*Micrasterias sp.*)

FERN
Tree fern
(*Dicksonia antarctica*)

Pyrenoid
(*small protein
body*)

Chloroplast

Sinus
(*division between
two halves of cell*)

Cell wall

Rachis
(*main axis
of pinnate leaf*)

BRYOPHYTE
Moss
(*Bryum sp.*)

Seta
(*stalk*)

Immature capsule

Petiole
(*leaf stalk*)

Ramentum
(*brown scale*)

Sporophyte
(*spore-
producing
plant*)

Capsule
(*site of spore
production*)

*Base of dead
frond (leaf)*

Trunk

"Leaf"

Gametophyte
(*gamete-producing
plant*)

*Adventitious
root*

*Epiphytic
fern growing
at base*

FLOWERING PLANT
Succulent
(*Kedrostis africana*)

*Petiole
(leaf stalk)*

Leaf

Spine *Flower*

*Bract
(leaf-like structure)*

Inflorescence

FLOWERING PLANT
Micrograph of cross section
through leaf of marram grass
(*Ammophila arenaria*)

*Sclerenchyma
(strengthening
tissue)*

*Cuticle
(waterproof
covering)*

Stem

Xylem

Phloem

*Vascular
tissue*

*Stiff trichome
(hair)*

*Interlocked
trichomes (hairs)*

*Epidermis
(outer layer
of cells)*

*Caudex
(swollen
stem
base)*

*Hinge cells
(cause curling of leaf to
reduce water loss)*

*Mesophyll
(photosynthetic
tissue)*

Stem

FLOWERING PLANT
Couch grass
(*Agropyron repens*)

Root

*Caryopsis
(type of
dry fruit)*

FLOWERING PLANT
Pitcher plant
(*Sarracenia purpurea*)

Sepal

*Fruit
surrounded
by floral parts*

*Pinna
(leaflet)*

*Rachis
(main axis of
grass inflorescence)*

*Umbrella
of style*

*Pitcher (leaf
modified to trap
insects)*

Frond (leaf)

*Pedicel
(flower
stalk)*

Node

Hood

*Downward-pointing
hair (encourages
insect prey into
pitcher)*

*Midrib of
pinna (leaflet)*

Wing

*Lamina
(blade)*

*Round, hollow
stem*

*Sheathing
leaf base*

*Adventitious
root*

*Immature
pitcher*

113

Fungi and lichens

FUNGI WERE ONCE THOUGHT OF AS PLANTS but are now classified as a separate kingdom. This kingdom includes not only the familiar mushrooms, puffballs, stinkhorns, and molds, but also yeasts, smuts, rusts, and lichens. Most fungi are multicellular, consisting of a mass of thread-like hyphae that together form a mycelium. However, the simpler fungi, like yeasts, are microscopic, single-celled organisms. Typically, fungi reproduce by means of spores. Most fungi feed on dead or decaying matter or on living organisms. A few fungi obtain their food from plants or algae, with which they have a symbiotic (mutually advantageous) relationship. Lichens are a symbiotic partnership between algae and fungi. Of the six types of lichens the three most common are crustose (flat and crusty), foliose (leafy), and fruticose (shrub-like). Some lichens (such as *Cladonia floerkeana*) are a combination of types. Lichens reproduce by means of spores or soredia (powdery vegetative fragments).

Emerging sporophore (spore-bearing structure)

Pileus (cap) continuous with stipe (stalk)

Bark of dead beech tree

Inrolled margin of pileus (cap)

Gill (site of spore production)

Sporophore (spore-bearing structure)

Stipe (stalk)

Hyphae (fungal filaments)

OYSTER FUNGUS
(*Pleurotus pulmonarius*)

EXAMPLES OF LICHENS

Secondary fruticose thallus

Branched, hollow stem

Apothecium (spore-producing body)

FRUTICOSE
Cladonia portentosa

Soredia (powdery vegetative fragments) produced at end of lobe

Tree bark

Foliose thallus

FOLIOSE
Hypogymnia physodes

Soredia (powdery vegetative fragments) released onto surface of squamulose thallus

Apothecium (spore-producing body)

Basal scale of primary squamulose thallus

Moss

Podetium (granular stalk) of secondary fruticose thallus

SQUAMULOSE (SCALY) AND FRUTICOSE THALLUS
Cladonia floerkeana

Gleba (spore-producing tissue found in this type of fungus)

Sporophore (spore-bearing structure)

Porous stipe (stalk)

Volva (remains of universal veil)

STINKHORN
(*Phallus impudicus*)

Toothed branchlet

Branch

Sporophore (spore-bearing structure)

Stipe (stalk)

RAMARIA FORMOSA

SECTION THROUGH FOLIOSE LICHEN SHOWING REPRODUCTION BY SOREDIA

Soredium (powdery vegetative fragment involved in propagation) released from lichen

Algal cell

Fungal hypha

Upper cortex

Algal layer

Medulla of fungal hyphae (mycelium)

Lower cortex

Rhizine (bundle of absorptive hyphae)

Soralium (pore in upper surface of thallus)

Upper surface of thallus

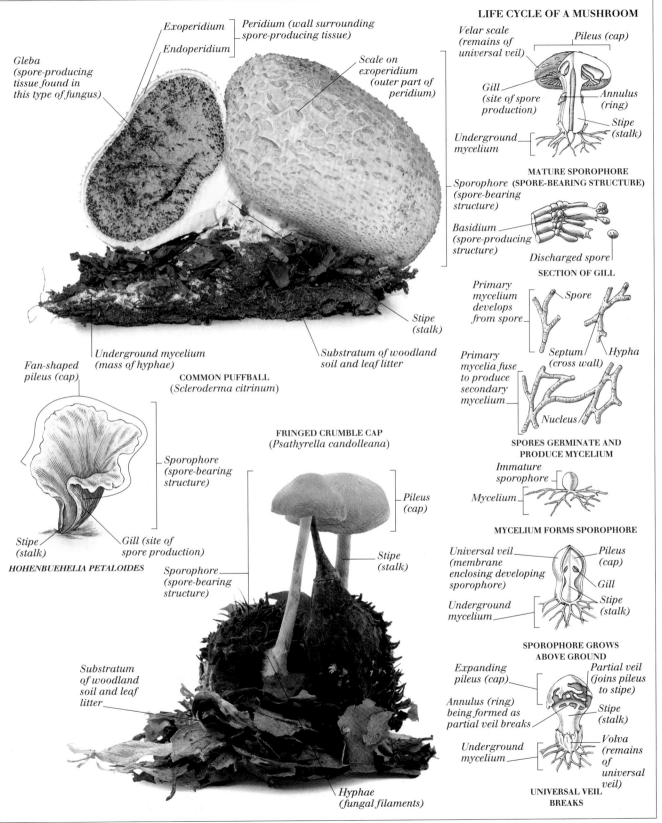

Gleba (spore-producing tissue found in this type of fungus)

Exoperidium

Endoperidium

Peridium (wall surrounding spore-producing tissue)

Scale on exoperidium (outer part of peridium)

Stipe (stalk)

Underground mycelium (mass of hyphae)

Substratum of woodland soil and leaf litter

COMMON PUFFBALL (Scleroderma citrinum)

Fan-shaped pileus (cap)

Sporophore (spore-bearing structure)

Stipe (stalk)

Gill (site of spore production)

HOHENBUEHELIA PETALOIDES

FRINGED CRUMBLE CAP (Psathyrella candolleana)

Sporophore (spore-bearing structure)

Pileus (cap)

Stipe (stalk)

Substratum of woodland soil and leaf litter

Hyphae (fungal filaments)

LIFE CYCLE OF A MUSHROOM

Velar scale (remains of universal veil)

Pileus (cap)

Gill (site of spore production)

Annulus (ring)

Stipe (stalk)

Underground mycelium

MATURE SPOROPHORE (SPORE-BEARING STRUCTURE)

Sporophore (spore-bearing structure)

Basidium (spore-producing structure)

Discharged spore

SECTION OF GILL

Primary mycelium develops from spore

Spore

Septum (cross wall)

Hypha

Primary mycelia fuse to produce secondary mycelium

Nucleus

SPORES GERMINATE AND PRODUCE MYCELIUM

Immature sporophore

Mycelium

MYCELIUM FORMS SPOROPHORE

Universal veil (membrane enclosing developing sporophore)

Pileus (cap)

Gill

Underground mycelium

Stipe (stalk)

SPOROPHORE GROWS ABOVE GROUND

Expanding pileus (cap)

Partial veil (joins pileus to stipe)

Annulus (ring) being formed as partial veil breaks

Stipe (stalk)

Underground mycelium

Volva (remains of universal veil)

UNIVERSAL VEIL BREAKS

115

Algae and seaweed

ALGAE ARE NOT TRUE PLANTS. They form a diverse group of plantlike organisms that belong to the kingdom Protista. Like plants, algae possess the green pigment chlorophyll and make their own food by photosynthesis (see pp. 138-139). Many algae also possess other pigments by which they can be classified. For example, the brown pigment fucoxanthin is found in brown algae. Some of the ten phyla of algae are exclusively unicellular (single-celled); others also contain aggregates of cells in filaments or colonies. Three phyla—the Chlorophyta (green algae), Rhodophyta (red algae), and Phaeophyta (brown algae)—contain larger, multicellular, thalloid (flat), marine organisms commonly known as seaweed.

Most algae can reproduce sexually. For example, in brown seaweed *Fucus vesiculosus*, gametes (sex cells) are produced in conceptacles (chambers) in the receptacles (fertile tips of fronds); after their release into the sea, antherozoids (male gametes) and oospheres (female gametes) fuse. The resulting zygote settles on a rock and develops into a new seaweed.

BROWN SEAWEED
Channeled wrack
(*Pelvetia canaliculata*)

Thallus (plant body)

Receptacle (fertile tip of frond)

Apical notch

Margin of lamina (blade) rolled inwards to form channel

Hapteron (holdfast)

BROWN SEAWEED
Spiral wrack
(*Fucus spiralis*)

Apical notch

Conceptacle (chamber)

Receptacle (fertile tip of frond)

Lamina (blade)

Smooth margin

Midrib

Thallus (plant body)

Hapteron (holdfast)

EXAMPLES OF ALGAE

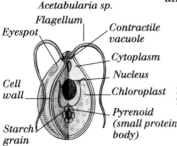

Cap

Reproductive chamber

Sterile whorl

Cell wall

Stalk

Rhizoid

GREEN ALGA
Acetabularia sp.

Flagellum

Eyespot

Contractile vacuole

Cytoplasm

Nucleus

Cell wall

Chloroplast

Pyrenoid (small protein body)

Starch grain

GREEN ALGA
Chlamydomonas sp.

Coenobium (colony of cells)

Daughter coenobium

Girdle

Gelatinous sheath

Nucleus

Biflagellate cell

GREEN ALGA
Volvox sp.

Spine

Cytoplasm

Vacuole

Plastid (photosynthetic organelle)

Nucleus

DIATOM
Thalassiosira sp.

Apical notch

Receptacle (fertile tip of frond)

Conceptacle (chamber) containing reproductive structures

Lamina (blade)

Midrib

RECEPTACLE
Spiral wrack
(*Fucus spiralis*)

BROWN SEAWEED
Oarweed
(*Laminaria digitata*)

Thallus (plant body)

Lamina (blade) palmately divided

GREEN SEAWEED
Enteromorpha linza

Crinkled margin

Thallus
(plant
body)

Unbranched,
spirally twisted
frond

Small hapteron
(holdfast) attaching
seaweed to mussel

RED SEAWEED
Corallina officinalis

Branch

Male
receptacle

Branched,
hard thallus
(plant body)

Hapteron
(holdfast)

Main
stem

LIFE CYCLE OF BROWN SEAWEED
Bladder wrack
(*Fucus vesiculosus*)

Female
receptacle

Air bladder

Lamina
(blade)

Hapteron
(holdfast)

Stipe
(stalk)

MALE AND FEMALE SEAWEEDS

Male
receptacle

Female
receptacle

Conceptacle

Ostiole
(opening to
conceptacle)

MALE AND FEMALE RECEPTACLES

Paraphysis
(sterile hair)

Ostiole
(opening to
conceptacle)

Antheridium
(male sex
organ)

Oogonium
(female sex organ)

**SECTIONS THROUGH MALE AND FEMALE
CONCEPTACLES**

Antherozoid
(male gamete)

Oogonium

Antheridium
(male sex organ)

Oosphere
(female
gamete)

PRODUCTION OF GAMETES

RED SEAWEED
Dilsea carnosa

Thallus
(plant
body)

Lamina
(blade)

Hapteron
(holdfast)

Antherozoid (male
gamete) swims
toward oosphere

Flagellum

Oosphere
(female
gamete) is
fertilized by
antherozoid
to produce
a zygote

FERTILIZATION

GREEN ALGA
Spirogyra sp.

Cytoplasm

Cell (cylindrical)

Cell wall

End wall
of cell

Filament
(strand of
linked cells)

Two filaments
linked for
conjugation
(sexual
reproduction)

Spirally
wound
chloroplast

Conjugation
tube

End wall of conjugation
tube still in place

Flexible stipe
(stalk)

Hapteron
(holdfast)

Young thallus
(plant body)

Hapteron
(holdfast)

**ZYGOTE DEVELOPS INTO
A YOUNG SEAWEED**

117

Liverworts and mosses

"Stem"

"Leaf"

Rhizoid

LIVERWORTS AND MOSSES ARE SMALL, LOW-GROWING PLANTS that belong to the phylum Bryophyta. Bryophytes do not have true stems, leaves, or roots (they are anchored to the ground by rhizoids), nor do they have the vascular tissues (xylem and phloem) that transport water and nutrients in higher plants. With no outer, waterproof cuticle, bryophytes are susceptible to dehydration, and most grow in moist habitats. The bryophyte life cycle has two stages. In stage one, the green plant (gametophyte) produces male and female gametes (sex cells), which fuse to form a zygote. In stage two, the zygote develops into a sporophyte that remains attached to the gametophyte. The sporophyte produces spores, which are released and germinate into new green plants. Liverworts (class Hepaticae) grow horizontally and may be thalloid (flat and ribbon-like) or "leafy." Mosses (class Musci) typically have an upright "stem" with spirally arranged "leaves."

A THALLOID LIVERWORT
Marchantia polymorpha

Gemma cup

Gemma (detachable tissue that produces new plants)

Thallus (plant body)

Toothed margin of cup

DETAIL OF GEMMA CUP

Archegoniophore (stalked structure carrying archegonia)
— Disk
— Lobe
— Stalk

Thallus (plant body)

Apical notch

Rhizoid

FEMALE GAMETOPHYTE

Disk
Lobe
Stalk

SIDE VIEW OF ARCHEGONIOPHORE

Lobe
Disk

Ray (radial groove)
Stalk

ARCHEGONIOPHORE FROM BELOW

Pore

Ray (radial groove)

MICROGRAPH OF LOBE

Gemma cup

Thallus (plant body)

Midrib

Archegoniophore (stalked structure carrying archegonia)

MICROGRAPH OF THALLUS
Conocephalum conicum

Position of air chamber

Pore for exchange of gases

Upper surface

Rhizoid

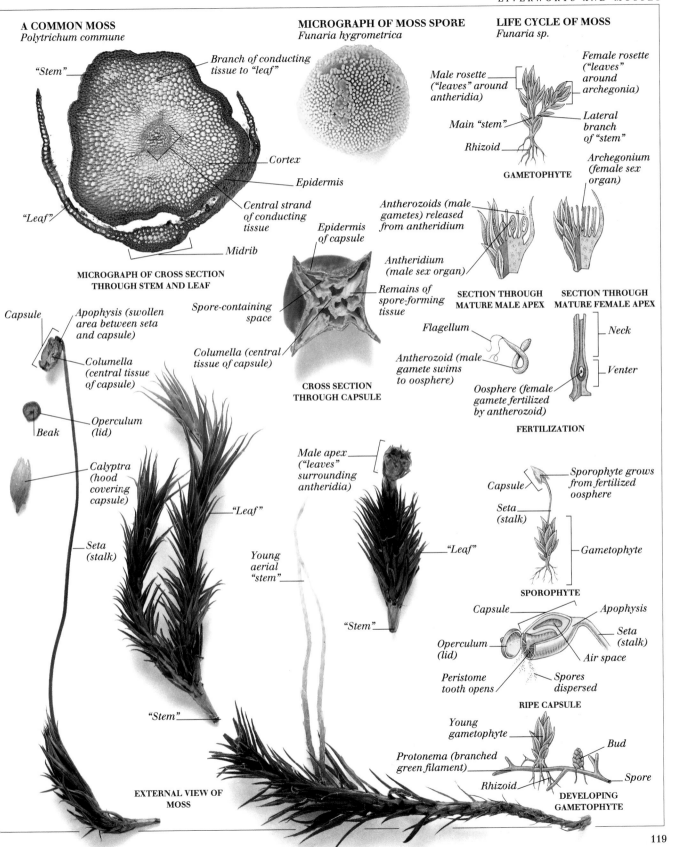

A COMMON MOSS
Polytrichum commune

"Stem"

Branch of conducting
tissue to "leaf"

Cortex

Epidermis

Central strand
of conducting
tissue

"Leaf"

Midrib

**MICROGRAPH OF CROSS SECTION
THROUGH STEM AND LEAF**

MICROGRAPH OF MOSS SPORE
Funaria hygrometrica

LIFE CYCLE OF MOSS
Funaria sp.

Male rosette
("leaves" around
antheridia)

Female rosette
("leaves"
around
archegonia)

Main "stem"

Lateral
branch
of "stem"

Rhizoid

GAMETOPHYTE

Archegonium
(female sex
organ)

Antherozoids (male
gametes) released
from antheridium

Antheridium
(male sex organ)

**SECTION THROUGH
MATURE MALE APEX**

**SECTION THROUGH
MATURE FEMALE APEX**

Neck

Venter

Flagellum

Antherozoid (male
gamete swims
to oosphere)

Oosphere (female
gamete fertilized
by antherozoid)

FERTILIZATION

Epidermis
of capsule

Spore-containing
space

Columella (central
tissue of capsule)

Remains of
spore-forming
tissue

**CROSS SECTION
THROUGH CAPSULE**

Capsule

Apophysis (swollen
area between seta
and capsule)

Columella
(central tissue
of capsule)

Operculum
(lid)

Beak

Calyptra
(hood
covering
capsule)

Seta
(stalk)

"Leaf"

"Stem"

Young
aerial
"stem"

Male apex
("leaves"
surrounding
antheridia)

"Leaf"

"Stem"

Capsule

Sporophyte grows
from fertilized
oosphere

Seta
(stalk)

Gametophyte

SPOROPHYTE

Capsule

Apophysis

Operculum
(lid)

Seta
(stalk)

Air space

Peristome
tooth opens

Spores
dispersed

RIPE CAPSULE

Young
gametophyte

Protonema (branched
green filament)

Bud

Spore

Rhizoid

**DEVELOPING
GAMETOPHYTE**

**EXTERNAL VIEW OF
MOSS**

Horsetails, club mosses, and ferns

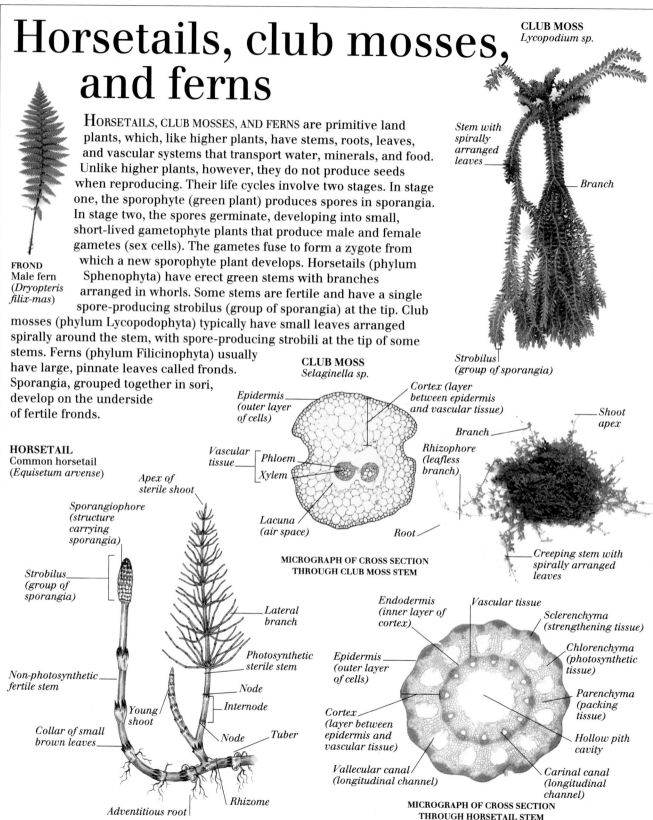

CLUB MOSS
Lycopodium sp.

HORSETAILS, CLUB MOSSES, AND FERNS are primitive land plants, which, like higher plants, have stems, roots, leaves, and vascular systems that transport water, minerals, and food. Unlike higher plants, however, they do not produce seeds when reproducing. Their life cycles involve two stages. In stage one, the sporophyte (green plant) produces spores in sporangia. In stage two, the spores germinate, developing into small, short-lived gametophyte plants that produce male and female gametes (sex cells). The gametes fuse to form a zygote from which a new sporophyte plant develops. Horsetails (phylum Sphenophyta) have erect green stems with branches arranged in whorls. Some stems are fertile and have a single spore-producing strobilus (group of sporangia) at the tip. Club mosses (phylum Lycopodophyta) typically have small leaves arranged spirally around the stem, with spore-producing strobili at the tip of some stems. Ferns (phylum Filicinophyta) usually have large, pinnate leaves called fronds. Sporangia, grouped together in sori, develop on the underside of fertile fronds.

FROND
Male fern
(*Dryopteris filix-mas*)

CLUB MOSS
Selaginella sp.

Stem with spirally arranged leaves

Branch

Strobilus (group of sporangia)

Epidermis (outer layer of cells)

Cortex (layer between epidermis and vascular tissue)

Vascular tissue
Phloem
Xylem

Lacuna (air space)

HORSETAIL
Common horsetail
(*Equisetum arvense*)

Apex of sterile shoot

Sporangiophore (structure carrying sporangia)

Strobilus (group of sporangia)

Non-photosynthetic fertile stem

Collar of small brown leaves

Young shoot

Node

Internode

Node

Tuber

Lateral branch

Photosynthetic sterile stem

Rhizome

Adventitious root

Branch

Rhizophore (leafless branch)

Shoot apex

Root

Creeping stem with spirally arranged leaves

MICROGRAPH OF CROSS SECTION THROUGH CLUB MOSS STEM

Endodermis (inner layer of cortex)

Vascular tissue

Sclerenchyma (strengthening tissue)

Epidermis (outer layer of cells)

Chlorenchyma (photosynthetic tissue)

Parenchyma (packing tissue)

Cortex (layer between epidermis and vascular tissue)

Hollow pith cavity

Vallecular canal (longitudinal channel)

Carinal canal (longitudinal channel)

MICROGRAPH OF CROSS SECTION THROUGH HORSETAIL STEM

SPORE PRODUCTION IN FERN
Bracken
(*Pteridium aquilinum*)

Apex of pinnule

Sporangium (spore-producing structure)

Pinnule (leaflet of pinna)

Spore inside dehisced (split open) sporangium

Abaxial (lower) surface of pinnule

Midrib of pinnule

Sorus (group of sporangia)

MICROGRAPH OF LOWER SURFACE OF FERTILE PINNULE

Sporangium (spore-producing structure)

Spore

Annulus (ring of cells around sporangium)

Midrib of pinnule

MICROGRAPH OF SPORANGIA ON LOWER SURFACE OF FERTILE PINNULE

LIFE CYCLE OF FERN

Pinna (leaflet)

Pinnule (leaflet of pinna)

Frond (leaf)

Rolled immature frond

SPOROPHYTE

Rhizome

Pinnule (leaflet of pinna)

Placenta

Indusium (flap protecting sorus)

Sporangium (spore-producing structure)

Sorus (group of sporangia)

SECTION THROUGH MATURE PINNULE

Sporangium splits and releases spores

Annulus ruptures at weak point

Spore

RELEASE OF SPORES FROM SPORANGIUM

Spore

Filament develops into prothallus

Rhizoid

GERMINATION OF SPORE

Antheridium (male sex organ)

Archegonium (female sex organ)

Prothallus (free-living gametophyte)

Rhizoid

GAMETOPHYTE PRODUCES GAMETES

Antheridium (male sex organ)

Oosphere (female gamete)

Antherozoid (male gamete) swims to oosphere

Archegonium (female sex organ)

FERTILIZATION

Primary leaf of growing sporophyte

Remains of gametophyte

FERTILIZED OOSPHERE GROWS INTO NEW SPOROPHYTE PLANT

FERN
Male fern
(*Dryopteris filix-mas*)

Midrib of pinna (leaflet)

Apex of frond (leaf)

Pinna (leaflet)

Pinnule (leaflet of pinna)

Frond (leaf)

Young frond (leaf)

Rachis (main axis of pinnate leaf)

Base of old dead frond (leaf)

Young frond (leaf) rolled and covered by ramenta

Ramentum (brown scale)

Rhizome

Vascular bundle

Sclerenchyma (strengthening tissue)

Phloem

Xylem

Vascular tissue

Epidermis (outer layer of cells)

Parenchyma (packing tissue)

MICROGRAPH OF CROSS SECTION THROUGH FERN RACHIS

Adventitious root

Gymnosperms 1

THE GYMNOSPERMS ARE FOUR RELATED PHYLA of seed-producing plants: Their seeds, however, lack the protective outer covering which surrounds the seeds of flowering plants. Typically, gymnosperms are woody, perennial shrubs or trees, with stems, leaves, roots, and a well-developed vascular (transport) system. The reproductive structures in most gymnosperms are cones. Male cones produce microspores in which male gametes (sex cells) develop; female cones produce megaspores in which female gametes develop. Microspores are blown by the wind to female cones, male and female gametes fuse during fertilization, and a seed develops. The four gymnosperm phyla are the conifers (phylum Coniferophyta), mostly tall trees; cycads (phylum Cycadophyta), small palm-like trees; the ginkgo or maidenhair tree (phylum Ginkgophyta), a tall tree with bilobed leaves; and gnetophytes (phylum Gnetophyta), a diverse group of plants, mainly shrubs, but also including the horizontally growing welwitschia.

LIFE CYCLE OF SCOTS PINE
(*Pinus sylvestris*)

Needle (foliage leaf)

Cone

Ovuliferous scale (ovule-/seed-bearing structure)

MALE CONES   **YOUNG FEMALE CONE**

Pollen grain in micropyle (entrance to ovule)

Ovuliferous scale

Pollen grain

Nucleus

Air sac

Ovule (contains female gamete)

POLLINATION

Integument (outer part of ovule)

Pollen tube (carries male gamete from pollen grain to ovum)

Archegonium (containing female gamete)

FERTILIZATION

SCALE AND SEEDS
Pine
(*Pinus sp.*)

Ovuliferous scale (ovule-/seed-bearing structure)

Wing scar

Wing of seed derived from ovuliferous scale

Seed

Seed

Seed scar

Point of attachment to axis of cone

OVULIFEROUS SCALE FROM THIRD-YEAR FEMALE CONE

Seed

Seed

Ovuliferous scale (ovule-/seed-bearing structure)

Wing

MATURE FEMALE CONE AND WINGED SEED

Microsporangium (structure in which pollen grains are formed)

Microsporophyll (modified leaf carrying microsporangia)

Ovule (contains female gametes)

Bract scale

Scale leaf

Axis of cone

Ovuliferous scale (ovule-/seed-bearing structure)

Axis of cone

MICROGRAPH OF LONGITUDINAL SECTION THROUGH YOUNG MALE CONE

MICROGRAPH OF LONGITUDINAL SECTION THROUGH SECOND-YEAR FEMALE CONE

Plumule (embryonic shoot)

Cotyledon (seed leaf)

Root

GERMINATION OF PINE SEEDLING

WELWITSCHIA
(*Welwitschia mirabilis*)

Frayed end of leaf

SMOOTH CYPRESS
(*Cupressus glabra*)

Immature female cone

Ovuliferous scale (ovule-/seed-bearing structure)

Scalelike leaf

Mature female cone

Immature male cone

Ovuliferous scale

Ovule (contains female gamete)

CROSS SECTION THROUGH IMMATURE CONE

Ovuliferous scale (ovule-/seed-bearing structure)

Seed

CROSS SECTION THROUGH MATURE CONE

Woody scale

Opening between woody scales through which seeds are released

DISCARDED CONE

YEW
(*Taxus baccata*)

Single ovule (contains female gamete)

Scale

Female "cone"

Scale

Developing seed

Scale

FEMALE "CONES" AT VARIOUS STAGES OF DEVELOPMENT

Seed

Aril (fleshy outgrowth from seed)

Stem

Needle (foliage leaf)

CYCAD
Sago palm
(*Cycas revoluta*)

Pinnate leaf

Scale leaf

Pinna (leaflet)

Old leaf base

Stem covered by scale leaves

GINKGO
(*Ginkgo biloba*)

Stem

Girdle scar

Petiole (leaf stalk)

Bilobed leaf

Continuously growing leaf

Site of cone growth

Immature cone

Stalk scar

Woody stem

Adaxial (upper) surface of leaf

Abaxial (lower) surface of leaf

Frayed end of leaf

Gymnosperms 2

BRANCH OF BISHOP PINE
(*Pinus muricata*)

Second-year female cone

Ovuliferous scale
(ovule-/seed-bearing
structure)

*Needle
(foliage leaf)*

*Ovuliferous scale
(ovule-/seed-bearing
structure)*

*Bud
scale*

Cone

Cone stalk

Stem

Dwarf shoot

Scale leaf scar

FEMALE CONE (FIRST YEAR)

Apical bud

Stem

Needle (foliage leaf)

Dwarf shoot

Male cone

*Scar of
dwarf shoot*

*Margin
of needle
(foliage leaf)*

*Upper surface
of needle
(foliage leaf)*

*Needle
(foliage leaf)*

Apical bud

Stem

Dwarf shoot

TERMINAL ZONE OF BRANCH

*Stoma
(pore)*

*Female
cone*

*Woody ovuliferous
scale (ovule-/seed-
bearing structure)*

FEMALE CONE (THIRD YEAR)

Vascular tissue

Phloem   *Xylem*

*Mesophyll
(photosynthetic tissue)*

*Stoma
(pore)*

*Epidermis
(outer
layer of
cells)*

*Endodermis
(inner layer
of cortex)*

Resin canal

*Cuticle
(waterproof
covering)*

**MICROGRAPH OF CROSS SECTION
THROUGH NEEDLE (FOLIAGE LEAF)**

**MICROGRAPH OF NEEDLE
(FOLIAGE LEAF) OF PINE**
(*Pinus sp.*)

124

CROSS SECTION THROUGH
MATURE STEM OF BISHOP PINE
(*Pinus muricata*)

Apical bud scale

Apical bud

Shoot apex

Needle (foliage leaf) bud

Bud scale

Scale leaf

Immature needle (foliage leaf)

**MICROGRAPH OF LONGITUDINAL SECTION
THROUGH SHOOT APEX OF PINE
(*Pinus sp.*)**

Annual ring

Heartwood (supportive, inactive secondary xylem)

Branch trace (vascular bundle supplying branch)

Pith

Sapwood (active secondary xylem)

Bark

Phloem

Periderm (outer layer of bark)

Medullary ray (extension of pith)

Pith

Hypodermis (cell layer below epidermis)

Cortex (layer between epidermis and vascular tissue)

Base of dwarf shoot

Dwarf shoot trace (vascular bundle supplying dwarf shoot)

Epidermis (outer layer of cells)

Secondary xylem

Vascular tissue

Phloem

Primary xylem

Resin canal

**MICROGRAPH OF CROSS SECTION
THROUGH YOUNG STEM OF PINE
(*Pinus sp.*)**

Cortex (layer between phellem and vascular tissue)

Resin canal

Endodermis (inner layer of cortex)

Phloem

Phellem (protective outer layer)

Secondary xylem

Primary xylem

**MICROGRAPH OF CROSS SECTION
THROUGH YOUNG ROOT OF PINE
(*Pinus sp.*)**

Cortex (layer between phellem and vascular tissue)

Secondary xylem

Phellem (protective outer layer)

Primary xylem

Resin canal

Phloem

**MICROGRAPH OF CROSS SECTION
THROUGH MATURE ROOT OF PINE
(*Pinus sp.*)**

Monocotyledons and dicotyledons

FLOWERING PLANTS (PHYLUM ANGIOSPERMOPHYTA) are divided into two classes: monocotyledons (class Monocotyledoneae) and dicotyledons (class Dicotyledoneae). Typically, monocotyledons have seeds with one cotyledon (seed leaf); their foliage leaves are narrow with parallel veins; the flower components occur in multiples of three; sepals and petals are indistinguishable and are known as tepals; vascular (transport) tissues are scattered in random bundles throughout the stem; and, because they lack stem cambium (actively dividing cells that produce wood), most monocotyledons are herbaceous (see pp. 128-129).

CROSS SECTION THROUGH MONOCOTYLEDONOUS LEAF BASES

Dicotyledons have seeds with two cotyledons; leaves are broad with a central midrib and branched veins; flower parts occur in multiples of four or five; sepals are generally small and green; petals are large and colorful; vascular bundles are arranged in a ring around the edge of the stem; and, because many dicotyledons possess wood-producing stem cambium, there are woody forms (see pp. 130-131) as well as herbaceous ones.

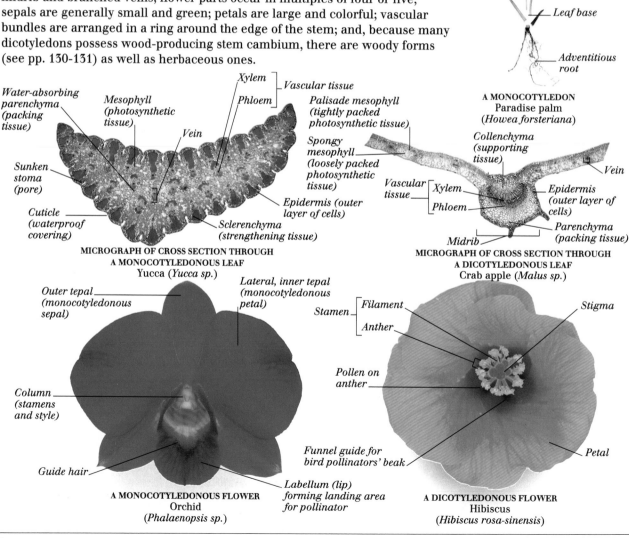

A MONOCOTYLEDON
Paradise palm
(*Howea forsteriana*)

MICROGRAPH OF CROSS SECTION THROUGH
A MONOCOTYLEDONOUS LEAF
Yucca (*Yucca sp.*)

MICROGRAPH OF CROSS SECTION THROUGH
A DICOTYLEDONOUS LEAF
Crab apple (*Malus sp.*)

A MONOCOTYLEDONOUS FLOWER
Orchid
(*Phalaenopsis sp.*)

A DICOTYLEDONOUS FLOWER
Hibiscus
(*Hibiscus rosa-sinensis*)

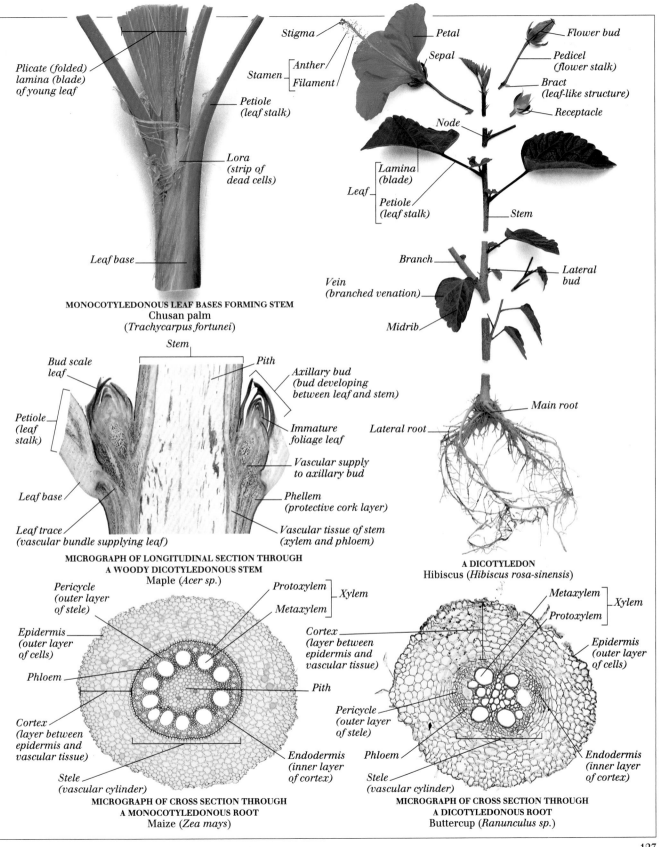

Plicate (folded) lamina (blade) of young leaf

Petiole (leaf stalk)

Lora (strip of dead cells)

Leaf base

MONOCOTYLEDONOUS LEAF BASES FORMING STEM
Chusan palm
(*Trachycarpus fortunei*)

Stigma

Petal

Stamen { Anther / Filament

Sepal

Flower bud

Pedicel (flower stalk)

Bract (leaf-like structure)

Receptacle

Node

Leaf { Lamina (blade) / Petiole (leaf stalk)

Stem

Branch

Lateral bud

Vein (branched venation)

Midrib

A DICOTYLEDON
Hibiscus (*Hibiscus rosa-sinensis*)

Stem

Pith

Bud scale leaf

Axillary bud (bud developing between leaf and stem)

Petiole (leaf stalk)

Immature foliage leaf

Vascular supply to axillary bud

Leaf base

Leaf trace (vascular bundle supplying leaf)

Phellem (protective cork layer)

Vascular tissue of stem (xylem and phloem)

MICROGRAPH OF LONGITUDINAL SECTION THROUGH A WOODY DICOTYLEDONOUS STEM
Maple (*Acer sp.*)

Main root

Lateral root

Pericycle (outer layer of stele)

Protoxylem } Xylem
Metaxylem

Epidermis (outer layer of cells)

Phloem

Cortex (layer between epidermis and vascular tissue)

Pith

Cortex (layer between epidermis and vascular tissue)

Stele (vascular cylinder)

Endodermis (inner layer of cortex)

MICROGRAPH OF CROSS SECTION THROUGH A MONOCOTYLEDONOUS ROOT
Maize (*Zea mays*)

Metaxylem } Xylem
Protoxylem

Epidermis (outer layer of cells)

Cortex (layer between epidermis and vascular tissue)

Pericycle (outer layer of stele)

Phloem

Stele (vascular cylinder)

Endodermis (inner layer of cortex)

MICROGRAPH OF CROSS SECTION THROUGH A DICOTYLEDONOUS ROOT
Buttercup (*Ranunculus sp.*)

Herbaceous flowering plants

HERBACEOUS FLOWERING PLANTS TYPICALLY HAVE GREEN NON-WOODY STEMS, and tend to be relatively short-lived. Many herbaceous plants live for only one or two years. Annuals (such as sweet peas) grow from seed, produce flowers and then seeds, and die within a single year. Biennials (like carrots) have a two-year life cycle. In the first year, seeds grow into plants, which produce leaves and store food in underground storage organs; the stems and foliage then die in winter. In the second year, new stems grow from the storage organs, produce leaves, flowers, and seeds, and then die. Some herbaceous plants (such as potatoes) are perennial. They grow back year after year, producing shoots and flowers in spring, storing food in underground tubers or rhizomes during summer, dying in autumn, and surviving underground during winter.

Young plant forming

Petiole (stalk) of young leaf

Lateral root

Stipule (structure at base of leaf)

Trifoliate leaf

Node

Simple ovate leaflet

Root nodule

Main root

SWEET PEA
(*Lathyrus odoratus*)

STRAWBERRY
(*Fragaria x ananassa*)

Runner (creeping stem)

Remains of leaves

Lateral root scar

Leaf scar

Stem

Rib

Lateral root

Tap root

CARROT
(*Daucus carota*)

Leaf base

Leaf scar

Petiole (leaf stalk)

Spine (modified leaf)

Slender rhizome

Stem tuber

Adventitious root

Stem

Narrow, succulent leaf

Simple deltoid leaf

POTATO
(*Solanum tuberosum*)

ROCK STONECROP
(*Sedum rupestre*)

Adventitious root

PARTS OF HERBACEOUS FLOWERING PLANTS

Bract
(leaf-like
structure)

Bracteole
(small bract)

Cyme (type of
inflorescence)

Midrib

Succulent,
simple ovate
leaf

Inner, tubular
disk floret

Outer, ligulate
ray floret

Flower bud

Node

Peduncle
(inflorescence stalk)

Dentate
margin

Internode

Capitulum (type
of inflorescence)

Leaf

Peduncle
(inflorescence
stalk)

Flower
bud

SHOWY STONECROP
(*Sedum spectabile*)

Simple lobed
leaf

Petiole
(leaf stalk)

Petiole
(leaf
stalk)

Leaf base

Stem

Succulent
stem

Leaf
scar

Lateral
bud

Prickle

FLORISTS' CHRYSANTHEMUM
(*Chrysanthemum morifolium*)

Linear
leaf

**CEREOID
CACTUS**

BEGONIA
(*Begonia* x
tuberhybrida)

Bract
(leaf-like
structure)

Capitulum (type
of inflorescence)

Hollow
stem

Sheath formed
from leaf base

TOADFLAX
(*Linaria* sp.)

Spinose-dentate
margin

Dentate
margin

Unwinged rachis
(main axis of
pinnate leaf)

Winged
stem

Rachis (main
axis of pinnate
leaf)

SLENDER THISTLE
(*Carduus tenuiflorus*)

Tendril

Stipule
(structure at
base of leaf)

Stem
segment

Winged
rachis
(main
axis of
pinnate
leaf)

Peduncle
(inflorescence
stalk)

Flower bud

Pinna
(leaflet)

HOGWEED
(*Heracleum sphondylium*)

Petiole
(leaf stalk)

Margin of
cladode

Toothed
notch

Bract
(leaflike
structure)

Tepal

Peduncle
(inflorescence
stalk)

Cladode
(flattened stem)

Stem
branch

PERUVIAN LILY
(*Alstroemeria aurea*)

Raceme (type
of inflorescence)

Petal

Sepal

CRAB CACTUS
(*Schlumbergera truncata*)

EVERLASTING PEA
(*Lathyrus latifolius*)

Woody flowering plants

WOODY FLOWERING PLANTS ARE PERENNIAL: They continue to grow and reproduce for many years. They have one or more permanent stems above ground and numerous smaller branches. The stems and branches have a strong woody core that supports the plant and contains vascular tissue for transporting water and nutrients. Outside the woody core is a layer of tough, protective bark, which has lenticels (tiny pores) to allow gases to pass through. Woody flowering plants may be shrubs, which have several stems rising from the soil; bushes, which are shrubs with dense branching and foliage; or trees, which typically have a single upright stem (the trunk) that bears branches. Deciduous woody plants (like roses) shed all their leaves once a year and remain leafless during winter. Evergreen woody plants (such as holly) shed their leaves gradually, so they retain full leaf cover throughout the year.

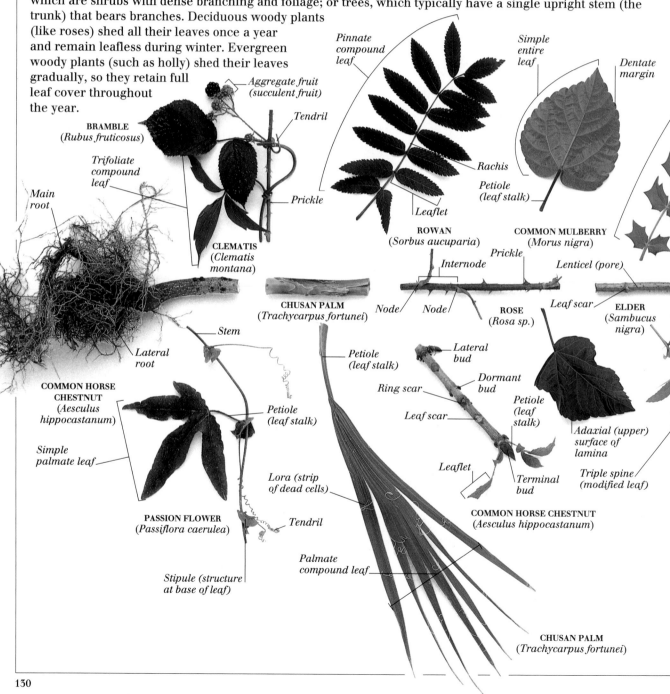

Pinnate compound leaf

Simple entire leaf

Dentate margin

Aggregate fruit (succulent fruit)

Tendril

BRAMBLE
(*Rubus fruticosus*)

Trifoliate compound leaf

Prickle

Rachis

Petiole (leaf stalk)

Leaflet

ROWAN
(*Sorbus aucuparia*)

COMMON MULBERRY
(*Morus nigra*)

Main root

CLEMATIS
(*Clematis montana*)

Internode

Prickle

Lenticel (pore)

Node

Node

Leaf scar

CHUSAN PALM
(*Trachycarpus fortunei*)

ROSE
(*Rosa sp.*)

ELDER
(*Sambucus nigra*)

Stem

Lateral root

COMMON HORSE CHESTNUT
(*Aesculus hippocastanum*)

Petiole (leaf stalk)

Petiole (leaf stalk)

Lateral bud

Dormant bud

Ring scar

Leaf scar

Petiole (leaf stalk)

Adaxial (upper) surface of lamina

Simple palmate leaf

Lora (strip of dead cells)

Leaflet

Terminal bud

Triple spine (modified leaf)

PASSION FLOWER
(*Passiflora caerulea*)

Tendril

COMMON HORSE CHESTNUT
(*Aesculus hippocastanum*)

Stipule (structure at base of leaf)

Palmate compound leaf

CHUSAN PALM
(*Trachycarpus fortunei*)

PARTS OF WOODY FLOWERING PLANTS

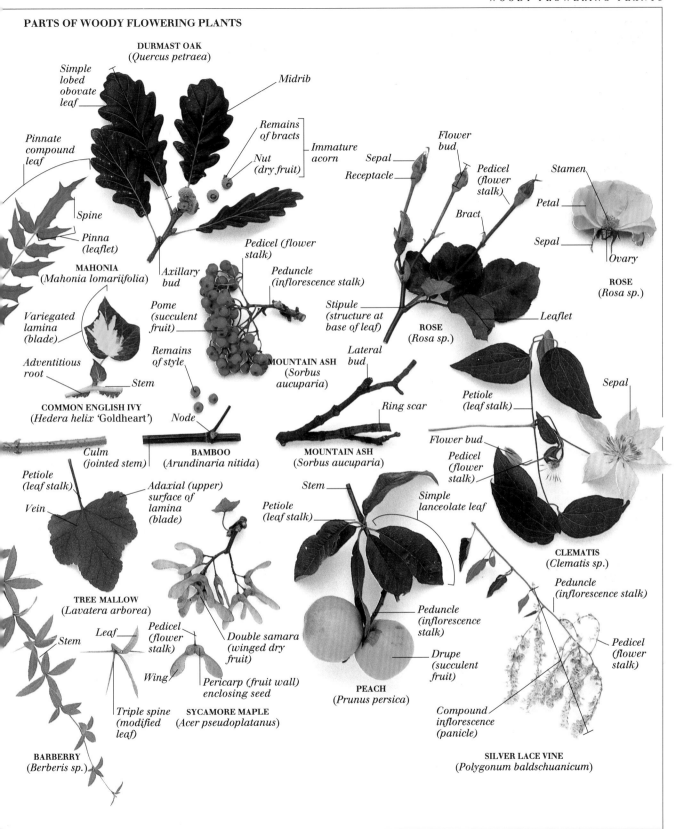

DURMAST OAK
(*Quercus petraea*)

Simple lobed obovate leaf

Midrib

Pinnate compound leaf

Remains of bracts

Nut (dry fruit)

Immature acorn

Spine

Pinna (leaflet)

MAHONIA
(*Mahonia lomariifolia*)

Axillary bud

Pedicel (flower stalk)

Peduncle (inflorescence stalk)

Flower bud

Sepal

Receptacle

Pedicel (flower stalk)

Stamen

Petal

Bract

Sepal

Ovary

ROSE
(*Rosa sp.*)

Variegated lamina (blade)

Pome (succulent fruit)

Adventitious root

Stem

Remains of style

COMMON ENGLISH IVY
(*Hedera helix* 'Goldheart')

Node

MOUNTAIN ASH
(*Sorbus aucuparia*)

Stipule (structure at base of leaf)

Leaflet

ROSE
(*Rosa sp.*)

Lateral bud

Petiole (leaf stalk)

Sepal

Culm (jointed stem)

BAMBOO
(*Arundinaria nitida*)

Ring scar

MOUNTAIN ASH
(*Sorbus aucuparia*)

Flower bud

Pedicel (flower stalk)

CLEMATIS
(*Clematis sp.*)

Petiole (leaf stalk)

Vein

Adaxial (upper) surface of lamina (blade)

Stem

Petiole (leaf stalk)

Simple lanceolate leaf

Peduncle (inflorescence stalk)

Peduncle (inflorescence stalk)

Pedicel (flower stalk)

TREE MALLOW
(*Lavatera arborea*)

Stem

Leaf

Pedicel (flower stalk)

Wing

Double samara (winged dry fruit)

Pericarp (fruit wall) enclosing seed

Drupe (succulent fruit)

Triple spine (modified leaf)

SYCAMORE MAPLE
(*Acer pseudoplatanus*)

PEACH
(*Prunus persica*)

Compound inflorescence (panicle)

BARBERRY
(*Berberis sp.*)

SILVER LACE VINE
(*Polygonum baldschuanicum*)

Roots

ROOTS ARE THE UNDERGROUND PARTS OF PLANTS. They have
three main functions. First, they anchor the plant in the soil.
Second, they absorb water and minerals from the spaces
between soil particles. The roots' absorptive properties
are increased by root hairs, which grow behind the root tip,
allowing maximum absorption of vital substances. Third, the
root is part of the plant's transport system. Xylem carries
water and minerals from the roots to the stem and leaves,
and phloem carries nutrients from the leaves to all parts of
the root system. In addition, some roots (like carrots) are food
stores. Roots have an outer epidermis covering a cortex of parenchyma
(packing tissue), and a central cylinder of vascular tissue. This arrangement
helps the roots resist the forces of compression as they grow through the soil.

MICROGRAPH OF PRIMARY ROOT DEVELOPMENT
Cabbage (*Brassica sp.*)

Split in testa
as seed
germinates

Cotyledon
(seed leaf)

Primary root

Testa
(seed coat)

Root hair

Root tip
(region of
cell division)

CARROT
(*Daucus carota*)

FEATURES OF A TYPICAL ROOT
Buttercup
(*Ranunculus sp.*)

Pericycle
(outer layer
of stele)

Root hair

Air space
(allowing gas
diffusion in
the root)

Stele
(vascular cylinder)

Phloem sieve tube
(through which
nutrients are
transported)

Companion cell
(cell associated
with phloem
sieve tube)

Cortex
(layer between
epidermis and
vascular tissue)

Root hair

Epidermis
(outer layer
of cells)

Xylem vessel
(through which water
and minerals are transported)

Endodermis
(inner layer
of cortex)

Cell wall

Nucleus

Cytoplasm

Parenchyma
(packing) cell

PRIMARY ROOT AND MICROGRAPHS OF SECTIONS THROUGH ROOTS

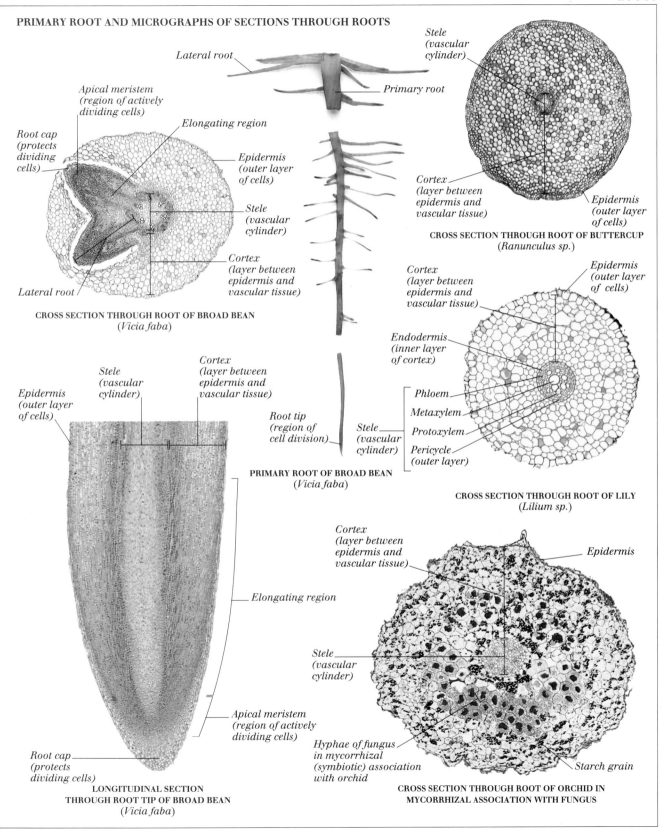

Lateral root

Primary root

Apical meristem
(region of actively
dividing cells)

Elongating region

Root cap
(protects
dividing
cells)

Epidermis
(outer layer
of cells)

Stele
(vascular
cylinder)

Cortex
(layer between
epidermis and
vascular tissue)

Lateral root

CROSS SECTION THROUGH ROOT OF BROAD BEAN
(*Vicia faba*)

Stele
(vascular
cylinder)

Cortex
(layer between
epidermis and
vascular tissue)

Epidermis
(outer layer
of cells)

CROSS SECTION THROUGH ROOT OF BUTTERCUP
(*Ranunculus sp.*)

Cortex
(layer between
epidermis and
vascular tissue)

Epidermis
(outer layer
of cells)

Endodermis
(inner layer
of cortex)

Phloem

Metaxylem

Protoxylem

Pericycle
(outer layer)

Stele
(vascular
cylinder)

CROSS SECTION THROUGH ROOT OF LILY
(*Lilium sp.*)

Root tip
(region of
cell division)

Stele
(vascular
cylinder)

PRIMARY ROOT OF BROAD BEAN
(*Vicia faba*)

Stele
(vascular
cylinder)

Cortex
(layer between
epidermis and
vascular tissue)

Epidermis
(outer layer
of cells)

Elongating region

Apical meristem
(region of actively
dividing cells)

Root cap
(protects
dividing cells)

**LONGITUDINAL SECTION
THROUGH ROOT TIP OF BROAD BEAN**
(*Vicia faba*)

Cortex
(layer between
epidermis and
vascular tissue)

Epidermis

Stele
(vascular
cylinder)

Hyphae of fungus
in mycorrhizal
(symbiotic) association
with orchid

Starch grain

**CROSS SECTION THROUGH ROOT OF ORCHID IN
MYCORRHIZAL ASSOCIATION WITH FUNGUS**

Stems

THE STEM IS THE MAIN SUPPORTIVE PART OF A PLANT that grows above ground. Stems bear leaves (organs of photosynthesis), which grow at nodes; buds (shoots covered by protective scales), which grow at the stem tip (apical or terminal buds) and in the angle between a leaf and the stem (axillary or lateral buds); and flowers (reproductive structures). The stem forms part of the plant's transport system. Xylem tissue in the stem transports water and minerals from the roots to the aerial parts of the plant, and phloem tissue transports nutrients manufactured in the leaves to other parts of the plant. Stem tissues are also used for storing water and food. Herbaceous (nonwoody) stems have an outer protective epidermis covering a cortex that consists mainly of parenchyma (packing tissue) but also has some collenchyma (supporting tissue). The vascular tissue of such stems is arranged in bundles, each of which consists of xylem, phloem, and sclerenchyma (strengthening tissue). Woody stems have an outer protective layer of tough bark, which is perforated with lenticels (pores) to allow gas exchange. Inside the bark is a ring of secondary phloem, which surrounds an inner core of secondary xylem.

MICROGRAPH OF LONGITUDINAL SECTION THROUGH APEX OF STEM
Coleus sp.

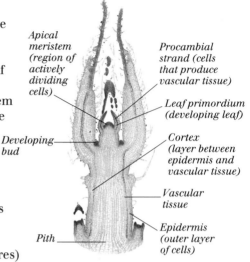

Apical meristem (region of actively dividing cells)

Procambial strand (cells that produce vascular tissue)

Leaf primordium (developing leaf)

Developing bud

Cortex (layer between epidermis and vascular tissue)

Vascular tissue

Epidermis (outer layer of cells)

Pith

YOUNG WOODY STEM
Linden
(*Tilia sp.*)

EMERGENT BUDS
Maple
(*Acer*)

Secondary phloem

Pith

Phellem (protective cork layer)

Cortex (layer between phellem and vascular tissue)

Xylem vessel (through which water and minerals are transported)

Xylem fiber (supporting tissue)

Ray (parenchyma cells)

Phloem sieve tube (through which nutrients are transported)

Phloem fiber (supporting tissue)

Lenticel (pore)

Vascular cambium (actively dividing cells that produce xylem and phloem)

Summer wood

Secondary xylem

Spring wood

Companion cell (cell associated with phloem sieve tube)

Young leaves emerging

Terminal bud

Lateral bud

Node

Internode

Inner bud scale

Secondary xylem

Outer bud scale

Node

Leaf scar

Lenticel (pore)

Woody stem

MICROGRAPHS OF CROSS SECTIONS THROUGH VARIOUS STEMS

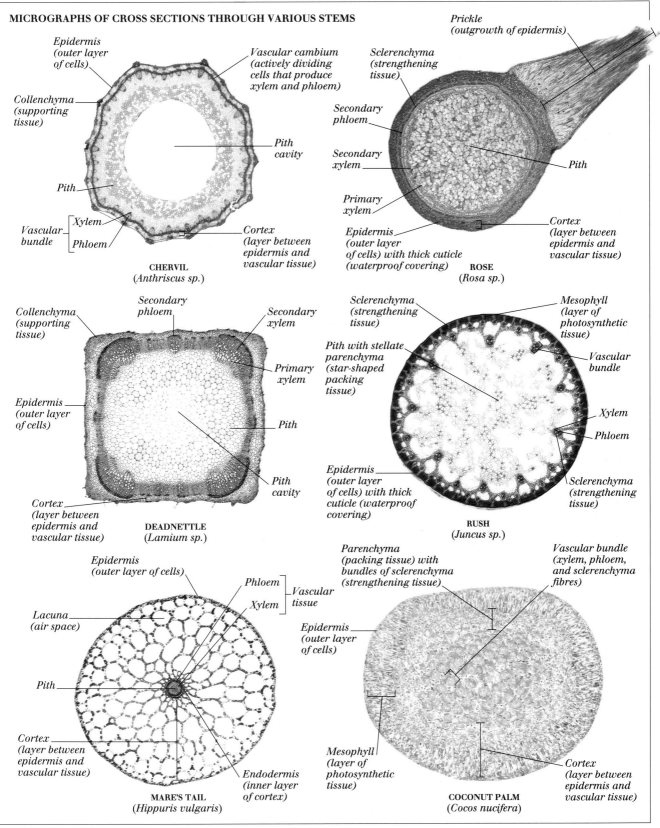

Epidermis (outer layer of cells)

Collenchyma (supporting tissue)

Pith

Vascular bundle [Xylem / Phloem]

Vascular cambium (actively dividing cells that produce xylem and phloem)

Pith cavity

Cortex (layer between epidermis and vascular tissue)

CHERVIL (*Anthriscus sp.*)

Prickle (outgrowth of epidermis)

Sclerenchyma (strengthening tissue)

Secondary phloem

Secondary xylem

Primary xylem

Epidermis (outer layer of cells) with thick cuticle (waterproof covering)

Pith

Cortex (layer between epidermis and vascular tissue)

ROSE (*Rosa sp.*)

Collenchyma (supporting tissue)

Secondary phloem

Secondary xylem

Primary xylem

Epidermis (outer layer of cells)

Pith

Pith cavity

Cortex (layer between epidermis and vascular tissue)

DEADNETTLE (*Lamium sp.*)

Sclerenchyma (strengthening tissue)

Pith with stellate parenchyma (star-shaped packing tissue)

Epidermis (outer layer of cells) with thick cuticle (waterproof covering)

Mesophyll (layer of photosynthetic tissue)

Vascular bundle

Xylem

Phloem

Sclerenchyma (strengthening tissue)

RUSH (*Juncus sp.*)

Epidermis (outer layer of cells)

Lacuna (air space)

Pith

Cortex (layer between epidermis and vascular tissue)

Phloem / Xylem] Vascular tissue

Endodermis (inner layer of cortex)

MARE'S TAIL (*Hippuris vulgaris*)

Parenchyma (packing tissue) with bundles of sclerenchyma (strengthening tissue)

Epidermis (outer layer of cells)

Mesophyll (layer of photosynthetic tissue)

Vascular bundle (xylem, phloem, and sclerenchyma fibres)

Cortex (layer between epidermis and vascular tissue)

COCONUT PALM (*Cocos nucifera*)

135

Leaves

LEAVES ARE THE MAIN SITES OF PHOTOSYNTHESIS (see pp. 138-139) and transpiration (water loss by evaporation) in plants. A typical leaf consists of a thin, flat lamina (blade) supported by a network of veins; a petiole (leaf stalk); and a leaf base, where the petiole joins the stem. Leaves can be classified as simple, in which the lamina is a single unit, or compound, in which the lamina is divided into separate leaflets. Compound leaves may be pinnate, with pinnae (leaflets) on both sides of a rachis (main axis), or palmate, with leaflets arising from a single point at the tip of the petiole. Leaves can be classified further by the overall shape of the lamina, and by the shape of the lamina's apex, margin, and base.

CHECKERBLOOM
(*Sidalcea malviflora*)

SIMPLE LEAF SHAPES

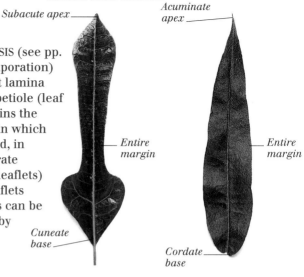

Subacute apex

Acuminate apex

Entire margin

Entire margin

Cuneate base

Cordate base

PANDURIFORM
Croton
(*Codiaeum variegatum*)

LANCEOLATE
Sea buckthorn
(*Hippophae rhamnoides*)

GENERAL LEAF FEATURES

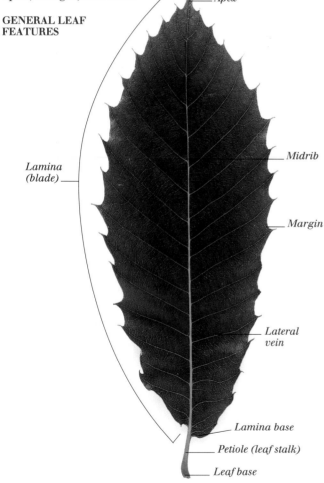

Apex

Lamina (blade)

Midrib

Margin

Lateral vein

Lamina base

Petiole (leaf stalk)

Leaf base

Spanish chestnut
(*Castanea sativa*)

COMPOUND LEAF SHAPES

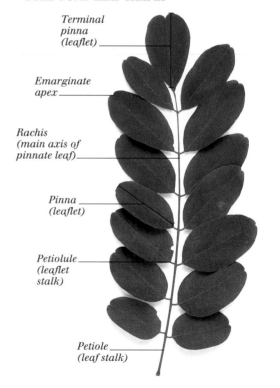

Terminal pinna (leaflet)

Emarginate apex

Rachis (main axis of pinnate leaf)

Pinna (leaflet)

Petiolule (leaflet stalk)

Petiole (leaf stalk)

ODD PINNATE
Black locust
(*Robinia pseudoacacia*)

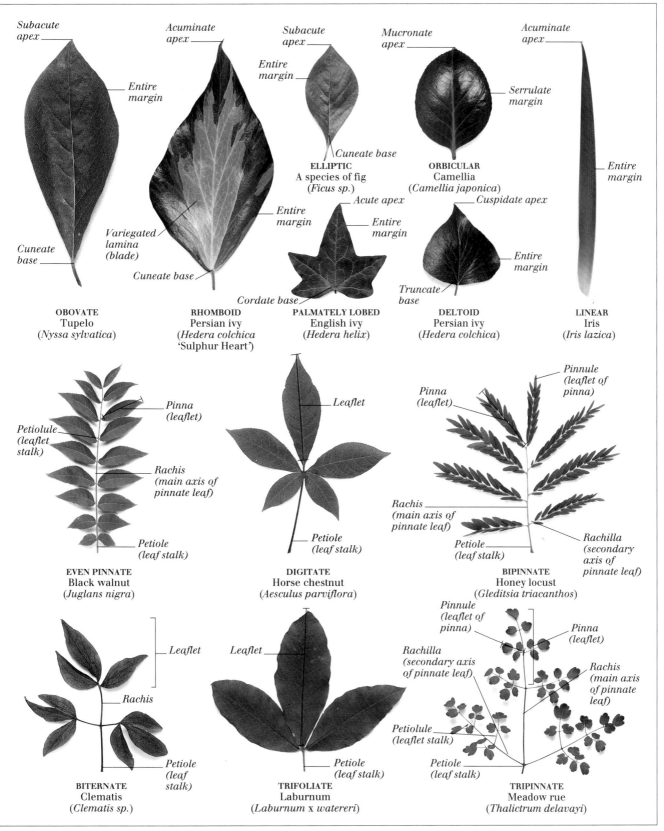

Subacute apex

Acuminate apex

Subacute apex

Entire margin

Entire margin

Mucronate apex

Serrulate margin

Acuminate apex

Cuneate base

ELLIPTIC
A species of fig
(*Ficus sp.*)

ORBICULAR
Camellia
(*Camellia japonica*)

Entire margin

Entire margin

Variegated lamina (blade)

Entire margin

Acute apex

Entire margin

Cuspidate apex

Entire margin

Cuneate base

Cuneate base

Cordate base

Truncate base

OBOVATE
Tupelo
(*Nyssa sylvatica*)

RHOMBOID
Persian ivy
(*Hedera colchica* 'Sulphur Heart')

PALMATELY LOBED
English ivy
(*Hedera helix*)

DELTOID
Persian ivy
(*Hedera colchica*)

LINEAR
Iris
(*Iris lazica*)

Pinna (leaflet)

Petiolule (leaflet stalk)

Rachis (main axis of pinnate leaf)

Petiole (leaf stalk)

Leaflet

Petiole (leaf stalk)

Pinnule (leaflet of pinna)

Pinna (leaflet)

Rachis (main axis of pinnate leaf)

Petiole (leaf stalk)

Rachilla (secondary axis of pinnate leaf)

EVEN PINNATE
Black walnut
(*Juglans nigra*)

DIGITATE
Horse chestnut
(*Aesculus parviflora*)

BIPINNATE
Honey locust
(*Gleditsia triacanthos*)

Leaflet

Rachis

Petiole (leaf stalk)

Leaflet

Petiole (leaf stalk)

Pinnule (leaflet of pinna)

Rachilla (secondary axis of pinnate leaf)

Pinna (leaflet)

Rachis (main axis of pinnate leaf)

Petiolule (leaflet stalk)

Petiole (leaf stalk)

BITERNATE
Clematis
(*Clematis sp.*)

TRIFOLIATE
Laburnum
(*Laburnum* x *watereri*)

TRIPINNATE
Meadow rue
(*Thalictrum delavayi*)

Photosynthesis

PHOTOSYNTHESIS IS THE PROCESS by which plants make their food using sunlight, water, and carbon dioxide. It takes place inside special structures in leaf cells called chloroplasts. The chloroplasts contain chlorophyll, a green pigment that absorbs energy from sunlight. During photosynthesis, the absorbed energy is used to join together carbon dioxide and water to form the sugar glucose, which is the energy source for the whole plant. Oxygen, a waste product, is released into the air. Leaves are the main sites of photosynthesis and have various adaptations for that purpose. Flat laminae (blades) provide a large surface for absorbing sunlight; stomata (pores) in the lower surface of the laminae allow gases (carbon dioxide and oxygen) to pass into and out of the leaves; and an extensive network of veins brings water into the leaves and transports the glucose produced by photosynthesis to the rest of the plant.

MICROGRAPH OF LEAF
Lily (*Lilium sp.*)

Stoma (pore) | Guard cell (controls opening and closing of stoma) | Lower surface of lamina (blade)

THE PROCESS OF PHOTOSYNTHESIS

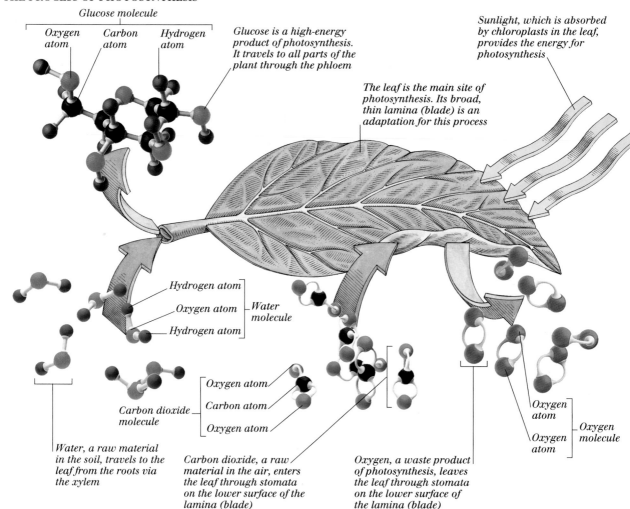

Glucose molecule

Oxygen atom | Carbon atom | Hydrogen atom

Glucose is a high-energy product of photosynthesis. It travels to all parts of the plant through the phloem

Sunlight, which is absorbed by chloroplasts in the leaf, provides the energy for photosynthesis

The leaf is the main site of photosynthesis. Its broad, thin lamina (blade) is an adaptation for this process

Hydrogen atom
Oxygen atom — Water molecule
Hydrogen atom

Carbon dioxide molecule

Oxygen atom
Carbon atom
Oxygen atom

Oxygen atom
Oxygen atom — Oxygen molecule

Water, a raw material in the soil, travels to the leaf from the roots via the xylem

Carbon dioxide, a raw material in the air, enters the leaf through stomata on the lower surface of the lamina (blade)

Oxygen, a waste product of photosynthesis, leaves the leaf through stomata on the lower surface of the lamina (blade)

138

CROSS SECTION THROUGH LEAF
Christmas rose
(*Helleborus niger*)

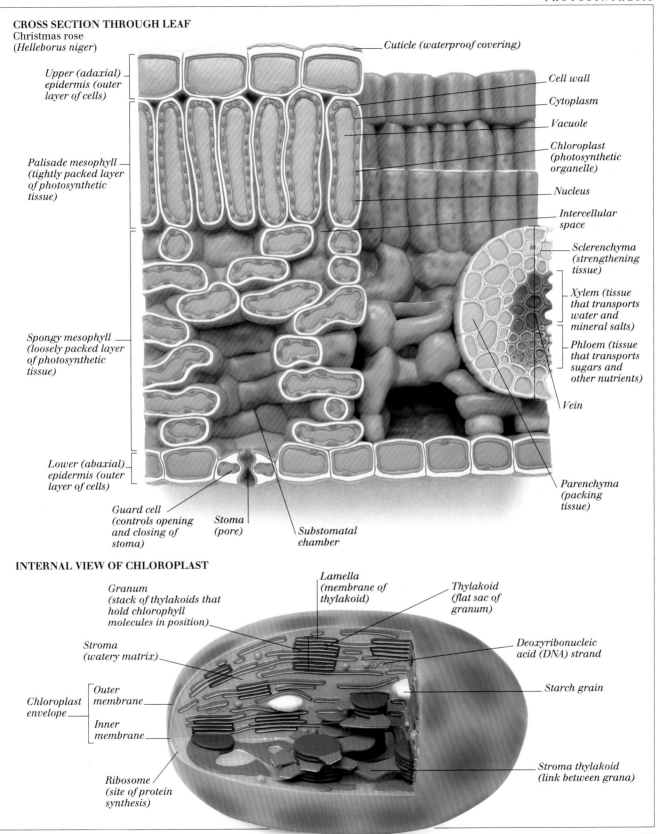

Cuticle (waterproof covering)

Upper (adaxial) epidermis (outer layer of cells)

Cell wall

Cytoplasm

Vacuole

Chloroplast (photosynthetic organelle)

Palisade mesophyll (tightly packed layer of photosynthetic tissue)

Nucleus

Intercellular space

Sclerenchyma (strengthening tissue)

Xylem (tissue that transports water and mineral salts)

Phloem (tissue that transports sugars and other nutrients)

Spongy mesophyll (loosely packed layer of photosynthetic tissue)

Vein

Lower (abaxial) epidermis (outer layer of cells)

Parenchyma (packing tissue)

Guard cell (controls opening and closing of stoma)

Stoma (pore)

Substomatal chamber

INTERNAL VIEW OF CHLOROPLAST

Granum (stack of thylakoids that hold chlorophyll molecules in position)

Lamella (membrane of thylakoid)

Thylakoid (flat sac of granum)

Stroma (watery matrix)

Deoxyribonucleic acid (DNA) strand

Chloroplast envelope

Outer membrane

Inner membrane

Starch grain

Ribosome (site of protein synthesis)

Stroma thylakoid (link between grana)

139

Flowers 1

FLOWERS ARE THE SITES OF SEXUAL REPRODUCTION in flowering plants. Their component parts are arranged in whorls around the receptacle (tip of the flower stalk). The sepals (collectively called the calyx) are outermost; typically small and green, they protect the developing flower. The petals (collectively called the corolla) are typically large and brightly colored; they are found inside the sepals. In monocotyledonous flowers (see pp. 126-127), sepals and petals are indistinguishable; individually they are called tepals (collectively called the perianth). The petals surround the male and female reproductive structures (androecium and gynoecium). The androecium consists of stamens (male organs); each stamen is made up of a filament (stalk) and anther. The gynoecium has one or more carpels (female organs); each carpel consists of an ovary, style, and stigma. Some flowers (like the lily) occur singly on a pedicel (flower stalk); others (such as elder, sunflower) are arranged in a group (inflorescence) on a peduncle (inflorescence stalk).

Inner tepal (monocotyledonous petal)

Honey guide

Groove secreting nectar

Filament

Style

Outer tepal (monocotyledonous sepal)

Stigma

Anther

EXTERNAL VIEW

A MONOCOTYLEDONOUS FLOWER
Lily
(*Lilium sp.*)

Syncarpous (fused carpels) gynoecium

Ovary

Stigma

Style

Inner tepal (monocotyledonous petal)

Honey guide

Outer tepal (monocotyledonous sepal)

Tepal scar

Receptacle

Stamen

Anther

Filament

Ovary wall

Ovule

Pollen on anther

Pedicel (flower stalk)

Papilla (fleshy hair)

Outer tepal sheath

Style

Folded inner tepal (monocotyledonous petal)

Stigma

Ovary

Receptacle

Anther

Pedicel (flower stalk)

Filament

LONGITUDINAL SECTION THROUGH FLOWER BUD

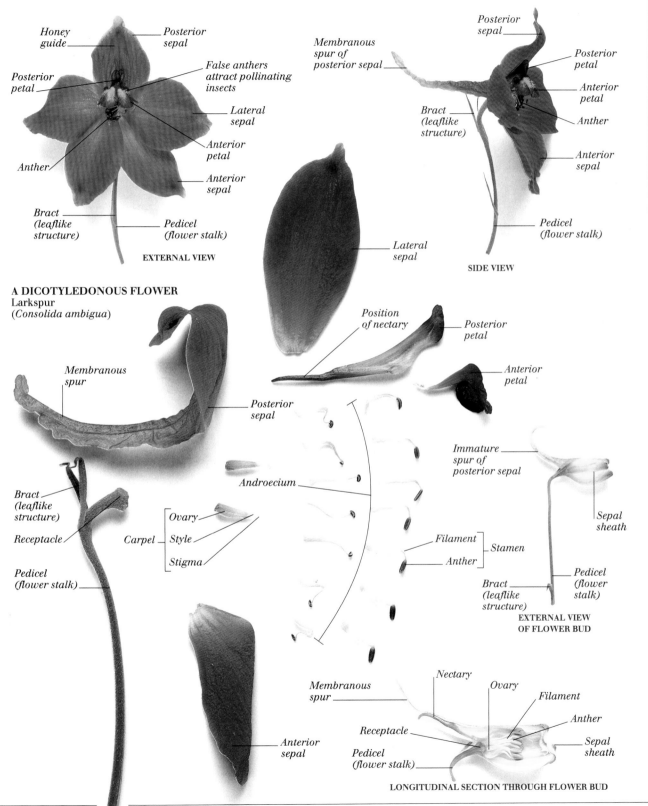

A DICOTYLEDONOUS FLOWER
Larkspur
(*Consolida ambigua*)

Honey guide

Posterior sepal

False anthers attract pollinating insects

Posterior petal

Lateral sepal

Anterior petal

Anterior sepal

Anther

Bract (leaflike structure)

Pedicel (flower stalk)

EXTERNAL VIEW

Membranous spur of posterior sepal

Posterior sepal

Posterior petal

Anterior petal

Anther

Bract (leaflike structure)

Anterior sepal

Pedicel (flower stalk)

SIDE VIEW

Lateral sepal

Membranous spur

Posterior sepal

Position of nectary

Posterior petal

Anterior petal

Bract (leaflike structure)

Receptacle

Androecium

Pedicel (flower stalk)

Carpel
Ovary
Style
Stigma

Filament
Anther
Stamen

Immature spur of posterior sepal

Sepal sheath

Bract (leaflike structure)

Pedicel (flower stalk)

EXTERNAL VIEW OF FLOWER BUD

Anterior sepal

Membranous spur

Nectary

Ovary

Filament

Anther

Receptacle

Sepal sheath

Pedicel (flower stalk)

LONGITUDINAL SECTION THROUGH FLOWER BUD

141

Flowers 2

COMPOUND INFLORESCENCE (CAPITULUM)
Sunflower
(*Helianthus annuus*)

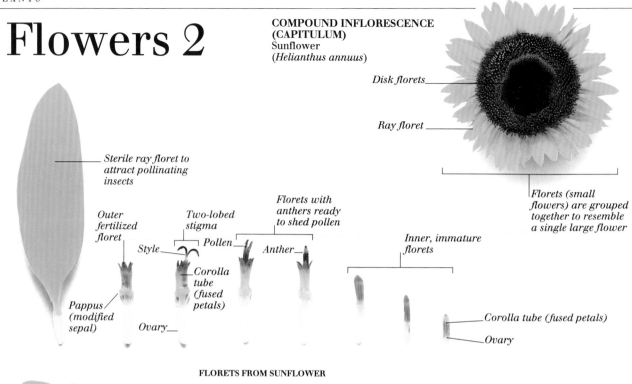

Disk florets

Ray floret

Florets (small flowers) are grouped together to resemble a single large flower

Sterile ray floret to attract pollinating insects

Outer fertilized floret

Two-lobed stigma

Florets with anthers ready to shed pollen

Style

Pollen

Anther

Inner, immature florets

Corolla tube (fused petals)

Pappus (modified sepal)

Ovary

Corolla tube (fused petals)

Ovary

FLORETS FROM SUNFLOWER

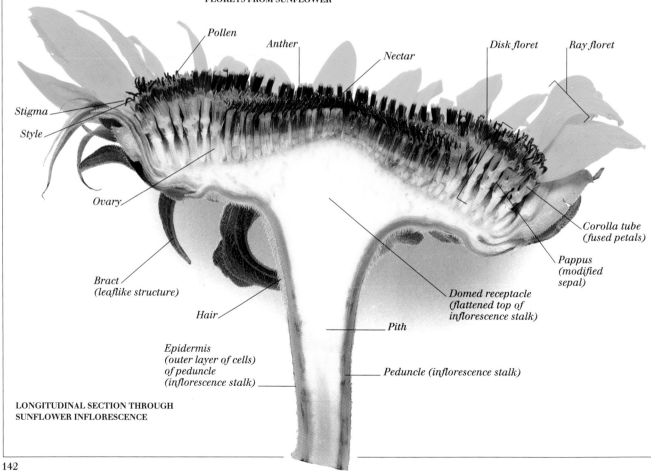

Pollen

Anther

Nectar

Disk floret

Ray floret

Stigma

Style

Ovary

Corolla tube (fused petals)

Pappus (modified sepal)

Bract (leaflike structure)

Hair

Domed receptacle (flattened top of inflorescence stalk)

Pith

Epidermis (outer layer of cells) of peduncle (inflorescence stalk)

Peduncle (inflorescence stalk)

LONGITUDINAL SECTION THROUGH SUNFLOWER INFLORESCENCE

ARRANGEMENT OF FLOWERS ON STEM

Bract
(leaflike
structure)

Flower

Ovary

Peduncle
(inflorescence
stalk)

Remains of tepals
(monocotyledonous
petals and sepals)

INFLORESCENCE (SPIKE)
Heliconia peruviana

Flower

Petal

Peduncle
(inflorescence
stalk)

Pedicel
(flower
stalk)

**INFLORESCENCE
(COMPOUND UMBEL)**
European elder
(*Sambucus nigra*)

Spathe
(large bract) to
attract pollinating
insects

Spadix (fleshy
axis) carrying
male and female
flowers

Peduncle
(inflorescence
stalk)

INFLORESCENCE (SPADIX)
Flamingo Flower
(*Anthurium andreanum*)

Stigma

Style

Anther
Filament

Stamen

Flower
bud

Pedicel
(flower
stalk)

Bract
(leaflike
structure)

Peduncle
(inflorescence
stalk) fused
to bract

**INFLORESCENCE
(DICHASIAL CYME)**
Common linden
(*Tilia x europaea*)

Three-lobed
stigma

Style

Ovary

Inner tepal
(monocotyledonous
petal)

Filament
Anther

Stamen

Outer tepal
(monocotyledonous
sepal)

Pedicel
(flower stalk)

SINGLE FLOWER
Glory lily
(*Gloriosa superba*)

Flower

Peduncle
(inflorescence
stalk)

Corolla

Calyx

Bract
(leaflike
structure)

**SINGLE
FLOWER**

**INFLORESCENCE
(SPHERICAL UMBEL)**
Echinops sp.

Pollination

POLLINATION IS THE TRANSFER OF POLLEN (which contains the male sex cells) from an anther (part of the male reproductive organ) to a stigma (part of the female reproductive organ). This process precedes fertilization (see pp. 146-147). Pollination may occur within the same flower (self-pollination), or between flowers on separate plants of the same species (cross-pollination). In most plants, pollination is carried out either by insects (entomophilous pollination) or by the wind (anemophilous pollination). Less commonly, birds, bats, or water are the agents of pollination. Insect-pollinated flowers are typically scented and brightly colored. They also produce nectar, on which insects feed. Such flowers also tend to have patterns that are visible only in ultraviolet light, which many insects can see but which humans cannot. These features attract insects, which become covered with the sticky pollen grains when they visit one flower, and then transfer the pollen to the next flower they visit. Wind-pollinated flowers are generally small, relatively inconspicuous, and unscented. They produce large quantities of light pollen grains that are easily blown by the wind to other flowers.

REPRODUCTIVE STRUCTURES IN WIND-POLLINATED PLANT
Sweet chestnut
(*Castanea sativa*)

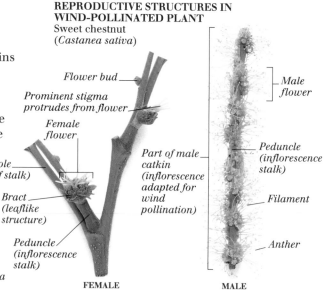

Flower bud

Prominent stigma protrudes from flower

Female flower

Petiole (leaf stalk)

Bract (leaflike structure)

Peduncle (inflorescence stalk)

Part of male catkin (inflorescence adapted for wind pollination)

Male flower

Peduncle (inflorescence stalk)

Filament

Anther

FEMALE

MALE

REPRODUCTIVE STRUCTURES IN INSECT-POLLINATED PLANTS

Stigma

Style

Dehisced (split open) pollen sac

Boundary between two fused carpels (each carpel consists of a stigma, style, and ovary)

Ovary

Endothecium (pollen sac wall)

Pollen grain

Anther

Stamen

Filament

Calyx (whorl of sepals)

MICROGRAPHS OF POLLEN GRAINS

Exine (outer coat of pollen grain)

Pore

EUROPEAN FIELD ELM
(*Ulmus minor*)

MICROGRAPH OF CARPELS (FEMALE ORGANS)
Yellow-wort
(*Blackstonia perfoliata*)

Colpus (furrow-shaped aperture)

Exine (outer coat of pollen grain)

JUSTICIA AUREA

Exine (outer coat of pollen grain)

Pore

Baculum (rod-shaped structure)

MEADOW CRANESBILL
(*Geranium pratense*)

MICROGRAPH OF STAMENS (MALE ORGANS)
Common centaury
(*Centaurium erythraea*)

Colpus (furrow-shaped aperture)

Exine (outer coat of pollen grain)

Equatorial furrow

BOX-LEAVED MILKWORT
(*Polygala chamaebuxus*)

INSECT POLLINATION OF MEADOW SAGE

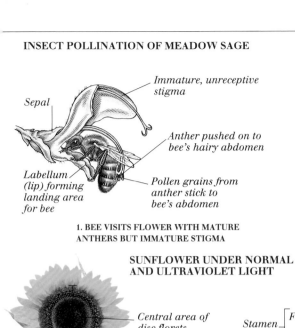

Sepal

Immature, unreceptive stigma

Anther pushed on to bee's hairy abdomen

Labellum (lip) forming landing area for bee

Pollen grains from anther stick to bee's abdomen

1. BEE VISITS FLOWER WITH MATURE ANTHERS BUT IMMATURE STIGMA

Pollen grains attached to hairy abdomen

2. BEE FLIES TO OTHER FLOWERS

Long style curves downward when bee enters flower

Sepal

Mature, receptive stigma touches bee's abdomen, picking up pollen

Labellum (lip) forming landing area for bee

3. BEE VISITS FLOWER WHERE THE ANTHERS HAVE WITHERED AND THE STIGMA IS MATURE

SUNFLOWER UNDER NORMAL AND ULTRAVIOLET LIGHT

Central area of disc florets

Ray floret

NORMAL LIGHT

Petal

Ovary

Stigma

Stamen
- Filament
- Anther

NORMAL LIGHT

ST JOHN'S WORT UNDER NORMAL AND ULTRAVIOLET LIGHT

Honey guide directs insects to dark, central part of flower

Lighter, outer part of ray floret

Darker, inner part of ray floret

Insects attracted to darkest, central part of flower, which contains nectaries, anthers, and stigmas

Dark central area containing nectaries, anthers, and stigmas

ULTRAVIOLET LIGHT

ULTRAVIOLET LIGHT

Pore

Exine (outer coat of pollen grain)

Exine (outer coat of pollen grain)

Trilete mark (development scar)

Exine (outer coat of pollen grain)

Columella (small column-shaped structure)

Colpus (furrow-shaped aperture)

Exine (outer coat of pollen grain)

Tricolpate (three colpae) pollen grain

MIMULOPSIS SOLMSII

THESIUM ALPINIUM

RUELLIA GRANDIFLORA

CROSSANDRA NILOTICA

Fertilization

FERTILIZATION IS THE FUSION of male and female gametes (sex cells) to produce a zygote (embryo). Following pollination (see pp. 144-145), the pollen grains that contain the male gametes are on the stigma, some distance from the female gamete (ovum) inside the ovule. To enable the gametes to meet, the pollen grain germinates and produces a pollen tube, which grows down and enters the embryo sac (the inner part of the ovule that contains the ovum). Two male gametes, traveling at the tip of the pollen tube, enter the embryo sac. One gamete fuses with the ovum to produce a zygote that will develop into an embryo plant. The other male gamete fuses with two polar nuclei to produce the endosperm, which acts as a food supply for the developing embryo. Fertilization also initiates other changes: the integument (outer part of ovule) forms a testa (seed coat) around the embryo and endosperm; the petals fall off; the stigma and style wither; and the ovary wall forms a layer (called the pericarp) around the seed. Together, the pericarp and seed form the fruit, which may be succulent (see pp. 148-149) or dry (see pp. 150-151). In some species (such as blackberry), apomixis can occur: The seed develops without fertilization of the ovum by a male gamete, but endosperm formation and fruit development take place as in other species.

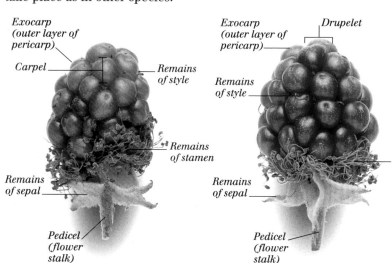

BANANA
(*Musa 'Lacatan'*)

DEVELOPMENT OF A SUCCULENT FRUIT
Blackberry
(*Rubus fruticosus*)

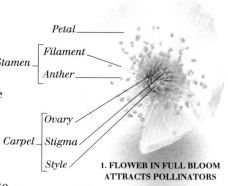

Petal

Stamen
Filament
Anther

Carpel
Ovary
Stigma
Style

**1. FLOWER IN FULL BLOOM
ATTRACTS POLLINATORS**

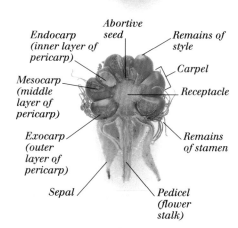

Endocarp (inner layer of pericarp)

Mesocarp (middle layer of pericarp)

Exocarp (outer layer of pericarp)

Sepal

Abortive seed

Remains of style

Carpel

Receptacle

Remains of stamen

Pedicel (flower stalk)

**4. PERICARP FORMS
FLESH, SKIN, AND A HARD INNER
LAYER (SHOWN IN CROSS SECTION)**

Exocarp (outer layer of pericarp)

Carpel

Remains of style

Remains of sepal

Remains of stamen

Pedicel (flower stalk)

**7. MESOCARP (FLESHY PART OF PERICARP)
OF EACH CARPEL STARTS TO
CHANGE COLOR**

Exocarp (outer layer of pericarp)

Drupelet

Remains of style

Remains of sepal

Remains of stamen

Pedicel (flower stalk)

**8. CARPELS MATURE INTO DRUPELETS
(SMALL FLESHY FRUITS WITH SINGLE SEEDS
SURROUNDED BY HARD ENDOCARP)**

Exocarp (outer layer of pericarp)

Drupelet

Remains of style

Remains of sepal

Remains of stamen

Pedicel (flower stalk)

**9. MESOCARP OF DRUPELET BECOMES
DARKER AND SWEETER**

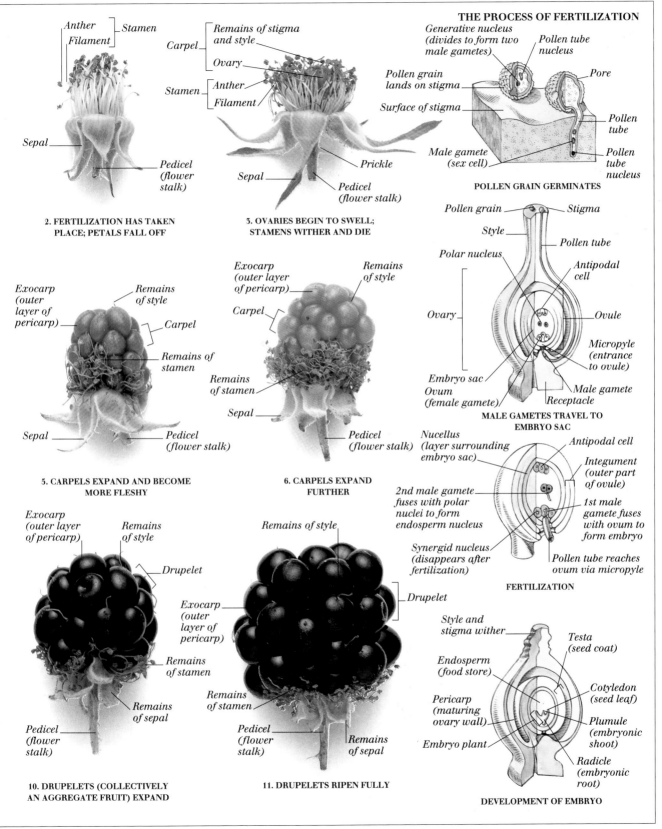

2. FERTILIZATION HAS TAKEN PLACE; PETALS FALL OFF

Stamen
Anther
Filament
Sepal
Pedicel (flower stalk)

3. OVARIES BEGIN TO SWELL; STAMENS WITHER AND DIE

Carpel
Remains of stigma and style
Ovary
Stamen
Anther
Filament
Sepal
Pedicel (flower stalk)
Prickle

THE PROCESS OF FERTILIZATION

Generative nucleus (divides to form two male gametes)
Pollen tube nucleus
Pollen grain lands on stigma
Pore
Surface of stigma
Pollen tube
Male gamete (sex cell)
Pollen tube nucleus

POLLEN GRAIN GERMINATES

5. CARPELS EXPAND AND BECOME MORE FLESHY

Exocarp (outer layer of pericarp)
Remains of style
Carpel
Remains of stamen
Sepal
Pedicel (flower stalk)

6. CARPELS EXPAND FURTHER

Exocarp (outer layer of pericarp)
Remains of style
Carpel
Remains of stamen
Sepal
Pedicel (flower stalk)

Pollen grain
Stigma
Style
Pollen tube
Polar nucleus
Antipodal cell
Ovary
Ovule
Micropyle (entrance to ovule)
Embryo sac
Ovum (female gamete)
Male gamete
Receptacle

MALE GAMETES TRAVEL TO EMBRYO SAC

Nucellus (layer surrounding embryo sac)
Antipodal cell
Integument (outer part of ovule)
2nd male gamete fuses with polar nuclei to form endosperm nucleus
1st male gamete fuses with ovum to form embryo
Synergid nucleus (disappears after fertilization)
Pollen tube reaches ovum via micropyle

FERTILIZATION

10. DRUPELETS (COLLECTIVELY AN AGGREGATE FRUIT) EXPAND

Exocarp (outer layer of pericarp)
Remains of style
Drupelet
Remains of stamen
Remains of sepal
Pedicel (flower stalk)

11. DRUPELETS RIPEN FULLY

Remains of style
Drupelet
Exocarp (outer layer of pericarp)
Remains of stamen
Pedicel (flower stalk)
Remains of sepal

Style and stigma wither
Testa (seed coat)
Endosperm (food store)
Cotyledon (seed leaf)
Pericarp (maturing ovary wall)
Plumule (embryonic shoot)
Embryo plant
Radicle (embryonic root)

DEVELOPMENT OF EMBRYO

147

Succulent fruits

A FRUIT IS A FULLY DEVELOPED and ripened ovary—the seed-producing part of a plant's female reproductive organs. Fruits may be succulent or dry (see pp. 150-151). Succulent fruits are fleshy and brightly colored, making them attractive to animals, which eat them and disperse the seeds away from the parent plant. The wall (pericarp) of a succulent fruit has three layers: an outer exocarp, a middle mesocarp, and an inner endocarp. These three layers vary in thickness and texture in different types of fruits and may blend into each other. Succulent fruits can be classed as simple (derived from one ovary) or compound (derived from several ovaries). Simple succulent fruits include berries, which typically have many seeds, and drupes, which typically have a single stone or pit (such as cherry and peach). Compound succulent fruits include aggregate fruits, which are formed from many ovaries in one flower, and multiple fruits, which develop from the ovaries of many flowers. Some fruits, known as false fruits or pseudocarps, develop from parts of the flower in addition to the ovaries. For example, the flesh of the apple is formed from the receptacle (the upper end of the flower stalk).

BERRY
Cocoa
(*Theobroma cacao*)

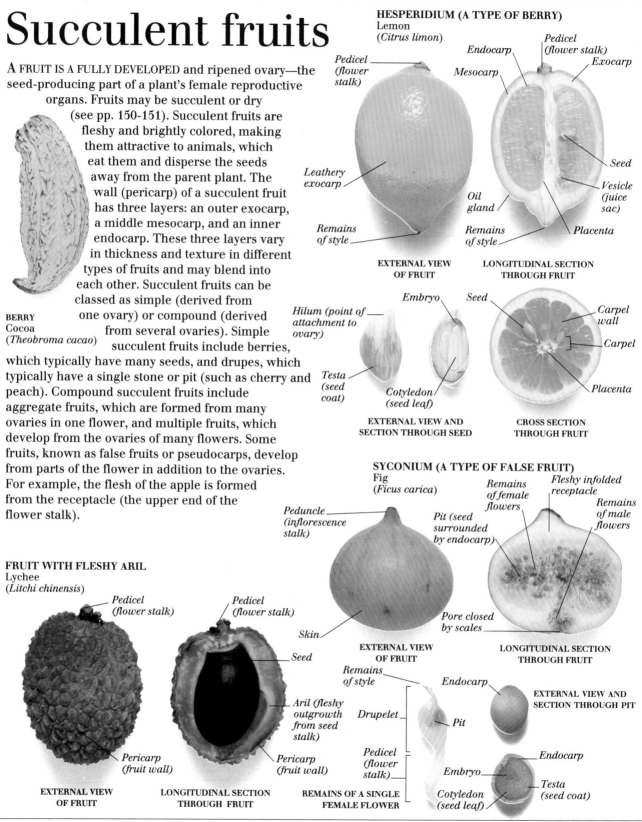

HESPERIDIUM (A TYPE OF BERRY)
Lemon
(*Citrus limon*)

Pedicel (flower stalk)
Endocarp
Mesocarp
Pedicel (flower stalk)
Exocarp
Leathery exocarp
Seed
Oil gland
Vesicle (juice sac)
Remains of style
Remains of style
Placenta

EXTERNAL VIEW OF FRUIT

LONGITUDINAL SECTION THROUGH FRUIT

Hilum (point of attachment to ovary)
Embryo
Seed
Carpel wall
Carpel
Testa (seed coat)
Cotyledon (seed leaf)
Placenta

EXTERNAL VIEW AND SECTION THROUGH SEED

CROSS SECTION THROUGH FRUIT

SYCONIUM (A TYPE OF FALSE FRUIT)
Fig
(*Ficus carica*)

Peduncle (inflorescence stalk)
Remains of female flowers
Fleshy infolded receptacle
Remains of male flowers
Pit (seed surrounded by endocarp)
Skin
Pore closed by scales

EXTERNAL VIEW OF FRUIT

LONGITUDINAL SECTION THROUGH FRUIT

FRUIT WITH FLESHY ARIL
Lychee
(*Litchi chinensis*)

Pedicel (flower stalk)
Pedicel (flower stalk)
Skin
Seed
Aril (fleshy outgrowth from seed stalk)
Pericarp (fruit wall)
Pericarp (fruit wall)

Remains of style
Drupelet
Pit
Pedicel (flower stalk)
Endocarp
Embryo
Cotyledon (seed leaf)
Endocarp
Testa (seed coat)

EXTERNAL VIEW AND SECTION THROUGH PIT

EXTERNAL VIEW OF FRUIT

LONGITUDINAL SECTION THROUGH FRUIT

REMAINS OF A SINGLE FEMALE FLOWER

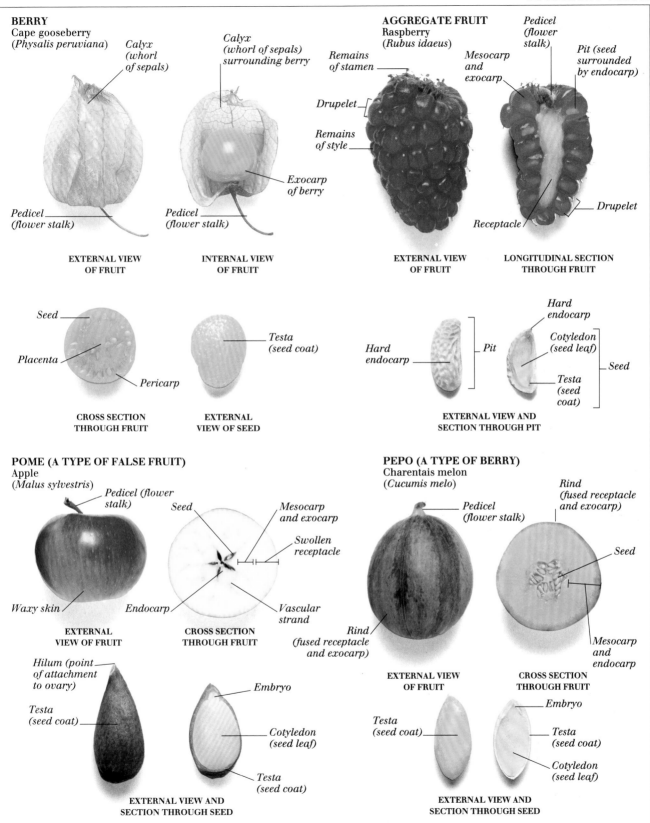

BERRY
Cape gooseberry
(*Physalis peruviana*)

Calyx (whorl of sepals)

Calyx (whorl of sepals) surrounding berry

Pedicel (flower stalk)

Pedicel (flower stalk)

Exocarp of berry

EXTERNAL VIEW
OF FRUIT

INTERNAL VIEW
OF FRUIT

Seed

Placenta

Pericarp

Testa (seed coat)

CROSS SECTION
THROUGH FRUIT

EXTERNAL
VIEW OF SEED

AGGREGATE FRUIT
Raspberry
(*Rubus idaeus*)

Pedicel (flower stalk)

Pit (seed surrounded by endocarp)

Remains of stamen

Mesocarp and exocarp

Drupelet

Remains of style

Receptacle

Drupelet

EXTERNAL VIEW
OF FRUIT

LONGITUDINAL SECTION
THROUGH FRUIT

Hard endocarp

Hard endocarp

Cotyledon (seed leaf)

Testa (seed coat)

Pit

Seed

EXTERNAL VIEW AND
SECTION THROUGH PIT

POME (A TYPE OF FALSE FRUIT)
Apple
(*Malus sylvestris*)

Pedicel (flower stalk)

Seed

Mesocarp and exocarp

Swollen receptacle

Waxy skin

Endocarp

Vascular strand

EXTERNAL
VIEW OF FRUIT

CROSS SECTION
THROUGH FRUIT

Hilum (point of attachment to ovary)

Testa (seed coat)

Embryo

Cotyledon (seed leaf)

Testa (seed coat)

EXTERNAL VIEW AND
SECTION THROUGH SEED

PEPO (A TYPE OF BERRY)
Charentais melon
(*Cucumis melo*)

Rind (fused receptacle and exocarp)

Pedicel (flower stalk)

Seed

Rind (fused receptacle and exocarp)

Mesocarp and endocarp

EXTERNAL VIEW
OF FRUIT

CROSS SECTION
THROUGH FRUIT

Testa (seed coat)

Embryo

Testa (seed coat)

Cotyledon (seed leaf)

EXTERNAL VIEW AND
SECTION THROUGH SEED

149

Dry fruits

DRY FRUITS HAVE A HARD, DRY PERICARP (fruit wall) around their seeds, unlike succulent fruits, which have fleshy pericarps (see pp. 148-149). Dry fruits are divided into three types: dehiscent, in which the pericarp splits open to release the seeds; indehiscent, which do not split open; and schizocarpic, in which the fruit splits but the seeds are not exposed. Dehiscent dry fruits include capsules (for example, love-in-a-mist), follicles (delphinium), legumes (pea), and silicles (honesty). Typically, the seeds of dehiscent fruits are dispersed by the wind. Indehiscent dry fruits include nuts (sweet chestnut), nutlets (goose grass), achenes (strawberry), caryopses (wheat), samaras (elm), and cypselas (dandelion). Some indehiscent dry fruits are dispersed by the wind, assisted by "wings" (elm) or "parachutes" (dandelion); others (goose grass) have hooked pericarps to aid dispersal on animals' fur. Schizocarpic dry fruits include cremocarps (hogweed), and double samaras (sycamore maple); these are dispersed by the wind.

NUTLET
Goose grass
(*Galium aparine*)

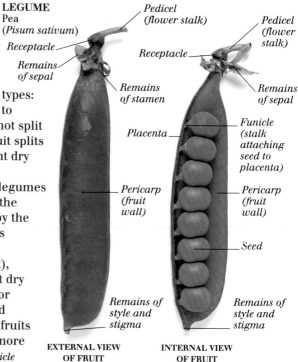

LEGUME
Pea
(*Pisum sativum*)

- Pedicel (flower stalk)
- Receptacle
- Remains of sepal
- Remains of stamen
- Placenta
- Pericarp (fruit wall)
- Remains of style and stigma

- Pedicel (flower stalk)
- Receptacle
- Remains of sepal
- Funicle (stalk attaching seed to placenta)
- Pericarp (fruit wall)
- Seed
- Remains of style and stigma

EXTERNAL VIEW OF FRUIT

INTERNAL VIEW OF FRUIT

- Funicle (stalk attaching seed to placenta)
- Micropyle (pore for water absorption)
- Testa (seed coat)

- Cotyledon (seed leaf)
- Radicle (embryonic root)
- Testa (seed coat)
- Plumule (embryonic shoot)

EXTERIOR VIEW AND SECTION THROUGH SEED

NUT
Spanish chestnut
(*Castanea sativa*)

- Line of splitting between valves of cupule
- Peduncle (inflorescence stalk)
- Remains of male inflorescence
- Nut (indehiscent fruit)
- Spiky cupule (husk around fruit formed from bracts)

EXTERNAL VIEW OF FRUIT WITH SURROUNDING CUPULE

- Remains of stigma
- Remains of style
- Remains of stigma
- Remains of style
- Nut (indehiscent fruit)
- Embryo
- Cotyledon (seed leaf)
- Testa (seed coat)
- Woody pericarp (fruit wall)
- Woody pericarp (fruit wall)

EXTERNAL VIEW AND SECTION THROUGH FRUIT

ACHENE
Strawberry
(*Fragaria* x *ananassa*)

- Sepal
- Pedicel (flower stalk)
- Swollen receptacle
- Remains of stigma and style
- Achene (one-seeded dry fruit)

- Sepal
- Pedicel (flower stalk)
- Swollen fleshy tissues of receptacle

EXTERNAL VIEW OF FRUIT

LONGITUDINAL SECTION THROUGH FRUIT

- Pericarp (fruit wall)
- Pericarp (fruit wall)
- Cotyledon (seed leaf)
- Testa (seed coat)

EXTERNAL VIEW AND SECTION THROUGH SEED

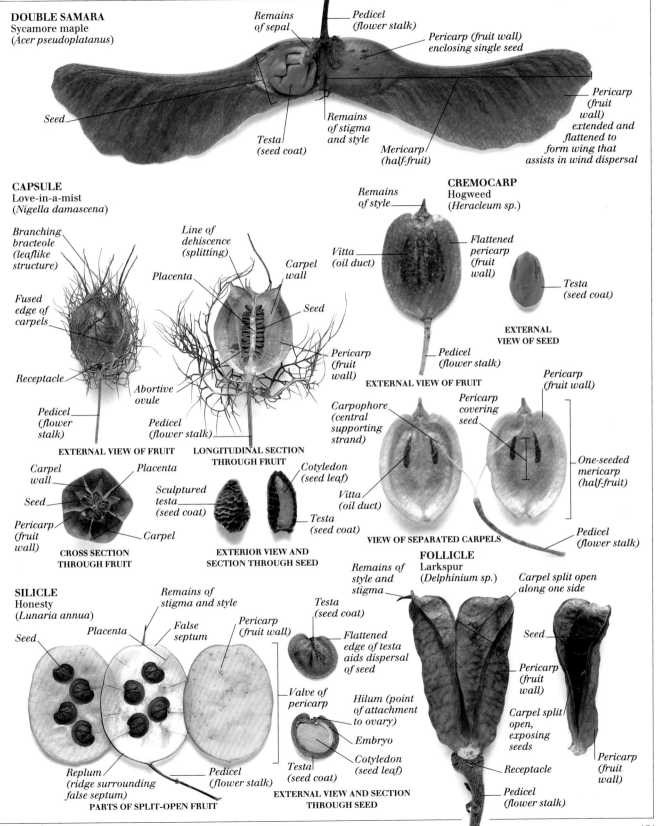

DOUBLE SAMARA
Sycamore maple
(*Acer pseudoplatanus*)

Remains of sepal

Pedicel (flower stalk)

Pericarp (fruit wall) enclosing single seed

Seed

Testa (seed coat)

Remains of stigma and style

Mericarp (half-fruit)

Pericarp (fruit wall) extended and flattened to form wing that assists in wind dispersal

CAPSULE
Love-in-a-mist
(*Nigella damascena*)

Branching bracteole (leaflike structure)

Fused edge of carpels

Receptacle

Pedicel (flower stalk)

Line of dehiscence (splitting)

Placenta

Carpel wall

Seed

Pericarp (fruit wall)

Abortive ovule

Pedicel (flower stalk)

EXTERNAL VIEW OF FRUIT

LONGITUDINAL SECTION THROUGH FRUIT

Carpel wall

Placenta

Seed

Pericarp (fruit wall)

Carpel

CROSS SECTION THROUGH FRUIT

Sculptured testa (seed coat)

Cotyledon (seed leaf)

Testa (seed coat)

EXTERIOR VIEW AND SECTION THROUGH SEED

CREMOCARP
Hogweed
(*Heracleum sp.*)

Remains of style

Vitta (oil duct)

Flattened pericarp (fruit wall)

Testa (seed coat)

EXTERNAL VIEW OF SEED

Pedicel (flower stalk)

EXTERNAL VIEW OF FRUIT

Carpophore (central supporting strand)

Pericarp covering seed

Pericarp (fruit wall)

Vitta (oil duct)

One-seeded mericarp (half-fruit)

Pedicel (flower stalk)

VIEW OF SEPARATED CARPELS

SILICLE
Honesty
(*Lunaria annua*)

Remains of stigma and style

False septum

Pericarp (fruit wall)

Seed

Placenta

Replum (ridge surrounding false septum)

Pedicel (flower stalk)

Valve of pericarp

PARTS OF SPLIT-OPEN FRUIT

Testa (seed coat)

Flattened edge of testa aids dispersal of seed

Hilum (point of attachment to ovary)

Embryo

Cotyledon (seed leaf)

Testa (seed coat)

EXTERNAL VIEW AND SECTION THROUGH SEED

FOLLICLE
Larkspur
(*Delphinium sp.*)

Remains of style and stigma

Carpel split open along one side

Seed

Pericarp (fruit wall)

Carpel split open, exposing seeds

Receptacle

Pedicel (flower stalk)

Pericarp (fruit wall)

151

Germination

GERMINATION IS THE GROWTH OF SEEDS INTO SEEDLINGS. It starts when seeds become active below ground, and ends when the first foliage leaves appear above ground. A seed consists of an embryo and its food supply, surrounded by a testa (seed coat). The embryo is made up of one or two cotyledons (seed leaves) attached to a central axis. The upper part of the axis consists of an epicotyl, which has a plumule (embryonic shoot) at its tip. The lower part of the axis consists of a hypocotyl and a radicle (embryonic root). After dispersal from the parent plant, the seeds dehydrate and enter a period of dormancy. Germination begins, following this dormant period, as long as the seeds have enough water, oxygen, warmth, and, in some cases, light. In the first stages of germination, the seed takes in water; the embryo starts to use its food store; and the radicle swells, breaks through the testa, and grows downward. Germination then proceeds in one of two ways, depending on the type of seed. In epigeal germination, the hypocotyl lengthens, pulling the plumule and its protective cotyledons out of the soil. In hypogeal germination, the cotyledons remain below ground and the epicotyl lengthens, pushing the plumule upward.

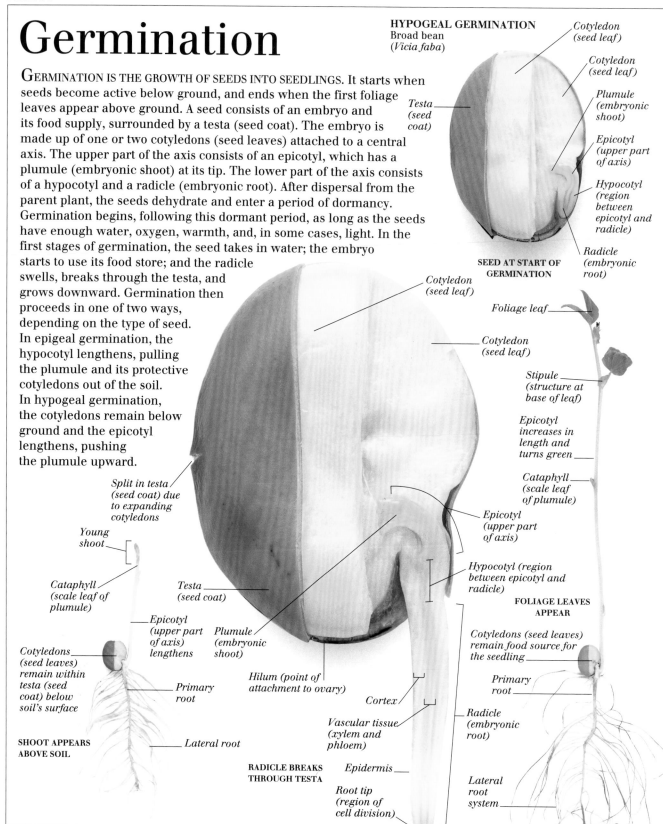

HYPOGEAL GERMINATION
Broad bean
(Vicia faba)

Cotyledon (seed leaf)

Cotyledon (seed leaf)

Testa (seed coat)

Plumule (embryonic shoot)

Epicotyl (upper part of axis)

Hypocotyl (region between epicotyl and radicle)

Radicle (embryonic root)

SEED AT START OF GERMINATION

Cotyledon (seed leaf)

Foliage leaf

Cotyledon (seed leaf)

Stipule (structure at base of leaf)

Epicotyl increases in length and turns green

Cataphyll (scale leaf of plumule)

Epicotyl (upper part of axis)

Hypocotyl (region between epicotyl and radicle)

FOLIAGE LEAVES APPEAR

Cotyledons (seed leaves) remain food source for the seedling

Primary root

Radicle (embryonic root)

Lateral root system

Split in testa (seed coat) due to expanding cotyledons

Young shoot

Cataphyll (scale leaf of plumule)

Cotyledons (seed leaves) remain within testa (seed coat) below soil's surface

SHOOT APPEARS ABOVE SOIL

Epicotyl (upper part of axis) lengthens

Testa (seed coat)

Plumule (embryonic shoot)

Primary root

Lateral root

Hilum (point of attachment to ovary)

Cortex

Vascular tissue (xylem and phloem)

RADICLE BREAKS THROUGH TESTA

Epidermis

Root tip (region of cell division)

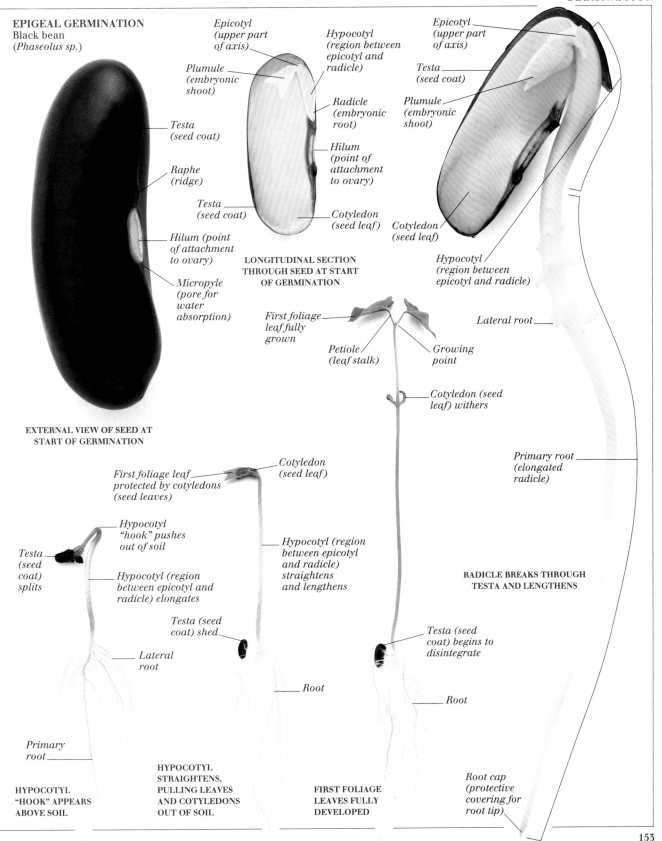

EPIGEAL GERMINATION
Black bean
(*Phaseolus sp.*)

Testa (seed coat)

Raphe (ridge)

Hilum (point of attachment to ovary)

Micropyle (pore for water absorption)

EXTERNAL VIEW OF SEED AT START OF GERMINATION

Epicotyl (upper part of axis)

Plumule (embryonic shoot)

Hypocotyl (region between epicotyl and radicle)

Radicle (embryonic root)

Hilum (point of attachment to ovary)

Testa (seed coat)

Cotyledon (seed leaf)

LONGITUDINAL SECTION THROUGH SEED AT START OF GERMINATION

Epicotyl (upper part of axis)

Testa (seed coat)

Plumule (embryonic shoot)

Cotyledon (seed leaf)

Hypocotyl (region between epicotyl and radicle)

First foliage leaf fully grown

Petiole (leaf stalk)

Growing point

Cotyledon (seed leaf) withers

Lateral root

Primary root (elongated radicle)

RADICLE BREAKS THROUGH TESTA AND LENGTHENS

First foliage leaf protected by cotyledons (seed leaves)

Cotyledon (seed leaf)

Testa (seed coat) splits

Hypocotyl "hook" pushes out of soil

Hypocotyl (region between epicotyl and radicle) elongates

Hypocotyl (region between epicotyl and radicle) straightens and lengthens

Testa (seed coat) shed

Lateral root

Primary root

HYPOCOTYL "HOOK" APPEARS ABOVE SOIL

Root

HYPOCOTYL STRAIGHTENS, PULLING LEAVES AND COTYLEDONS OUT OF SOIL

FIRST FOLIAGE LEAVES FULLY DEVELOPED

Testa (seed coat) begins to disintegrate

Root

Root cap (protective covering for root tip)

153

Vegetative reproduction

MANY PLANTS CAN PROPAGATE THEMSELVES by vegetative reproduction. In this process, part of a plant separates, takes root, and grows into a new plant. Vegetative reproduction is a type of asexual reproduction; it involves only one parent and there is no fusion of gametes (sex cells). Plants use various structures to reproduce vegetatively. Some plants use underground storage organs. Such organs include rhizomes (horizontal, underground stems), the branches of which produce new plants; bulbs (swollen leaf bases) and corms (swollen stems), which produce daughter bulbs or corms that separate from the parent; and stem tubers (thickened underground stems) and root tubers (swollen adventitious roots), which also separate from the parent. Other propagative structures include runners and stolons, creeping horizontal stems that take root and produce new plants; bulbils, small bulbs that develop on the stem or in the place of flowers, and then drop off and grow into new plants; and adventitious buds, miniature plants that form on leaf margins before dropping to the ground and growing into mature plants.

CORM
Gladiolus
(*Gladiolus sp.*)

ADVENTITIOUS BUD
Mexican hat plant
(*Kalanchoe daigremontiana*)

Apex of leaf

Lamina (blade) of leaf

Leaf margin

Notch in leaf margin containing meristematic (actively dividing) cells

Adventitious bud (detachable bud with adventitious roots) drops from leaf

Petiole (leaf stalk)

BULBIL IN PLACE OF FLOWER
Orange lily
(*Lilium bulbiferum*)

Scar left by flower

Leaf

Pedicel (flower stalk)

Detachable bulbil formed in place of flower

Peduncle (inflorescence stalk)

STOLON
Ground ivy
(*Glechoma hederacea*)

Internode

Terminal bud

Node

Node

Parent plant

Stolon (creeping stem)

Adventitious root of daughter plant

Daughter plant developed from lateral bud

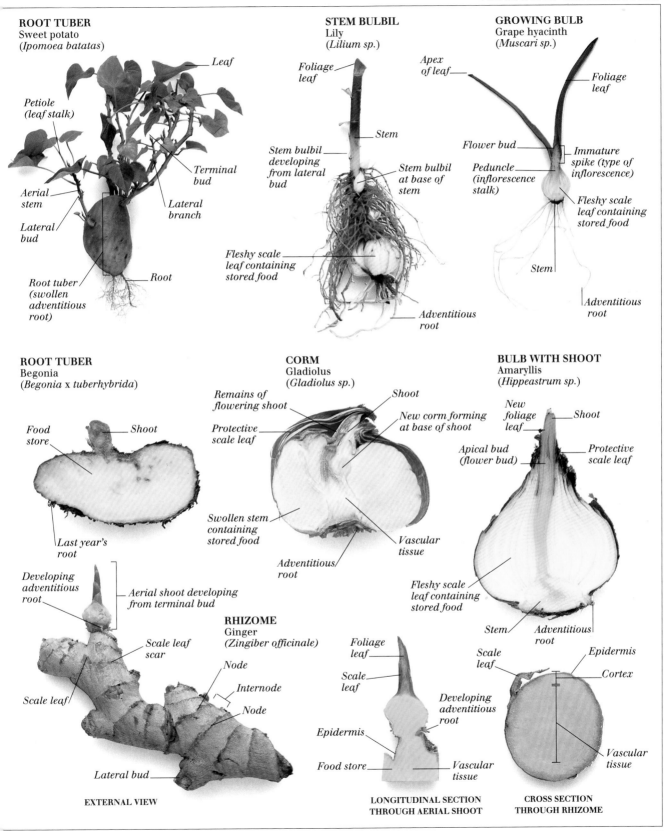

ROOT TUBER
Sweet potato
(*Ipomoea batatas*)

Leaf

Petiole
(leaf stalk)

Terminal
bud

Aerial
stem

Lateral
branch

Lateral
bud

Root tuber
(swollen
adventitious
root)

Root

STEM BULBIL
Lily
(*Lilium sp.*)

Foliage
leaf

Stem

Stem bulbil
developing
from lateral
bud

Stem bulbil
at base of
stem

Fleshy scale
leaf containing
stored food

Adventitious
root

GROWING BULB
Grape hyacinth
(*Muscari sp.*)

Apex
of leaf

Foliage
leaf

Flower bud

Immature
spike (type of
inflorescence)

Peduncle
(inflorescence
stalk)

Fleshy scale
leaf containing
stored food

Stem

Adventitious
root

ROOT TUBER
Begonia
(*Begonia* x *tuberhybrida*)

Food
store

Shoot

Last year's
root

Developing
adventitious
root

Aerial shoot developing
from terminal bud

Scale leaf
scar

Node

Internode

Node

Scale leaf

Lateral bud

EXTERNAL VIEW

CORM
Gladiolus
(*Gladiolus sp.*)

Remains of
flowering shoot

Shoot

Protective
scale leaf

New corm forming
at base of shoot

Swollen stem
containing
stored food

Vascular
tissue

Adventitious
root

RHIZOME
Ginger
(*Zingiber officinale*)

Foliage
leaf

Scale
leaf

Developing
adventitious
root

Epidermis

Food store

Vascular
tissue

**LONGITUDINAL SECTION
THROUGH AERIAL SHOOT**

BULB WITH SHOOT
Amaryllis
(*Hippeastrum sp.*)

New
foliage
leaf

Shoot

Apical bud
(flower bud)

Protective
scale leaf

Fleshy scale
leaf containing
stored food

Stem

Adventitious
root

Scale
leaf

Epidermis

Cortex

Vascular
tissue

**CROSS SECTION
THROUGH RHIZOME**

155

Dryland plants

DRYLAND PLANTS (XEROPHYTES) are able to survive in unfavorable habitats. All are found in places where little water is available; some live in high temperatures that cause excessive loss of water from the leaves. Xerophytes show a number of adaptations to dry conditions. These include reduced leaf area, rolled leaves, sunken stomata, hairs, spines, and thick cuticles. One group, succulent plants, stores water in specially enlarged spongy tissues found in leaves, roots, or stems. Leaf succulents have enlarged, fleshy, water-storing leaves. Root succulents have a large underground water-storage organ with short-lived stems and leaves above ground. Stem succulents are represented by the cacti (family Cactaceae). Cacti stems are fleshy, green, and photosynthetic. They are typically ribbed or covered by tubercles in rows, with leaves being reduced to spines or entirely absent.

LEAF SUCCULENT
Lithops sp.

STEM SUCCULENT
Golden barrel cactus
(*Echinocactus grusonii*)

Areole (modified lateral shoot)

Trichome (hair)

Spine (modified leaf)

Spine (modified leaf)

Tubercle (projection from stem surface)

Root

EXTERNAL VIEW

Waxy cuticle (waterproof covering)

Water-storing parenchyma (packing tissue)

Sinuous (wavy) cell wall

Stoma (pore) controlling exchange of gases

MICROGRAPH OF STEM SURFACE

Tubercle (projection from stem surface)

Vascular cylinder (transport tissue)

Root

Spine (modified leaf)

Areole (modified lateral shoot)

Tubercle (projection from stem surface)

Waxy cuticle (waterproof covering)

DETAIL OF STEM SURFACE

LONGITUDINAL SECTION THROUGH STEM

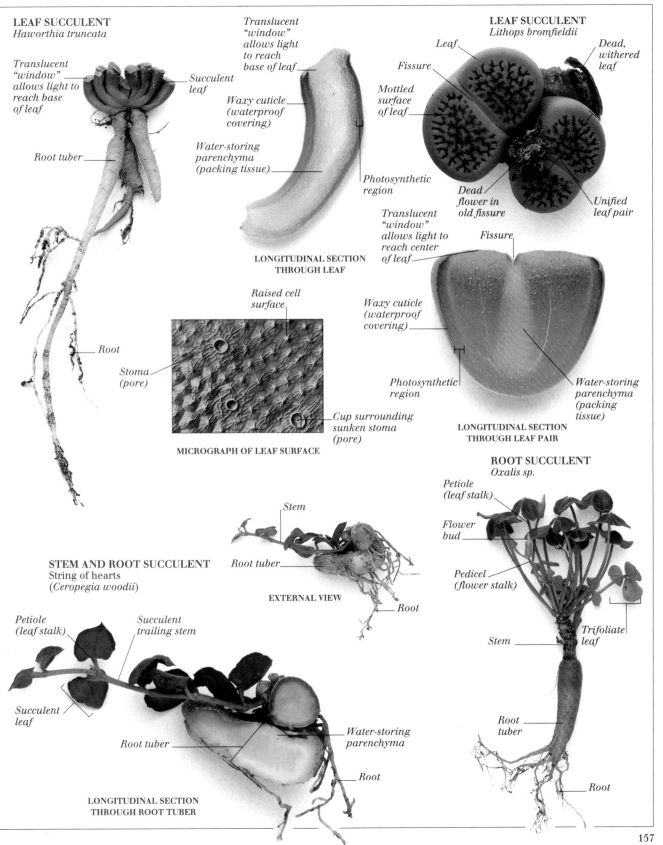

LEAF SUCCULENT
Haworthia truncata

Translucent
"window"
allows light to
reach base
of leaf

Succulent
leaf

Root tuber

Root

Translucent
"window"
allows light
to reach
base of leaf

Waxy cuticle
(waterproof
covering)

Water-storing
parenchyma
(packing tissue)

Photosynthetic
region

**LONGITUDINAL SECTION
THROUGH LEAF**

Raised cell
surface

Stoma
(pore)

Cup surrounding
sunken stoma
(pore)

MICROGRAPH OF LEAF SURFACE

LEAF SUCCULENT
Lithops bromfieldii

Leaf

Fissure

Mottled
surface
of leaf

Dead,
withered
leaf

Dead
flower in
old fissure

Unified
leaf pair

Translucent
"window"
allows light to
reach center
of leaf

Fissure

Waxy cuticle
(waterproof
covering)

Photosynthetic
region

Water-storing
parenchyma
(packing
tissue)

**LONGITUDINAL SECTION
THROUGH LEAF PAIR**

ROOT SUCCULENT
Oxalis sp.

Petiole
(leaf stalk)

Flower
bud

Pedicel
(flower stalk)

Stem

Trifoliate
leaf

Root
tuber

Root

STEM AND ROOT SUCCULENT
String of hearts
(*Ceropegia woodii*)

Stem

Root tuber

Root

EXTERNAL VIEW

Petiole
(leaf stalk)

Succulent
trailing stem

Succulent
leaf

Root tuber

Water-storing
parenchyma

Root

**LONGITUDINAL SECTION
THROUGH ROOT TUBER**

Wetland plants

WETLAND PLANTS GROW SUBMERGED IN WATER, either partially, like the water hyacinth, or completely, like the pondweeds, and show various adaptations to this habitat. Typically, there are numerous air spaces inside the stems, leaves, and roots; these aid gas exchange and buoyancy. Submerged parts generally have no cuticle (waterproof covering), allowing the plants to absorb minerals and gases directly from the water. Also, because they are supported by the water, wetland plants need little of the supportive tissue found in land plants. Stomata, the gas exchange pores, are absent from plants that are completely submerged. In partially submerged plants with floating leaves, such as water lilies, stomata are found on the upper leaf surfaces, where they cannot be flooded.

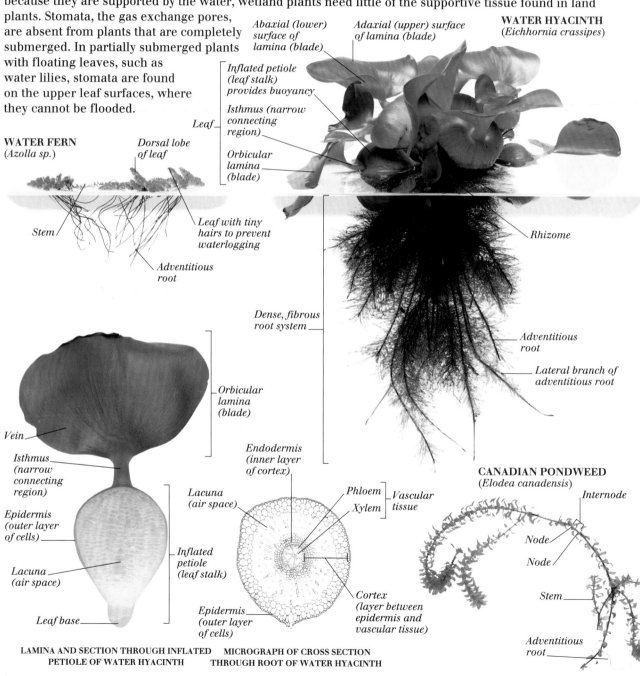

WATER HYACINTH
(Eichhornia crassipes)

Abaxial (lower) surface of lamina (blade)

Adaxial (upper) surface of lamina (blade)

Inflated petiole (leaf stalk) provides buoyancy

Isthmus (narrow connecting region)

Leaf

Orbicular lamina (blade)

Rhizome

Adventitious root

Lateral branch of adventitious root

Dense, fibrous root system

WATER FERN
(Azolla sp.)

Dorsal lobe of leaf

Stem

Leaf with tiny hairs to prevent waterlogging

Adventitious root

CANADIAN PONDWEED
(Elodea canadensis)

Internode

Node

Node

Stem

Adventitious root

Vein

Isthmus (narrow connecting region)

Epidermis (outer layer of cells)

Lacuna (air space)

Leaf base

Orbicular lamina (blade)

Endodermis (inner layer of cortex)

Lacuna (air space)

Phloem

Xylem

Vascular tissue

Inflated petiole (leaf stalk)

Epidermis (outer layer of cells)

Cortex (layer between epidermis and vascular tissue)

LAMINA AND SECTION THROUGH INFLATED PETIOLE OF WATER HYACINTH

MICROGRAPH OF CROSS SECTION THROUGH ROOT OF WATER HYACINTH

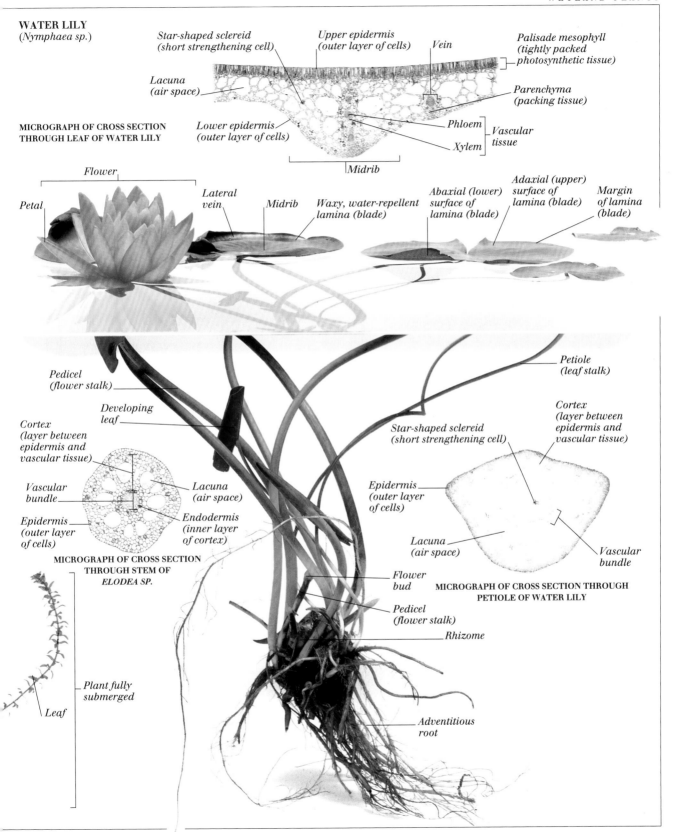

WATER LILY
(*Nymphaea sp.*)

Star-shaped sclereid
(short strengthening cell)

Upper epidermis
(outer layer of cells)

Vein

Palisade mesophyll
(tightly packed
photosynthetic tissue)

Lacuna
(air space)

Parenchyma
(packing tissue)

**MICROGRAPH OF CROSS SECTION
THROUGH LEAF OF WATER LILY**

Lower epidermis
(outer layer of cells)

Phloem | Vascular
tissue

Xylem

Midrib

Flower

Lateral
vein

Midrib

Waxy, water-repellent
lamina (blade)

Abaxial (lower)
surface of
lamina (blade)

Adaxial (upper)
surface of
lamina (blade)

Margin
of lamina
(blade)

Petal

Pedicel
(flower stalk)

Petiole
(leaf stalk)

Developing
leaf

Cortex
(layer between
epidermis and
vascular tissue)

Star-shaped sclereid
(short strengthening cell)

Cortex
(layer between
epidermis and
vascular tissue)

Vascular
bundle

Lacuna
(air space)

Epidermis
(outer layer
of cells)

Epidermis
(outer layer
of cells)

Endodermis
(inner layer
of cortex)

Lacuna
(air space)

Vascular
bundle

**MICROGRAPH OF CROSS SECTION
THROUGH STEM OF
ELODEA SP.**

**MICROGRAPH OF CROSS SECTION THROUGH
PETIOLE OF WATER LILY**

Flower
bud

Pedicel
(flower stalk)

Rhizome

Plant fully
submerged

Leaf

Adventitious
root

Carnivorous plants

A PITCHER PLANT
Cobra lily (*Darlingtonia californica*)

Areola ("window" of transparent tissue)

Fishtail nectary

Hood

Wing

Pitcher

Tubular petiole (leaf stalk)

Areola ("window" of transparent tissue)

CARNIVOROUS (INSECTIVOROUS) PLANTS FEED ON INSECTS and other small animals in addition to producing food in their leaves by photosynthesis. The nutrients absorbed from trapped insects allow carnivorous plants to thrive in acid, boggy soils that lack essential minerals, especially nitrates, where most other plants could not survive.

All carnivorous plants have some leaves modified as traps. Many use bright colors and scented nectar to attract prey, and most use enzymes to digest the prey. There are three types of traps. Pitcher plants, such as the monkey cup and cobra lily, have leaves modified as pitcher-shaped pitfall traps, half-filled with water. Once lured inside the mouth of the trap, insects lose their footing on the slippery surface, fall into the liquid, and either decompose or are digested. Venus fly-traps use a spring-trap mechanism; when an insect touches trigger hairs on the inner surfaces of the leaves, the two lobes of the trap snap shut. Butterworts and sundews entangle prey by sticky droplets on the leaf surface, while the edges of the leaves slowly curl over to envelop and digest the prey.

Dome-shaped hood develops

Smooth surface

Nectar roll

Fishtail nectary appears

Mouth

Immature pitcher

Wing

Downward-pointing hair

DEVELOPMENT OF MODIFIED LEAF IN COBRA LILY

Immature trap

Interlocked teeth

Closed trap

Red color of trap attracts insects

VENUS FLYTRAP
(*Dionaea muscipula*)

Phyllode (flattened petiole)

Summer petiole (leaf stalk)

Trigger hair

Sensory hinge

Nectary zone (glands secrete nectar)

Inner surface of trap

Digestive zone (glands secrete digestive enzymes)

Lobe of trap

Trap (twin-lobed leaf blade)

Midrib (hinge of trap)

Tooth

Spring petiole (leaf stalk)

Digestive gland

Trigger hair

MICROGRAPH OF LOBE OF VENUS FLYTRAP

PITCHER PLANT
Monkey cup
(*Nepenthes mirabalis*)

Lamina
(blade)

Tendril

Immature
pitcher

Lid

Rim of
pitcher

Mouth
of pitcher

Pitcher

Inner surface
of pitcher

Digestive
gland

Outer surface
of pitcher

MICROGRAPH OF WALL OF PITCHER

Lamina
(blade)

Nectar-
secreting
gland

Midrib

Lid (attracts insects
and stops rainwater
from flooding pitcher)

Rim of pitcher
(containing
nectar
glands)

Spur

Tendril

Waxy
zone (no
foothold
for insects)

Digestive
zone
(normally
containing
digestive
fluid)

Partly
digested
insects

Digestive
gland

Lid
opens

Mouth of
pitcher

Recently
formed leaf

Lid remains
firmly closed as
pitcher develops

Tendril
elongates

Frontal
rib

Tendril at tip of
recently formed leaf

Swelling forms
at tip of tendril

Immature pitcher
fills with air

Mature
pitcher

**DEVELOPMENT OF MODIFIED LEAF
IN PITCHER PLANT**

**SECTION THROUGH
PITCHER**

BUTTERWORT
(*Pinguicula caudata*)

Stalked secretory
gland (produces
sticky, mucus-like
substance)

Digestive gland
(produces enzymes)

Adaxial
(upper) surface
of leaf

Abaxial
(lower) surface
of leaf

**MICROGRAPH OF
BUTTERWORT LEAF**

Flattened
lamina
(blade)

Insect
trapped
on sticky
surface
of lamina
(blade)

Margin of
lamina (blade)
rolled inwards

Immature
leaf

Epiphytic and parasitic plants

EPIPHYTIC AND PARASITIC PLANTS GROW ON OTHER LIVING PLANTS. Typically, epiphytic plants are not rooted in the soil. Instead, they live above ground level on the stems and branches of other plants. Epiphytes obtain water from trapped rainwater and from moisture in the air. They obtain minerals from organic matter that has accumulated on the surface of the plant on which they are growing. Like other green plants, epiphytes produce their food by photosynthesis. Epiphytes include tropical orchids and bromeliads (air plants) and some mosses that live in temperate regions. Parasitic plants obtain all their nutrient requirements from the host plants on which they grow. The parasites produce haustoria, root-like organs that penetrate the stem or roots of the host and grow inward to merge with the host's vascular tissue. These extract water, minerals, and manufactured nutrients. Because they have no need to produce their own food, parasitic plants lack chlorophyll, the green photosynthetic pigment, and they have no foliage leaves. Partial parasitic plants, like mistletoe, obtain water and minerals from the host plant but have green leaves and stems and are therefore able to produce their own food by photosynthesis.

EPIPHYTIC BROMELIAD
Aechmea miniata

Inflorescence (spike)

Peduncle (inflorescence stalk)

Flower bud

Strap-shaped arching leaf (part of rosette of leaves)

Leaf margin with spines

Overlapping leaf bases in which rainwater is trapped

Mass of adventitious roots

Stem

Bark of tree to which epiphyte is attached

EPIPHYTIC ORCHID
Brassavola nodosa

Peduncle (inflorescence stalk)

Pedicel (flower stalk)

Flower

Scale leaf

Leaf

Aerial root

Node

Stem

Bark of tree to which epiphyte is attached

Velamen (multilayered epidermis capable of absorbing water from rain or condensation)

Exodermis (outer layer of cortex)

Cortex (layer between epidermis and vascular tissue)

Cortex cell containing chloroplasts

Pith

Vascular tissue { Xylem / Phloem }

Endodermis (inner layer of cortex)

MICROGRAPH OF CROSS SECTION THROUGH AERIAL ROOT OF EPIPHYTIC ORCHID

LONGITUDINAL SECTION THROUGH EPIPHYTIC BROMELIAD
Scarlet star
(*Guzmania
lingulata*)

*Bract
(leaflike
structure)*

*Leaf (part of
rosette of leaves)*

*Immature
bracts*

*Overlapping leaf bases
in which rainwater is
trapped*

Stem

*Immature
flowers*

Swollen stem base

ROOT PARASITE
Broomrape
(*Orobanche sp.*)

Stem of host plant

*Flower bud
of broomrape*

*Flower of
broomrape*

*Stem of
broomrape*

*Tuber of broomrape attached to
host plant's roots through
haustoria (penetrating organs
that absorb nutrients from host's
vascular tissue)*

*Leaf of
host plant*

*Shoot of
broomrape*

*Main root
of host plant*

*Lateral root of
host plant*

STEM PARASITE
Dodder
(*Cuscuta europaea*)

*Tip of dodder
stem showing
circular
movement
around
host plant*

*Inflorescence
(spike) of dodder
flowers*

*Point of
attachment
of dodder stem
to host stem*

*Leaf of
host plant*

*Thread-like
stem of dodder
twined around
stem of host
plant*

*Stem of
host plant*

**EXTERNAL VIEW OF PLANT
PARASITIZED BY DODDER**

*Haustorium
(penetrating organ that
absorbs nutrients from
host's vascular tissue)*

*Vascular tissue
of dodder*

*Union of host and dodder
vascular systems*

*Stem of
dodder*

*Vascular
tissue
of host plant*

Phloem

Xylem

*Stem of
host plant*

**MICROGRAPH OF CROSS SECTION THROUGH STEM
OF PLANT PARASITIZED BY DODDER**

163

ANIMALS

Sponges, jellyfish, and sea anemones

SPONGES ARE MAINLY MARINE animals that make up the phylum Porifera. They are among the simplest of all animals, having no tissues or organs. Their bodies consist of two layers of cells separated by a jelly-like layer (mesohyal) that is strengthened by mineral spicules or protein fibers. The body is perforated by a system of pores and water channels called the aquiferous system. Special cells (choanocytes) with whip-like structures (flagella) draw water through the aquiferous system, thereby bringing tiny food particles to the sponge's cells. Jellyfish (class Scyphozoa), sea anemones (class Anthozoa), and corals (also class Anthozoa) belong to the phylum Cnidaria, also known as Coelenterata. More complex than sponges, coelenterates have simple tissues, such as nervous tissue; a radially symmetrical body; and a mouth surrounded by tentacles with unique stinging cells (cnidocytes).

INTERNAL ANATOMY OF A SPONGE

Amebocyte

Osculum (excurrent pore)

Choanocyte (collar cell)

Ostium (incurrent pore)

Porocyte (pore cell)

Mesohyal

Spongocoel (atrium; paragaster)

Spicule

Pinacocyte (epidermal cell)

Ostium (incurrent pore)

SKELETON OF A SPONGE

Protein matrix

Pore

EXTERNAL FEATURES OF A SEA ANEMONE

Tentacle

EXAMPLES OF SEA ANEMONES

JEWEL ANEMONE
(Corynactis viridis)

PARASITIC ANEMONE
(Calliactis parasitica)

PLUMOSE ANEMONE
(Metridium senile)

MEDITERRANEAN SEA ANEMONE
(Condylactis sp.)

GREEN SNAKELOCK ANEMONE
(Anemonia viridis)

BEADLET ANEMONE
(Actinia equina)

GHOST ANEMONE
(Actinothoe sphyrodeta)

Sagartia elegans

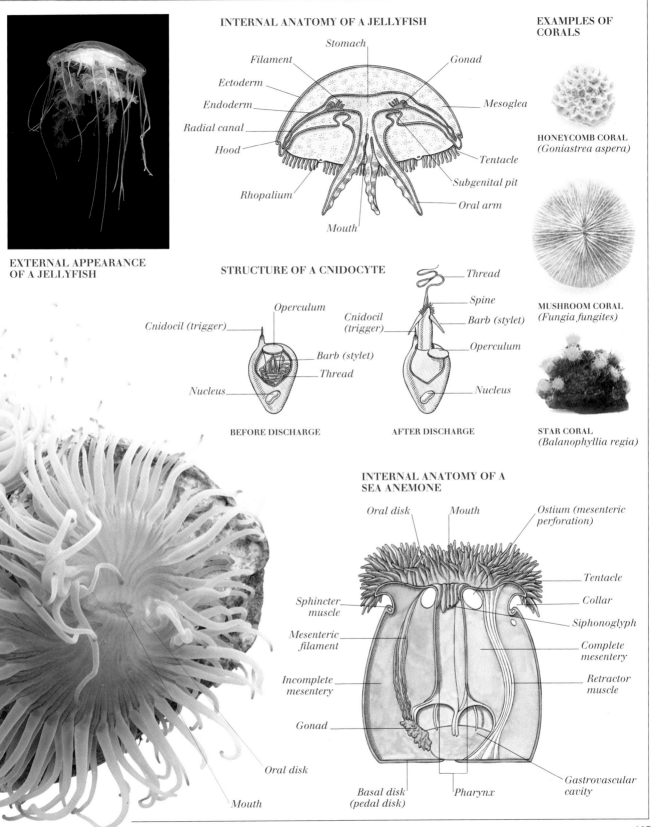

**EXTERNAL APPEARANCE
OF A JELLYFISH**

INTERNAL ANATOMY OF A JELLYFISH

Stomach

Filament

Gonad

Ectoderm

Endoderm

Mesoglea

Radial canal

Hood

Tentacle

Subgenital pit

Rhopalium

Oral arm

Mouth

**EXAMPLES OF
CORALS**

HONEYCOMB CORAL
(*Goniastrea aspera*)

MUSHROOM CORAL
(*Fungia fungites*)

STAR CORAL
(*Balanophyllia regia*)

STRUCTURE OF A CNIDOCYTE

Operculum

Thread

Spine

Cnidocil (trigger)

Cnidocil
(trigger)

Barb (stylet)

Operculum

Barb (stylet)

Thread

Nucleus

Nucleus

BEFORE DISCHARGE

AFTER DISCHARGE

**INTERNAL ANATOMY OF A
SEA ANEMONE**

Oral disk

Mouth

Ostium (mesenteric
perforation)

Sphincter
muscle

Tentacle

Collar

Mesenteric
filament

Siphonoglyph

Incomplete
mesentery

Complete
mesentery

Gonad

Retractor
muscle

Oral disk

Basal disk
(pedal disk)

Pharynx

Gastrovascular
cavity

Mouth

Insects

PUPA (CHRYSALIS)

THE WORD INSECT REFERS to small invertebrate creatures, especially those with bodies divided into sections. Insects, including beetles, ants, bees, butterflies, and moths, belong to various orders in the class Insecta, which is a division of the phylum Arthropoda. Features common to all insects are an exoskeleton (external skeleton); three pairs of jointed legs; three body sections (head, thorax, and abdomen); and one pair of sensory antennae. Beetles (order Coleoptera) are the biggest group of insects, with about 300,000 species (about 30 percent of all known insects). They have a pair of hard elytra (wing cases), which are modified front wings. The principal function of the elytra is to protect the hind wings, which are used for flying. Ants, together with bees and wasps, form the order Hymenoptera, which contains about 200,000 species. This group is characterized by a marked narrowing between the thorax and abdomen. Butterflies and moths form the order Lepidoptera, which has about 150,000 species. They have wings covered with tiny scales, hence the name of their order (Lepidoptera means "scale wings"). The separation of lepidopterans into butterflies and moths is largely artificial as there are no features that categorically distinguish one group from the other. In general, however, most butterflies fly by day, whereas most moths are night flyers. Some insects, including butterflies and moths, undergo complete metamorphosis (transformation) during their life cycle. A butterfly metamorphoses from an egg to a larva (caterpillar), then to a pupa (chrysalis), and finally to an imago (adult).

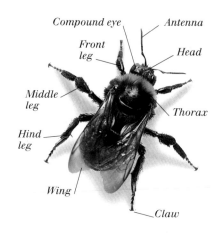

EXAMPLES OF INSECTS

Compound eye · Antenna · Front leg · Head · Middle leg · Thorax · Hind leg · Wing · Claw

BUMBLEBEE

Compound eye · Stigma (spot) · Vein · Abdomen

DAMSELFLY

EXTERNAL FEATURES OF A BEETLE

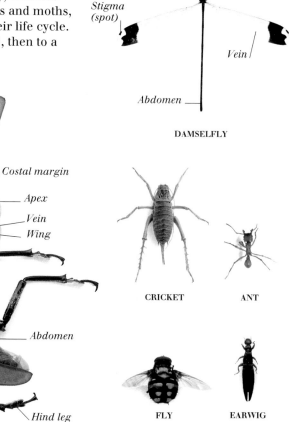

Elytron · Tarsus · Claw · Tibia · Costal margin · Pedicel · Apex · Femur · Vein · Trochanter · Wing · Flagellum · Mandible · Scape · Coxa · Labrum · Labial palpus · Abdomen · Compound eye · Head · Prothorax · Mesothorax · Front leg · Scutellum · Hind leg · Metathorax · Middle leg

CRICKET · **ANT**

FLY · **EARWIG**

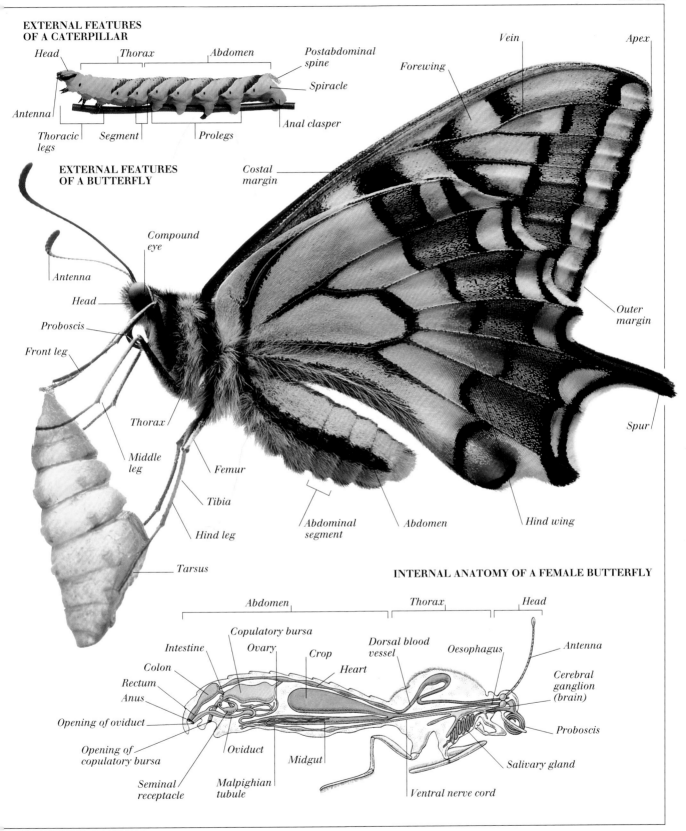

**EXTERNAL FEATURES
OF A CATERPILLAR**

Head

Thorax

Abdomen

*Postabdominal
spine*

Spiracle

Antenna

*Thoracic
legs*

Segment

Prolegs

Anal clasper

Vein

Apex

Forewing

*Costal
margin*

**EXTERNAL FEATURES
OF A BUTTERFLY**

*Compound
eye*

Antenna

Head

Proboscis

Front leg

*Outer
margin*

Thorax

*Middle
leg*

Femur

Tibia

Hind leg

*Abdominal
segment*

Abdomen

Spur

Hind wing

Tarsus

INTERNAL ANATOMY OF A FEMALE BUTTERFLY

Abdomen

Thorax

Head

Copulatory bursa

Intestine

Ovary

Crop

*Dorsal blood
vessel*

Oesophagus

Antenna

Colon

Heart

*Cerebral
ganglion
(brain)*

Rectum

Anus

Opening of oviduct

Proboscis

*Opening of
copulatory bursa*

Oviduct

Salivary gland

*Seminal
receptacle*

*Malpighian
tubule*

Midgut

Ventral nerve cord

Arachnids

THE CLASS ARACHNIDA INCLUDES SPIDERS (order Araneae) and scorpions (order Scorpiones). The class is part of the phylum Arthropoda, which also includes insects and crustaceans. Spiders and scorpions are characterized by having four pairs of walking legs; a pair of pincer-like mouthparts called chelicerae; another pair of frontal appendages called pedipalps, which are sensory in spiders but used for grasping in scorpions; and a body divided into two sections (a combined head and thorax called a cephalothorax, or prosoma, and an abdomen, or opisthosoma). Unlike other arthropods, spiders and scorpions lack antennae. Spiders and scorpions are carnivorous. Spiders poison prey by biting with the fanged chelicerae, scorpions by stinging with the end of the metasoma (tail).

MEXICAN TRUE RED-LEGGED TARANTULA
(Euathlus emilia)

INTERNAL ANATOMY OF A FEMALE SPIDER

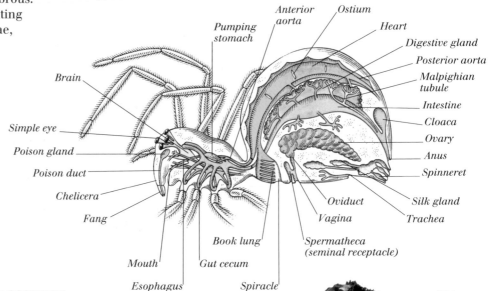

EXTERNAL FEATURES OF A SCORPION

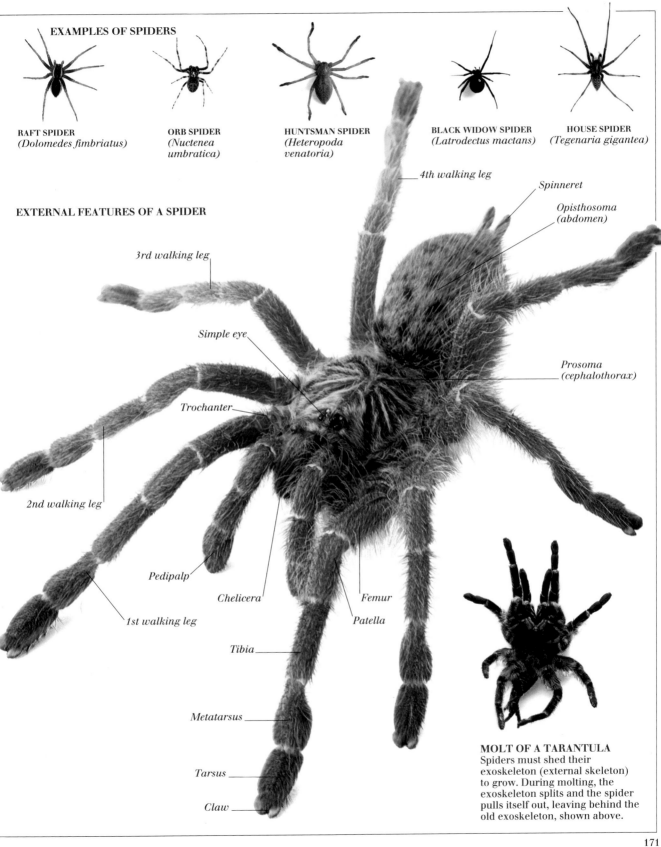

EXAMPLES OF SPIDERS

RAFT SPIDER
(Dolomedes fimbriatus)

ORB SPIDER
(Nuctenea umbratica)

HUNTSMAN SPIDER
(Heteropoda venatoria)

BLACK WIDOW SPIDER
(Latrodectus mactans)

HOUSE SPIDER
(Tegenaria gigantea)

EXTERNAL FEATURES OF A SPIDER

4th walking leg

Spinneret

Opisthosoma (abdomen)

3rd walking leg

Simple eye

Prosoma (cephalothorax)

Trochanter

2nd walking leg

Pedipalp

Femur

Chelicera

1st walking leg

Patella

Tibia

Metatarsus

Tarsus

Claw

MOLT OF A TARANTULA
Spiders must shed their exoskeleton (external skeleton) to grow. During molting, the exoskeleton splits and the spider pulls itself out, leaving behind the old exoskeleton, shown above.

Crustaceans

THE SUBPHYLUM CRUSTACEA is one of the largest groups in the phylum Arthropoda. The subphylum is divided into several classes, the most important of which are Malacostraca and Cirripedia. The class Malacostraca includes crayfish, crabs, lobsters, and shrimps. Typical features of malacostracans include a body divided into two sections (a combined head and thorax called a cephalothorax, and an abdomen); an exoskeleton (external skeleton) with a large plate (carapace) covering the cephalothorax; stalked, compound eyes; and two pairs of antennae. The class Cirripedia includes barnacles, which, unlike other crustaceans, spend their adult lives attached to a surface, such as a rock. Other characteristics of cirripedes include an exoskeleton of overlapping calcareous plates; a body consisting almost entirely of thorax (the abdomen and head are minute); and six pairs of thoracic appendages (cirri) used for filter feeding.

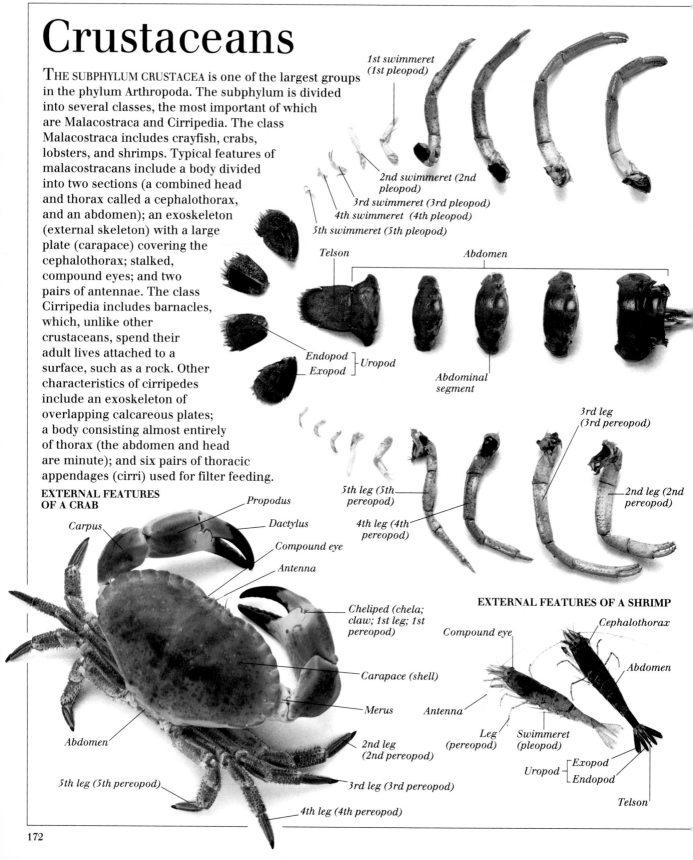

1st swimmeret (1st pleopod)

2nd swimmeret (2nd pleopod)

3rd swimmeret (3rd pleopod)

4th swimmeret (4th pleopod)

5th swimmeret (5th pleopod)

Telson

Abdomen

Endopod ⎤ Uropod
Exopod ⎦

Abdominal segment

3rd leg (3rd pereopod)

2nd leg (2nd pereopod)

5th leg (5th pereopod)

4th leg (4th pereopod)

EXTERNAL FEATURES OF A CRAB

Propodus

Dactylus

Compound eye

Antenna

Carpus

Cheliped (chela; claw; 1st leg; 1st pereopod)

Carapace (shell)

Merus

2nd leg (2nd pereopod)

3rd leg (3rd pereopod)

4th leg (4th pereopod)

5th leg (5th pereopod)

Abdomen

EXTERNAL FEATURES OF A SHRIMP

Compound eye

Cephalothorax

Abdomen

Antenna

Leg (pereopod)

Swimmeret (pleopod)

Uropod ⎡ Exopod
        ⎣ Endopod

Telson

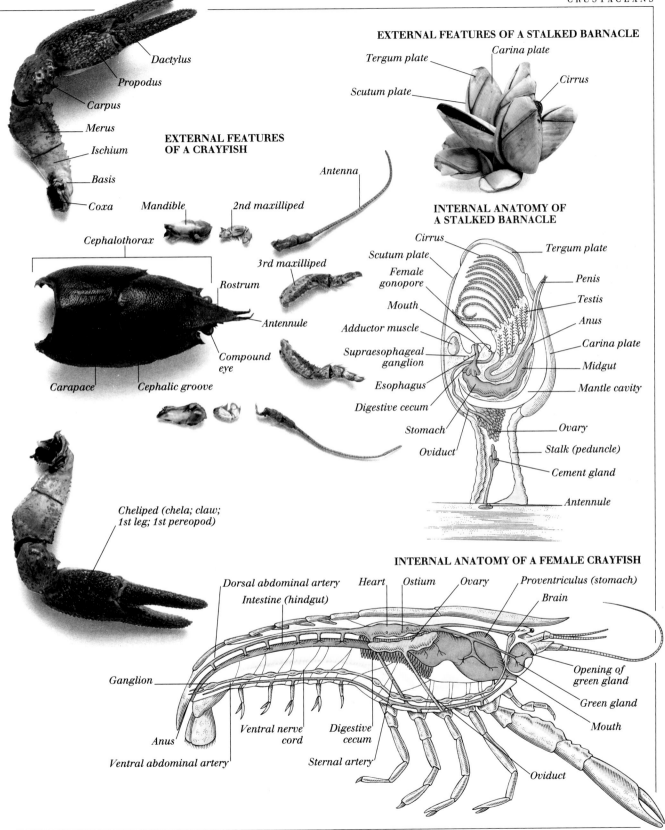

EXTERNAL FEATURES OF A STALKED BARNACLE

Tergum plate

Carina plate

Cirrus

Scutum plate

Dactylus

Propodus

Carpus

Merus

Ischium

Basis

Coxa

EXTERNAL FEATURES OF A CRAYFISH

Mandible

2nd maxilliped

Antenna

INTERNAL ANATOMY OF A STALKED BARNACLE

Cephalothorax

3rd maxilliped

Rostrum

Antennule

Compound eye

Carapace

Cephalic groove

Cirrus

Scutum plate

Female gonopore

Mouth

Adductor muscle

Supraesophageal ganglion

Esophagus

Digestive cecum

Stomach

Oviduct

Tergum plate

Penis

Testis

Anus

Carina plate

Midgut

Mantle cavity

Ovary

Stalk (peduncle)

Cement gland

Antennule

Cheliped (chela; claw; 1st leg; 1st pereopod)

INTERNAL ANATOMY OF A FEMALE CRAYFISH

Dorsal abdominal artery

Intestine (hindgut)

Heart

Ostium

Ovary

Proventriculus (stomach)

Brain

Ganglion

Opening of green gland

Green gland

Mouth

Anus

Ventral nerve cord

Digestive cecum

Sternal artery

Oviduct

Ventral abdominal artery

173

Starfish and sea urchins

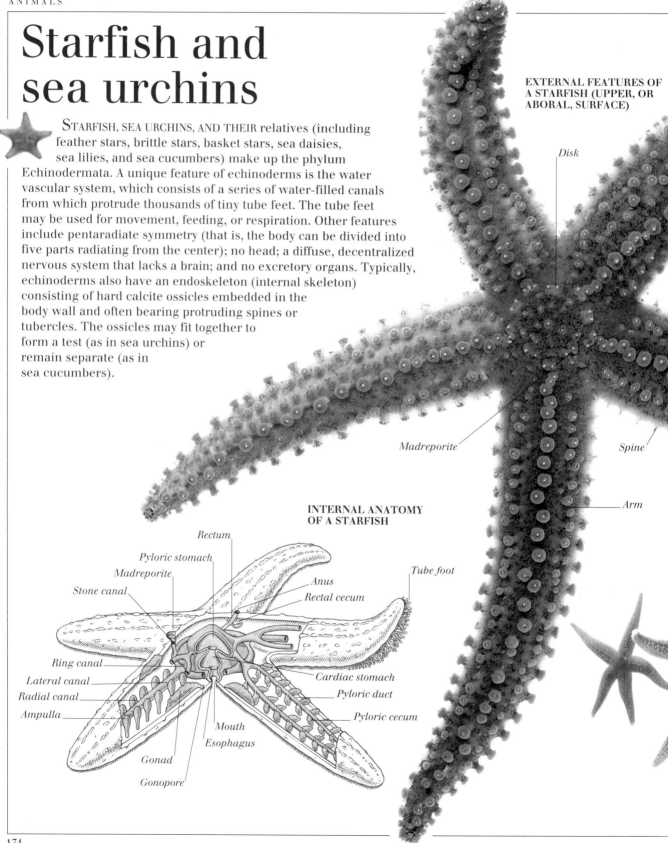

STARFISH, SEA URCHINS, AND THEIR relatives (including feather stars, brittle stars, basket stars, sea daisies, sea lilies, and sea cucumbers) make up the phylum Echinodermata. A unique feature of echinoderms is the water vascular system, which consists of a series of water-filled canals from which protrude thousands of tiny tube feet. The tube feet may be used for movement, feeding, or respiration. Other features include pentaradiate symmetry (that is, the body can be divided into five parts radiating from the center); no head; a diffuse, decentralized nervous system that lacks a brain; and no excretory organs. Typically, echinoderms also have an endoskeleton (internal skeleton) consisting of hard calcite ossicles embedded in the body wall and often bearing protruding spines or tubercles. The ossicles may fit together to form a test (as in sea urchins) or remain separate (as in sea cucumbers).

EXTERNAL FEATURES OF A STARFISH (UPPER, OR ABORAL, SURFACE)

Disk

Madreporite

Spine

Arm

INTERNAL ANATOMY OF A STARFISH

Rectum

Pyloric stomach

Madreporite

Stone canal

Anus

Rectal cecum

Tube foot

Ring canal

Lateral canal

Radial canal

Ampulla

Cardiac stomach

Pyloric duct

Pyloric cecum

Mouth

Esophagus

Gonad

Gonopore

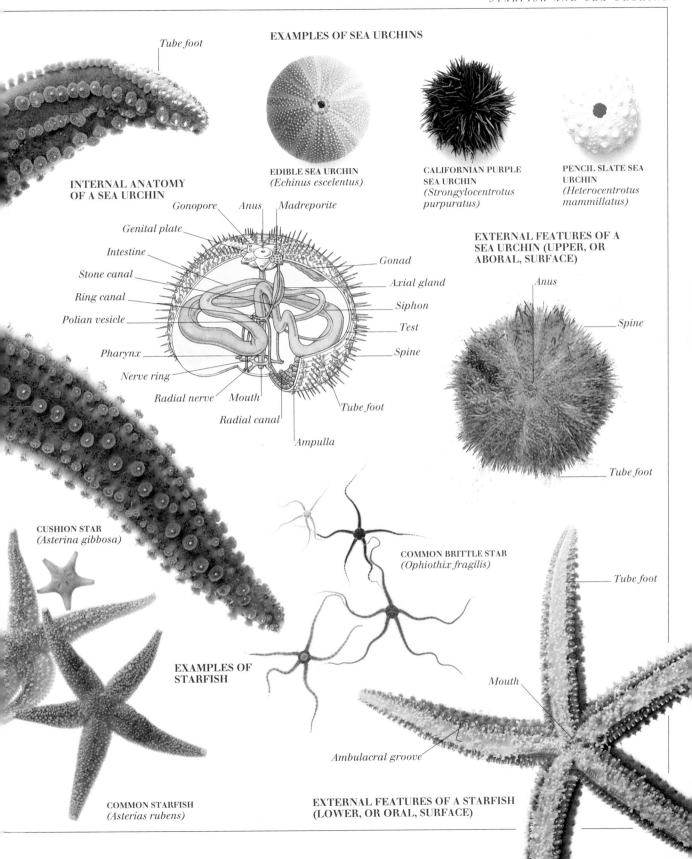

Tube foot

EXAMPLES OF SEA URCHINS

EDIBLE SEA URCHIN
(*Echinus escelentus*)

**CALIFORNIAN PURPLE
SEA URCHIN**
(*Strongylocentrotus
purpuratus*)

**PENCIL SLATE SEA
URCHIN**
(*Heterocentrotus
mammillatus*)

**INTERNAL ANATOMY
OF A SEA URCHIN**

Gonopore　*Anus*　*Madreporite*

Genital plate

Intestine

Stone canal

Ring canal

Polian vesicle

Pharynx

Nerve ring

Radial nerve　*Mouth*

Radial canal

Ampulla

Gonad

Axial gland

Siphon

Test

Spine

Tube foot

**EXTERNAL FEATURES OF A
SEA URCHIN (UPPER, OR
ABORAL, SURFACE)**

Anus

Spine

Tube foot

CUSHION STAR
(*Asterina gibbosa*)

COMMON BRITTLE STAR
(*Ophiothrix fragilis*)

Tube foot

**EXAMPLES OF
STARFISH**

Mouth

Ambulacral groove

COMMON STARFISH
(*Asterias rubens*)

**EXTERNAL FEATURES OF A STARFISH
(LOWER, OR ORAL, SURFACE)**

Mollusks

THE PHYLUM MOLLUSCA (MOLLUSKS) is a large group of animals that includes octopuses, snails, and scallops. Octopuses and their relatives —including squid and cuttlefish—form the class Cephalopoda. Cephalopods typically have a head with a radula (a file-like feeding organ) and beak; a well-developed nervous system; sucker-bearing tentacles; a muscular mantle (part of the body wall) that can expel water through the siphon, enabling movement by jet propulsion; and a small shell or no shell. Snails and their relatives—including slugs, limpets, and abalones—make up the class Gastropoda. Gastropods typically have a coiled external shell, although some, such as slugs, have a small internal shell or no shell; a flat foot; and a head with tentacles and a radula. Scallops and their relatives—including clams, mussels, and oysters—make up the class Bivalvia (also called Pelecypoda). Features of bivalves include a shell with two halves (valves); large gills that are used for breathing and filter feeding; and no radula.

EXTERNAL FEATURES OF A SCALLOP

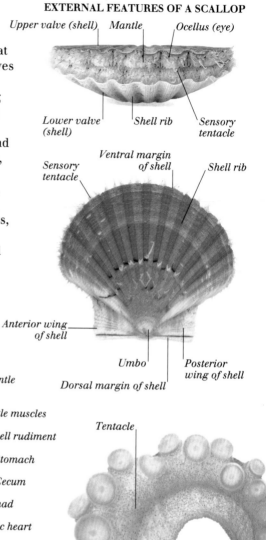

Upper valve (shell)   Mantle   Ocellus (eye)

Lower valve (shell)   Shell rib   Sensory tentacle

Sensory tentacle   Ventral margin of shell   Shell rib

Anterior wing of shell

Umbo   Posterior wing of shell

Dorsal margin of shell

INTERNAL ANATOMY OF AN OCTOPUS

Cephalic vein   Poison gland   Digestive cecum

Skull   Crop   Dorsal mantle cavity

Brain

Siphon (funnel)   Mantle muscles

Buccal mass   Shell rudiment

Beak   Stomach

Cecum

Gonad

Systemic heart

Kidney

Branchial heart

Anus   Ctenidium

Ink sac

Muscular septum

Tentacle

Sucker

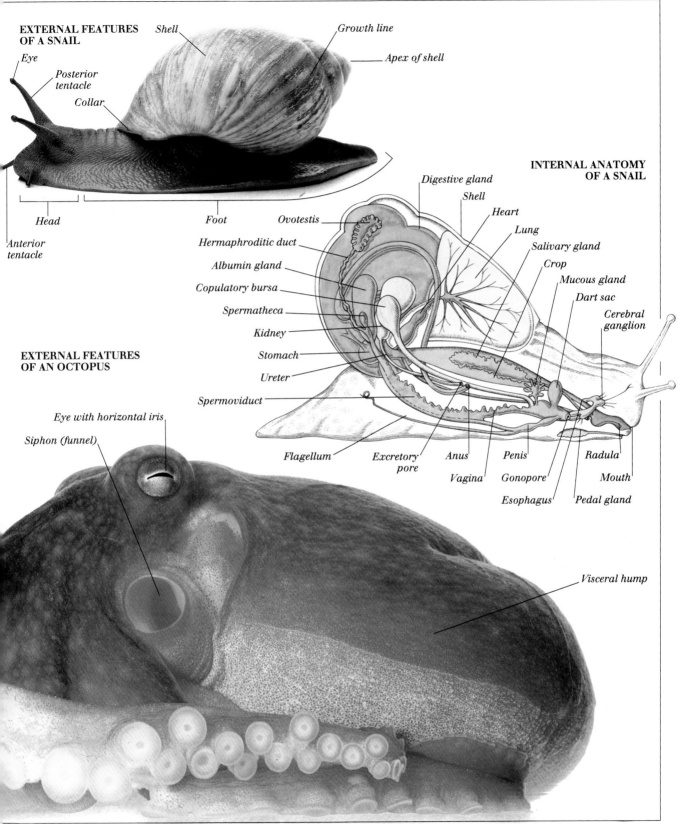

EXTERNAL FEATURES OF A SNAIL

Eye
Posterior tentacle
Collar
Shell
Growth line
Apex of shell
Head
Foot
Anterior tentacle

INTERNAL ANATOMY OF A SNAIL

Digestive gland
Shell
Heart
Lung
Salivary gland
Crop
Mucous gland
Dart sac
Cerebral ganglion
Ovotestis
Hermaphroditic duct
Albumin gland
Copulatory bursa
Spermatheca
Kidney
Stomach
Ureter
Spermoviduct
Flagellum
Excretory pore
Anus
Penis
Radula
Vagina
Gonopore
Mouth
Esophagus
Pedal gland

EXTERNAL FEATURES OF AN OCTOPUS

Eye with horizontal iris
Siphon (funnel)
Visceral hump

Sharks and jawless fish

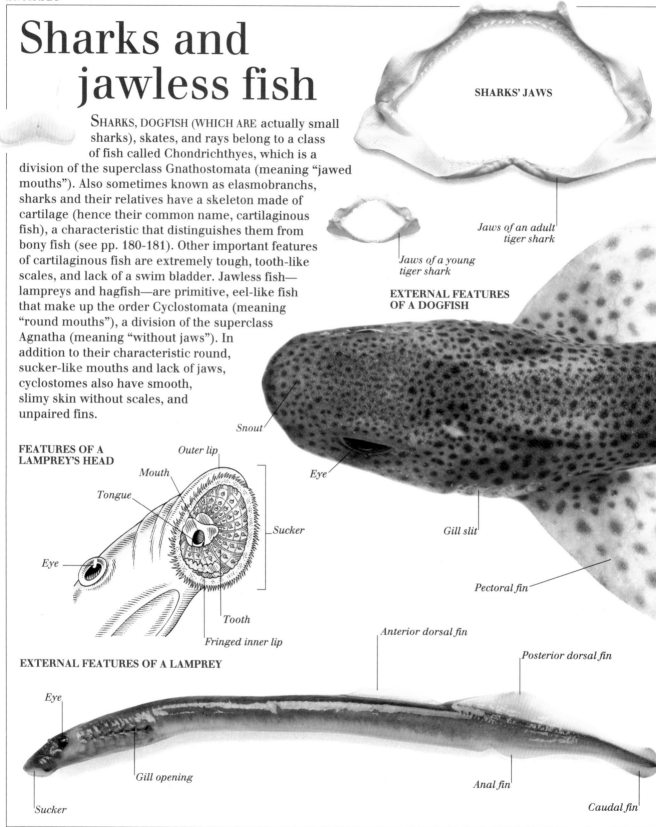

SHARKS, DOGFISH (WHICH ARE actually small sharks), skates, and rays belong to a class of fish called Chondrichthyes, which is a division of the superclass Gnathostomata (meaning "jawed mouths"). Also sometimes known as elasmobranchs, sharks and their relatives have a skeleton made of cartilage (hence their common name, cartilaginous fish), a characteristic that distinguishes them from bony fish (see pp. 180-181). Other important features of cartilaginous fish are extremely tough, tooth-like scales, and lack of a swim bladder. Jawless fish—lampreys and hagfish—are primitive, eel-like fish that make up the order Cyclostomata (meaning "round mouths"), a division of the superclass Agnatha (meaning "without jaws"). In addition to their characteristic round, sucker-like mouths and lack of jaws, cyclostomes also have smooth, slimy skin without scales, and unpaired fins.

SHARKS' JAWS

Jaws of an adult tiger shark

Jaws of a young tiger shark

EXTERNAL FEATURES OF A DOGFISH

Snout

Eye

Gill slit

Pectoral fin

FEATURES OF A LAMPREY'S HEAD

Outer lip

Mouth

Tongue

Eye

Sucker

Tooth

Fringed inner lip

EXTERNAL FEATURES OF A LAMPREY

Eye

Anterior dorsal fin

Posterior dorsal fin

Gill opening

Anal fin

Sucker

Caudal fin

EXAMPLES OF CARTILAGINOUS FISH

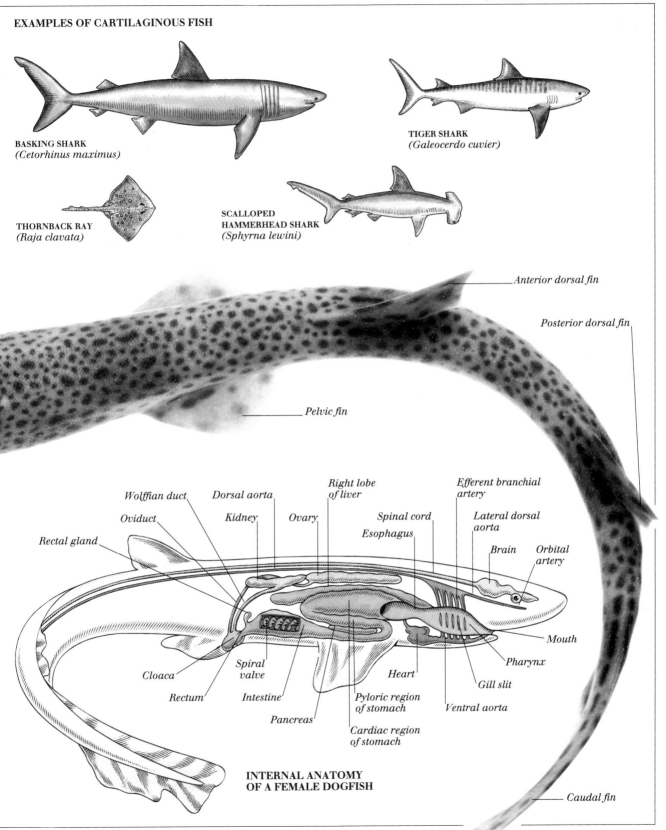

BASKING SHARK
(*Cetorhinus maximus*)

TIGER SHARK
(*Galeocerdo cuvier*)

THORNBACK RAY
(*Raja clavata*)

**SCALLOPED
HAMMERHEAD SHARK**
(*Sphyrna lewini*)

Anterior dorsal fin

Posterior dorsal fin

Pelvic fin

Wolffian duct

Oviduct

Rectal gland

Dorsal aorta

Kidney

Ovary

Right lobe
of liver

Spinal cord

Esophagus

Efferent branchial
artery

Lateral dorsal
aorta

Brain

Orbital
artery

Mouth

Pharynx

Gill slit

Ventral aorta

Heart

Cardiac region
of stomach

Pyloric region
of stomach

Pancreas

Intestine

Rectum

Spiral
valve

Cloaca

**INTERNAL ANATOMY
OF A FEMALE DOGFISH**

Caudal fin

Bony fish

BONY FISH, SUCH AS CARP, TROUT, SALMON, perch, and cod, are by far the best known and largest group of fish, with more than 20,000 species (over 95 percent of all known fish). As their name suggests, bony fish have skeletons made of bone, in contrast to the cartilaginous skeletons of sharks, jawless fish, and their relatives (see pp. 178-179). Other typical features of bony fish include a swim bladder, which functions as a variable-buoyancy organ, enabling a fish to remain effortlessly at whatever depth it is swimming; relatively thin, bone-like scales; a flap (called an operculum) covering the gills; and paired pelvic and pectoral fins. Scientifically, bony fish belong to the class Osteichthyes, which is a division of the superclass Gnathostomata (meaning "jawed mouths").

HOW FISH BREATHE

Fish "breathe" by extracting oxygen from water through their gills. Water is sucked in through the mouth; simultaneously, the opercula close to prevent the water from escaping. The mouth is then closed, and muscles in the walls of the mouth, pharynx, and opercular cavity contract to pump the water inside over the gills and out through the opercula. Some fish rely on swimming with their mouths open to keep water flowing over the gills.

Gill raker

Pharynx

Water out

Gill slit

Mouth

Water in

Gill filament

Operculum

EXAMPLES OF BONY FISH

MANDARINFISH
(Synchiropus splendidus)

ANGLERFISH
(Caulophryne jordani)

OCEANIC SEAHORSE
(Hippocampus kuda)

LIONFISH
(Pterois volitans)

STURGEON
(Acipenser sturio)

Vertebra

Neural spine

Hypural

Hemal spine

Caudal fin ray

Anal fin ray

Radial cartilage

SNOWFLAKE MORAY EEL
(Echidna nebulosa)

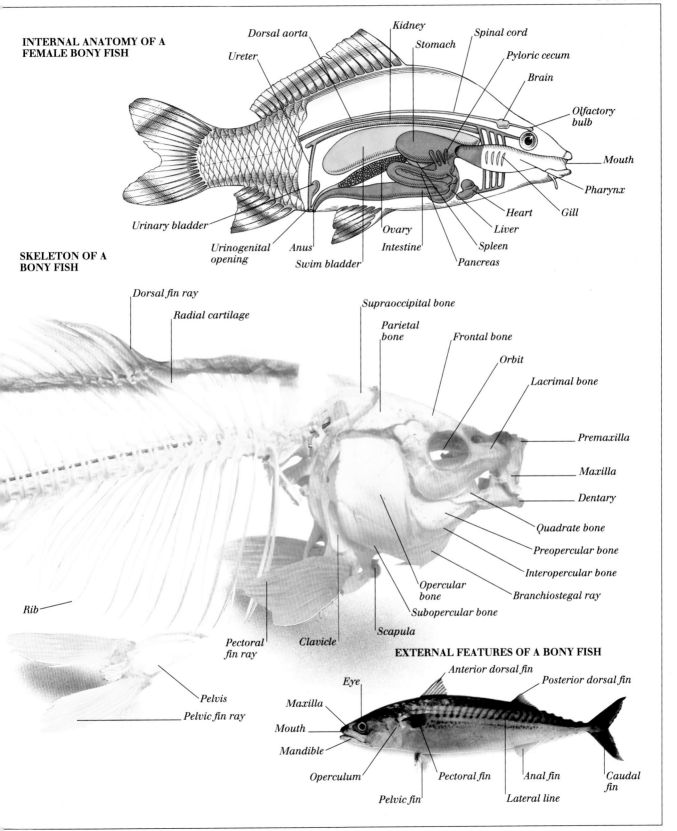

INTERNAL ANATOMY OF A FEMALE BONY FISH

Dorsal aorta

Ureter

Kidney

Stomach

Spinal cord

Pyloric cecum

Brain

Olfactory bulb

Mouth

Pharynx

Gill

Heart

Liver

Spleen

Pancreas

Intestine

Swim bladder

Ovary

Anus

Urinogenital opening

Urinary bladder

SKELETON OF A BONY FISH

Dorsal fin ray

Radial cartilage

Supraoccipital bone

Parietal bone

Frontal bone

Orbit

Lacrimal bone

Premaxilla

Maxilla

Dentary

Quadrate bone

Preopercular bone

Interopercular bone

Branchiostegal ray

Subopercular bone

Opercular bone

Scapula

Clavicle

Pectoral fin ray

Rib

Pelvis

Pelvic fin ray

EXTERNAL FEATURES OF A BONY FISH

Anterior dorsal fin

Posterior dorsal fin

Eye

Maxilla

Mouth

Mandible

Operculum

Pelvic fin

Pectoral fin

Lateral line

Anal fin

Caudal fin

181

Amphibians

THE CLASS AMPHIBIA INCLUDES FROGS and toads (which make up the order Anura) and newts and salamanders (which make up the order Urodela). Amphibians typically have moist, scaleless, hairless skin; lungs; and are cold-blooded. They also undergo complete metamorphosis, from eggs laid in water through various water-living larval stages (such as the tadpole stage) to land-living adults. Typical features of adult frogs and toads include a squat body with no tail; long, powerful hind legs; and large, often bulging, eyes. Adult newts and salamanders typically have a long body with a well-developed tail; and relatively short legs of equal size. However, newts and salamanders show considerable variation; for example, in some species the adults have minute legs, external gills rather than lungs, and spend their entire lives in water.

INTERNAL ANATOMY OF A FEMALE FROG

Larynx

Stomach

Right bronchus

Right lung

Heart

Liver

Posterior vena cava

Right kidney

Dorsal aorta

Cloaca

Rectum

Pulmonary artery

Left lung

Pancreas

Duodenum

Spleen

Left kidney

Mesentery

Small intestine (ileum)

Left ureter

EXTERNAL FEATURES OF A FROG

Hind limb

Trunk

Head

Forelimb

5 digits

Tympanum (eardrum)

4 digits

Web

External nostril

Mouth

Eye

EXTERNAL FEATURES OF A SALAMANDER

Eye

Tail

Forelimb

Hind limb

Digit

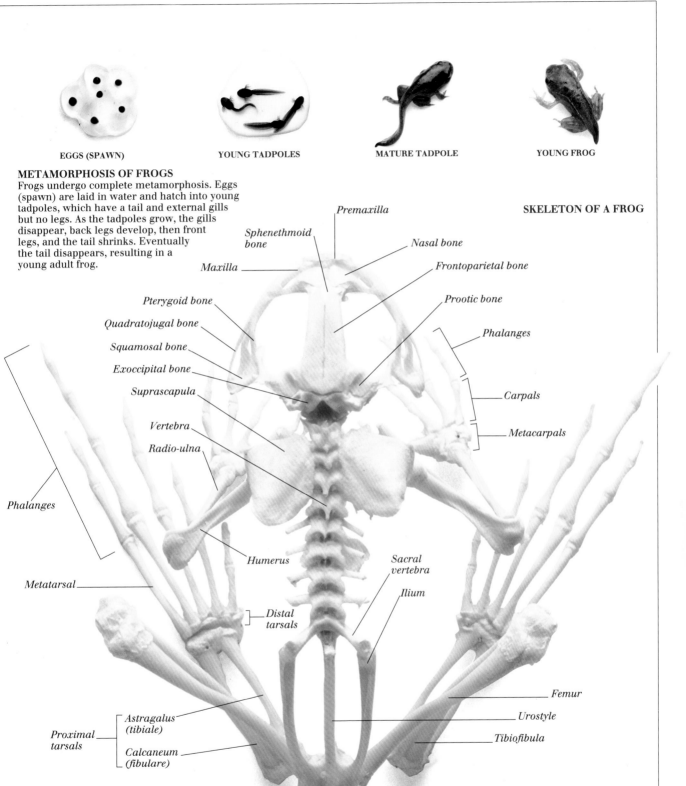

EGGS (SPAWN)

YOUNG TADPOLES

MATURE TADPOLE

YOUNG FROG

METAMORPHOSIS OF FROGS

Frogs undergo complete metamorphosis. Eggs (spawn) are laid in water and hatch into young tadpoles, which have a tail and external gills but no legs. As the tadpoles grow, the gills disappear, back legs develop, then front legs, and the tail shrinks. Eventually the tail disappears, resulting in a young adult frog.

SKELETON OF A FROG

Premaxilla

Sphenethmoid bone

Nasal bone

Maxilla

Frontoparietal bone

Pterygoid bone

Prootic bone

Quadratojugal bone

Phalanges

Squamosal bone

Exoccipital bone

Carpals

Suprascapula

Metacarpals

Vertebra

Radio-ulna

Phalanges

Humerus

Sacral vertebra

Metatarsal

Ilium

Distal tarsals

Femur

Astragalus (tibiale)

Urostyle

Proximal tarsals

Tibiofibula

Calcaneum (fibulare)

Ischium

Lizards and snakes

LIZARDS AND SNAKES BELONG to the order Squamata, a division of the class Reptilia. Characteristic reptilian features include scaly skin, lungs, and cold-bloodedness. Most reptiles lay leathery-shelled eggs, although some hatch the eggs inside their bodies and give birth to live young. Lizards belong to the suborder Lacertilia. Typically, they have long tails, and shed their skin in several pieces. Many lizards can regenerate a tail if it is lost; some can change color; and some are limbless. Snakes make up the suborder Ophidia (also called Serpentes). All snakes have long, limbless bodies; can dislocate their lower jaw to swallow large prey; and have eyelids that are joined together to form a single transparent covering over the front of the eye. Most snakes shed their skin in a single piece. Constrictor snakes kill their prey by squeezing; venomous snakes poison their prey.

EXAMPLES OF SNAKES

MEXICAN MOUNTAIN KING SNAKE (*Lampropeltis triangulum annulata*)

EXTERNAL FEATURES OF A LIZARD

BANDED MILK SNAKE (*Lampropeltis ruthveni*)

Eye

Mouth

Crest

Eardrum

Masseteric scale

Dorsal scale

External nostril

Dewlap

Foreleg

Belly

Ventral scale

SKELETON OF A LIZARD

Skull

Orbit

Scapula

Cervical vertebrae

Phalanges

Carpals

Metacarpal

Humerus

Ulna

Radius

Rib

Thoracolumbar vertebrae

Pelvis

Sacrum

Femur

Tibia

Fibula

Tarsals

Metatarsal

Caudal vertebrae

Phalanges

Toe

Claw

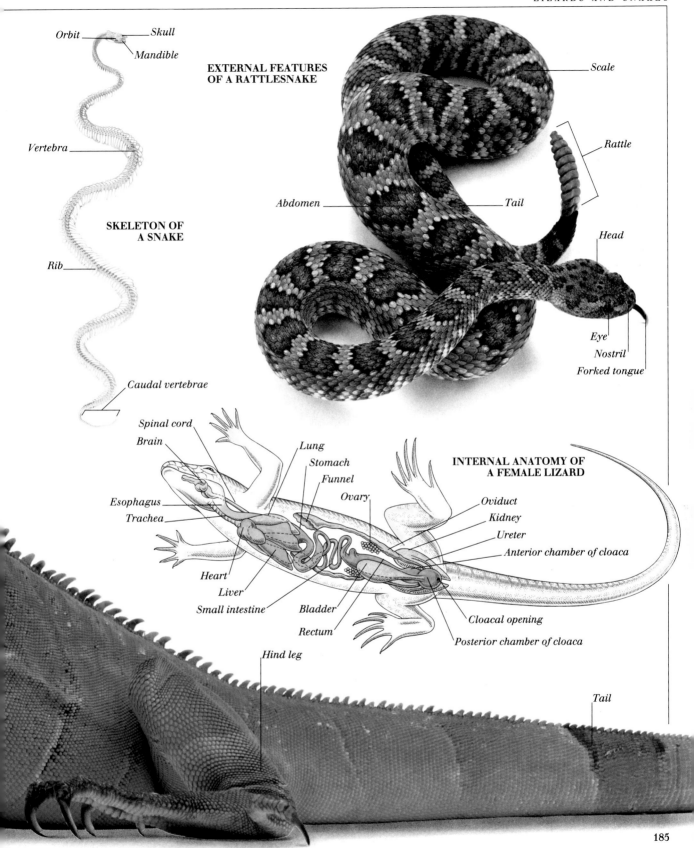

Orbit
Skull
Mandible

EXTERNAL FEATURES OF A RATTLESNAKE

Scale

Vertebra

Rattle

SKELETON OF A SNAKE

Abdomen
Tail

Head

Rib

Eye
Nostril
Forked tongue

Caudal vertebrae

Spinal cord
Brain

Lung
Stomach
Funnel
Ovary

INTERNAL ANATOMY OF A FEMALE LIZARD

Oviduct
Kidney
Ureter
Anterior chamber of cloaca

Esophagus
Trachea

Heart
Liver
Small intestine

Bladder
Rectum

Cloacal opening
Posterior chamber of cloaca

Hind leg

Tail

185

Crocodilians and turtles

CROCODILIANS AND TURTLES BELONG to different orders in the class Reptilia. The order Crocodilia includes crocodiles, alligators, caimans, and gharials. Typically, crocodilians are carnivores (flesh-eaters), and have a long snout, sharp teeth for gripping prey, and hard, square scales. All crocodilians are adapted to living on land and in water: they have four strong legs for moving on land; a powerful tail for swimming; and their eyes and nostrils are high on the head so that they stay above water while the rest of the body is submerged. The order Chelonia includes marine turtles, freshwater turtles (terrapins), and land turtles (tortoises). Characteristically, chelonians have a short, broad body encased in a bony shell with an outer horny covering, into which the head and limbs can be withdrawn; and a horny beak instead of teeth.

SKULLS OF CROCODILIANS

GHARIAL
(*Gavialis gangeticus*)

NILE CROCODILE
(*Crocodylus niloticus*)

MISSISSIPPI ALLIGATOR
(*Alligator mississippiensis*)

SKELETON OF A CROCODILE

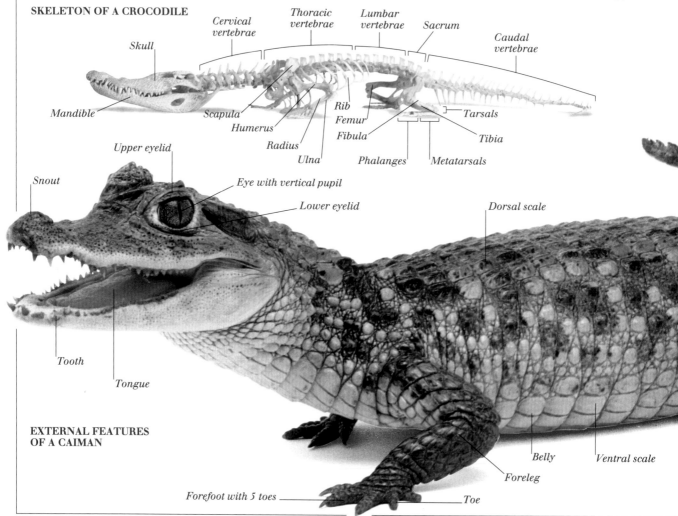

EXTERNAL FEATURES OF A CAIMAN

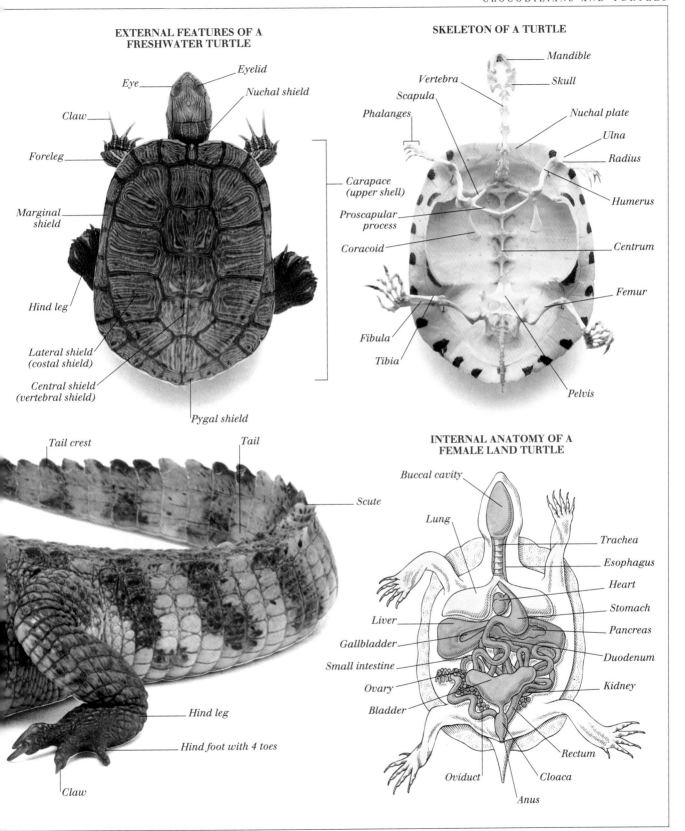

EXTERNAL FEATURES OF A FRESHWATER TURTLE

Eye
Eyelid
Nuchal shield
Claw
Foreleg
Marginal shield
Hind leg
Lateral shield (costal shield)
Central shield (vertebral shield)
Pygal shield
Carapace (upper shell)

SKELETON OF A TURTLE

Mandible
Skull
Vertebra
Scapula
Phalanges
Nuchal plate
Ulna
Radius
Humerus
Proscapular process
Coracoid
Centrum
Femur
Fibula
Tibia
Pelvis

Tail crest
Tail
Scute
Hind leg
Hind foot with 4 toes
Claw

INTERNAL ANATOMY OF A FEMALE LAND TURTLE

Buccal cavity
Lung
Trachea
Esophagus
Heart
Stomach
Pancreas
Duodenum
Kidney
Liver
Gallbladder
Small intestine
Ovary
Bladder
Rectum
Cloaca
Oviduct
Anus

Birds 1

Birds MAKE UP THE CLASS AVES. There are more than 9,000 species, almost all of which can fly (the only flightless birds are penguins, ostriches, rheas, cassowaries, and kiwis). The ability to fly is reflected in the typical bird features: forelimbs modified as wings, a streamlined body, and hollow bones to reduce weight. All birds lay hard-shelled eggs, which the parents incubate. Birds' beaks and feet vary according to diet and way of life. Beaks range from general purpose types suitable for a mixed diet (those of thrushes, for example), to types specialized for particular foods (such as the large, curved, sieving beaks of flamingos). Feet range from the webbed "paddles" of ducks, to the talons of birds of prey. Plumage also varies widely, and in many species the male is brightly colored for courtship display whereas the female is drab.

EXTERNAL FEATURES OF A BIRD

Forehead Eye Crown
Nostril Nape
Upper mandible
Beak
Lower mandible
Chin
Throat

EXAMPLES OF BIRDS

MALE TUFTED DUCK
(*Aythya fuligula*)

WHITE STORK
(*Ciconia ciconia*)

MALE OSTRICH
(*Struthio camelus*)

Minor coverts — Lesser wing coverts
Median wing coverts

Greater wing coverts (major coverts)

Secondary flight feathers (secondary remiges)

Primary flight feathers (primary remiges)

Breast
Belly
Flank
Thigh
Under tail coverts
Claw
Toe
Tarsus
Tail feathers (retrices)

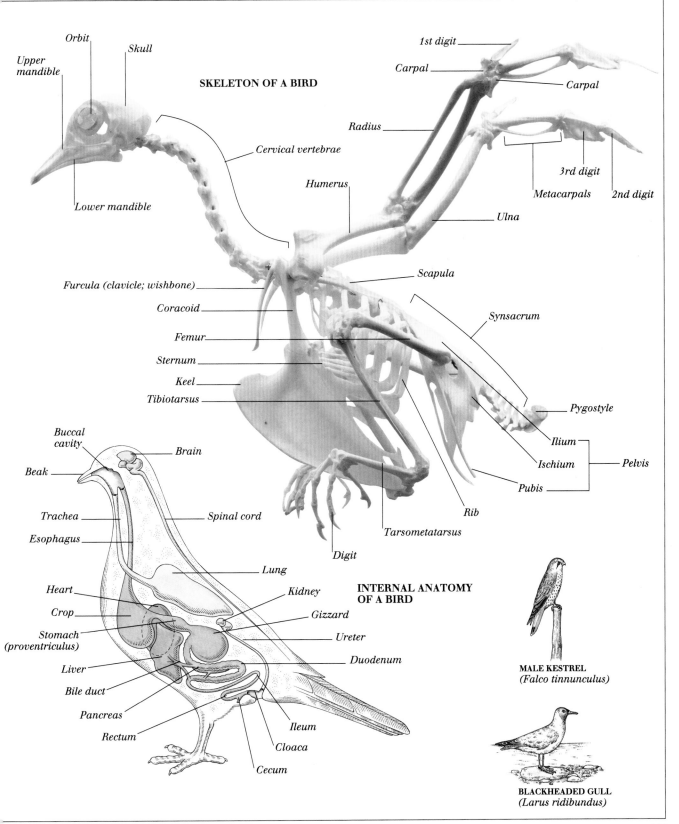

Orbit

Skull

Upper mandible

SKELETON OF A BIRD

1st digit

Carpal

Carpal

Radius

Cervical vertebrae

Humerus

3rd digit

Metacarpals

2nd digit

Ulna

Lower mandible

Scapula

Furcula (clavicle; wishbone)

Synsacrum

Coracoid

Femur

Sternum

Keel

Tibiotarsus

Pygostyle

Ilium

Ischium

Pelvis

Pubis

Rib

Tarsometatarsus

Buccal cavity

Brain

Beak

Spinal cord

Digit

Trachea

Esophagus

Lung

INTERNAL ANATOMY OF A BIRD

Heart

Kidney

Crop

Gizzard

Stomach (proventriculus)

Ureter

Liver

Duodenum

Bile duct

Pancreas

Ileum

Rectum

Cloaca

Cecum

MALE KESTREL
(Falco tinnunculus)

BLACKHEADED GULL
(Larus ridibundus)

189

Birds 2

EXAMPLES OF BIRDS' FEET

KITTIWAKE
(Rissa tridactyla)
The webbed feet are
adapted for paddling
through water.

TAWNY OWL
(Strix aluco)
The clawed feet are adapted
for gripping prey.

LITTLE GREBE
(Tachybaptus ruficollis)
The lobed, flattened feet
are adapted for swimming
underwater.

EXAMPLES OF BIRDS' BEAKS

GREATER FLAMINGO
(Phoenicopterus ruber)
In the living bird, the large,
curved beak contains a
cartilaginous "sieve" for
filtering food particles
from water.

MAVIS, OR MISTLE THRUSH
(Turdus viscivorus)
The all-purpose beak is suitable
for gathering a wide range of
animal and plant foods.

KING VULTURE
(Sarcorhamphus papa)
The hooked beak is adapted
for pulling apart flesh.

BLUE-AND-YELLOW MACAW
(Ara ararauna)
The broad, powerful, hooked beak
is adapted for crushing seeds and
eating fruit.

BONES OF A BIRD'S WING

1st digit

Carpal

Radius

3rd digit

Metacarpals

Humerus

Carpal

2nd digit

Ulna

Alula (spurious wing)

FEATHERS OF A BIRD'S WING

Minor coverts

Major coverts

Secondary flight feathers (secondary remiges)

Downcurved edge

Primary flight feathers (primary remiges)

STRUCTURE OF A FEATHER

Rachis (shaft)

Outer vane

Tip

Quill (calamus)

Upcurved edge

Inner vane

Eggs

AN EGG IS A SINGLE CELL, produced by the female, with the capacity to develop into a new individual. Development may take place inside the mother's body (as in most mammals) or outside, in which case the egg has a protective covering such as a shell. Egg yolk nourishes the growing young. Eggs developing inside the mother generally have little yolk, because the young are nourished from her body. Eggs developing outside may also have little yolk if they are produced by animals whose young go through a larval stage (such as a caterpillar) that feeds itself while developing into the adult form. The shelled eggs of birds and reptiles contain enough yolk to sustain the young until it hatches into a juvenile version of the adult.

SECTION THROUGH A CHICKEN'S EGG

Yolk
Yolk sac
Shell
Allantoic fluid
Allantois
Chorioallantoic membrane
Air sac
Albumen (egg white)
Amnion
Amniotic fluid
Developing chick
Developing wing
Shell membrane

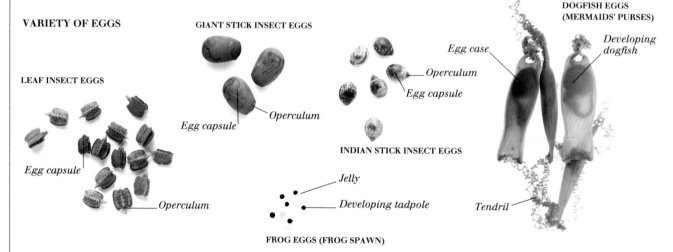

VARIETY OF EGGS

LEAF INSECT EGGS
Egg capsule
Operculum

GIANT STICK INSECT EGGS
Egg capsule
Operculum

INDIAN STICK INSECT EGGS
Operculum
Egg capsule

FROG EGGS (FROG SPAWN)
Jelly
Developing tadpole

DOGFISH EGGS (MERMAIDS' PURSES)
Egg case
Developing dogfish
Tendril

HATCHING OF A QUAIL'S EGG

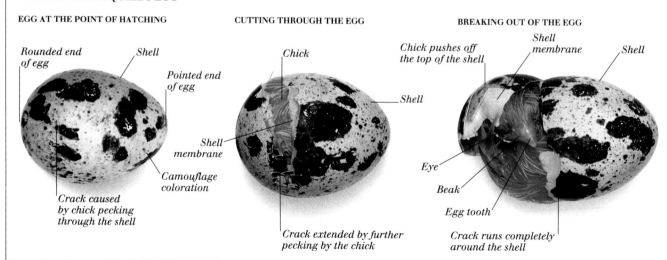

EGG AT THE POINT OF HATCHING
Rounded end of egg
Shell
Pointed end of egg
Camouflage coloration
Crack caused by chick pecking through the shell

CUTTING THROUGH THE EGG
Chick
Shell
Shell membrane
Crack extended by further pecking by the chick

BREAKING OUT OF THE EGG
Chick pushes off the top of the shell
Shell membrane
Shell
Eye
Beak
Egg tooth
Crack runs completely around the shell

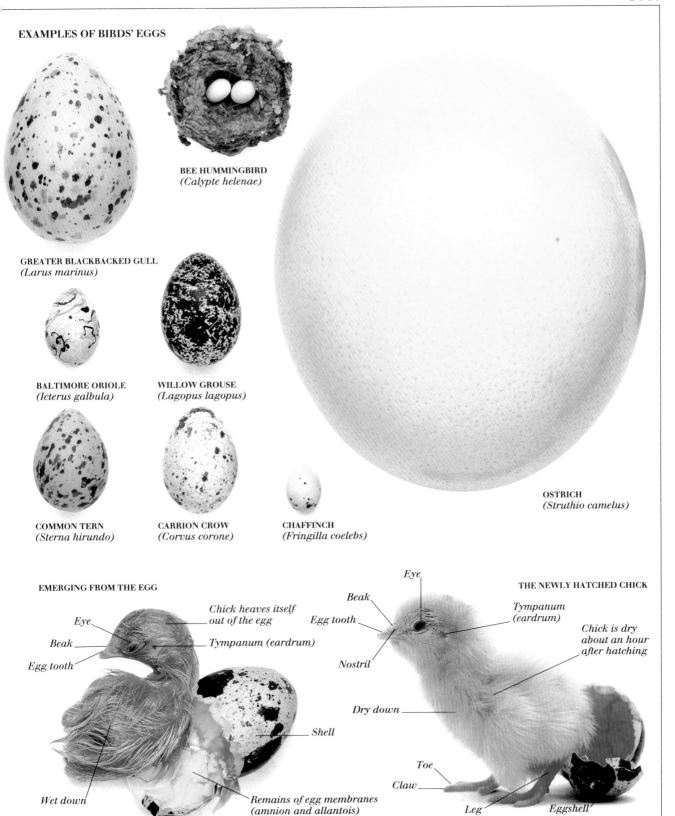

EXAMPLES OF BIRDS' EGGS

BEE HUMMINGBIRD
(Calypte helenae)

GREATER BLACKBACKED GULL
(Larus marinus)

BALTIMORE ORIOLE
(Icterus galbula)

WILLOW GROUSE
(Lagopus lagopus)

COMMON TERN
(Sterna hirundo)

CARRION CROW
(Corvus corone)

CHAFFINCH
(Fringilla coelebs)

OSTRICH
(Struthio camelus)

EMERGING FROM THE EGG

Eye

Beak

Egg tooth

Chick heaves itself
out of the egg

Tympanum (eardrum)

Shell

Wet down

Remains of egg membranes
(amnion and allantois)

THE NEWLY HATCHED CHICK

Eye

Beak

Egg tooth

Nostril

Tympanum
(eardrum)

Chick is dry
about an hour
after hatching

Dry down

Toe

Claw

Leg

Eggshell

Carnivores

THE MAMMALIAN ORDER CARNIVORA includes cats, dogs, bears, raccoons, pandas, weasels, badgers, skunks, otters, civets, mongooses, and hyenas. The order's name is derived from the fact that most of its members are carnivores (flesh-eaters). Typical carnivore features therefore reflect a hunting lifestyle: speed and agility; sharp claws and well-developed canine teeth for holding and killing prey; carnassial teeth (cheek teeth) for cutting flesh; and forward-facing eyes for good distance judgment. However, some members of the order—bears, badgers, and foxes, for example—have a more mixed diet, and a few are entirely herbivorous (plant-eating), notably pandas. Such animals have no carnassial teeth and tend to be slower-moving than pure flesh-eaters.

EXTERNAL FEATURES OF A MALE LION

Nose

Eye

Mane

Nostril

Vibrissa (whisker)

Tongue

Canine tooth

Incisor tooth

Chest

Elbow

Lower arm

Toe

SKULL OF A LION

Zygomatic arch

Coronoid process

Sagittal crest

Orbit

Nasal bone

Maxilla

Upper premolars

Upper canine

Lower canine

Mandible

Lower premolars

Occipital condyle

Tympanic bulla

Condyle

Angular process

Upper carnassial tooth (4th upper premolar)

SKULL OF A BEAR

Sagittal crest

Occipital condyle

Zygomatic arch

Orbit

Upper molars

Nasal bone

Upper premolars

Maxilla

Upper canine

Upper incisor

Lower incisor

Lower canine

Mandible

Lower premolars

Lower molars

Tympanic bulla

Angular process

Condyle

EXAMPLES OF CARNIVORES

GERMAN SHEPHERD DOG
(Canis familiaris)

MANED WOLF
(Chrysocyon brachyurus)

RACCOON
(Procyon lotor)

AMERICAN BLACK BEAR
(Ursus americanus)

SKELETON OF A DOMESTIC CAT

Back

Rump

Hip

Rib cage

Caudal vertebrae

Sacrum

Lumbar vertebrae

Thoracic vertebrae

Cervical vertebrae

Skull

Pelvis

Femur

Scapula

Sternum

Humerus

Patella

Rib

Fibula

Ulna

Tibia

Radius

Metatarsals

Carpals

Tarsals

Metacarpals

Belly

Thigh

Knee

Phalanges

Hock

Paw

Tail

INTERNAL ANATOMY OF A MALE DOMESTIC CAT

Brain

Spinal cord

Stomach

Kidney

Diaphragm

Liver

Ureter

Large intestine

Nasal cavity

Small intestine

Buccal cavity

Anus

Nostril

Testis

Tongue

Trachea

Esophagus

Lung

Heart

Gallbladder

Pancreas

Spleen

Bladder

Urethra

Vas deferens (sperm duct)

Rabbits and rodents

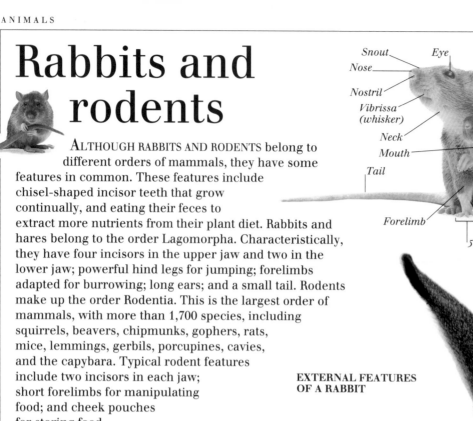

Snout
Eye
Ear
Nose
Nostril
Vibrissa (whisker)
Neck
Mouth
Tail
Pinna (ear flap)
Forelimb
5 digits
Hind limb
5 digits

ALTHOUGH RABBITS AND RODENTS belong to different orders of mammals, they have some features in common. These features include chisel-shaped incisor teeth that grow continually, and eating their feces to extract more nutrients from their plant diet. Rabbits and hares belong to the order Lagomorpha. Characteristically, they have four incisors in the upper jaw and two in the lower jaw; powerful hind legs for jumping; forelimbs adapted for burrowing; long ears; and a small tail. Rodents make up the order Rodentia. This is the largest order of mammals, with more than 1,700 species, including squirrels, beavers, chipmunks, gophers, rats, mice, lemmings, gerbils, porcupines, cavies, and the capybara. Typical rodent features include two incisors in each jaw; short forelimbs for manipulating food; and cheek pouches for storing food.

EXTERNAL FEATURES OF A RABBIT

Pinna (ear flap)
Ear
Shoulder
Eye
Nose
Nostril
Vibrissa (whisker)
Forelimb
5 digits

INTERNAL ANATOMY OF A MALE RABBIT

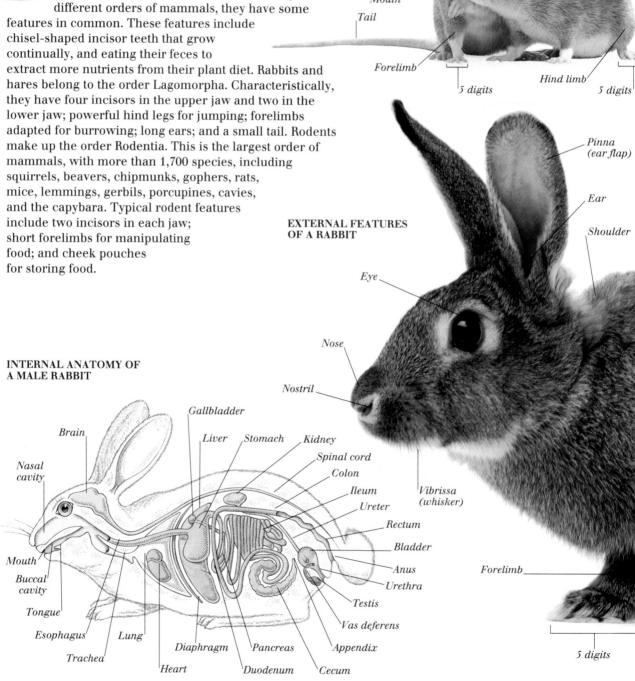

Brain
Gallbladder
Liver
Stomach
Kidney
Spinal cord
Colon
Ileum
Ureter
Rectum
Bladder
Anus
Urethra
Testis
Vas deferens
Appendix
Cecum
Duodenum
Pancreas
Diaphragm
Heart
Lung
Trachea
Esophagus
Tongue
Buccal cavity
Mouth
Nasal cavity

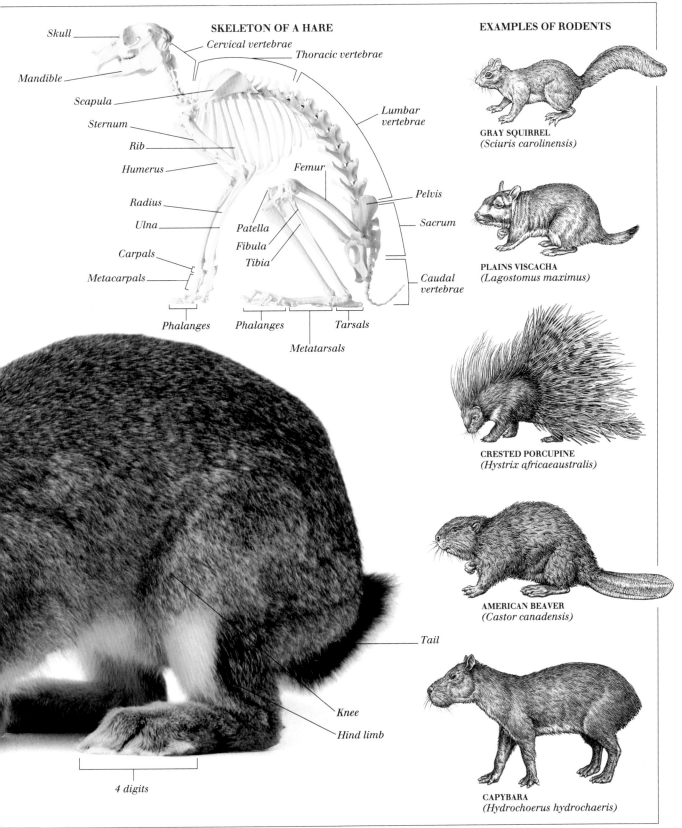

SKELETON OF A HARE

Skull

Mandible

Scapula

Sternum

Rib

Humerus

Radius

Ulna

Carpals

Metacarpals

Cervical vertebrae

Thoracic vertebrae

Lumbar vertebrae

Femur

Patella

Fibula

Tibia

Pelvis

Sacrum

Caudal vertebrae

Phalanges

Phalanges

Metatarsals

Tarsals

4 digits

Tail

Knee

Hind limb

EXAMPLES OF RODENTS

GRAY SQUIRREL
(*Sciuris carolinensis*)

PLAINS VISCACHA
(*Lagostomus maximus*)

CRESTED PORCUPINE
(*Hystrix africaeaustralis*)

AMERICAN BEAVER
(*Castor canadensis*)

CAPYBARA
(*Hydrochoerus hydrochaeris*)

Ungulates

UNGULATES IS A GENERAL TERM FOR a large, varied group
of mammals that includes horses, cattle, and their
relatives. The ungulates are divided into two orders
on the basis of the number of toes. Members of the
order Perissodactyla (odd-toed ungulates) have
one or three toes. Perissodactyls include horses,
asses, and zebras (all of which are one-toed), and
rhinoceroses and tapirs (which are three-toed).
Members of the order Artiodactyla (even-toed
ungulates) have two or four toes. Most artiodactyls
have two toes, which are typically encased in hooves to
give the so-called cloven hoof. Two-toed, cloven-hoofed
artiodactyls include cows and other cattle, sheep, goats,
antelopes, deer, and giraffes. The other main two-toed
artiodactyls are camels and llamas. Most two-toed
artiodactyls are ruminants; that is, they have a
four-chambered stomach and chew the cud.
The principal four-toed artiodactyls are hogs
and hippopotamuses.

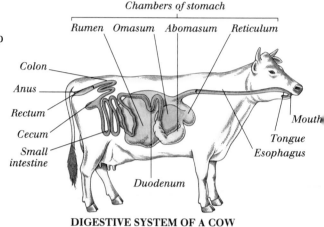

DIGESTIVE SYSTEM OF A COW

**COMPARISON OF THE FRONT FEET
OF A HORSE AND A COW**

**SKELETON OF THE LEFT
FRONT FOOT OF A HORSE**

**SKELETON OF THE RIGHT
FRONT FOOT OF A COW**

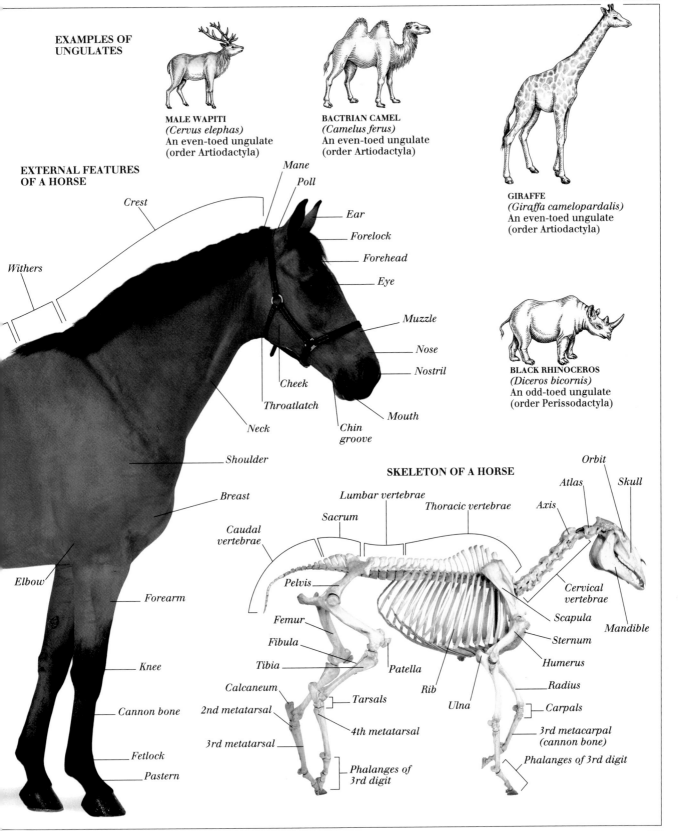

**EXAMPLES OF
UNGULATES**

MALE WAPITI
(Cervus elephas)
An even-toed ungulate
(order Artiodactyla)

BACTRIAN CAMEL
(Camelus ferus)
An even-toed ungulate
(order Artiodactyla)

GIRAFFE
(Giraffa camelopardalis)
An even-toed ungulate
(order Artiodactyla)

BLACK RHINOCEROS
(Diceros bicornis)
An odd-toed ungulate
(order Perissodactyla)

**EXTERNAL FEATURES
OF A HORSE**

Mane

Poll

Ear

Forelock

Forehead

Eye

Crest

Muzzle

Nose

Withers

Nostril

Cheek

Throatlatch

Mouth

Neck

*Chin
groove*

Shoulder

SKELETON OF A HORSE

Orbit

Atlas

Skull

Breast

Lumbar vertebrae

Thoracic vertebrae

Axis

*Caudal
vertebrae*

Sacrum

*Cervical
vertebrae*

Pelvis

Elbow

Scapula

Mandible

Forearm

Femur

Sternum

Fibula

Humerus

Tibia

Knee

Patella

Rib

Radius

Calcaneum

Ulna

Tarsals

Carpals

2nd metatarsal

Cannon bone

4th metatarsal

*3rd metacarpal
(cannon bone)*

3rd metatarsal

Phalanges of 3rd digit

Fetlock

*Phalanges of
3rd digit*

Pastern

Elephants

THE TWO SPECIES OF elephants—African and Asian—are the only members of the mammalian order Proboscidea. The bigger African elephant is the largest land animal: a fully grown male may be up to 13 ft (4m) tall and weigh as much as 7.7 tons (7 tonnes). A fully grown male Asian elephant may be 11 ft (3.3 m) tall and weigh 6 tons (5.4 tonnes). The muscular trunk—an extension of the nose and upper lip—is the elephant's most obvious feature. It is used for manipulating and lifting, feeding, drinking and spraying water, smelling, touching, and producing trumpeting sounds. Other characteristic features of this mighty plant-eater include a pair of ivory tusks, used for defense and for crushing vegetation; thick, pillar-like legs and broad feet to support the massive body; and large ear flaps that act as radiators to keep the elephant cool.

DIFFERENCES BETWEEN AFRICAN AND ASIAN ELEPHANTS

Flat forehead
Very large ears
2 "lips" at the end of the trunk
4 toenails
Concave back
3 toenails

AFRICAN ELEPHANT
(Loxodonta africana)

Twin-domed forehead
Smaller ears
1 "lip" at the end of the trunk
5 toenails
Arched back
4 toenails

ASIAN ELEPHANT
(Elephas maximus)

INTERNAL ANATOMY OF A FEMALE ELEPHANT

Spinal cord
Heart
Stomach
Duodenum
Kidney
Ureter
Uterus
Rectum
Bladder
Anal flap
Anus
Vagina
Rump
Brain
Nasal cavity
Buccal cavity
Mouth
Tongue
Tusk
Epiglottis
Esophagus
Trachea
Lung
Diaphragm
Nasal passage
Nostril
Spleen
Vulva
Small intestine
Hind leg
Toenail

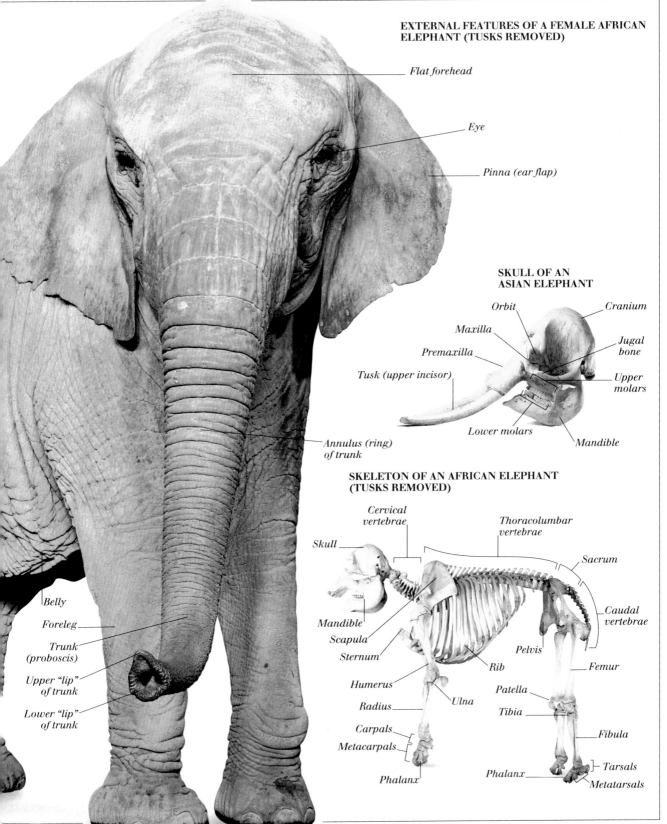

EXTERNAL FEATURES OF A FEMALE AFRICAN ELEPHANT (TUSKS REMOVED)

Flat forehead

Eye

Pinna (ear flap)

Belly

Foreleg

Trunk (proboscis)

Upper "lip" of trunk

Lower "lip" of trunk

Annulus (ring) of trunk

SKULL OF AN ASIAN ELEPHANT

Orbit

Cranium

Maxilla

Jugal bone

Premaxilla

Upper molars

Tusk (upper incisor)

Lower molars

Mandible

SKELETON OF AN AFRICAN ELEPHANT (TUSKS REMOVED)

Cervical vertebrae

Thoracolumbar vertebrae

Skull

Sacrum

Mandible

Caudal vertebrae

Scapula

Sternum

Pelvis

Humerus

Rib

Femur

Radius

Ulna

Patella

Carpals

Tibia

Metacarpals

Fibula

Phalanx

Phalanx

Tarsals

Metatarsals

Primates

THE MAMMALIAN ORDER PRIMATES consists of monkeys, apes, and their relatives (including humans). There are two suborders of primates: Prosimii, the primitive primates, which include lemurs, tarsiers, and lorises; and Anthropoidea, the advanced primates, which include monkeys, apes, and humans. The anthropoids are divided into New World monkeys, Old World monkeys, and hominids. New World monkeys typically have widespread nostrils that open to the side; and long tails, which are prehensile (grasping) in some species. This group of monkeys lives in South America, and includes marmosets, tamarins, and howler monkeys. Old World monkeys typically have close-set nostrils that open forward or downward and nonprehensile tails. This group of monkeys lives in Africa and Asia, and includes langurs, mandrills, macaques, and baboons. Hominids typically have large brains and no tail. This group includes the apes—chimpanzees, gibbons, gorillas, and orangutans—and humans.

INTERNAL ANATOMY OF A FEMALE CHIMPANZEE

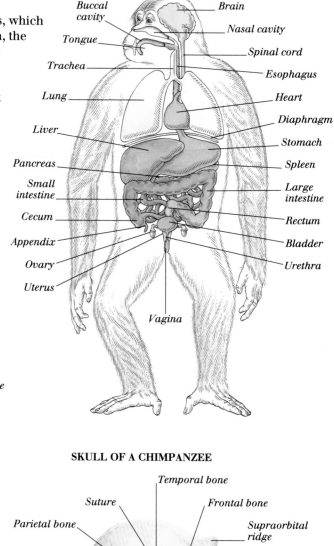

SKELETON OF A RHESUS MONKEY

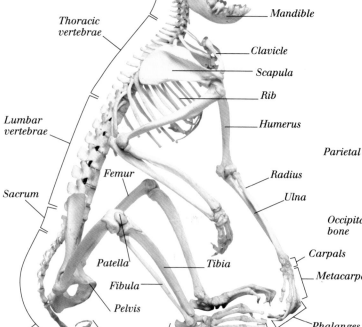

SKULL OF A CHIMPANZEE

EXAMPLES OF PRIMATES

RING-TAILED LEMUR
(Lemur catta)
A prosimian

MALE RED HOWLER MONKEY
(Alouatta seniculus)
A New World monkey

MALE MANDRILL
(Mandrillus sphinx)
An Old World monkey

CHIMPANZEE
(Pan troglodytes)
An ape

EXTERNAL FEATURES OF
A YOUNG GORILLA

GOLDEN LION TAMARIN
(Leontopithecus rosalia)
A New World monkey

Pinna (ear flap)

Shoulder

Brow ridge

Eye

Nostril

Mouth

Upper arm

Thigh

Forearm

Chest

Knee

Elbow

Lower leg

Hand

Foot

Finger

Toe

Toenail

Dolphins, whales, and seals

DOLPHINS, WHALES, AND SEALS belong to two orders of mammals adapted to living in water. Dolphins and whales make up the order Cetacea. Typical cetacean features include a streamlined, fish-like shape; forelimbs in the form of flippers; no visible hind limbs; a horizontally flattened tail; and thick blubber under the skin. There are two groups of cetaceans: toothed whales, including sperm whales, white whales, beaked whales, dolphins, and porpoises; and the larger whalebone (baleen) whales, including rorquals, gray whales, and right whales. The blue whale—a rorqual—is the largest living animal: an adult may be up to 100 ft (30m) long and weigh 145 tons (130 tonnes). Seals and their relatives—sea lions and walruses—make up the order Pinnipedia. Characteristically, they have a streamlined, torpedo-shaped body; forelimbs and hind limbs modified as flippers; thick blubber; and no external ears.

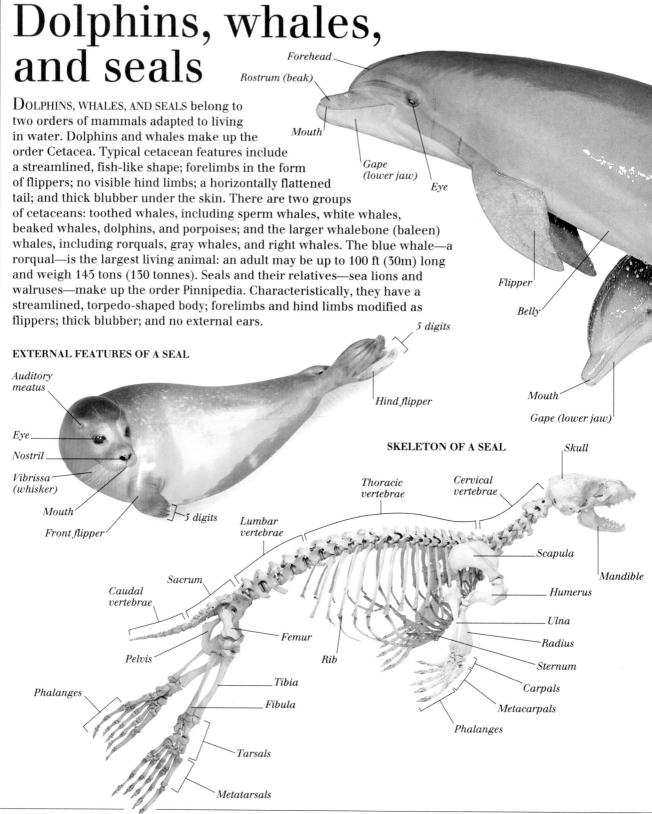

Forehead

Rostrum (beak)

Mouth

Gape (lower jaw)

Eye

Flipper

Belly

Mouth

Gape (lower jaw)

EXTERNAL FEATURES OF A SEAL

Auditory meatus

Eye

Nostril

Vibrissa (whisker)

Mouth

Front flipper

5 digits

Hind flipper

5 digits

SKELETON OF A SEAL

Skull

Cervical vertebrae

Thoracic vertebrae

Lumbar vertebrae

Scapula

Mandible

Humerus

Ulna

Radius

Sternum

Carpals

Metacarpals

Phalanges

Sacrum

Caudal vertebrae

Femur

Rib

Pelvis

Tibia

Fibula

Phalanges

Tarsals

Metatarsals

EXAMPLES OF CETACEANS

**EXTERNAL FEATURES
OF A DOLPHIN**

Dorsal fin

Tail

Tail fluke

BLUE WHALE
(Balaenoptera musculus)

SPERM WHALE
(Physeter catodon)

MALE BAIRD'S BEAKED WHALE
(Berardius bairdi)

MALE KILLER WHALE
(Orcinus orca)

MALE NARWHAL
(Monodon monoceros)

**INTERNAL ANATOMY OF
A MALE DOLPHIN**

Spinal cord

Stomach

Kidney

Blowhole (nostril)

Brain

Aorta

Intestine

Bladder

Nasal plug

Buccal cavity

Anus

Rectum

Tongue

Penis

Esophagus

Testis

Trachea

Urinogenital opening

Heart

Lung

Liver

205

Marsupials and Monotremes

MARSUPIALS AND MONOTREMES are two orders of mammals that differ from other mammalian groups in the ways that their young develop. The order Marsupalia, the pouched mammals, is made up of kangaroos and their relatives. Typically, marsupials give birth to their young at a very early stage of development. The young then crawls to the mother's pouch (which is on the outside of her abdomen), where it attaches itself to a nipple and remains until fully developed. Most marsupials live in Australia, although the opossums—which are classified as marsupials despite not having a pouch—live in the Americas. The order Monotremata is made up of the platypus and its relatives (the echidnas, or spiny anteaters). The monotremes are primitive mammals that lay eggs, which the mother incubates. The monotremes are found only in Australia and New Guinea.

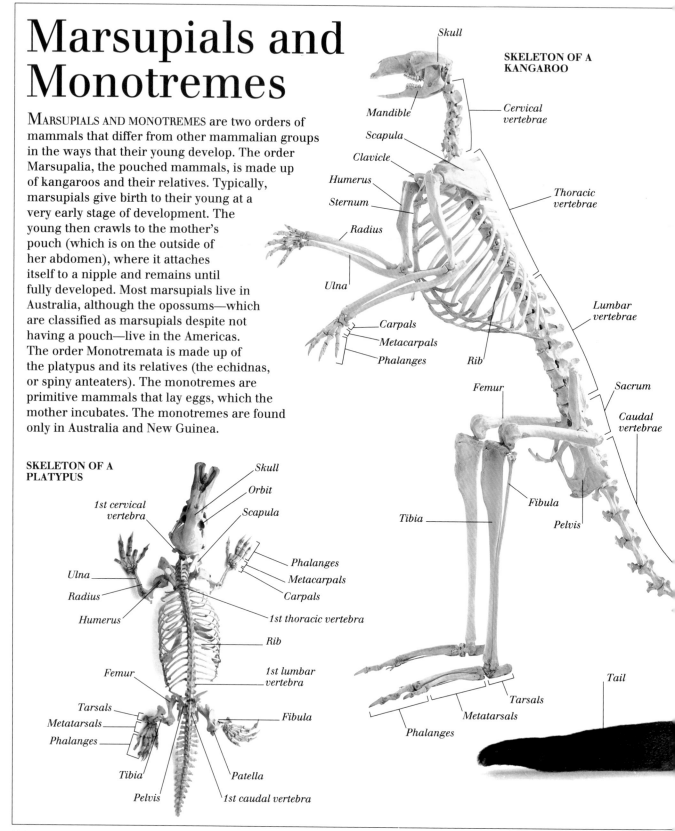

SKELETON OF A KANGAROO

Skull
Mandible
Scapula
Clavicle
Humerus
Sternum
Radius
Ulna
Carpals
Metacarpals
Phalanges
Rib
Femur
Tibia
Fibula
Pelvis
Cervical vertebrae
Thoracic vertebrae
Lumbar vertebrae
Sacrum
Caudal vertebrae
Tarsals
Metatarsals
Phalanges
Tail

SKELETON OF A PLATYPUS

Skull
Orbit
Scapula
1st cervical vertebra
Ulna
Radius
Humerus
Phalanges
Metacarpals
Carpals
1st thoracic vertebra
Rib
Femur
1st lumbar vertebra
Tarsals
Metatarsals
Phalanges
Fibula
Tibia
Patella
Pelvis
1st caudal vertebra

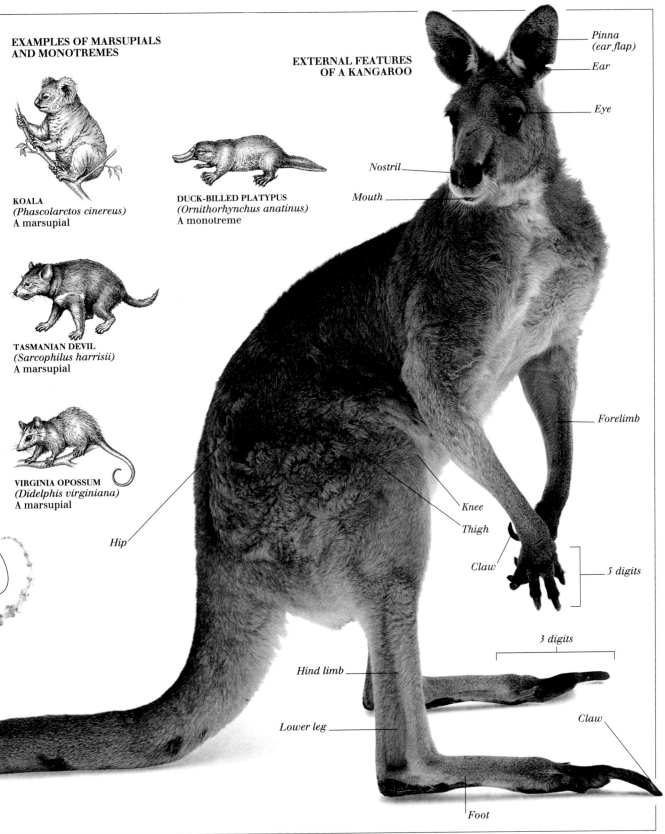

EXAMPLES OF MARSUPIALS AND MONOTREMES

EXTERNAL FEATURES OF A KANGAROO

KOALA
(Phascolarctos cinereus)
A marsupial

DUCK-BILLED PLATYPUS
(Ornithorhynchus anatinus)
A monotreme

TASMANIAN DEVIL
(Sarcophilus harrisii)
A marsupial

VIRGINIA OPOSSUM
(Didelphis virginiana)
A marsupial

Pinna (ear flap)

Ear

Eye

Nostril

Mouth

Forelimb

Hip

Knee

Thigh

Claw

5 digits

3 digits

Hind limb

Lower leg

Claw

Foot

207

THE HUMAN BODY

Body features

ALTHOUGH THERE IS enormous variation between the external appearances of humans, all bodies contain the same basic features. The outward form of the human body depends on the size of the skeleton, the shape of the muscles, the thickness of the fat layer beneath the skin, the elasticity or sagginess of the skin, and the person's age and gender. Males tend to be taller than females, with broader shoulders, more body hair, and a different pattern of fat deposits under the skin; the female body tends to be less muscular and has a shallower and wider pelvis to allow for childbirth.

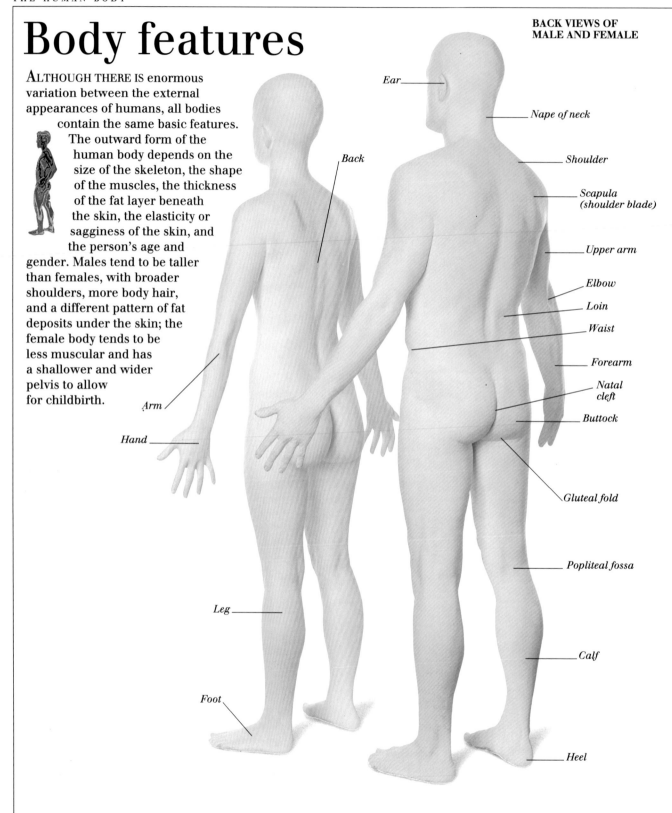

Ear

Nape of neck

Shoulder

Scapula
(shoulder blade)

Upper arm

Elbow

Loin

Waist

Forearm

Natal
cleft

Buttock

Gluteal fold

Popliteal fossa

Calf

Heel

Back

Arm

Hand

Leg

Foot

**FRONT VIEWS OF
MALE AND FEMALE**

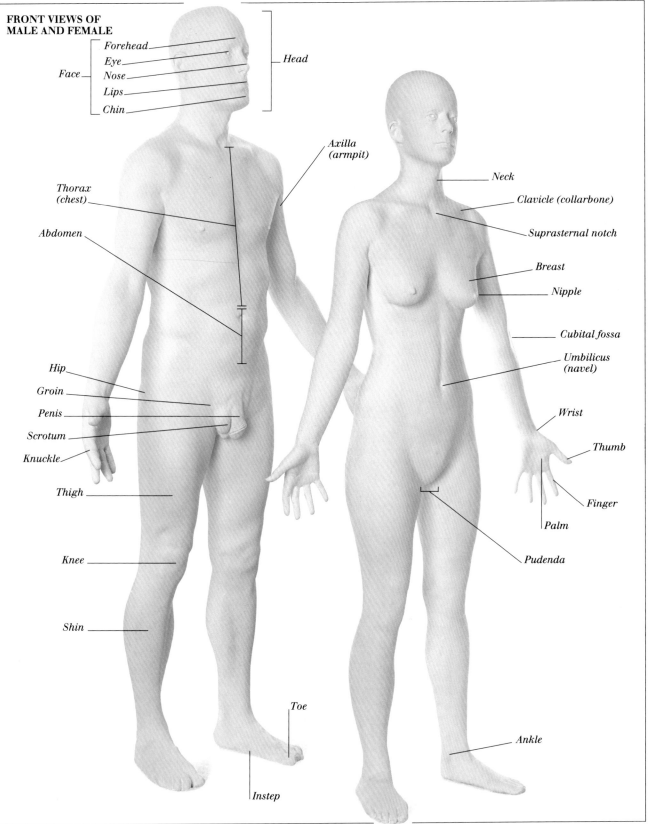

Forehead

Eye

Face — Nose

Lips

Chin

Head

Thorax
(chest)

Abdomen

Hip

Groin

Penis

Scrotum

Knuckle

Thigh

Knee

Shin

Toe

Instep

Axilla
(armpit)

Neck

Clavicle (collarbone)

Suprasternal notch

Breast

Nipple

Cubital fossa

Umbilicus
(navel)

Wrist

Thumb

Finger

Palm

Pudenda

Ankle

Head

IN A NEWBORN BABY, the head accounts for one quarter of the total body length; by adulthood, the proportion has reduced to one eighth. Contained in the head are the body's main sense organs: eyes, ears, olfactory nerves that detect smells, and the taste buds of the tongue. Signals from these organs pass to the body's great coordination center: the brain, housed in the protective, bony dome of the skull. Hair on the head insulates against heat loss, and adult males also grow thick facial hair. The face has three important openings: two nostrils through which air passes, and the mouth, which takes in nourishment and helps form speech. Although all heads are basically similar, differences in the size, shape, and color of features produce an infinite variety of appearances.

SIDE VIEW OF EXTERNAL FEATURES OF HEAD

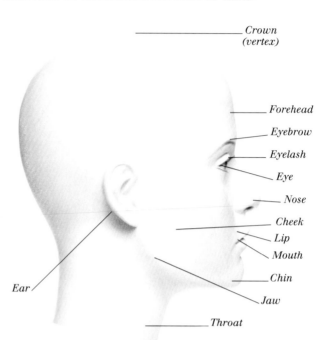

Crown (vertex)

Forehead

Eyebrow

Eyelash

Eye

Nose

Cheek

Lip

Mouth

Chin

Jaw

Throat

Ear

SECTION THROUGH HEAD

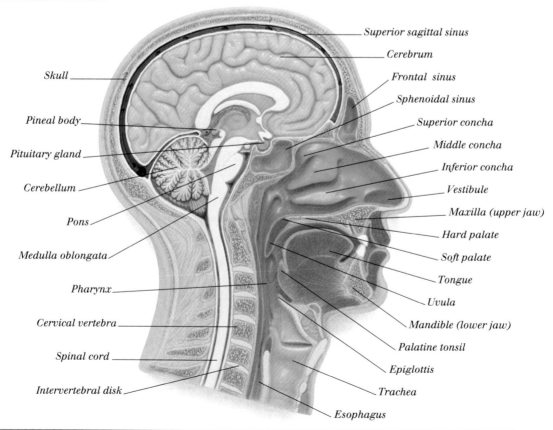

Superior sagittal sinus

Cerebrum

Frontal sinus

Sphenoidal sinus

Superior concha

Middle concha

Inferior concha

Vestibule

Maxilla (upper jaw)

Hard palate

Soft palate

Tongue

Uvula

Mandible (lower jaw)

Palatine tonsil

Epiglottis

Trachea

Esophagus

Skull

Pineal body

Pituitary gland

Cerebellum

Pons

Medulla oblongata

Pharynx

Cervical vertebra

Spinal cord

Intervertebral disk

**FRONT VIEW OF EXTERNAL
FEATURES OF HEAD**

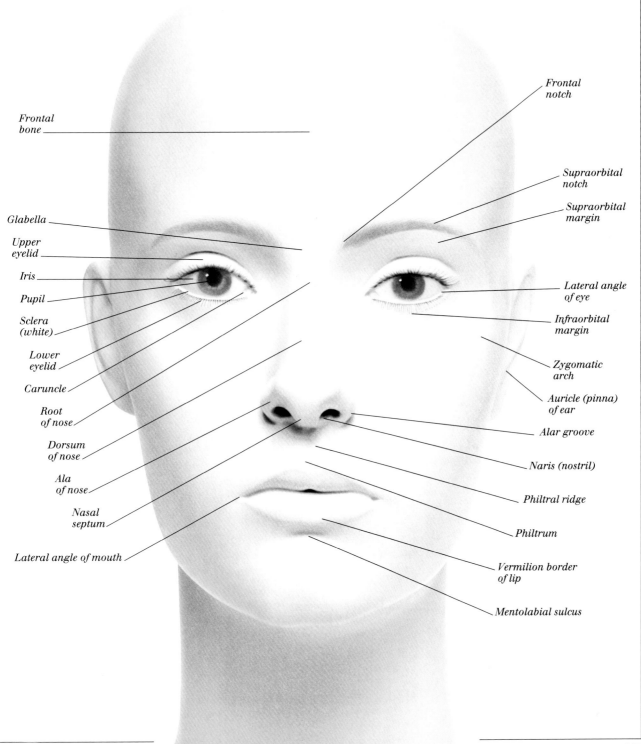

*Frontal
notch*

*Frontal
bone*

*Supraorbital
notch*

*Supraorbital
margin*

Glabella

*Upper
eyelid*

Iris

Pupil

*Lateral angle
of eye*

*Sclera
(white)*

*Infraorbital
margin*

*Lower
eyelid*

*Zygomatic
arch*

Caruncle

*Auricle (pinna)
of ear*

*Root
of nose*

Alar groove

*Dorsum
of nose*

Naris (nostril)

*Ala
of nose*

Philtral ridge

*Nasal
septum*

Philtrum

Lateral angle of mouth

*Vermilion border
of lip*

Mentolabial sulcus

Body organs

ALL THE VITAL BODY ORGANS except for the brain are enclosed within the trunk or torso (the body apart from the head and limbs). The trunk contains two large cavities separated by a muscular sheet called the diaphragm. The upper cavity, known as the thorax or chest cavity, contains the heart and lungs. The lower cavity, called the abdominal cavity, contains the stomach, intestines, liver, and pancreas, which all play a role in digesting food. Also within the trunk are the kidneys and bladder, which are part of the urinary system, and the reproductive organs, which hold the seeds of new human life. Modern imaging techniques, such as contrast X-rays and different types of scans, make it possible to see and study body organs without the need to cut through their protective coverings of skin, fat, muscle, and bone.

MAJOR INTERNAL STRUCTURES

Thyroid gland

Larynx

Heart

Right lung

Left lung

Diaphragm

Liver

Stomach

Large intestine

Small intestine

Greater omentum

IMAGING THE BODY

SCINTIGRAM OF HEART CHAMBERS

ANGIOGRAM OF RIGHT LUNG

CONTRAST X-RAY OF GALLBLADDER

SCINTIGRAM OF NERVOUS SYSTEM

DOUBLE CONTRAST X-RAY OF COLON

ULTRASOUND SCAN OF TWINS IN UTERUS

ANGIOGRAM OF KIDNEYS

ANGIOGRAM OF ARTERIES OF HEAD

CT SCAN THROUGH FEMALE CHEST

THERMOGRAM OF CHEST REGION

ANGIOGRAM OF ARTERIES OF HEART

MRI SCAN THROUGH HEAD AT EYE LEVEL

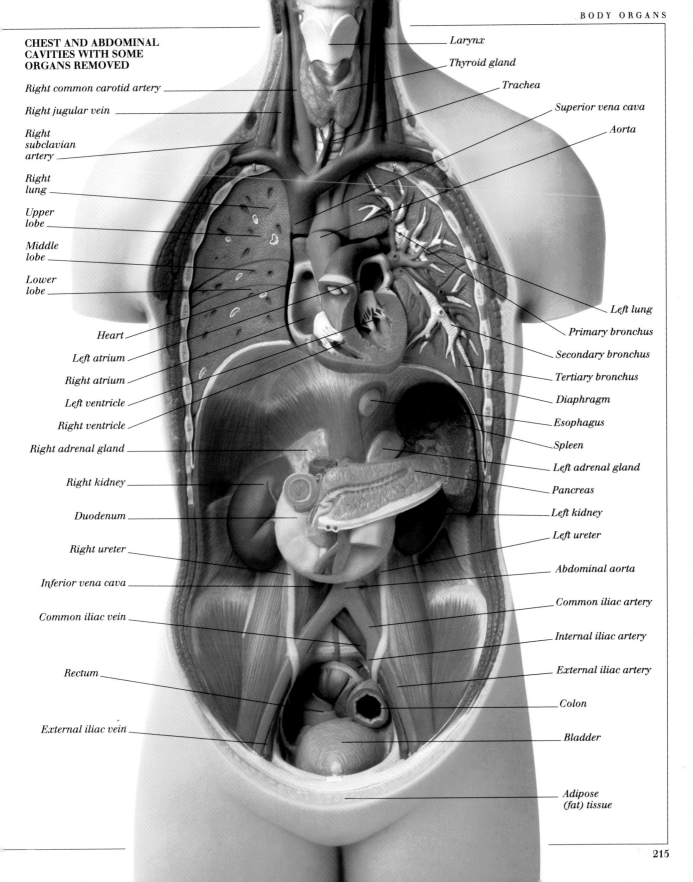

CHEST AND ABDOMINAL CAVITIES WITH SOME ORGANS REMOVED

Right common carotid artery

Right jugular vein

Right subclavian artery

Right lung

Upper lobe

Middle lobe

Lower lobe

Heart

Left atrium

Right atrium

Left ventricle

Right ventricle

Right adrenal gland

Right kidney

Duodenum

Right ureter

Inferior vena cava

Common iliac vein

Rectum

External iliac vein

Larynx

Thyroid gland

Trachea

Superior vena cava

Aorta

Left lung

Primary bronchus

Secondary bronchus

Tertiary bronchus

Diaphragm

Esophagus

Spleen

Left adrenal gland

Pancreas

Left kidney

Left ureter

Abdominal aorta

Common iliac artery

Internal iliac artery

External iliac artery

Colon

Bladder

Adipose (fat) tissue

215

Body cells

EVERYONE IS MADE UP OF BILLIONS OF CELLS, which are the basic structural units of the body. Bones, muscles, nerves, skin, blood, and all other body tissues are formed from different types of cells. Each cell has a specific function but works with other types of cells to perform the enormous number of tasks needed to sustain life. Most body cells have a similar basic structure. Each cell has an outer layer (called the cell membrane) and contains a fluid material (cytoplasm). Within the cytoplasm are many specialized structures (organelles). The most important organelle is the nucleus, which contains vital genetic material and acts as the cell's control center.

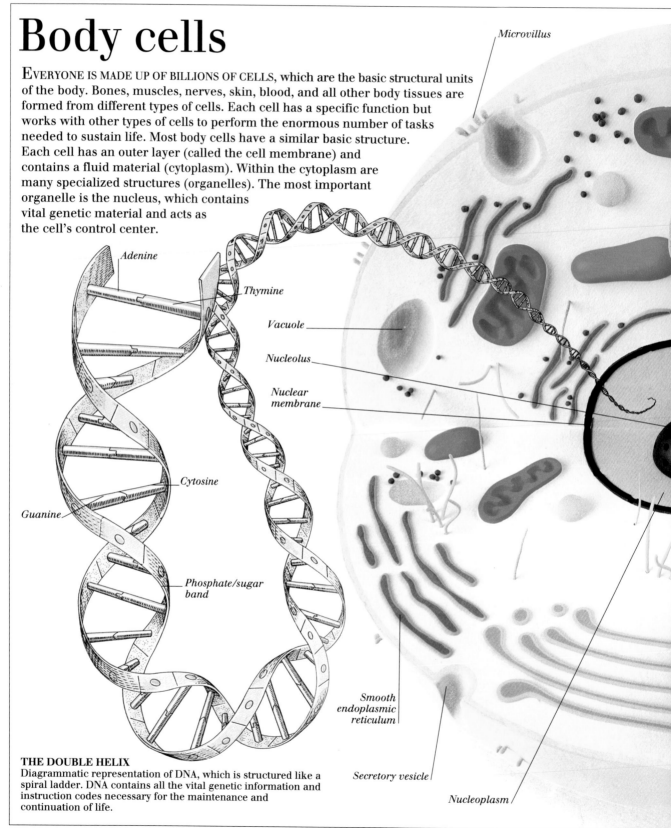

Microvillus

Adenine

Thymine

Vacuole

Nucleolus

Nuclear membrane

Cytosine

Guanine

Phosphate/sugar band

Smooth endoplasmic reticulum

Secretory vesicle

Nucleoplasm

THE DOUBLE HELIX
Diagrammatic representation of DNA, which is structured like a spiral ladder. DNA contains all the vital genetic information and instruction codes necessary for the maintenance and continuation of life.

GENERALIZED HUMAN CELL

Cytoplasm

Lysosome

Cell membrane

Mitochondrial crista

Nucleus

Rough endoplasmic reticulum

Microfilament

Pore of nuclear membrane

Ribosome

Centriole

Mitochondrion

Microtubule

Peroxisome

Pinocytotic vesicle

Golgi complex (Golgi apparatus; Golgi body)

TYPES OF CELLS

BONE-FORMING CELL

NERVE CELLS IN SPINAL CORD

SPERM CELLS IN SEMEN

SECRETORY THYROID GLAND CELLS

ACID-SECRETING STOMACH CELLS

CONNECTIVE TISSUE CELLS

MUCUS-SECRETING DUODENAL CELLS

RED AND TWO WHITE BLOOD CELLS

FAT CELLS IN ADIPOSE TISSUE

EPITHELIAL CELLS IN CHEEK

Skeleton

THE SKELETON IS A MOBILE FRAMEWORK made up of 206 bones, approximately half of which are in the hands and feet. Although individual bones are rigid, the skeleton as a whole is remarkably flexible and allows the human body a huge range of movement. The skeleton serves as an anchorage for the skeletal muscles, and as a protective cage for the body's internal organs. Female bones are usually smaller and lighter than male bones, and the female pelvis is shallower and has a wider cavity.

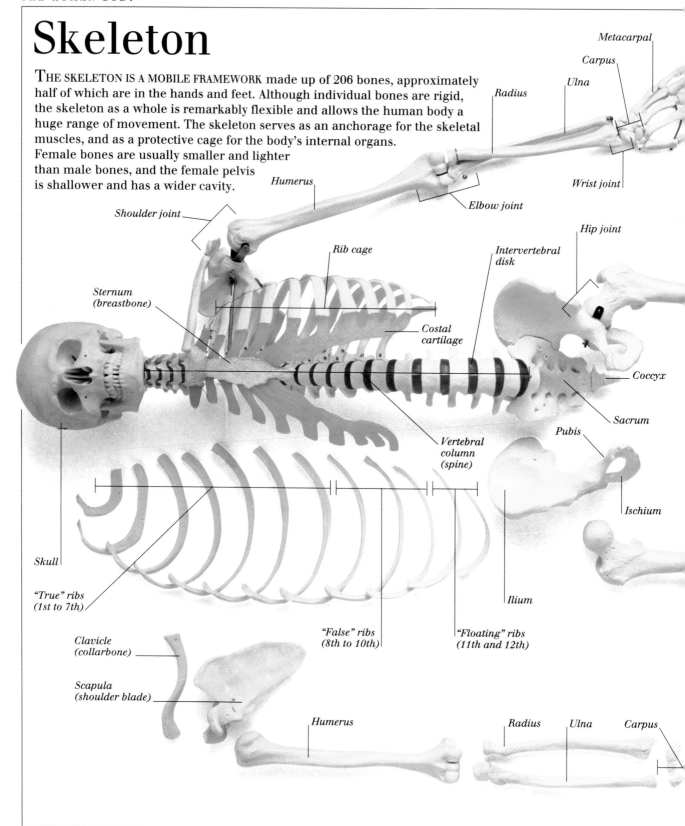

Metacarpal

Carpus

Ulna

Radius

Humerus

Elbow joint

Wrist joint

Shoulder joint

Rib cage

Intervertebral disk

Hip joint

Sternum (breastbone)

Costal cartilage

Coccyx

Sacrum

Pubis

Ischium

Vertebral column (spine)

Skull

Ilium

"True" ribs (1st to 7th)

"False" ribs (8th to 10th)

"Floating" ribs (11th and 12th)

Clavicle (collarbone)

Scapula (shoulder blade)

Humerus

Radius

Ulna

Carpus

Distal phalanx

Middle phalanx

Proximal phalanx

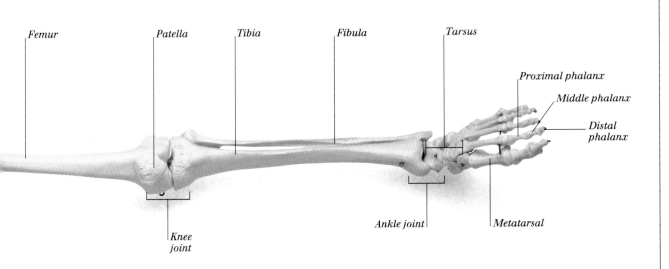

Femur

Patella

Tibia

Fibula

Tarsus

Proximal phalanx

Middle phalanx

Distal phalanx

Knee joint

Ankle joint

Metatarsal

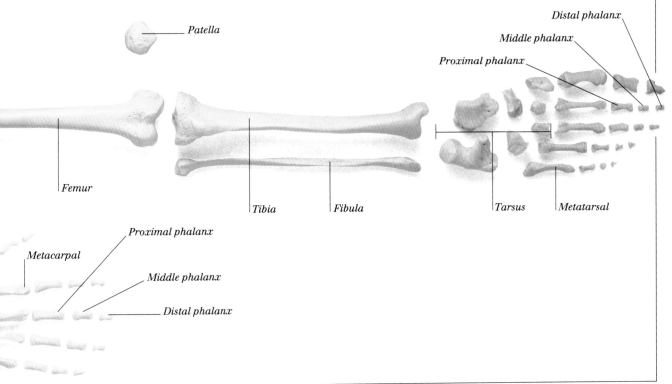

Patella

Distal phalanx

Middle phalanx

Proximal phalanx

Femur

Tibia

Fibula

Tarsus

Metatarsal

Metacarpal

Proximal phalanx

Middle phalanx

Distal phalanx

219

Skull

THE SKULL is the most complicated bony structure of the body—but every feature serves a purpose. Internally, the main hollow chamber of the skull has three levels that support the brain, with every bump and hollow corresponding to the shape of the brain. Underneath and toward the back of the skull is a large round hole, called the foramen magnum, through which the spinal cord passes. To the front of this are many smaller openings through which nerves, arteries, and veins pass to and from the brain. The roof of the skull is formed from four thin, curved bones that are firmly fixed together from the age of about two years. At the front of the skull are two orbits, which contain the eyeballs, and a central hole for the airway of the nose. The jawbone hinges on either side of the skull at ear level.

RIGHT SIDE VIEW OF A FETAL SKULL

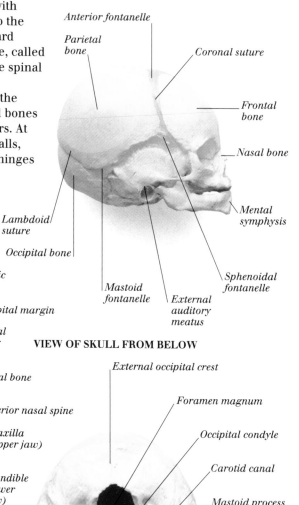

Anterior fontanelle

Parietal bone

Coronal suture

Frontal bone

Nasal bone

Mental symphysis

Lambdoid suture

Occipital bone

Sphenoidal fontanelle

Mastoid fontanelle

External auditory meatus

RIGHT SIDE VIEW OF SKULL

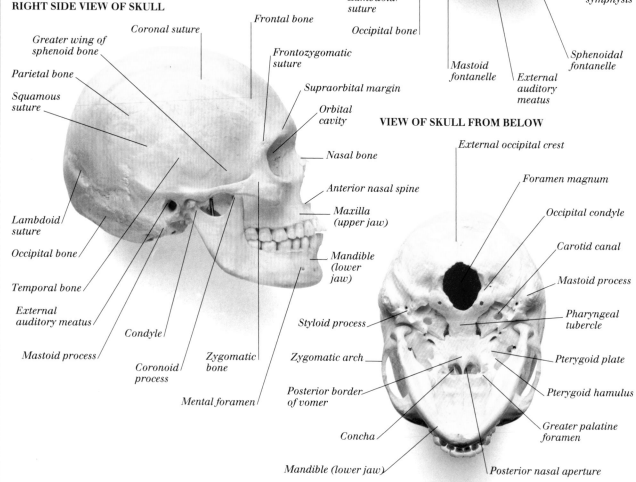

Greater wing of sphenoid bone

Coronal suture

Frontal bone

Frontozygomatic suture

Parietal bone

Squamous suture

Supraorbital margin

Orbital cavity

Nasal bone

Anterior nasal spine

Maxilla (upper jaw)

Lambdoid suture

Occipital bone

Temporal bone

External auditory meatus

Mandible (lower jaw)

Mastoid process

Condyle

Coronoid process

Zygomatic bone

Styloid process

Mental foramen

VIEW OF SKULL FROM BELOW

External occipital crest

Foramen magnum

Occipital condyle

Carotid canal

Mastoid process

Pharyngeal tubercle

Pterygoid plate

Zygomatic arch

Posterior border of vomer

Pterygoid hamulus

Greater palatine foramen

Concha

Posterior nasal aperture

Mandible (lower jaw)

FRONT VIEW OF SKULL

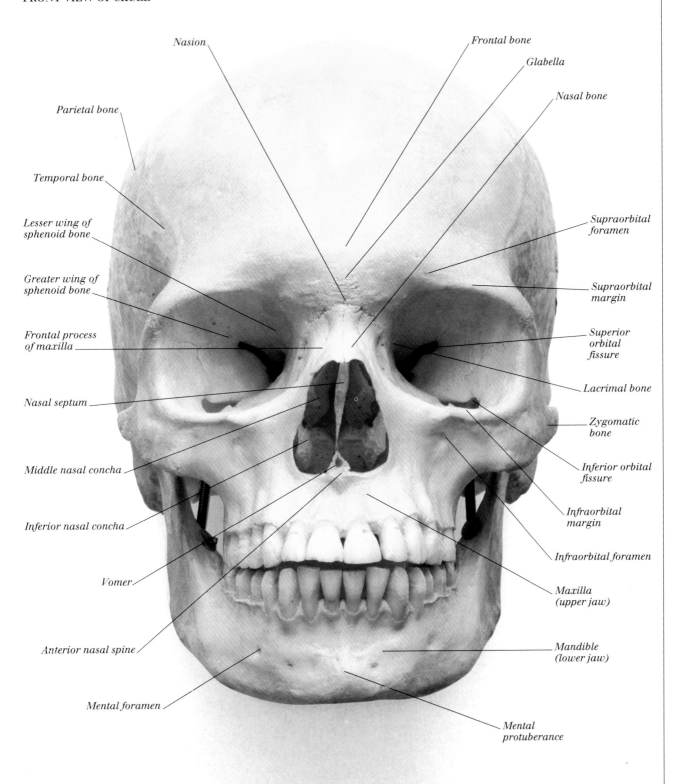

Nasion

Frontal bone

Glabella

Nasal bone

Parietal bone

Temporal bone

Lesser wing of
sphenoid bone

Greater wing of
sphenoid bone

Frontal process
of maxilla

Nasal septum

Middle nasal concha

Inferior nasal concha

Vomer

Anterior nasal spine

Mental foramen

Supraorbital
foramen

Supraorbital
margin

Superior
orbital
fissure

Lacrimal bone

Zygomatic
bone

Inferior orbital
fissure

Infraorbital
margin

Infraorbital foramen

Maxilla
(upper jaw)

Mandible
(lower jaw)

Mental
protuberance

Spine

THE SPINE (OR VERTEBRAL COLUMN) has two main functions: it serves as a protective surrounding for the delicate spinal cord and forms the supporting back bone of the skeleton. The spine consists of 24 separate differently shaped bones (vertebrae) with a curved, triangular bone (the sacrum) at the bottom. The sacrum is made up of fused vertebrae; at its lower end is a small tail-like structure made up of tiny bones collectively called the coccyx. Between each pair of vertebrae is a disc of cartilage that cushions the bones during movement. The top two vertebrae differ in appearance from the others and work as a pair: the first, called the atlas, rotates around a stout vertical peg on the second, the axis. This arrangement allows the skull to move freely up and down, and from side to side.

SPINE DIVIDED INTO VERTEBRAL SECTIONS

FRONT

- Cervical vertebrae
- Thoracic vertebrae
- Lumbar vertebrae
- Sacral vertebrae
- Coccygeal vertebrae

TYPES OF VERTEBRAE (VIEWED FROM ABOVE)

ATLAS

- Lateral mass with superior articular facet
- Anterior arch
- Posterior arch
- Anterior tubercle
- Posterior tubercle
- Vertebral foramen
- Transverse foramen
- Transverse process

AXIS

- Vertebral foramen
- Facet
- Spinous process
- Dens
- Lamina
- Transverse process and foramen

CERVICAL VERTEBRA

- Body
- Superior articular process
- Anterior tubercle
- Spinous process
- Vertebral foramen
- Posterior tubercle
- Transverse foramen

SKULL AND SPINE

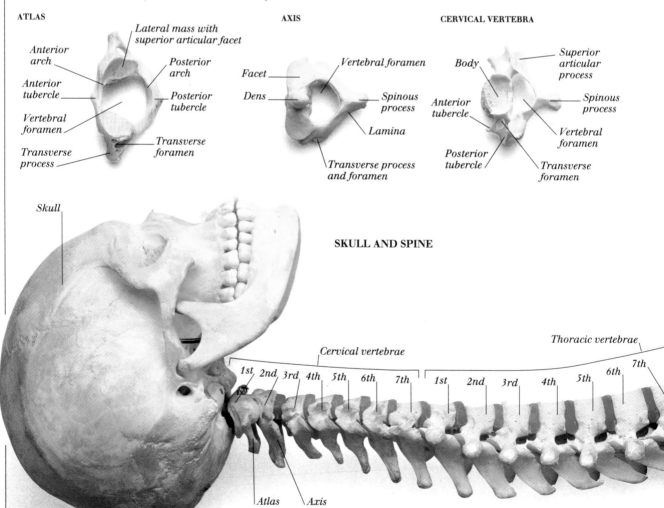

- Skull
- Cervical vertebrae
- Thoracic vertebrae
- 1st 2nd 3rd 4th 5th 6th 7th
- 1st 2nd 3rd 4th 5th 6th 7th
- Atlas
- Axis

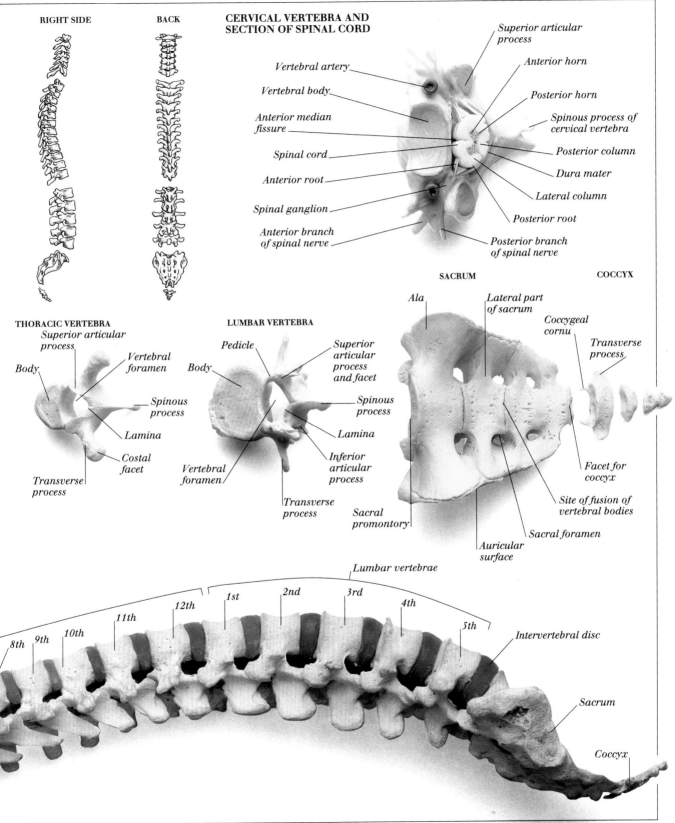

RIGHT SIDE

BACK

CERVICAL VERTEBRA AND SECTION OF SPINAL CORD

Superior articular process

Vertebral artery

Anterior horn

Vertebral body

Posterior horn

Anterior median fissure

Spinous process of cervical vertebra

Spinal cord

Posterior column

Anterior root

Dura mater

Lateral column

Spinal ganglion

Posterior root

Anterior branch of spinal nerve

Posterior branch of spinal nerve

SACRUM

COCCYX

Ala

Lateral part of sacrum

Coccygeal cornu

Transverse process

THORACIC VERTEBRA

Superior articular process

Vertebral foramen

Body

Spinous process

Lamina

Costal facet

Transverse process

LUMBAR VERTEBRA

Pedicle

Body

Superior articular process and facet

Spinous process

Lamina

Inferior articular process

Vertebral foramen

Transverse process

Sacral promontory

Auricular surface

Facet for coccyx

Site of fusion of vertebral bodies

Sacral foramen

Lumbar vertebrae

8th 9th 10th 11th 12th 1st 2nd 3rd 4th 5th

Intervertebral disc

Sacrum

Coccyx

Bones and joints

BONES FORM the body's hard, strong skeletal framework. Each bone has a hard, compact exterior surrounding a spongy, lighter interior. The long bones of the arms and legs, such as the femur (thigh bone), have a central cavity containing bone marrow. Bones are composed chiefly of calcium, phosphorus, and a fibrous substance known as collagen. Bones meet at joints, which are of several different types. For example, the hip is a ball-and-socket joint that allows the femur a wide range of movement, whereas finger joints are simple hinge joints that allow only bending and straightening. Joints are held in place by bands of tissue called ligaments. Movement of joints is facilitated by the smooth hyaline cartilage that covers the bone ends and by the synovial membrane that lines and lubricates the joint.

LIGAMENTS SURROUNDING HIP JOINT

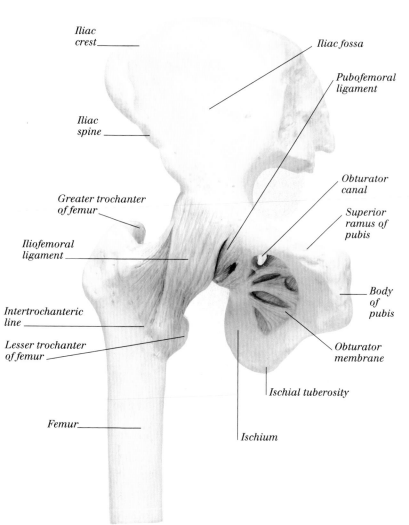

Iliac crest
Iliac fossa
Pubofemoral ligament
Iliac spine
Obturator canal
Greater trochanter of femur
Superior ramus of pubis
Iliofemoral ligament
Body of pubis
Intertrochanteric line
Obturator membrane
Lesser trochanter of femur
Ischial tuberosity
Femur
Ischium

SECTION THROUGH LEFT FEMUR

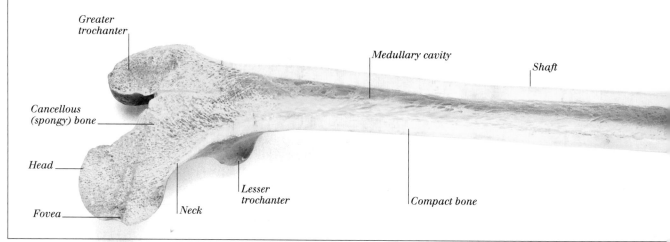

Greater trochanter
Medullary cavity
Shaft
Cancellous (spongy) bone
Head
Lesser trochanter
Neck
Compact bone
Fovea

SECTION THROUGH HIP JOINT

Psoas major muscle

Iliacus muscle

Iliac crest

External
iliac artery

Hyaline cartilage
of acetabulum

Hyaline cartilage
of head of femur

Ligament of
head of femur

Femoral
artery

Articular
cavity

Gluteus
minimus muscle

Gluteus
medius muscle

Acetabular
labrum

Head
of femur

Greater
trochanter
of femur

Neck of
femur

Vastus
lateralis
muscle

Shaft
of femur

Pectineus
muscle

Adductor
longus muscle

Iliacus
muscle

Vastus
medialis muscle

SECTION OF COMPACT BONE

Parallel rows of concentric
bony layers make up this
strong material.

BONE MARROW CELLS

Composed mainly of red and
white blood cells, marrow fills
the cavities of bones.

Lateral
epicondyle

Patellar
surface

Adductor tubercle

Medial
epicondyle

SECTION THROUGH LONG BONE

Osteon
(haversian system)

Haversian lamella

Outer lamella

Sharpey's
fiber

Osteocyte
(bone cell)

Intermediate
lamella

Endosteum

Periosteum

Haversian canal

Volkmann's vessel

Lacuna

Muscles 1

THERE ARE THREE MAIN TYPES OF MUSCLE: skeletal muscle (also called voluntary muscle because it can be consciously controlled); smooth muscle (also called involuntary muscle because it is not under voluntary control); and the specialized muscle tissue of the heart. Humans have more than 600 skeletal muscles, which differ in size and shape according to the jobs they do. Skeletal muscles are attached either directly or indirectly (via tendons) to bones, and work in opposing pairs (one muscle in the pair contracts while the other relaxes) to produce body movements as diverse as walking, threading a needle, and an array of facial expressions. Smooth muscles occur in the walls of internal body organs and perform actions such as forcing food through the intestines, contracting the uterus (womb) in childbirth, and pumping blood through the blood vessels.

SOME OTHER MUSCLES IN THE BODY

Iris

Pupil

IRIS
The muscle fibers contract and dilate (expand) to alter pupil size.

TONGUE
Interlacing layers of muscle allow great mobility.

ILEUM
Opposing muscle layers transport semidigested food.

SUPERFICIAL SKELETAL MUSCLES

FRONT VIEW

Brachioradialis

Flexors of forearm

Frontalis

Brachialis

Orbicularis oculi

Temporalis

Sternocleidomastoid

Trapezius

Pectoralis major

Deltoid

Serratus anterior

Rectus abdominis

Biceps brachii

Linea alba

External oblique

Tensor fasciae latae

Iliopsoas

Pectineus

Adductor longus

Vastus lateralis

Rectus femoris

Gracilis

Sartorius

Vastus medialis

Gastrocnemius

Tibialis anterior

BACK VIEW

Extensors of hand

Flexors of hand

Temporalis

Sternocleidomastoid

Trapezius

Deltoid

Triceps brachii

Teres minor

Teres major

Infraspinatus

Rhomboideus major

Latissimus dorsi

Gluteus maximus

Adductor magnus

Gracilis

Biceps femoris

Semitendinosus

Gastrocnemius

Soleus

Peroneus brevis

MOVEMENT OF THE FOREARM
Controlled movement of the limbs relies on coordinated relaxation and contraction of opposing muscles. To raise the forearm, the biceps (two-rooted muscle) contracts and shortens while the triceps (three-rooted muscle) relaxes; the reverse occurs when the forearm is lowered.

Triceps in resting phase

Biceps in resting phase

Forearm at rest

Triceps relaxes

Biceps contracts

Forearm half raised

Triceps fully relaxed

Biceps fully contracted

Forearm fully raised

Triceps contracts

Biceps relaxes

Forearm half lowered

Triceps back in resting phase

Biceps back in resting phase

Forearm back at rest

Muscles 2

SKELETAL MUSCLE FIBER

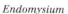

Myofibril

Sarcomere

*Motor
end plate*

Nucleus

*Synaptic
knob*

*Sarcoplasmic
reticulum*

*Schwann
cell*

Sarcolemma

*Motor
neuron*

Endomysium

*Node of
Ranvier*

MUSCLES OF FACIAL EXPRESSION

A single expression is the result of movement of many muscles; the main muscles of expression are shown in action below.

FRONTALIS

**CORRUGATOR
SUPERCILII**

ORBICULARIS ORIS

**ZYGOMATICUS
MAJOR**

**DEPRESSOR ANGULI
ORIS**

TYPES OF MUSCLE

CARDIAC MUSCLE

SKELETAL MUSCLE

SMOOTH MUSCLE

CONTRACTION OF SKELETAL MUSCLE

RELAXED STATE

CONTRACTED STATE

**MUSCLES OF
HEAD AND NECK**

Frontalis

Procerus

Temporalis

Corrugator
supercilii

Orbicularis
oculi

Levator labii
superioris

Zygomaticus
major

Nasalis

Orbicularis oris

Buccinator

Masseter

Risorius

Levator anguli oris

Depressor labii
inferioris

Platysma

Mentalis

Depressor anguli oris

Thyrohyoid

Scalenus medius

Sternocleidomastoid

Sternohyoid

Omohyoid

Cricothyroid

Trapezius

Hands

THE HUMAN HAND is an extremely versatile tool, capable of delicate manipulation as well as powerful gripping actions. The arrangement of its 27 small bones, moved by 37 skeletal muscles that are connected to the bones by tendons, allows a wide range of movements. Our ability to bring the tips of our thumbs and fingers together, combined with the extraordinary sensitivity of our fingertips due to their rich supply of nerve endings, makes our hands uniquely dextrous.

X-RAY OF LEFT HAND OF A YOUNG CHILD

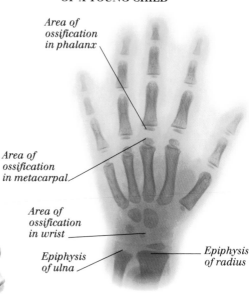

Area of ossification in phalanx

Area of ossification in metacarpal

Area of ossification in wrist

Epiphysis of ulna

Epiphysis of radius

Areas of cartilage in the wrist and at the ends of the finger bones are the sites of growth and have still to ossify.

BONES OF HAND

Ring finger

Middle finger

Index finger

Little finger

Distal phalanx

Middle phalanx

Proximal phalanx

2nd metacarpal

3rd metacarpal

4th metacarpal

5th metacarpal

Hamate

Pisiform

Capitate

Triquetral

Lunate

Ulna

Head

Shaft

Base

Trapezium

Trapezoid

Scaphoid

Radius

Distal phalanx of thumb

Proximal phalanx of thumb

1st metacarpal

230

STRUCTURES UNDERLYING SKIN OF PALM OF HAND

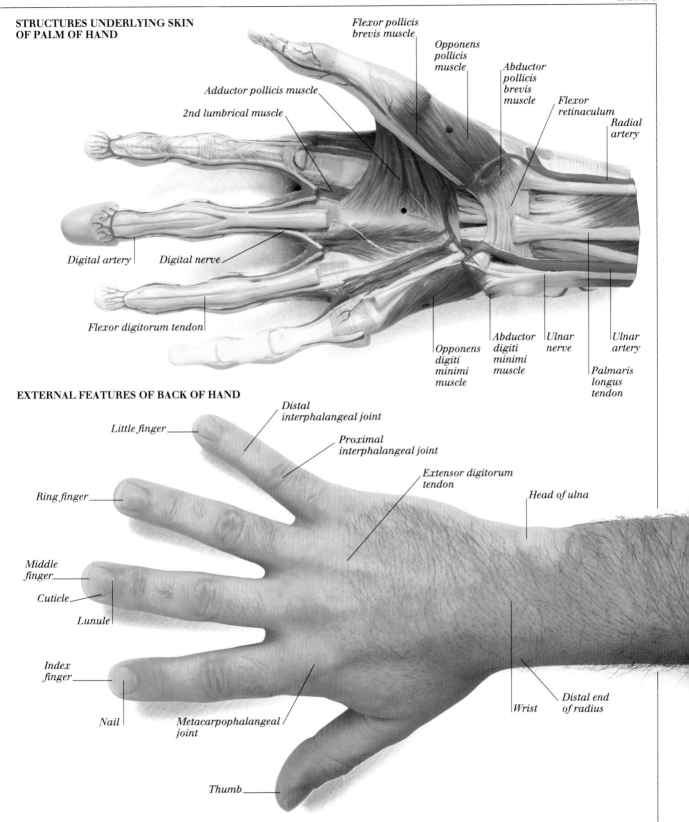

Flexor pollicis brevis muscle

Opponens pollicis muscle

Abductor pollicis brevis muscle

Flexor retinaculum

Radial artery

Adductor pollicis muscle

2nd lumbrical muscle

Digital artery

Digital nerve

Flexor digitorum tendon

Opponens digiti minimi muscle

Abductor digiti minimi muscle

Ulnar nerve

Ulnar artery

Palmaris longus tendon

EXTERNAL FEATURES OF BACK OF HAND

Distal interphalangeal joint

Little finger

Proximal interphalangeal joint

Extensor digitorum tendon

Head of ulna

Ring finger

Middle finger

Cuticle

Lunule

Index finger

Nail

Metacarpophalangeal joint

Wrist

Distal end of radius

Thumb

Feet

THE FEET AND TOES are essential elements in body movement. They bear and propel the weight of the body during walking and running, and also help to maintain balance during changes of body position. Each foot has 26 bones, more than 100 ligaments, and 33 muscles, some of which are attached to the lower leg. The heel pad and the arch of the foot act as shock absorbers, providing a cushion against the jolts that occur with every step.

BONES OF FOOT

LIGAMENTS OF FOOT

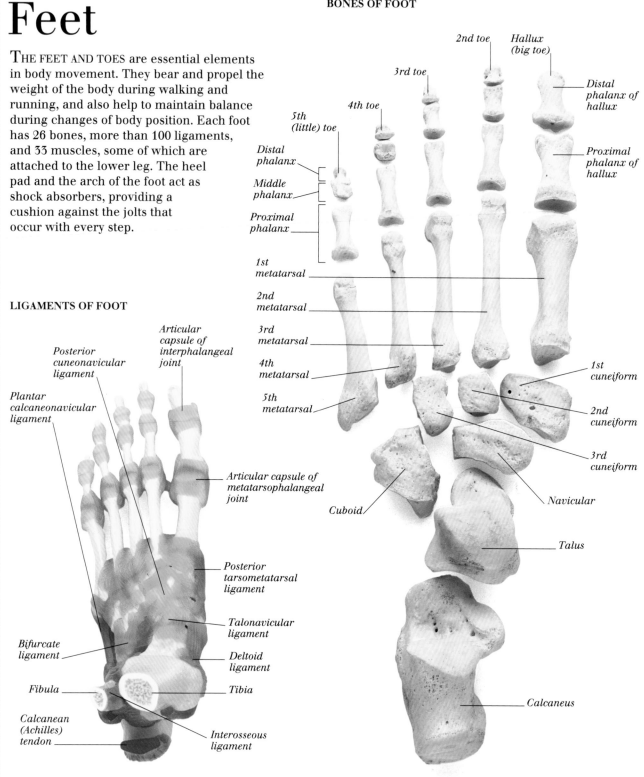

2nd toe
Hallux (big toe)
3rd toe
4th toe
5th (little) toe
Distal phalanx of hallux
Distal phalanx
Middle phalanx
Proximal phalanx
Proximal phalanx of hallux
1st metatarsal
2nd metatarsal
3rd metatarsal
4th metatarsal
5th metatarsal
1st cuneiform
2nd cuneiform
3rd cuneiform
Cuboid
Navicular
Talus
Calcaneus

Articular capsule of interphalangeal joint
Posterior cuneonavicular ligament
Plantar calcaneonavicular ligament
Articular capsule of metatarsophalangeal joint
Posterior tarsometatarsal ligament
Talonavicular ligament
Bifurcate ligament
Deltoid ligament
Fibula
Tibia
Calcanean (Achilles) tendon
Interosseous ligament

STRUCTURES UNDERLYING SKIN OF FOOT

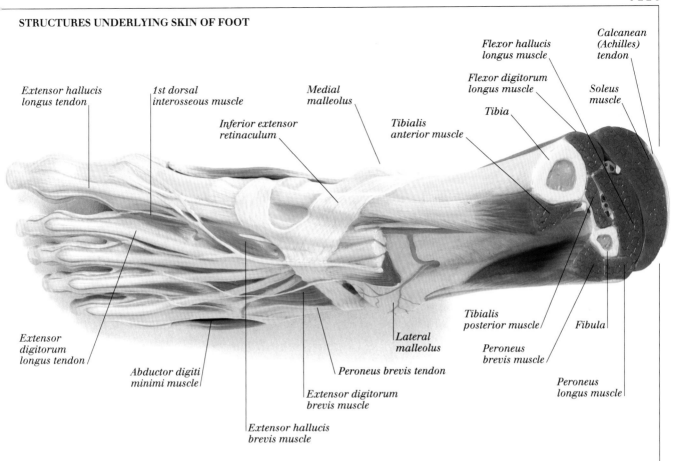

Extensor hallucis
longus tendon

1st dorsal
interosseous muscle

Inferior extensor
retinaculum

Medial
malleolus

Tibialis
anterior muscle

Flexor hallucis
longus muscle

Flexor digitorum
longus muscle

Tibia

Calcanean
(Achilles)
tendon

Soleus
muscle

Extensor
digitorum
longus tendon

Abductor digiti
minimi muscle

Extensor hallucis
brevis muscle

Extensor digitorum
brevis muscle

Peroneus brevis tendon

Lateral
malleolus

Tibialis
posterior muscle

Peroneus
brevis muscle

Fibula

Peroneus
longus muscle

EXTERNAL FEATURES OF FOOT

Toenail

Hallux
(big toe)

Interphalangeal
joint

Extensor hallucis
longus tendon

Extensor digitorum
longus tendon

Medial malleolus

2nd toe

3rd toe

4th toe

5th
(little) toe

Lateral malleolus

Skin and hair

SKIN IS THE BODY'S LARGEST ORGAN, a waterproof barrier that protects the internal organs against infection, injury, and harmful sun rays. The skin is also an important sensory organ and helps to control body temperature. The outer layer of the skin, known as the epidermis, is coated with keratin, a tough, horny protein that is also the chief constituent of hair and nails. Dead cells are shed from the skin's surface and are replaced by new cells from the base of the epidermis, the region that also produces the skin pigment, melanin. The dermis contains most of the skin's living structures, and includes nerve endings, blood vessels, elastic fibers, sweat glands that cool the skin, and sebaceous glands that produce oil to keep the skin supple. Beneath the dermis lies the subcutaneous tissue (hypodermis), which is rich in fat and blood vessels. Hair shafts grow from hair follicles situated in the dermis and subcutaneous tissue. Hair grows on every part of the skin apart from the palms of the hands and soles of the feet.

SECTION OF HAIR

- Medulla
- Cortex
- Melanin granule
- Cell nucleus residue
- Macrofibril
- Cuticle

SECTIONS OF DIFFERENT TYPES OF SKIN

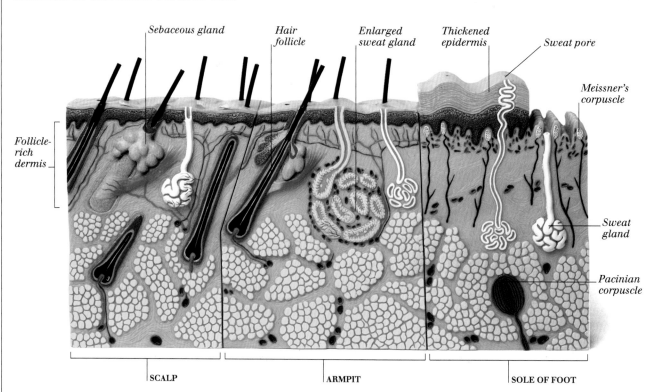

- Sebaceous gland
- Hair follicle
- Enlarged sweat gland
- Thickened epidermis
- Sweat pore
- Meissner's corpuscle
- Follicle-rich dermis
- Sweat gland
- Pacinian corpuscle

SCALP

ARMPIT

SOLE OF FOOT

SECTION OF SKIN

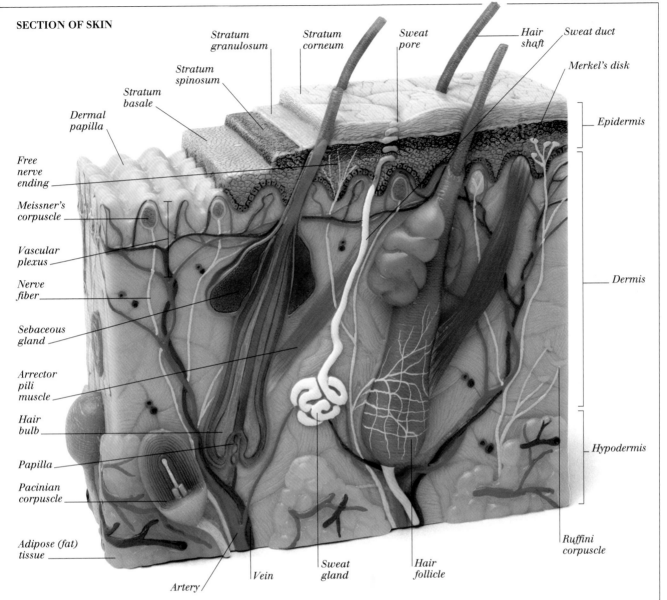

Stratum
granulosum

Stratum
corneum

Sweat
pore

Hair
shaft

Sweat duct

Stratum
spinosum

Merkel's disk

Stratum
basale

Epidermis

Dermal
papilla

Free
nerve
ending

Meissner's
corpuscle

Vascular
plexus

Dermis

Nerve
fiber

Sebaceous
gland

Arrector
pili
muscle

Hair
bulb

Hypodermis

Papilla

Pacinian
corpuscle

Adipose (fat)
tissue

Ruffini
corpuscle

Artery

Vein

Sweat
gland

Hair
follicle

PHOTOMICROGRAPHS OF SKIN AND HAIR

SECTION OF SKIN
The flaky cells at the skin's
surface are shed continuously.

SWEAT PORE
This allows loss of fluid as part
of temperature control.

SKIN HAIR
Two hairs pushing through the
outer layer of skin.

HEAD HAIR
The root and part of the shaft of
a hair from the scalp.

Brain

THE BRAIN IS THE MAJOR ORGAN of the central nervous system and the control center for all the body's voluntary and involuntary activities. It is also responsible for the complexities of thought, memory, emotion, and language. In adults, this complex organ is a mere 3 lb (1.4 kg) in weight, containing over 10 thousand million nerve cells. Three distinct regions can easily be seen—the brainstem, the cerebellum, and the large cerebrum. The brainstem controls vital body functions, such as breathing and digestion. The cerebellum's main functions are the maintenance of posture and the coordination of body movements. The cerebrum, which consists of the right and left cerebral hemispheres joined by the corpus callosum, is the site of most conscious and intelligent activities.

MRI SCAN OF TRANSVERSE SECTION THROUGH BRAIN

White matter

Gray matter

Skull

Scalp

Longitudinal fissure

Lateral ventricle

Coronal section

Sagittal section

SAGITTAL SECTION THROUGH BRAIN

Central sulcus

Fornix

Cerebrum

Parietal lobe

Corpus callosum

Parieto-occipital sulcus

Thalamus

Pineal body

Occipital lobe

Frontal lobe

Aqueduct

Hypothalamus

Cerebellum

Optic chiasma

4th ventricle

Pituitary gland

Mesencephalon (midbrain)

Pons

Brainstem

Spinal cord

Medulla oblongata

SECTION THROUGH SKULL AND BRAIN

Scalp
Epicranial
aponeurosis
Arachnoid
granulation
Pericranium
Skull
Dura mater
Lateral
lacuna
Arachnoid
mater
Superior
sagittal
sinus
Pia mater
Falx
cerebri
Subarachnoid
space
Cerebral
vessel
Cerebrum
Gray matter
White matter

EXTERNAL ANATOMY OF BRAIN

Parietal lobe
Parieto-occipital
sulcus
Precentral gyrus
Postcentral gyrus
Central sulcus
Frontal lobe
Lateral sulcus
Temporal lobe
Occipital
lobe
Cerebellum

SPECIFIC ROLES OF AREAS OF CEREBRUM

Skilled
movements
Basic
movements
Sensation
Visual
recognition
Behavior and
emotion
Speech
Hearing
Vision
Balance
and muscle
coordination

CORONAL SECTION THROUGH BRAIN

Corpus
callosum
Longitudinal
fissure
Gray matter
White matter
Cerebrum
Caudate
nucleus
Lateral
ventricle
Fornix
Lentiform
nucleus
Internal
capsule
Thalamus
Crus
cerebri of
midbrain
3rd
ventricle
Pons
Medulla oblongata
Cerebellum

NERVE CELLS IN BRAIN

The dark cells are Purkinje cells, which are among the largest nerve cells in the body.

Nervous system

THE NERVOUS SYSTEM IS THE BODY'S internal, electrochemical, communications network. Its main parts are the brain, spinal cord, and nerves. The brain and spinal cord form the central nervous system (CNS), the body's chief controlling and coordinating centers. Billions of long neurons, many grouped as nerves, make up the peripheral nervous system, transmitting nerve impulses between the CNS and other regions of the body. Each neuron has three parts: a cell body, branching dendrites that receive chemical signals from other neurons, and a tube-like axon that conveys these signals as electrical impulses.

CENTRAL AND PERIPHERAL NERVOUS SYSTEMS

Cranial nerves
Cerebrum
Cerebellum
Cervical nerves
Brachial plexus
Thoracic nerves
Spinal cord
Radial nerve
Median nerve
Ulnar nerve
Lumbar nerves
Sacral nerves
Sacral plexus
Femoral nerve
Pudendal nerve
Sciatic nerve
Cutaneous nerve
Common peroneal nerve
Posterior tibial nerve
Superficial peroneal nerve
Deep peroneal nerve

SECTION THROUGH SPINAL CORD

Spinal ganglion
Gray matter
Central canal
Posterior root of spinal nerve
Spinal nerve
White matter
Anterior median fissure
Anterior root of spinal nerve

STRUCTURE OF A MOTOR NEURON

Cell body

Nucleus

Synaptic knob

Axon hillock

Axon

Dendrite

Nucleolus

Nissl body

Schwann cell

Node of Ranvier

Mitochondrion

Myelin sheath

TYPES OF NERVE ENDING

STRUCTURE OF A SYNAPTIC KNOB

Presynaptic axon

Microtubule

Neurofilament

Endoplasmic reticulum

Mitochondrion

Synaptic vesicle

Neurotransmitter

Presynaptic membrane

Myelin sheath

Axon

Cell body

Nucleus

Dendrite

TYPES OF NEURON

MULTIPOLAR

Motor end plate

Node of Ranvier

Schwann cell

Cell body

Nucleus

Receptor

UNIPOLAR

Dendrite

Axon

Cell body

Nucleus

BIPOLAR

Dendrite

Axon

Cell body

Nucleus

Dendrite

FREE NERVE ENDING

MEISSNER'S CORPUSCLE

MERKEL'S DISK

RUFFINI CORPUSCLE

PACINIAN CORPUSCLE

Eye

THE EYE IS THE ORGAN OF SIGHT. The two eyeballs, protected within bony sockets called orbits and on the outside by the eyelids, eyebrows, and tear film, are directly connected to the brain by the optic nerves. Each eye is moved by six muscles, which are attached around the eyeball. Light rays entering the eye through the pupil are focused by the cornea and lens to form an image on the retina. The retina contains millions of light-sensitive cells, called rods and cones, which convert the image into a pattern of nerve impulses. These impulses are transmitted along the optic nerve to the brain. Information from the two optic nerves is processed in the brain to produce a single coordinated image.

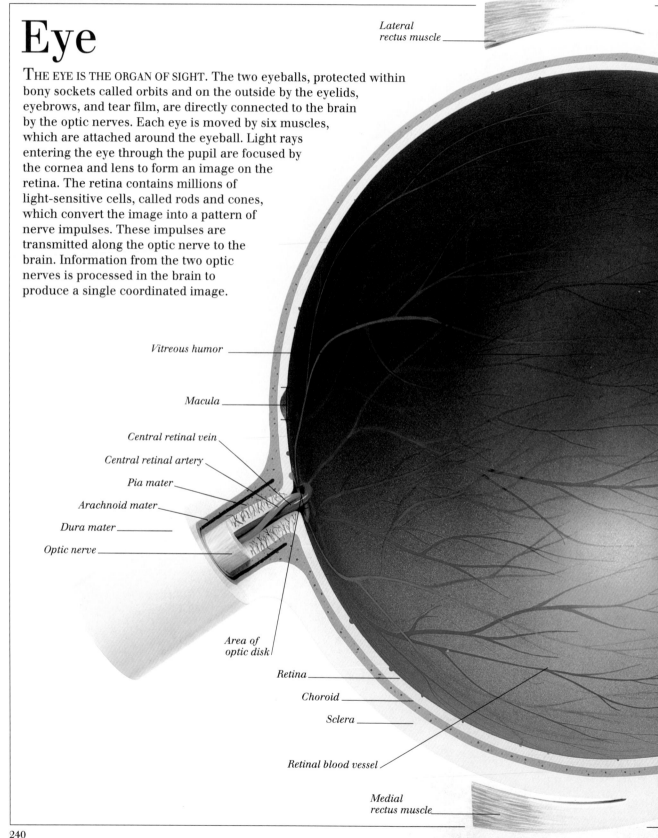

Lateral rectus muscle

Vitreous humor

Macula

Central retinal vein

Central retinal artery

Pia mater

Arachnoid mater

Dura mater

Optic nerve

Area of optic disk

Retina

Choroid

Sclera

Retinal blood vessel

Medial rectus muscle

SECTION THROUGH LEFT EYE

LACRIMAL (TEAR-PRODUCING) APPARATUS

Lacrimal sac   *Lacrimal canaliculus*   *Lacrimal gland*

Middle meatus

Middle nasal concha

Nasal septum

Inferior nasal concha

Nasolacrimal duct

Lacrimal punctum

Iris

Anterior chamber
Posterior chamber
   } *Aqueous humor*

Conjunctiva

Pupil

Cornea

Lens

Sphincter muscle

Dilator muscle

Zonular ligament

Sinus venosus sclerae

Iridocorneal angle

Ciliary body

Ora serrata

OPHTHALMOSCOPIC VIEW OF RETINA

Retinal blood vessel

Optic disk

Macula

The blind spot, where the optic nerve leaves the eye, can be clearly seen as a light circular area toward the center of the image.

MUSCLES SURROUNDING RIGHT EYE

Medial rectus

Superior oblique

Trochlea

Superior rectus

Levator palpebrae superioris

Annular tendon

Inferior rectus

Lateral rectus

Inferior oblique

Ear

THE EAR IS THE ORGAN OF HEARING AND BALANCE. The outer ear consists of a flap called the auricle or pinna and the auditory canal. The main functional parts—the middle and inner ears—are enclosed within the skull. The middle ear consists of three tiny bones, known as auditory ossicles, and the eustachian tube, which links the ear to the back of the nose. The inner ear consists of the spiral-shaped cochlea, and also the semicircular canals and the vestibule, which are the organs of balance. Sound waves entering the ear travel through the auditory canal to the tympanic membrane (eardrum), where they are converted to vibrations that are transmitted via the ossicles to the cochlea. Here, the vibrations are converted by millions of microscopic hairs into electrical nerve signals to be interpreted by the brain.

RIGHT AURICLE (PINNA)

Scaphoid fossa

Helix

Antihelix

Antitragus

External auditory meatus

Upper crux of antihelix

Triangular fossa

Lower crux of antihelix

Concha

Tragus

Intertragic notch

Lobule

Auricle (pinna)

Auditory canal

Temporal bone

Cartilage of auricle

Mastoid process

Cartilaginous part of meatus

Lobule

OSSICLES OF MIDDLE EAR

MALLEUS (HAMMER) **INCUS (ANVIL)** **STAPES (STIRRUP)**

These three tiny bones connect to form a bridge between the tympanic membrane and the oval window. With a system of membranes they convey sound vibrations to the inner ear.

INTERNAL STRUCTURE OF AMPULLA

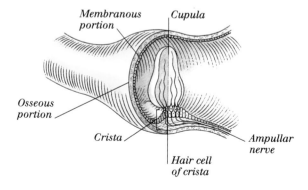

Membranous portion

Cupula

Osseous portion

Crista

Hair cell of crista

Ampullar nerve

LABYRINTH

Osseous (bony) part of meatus

Tympanic membrane (eardrum)

Semicircular canal

Cochlea

Vestibulocochlear nerve

Tensor tympani muscle

Utricle

Common crus

Anterior semicircular canal

Lateral semicircular canal

Ampulla

Saccule

Vestibular nerve

Tympanic canal

Median canal

Vestibular canal

Cochlea

Cochlear nerve

Oval window

Posterior semicircular canal

Internal carotid artery

Eustachian tube

Styloid process

SECTION THROUGH COCHLEA

Vestibular canal

Organ of Corti

Median canal

Vestibular membrane

Spiral ganglion

Cochlear nerve

Hair cells

Tympanic canal

Basilar membrane

Nose, mouth, and throat

WITH EVERY BREATH, air passes through the nasal cavity down the pharynx (throat), larynx ("voice box"), and trachea (windpipe) to the lungs. The nasal cavity warms and moistens air, and the tiny layers in its lining protect the airway against damage by foreign bodies. During swallowing, the tongue moves up and back, the larynx rises, the epiglottis closes off the entrance to the trachea, and the soft palate separates the nasal cavity from the pharynx. Saliva, secreted from three pairs of salivary glands, lubricates food to make swallowing easier; it also begins the chemical breakdown of food, and helps to produce taste. The senses of taste and smell are closely linked. Both depend on the detection of dissolved molecules by sensory receptors in the olfactory nerve endings of the nose and in the taste buds of the tongue.

STRUCTURE OF TONGUE

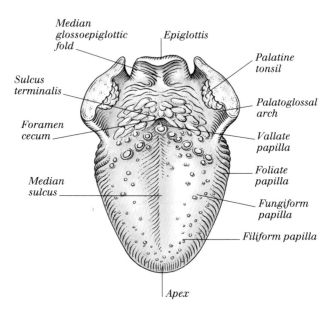

Median glossoepiglottic fold

Epiglottis

Palatine tonsil

Sulcus terminalis

Foramen cecum

Palatoglossal arch

Vallate papilla

Foliate papilla

Median sulcus

Fungiform papilla

Filiform papilla

Apex

TASTE AREAS ON TONGUE

STRUCTURES SURROUNDING PHARYNX

Lingual nerve

Tongue

Styloglossus muscle

Hyoglossus muscle

Hypoglossal nerve

Sublingual gland

Mandible (lower jaw)

Superior laryngeal nerve

Submandibular gland

Superior thyroid artery

Hyoid bone

Laryngeal prominence (Adam's apple)

Thyrohyoid muscle

Thyrohyoid membrane

Cricothyroid muscle

Cricothyroid ligament

Thyroid gland

Trachea

Bitter

Sour

Salt

Sweet

TYPES OF PAPILLAE

FILIFORM PAPILLAE　　**FUNGIFORM PAPILLAE**　　**VALLATE PAPILLAE**

**SECTION THROUGH NOSE,
MOUTH, AND THROAT**

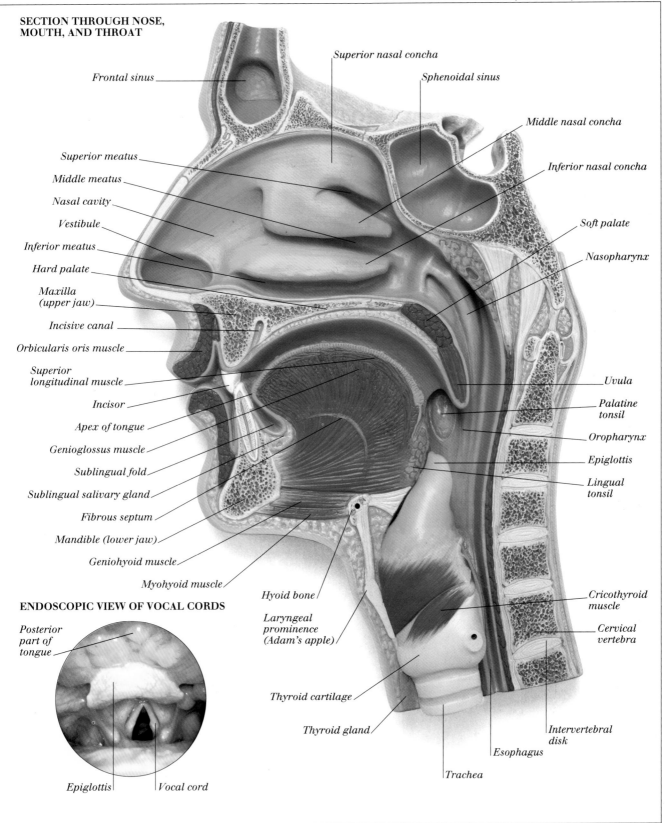

Frontal sinus

Superior nasal concha

Sphenoidal sinus

Middle nasal concha

Inferior nasal concha

Superior meatus

Middle meatus

Nasal cavity

Vestibule

Inferior meatus

Hard palate

Soft palate

Nasopharynx

Maxilla
(upper jaw)

Incisive canal

Orbicularis oris muscle

Superior
longitudinal muscle

Incisor

Apex of tongue

Genioglossus muscle

Sublingual fold

Sublingual salivary gland

Fibrous septum

Mandible (lower jaw)

Geniohyoid muscle

Myohyoid muscle

Uvula

Palatine
tonsil

Oropharynx

Epiglottis

Lingual
tonsil

Cricothyroid
muscle

Cervical
vertebra

ENDOSCOPIC VIEW OF VOCAL CORDS

Posterior
part of
tongue

Epiglottis

Vocal cord

Hyoid bone

Laryngeal
prominence
(Adam's apple)

Thyroid cartilage

Thyroid gland

Intervertebral
disk

Esophagus

Trachea

245

Teeth

THE 20 PRIMARY TEETH (also called deciduous or milk teeth) usually begin to erupt when a baby is about six months old. They start to be replaced by the permanent teeth when the child is about six years old. By the age of 20, most adults have a full set of 32 teeth although the third molars (commonly called wisdom teeth) may never erupt. While teeth help people to speak clearly and give shape to the face, their main function is the chewing of food. Incisors and canines shear and tear the food into pieces; premolars and molars crush and grind it further. Although tooth enamel is the hardest substance in the body, it tends to be eroded and destroyed by acid produced in the mouth during the breakdown of food.

DEVELOPMENT OF TEETH IN A FETUS

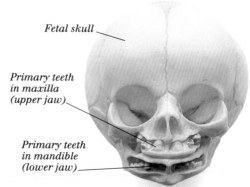

Fetal skull

Primary teeth in maxilla (upper jaw)

Primary teeth in mandible (lower jaw)

FETAL JAWS
By the sixth week of embryonic development areas of thickening occur in each jaw; these areas give rise to tooth buds. By the time the fetus is six months old, enamel has formed on the tooth buds.

DEVELOPMENT OF JAW AND TEETH

Maxilla (upper jaw)

Mandible (lower jaw)

A NEWBORN BABY'S JAWS
The primary teeth can be seen developing in the jawbones; they begin to erupt around the age of six months.

A FIVE-YEAR-OLD CHILD'S TEETH
There is a full set of 20 erupted primary teeth; the permanent teeth can be seen developing in the upper and lower jaws.

A NINE-YEAR-OLD CHILD'S TEETH
Most of the teeth are primary teeth but the permanent incisors and first molars have now emerged.

AN ADULT'S TEETH
By the age of 20, the full set of 32 permanent teeth (including the wisdom teeth) should be in position.

THE PERMANENT TEETH

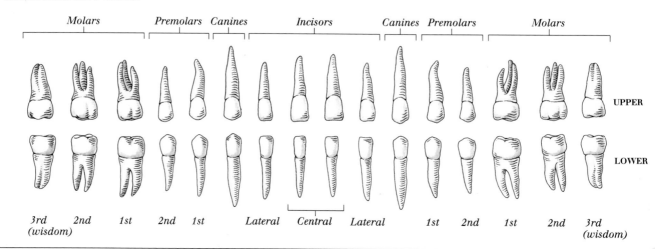

Molars   *Premolars*   *Canines*   *Incisors*   *Canines*   *Premolars*   *Molars*

UPPER

LOWER

3rd (wisdom)   2nd   1st   2nd   1st   Lateral   Central   Lateral   1st   2nd   1st   2nd   3rd (wisdom)

STRUCTURE OF A TOOTH

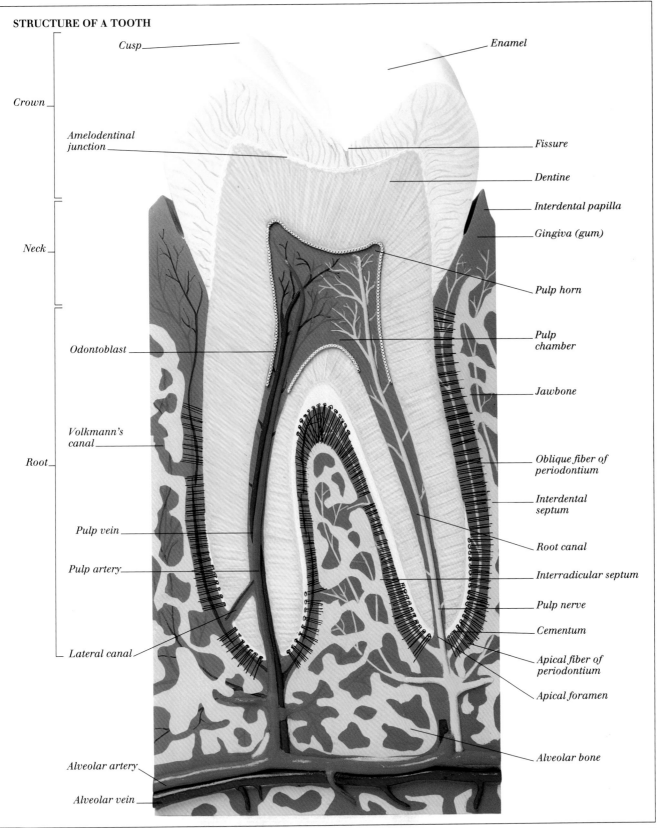

Cusp

Enamel

Crown

Amelodentinal
junction

Fissure

Dentine

Interdental papilla

Neck

Gingiva (gum)

Pulp horn

Pulp
chamber

Odontoblast

Jawbone

Volkmann's
canal

Oblique fiber of
periodontium

Interdental
septum

Root

Pulp vein

Root canal

Pulp artery

Interradicular septum

Pulp nerve

Cementum

Lateral canal

Apical fiber of
periodontium

Apical foramen

Alveolar bone

Alveolar artery

Alveolar vein

Digestive system

THE DIGESTIVE SYSTEM BREAKS DOWN FOOD into particles so tiny that blood can take nourishment to all parts of the body. The system's main part is a 30-foot (9 m) tube from mouth to rectum; muscles in this alimentary canal force food along. Chewed food first travels through the esophagus to the stomach, which churns and liquidizes food before it passes through the duodenum, jejunum, and ileum—the three parts of the long, convoluted small intestine. Here, digestive juices from the gallbladder and pancreas break down food particles; many filter out into the blood through tiny fingerlike villi that line the small intestine's inner wall. Undigested food in the colon forms feces that leave the body through the anus.

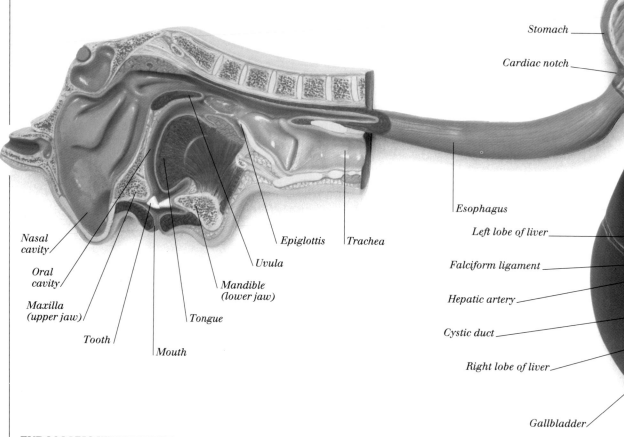

Stomach

Cardiac notch

Nasal cavity

Oral cavity

Maxilla (upper jaw)

Tooth

Mouth

Tongue

Mandible (lower jaw)

Uvula

Epiglottis

Trachea

Esophagus

Left lobe of liver

Falciform ligament

Hepatic artery

Cystic duct

Right lobe of liver

Gallbladder

ENDOSCOPIC VIEWS INSIDE ALIMENTARY CANAL

ESOPHAGUS

Mucosa

STOMACH ENTRANCE

Cardiac orifice

STOMACH

Ruga

STOMACH EXIT

Pylorus

ALIMENTARY CANAL

Fold of mucous membrane

Angular notch

Spleen

Pancreas

Peritoneum

Transverse colon

Tenia colica

Descending colon

Small intestine (jejunum and ileum)

Haustration of colon

Sigmoid colon

Anal sphincter muscle

Rectum

Anal canal

Anus

Terminal ileum

Appendix

Appendix orifice

Cecum

Ileocecal fold

Semilunar fold

Ascending colon

Pyloric sphincter muscle

Duodenum

Bile duct

Plica circulare

DUODENUM

Plica circulare

ILEUM

Villi of mucosa

COLON

Semilunar fold

Blood vessel

RECTUM

Mucosa

Heart

THE HEART IS A HOLLOW MUSCLE in the middle of the chest that pumps blood around the body, supplying cells with oxygen and nutrients. A muscular wall, called the septum, divides the heart lengthwise into left and right sides. A valve divides each side into two chambers: an upper atrium and a lower ventricle. When the heart muscle contracts, it squeezes blood through the atria and then through the ventricles. Oxygenated blood from the lungs flows from the pulmonary veins into the left atrium, through the left ventricle, and then out via the aorta to all parts of the body. Deoxygenated blood returning from the body flows from the vena cava into the right atrium, through the right ventricle, and then out via the pulmonary artery to the lungs for reoxygenation. At rest the heart beats between 60 and 80 times a minute; during exercise or at times of stress or excitement the rate may increase to 200 beats a minute.

ARTERIES AND VEINS SURROUNDING HEART

Aorta

Left coronary artery

Cardiac vein

Right coronary artery

Coronary sinus

Main branch of left coronary artery

SECTION THROUGH HEART WALL

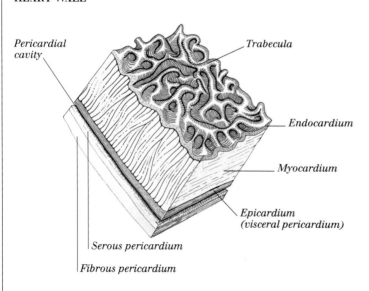

Pericardial cavity

Trabecula

Endocardium

Myocardium

Epicardium (visceral pericardium)

Serous pericardium

Fibrous pericardium

HEARTBEAT SEQUENCE

ATRIAL DIASTOLE

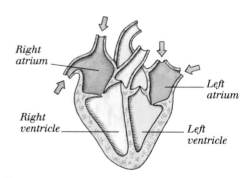

Right atrium

Left atrium

Right ventricle

Left ventricle

Deoxygenated blood enters the right atrium while the left atrium receives oxygenated blood.

STRUCTURE OF HEART

Brachiocephalic trunk

Left subclavian artery

Left common carotid artery

Superior vena cava

Ascending aorta

Left pulmonary vein

Right pulmonary artery

Pulmonary trunk

Fossa ovalis

Pulmonary semilunar valve

Coronary artery

Right pulmonary vein

Right atrium

Chordae tendineae

Opening of inferior vena cava

Muscular part of interventricular septum

Branch of coronary artery

Left ventricle

Papillary muscle

Tricuspid valve

Chordae tendineae

Myocardium of left ventricle

Right ventricle

Trabecula

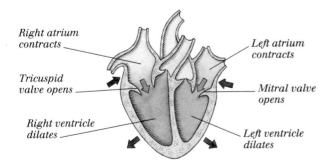

ATRIAL SYSTOLE (VENTRICULAR DIASTOLE)

Right atrium contracts

Left atrium contracts

Tricuspid valve opens

Mitral valve opens

Right ventricle dilates

Left ventricle dilates

Left and right atria contract, forcing blood into the relaxed ventricles.

VENTRICULAR SYSTOLE

Pulmonary artery

Aorta

Pulmonary valve opens

Aortic valve opens

Tricuspid valve closes

Mitral valve closes

Right ventricle contracts

Left ventricle contracts

Ventricles contract and force blood to the lungs for oxygenation and via the aorta to the rest of the body.

Circulatory system

THE CIRCULATORY SYSTEM consists of the heart and blood vessels, which together maintain a continuous flow of blood around the body. The heart pumps oxygen-rich blood from the lungs to all parts of the body through a network of tubes called arteries, and smaller branches called arterioles. Blood returns to the heart via small vessels called venules, which lead in turn into larger tubes called veins. Arterioles and venules are linked by a network of tiny vessels called capillaries, where the exchange of oxygen and carbon dioxide between blood and body cells takes place. Blood has four main components: red blood cells, white blood cells, platelets, and liquid plasma.

ARTERIAL SYSTEM OF BRAIN

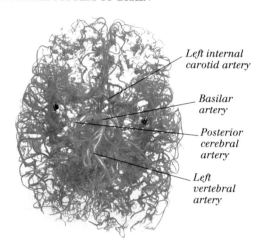

Left internal carotid artery

Basilar artery

Posterior cerebral artery

Left vertebral artery

CIRCULATORY SYSTEM OF LIVER

Inferior vena cava

Portal vein

Common bile duct

Hepatic artery

Gallbladder

CIRCULATORY SYSTEM OF HEART AND LUNGS

Superior vena cava

Aorta

Right ventricle

Left ventricle

SECTION OF MAIN ARTERY

Tunica media

Collagen and elastic fibers

External elastic lamina

Tunica adventitia

Internal elastic lamina

Tunica intima

Endothelium

Arteriole

SECTION OF MAIN VEIN

Tunica media

Collagen and elastic fibers

External elastic lamina

Tunica adventitia

Valve cusp

Internal elastic lamina

Tunica intima

Endothelium

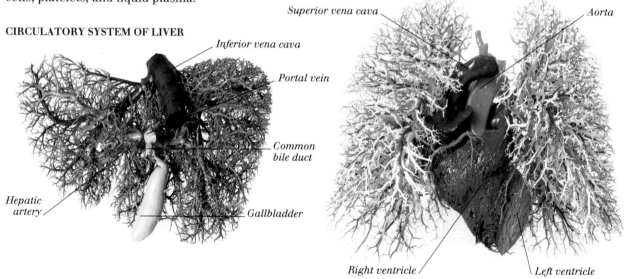

PRINCIPAL ARTERIES AND VEINS OF CIRCULATORY SYSTEM

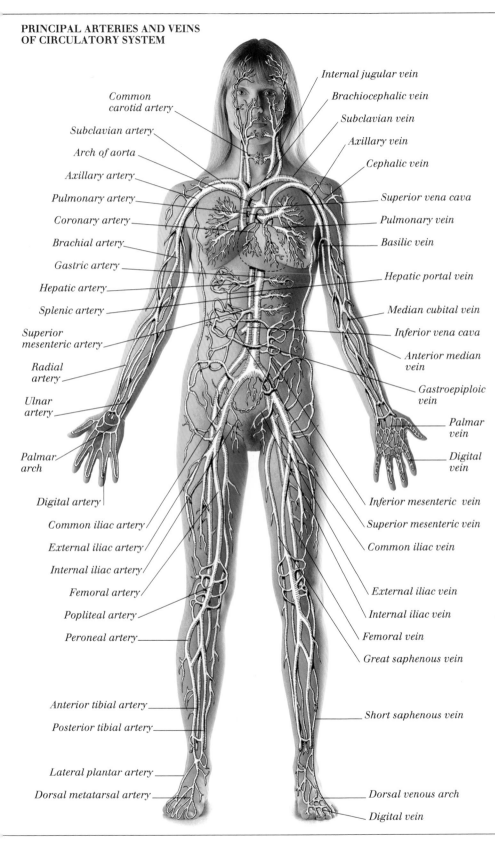

Common carotid artery

Subclavian artery

Arch of aorta

Axillary artery

Pulmonary artery

Coronary artery

Brachial artery

Gastric artery

Hepatic artery

Splenic artery

Superior mesenteric artery

Radial artery

Ulnar artery

Palmar arch

Digital artery

Common iliac artery

External iliac artery

Internal iliac artery

Femoral artery

Popliteal artery

Peroneal artery

Anterior tibial artery

Posterior tibial artery

Lateral plantar artery

Dorsal metatarsal artery

Internal jugular vein

Brachiocephalic vein

Subclavian vein

Axillary vein

Cephalic vein

Superior vena cava

Pulmonary vein

Basilic vein

Hepatic portal vein

Median cubital vein

Inferior vena cava

Anterior median vein

Gastroepiploic vein

Palmar vein

Digital vein

Inferior mesenteric vein

Superior mesenteric vein

Common iliac vein

External iliac vein

Internal iliac vein

Femoral vein

Great saphenous vein

Short saphenous vein

Dorsal venous arch

Digital vein

TYPES OF BLOOD CELLS

RED BLOOD CELLS
These cells are biconcave in shape to maximize their oxygen-carrying capacity.

WHITE BLOOD CELLS
Lymphocytes are the smallest white blood cells; they form antibodies against disease.

PLATELETS
Tiny cells that are activated whenever blood clotting or repair to vessels is necessary.

BLOOD CLOTTING

Filaments of fibrin enmesh red blood cells as part of the process of blood clotting.

Respiratory system

THE RESPIRATORY SYSTEM supplies the oxygen needed by body cells and carries off their carbon dioxide waste. Inhaled air passes via the trachea (windpipe) through two narrower tubes, the bronchi, to the lungs. Each lung comprises many fine, branching tubes called bronchioles that end in tiny clustered chambers called alveoli. Gases cross the thin alveolar walls to and from a network of tiny blood vessels. Intercostal (rib) muscles and the muscular diaphragm below the lungs operate the lungs like bellows, drawing air in and forcing it out at regular intervals.

BRONCHIOLE AND ALVEOLI

Bronchial nerve

Visceral cartilage

Branch of pulmonary vein

Mucosal gland

Terminal bronchiole

Bronchial vein

Branch of pulmonary artery

Elastic fibers

Interalveolar septum

Alveolus

Connective tissue

Capillary network

Epithelium

SEGMENTS OF BRONCHIAL TREE

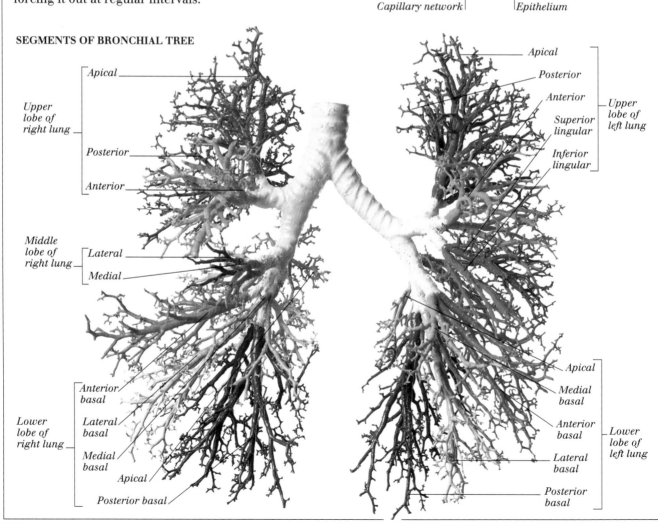

Apical

Posterior

Anterior

Upper lobe of left lung

Superior lingular

Inferior lingular

Upper lobe of right lung

Apical

Posterior

Anterior

Middle lobe of right lung

Lateral

Medial

Lower lobe of right lung

Anterior basal

Lateral basal

Medial basal

Apical

Posterior basal

Apical

Medial basal

Anterior basal

Lower lobe of left lung

Lateral basal

Posterior basal

STRUCTURES OF THORACIC CAVITY

Epiglottis

Hyoid bone

Thyroid cartilage

Thyroid gland

Apex of lung

Superior vena cava

Upper lobe of right lung

Horizontal fissure

Oblique fissure

Cricoid cartilage

Trachea

Aorta

Upper lobe of left lung

Pulmonary trunk

Left pulmonary artery

Heart

Lower lobe of left lung

Secondary bronchus

Tertiary bronchus

Lower lobe of right lung

Middle lobe of right lung

Right crus of diaphragm

Abdominal aorta

Left crus of diaphragm

Esophagus

Muscular wall of diaphragm

GASEOUS EXCHANGE IN ALVEOLUS

Oxygen diffuses into blood

Oxygenated blood

Alveolus

Deoxygenated blood rich in carbon dioxide

Carbon dioxide diffuses from blood into alveolus

MECHANISM OF RESPIRATION
INSPIRATION

Lung expands

Air drawn into lungs

Diaphragm contracts and flattens

Intercostal muscles contract

EXPIRATION

Lung contracts

Air forced out of lungs

Diaphragm relaxes and moves up

Intercostal muscles relax

Urinary system

THE URINARY SYSTEM FILTERS WASTE PRODUCTS from the blood and removes them from the body via a system of tubes. Blood is filtered in the two kidneys, which are fist-sized, bean-shaped organs. The renal arteries carry blood to the kidneys; the renal veins remove blood after filtering. Each kidney contains about one million tiny units called nephrons. Each nephron is made up of a tubule and a filtering unit called a glomerulus, which consists of a collection of tiny blood vessels surrounded by the hollow Bowman's capsule. The filtering process produces a watery fluid that leaves the kidney as urine. The urine is carried via two tubes called ureters to the bladder, where it is stored until its release from the body through another tube called the urethra.

ARTERIAL SYSTEM OF KIDNEYS

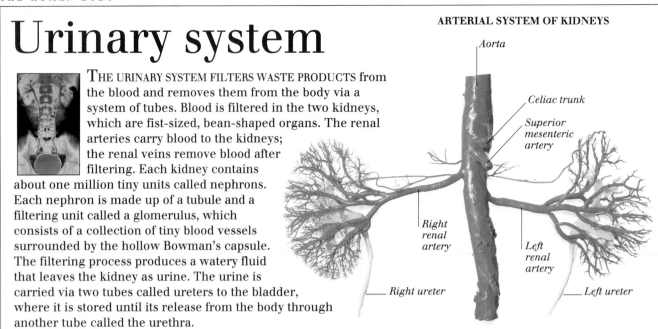

Aorta

Celiac trunk

Superior mesenteric artery

Right renal artery

Left renal artery

Right ureter

Left ureter

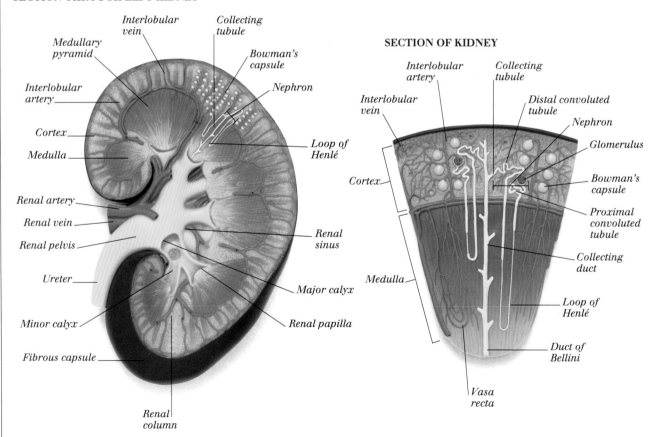

SECTION THROUGH LEFT KIDNEY

Interlobular vein

Collecting tubule

Medullary pyramid

Bowman's capsule

Interlobular artery

Nephron

Cortex

Medulla

Loop of Henlé

Renal artery

Renal vein

Renal pelvis

Renal sinus

Ureter

Major calyx

Minor calyx

Renal papilla

Fibrous capsule

Renal column

SECTION OF KIDNEY

Interlobular artery

Collecting tubule

Interlobular vein

Distal convoluted tubule

Nephron

Cortex

Glomerulus

Bowman's capsule

Proximal convoluted tubule

Medulla

Collecting duct

Loop of Henlé

Duct of Bellini

Vasa recta

MALE URINARY TRACT

Superior mesenteric artery

Celiac trunk

Left adrenal (suprarenal) gland

Right adrenal (suprarenal) gland

Left suprarenal vein

Inferior vena cava

Left renal artery

Renal artery

Left renal vein

Renal vein

Left kidney

Right kidney

Left ureter

Vertebral column

Psoas muscle

Aorta

Left common iliac artery

Right ureter

Left common iliac vein

Testicular vein and artery

Bladder

Superior pubic ramus

SECTION THROUGH BOWMAN'S CAPSULE

Distal convoluted tubule

Efferent arteriole

Afferent arteriole

Basement membrane of Bowman's capsule

Bowman's space

Bowman's capsule

Glomerulus

Proximal convoluted tubule

SECTION THROUGH MALE BLADDER

Right ureter

Peritoneum

Urachus

Left ureter

Transitional cell mucosa

Muscle layer

Right ureteric orifice

Internal urethral orifice

Left ureteric orifice

Prostate gland

Trigone

Internal urethral sphincter muscle

Urethra

257

Reproductive system

SEX ORGANS LOCATED IN THE PELVIS create new human lives. Each month a ripe egg is released from one of the female's ovaries into a fallopian tube leading to the uterus (womb), a muscular pear-sized organ. A male produces minute tadpole-like sperm in two oval glands called testes. When the male is ready to release sperm into the female's vagina, many millions pass into his urethra and leave his body through the fleshy penis. The sperm travel up through the vagina into the uterus and one sperm may enter and fertilize an egg. The fertilized egg becomes embedded in the uterus wall and starts to grow into a new human being.

SECTION THROUGH OVARY

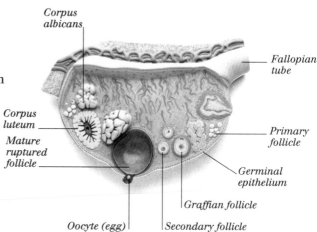

- *Corpus albicans*
- *Fallopian tube*
- *Corpus luteum*
- *Mature ruptured follicle*
- *Primary follicle*
- *Germinal epithelium*
- *Graffian follicle*
- *Secondary follicle*
- *Oocyte (egg)*

SECTION THROUGH FEMALE PELVIC REGION

- *Ureter*
- *Ampulla of fallopian tube*
- *Fimbria of fallopian tube*
- *Isthmus of fallopian tube*
- *Ovary*
- *Fundus of uterus*
- *Uterus (womb)*
- *Cervix (neck of uterus)*
- *Os*
- *Rectum*
- *Vagina*
- *Anus*
- *Perineum*
- *Bladder*
- *Pubic symphysis*
- *Urethra*
- *Clitoris*
- *External urinary meatus*
- *Labia minora*
- *Labia majora*
- *Introitus (vaginal opening)*

FEMALE REPRODUCTIVE ORGANS

Fallopian tube

Fundus of uterus

Isthmus of fallopian tube

Ampulla of fallopian tube

Ovarian ligament

Ovary

Body of uterus (womb)

Os

Vagina

Cervix (neck of uterus)

Fimbria of fallopian tube

MALE REPRODUCTIVE ORGANS

External spermatic fascia

Prostate gland

Ductus vas deferens

Seminal vesicle

Cremasteric fascia

Bulbourethral gland

Internal spermatic fascia

Urethra

Corpus spongiosum

Epididymis

Corpus cavernosum

Testis (testicle)

Scrotum

Prepuce (foreskin)

Glans penis

Urethral opening

SECTION THROUGH MALE PELVIC REGION

Intervertebral disk

Ureter

EXTERNAL STRUCTURE OF SPERM

Acrosomal cap

Head

Mitochondrial sheath

Terminal ring

Tailpiece

Flagellum

Colon

Sacrum

Seminal vesicle

Ejaculatory duct

Bladder

Pubis of pelvis

Prostate gland

Penis

Corpus cavernosum

Corpus spongiosum

Urethra

Epididymis

Glans penis

Testis (testicle)

Scrotum

259

Development of a baby

A FERTILIZED EGG IS NOURISHED AND PROTECTED as it develops into an embryo and then a fetus during the 40 weeks of pregnancy. The placenta, a mass of blood vessels implanted in the uterus lining, delivers nourishment and oxygen, and removes waste through the umbilical cord. Meanwhile, the fetus lies snugly in its amniotic sac, a bag of fluid that protects it against any sudden jolts. In the last weeks of the pregnancy, the rapidly growing fetus turns head down: a baby ready to be born.

EMBRYO AT FIVE WEEKS

Rudimentary ear

Rudimentary eye

Rudimentary mouth

Heart bulge

Arm bud

Rudimentary liver

Tail bud

Leg bud

Rudimentary vertebra

Amniotic fluid

Umbilicus (navel)

Uterine wall

Fetus

SECTION THROUGH PLACENTA

Umbilical cord

Umbilical vein

Umbilical artery

Amnion

Fetal blood vessels

Chorionic plate

Chorion

Trophoblast

Chorionic villus

Pool of maternal blood

Septum

Decidual plate

Maternal blood vessel

Myometrium

**SECTION THROUGH PELVIS IN
NINTH MONTH OF PREGNANCY**

THE DEVELOPING FETUS

Placenta

Uterine wall

*Fallopian
tube*

SECOND MONTH
All the internal
organs have
developed by
this stage.

Fetus

*Intervertebral
disk*

*Umbilical
cord*

THIRD MONTH
The fetus is
fully formed
and now
begins a
period of rapid
growth.

Vertebra

Spinal cord

FIFTH MONTH
Although the fetus
here is in breech
(bottom down)
position, it
will probably
turn by 180°
before birth. By
the fifth month
the baby is moving
actively and responds
to sound.

Cervix

SEVENTH MONTH
The internal organs
are maturing in
preparation for life
outside the uterus.
The baby has grown
to such a size that
there is less room
for movement
within the uterus.

Bladder

Cervix

Rectum

Anus

*Pubic
bone*

Placenta

Vagina

Urethra

GEOLOGY, GEOGRAPHY, AND METEOROLGY

Earth's physical features

MOST OF THE EARTH'S SURFACE (about 70 percent) is covered with water. The largest single body of water, the Pacific Ocean, alone covers about 30 percent of the surface. Most of the land is distributed as seven continents; these are (from largest to smallest) Asia, Africa, North America, South America, Antarctica, Europe, and Australasia. The physical features of the land are remarkably varied. Among the most notable are mountain ranges, rivers, and deserts. The largest mountain ranges—the Himalayas in Asia and the Andes in South America—extend for thousands of miles. The Himalayas include the world's highest mountain, Mount Everest (29,029 feet). The longest rivers are the River Nile in Africa (4,160 miles) and the Amazon River in South America (4,000 miles). Deserts cover about 20 percent of the total land area. The largest is the Sahara, which covers nearly a third of Africa. The Earth's surface features can be represented in various ways. Only a globe can correctly represent areas, shapes, sizes, and directions, because there is always distortion when a spherical surface like the Earth's is projected onto the flat surface of a map. Each map projection is therefore a compromise: some aspects of global features are shown accurately by allowing others to be distorted. Even satellite mapping does not produce completely accurate maps, although they can show physical features with great clarity.

EXAMPLES OF MAP PROJECTIONS

CYLINDRICAL PROJECTION

CYLINDRICAL-PROJECTION MAP

180° 160° 120° 80°

Great Slave Lake
Great Bear Lake
Lake Superior
Greenland
Mackenzie-Peace River
Baffin Island
Bering Sea
Hudson Bay
NORTH AMERICA
Rocky Mountains
Lake Huron
Lake Ontario
Mississippi-Missouri River
Lake Erie
Lake Michigan
Sonoran Desert
Appalachian Mountains
Sierra Madre
ATLANTIC OCEAN
Gulf of Mexico
Chihuahuan Desert
Caribbean Sea
Guiana Highlands
Amazon River
Brazil Highla
Andes
PACIFIC OCEAN
Atacama Desert
Gran Chaco
Mato Gross
Parana River
Pampas
Patagonia

SATELLITE MAPPING OF THE EARTH

Satellite takes photographs of the Earth

Solar panel

Earth's rotation

Antenna

Earth

Polar orbit of satellite

Area of Earth's surface on each photograph

Composite picture of Earth created from thousands of separate images

180° 160° 120° 80°

WEST OF GREENWICH MERIDIAN

CONICAL
PROJECTION

CONICAL-
PROJECTION MAP

AZIMUTHAL
PROJECTION

AZIMUTHAL-
PROJECTION MAP

MODIFIED
AZIMUTHAL-PROJECTION MAP

SATELLITE MAP OF THE EARTH

160°   180°
120°
80°
40°
0°

*ARCTIC
OCEAN*

Carpathians
Alps

Pyrenees

Aral Sea   Caucasus

Ural
Mountains

Kara
Kum

River
Ob-Irtysh

River
Lena

ARCTIC CIRCLE
(66° 52'N)

EUROPE

Black Sea

ASIA

River
Amur

Lake Baikal

Sea of
Japan

Honshu

us
untains

ara

*Mediterranean
Sea*

Red
Sea

AFRICA

Pamirs

Caspian
Sea

Thar
Desert

Himalayas

Takla Makan
Desert

Gobi Desert

Yellow River
(Huang He)

Yangtze
River (Chang
Jiang)

South
China
Sea

River
Mekong

*PACIFIC
OCEAN*

TROPIC OF
CANCER
(25° 30'N)

Arabian
Desert

River Nile

River Congo
(Zaire)

Lake Victoria

Lake
Tanganyika

Sumatra

Borneo

New Guinea

EQUATOR
(0°)

Madagascar

*INDIAN
OCEAN*

Australian
Desert

AUSTRALASIA

Namib
Desert

Lake Nyasa

Kalahari
Desert

Drakensberg

TROPIC OF
CAPRICORN
(25° 30'S)

New Zealand

ANTARCTIC CIRCLE
(66° 52'S)

ANTARCTICA

0°
40°
80°
120°
160°   180°

GREENWICH
MERIDIAN

EAST OF GREENWICH
MERIDIAN

265

The rock cycle

THE ROCK CYCLE IS A CONTINUOUS PROCESS through which old rocks are transformed into new ones. Rocks can be divided into three main groups: igneous, sedimentary, and metamorphic. Igneous rocks are formed when magma (molten rock) from the Earth's interior cools and solidifies (see pp. 274-275). Sedimentary rocks are formed when sediment (rock particles, for example) becomes compressed and cemented together in a process known as lithification (see pp. 276-277). Metamorphic rocks are formed when igneous, sedimentary, or other metamorphic rocks are changed by heat or pressure (see pp. 274-275). Rocks are added to the Earth's surface by crustal movements and volcanic activity. Once exposed on the surface, the rocks are broken down into rock particles by weathering (see pp. 282-283). The particles are then transported by glaciers, rivers, and wind and are deposited as sediment in lakes, deltas, deserts, and on the ocean floor. Some of this sediment undergoes lithification and forms sedimentary rock. This rock may be thrust back to the surface by crustal movements or forced deeper into the Earth's interior, where heat and pressure transform it into metamorphic rock. The metamorphic rock in turn may be pushed up to the surface or may be melted to form magma. Eventually, the magma cools and solidifies—below or on the surface—forming igneous rock. When the sedimentary, igneous, and metamorphic rocks are exposed once more on the Earth's surface, the cycle begins again.

HEXAGONAL BASALT COLUMNS, ICELAND

THE ROCK CYCLE

Igneous rock

Weathering, transport, and deposition

Sediment

Cooling and solidification (crystallization)

Heat and pressure (metamorphism)

Weathering, transport, and deposition

Weathering, transport, and deposition

Compression and cementation (lithification)

Magma

Melting

Metamorphic rock

Heat and pressure (metamorphism)

Sedimentary rock

STAGES IN THE ROCK CYCLE

Magma extruded as lava, which solidifies to form igneous rock

Lava flow

Vent

Main conduit

Secondary conduit

Lava

Ash

Rock surrounding magma changed by heat to form metamorphic rock

Intense heat of rising magma melts some of the surrounding rock

Sedimentary rock crushed and folded to form metamorphic rock

IGNEOUS ROCK

Pyroxene crystal

Olivine crystal

Plagioclase feldspar

Dark pyroxene crystal

Coarse-grained texture

PHOTOMICROGRAPH OF GABBRO

PIECE OF GABBRO

SEDIMENTARY ROCK

Mud groundmass (matrix)

Brown coloring from iron oxides

Fine-grained texture

Ammonite shell embedded in rock

Ammonite shell

PHOTOMICROGRAPH OF SHELLY LIMESTONE

PIECE OF SHELLY LIMESTONE

METAMORPHIC ROCK

Garnet crystal (pink)

Quartz and feldspar crystal (gray)

Red garnet crystal

Wavy foliation

PHOTOMICROGRAPH OF GARNET-MICA SCHIST

PIECE OF GARNET-MICA SCHIST

Mountain

Glacier erodes rocks and carries rock particles to river

Waterfall erodes rock

River erodes valley floor and carries rock particles downstream

Rock particles deposited as sediment in lake

Rock particles deposited by wind to form sand dunes

Rock particles deposited in delta

Larger rock particles deposited on continental shelf

Continental shelf

Continental slope

Finer rock particles collect on ocean floor to form layers of sediment

Layers of sediment compressed and cemented to form sedimentary rock

Minerals

A MINERAL IS A NATURALLY OCCURRING SUBSTANCE that has a characteristic chemical composition and specific physical properties, such as habit and streak (see pp. 270-271). A rock, by comparison, is an aggregate of minerals and need not have a specific chemical composition. Minerals are made up of elements (substances that cannot be broken down chemically into simpler substances), each of which can be represented by a chemical symbol. Minerals can be divided into two main groups: native elements and compounds. Native elements are made up of a pure element. Examples include gold (chemical symbol Au), silver (Ag), copper (Cu), and carbon (C); carbon occurs as a native element in two forms, diamond and graphite. Compounds are combinations of two or more elements. For example, sulfides are compounds of sulfur (S) and one or more other elements, such as lead (Pb) in the mineral galena, or antimony (Sb) in the mineral stibnite.

NATIVE ELEMENTS

Dendritic (branching) copper

Limonite groundmass (matrix)

COPPER
(Cu)

SULFIDES

Cubic galena crystal

GALENA
(PbS)

Dendritic (branching) gold

Quartz vein

GOLD
(Au)

White diamond

Kimberlite groundmass (matrix)

DIAMOND
(C)

Hexagonal graphite crystal

GRAPHITE
(C)

OXIDES/HYDROXIDES

Milky quartz groundmass (matrix)

Smoky quartz crystal

SMOKY QUARTZ
(SiO$_2$)

Rounded bauxite grains in groundmass (matrix)

BAUXITE
(FeO(OH) and Al$_2$O$_3$.2H$_2$O)

Mass of specular hematite crystals

SPECULAR HEMATITE
(Fe$_2$O$_3$)

Prismatic stibnite crystal

Quartz groundmass (matrix)

STIBNITE
(Sb$_2$S$_5$)

Perfect octahedral pyrites crystal

Quartz crystal

PYRITES
(FeS$_2$)

Parallel bands of onyx

ONYX
(SiO$_2$)

Kidney ore hematite

Specular crystals of hematite

KIDNEY ORE HEMATITE
(Fe$_2$O$_3$)

PHOSPHATES

Limonite groundmass (matrix)

Rock groundmass (matrix)

Radiating wavellite crystals

Prismatic pyromorphite crystals

WAVELLITE
$(Al_5(PO_4)_2(OH,F)_5.5H_2O)$

PYROMORPHITE
$(Pb_5(PO_4)_5Cl)$

CARBONATES

Striated cerussite crystal

Dog tooth calcite crystal

CERUSSITE
$(PbCO_5)$

CALCITE
$(CaCO_5)$

SULFATES

Rock groundmass (matrix)

Radiating crystal mass of daisy gypsum

Radiating cyanotrichite crystals

CYANOTRICHITE
$(Cu_4Al_2(SO_4)(OH)_{12}.2H_2O)$

DAISY GYPSUM
$(CaSO_4.2H_2O)$

MOLYBDATE

Tabular wulfenite crystal

Dark rock groundmass (matrix)

WULFENITE
$(PbMoO_4)$

SILICATES

Feldspar groundmass (matrix)

Transparent bicolored tourmaline crystal

Dodecahedral sodalite crystal

SODALITE
$(Na_8Al_6Si_6O_{24}Cl_2)$

Striated surface of olivine crystal

TOURMALINE
$(Na(Mg,Fe,Li,Mn,Al)_5Al_6(BO_5)_5Si_6.O_{18}(OH,F)_4)$

OLIVINE
$(Fe_2SiO_4 - Mg_2SiO_4)$

Striated prismatic epidote crystal

Tabular muscovite crystal

EPIDOTE
$(Ca_2(Al,Fe)_5(SiO_4)_5(OH))$

Orthoclase crystal

MUSCOVITE
$(KAl_2(Si_5Al)O_{10}(OH,F)_2)$

ORTHOCLASE
$(KAlSi_5O_8)$

HALIDES

Cubic rock salt crystal

Cubic fluorite crystal

GREEN FLUORITE
(CaF_2)

ORANGE HALITE (ROCK SALT)
$(NaCl)$

Mineral features

MINERALS CAN BE IDENTIFIED BY STUDYING features such as fracture, cleavage, crystal system, habit, hardness, color, and streak. Minerals can break in different ways. If a mineral breaks in an irregular way, leaving rough surfaces, it possesses fracture. If a mineral breaks along well-defined planes of weakness, it possesses cleavage. Specific minerals have distinctive patterns of cleavage. For example, mica cleaves along one plane. Most minerals form crystals that can be categorized into crystal systems according to their symmetry and number of faces. Within each system, several different but related forms of crystal are possible; for example, a cubic crystal can have six, eight, or twelve sides. A mineral's habit is the typical form taken by an aggregate of its crystals. Examples of habit include botryoidal (like a bunch of grapes) and massive (no definite form). The relative hardness of a mineral may be assessed by testing its resistance to scratching. This property is usually measured using Mohs' scale, which increases in hardness from 1 (talc) to 10 (diamond). The color of a mineral is not a dependable guide to its identity as some minerals have a range of colors. Streak (the color the powdered mineral makes when rubbed across an unglazed tile) is a more reliable indicator.

CLEAVAGE

Cleavage in one direction

CLEAVAGE ALONG ONE PLANE

Cleavage in three directions, forming a block cube

CLEAVAGE ALONG THREE PLANES

Horizontal cleavage

Vertical cleavage

CLEAVAGE ALONG TWO PLANES

Cleavage in four directions, forming a double-pyramid crystal

CLEAVAGE ALONG FOUR PLANES

CRYSTAL SYSTEMS

Cubic iron pyrites crystal

Tetragonal idocrase crystal

Representation of tetragonal system

TETRAGONAL SYSTEM

CUBIC SYSTEM

Representation of cubic system

Hexagonal beryl crystal

Representation of hexagonal/trigonal system

HEXAGONAL/TRIGONAL SYSTEM

Orthorhombic barite crystal

Representation of orthorhombic system

ORTHORHOMBIC SYSTEM

FRACTURE

Fire opal with conchoidal (shell-like) fracture

Nickel-iron with hackly (jagged) fracture

CONCHOIDAL FRACTURE

HACKLY FRACTURE

Orpiment with uneven fracture

Garnierite with splintery fracture

UNEVEN FRACTURE

SPLINTERY FRACTURE

Monoclinic selenite crystal

Representation of monoclinic system

MONOCLINIC SYSTEM

Triclinic axinite crystal

Representation of triclinic system

TRICLINIC SYSTEM

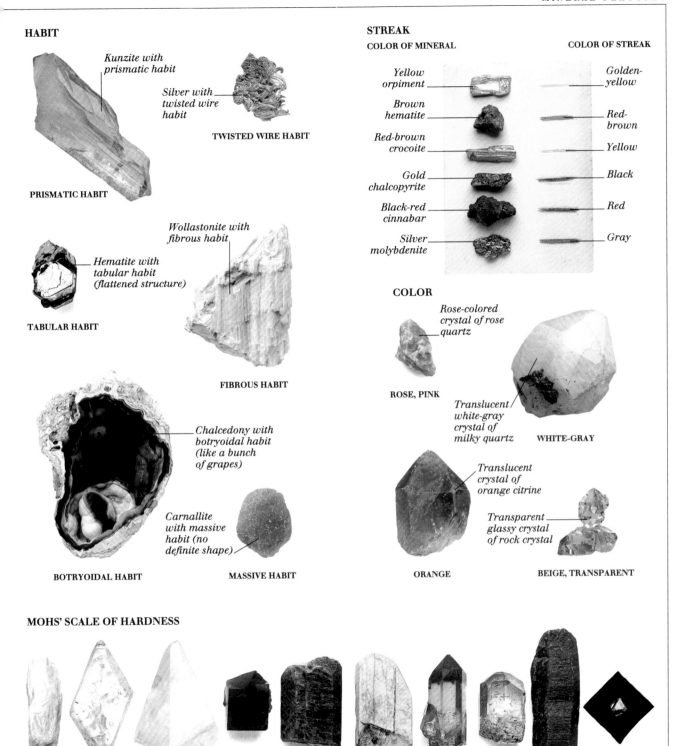

HABIT

Kunzite with prismatic habit

Silver with twisted wire habit

TWISTED WIRE HABIT

PRISMATIC HABIT

Wollastonite with fibrous habit

Hematite with tabular habit (flattened structure)

TABULAR HABIT

FIBROUS HABIT

Chalcedony with botryoidal habit (like a bunch of grapes)

Carnallite with massive habit (no definite shape)

BOTRYOIDAL HABIT

MASSIVE HABIT

STREAK

COLOR OF MINERAL

Yellow orpiment

Brown hematite

Red-brown crocoite

Gold chalcopyrite

Black-red cinnabar

Silver molybdenite

COLOR OF STREAK

Golden-yellow

Red-brown

Yellow

Black

Red

Gray

COLOR

Rose-colored crystal of rose quartz

ROSE, PINK

Translucent white-gray crystal of milky quartz

WHITE-GRAY

Translucent crystal of orange citrine

Transparent glassy crystal of rock crystal

ORANGE

BEIGE, TRANSPARENT

MOHS' SCALE OF HARDNESS

TALC	GYPSUM	CALCITE	FLUORITE	APATITE	ORTHOCLASE	QUARTZ	TOPAZ	CORUNDUM	DIAMOND
1	2	3	4	5	6	7	8	9	10

Volcanoes

Folded, rope-
like surface

VOLCANOES ARE VENTS OR FISSURES IN THE EARTH'S crust through which magma (molten rock that originates from deep beneath the crust) is forced onto the surface as lava. They occur most commonly along the boundaries of crustal plates; most volcanoes lie in a belt called the "Ring of Fire," which runs along the edge of the Pacific Ocean. Volcanoes can be classified according to the violence and frequency of their eruptions.

HORU GEYSER,
NEW ZEALAND

Nonexplosive volcanic eruptions generally occur where crustal plates pull apart. These eruptions produce runny basaltic lava that spreads quickly over a wide area to form relatively flat cones. The most violent eruptions take place where plates collide. Such eruptions produce thick rhyolitic lava and may also blast out clouds of dust and pyroclasts (lava fragments). The lava does not flow far before cooling and therefore builds up steep-sided, conical volcanoes. Some volcanoes produce lava and ash eruptions, which build up composite volcanic cones. Volcanoes that erupt frequently are described as active, those that erupt rarely are termed dormant, and those that have stopped erupting altogether are termed extinct. Besides the volcanoes themselves, other features associated with volcanic regions include geysers, hot mineral springs, solfataras, fumaroles, and bubbling mud pools.

PAHOEHOE
(ROPY LAVA)

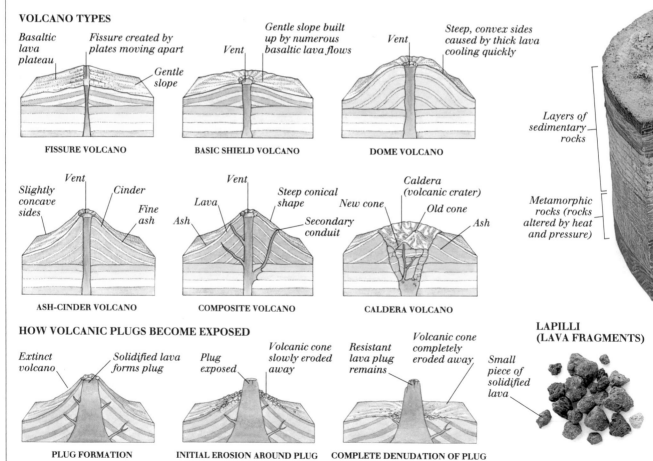

VOLCANO TYPES

Basaltic lava plateau — Fissure created by plates moving apart — Gentle slope

FISSURE VOLCANO

Gentle slope built up by numerous basaltic lava flows — Vent

BASIC SHIELD VOLCANO

Vent — Steep, convex sides caused by thick lava cooling quickly

DOME VOLCANO

Slightly concave sides — Vent — Cinder — Fine ash

ASH-CINDER VOLCANO

Vent — Lava — Ash — Steep conical shape — Secondary conduit

COMPOSITE VOLCANO

Caldera (volcanic crater) — New cone — Old cone — Ash

CALDERA VOLCANO

Layers of sedimentary rocks

Metamorphic rocks (rocks altered by heat and pressure)

HOW VOLCANIC PLUGS BECOME EXPOSED

Extinct volcano — Solidified lava forms plug

PLUG FORMATION

Plug exposed — Volcanic cone slowly eroded away

INITIAL EROSION AROUND PLUG

Resistant lava plug remains — Volcanic cone completely eroded away

COMPLETE DENUDATION OF PLUG

**LAPILLI
(LAVA FRAGMENTS)**

Small piece of solidified lava

TYPES OF LAVA

Scoria (sharp, angular chunks)

Driblets of lava from roof of tunnel

AA (BLOCKY LAVA)

REMELTED LAVA

LOCATION OF VOLCANOES

▲ Volcano ⊢┼┼┼ Plate boundary

STRUCTURE OF A VOLCANO

Steeply sloping cone consisting of numerous layers of ash and lava

Vent

Plug (solidified lava)

Main conduit

Volcanic ash

Cinder cone

Parasitic cone

Mineral spring

Laccolith

Secondary conduit

Magma reservoir

Lava flow

Groundwater

VOLCANIC FEATURES

Sulfurous gases

Jet of hot water and steam

Water heated by hot rocks

Steam pressure builds up

Hot water

Mud and surface deposits mixed with hot water

Superheated water

Steam

SOLFATARA

GEYSER

MUD POOL

FUMAROLE

273

Igneous and metamorphic rocks

IGNEOUS ROCKS ARE FORMED WHEN MAGMA (molten rock that originates from deep beneath the Earth's crust) cools and solidifies. There are two main types of igneous rock: intrusive and extrusive. Intrusive rocks are formed deep underground, where magma is forced into cracks or between rock layers to form structures including sills, dikes, and batholiths. The magma cools slowly to form coarse-grained rocks such as gabbro and pegmatite. Extrusive rocks are formed above the Earth's surface from lava (magma that has been ejected in a volcanic eruption). The molten lava cools quickly, producing fine-grained rocks such as rhyolite and basalt. Metamorphic rocks are those that have been altered by intense heat (contact metamorphism) or extreme pressure (regional metamorphism). Contact metamorphism occurs when rocks are changed by heat from, for example, an igneous intrusion or lava flow. Regional metamorphism occurs when rock is crushed in the middle of a folding mountain range. Metamorphic rocks can be formed from igneous rocks, sedimentary rocks, or even other metamorphic rocks.

Cinder cone

Large eroded lava flow

Cedar tree laccolith

Butte

Plug

Cone sheet

Ring dike

Batholith

Dike

Sill

Dike swarm

Lopolith

IGNEOUS ROCK STRUCTURES

CONTACT METAMORPHISM

Metamorphic aureole (region where contact metamorphism occurs)

Hot igneous intrusion

Limestone

Shale

Marble (metamorphosed limestone)

Slate (metamorphosed shale)

REGIONAL METAMORPHISM

Mountain range

Slate, formed under low pressure and temperature

Compression

Compression

Schist, formed under medium pressure and temperature

Crust

Gneiss, formed under high pressure and temperature

Mantle

Magma

EXAMPLES OF METAMORPHIC ROCKS

Pale feldspar

Dark mica

Dark mineral band

Pale calcite

GNEISS

FOLDED SCHIST

SKARN

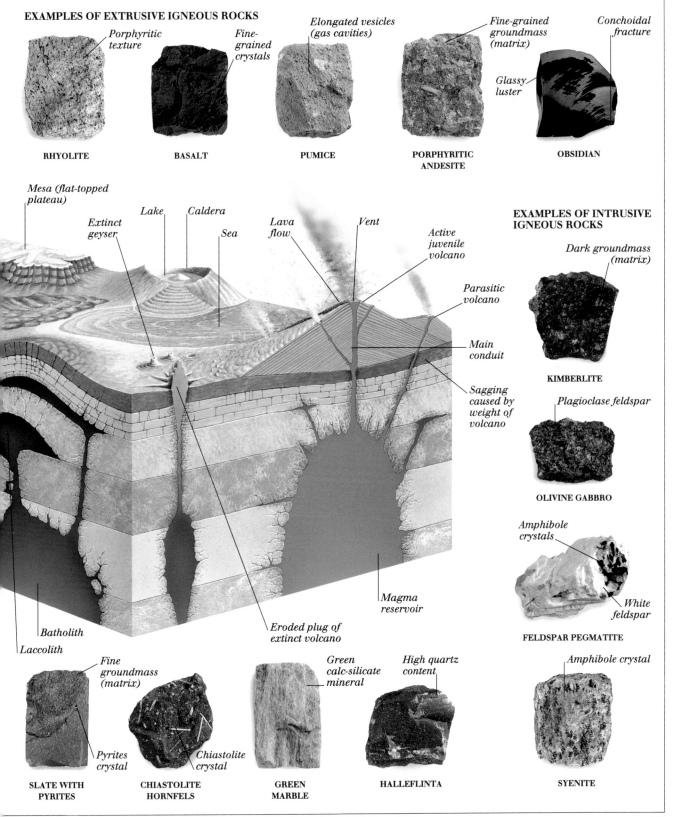

EXAMPLES OF EXTRUSIVE IGNEOUS ROCKS

Porphyritic texture

Fine-grained crystals

Elongated vesicles (gas cavities)

Fine-grained groundmass (matrix)

Conchoidal fracture

Glassy luster

RHYOLITE

BASALT

PUMICE

PORPHYRITIC ANDESITE

OBSIDIAN

Mesa (flat-topped plateau)

Lake

Caldera

Extinct geyser

Sea

Lava flow

Vent

Active juvenile volcano

Parasitic volcano

EXAMPLES OF INTRUSIVE IGNEOUS ROCKS

Dark groundmass (matrix)

Main conduit

Sagging caused by weight of volcano

KIMBERLITE

Plagioclase feldspar

OLIVINE GABBRO

Amphibole crystals

White feldspar

Batholith

Laccolith

Eroded plug of extinct volcano

Magma reservoir

FELDSPAR PEGMATITE

Fine groundmass (matrix)

Green calc-silicate mineral

High quartz content

Amphibole crystal

Pyrites crystal

Chiastolite crystal

SLATE WITH PYRITES

CHIASTOLITE HORNFELS

GREEN MARBLE

HALLEFLINTA

SYENITE

Sedimentary rocks

SEDIMENTARY ROCKS ARE FORMED BY THE ACCUMULATION and consolidation of sediments (see pp. 266-267). There are three main types of sedimentary rock: clastic sedimentary rocks, such as breccia or sandstone, are formed from other rocks that have been broken down into fragments by weathering (see pp. 282-283), which have then been transported and deposited elsewhere; organic sedimentary rocks, such as coal (see pp. 280-281), are derived from plant and animal remains; and chemical sedimentary rocks are formed by chemical processes. For example, rock salt is formed when salt dissolved in water is deposited as the water evaporates. Sedimentary rocks are laid down in layers called beds, or strata. Each new layer is laid down horizontally over older ones. There are usually some gaps in the sequence, called unconformities. These represent periods in which no new sediments were being laid down, or when earlier sedimentary layers were raised above sea level and eroded away.

THE GRAND CANYON, U.S.A.

EXAMPLES OF UNCONFORMITIES

Early beds tilted and eroded

Later beds horizontal

ANGULAR UNCONFORMITY

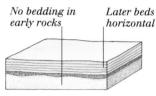

No bedding in early rocks

Later beds horizontal

NONCONFORMITY

Early beds folded and eroded

Later beds horizontal

DISCONFORMITY

SEDIMENTARY LAYERS OF THE GRAND CANYON REGION

Wasatch formation

Kaiparowits formation

Wahweap sandstone

Tropic formation

Dakota sandstone

Carmel formation

Pink Cliffs

Bryce Canyon

Zion Canyon

Gray Cliffs

Sevier fault

White Cliffs

Pipe Spring

Temple Cap sandstone

Navajo sandstone

Kayenta formation

Moenave formation

Chinle formation

Shinarump member

Moenkopi formation

Kaibab limestone

Toroweap formation

Coconino sandstone

Hermit shale

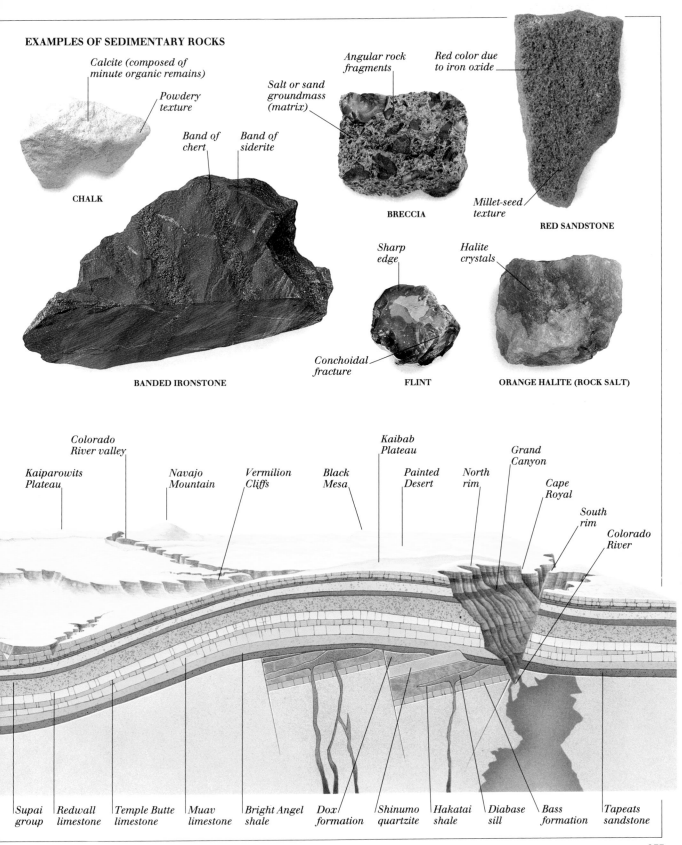

EXAMPLES OF SEDIMENTARY ROCKS

Calcite (composed of minute organic remains)

Powdery texture

CHALK

Band of chert

Band of siderite

BANDED IRONSTONE

Angular rock fragments

Salt or sand groundmass (matrix)

BRECCIA

Red color due to iron oxide

Millet-seed texture

RED SANDSTONE

Sharp edge

Conchoidal fracture

FLINT

Halite crystals

ORANGE HALITE (ROCK SALT)

Kaiparowits Plateau

Colorado River valley

Navajo Mountain

Vermilion Cliffs

Black Mesa

Kaibab Plateau

Painted Desert

North rim

Grand Canyon

Cape Royal

South rim

Colorado River

Supai group

Redwall limestone

Temple Butte limestone

Muav limestone

Bright Angel shale

Dox formation

Shinumo quartzite

Hakatai shale

Diabase sill

Bass formation

Tapeats sandstone

277

Fossils

FOSSILS ARE THE REMAINS of plants and animals that have been preserved in rock. A fossil may be the preserved remains of an organism itself, an impression of it in rock, or preserved traces (known as trace fossils) left by an organism while it was alive, such as organic carbon outlines, fossilized footprints, or droppings. Most dead organisms soon rot away or are eaten by scavengers. For fossilization to occur, rapid burial by sediment is necessary. The organism decays, but the harder parts—bones, teeth, and shells, for example—may be preserved and hardened by minerals from the surrounding sediment. Fossilization may also occur even when the hard parts of an organism are dissolved away to leave an impression called a mold. The mold is filled by minerals, thereby creating a cast of the organism. The study of fossils (paleontology) not only can show how living things have evolved, but can also help reveal the Earth's geological history—for example, by aiding in the dating of rock strata.

PROCESS OF FOSSILIZATION

ANIMAL DIES

SOFT PARTS ROT

SHELL BURIED

SHELL FOSSILIZED

EXAMPLES OF FOSSILS

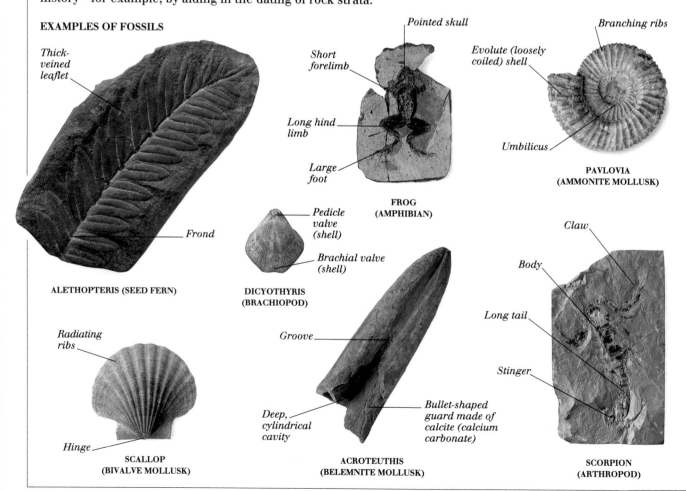

ALETHOPTERIS (SEED FERN)

FROG (AMPHIBIAN)

PAVLOVIA (AMMONITE MOLLUSK)

DICYOTHYRIS (BRACHIOPOD)

SCALLOP (BIVALVE MOLLUSK)

ACROTEUTHIS (BELEMNITE MOLLUSK)

SCORPION (ARTHROPOD)

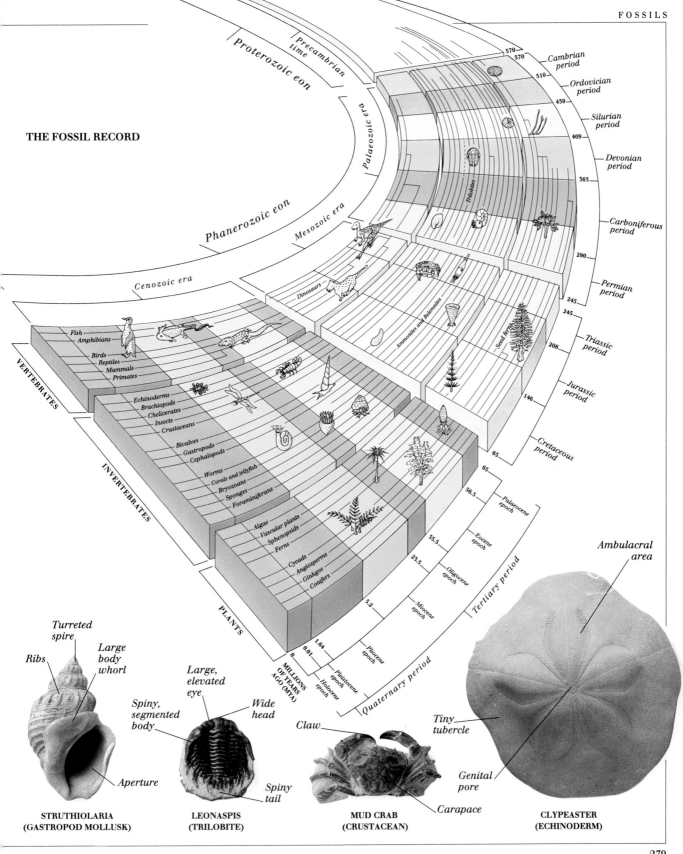

THE FOSSIL RECORD

Precambrian time

Proterozoic eon

Palaeozoic era

Phanerozoic eon

Mesozoic era

Cenozoic era

Cambrian period

Ordovician period

Silurian period

Devonian period

Carboniferous period

Permian period

Triassic period

Jurassic period

Cretaceous period

570
570
510
459
409
363
290
245
245
208
146
65

Dinosaurs

Ammonites and Belemnites

Seed ferns

Trilobite

VERTEBRATES

INVERTEBRATES

PLANTS

Fish
Amphibians
Birds
Reptiles
Mammals
Primates

Echinoderms
Brachiopods
Chelicerates
Insects
Crustaceans
Bivalves
Gastropods
Cephalopods
Worms
Corals and jellyfish
Bryozoans
Sponges
Foraminiferans

Algae
Vascular plants
Sphenopsids
Ferns
Cycads
Angiosperms
Ginkgos
Conifers

65
56.5
55.5
23.5
5.2
1.64
0.01

Palaeocene epoch
Eocene epoch
Oligocene epoch
Miocene epoch
Pliocene epoch
Pleistocene epoch
Holocene epoch

Tertiary period

Quaternary period

MILLIONS OF YEARS AGO (MYA)

Ambulacral area

Turreted spire

Ribs

Large body whorl

Aperture

STRUTHIOLARIA (GASTROPOD MOLLUSK)

Large, elevated eye

Spiny, segmented body

Wide head

Spiny tail

LEONASPIS (TRILOBITE)

Claw

Carapace

MUD CRAB (CRUSTACEAN)

Tiny tubercle

Genital pore

CLYPEASTER (ECHINODERM)

279

Mineral resources

Stalk

Leaf

PLANT MATTER

MINERAL RESOURCES CAN BE DEFINED AS naturally occurring substances that can be extracted from the Earth and are useful as fuels and raw materials. Coal, oil, and gas—collectively called fossil fuels—are commonly included in this group, but are not strictly minerals, because they are of organic origin. Coal formation begins when vegetation is buried and partly decomposed to form peat. Overlying sediments compress the peat and transform it into lignite (soft brown coal). As the overlying sediments accumulate, increasing pressure and temperature eventually transform the lignite into bituminous and hard anthracite coals. Oil and gas are usually formed from organic molecules that were deposited in marine sediments. Under the effects of heat and pressure, the compressed organic molecules undergo complex chemical changes to form oil and gas. The oil and gas percolate upward through water-saturated permeable rocks. They may rise to the Earth's surface, or accumulate below an impermeable layer of rock that has been folded or faulted to form a trap—an anticline (upfold) trap, for example. Minerals are inorganic substances that may consist of a single chemical element, such as gold, silver, or copper, or combinations of elements (see pp. 268-269). Some minerals are concentrated in mineralization zones in rock associated with crustal movements or volcanic activity. Others may be found in sediments as placer deposits— accumulations of high-density minerals that have been weathered out of rocks, transported, and deposited (on riverbeds, for example).

OIL RIG, NORTH SEA

Decayed plant matter

About 60% carbon

PEAT

About 70% carbon

Crumbly texture

LIGNITE (BROWN COAL)

Powdery texture

About 80% carbon

HOW COAL IS FORMED

Increasing layers of overlying sediment

Vegetation

Increasing layers of overlying sediment

Increasing pressure and temperature

Increasing pressure and temperature

Peat (about 60% carbon)

PEAT

Lignite (about 70% carbon)

LIGNITE (BROWN COAL)

Bituminous coal (about 80% carbon)

BITUMINOUS COAL

Shiny surface

BITUMINOUS COAL

About 95% carbon

ANTHRACITE COAL

EXAMPLES OF OIL AND GAS TRAPS

Impermeable rock
Oil
Folded impermeable rock
Water-saturated permeable rock
Fault

FAULT TRAP

Pinch-out
Water-saturated permeable rock
Fault
Gas
Oil

PINCH-OUT TRAP

Folded impermeable rock
Anticline
Water-saturated permeable rock
Gas
Oil

ANTICLINE TRAP

Folded impermeable rock
Water-saturated permeable rock
Oil
Impermeable salt dome

SALT-DOME TRAP

MAJOR COAL, OIL, AND GAS DEPOSITS

● Coal   ● Oil and gas

HOW AN ANTICLINE TRAP IS FORMED

Layer of sediment containing decayed plant and animal matter
Sea
Old seabed

DEPOSITION OF ORGANIC MATERIAL

Increasing layers of overlying sediment
Sea
Oil and gas formed by chemical reactions, heat, and pressure

FORMATION OF OIL AND GAS

Land
Sea
Anticline
Impermeable rock layer folded to form oil and gas trap
Gas
Oil
Water-saturated permeable rock

COLLECTION OF OIL AND GAS IN ANTICLINE TRAP

MINERALIZATION ZONES

Continental crust
Volcano
Subduction zone
Oceanic crust
Midocean ridge

Tin, tungsten, bismuth, and copper
Copper, zinc, gold, and chromium
Copper, gold, silver, tin, lead, and mercury
Lead, zinc, and copper
Chromium
Manganese, cobalt, and nickel
Copper and zinc

Weathering and erosion

WEATHERING IS THE BREAKING DOWN of rocks on the Earth's surface. There are two main types: physical (or mechanical), and chemical. Physical weathering may be caused by temperature changes, such as freezing and thawing, or by abrasion from material carried by winds, rivers, or glaciers. Rocks may also be broken down by the actions of animals and plants, such as the burrowing of animals and the growth of roots. Chemical weathering causes rocks to decompose by changing their chemical composition. For example, rainwater may dissolve certain minerals in a rock. Erosion is the wearing away and removal of land surfaces by water, wind, or ice. It is greatest in areas of little or no surface vegetation, such as deserts, where sand dunes may form.

FORMATION OF A ROCK PAVEMENT (HAMADA)

Wind blows away small particles

Larger particles aggregate

Rock pavement forms

FIRST STAGE

SECOND STAGE

FINAL STAGE

FEATURES PRODUCED BY WIND ACTION

Wind-blown sand

Mushroom-shaped rock

Neck

Rock base eroded by wind-blown sand

ROCK PEDESTAL

Wind-blown sand

Widened joint

Soft rock

Hard rock

ZEUGEN

Wind-blown sand

Furrow

Hard rock

Soft rock eroded by wind-blown sand

YARDANG

FEATURES OF WEATHERING AND EROSION

Mesa (flat-topped plateau)

Canyon

Zeugen

Joint

Hard rock

Soft rock

Shelf formed of hard rock

Talus (scree)

Alluvial fan (alluvial cone)

Bahada (gentle slope covered with loose rock)

Bolson (alluvium-filled basin)

EXAMPLES OF PHYSICAL WEATHERING PROCESSES

Heated rock surface expands

Exfoliation dome

Flaking rock

Fallen debris

EXFOLIATION (ONION-SKIN WEATHERING)

Joint expands and contracts due to temperature changes

Block of fallen rock

BLOCK DISINTEGRATION

Talus (scree)

Joint widened by frozen water

FROST WEDGING

Trunk

Crack widened by tree root

TREE ROOT ACTION

SECTION THROUGH A BARKHAN DUNE

Strong wind
Weak wind
Windward face
Direction of wind-blown sand
Direction of sand movement
Slip face
Foreset strata
Cross-bed set
Topset strata
Bottomset strata

EXAMPLES OF SAND DUNES

Wind direction
Crescent-shaped dune
BARKHAN DUNE

Wind direction
Dune at right angle to wind
TRANSVERSE DUNE

Wind direction
Point where sand ridges meet
STAR DUNE

Wind direction
Parallel dunes
SEIF (LINEAR) DUNE

Canyon
Wadi (dry wash)
Mesa (flat-topped plateau)
Talus (scree)
Butte (flat-topped mesa remnant)
Eroded arch
Residual hill on pediment
Rock pavement (hamada)
Rock pedestal
Barkhan dune
Parabolic dune
Transverse dune
Seif (linear) dune
Inselberg (isolated, steep-sided hill)

Playa (dry lake bed of salt or desiccated clay)
Faultline
Freshwater lake
Fertile oasis
Deflation hollow (created by wind erosion)
Hogback (steep ridge)
Hard sandstone
Fault plane
Cuesta (asymmetric ridge)
Hard granite

283

Caves

CAVES COMMONLY FORM in areas of limestone, although on coastlines they also occur in other rocks. Limestone is made of calcite (calcium carbonate), which dissolves in the carbonic acid naturally present in rainwater, and in humic acids from the decay of vegetation. The acidic water trickles down through cracks and joints in the limestone and between rock layers, breaking up the surface terrain into clints (blocks of rock), separated by grikes (deep cracks), and punctuated by sinkholes (also called swallow holes or potholes) into which surface streams may disappear. Underground, the acidic water dissolves the rock around crevices, opening up a network of passages and caves, which can become large caverns if the roofs collapse. Various features are formed when the dissolved calcite is redeposited. For example, it may be redeposited along an underground stream to form a gour (series of calcite ridges), or in caves and passages to form stalactites and stalagmites. Stalactites develop where calcite is left behind as water drips from the roof; where the drops land, stalagmites build up.

MERGED STALACTITE

STALACTITE WITH RING MARKS

Ring mark

SURFACE TOPOGRAPHY OF A CAVE SYSTEM

Doline (depression caused by collapse of cave roof)

Sinkhole

Gorge where cave roof has fallen in

Porous limestone

Resurgence

Limestone terrain with clints and grikes

Impermeable rock

STALAGMITE FORMATIONS

Calcite (calcium carbonate) crystalized under water

CRYSTALLINE STALAGMITIC FLOOR

Thin encrustations of calcite (calcium carbonate)

CALCAREOUS TUFA

Encrustations on dead stems of small plants

Calcite (calcium carbonate)

Calcite (calcium carbonate)

STALAGMITIC FLOOR

Calcite (calcium carbonate)

Encrustations with fungoid structure

STALAGMITIC BOSS

Scar of bare rock

Former water table

Permeable limestone

Resurgence

Layer of impermeable rock

Present water table

DEVELOPMENT OF A CAVE SYSTEM

Impermeable rock

Joint

Bedding plane

Impermeable rock

Permeable limestone

STRUCTURE OF LIMESTONE STRATA

Water seeps through cracks in rock

Calcite (calcium carbonate) deposits begin to form

Stream enters permeable rock

Resurgence

Tunnel

Underground stream

INITIAL CAVE

Doline caused by collapse of cave roof

Sinkhole

Stalactite

Stalagmite

Gorge

Resurgence

Dry gallery

Cave

EXTENDED CAVE SYSTEM

INTERCONNECTED CAVE SYSTEM

Stalactite

Pillar (column)

Gorge

Stalactite

Dry gallery (former course of underground stream)

Gour (series of calcite ridges) deposited by running water

Stalagmite

Joint in rock enlarged by water

Bedding plane

Curtain of deposited calcite (calcium carbonate)

Tunnel

Cave

Passage

Cavern

Gour (series of calcite ridges)

Glaciers

GLACIER BAY, ALASKA

A VALLEY GLACIER IS A LARGE MASS OF ICE that forms on land and moves slowly downhill under its own weight. It is formed from snow that collects in cirques (mountain hollows also known as corries), compressing into ice as more and more snow accumulates. The cirque is deepened by frost wedging and abrasion (see pp. 282-283), and arêtes (sharp ridges) develop between adjacent cirques. Eventually, so much ice builds up that the glacier begins to flow. As the glacier moves it collects moraine (debris), which may range in size from particles of dust to large boulders. The rocks at the base of the glacier erode the glacial valley, giving it a U-shaped cross section. Under the glacier, *roches moutonnées* (eroded outcrops of hard rock) and drumlins (rounded mounds of rock and clay) are left behind on the valley floor. The glacier ends at a terminus (the snout), where the ice melts as fast as it arrives. If the temperature increases, the ice melts faster than it arrives, and the glacier retreats. The retreating glacier leaves behind its moraine and also erratics (isolated single boulders). Glacial streams from the melting glacier deposit eskers and kames (ridges and mounds of sand and gravel) but carry away the finer sediment to form a stratified outwash plain. Lumps of ice carried on to this plain melt, creating holes called kettles.

VALLEY GLACIER

Lateral moraine
Meltwater pool
Medial moraine
Suspended erratic
Horn
Arête (ridge)
Englacial stream
Cave
Hanging valley
Stream
Melting glacier
Ice margin lake
Waterfall
Terminal moraine
Steep side of U-shaped valley
Braided stream
Boulder clay
Terminal lake
Meltwater stream
Roche moutonnée
Lake

POST-GLACIAL VALLEY

Collapsed sediment
Drumlin
Exposed valley floor
Roche moutonnée
Horn of mountain
Arête (ridge)
Kame terrace
Esker
Erratic
Lacustrine terrace
Post-glacial stream
Kame delta
Kettle
Terminal moraine
Kettle lake
Outwash terrace
Boulder clay
Kame
Roche moutonnée
Outwash fan
Steep side of U-shaped valley

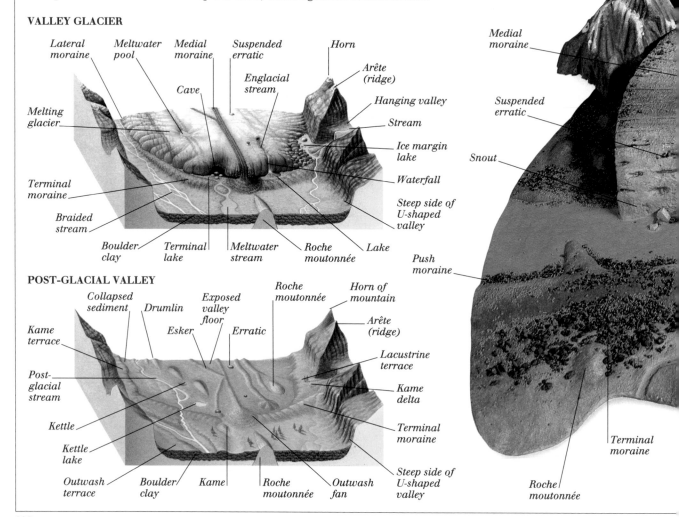

Medial moraine
Suspended erratic
Snout
Push moraine
Terminal moraine
Roche moutonnée

FEATURES OF A GLACIER

Firn (compressed snow)

Tributary glacier

Moving ice

U-shaped valley

Medial moraine

Lateral moraine

Cirque (corrie)

Arête (ridge)

Tributary moraine joins medial moraine

Subglacial stream

Rock being eroded by ice

Brittle surface ice

Viscous flowing ice

Englacial moraine

Crevasse

Ribbon lake

Sediment deposited by meltwater

Outwash plain

Meltwater

Stream

ICE-FALL

Gentle slope

Smooth surface

Steep slope

Slope flattens

Rougher surface

Crevasse deepens and widens

Ice breaks into blocks

Ice block tilts and twists

Ice recompresses

CIRQUE FORMATION

Firn (compressed snow)

Material loosened by frost wedging

Fresh snowfall

EARLY STAGE

Moraine pulled from ground

Steep back wall

Glacier

Base of cirque eroded by glacier's pivoting action

Rock lip

LATER STAGE

U-SHAPED VALLEY FORMATION

Arête (ridge)

Horn

Cirque overspills

Glacier

DURING GLACIATION

Deepened cirque

Deep U-shaped valley

Hanging valley

Tarn

AFTER GLACIATION

Rivers

RIVERS FORM PART of the water cycle—the continuous circulation of water between the land, sea, and atmosphere. The source of a river may be a mountain spring, or lake, or a melting glacier. The course that the river subsequently takes depends on the slope of the terrain and on the rock types and formations over which it flows. In its early, upland stages, a river tumbles steeply over rocks and boulders and cuts a steep-sided V-shaped valley. Farther downstream, it flows smoothly over sediments and forms winding meanders, eroding sideways to create broad valleys and plains. On reaching the coast, the river may deposit sediment, forming an estuary or delta (see pp. 290-291).

RIVER CAPTURE

EARLY STAGE

Tributary erodes headward

River

River

LATER STAGE

Dry valley

River captured by tributary

River flow decreases

River flow increases

THE WATER CYCLE

Precipitation falls on high ground

Water carried downstream by river

Wind

Water vapor released into atmosphere by trees and other plants

Wind

Water vapor forms clouds

Water evaporates from sea

Water stored in sea

River flows into sea

Water seeps underground and flows to sea

Water evaporates from lake

Water seeps underground and flows to sea

SATELLITE IMAGE OF GANGES RIVER DELTA, BANGLADESH

River Ganges

Ganges delta

Infertile swampland

Distributary

Large volume of sediment

RIVER DRAINAGE PATTERNS

RADIAL

CENTRIPETAL

PARALLEL

DENDRITIC

DERANGED

TRELLISED

ANNULAR

RECTANGULAR

Seabed

Sea

Sediment layers

STAGES IN A RIVER'S DEVELOPMENT

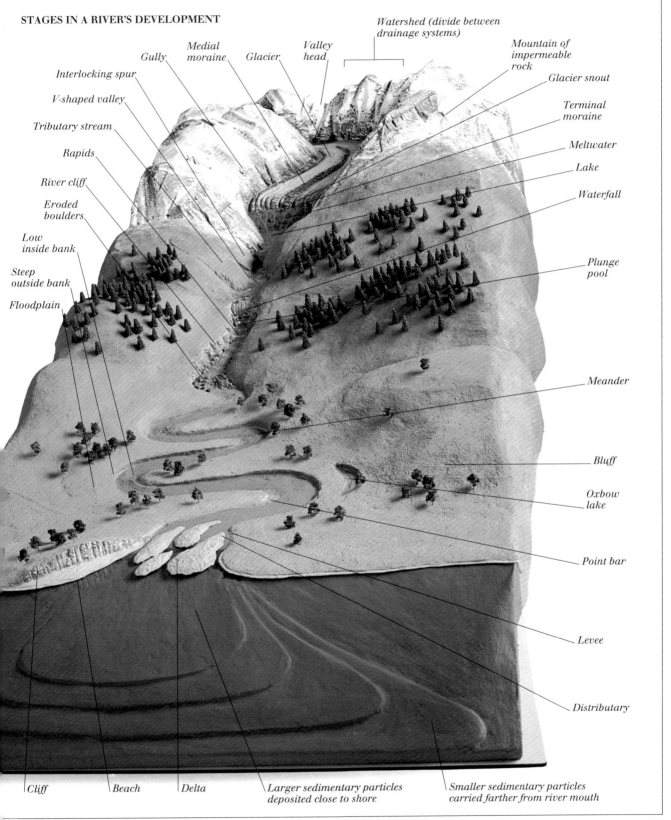

Watershed (divide between drainage systems)

Medial moraine

Gully

Glacier

Valley head

Interlocking spur

V-shaped valley

Tributary stream

Rapids

River cliff

Eroded boulders

Low inside bank

Steep outside bank

Floodplain

Mountain of impermeable rock

Glacier snout

Terminal moraine

Meltwater

Lake

Waterfall

Plunge pool

Meander

Bluff

Oxbow lake

Point bar

Levee

Distributary

Cliff

Beach

Delta

Larger sedimentary particles deposited close to shore

Smaller sedimentary particles carried farther from river mouth

River features

RIVERS ARE ONE OF THE MAJOR FORCES that shape the landscape. Near its source, a river is steep (see pp. 288-289). It erodes downward, carving out V-shaped valleys and deep gorges. Waterfalls and rapids are formed where the river flows from hard rock to softer, more easily eroded rock. Farther downstream, meanders may form and there is greater sideways erosion, resulting in a broad river valley. The river sometimes erodes through the neck of a meander to form an oxbow lake. Sediment deposited on the valley floor by meandering rivers and during floods helps to create a floodplain. Floods may also deposit sediment on the banks of the river to form levees. As a river spills into the sea or a lake, it deposits large amounts of sediment, and may form a delta. A delta is an area of sand bars, swamps and lagoons through which the river flows in several channels called distributaries—the Mississippi delta, for example. Often, a rise in sea level may have flooded the river mouth to form a broad estuary, a tidal section where seawater mixes with fresh water.

HOW WATERFALLS AND RAPIDS ARE FORMED

WATERFALL

RAPIDS

A RIVER VALLEY DRAINAGE SYSTEM

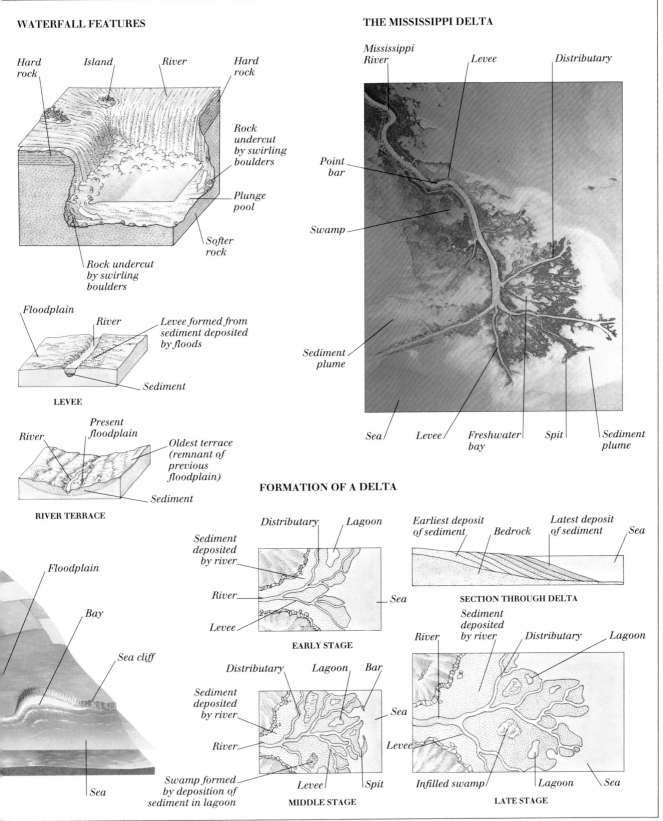

WATERFALL FEATURES

Hard rock

Island

River

Hard rock

Rock undercut by swirling boulders

Plunge pool

Softer rock

Rock undercut by swirling boulders

Floodplain

River

Levee formed from sediment deposited by floods

Sediment

LEVEE

River

Present floodplain

Oldest terrace (remnant of previous floodplain)

Sediment

RIVER TERRACE

Floodplain

Bay

Sea cliff

Sea

THE MISSISSIPPI DELTA

Mississippi River

Levee

Distributary

Point bar

Swamp

Sediment plume

Sea

Levee

Freshwater bay

Spit

Sediment plume

FORMATION OF A DELTA

Distributary

Lagoon

Sediment deposited by river

River

Sea

Levee

EARLY STAGE

Earliest deposit of sediment

Bedrock

Latest deposit of sediment

Sea

SECTION THROUGH DELTA

Distributary

Lagoon

Bar

Sediment deposited by river

Sea

River

Swamp formed by deposition of sediment in lagoon

Levee

Spit

MIDDLE STAGE

Sediment deposited by river

River

Distributary

Lagoon

Levee

Infilled swamp

Lagoon

Sea

LATE STAGE

291

Lakes and groundwater

NATURAL LAKES OCCUR WHERE a large quantity of water collects in a hollow in impermeable rock or is prevented from draining away by a barrier, such as moraine (glacial deposits) or solidified lava. Lakes are often relatively short-lived landscape features, because they tend to become silted up by sediment from the streams and rivers that feed them. Some of the more long-lasting lakes are found in deep rift valleys formed by vertical movements of the Earth's crust (see pp. 58-59)— for example, Lake Baikal in Russia, the world's largest freshwater lake, and the Dead Sea in the Middle East, one of the world's saltiest lakes. Where water is able to drain away, it sinks into the ground until it reaches a layer of impermeable rock, then accumulates in the permeable rock above it. This water-saturated permeable rock is called an aquifer. The saturated zone varies in depth according to seasonal and climatic changes. In wet conditions, the water stored underground builds up, while in dry periods it becomes depleted. Where the upper edge of the saturated zone—the water table—meets the ground surface, water emerges as springs. In an artesian basin, where the aquifer is below an aquiclude (layer of impermeable rock), the water table throughout the basin is determined by its height at the rim. At the center of such a basin, the water table is above ground level. The water in the basin is thus trapped below the water table and can rise under its own pressure along fault lines or well shafts.

LAKE BAIKAL, RUSSIA

(see pp. 58-59)

EXAMPLES OF SPRINGS

LIMESTONE SPRING

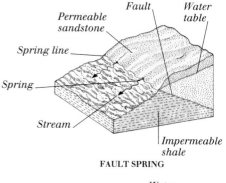

COASTAL (VALLEY) SPRING

FAULT SPRING

LAVA SPRING

STRUCTURE OF AN ARTESIAN BASIN

FEATURES OF A GROUNDWATER SYSTEM

Zone of aeration

Lake

Stream

Marsh

Layer of soil moisture

Zone of aeration

Capillary fringe

Water table

Saturated zone

CLOSE-UP OF SURFACE LAYER

Dry-season water table

Permanently saturated zone (saturated in wet and dry seasons)

Present water table (wet season)

Temporarily saturated zone (saturated only in wet season)

EXAMPLES OF LAKES

Glacial deposits

Lake in kettle (former site of ice block)

Oxbow lake (cut-off river meander)

River

KETTLE LAKE

OXBOW LAKE

Caldera (collapsed crater)

Volcanic lake

Movement along strike-slip (lateral) fault

Strike-slip (lateral) fault

Lake in elongated hollow

VOLCANIC LAKE

STRIKE-SLIP (LATERAL) FAULT LAKE

Rift valley

Steep back wall eroded by frost and ice

Moraine or rock lip damming lake

High valley walls

Sinking graben (block fault)

Tarn (circular mountain lake)

GRABEN (BLOCK-FAULT) LAKE

TARN

THE DEAD SEA, ISRAEL/JORDAN

River Jordan

Dead Sea

Steep rift-valley walls

Salt left by evaporation

Israel

Shallow flats

Jordan

Coastlines

COASTLINES ARE AMONG THE MOST RAPIDLY changing landscape features. Some are eroded by waves, wind, and rain, causing cliffs to be undercut and caves to be hollowed out of solid rock. Others are built up by waves transporting sand and small rocks in a process known as longshore drift and by rivers depositing sediment in deltas. Additional influences include the activities of living organisms such as coral, crustal movements, and sea-level variations due to climatic changes. Rising land or a drop in sea level creates an emergent coastline, with cliffs and beaches standing above the new shoreline. Sinking land or a rise in sea level produces a drowned coastline, typified by fjords (submerged glacial valleys) or submerged river valleys.

FEATURES OF A SEA CLIFF

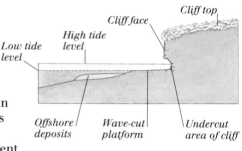

Cliff top
Cliff face
High tide level
Low tide level
Offshore deposits
Wave-cut platform
Undercut area of cliff

FEATURES OF WAVES

Wave height *Crest* *Wavelength* *Trough* *Shorter wavelength near beach*

Circular orbit of water and suspended particles

Orbit deformed into ellipse as water gets shallower

LONGSHORE DRIFT

Pebble *Backwash* *Movement of material along beach* *Buildup of material against groyne*

Beach

Groyne

Waves approaching shore at an oblique angle

Swash zone

Swash

Mature river

Headland

Bedding plane

Sea cliff

Remnants of former headland

Estuary

DEPOSITIONAL FEATURES OF COASTLINES

Bay head beach *Wave direction* *Headland*

Wave direction *Tombolo* *Island*

Wave direction *Cuspate foreland*

Wave direction *Barrier beach* *Lagoon*

BAY HEAD BEACH **TOMBOLO** **CUSPATE FORELAND** **BARRIER BEACH**

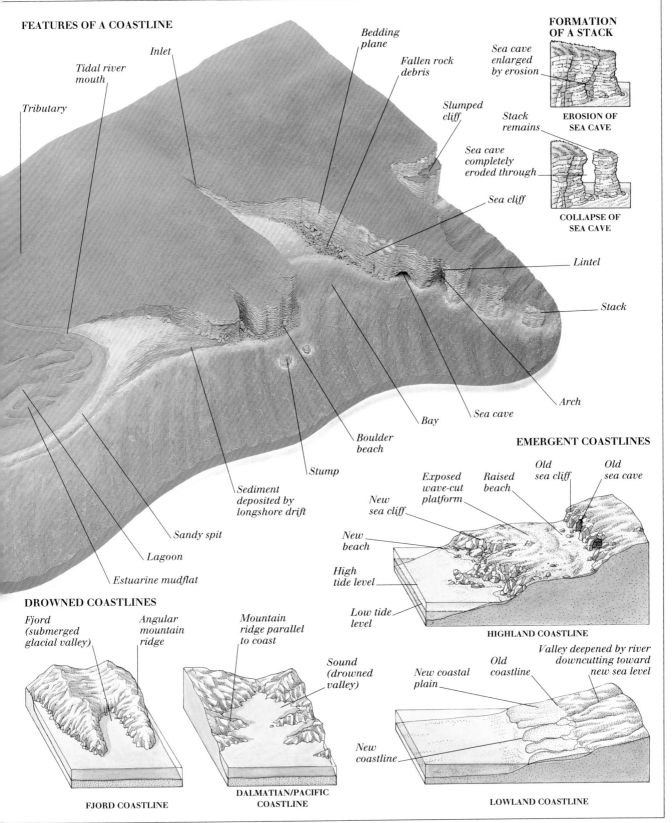

FEATURES OF A COASTLINE

Inlet

Tidal river mouth

Tributary

Bedding plane

Fallen rock debris

Slumped cliff

Sea cliff

Lintel

Stack

Arch

Sea cave

Bay

Boulder beach

Stump

Sediment deposited by longshore drift

Sandy spit

Lagoon

Estuarine mudflat

FORMATION OF A STACK

Sea cave enlarged by erosion

EROSION OF SEA CAVE

Stack remains

Sea cave completely eroded through

COLLAPSE OF SEA CAVE

EMERGENT COASTLINES

Exposed wave-cut platform

Raised beach

Old sea cliff

Old sea cave

New sea cliff

New beach

High tide level

Low tide level

HIGHLAND COASTLINE

Valley deepened by river downcutting toward new sea level

New coastal plain

Old coastline

New coastline

LOWLAND COASTLINE

DROWNED COASTLINES

Fjord (submerged glacial valley)

Angular mountain ridge

Mountain ridge parallel to coast

Sound (drowned valley)

FJORD COASTLINE

DALMATIAN/PACIFIC COASTLINE

Oceans and seas

OCEANS AND SEAS COVER ABOUT 70 PERCENT of the Earth's surface and account for about 97 percent of its total water. These oceans and seas play a crucial role in regulating temperature variations and determining climate. Their waters absorb heat from the Sun, especially in tropical regions, and the surface currents distribute it around the Earth, warming overlying air masses and neighboring land in winter and cooling them in summer. The oceans are never still. Differences in temperature and salinity drive deep current systems, while surface currents are generated by winds blowing over the oceans. All currents are deflected—to the right in the Northern Hemisphere, to the left in the Southern Hemisphere—as a result of the Earth's rotation. This deflective factor is known as the Coriolis force. A current that begins on the surface is immediately deflected. This current in turn generates a current in the layer of water beneath, which is also deflected. As the movement is transmitted downward, the deflections form an Ekman spiral. The waters of the oceans and seas are also moved by the constant ebb and flow of tides. These are caused by the gravitational pull of the Moon and Sun. The highest tides (Spring tides) occur at full and new Moon; the lowest tides (neap tides) occur at first and last quarter.

SURFACE CURRENTS

OFFSHORE CURRENTS

SALT CONTENT OF SEA WATER

Potassium 1.1%
Others 1.9%
Magnesium 3.7%
Calcium 1.2%
Sodium 30.2%
Sulfate 7.6%
Chloride 54.3%

Surface ocean current
Wind drives water along coast
Cold-water upwelling replaces warm surface water
Continental slope

COLD-WATER UPWELLING (SOUTHERN HEMISPHERE)

Surface ocean current
Pack ice formation increases water salinity and density
Cold, dense water sinks
Continental slope

POLAR BOTTOM WATER

EFFECT OF CORIOLIS FORCE

North Pole

Coriolis force

Winds and currents deflected to right in Northern Hemisphere

Equator

Winds and currents deflected to left in Southern Hemisphere

Original direction of wind or current

Actual direction of wind or current

South Pole

EKMAN SPIRAL (NORTHERN HEMISPHERE)

EQUATOR (0°)

Wind

Surface current caused by wind

Subsurface current slightly deflected by Coriolis force

Deep current at 180° to surface current

Midwater current further deflected by Coriolis force

ARCTIC CIRCLE (66° 32´N)

TROPIC OF CANCER (23° 30´N)

North Equatorial Current

Equatorial Countercurrent

South Equatorial Current

TROPIC OF CAPRICORN (23° 30´S)

East Australian Current

West Australian Current

SOUTH INDIAN GYRE

South Equatorial Current

Equatorial Countercurrent

North Equatorial Current

Northeast Monsoon Drift

Kuroshio Current

Oyashio Current

Agulhas Current

ANTARCTIC CIRCLE (66° 32´S)

HOW TIDES ARE CAUSED

HIGH SPRING TIDE

New Moon

LOW NEAP TIDE

Last quarter

Moon's gravitational pull

HIGH SPRING TIDE

Full Moon

Earth's orbit

Earth

Tidal bulge caused by Sun's gravitational pull

Tidal bulge caused by Moon's gravitational pull

Sun's gravitational pull

Sun's gravitational pull reinforces centrifugal effect, producing large tidal bulge

Equal and opposite tidal bulge produced by centrifugal effect due to Earth's spin

LOW NEAP TIDE

First quarter

Sun's gravitational pull diminishes Moon's effect

Sun

Tidal bulge where Moon's gravitational pull is strongest

Moon's orbit

Moon

The ocean floor

THE OCEAN FLOOR INCLUDES TWO SECTIONS: the continental shelf
and slope, and the deep-ocean floor. The continental shelf and slope are
part of the continental crust, but may extend far into the ocean. Sloping
quite gently to a depth of about 460 feet, the continental shelf is covered
in sandy deposits shaped by waves and tidal currents. At the edge of the
continental shelf, the seabed slopes down to the abyssal plain, which lies
at an average depth of about 12,500 feet. On this deep-ocean floor is a
layer of sediment made up of clays, fine oozes formed from the remains
of tiny sea creatures, and occasional mineral-rich deposits. Echo-
sounding and remote sensing from satellites has revealed that the
abyssal plain is divided by a world-circling system of mountain ranges,
far bigger than any on land—the midocean ridge. Here, magma
(molten rock) wells up from the Earth's interior and solidifies, widening
the ocean floor (see pp. 58-59). As the ocean floor spreads, volcanoes
that have formed over hot spots in the crust move away from their
magma source; they become extinct and are increasingly submerged
and eroded. Volcanoes eroded below sea level remain as seamounts
(underwater mountains). In warm waters, a volcano that projects
above the ocean surface often acquires a fringing coral reef, which
may develop into an atoll as the volcano becomes submerged.

CONTINENTAL-SHELF FLOOR

Bedrock
exposed by
tidal scour

Shoreline

Parallel strips
of coarse
material left
by strong
tidal currents

Sand
deposited
in wavy
pattern by
weaker
currents

Irregular patches of
fine sand deposited
by weakest currents

FEATURES OF THE OCEAN FLOOR

Sediment

Submarine
canyon

Continental
shelf

Course of
mud river

Continental
rise

Continental slope

Seamount
(underwater
mountain)

Guyot (flat-topped
seamount)

Abyssal
plain

Continental
crust

Ooze (sediment
consisting of remains
of tiny sea creatures)

Layer of
volcanic
rock

Pillow
lava

Volcanic
crystalline
rock

Oceanic
crust

DEEP-OCEAN FLOOR SEDIMENTS

KEY

- ☐ Calcareous ooze
- ☐ Pelagic clay
- ☐ Glacial sediments
- ☐ Siliceous ooze
- ☐ Terrigenous sediments
- ☐ Continental margin sediments
- ▨ Metalliferous muds
- ☐ Major nodule fields

ECHO-SOUND PROFILE OF OCEAN FLOOR

Sand wave

Event mark indicates synchronization of survey equipment

Sand wave

Seabed profile

Minor oscillations caused by ship's movement

Velocity of sound in water (1,493 m/sec; 4,898 ft/sec)

Reference code

Midocean ridge

Ocean trench

Magma (molten rock)

Sediment

DEVELOPMENT OF AN ATOLL

Volcanic island

Coral grows on shoreline

Sea level

FRINGING REEF

Lagoon

Eroded volcanic island subsides

Coral continues to grow, forming barrier reef

BARRIER REEF

Coral continues to grow where waves bring food

Lagoon

Dead coral

Volcanic island becomes submerged

ATOLL

Coral submerged too deeply to grow

Volcanic island is submerged further

SUBMERGED ATOLL

The atmosphere

JET STREAM

THE EARTH IS SURROUNDED BY ITS ATMOSPHERE, a blanket of gases that enables life to exist on the planet. This layer has no definite outer edge, gradually becoming thinner until it merges into space, but over 80 percent of atmospheric gases are held by gravity within about 10 miles of the Earth's surface. The atmosphere blocks out much harmful ultraviolet solar radiation, and insulates the Earth against extremes of temperature by limiting both incoming solar radiation and the escape of re-radiated heat into space. This natural balance may be distorted by the greenhouse effect, as gases such as carbon dioxide have built up in the atmosphere, trapping more heat. Close to the Earth's surface, differences in air temperature and pressure cause air to circulate between the equator and poles. This circulation, together with the Coriolis force, gives rise to the prevailing surface winds and the high-level jet streams.

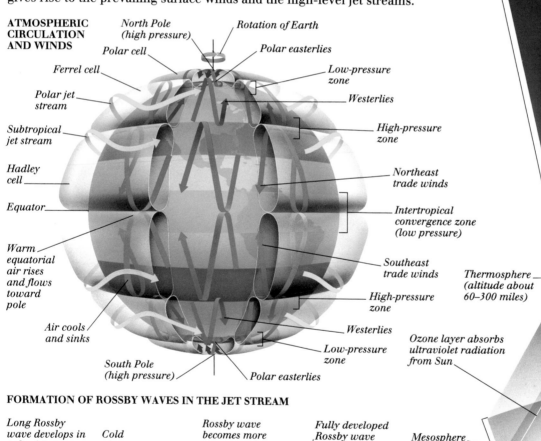

ATMOSPHERIC CIRCULATION AND WINDS

- North Pole (high pressure)
- Rotation of Earth
- Polar cell
- Polar easterlies
- Ferrel cell
- Low-pressure zone
- Polar jet stream
- Westerlies
- Subtropical jet stream
- High-pressure zone
- Hadley cell
- Northeast trade winds
- Equator
- Intertropical convergence zone (low pressure)
- Warm equatorial air rises and flows toward pole
- Southeast trade winds
- High-pressure zone
- Air cools and sinks
- Westerlies
- Low-pressure zone
- South Pole (high pressure)
- Polar easterlies

- Exosphere (altitude above about 300 miles)
- Corona
- Thermosphere (altitude about 60–300 miles)
- Ozone layer absorbs ultraviolet radiation from Sun
- Mesosphere (altitude about 30–60 miles)
- Stratosphere (altitude about 6–30 miles)
- Troposphere (altitude up to about 6 miles)

FORMATION OF ROSSBY WAVES IN THE JET STREAM

- Long Rossby wave develops in polar jet stream
- Cold air
- Rossby wave becomes more pronounced
- Fully developed Rossby wave
- Warm air

INITIAL UNDULATION　　**DEEPENING WAVE**　　**DEVELOPED WAVE**

STRUCTURE OF THE ATMOSPHERE

GLOBAL WARMING

Solar radiation re-radiated as heat

Some re-radiated heat escapes into space

Sun

Some re-radiated heat reflected back to Earth

Incoming solar radiation

Earth

Atmosphere

NATURALLY MODERATED GREENHOUSE EFFECT

Meteor (shooting star) burns up as it passes through atmosphere

Less re-radiated heat escapes

Solar radiation re-radiated as heat

More re-radiated heat reflected back to Earth

Aurora

Surface temperature rises

"Greenhouse gases" accumulate in atmosphere

UNBALANCED GREENHOUSE EFFECT

Incoming solar radiation

14% of incoming solar radiation absorbed by atmosphere

7% of incoming solar radiation reflected by atmosphere

COMPOSITION OF THE LOWER ATMOSPHERE

Other elements less than 0.1%

24% of incoming solar radiation reflected by clouds

Argon 0.93%

Cosmic rays (high-energy particles from space) penetrate to stratosphere

Oxygen 21%

Some absorbed heat re-radiated by atmosphere

4% of incoming solar radiation reflected by oceans and land

Nitrogen 78%

51% of incoming solar radiation absorbed by Earth's surface

Some absorbed heat re-radiated by clouds

Weather

WEATHER IS DEFINED AS THE ATMOSPHERIC CONDITIONS at a particular time and place; climate is the average weather conditions for a given region over time. Weather conditions include temperature, wind, cloud cover, and precipitation, such as rain or snow. Good weather is associated with high-pressure areas, where air is sinking. Cloudy, wet, changeable weather is common in low-pressure zones with rising, unstable air. Such conditions occur at temperate latitudes, where warm air meets cool air along the polar fronts. Here, spiraling low-pressure cells known as depressions (mid-latitude cyclones) often form. A depression usually contains a sector of warmer air, beginning at a warm front and ending at a cold front. If the two fronts merge, forming an occluded front, the warm air is pushed upward. An extreme form of low-pressure cell is a hurricane (also called a typhoon or tropical cyclone), which brings torrential rain, and exceptionally strong winds.

TYPES OF CLOUD

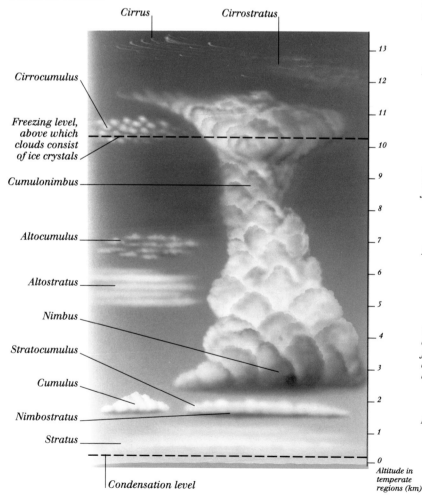

Cirrus

Cirrostratus

Cirrocumulus

Freezing level, above which clouds consist of ice crystals

Cumulonimbus

Altocumulus

Altostratus

Nimbus

Stratocumulus

Cumulus

Nimbostratus

Stratus

13
12
11
10
9
8
7
6
5
4
3
2
1
0

Altitude in temperate regions (km)

Condensation level

TYPES OF OCCLUDED FRONT

Advancing cold front rises up over warm front

Warm air

Warm front

Cool air

Cold air

WARM OCCLUSION

Cold air

Warm air

Cold front undercuts warm front

Warm front

Cool air

COLD OCCLUSION

FORMS OF PRECIPITATION

Water droplets less than 0.5 mm in diameter fall as drizzle

Water droplets coalesce to form raindrops 0.5–5.0 mm in diameter

Rising air

RAIN FROM CLOUDS NOT REACHING FREEZING LEVEL

Coalesced water droplets fall as rain

Ice crystal

Snowflakes grown from ice crystals fall as snow

Snowflakes melt to fall as rain

Rising air

RAIN AND SNOW FROM CLOUDS REACHING FREEZING LEVEL

Vertical air currents toss frozen water droplets up and down

Alternate freezing and melting builds up layers of ice

Rising air

Ice falls as hailstones

HAIL

STRUCTURE OF A HURRICANE

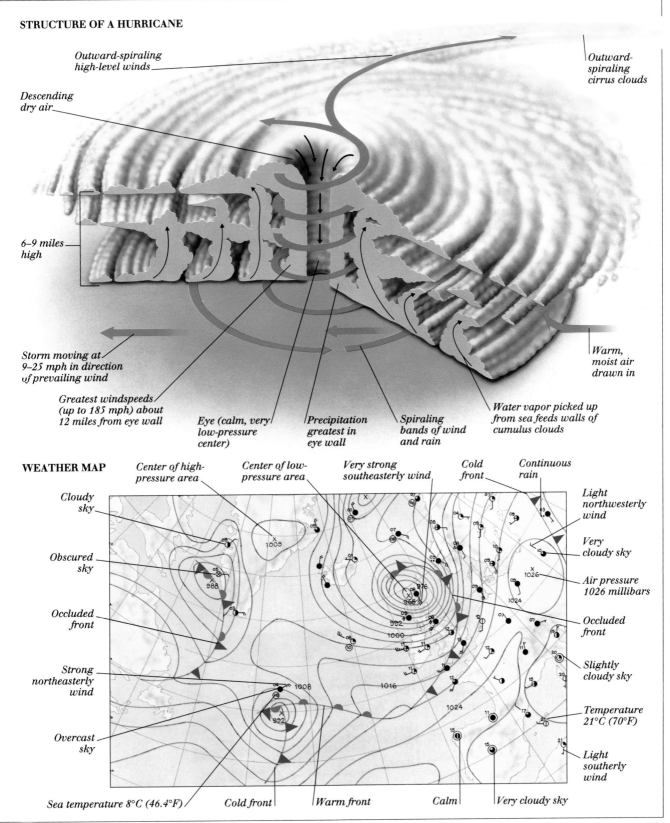

Outward-spiraling high-level winds

Outward-spiraling cirrus clouds

Descending dry air

6–9 miles high

Storm moving at 9–25 mph in direction of prevailing wind

Greatest windspeeds (up to 185 mph) about 12 miles from eye wall

Eye (calm, very low-pressure center)

Precipitation greatest in eye wall

Spiraling bands of wind and rain

Water vapor picked up from sea feeds walls of cumulus clouds

Warm, moist air drawn in

WEATHER MAP

Center of high-pressure area

Center of low-pressure area

Very strong southeasterly wind

Cold front

Continuous rain

Cloudy sky

Light northwesterly wind

Obscured sky

Very cloudy sky

Air pressure 1026 millibars

Occluded front

Occluded front

Strong northeasterly wind

Slightly cloudy sky

Overcast sky

Temperature 21°C (70°F)

Light southerly wind

Sea temperature 8°C (46.4°F)

Cold front

Warm front

Calm

Very cloudy sky

Physics and Chemistry

The variety of matter

**PLANT AND INSECT
(LIVING MATTER)**

MATTER IS ANYTHING THAT OCCUPIES SPACE. It includes everything from natural substances, such as minerals or living organisms, to synthetic materials. Matter can exist in three distinct states—solid, liquid, and gas. A solid is rigid and retains its shape. A liquid is fluid, has a definite volume, and will take the shape of its container. A gas (also fluid) fills a space, so its volume will be the same as the volume of its container. Most substances can exist as a solid, a liquid, or a gas: the state is determined by temperature. At very high temperatures, matter becomes plasma, often considered to be a fourth state of matter. All matter is composed of microscopic particles, such as atoms and molecules (see pp. 308-309). The arrangement and interactions of these particles give a substance its physical and chemical properties, by which matter can be identified. There is a huge variety of matter because particles can arrange themselves in countless ways, in one substance or by mixing with others. Natural glass, for example, seems to be a solid but is, in fact, a supercool liquid: the atoms are not locked into a pattern and can flow. Pure substances known as elements (see p. 310) combine to form compounds or mixtures. Mixtures called colloids are made up of larger particles of matter suspended in a solid, liquid, or gas, while a solution is one substance dissolved in another.

TYPES OF COLLOID

HAIR GEL (SOLID IN LIQUID)

**SHAVING CREAM
(AIR IN LIQUID)**

**MIST
(LIQUID IN GAS)**

EXAMPLES OF MATTER

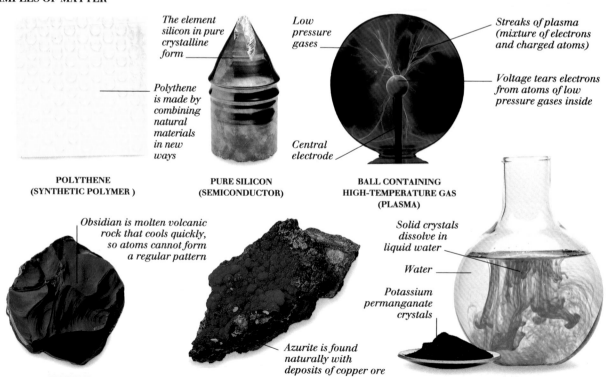

The element silicon in pure crystalline form

Polythene is made by combining natural materials in new ways

**POLYTHENE
(SYNTHETIC POLYMER)**

**PURE SILICON
(SEMICONDUCTOR)**

Low pressure gases

Central electrode

Streaks of plasma (mixture of electrons and charged atoms)

Voltage tears electrons from atoms of low pressure gases inside

**BALL CONTAINING
HIGH-TEMPERATURE GAS
(PLASMA)**

Obsidian is molten volcanic rock that cools quickly, so atoms cannot form a regular pattern

**OBSIDIAN
(NATURAL GLASS)**

Azurite is found naturally with deposits of copper ore

**AZURITE
(CRYSTALLINE MINERAL)**

Solid crystals dissolve in liquid water

Water

Potassium permanganate crystals

**POTASSIUM PERMANGANATE AND WATER
(SOLUTION)**

STATES OF MATTER

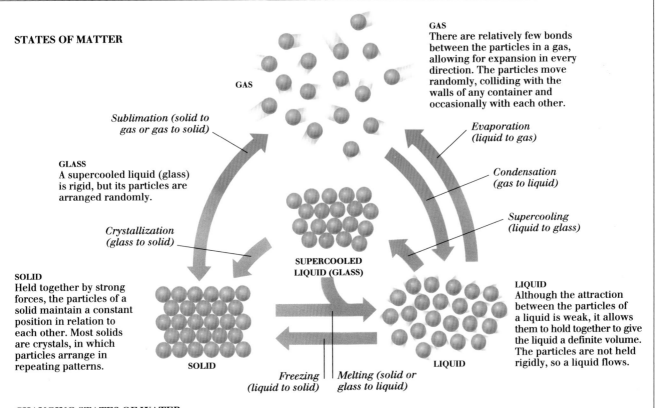

GAS

GAS
There are relatively few bonds between the particles in a gas, allowing for expansion in every direction. The particles move randomly, colliding with the walls of any container and occasionally with each other.

Sublimation (solid to gas or gas to solid)

Evaporation (liquid to gas)

GLASS
A supercooled liquid (glass) is rigid, but its particles are arranged randomly.

Condensation (gas to liquid)

Crystallization (glass to solid)

Supercooling (liquid to glass)

SUPERCOOLED LIQUID (GLASS)

SOLID
Held together by strong forces, the particles of a solid maintain a constant position in relation to each other. Most solids are crystals, in which particles arrange in repeating patterns.

LIQUID
Although the attraction between the particles of a liquid is weak, it allows them to hold together to give the liquid a definite volume. The particles are not held rigidly, so a liquid flows.

SOLID

LIQUID

Freezing (liquid to solid)

Melting (solid or glass to liquid)

CHANGING STATES OF WATER

Round-bottomed glass flask

Ice cubes have a definite shape

Liquid water

Liquid takes the shape of its container

Water remains liquid up to 212 °F (100 °C)

A gas will leave its container

Bubbles of steam form in boiling water

Steam turns back into liquid water where it meets cooler glass

Eventually, all the liquid will become a gas

SOLID STATE: ICE
The solid state of water, ice, forms when liquid water is cooled sufficiently. Ice cubes are rigid, with a definite shape and volume.

LIQUID STATE: WATER
When the temperature of a substance rises above its freezing point, it melts to become a liquid. Ice changes to water.

GASEOUS STATE: STEAM
Above its boiling point, a substance will become a gas. When heated sufficiently, liquid water turns to steam, a colorless gas.

Atoms and molecules

FALSE-COLOR IMAGE OF ACTUAL GOLD ATOMS

ATOMS ARE THE smallest individual parts of an element (see pp. 310-311). They are tiny, with diameters in the order of one ten-thousand-millionth of a meter (10^{-10} m). Two or more atoms join together (bond) to form a molecule of a substance known as a compound. For example, when atoms of the elements hydrogen and fluorine join together, they form a molecule of the compound hydrogen fluoride. So molecules are the smallest individual parts of a compound. Atoms themselves are not indivisible —they possess an internal structure. At their center is a dense nucleus consisting of protons, which have a positive electric charge (see p. 316), and neutrons, which are uncharged. Around the nucleus are negatively charged electrons. It is the electrons that give a substance most of its physical and chemical properties. They do not follow definite paths around the nucleus. Instead, electrons are said to be found within certain regions, called orbitals. These are arranged around the nucleus in "shells," each containing electrons of a particular energy. For example, the first shell (1) can hold up to two electrons, in a so-called s-orbital (1s). The second shell (2) can hold up to eight electrons in s-orbitals (2s) and p-orbitals (2p). If an atom loses an electron, it becomes a positive ion (cation). If an electron is gained, an atom becomes a negative ion (anion). Ions of opposite charges will attract and join together in a type of bonding known as ionic bonding. In covalent bonding, the atoms bond by sharing their electrons in what become molecular orbitals.

ATOMIC ORBITALS

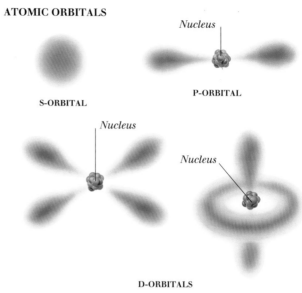

S-ORBITAL

P-ORBITAL

D-ORBITALS

Nucleus

MOLECULAR ORBITALS

π- (PI) ORBITAL

Σ- (SIGMA) ORBITAL

Nucleus

SP⁵-HYBRID ORBITAL

EXAMPLE OF IONIC BONDING

1s-orbital

1s-orbital   1s-orbital
Second shell holds seven electrons

2s-orbital

2p-orbital
2s-orbital   2p-orbital

2p-orbital

Electron transfer

Second shell now holds eight electrons, and is "filled"

Charged atoms (ions) held together by electrostatic forces

Li⁺ ion

F⁻ ion

Lithium atom loses 2s electron and becomes positively charged (Li⁺ ion)

Fluorine atom gains electron and becomes negatively charged (F⁻ ion)

1. NEUTRAL LITHIUM ATOM (Li)

NEUTRAL FLUORINE ATOM (F)

2. ELECTRON TRANSFER

3. IONIC BONDING: LITHIUM FLUORIDE MOLECULE (LiF)

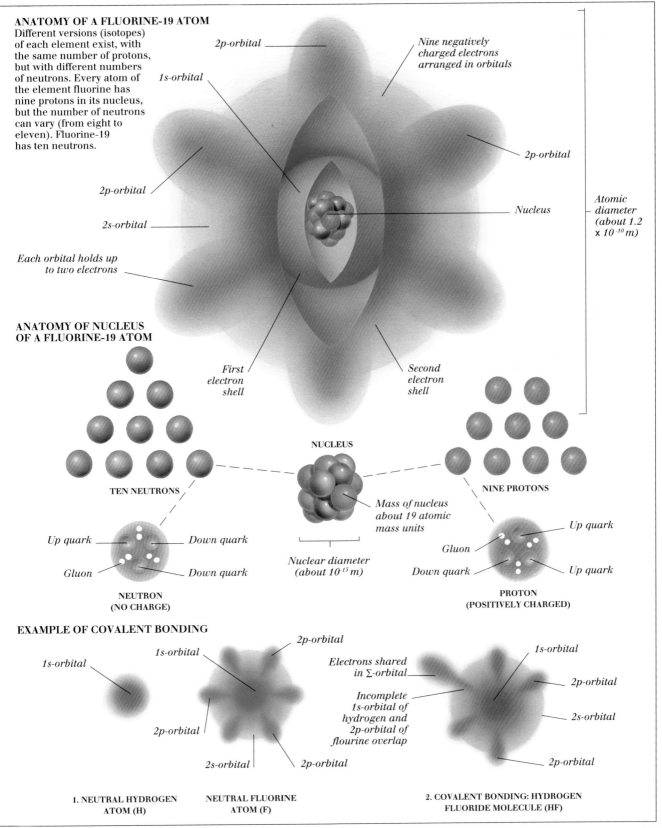

ANATOMY OF A FLUORINE-19 ATOM
Different versions (isotopes) of each element exist, with the same number of protons, but with different numbers of neutrons. Every atom of the element fluorine has nine protons in its nucleus, but the number of neutrons can vary (from eight to eleven). Fluorine-19 has ten neutrons.

2p-orbital

Nine negatively charged electrons arranged in orbitals

1s-orbital

2p-orbital

2p-orbital

Nucleus

2s-orbital

Atomic diameter (about 1.2 x 10^{-10} m)

Each orbital holds up to two electrons

ANATOMY OF NUCLEUS OF A FLUORINE-19 ATOM

First electron shell

Second electron shell

NUCLEUS

TEN NEUTRONS

NINE PROTONS

Mass of nucleus about 19 atomic mass units

Up quark

Down quark

Up quark

Gluon

Gluon

Down quark

Nuclear diameter (about 10^{-15} m)

Down quark

Up quark

NEUTRON (NO CHARGE)

PROTON (POSITIVELY CHARGED)

EXAMPLE OF COVALENT BONDING

1s-orbital

1s-orbital

2p-orbital

1s-orbital

Electrons shared in Σ-orbital

2p-orbital

2p-orbital

2s-orbital

Incomplete 1s-orbital of hydrogen and 2p-orbital of flourine overlap

2s-orbital

2p-orbital

2p-orbital

1. NEUTRAL HYDROGEN ATOM (H)

NEUTRAL FLUORINE ATOM (F)

2. COVALENT BONDING: HYDROGEN FLUORIDE MOLECULE (HF)

The periodic table

AN ELEMENT is a substance that consists of atoms of one type only. The 92 elements that occur naturally, and the 17 elements created artificially, are often arranged into a chart called the periodic table. Each element is defined by its atomic number—the number of protons in the nucleus of each of its atoms (it is also the number of electrons present). Atomic numbers increase along each row (period) and down each column (group). The shape of the table is determined by the way in which electrons arrange themselves around the nucleus: the positioning of elements in order of increasing atomic number brings together atoms with a similar pattern of orbiting electrons (orbitals). These appear in blocks. Electrons occupy shells of a certain energy (see pp. 308-309). Periods are ordered according to the filling of successive shells with electrons, while groups reflect the number of electrons in the outer shell (valency electrons). These outer electrons are important—they decide the chemical properties of the atom. Elements that appear in the same group have similar properties because they have the same number of electrons in their outer shell. Elements in Group 0 have filled shells, where the outer shell holds its maximum number of electrons, and are stable. Atoms of Group I elements have just one electron in their outer shell. This makes them unstable—and ready to react with other substances.

METALS AND NON-METALS

Elements at the left-hand side of each period are metals. Metals easily lose electrons and form positive ions. Non-metals, on the right of a period, tend to become negative ions. Semi-metals, which have properties of both metals and non-metals, are between the two.

TYPES OF ELEMENT KEY:

- Alkali metals
- Alkaline earth metals
- Transition metals
- Lanthanides (rare earths)
- Actinides
- Poor metals
- Semi-metals
- Non-metals
- Noble gases

Atomic number
Chemical symbol
Chemical name
Relative atomic mass

1
H
Hydrogen
1.0

RELATIVE ATOMIC MASS

Atomic mass (formerly atomic weight) is the mass of each atom of an element. It is equal to the number of protons plus the number of neutrons (electrons have negligible mass). The figures given are the averages for all the different versions (isotopes) of each element, measured relative to the mass of carbon-12.

Atomic number is number of protons in each nucleus

Atomic number goes up by one along each period

1st transition metals

Group I

1
H
Hydrogen
1.0

Group II

3	4
Li	**Be**
Lithium	Beryllium
6.9	9.0

11	12
Na	**Mg**
Sodium	Magnesium
23.0	24.3

19	20	21	22	23	24	25
K	**Ca**	**Sc**	**Ti**	**V**	**Cr**	**Mn**
Potassium	Calcium	Scandium	Titanium	Vanadium	Chromium	Manganese
39.1	40.1	45.0	47.9	50.9	52.0	54.9

37	38	39	40	41	42	43
Rb	**Sr**	**Y**	**Zr**	**Nb**	**Mo**	**Tc**
Rubidium	Strontium	Yttrium	Zirconium	Niobium	Molybdenum	Technetium
85.5	87.6	88.9	91.2	92.9	95.9	99.0

55	56	57-71	72	73	74	75
Cs	**Ba**		**Hf**	**Ta**	**W**	**Re**
Caesium	Barium		Hafnium	Tantalum	Tungsten	Rhenium
132.9	137.4		178.5	181.0	183.9	186.2

87	88	89-103	104	105	106	107
Fr	**Ra**		**Unq**	**Unp**	**Unh**	**Uns**
Francium	Radium		Unnilquadium	Unnilpentium	Unnilhexium	Unnilseptium
223.0	226.0		(261)	(262)	(263)	(262)

s-block

Two series always separated out from the table to give it a coherent shape

d-block

Soft, silvery, and highly reactive metal

SODIUM: GROUP 1 METAL

Silvery, reactive metal

MAGNESIUM: GROUP 2 METAL

Hard, silvery metal

CHROMIUM: 1ST TRANSITION METAL

Radioactive metal

PLUTONIUM: ACTINIDE SERIES METAL

57	58	59	60
La	**Ce**	**Pr**	**Nd**
Lanthanum	Cerium	Praseodymium	Neodymium
138.9	140.1	140.9	144.2

89	90	91	92
Ac	**Th**	**Pa**	**U**
Actinium	Thorium	Protactinium	Uranium
227.0	232.0	231.0	238.0

Bright yellow crystal

SULFUR: GROUP 6 SOLID NON-METAL

Purple-black solid turns to gas easily

IODINE: GROUP 7 SOLID NON-METAL

DIAMOND

ALLOTROPES OF CARBON
Some elements exist in more than one form —these are known as allotropes. Carbon powder, graphite, and diamond are allotropes of carbon. They all consist of carbon atoms, but have very different physical properties.

GRAPHITE

CARBON POWDER

Boron and carbon groups

Nitrogen and oxygen groups

Halogens

Group 0

			Group III	Group IV	Group V	Group VI	Group VII	**2** **He** Helium 4.0	Period
			5 **B** Boron 10.8	**6** **C** Carbon 12.0	**7** **N** Nitrogen 14.0	**8** **O** Oxygen 16.0	**9** **F** Fluorine 19.0	**10** **Ne** Neon 20.2	Short period
			13 **Al** Aluminum 27.0	**14** **Si** Silicon 28.1	**15** **P** Phosphorus 31.0	**16** **S** Sulfur 32.1	**17** **Cl** Chlorine 35.5	**18** **Ar** Argon 40.0	

2nd transition metals

3rd transition metals

26 **Fe** Iron 55.9	**27** **Co** Cobalt 58.9	**28** **Ni** Nickel 58.7	**29** **Cu** Copper 63.5	**30** **Zn** Zinc 65.4	**31** **Ga** Gallium 69.7	**32** **Ge** Germanium 72.6	**33** **As** Arsenic 74.9	**34** **Se** Selenium 79.0	**35** **Br** Bromine 79.9	**36** **Kr** Krypton 83.8	Long period
44 **Ru** Ruthenium 101.0	**45** **Rh** Rhodium 102.9	**46** **Pd** Palladium 106.4	**47** **Ag** Silver 107.9	**48** **Cd** Cadmium 112.4	**49** **In** Indium 114.8	**50** **Sn** Tin 118.7	**51** **Sb** Antimony 121.8	**52** **Te** Tellurium 127.6	**53** **I** Iodine 126.9	**54** **Xe** Xenon 131.3	
76 **Os** Osmium 190.2	**77** **Ir** Iridium 192.2	**78** **Pt** Platinum 195.1	**79** **Au** Gold 197.0	**80** **Hg** Mercury 200.6	**81** **Tl** Thallium 204.4	**82** **Pb** Lead 207.2	**83** **Bi** Bismuth 209.0	**84** **Po** Polonium 210.0	**85** **At** Astatine 210.0	**86** **Rn** Radon 222.0	
108 **Uno** Unniloctium (265)	**109** **Une** Unnilennium (266)										

d-block

p-block

Atomic mass is estimated, as element exists fleetingly

Unreactive, colorless gas glows red in discharge tube

NOBLE GASES
Group 0 contains elements that have a filled (complete) outer shell of electrons, which means the atoms do not need to lose or gain electrons by bonding with other atoms. This makes them stable and they do not easily form ions or react with other elements. Noble gases are also called rare or inert gases.

Yellow, unreactive precious metal

GOLD: 3RD TRANSITION METAL

Soft, shiny, reactive metal

TIN: GROUP 4 POOR METAL

Shiny semi-metal

ANTIMONY: GROUP 5 SEMI-METAL

NEON: GROUP 0 COLORLESS GAS

61 **Pm** Promethium 147.0	**62** **Sm** Samarium 150.4	**63** **Eu** Europium 152.0	**64** **Gd** Gadolinium 157.3	**65** **Tb** Terbium 158.9	**66** **Dy** Dysprosium 162.5	**67** **Ho** Holmium 164.9	**68** **Er** Erbium 167.3	**69** **Tm** Thulium 168.9	**70** **Yb** Ytterbium 173.0	**71** **Lu** Lutetium 175.0
93 **Np** Neptunium 237.0	**94** **Pu** Plutonium 242.0	**95** **Am** Americium 243.0	**96** **Cm** Curium 247.0	**97** **Bk** Berkelium 247.0	**98** **Cf** Californium 251.0	**99** **Es** Einsteinium 254.0	**100** **Fm** Fermium 253.0	**101** **Md** Mendelevium 256.0	**102** **No** Nobelium 254.0	**103** **Lr** Lawrencium 257.0

f-block

Chemical reactions

A CHEMICAL REACTION TAKES PLACE whenever bonds between
atoms are broken or made. In each case, atoms or groups of
atoms rearrange, making new substances (products) from the
original ones (reactants). Reactions happen naturally, or can be
made to happen; they may take years, or only an instant. Some
of the main types are shown here. A reaction usually involves
a change in energy (see pp. 314-315). In a burning reaction, for
example, the making of new bonds between atoms releases energy
as heat and light. This type of reaction, in which heat is given
off, is an exothermic reaction. Many reactions, like burning, are
irreversible, but some can take place in either direction, and are
said to be reversible. Reactions can be used to form solids from
solutions: in a double decomposition reaction, two compounds
in solution break down and re-form into two new substances,
often creating a precipitate (insoluble solid); in displacement,
an element (eg. copper) displaces another element (eg. silver)
from a solution. The rate (speed) of a reaction is determined by
many different factors, such as temperature, and the size and
shape of the reactants. To describe and keep track of reactions,
internationally recognized chemical symbols and equations
are used. Reactions are also used in the laboratory to identify
matter. An experiment with candle wax, for example,
demonstrates that it contains carbon and hydrogen.

SALT FORMATION (ACID ON METAL)

Glass beaker

Hydrogen gas (H_2) given off

Zinc (Zn) replaces hydrogen (H) in acid (HCl) to form zinc chloride solution ($ZnCl_2$)

Hydrogen in acid driven off when acid meets a reactive metal

Hydrochloric acid (HCl)

Effervescence

Zinc metal chippings (Zn)

Zinc metal chippings (Zn)

THE REACTION
Hydrochloric acid added to zinc
produces zinc chloride and hydrogen.
$Zn + 2HCl \rightarrow ZnCl_2 + H_2$

DISPLACEMENT

Copper metal (Cu)

Silver nitrate solution ($AgNO_3$)

Two metals compete for nitrate ions

Glass flask

Copper (Cu) ions displace silver (Ag) ions from silver nitrate solution ($AgNO_3$)

Blue solution of copper nitrate ($Cu(NO_3)_2$) forms

Needles of silver metal (Ag) form

THE REACTION
Copper metal added to silver nitrate solution
produces copper nitrate and silver metal.
$Cu + 2AgNO_3 \rightarrow Cu(NO_3)_2 + 2Ag$

BURNING MATTER

Ammonium dichromate ((NH_4)$_2$$Cr_2O_7$)

Flame

In this burning reaction, atoms form simpler substances and give off heat and light

Ammonium dichromate ((NH_4)$_2$$Cr_2O_7$) converts to chromium oxide (Cr_2O_3)

Nitrogen monoxide (NO) and water vapor (H_2O) given off as colorless gases

THE REACTION
When lit, ammonium
dichromate combines with oxygen from air.
$(NH_4)_2Cr_2O_7 + O_2 \rightarrow Cr_2O_3 + 4H_2O + 2NO$

A REVERSIBLE REACTION

Flat-bottomed glass flask

Potassium chromate solution (K_2CrO_4)

Bright yellow solution contains potassium and chromate ions

Pipette

Hydrochloric acid (HCl) added in drops

Acid causes reaction to take place

Chromate ions converted to orange dichromate ions

Potassium dichromate (KCr_2O_7) forms

Pipette

Sodium hydroxide (NaOH) added in drops

Sodium hydroxide (NaOH) neutralizes the acid

Solution turns to bright orange of potassium dichromate

Potassium dichromate (KCr_2O_7) re-forms to potassium chromate (K_2CrO_4)

Solution returns to original bright yellow color

1. THE REACTANT
Potassium chromate dissolves in water to
form potassium ions and chromate ions.
$K_2CrO_4 \rightarrow 2K^+ + CrO_4^{2-}$

2. THE REACTION
Addition of hydrochloric acid changes
chromate ions into dichromate ions.
$2CrO_4^{2-} \rightarrow Cr_2O_7^{2-}$

3. REVERSING
Addition of sodium hydroxide changes
dichromate ions back into chromate ions.
$Cr_2O_7^{2-} \rightarrow 2CrO_4^{2-}$

FERMENTATION

Yeast converts sugar into alcohol (C_2H_5OH) and carbon dioxide gas (CO_2)

Airtight stopper

Flat-bottomed glass flask

Yeast mixed with warm water and sugar ($C_6H_{12}O_6$)

Carbon dioxide bubbles (CO_2)

THE REACTION
Yeast converts sugar and warm water into alcohol and carbon dioxide.
$C_6H_{12}O_6 \rightarrow 2C_2H_5OH + 2CO_2$

DOUBLE DECOMPOSITION

Potassium iodide solution (KI)

Lead nitrate solution ($Pb(NO_3)_2$)

Potassium iodide solution added to lead nitrate solution

Two solutions swap partners

Lead iodide (PbI_2), a yellow solid, forms

Potassium nitrate solution (KNO_3) forms

1. THE REACTANTS
Potassium iodide in water (KI) and lead nitrate in water ($Pb(NO_3)_2$) each form colorless solutions.

2. THE REACTION
When the solutions are mixed, lead iodide, a precipitate, and potassium nitrate solution are formed.
$2KI + Pb(NO_3)_2 \rightarrow PbI_2 + 2KNO_3$

TESTING CANDLE WAX, AN ORGANIC COMPOUND

Clamp stand

Burning produces carbon dioxide gas (CO_2) and water vapor (H_2O)

Delivery tube

Delivery tube

Gases are trapped in funnel

Stopper

Stopper

Stopper

U-tube

Tube connection to pump that sucks gases through

Unburned carbon forms soot particles

Thistle funnel

Test tube

Flame

Burning candle wax

Water vapor condenses to form liquid water (H_2O)

Clamp

Carbon dioxide gas (CO_2) given off

Calcium hydroxide solution (lime water, $Ca(OH)_2$)

Water vapor trapped by solid drying agent, anhydrous copper sulfate ($CuSO_4$)

Anhydrous copper sulfate ($CuSO_4$)

Calcium hydroxide ($Ca(OH)_2$) and carbon dioxide (CO_2) form insoluble calcium carbonate ($CaCO_3$): lime water becomes milky

Candle wax ($C_{18}H_{38}$), a hydrocarbon, contains the elements carbon and hydrogen

Anhydrous copper sulfate crystals ($CuSO_4$) combine with water vapor (H_2O) to form darker blue hydrated copper sulfate ($CuSO_4 \cdot 10H_2O$)

1. THE BURNING REACTION
Burning wax produces carbon dioxide gas and water vapor.
$2C_{18}H_{38} + 55O_2 \rightarrow 36CO_2 + 38H_2O$

2. TESTING FOR WATER VAPOUR
A solid drying agent traps water vapor, proving the presence of hydrogen in the candle wax.
$CuSO_4 + 10H_2O \rightarrow CuSO_4 \cdot 10H_2O$

3. TESTING FOR CARBON DIOXIDE
Calcium hydroxide in solution reacts with carbon dioxide, forming a carbonate and turning milky.
$Ca(OH)_2 + CO_2 \rightarrow CaCO_3 + H_2O$

Energy

ANYTHING THAT HAPPENS—from a pin drop to an explosion
—requires energy. Energy is the capacity for doing work
(making something happen). Various forms of energy exist,
including light, heat, sound, electrical, chemical, nuclear,
kinetic, and potential energies. The Law of Conservation
of Energy states that the total amount of energy in the
Universe is fixed—energy cannot be created or destroyed,
it can only change from one form to another (energy
transfer). For example, potential energy is energy that
is stored, and can be used in the future. An object gains
potential energy when it is lifted; as the object is released,
potential energy changes into the energy of motion (kinetic
energy). During transference, some of the energy converts
into heat. A combined heat and power station can put some
of the "waste" heat to useful effect in local schools and
housing. Most of the Earth's energy is provided by the Sun,
in the form of electromagnetic radiation (see pp. 316-317).
Some of this energy transfers to plant and animal life, and
ultimately to fossil fuels, where it is stored in chemical
form. Our bodies obtain energy from the food we eat,
while energy needed for other tasks, such as heating and
transportation, can be obtained by burning fossil fuels
—or by harnessing natural forces like wind or moving
water—to generate electricity. Another source is nuclear
power, where energy is released by reactions in the nucleus
of an atom. All energy is measured by the international
unit, the joule (J). As a guide, one joule is about equal to
the amount of energy needed to lift an apple one yard.

SANKEY DIAGRAM SHOWING ENERGY FLOW IN A COAL-FIRED COMBINED HEAT AND POWER STATION

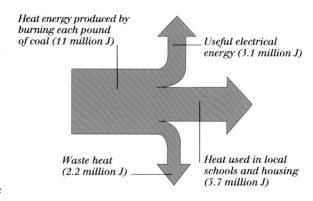

Heat energy produced by
burning each pound
of coal (11 million J)

Useful electrical
energy (3.1 million J)

Waste heat
(2.2 million J)

Heat used in local
schools and housing
(5.7 million J)

CROSS-SECTION OF HYDROELECTRIC POWER STATION WITH FRANCIS TURBINE

Transformer

Insulator

High voltage
cable

Switch gear
including
circuit braker

Bushing

Rotor house

Generator
unit

Gate

Generator rotor
turned by turbine

Shaft

Francis turbine

Curved blade

Gate

Afterbay

Screen

Water in
reservoir

Potential energy
of water intake
turns turbine

Penstock

Draft
tube

Tailrace

Water that flows
out has lost some
energy

CROSS-SECTION OF NUCLEAR POWER STATION WITH PRESSURIZED WATER REACTOR

Steam generator

Concrete
shielding

Water
pressurizer

Steel girder
framework

Control rod

Reactor core

Pump

Moderator
(water)

Enriched
uranium fuel

Coolant (water)
takes heat from
reactor core to
heat exchanger

Water in heat
exchanger turns
to steam

Steam drives
turbine

Heat
exchanger

Water pumped back into
steam generator

Turbine shaft
turns generator

Generator produces
electric current at
25,000 volts

Pump

Water cools used steam

Steam loses energy to turbine
and condenses back to water

Transformer
increases voltage
to 300,000 volts

High voltage
cable

Pylon carries
high voltage
electricity

Hot water to
cooling tower

Cold water
from cooling
tower

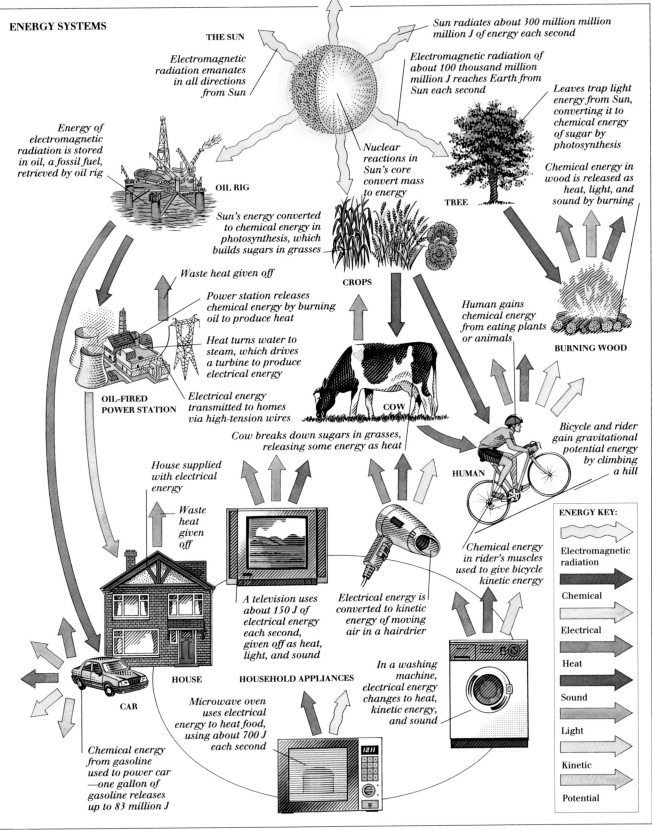

ENERGY SYSTEMS

THE SUN

Electromagnetic radiation emanates in all directions from Sun

Sun radiates about 300 million million million J of energy each second

Electromagnetic radiation of about 100 thousand million million J reaches Earth from Sun each second

Energy of electromagnetic radiation is stored in oil, a fossil fuel, retrieved by oil rig

OIL RIG

Nuclear reactions in Sun's core convert mass to energy

Leaves trap light energy from Sun, converting it to chemical energy of sugar by photosynthesis

Chemical energy in wood is released as heat, light, and sound by burning

TREE

Sun's energy converted to chemical energy in photosynthesis, which builds sugars in grasses

Waste heat given off

Power station releases chemical energy by burning oil to produce heat

Heat turns water to steam, which drives a turbine to produce electrical energy

Electrical energy transmitted to homes via high-tension wires

OIL-FIRED POWER STATION

CROPS

Human gains chemical energy from eating plants or animals

BURNING WOOD

Cow breaks down sugars in grasses, releasing some energy as heat

COW

House supplied with electrical energy

Waste heat given off

Bicycle and rider gain gravitational potential energy by climbing a hill

HUMAN

Chemical energy in rider's muscles used to give bicycle kinetic energy

A television uses about 150 J of electrical energy each second, given off as heat, light, and sound

Electrical energy is converted to kinetic energy of moving air in a hairdrier

HOUSE

HOUSEHOLD APPLIANCES

In a washing machine, electrical energy changes to heat, kinetic energy, and sound

CAR

Chemical energy from gasoline used to power car —one gallon of gasoline releases up to 83 million J

Microwave oven uses electrical energy to heat food, using about 700 J each second

ENERGY KEY:

Electromagnetic radiation

Chemical

Electrical

Heat

Sound

Light

Kinetic

Potential

Electricity and magnetism

ELECTRICAL EFFECTS result from an imbalance of electric charge. There are two types of electric charge: positive (carried by protons) and negative (carried by electrons). If charges are opposite (unlike), they attract one another, while like charges repel. These forces of attraction and repulsion (electrostatic forces) exist between any two charged particles. Matter is normally uncharged, but if electrons are gained, an object will gain an overall negative charge; if they are removed, it becomes positive. Objects with an overall negative or positive charge are said to have an imbalance of charge, and exert the same forces as individual negative and positive charges. On this larger scale, the forces will always act to regain the balance of charge. This causes static electricity. Lightning, for example, is produced by clouds discharging a huge excess of negative electrons. If charges are free—in a wire or material that allows electrons to pass through it—the forces cause a flow of charge called an electric current. Some substances exhibit the strange phenomenon of magnetism—which also produces attractive and repulsive forces. Magnetic substances consist of small regions called domains. Normally unmagnetized, they can be magnetized by being placed in a magnetic field. Magnetism and electricity are inextricably linked, a fact put to use in motors and generators.

LIGHTNING

VAN DE GRAAFF (ELECTROSTATIC) GENERATOR

Positive charges at many thousands of volts

Metal dome

Rotation of belt

Positively charged belt strips negative charges (electrons) from dome via metal comb, giving dome a positive charge

Pulley wheel

Moving rubber belt gains a positive charge

Insulating column prevents charges leaking away

Positive metal comb strips negative charges (electrons) from belt

Negatively charged metal plate

Connection to positive electrical supply

Pulley wheel

Rotation of belt

Connection to negative electrical supply

CURRENT ELECTRICITY

Crocodile clip connector

Junction

Direction of current, opposite to electron flow by convention

Four 1.5 volt cells (total of 6 volts)

Metal wire (conductor) coated with plastic (insulator)

Bulb receives 3 volts

Bulb holder

VOLTAGE
The higher the voltage, the greater the energy of electrical charges. One volt is one joule (unit of energy) per coulomb (unit of charge).

Bulb holder

Electrons flow from negative terminal to positive terminal

Negative terminal

Bulb receives 6 volts

Metal wire (conductor) coated with plastic (insulator)

Positive terminal

Bulb has high resistance

Bulb receives 3 volts

Switch completes or breaks circuit

Bulb holder

CURRENT
The greater the number of electrons moving around the circuit, the higher the current. Current is measured in amps (A). One amp equals one coulomb (unit of charge) per second.

RESISTANCE
For a given voltage, the flow of current depends upon the resistance of a circuit. Resistance is the degree to which a substance resists electrical current. It is measured in ohms (Ω).

SERIES ELECTRICAL CIRCUIT

SIMPLE ELECTRICAL CIRCUIT

MAGNETIC FIELDS AND FORCES

Iron filings
North-seeking pole
Profile of magnetic field
Bar magnet
North-seeking pole
South-seeking pole
Unlike poles attract

Like poles repel
North-seeking pole
South-seeking pole
Direction of force

Unlike poles attract
North-seeking pole
South-seeking pole
Like poles repel

South-seeking pole of electromagnet
Electromagnet
Wire to battery

MAGNETIC DOMAINS

Domain
Direction of magnetization within domain is random
Domain boundary

Direction of magnetization within domain has aligned
Domain aligned with magnetization has grown
Domain not aligned with magnetization has shrunk
Direction of overall magnetization

UNMAGNETIZED IRON

MAGNETIZED IRON IN A MAGNETIC FIELD

GENERATING MAGNETISM FROM ELECTRICITY

Direction of magnetic field (from north pole to south pole)
Electric current produces magnetic field
Magnetic field
Coil carries electric current
Direction of current
Metal wire (conductor) coated with plastic (insulator)
Negative terminal
Positive terminal
Four 1.5 volt cells (total of 6 volts)

CIRCUIT WITH ELECTROMAGNET

GENERATING ELECTRICITY FROM MAGNETISM

Terminal box
Coil of wire
Permanent magnet
Bearing
Non-drive end
Coil of wire

Terminal
Stator
Main rotor turns in magnetic field produced by coil of wire in stator
Fan
Drive end
Coil of wire
Shaft
Secondary (exciter) rotor

ELECTRIC GENERATOR
In a generator, the rotor rotates within the magnetic field of the stator to produce an electric current.

Coil of wire rotates within magnetic field of permanent magnet
Permanent magnet
Steel casing
Iron core
Coated copper winding
Commutator
Terminal
Spindle
End of shaft
Terminal

ELECTRIC MOTOR
In a motor, magnetic forces between the winding and permanent magnet produce a rotary motion.

317

Light

INFRARED IMAGE OF A HOUSE

LIGHT IS A FORM OF ENERGY. It is a type of electromagnetic radiation, like X rays or radio waves. All electromagnetic radiation is produced by electric charges (see pp. 316-317): it is caused by the effects of oscillating electric and magnetic fields as they travel through space. Electromagnetic radiation is considered to have both wave and particle properties. It can be thought of as a wave of electricity and magnetism. In that case, the difference between the various forms of radiation is their wavelength. Radiation can also be said to consist of particles, or packets of energy, called photons. The difference between light and X rays, for instance, is the amount of energy that each photon carries. The complete range of radiation is referred to as the electromagnetic spectrum, extending from low energy, long wavelength radio waves to high energy, short wavelength gamma rays. Light is the only part of the electromagnetic spectrum that is visible. White light from the Sun is made up of all the visible wavelengths of radiation, which can be seen when it is separated by using a prism. Light, like all forms of electromagnetic radiation, can be reflected (bounced back) and refracted (bent). Different parts of the electromagnetic spectrum are produced in different ways. Sometimes visible light—and infrared radiation—is generated by the vibrating particles of warm or hot objects. The emission of light in this way is called incandescence. Light can also be produced by fluorescence, a phenomenon in which electrons gain and lose energy within atoms.

MAXWELLIAN DIAGRAM OF ELECTROMAGNETIC RADIATION AS WAVES

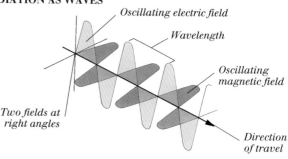

Oscillating electric field

Wavelength

Oscillating magnetic field

Two fields at right angles

Direction of travel

ELECTROMAGNETIC RADIATION AS PARTICLES

Photon thought of as wave packet of energy

Red light has long wavelength

Blue light has about twice the energy of red light

Blue light has shorter wavelength: waves are more tightly packed

PHOTON OF RED LIGHT   **PHOTON OF BLUE LIGHT**

SPLITTING WHITE LIGHT INTO THE SPECTRUM

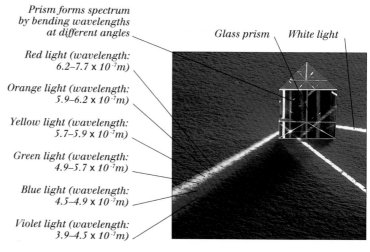

Prism forms spectrum by bending wavelengths at different angles

Glass prism   *White light*

Red light (wavelength: $6.2–7.7 \times 10^{-7}m$)

Orange light (wavelength: $5.9–6.2 \times 10^{-7}m$)

Yellow light (wavelength: $5.7–5.9 \times 10^{-7}m$)

Green light (wavelength: $4.9–5.7 \times 10^{-7}m$)

Blue light (wavelength: $4.5–4.9 \times 10^{-7}m$)

Violet light (wavelength: $3.9–4.5 \times 10^{-7}m$)

THE ELECTROMAGNETIC SPECTRUM

ENERGY (JOULES) 10^{-28} | 10^{-27} | 10^{-26} | 10^{-25} | 10^{-24} | 10^{-23} | 10^{-22} | 10^{-21} | 10^{-20} |

WAVELENGTH (METERS) 10^{4} | 10^{3} | 10^{2} | 10 | 1 | 10^{-1} | 10^{-2} | 10^{-3} | 10^{-4} | 10^{-5} |

Long-wave radio   *Medium-wave radio*   *Shortwave radio*   *Very high-frequency (VHF) radio*   *Microwaves*   *Infrared radiation*

Radio waves

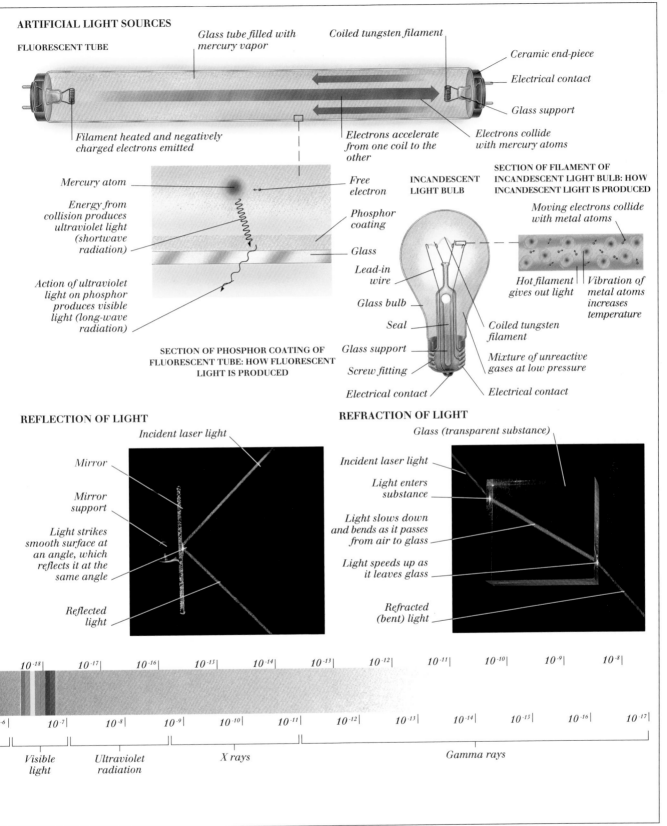

ARTIFICIAL LIGHT SOURCES

FLUORESCENT TUBE

Glass tube filled with mercury vapor

Coiled tungsten filament

Ceramic end-piece

Electrical contact

Glass support

Filament heated and negatively charged electrons emitted

Electrons accelerate from one coil to the other

Electrons collide with mercury atoms

Mercury atom

Free electron

Energy from collision produces ultraviolet light (shortwave radiation)

Action of ultraviolet light on phosphor produces visible light (long-wave radiation)

SECTION OF PHOSPHOR COATING OF FLUORESCENT TUBE: HOW FLUORESCENT LIGHT IS PRODUCED

INCANDESCENT LIGHT BULB

SECTION OF FILAMENT OF INCANDESCENT LIGHT BULB: HOW INCANDESCENT LIGHT IS PRODUCED

Phosphor coating

Glass

Lead-in wire

Glass bulb

Seal

Glass support

Screw fitting

Electrical contact

Coiled tungsten filament

Mixture of unreactive gases at low pressure

Electrical contact

Moving electrons collide with metal atoms

Hot filament gives out light

Vibration of metal atoms increases temperature

REFLECTION OF LIGHT

Incident laser light

Mirror

Mirror support

Light strikes smooth surface at an angle, which reflects it at the same angle

Reflected light

REFRACTION OF LIGHT

Glass (transparent substance)

Incident laser light

Light enters substance

Light slows down and bends as it passes from air to glass

Light speeds up as it leaves glass

Refracted (bent) light

10^{-18} | 10^{-17} | 10^{-16} | 10^{-15} | 10^{-14} | 10^{-13} | 10^{-12} | 10^{-11} | 10^{-10} | 10^{-9} | 10^{-8} |

10^{-6} | 10^{-7} | 10^{-8} | 10^{-9} | 10^{-10} | 10^{-11} | 10^{-12} | 10^{-13} | 10^{-14} | 10^{-15} | 10^{-16} | 10^{-17} |

Visible light

Ultraviolet radiation

X rays

Gamma rays

Force and motion

FORCES ARE PUSHES OR PULLS that change the motion of objects. To make a stationary object move, or a moving object stop, a force is needed. A force is also required to change the speed or direction of an object. This change in speed or direction is known as acceleration. Acceleration depends on the size (magnitude) of the force, and on the mass of the object. The effects of forces were first summarized by Isaac Newton in his three laws of motion. The international unit of force, named after him, is the newton (N), which is approximately equal to the weight of one apple. Gravity—the force of attraction between any two masses—can be measured using a newton meter (spring balance). Forces are put to useful effect in machines. A simple machine, such as a wheel and axle, is a device that changes the size or direction of an applied force. It allows an applied force (the effort) to produce another force (the load). A lever uses a bar that turns on a fulcrum to exert force. In all simple machines, there is a relationship between force and distance. A small force (in a compound pulley, for instance) moves through a large distance to lift a heavy object a small distance. This is called the Law of Simple Machines.

SIMPLE MACHINES

Single-pulley system (simple pulley)

Pulley wheel

Simple pulley only changes direction of a force

Effort is the same size as the load (10 N) and is pulled the same distance

One rope attached to load

Load of 10 N

Two-pulley system (simple pulley)

Pulley wheel

Effort is half the load (5 N), but the rope must be pulled twice the distance

Two ropes share the force and distance

Pulley wheel

Load of 10 N

Four-pulley system (compound pulley)

Two pulley wheels

Effort is one quarter of the load (2.5 N), but the rope must be pulled four times the distance

Four ropes share the force and distance

SIMPLE AND COMPOUND PULLEYS

Two pulley wheels

Load of 10 N

NEWTON METERS (SPRING BALANCES)

Weight is measured using a spring

When weight pulls downward, pointer moves along scale and measures force

Weight is 10 N

Weight is 20 N

Mass of 1 kg

Mass of 2 kg

WEIGHT AND MASS
The mass of an object is a measure of the quantity of matter that it possesses. Mass is usually measured in grams (g) or kilograms (kg). The weight of an object is the force exerted on the object's mass by gravity. Since weight is a force, its unit is the newton (N).

Wheel and axle multiplies the effort

Force is transmitted to the wheels by the chain

Pedal

Crank

A larger force, the load, is produced at the axle

WHEEL AND AXLE

Effort, provided by cyclist's muscles, is smaller than the load, but moves through a greater distance

A screw, acting like a wedge wrapped around a shaft, multiplies the effort

Effort, a turning force supplied through a screwdriver

Pitch (the angle of the screw thread)

The smaller the angle of pitch, the less force is required, but more turns are needed to move it through a greater distance

A larger force, the load, pulls the screw into wood

SCREW

Effort pushes axe into wood

Axe blade has wedge shape

Wedge multiplies effort

A larger force, the load, moves through a smaller distance to push wood apart

WEDGE

NEWTON'S THREE LAWS OF MOTION

NEWTON'S FIRST LAW
When no force acts on a body, it will continue in a state of rest or uniform motion.

Newton meter shows no applied force

Mass of 1 kg

Mass of trolley is negligible

Trolley is not in motion, and will remain at rest until a force acts

NO FORCE, NO ACCELERATION: STATE OF REST

Constant speed

Mass of 1 kg

Newton meter shows no applied force

Trolley is in motion, and will continue at a constant speed in a straight line until a force acts

NO FORCE, NO ACCELERATION: UNIFORM MOTION

NEWTON'S SECOND LAW
When a force acts on a body, the motion of the body will change. The size of the change will depend upon the mass of the object and the magnitude of the applied force.

Acceleration is 2 ms⁻²

Trolley and mass (1 kg) gain 2 meters per second of speed each second (2 ms⁻²)

Newton meter registers force of 2 N

Mass of 1 kg

Acceleration is 1 ms⁻²

Trolley and mass (2 kg) gain 1 meter per second of speed each second (1 ms⁻²)

Mass of 2 kg

Newton meter registers force of 2 N

With the same applied force, an object with 2 kg mass accelerates at half the rate of object with 1 kg mass

FORCE AND ACCELERATION: SMALL MASS, LARGE ACCELERATION   **FORCE AND ACCELERATION: LARGE MASS, SMALL ACCELERATION**

NEWTON'S THIRD LAW
If one object exerts a force on another, an equal and opposite force, called the reaction force, is applied by the second object on the first.

Newton meters pull on each other with equal and opposite forces

Acceleration: the trolley and mass accelerate at 2 ms⁻²

Newton meter registers force of 2 N to the left

Newton meter registers force of 2 N to the right

Mass of 1 kg

Person experiences a reaction force

ACTION AND REACTION

THREE CLASSES OF LEVER

Fulcrum, between effort and load

Effort

Load is greater than effort, but moves through smaller distance

CLASS 1 LEVER
Pliers consist of two class 1 levers.

Fulcrum

Load, between effort and fulcrum

Effort is smaller than load, but moves through greater distance

Load is smaller than effort, but moves through greater distance

CLASS 2 LEVER
Nutcrackers consist of two class 2 levers.

Load is applied at open end

Effort forces tongs together

Effort, between fulcrum and load

Fulcrum

CLASS 3 LEVER
Tongs consist of two class 3 levers.

RAIL AND ROAD

Steam locomotives

WAGONS THAT ARE PULLED along tracks have been used to transport material since the 16th century, but these trains were drawn by men or horses until the invention of the steam locomotive. Steam locomotives enabled the basic railroad system to realize its true potential. In 1804, Richard Trevithick built the world's first working steam locomotive in South Wales. It was not entirely successful, but it encouraged others to develop new designs. By 1829, the British engineer Robert Stephenson had built the Rocket, considered to be the forerunner of the modern locomotive. The Rocket was a self-sufficient unit, carrying coal to heat the boiler and a water supply for generating steam. Steam passed from the boiler to force the pistons back and forth, and this movement turned the driving wheels, propelling the train forward. Used steam was then expelled in characteristic puffs. Later steam locomotives, like Ellerman Lines and the Mallard, worked in a similar way, but on a much larger scale. The simple design and reliability of steam locomotives ensured that they changed very little in 120 years of use, before being replaced in the 1950s by more efficient diesel and electric power (see pp. 326-329).

ROCKET STEAM LOCOMOTIVE, 1829

Chimney

Smokebox

Leaf spring

Rocket nameplate

Pipe takes steam from boiler to cylinder

Regulator (throttle)

Wrought iron boiler

Remains of firebox

Valve chest

Valve setting control

Wooden buffer beam

Wooden driving wheel

Metal tire

Axle

Ballast

Rail chair

Wrought iron rail

Wooden sleeper

Piston rod

Cylinder

Carrying wheel

Driver's platform

ELLERMAN LINES, 1949 (CUTAWAY VIEW)

Stay

Vacuum reservoir

Water filler

Hand rail

Buffer

Panel brace

Panel sheeting

Water tank

Coal space

Tender hand brake

Cab

Firebox

Brick arch

Brake vacuum pipe

Wheel guard

Axle

Axle box

Tender wheel

Brake rigging

Water float to indicate water level

Water float lever

Axle box cover

Step

Footplate

Coupling

Coil spring

Trailing wheel

Grate

Fire drawn into fire tubes

TENDER

CAB INTERIOR OF MALLARD EXPRESS STEAM LOCOMOTIVE, 1938

Steam sanding control
Blower isolator valve
Pressure gauge isolator valve
Steam heating isolator valve
Vacuum brake isolator valve
Steam chest pressure gauge
Sliding roof vent
Boiler pressure gauge
Vacuum brake pressure gauge
Blower control
Gauge glass to show level of water in boiler
Regulator controls flow of steam to cylinders
Exhaust steam water injector control
Cab side window
Steam heating pressure gauge
Vacuum brake lever
Glass deflector
Live steam water injector control
Whistle lever
Manual sanding lever
Cylinder drain lever
Reverser handle
Control valve for hot water hose
Driver's seat
Fireman's seat
Steam-operated reversing shaft lock control
Oil can warming tray
Firebox
Firehole
Firebox door
Steam heat safety valve

Fire tube
Steam dome
Mechanical lubricator
Chimney
Thermal siphon
Regulator valve
Pipe takes steam from boiler to cylinder
Blast pipe
Superheater tube inside flue tube
Boiler
Smoke box
Smoke box door
Lubricating pipe
Piston valve
Buffer
Brake shoe
Expansion lever
Slide bar
Screw coupling
Brake rigging
Driving wheel
Crank
Connecting rod
Combination lever
Piston, linked to connecting rod
Leading wheel
Coupling rod
Cylinder

STEAM LOCOMOTIVE

Diesel trains

RUDOLF DIESEL FIRST DEMONSTRATED the diesel engine in Germany in 1898, but it was not until the 1940s that diesel locomotives were successfully established on both passenger and freight services in the U.S. Early diesel locomotives like the Union Pacific were more expensive to build than steam locomotives, but were more efficient and cheaper to operate, especially where oil was plentiful. One feature of diesel engines is that the power output cannot be coupled directly to the wheels. To convert the mechanical energy produced by diesel engines, a transmission system is needed. Almost all diesel locomotives have electric transmissions, and are known as diesel-electric locomotives. The diesel engine works by drawing air into the cylinders and compressing it to increase its temperature; a small quantity of diesel fuel is then injected into it. The resulting combustion drives the generator (more recently an alternator) to produce electricity, which is fed to electric motors connected to the wheels. Diesel-electric locomotives are essentially electric locomotives that carry their own power plants, and are used worldwide today. The Deltic diesel-electric locomotive, similar to the one shown here, replaced classic express steam locomotives, and ran at speeds up to 100 mph.

FRONT VIEW OF UNION PACIFIC DIESEL-ELECTRIC LOCOMOTIVE, 1950s

Exhaust vent · Windshield wiper · Horn · Cab front window · Headlight · Cab door · Name of operating railroad · Illuminated locomotive unit number · Railroad crest · Cab step · Step · Motor-driven bogie axle · Air-brake coupling hose · Center buckeye coupler

PROTOTYPE DELTIC DIESEL-ELECTRIC LOCOMOTIVE, 1956

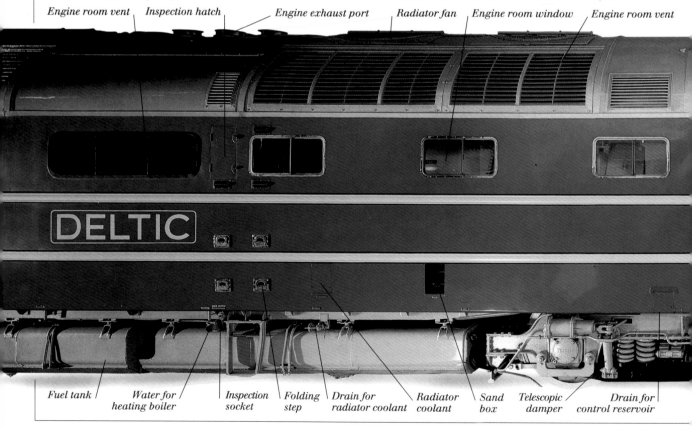

Engine room vent · Inspection hatch · Engine exhaust port · Radiator fan · Engine room window · Engine room vent

DELTIC

Fuel tank · Water for heating boiler · Inspection socket · Folding step · Drain for radiator coolant · Radiator coolant · Sand box · Telescopic damper · Drain for control reservoir

DIESEL ENGINE OF BRITISH RAIL CLASS 20 DIESEL-ELECTRIC LOCOMOTIVE

Exhaust vent

Cylinder head
(V-four configuration)

Turbo-charged diesel
engine drives generator

Generator
cooling fan

Generator
compartment
vent

Auxiliary
generator

Main generator
produces
electricity that
drives wheels

Main chassis
member

Innermost
wheel set on
cab-end bogie

Air brake pipe

Brake
rigging

Battery
box

Engine crankcase

Air reservoir and
isolator valves

Lubricating oil
primary pump and
fuel supply pump

Cab
door

Driver's seat

Cab

Warning horn

Windshield

Windshield wiper

Cab window

Manufacturer's
logo

Cab vent

Indicator
light

Sand box

Buffer

Brake cylinder

Roller-bearing
axle box

Brake
shoe

Brake
actuating chain

Transverse leaf spring
secondary suspension

Coil spring primary
suspension

EXAMPLES OF FREIGHT CARS

BOX CAR

HOPPER CAR

REFRIGERATOR CAR

LIVESTOCK CAR

FLAT CAR WITH BULKHEADS

AUTOMOBILE CAR

Electric and high-speed trains

THE FIRST ELECTRIC LOCOMOTIVE ran in 1879 in Berlin, Germany. In Europe, electric trains developed as a more efficient alternative to the steam locomotive and diesel-electric power. Like diesels, electric trains employ electric motors to drive the wheels but, unlike diesels, the electricity is generated externally at a power station. Electric current is picked up either from a catenary (overhead cable) via a pantograph, or from a third rail. Since it does not carry its own power-generating equipment, an electric locomotive has a better power-to-weight ratio and greater acceleration than its diesel-electric equivalent. This makes electric trains highly suitable for urban routes with many stops. They are also faster, quieter, and cause less pollution. The latest electric French TGV (Train à Grande Vitesse) reaches 186 mph; other trains, like the London to Paris and Brussels Eurostar, can run at several voltages and operate between different countries. Simpler electric trains perform special duties—the "People Mover" at Gatwick Airport, London, runs between terminals.

HOW ALTERNATING CURRENT (AC) ELECTRIC TRAINS WORK

Running rail for return current

Feeder station provides current

Catenary

Vacuum circuit breaker

Pantograph collects current

Thyristor converter converts current (ac) to direct current (dc)

Traction motor turns wheel

Control circuit

Transformer steps down voltage

Axle brush

FRONT VIEW OF PARIS METRO

Route number

Windshield wiper

Unit number

Operator's initials (Régie Autonome des Transports Parisien)

Rubber running wheel

Guard for rubber wheel

124

031

RATP

Door open/shut indicator light

Driver's seat

Handle

Front light (white)

Rear light (red)

Buffing pad

Rubber guide wheel

FRONT VIEW OF ITALIAN STATE RAILWAYS CLASS 402 ELECTRIC LOCOMOTIVE

Collector strip for electric current

Double-arm pantograph

Headlight

Windshield wiper

Italian State Railways crest

Number of electric (E) locomotive (class 402 No. 5)

Buffer

Jumper cable

Conventional hook-screw coupling

Front light (white)

Rear light (red)

SIDE VIEW OF GATWICK EXPRESS "PEOPLE MOVER"

Pneumatic rubber wheel

Concrete track

Automatic door

No driver (train controlled by central computer)

EUROSTAR MULTI-VOLTAGE ELECTRIC TRAIN

Cab window

Grill over warning horn

Rear light (red)

Headlight (white)

Fiberglass reinforced plastic cover

Fiberglass reinforced plastic cover

Aerofoil wheel guard

Aerofoil wheel guard

Sanding pipe

FRONT VIEW

Cab side window

Cab front window

Electric equipment compartment

Cab door

Side vent

Leading driven axle

Horizontal telescopic damper

Third (electric) rail collector shoe

Coil spring suspension

SIDE VIEW

TGV ELECTRIC HIGH-SPEED TRAIN

Luggage rack

Reading light

Double-glazed and tinted side window

Sliding curtain

Seat

Main overhead lighting

Automatic electric carriage end door

Antimacassar

Headrest

Armrest

Center gangway

INTERIOR OF TGV

Cab door

Hand rail

Side vent

Roof vent

Cab side window

Cab front window

Windshield wiper

Emergency exit door

Access panel for servicing

Nose air deflector dam

Vertical damper

Horizontal damper

SIDE VIEW OF TGV

Train equipment

MODERN RAILROAD TRACK consists of two parallel steel rails clipped onto a support called a sleeper. Sleepers are usually made of reinforced concrete, although wood and steel are still used. The distance between the inside edges of the rails is the track gauge. It evolved in Britain, which uses a gauge of 4 ft 8½ in (1,435 mm), known as the standard gauge. As engineering grew more sophisticated, narrower gauges were adopted because they cost less to build. The loading gauge, which is equally important, determines the size of the largest loaded vehicle that may pass through tunnels and under bridges with adequate clearance. Safe train operation relies on following a signaling system. At first, signaling was based on a simple time interval between trains, but it now depends on maintaining a safe distance between successive trains traveling in the same direction. Most modern signals are colored lights, but older mechanical semaphore signals are still used. On the latest high-speed lines, train drivers receive control instructions by electronic means. Signaling depends on reliable control of the train by effective braking. For fast, modern trains, which have considerable momentum, it is essential that each vehicle in the train can be braked by the driver or by a train control system, such as Automatic Train Protection (ATP). Braking is achieved by the brake shoe acting on the wheel rim (rim brakes), by disc brakes, or, increasingly, by electrical braking.

MECHANICAL SEMAPHORE SIGNAL

Red, square-ended arm in raised position means "all clear"

Red glass

Green glass

Actuating lever system

Motor operating "home" stop signal

Green glass

Yellow glass

Yellow, "distant" warning arm in horizontal position means "caution"

Tubular steel post

Ladder

Electrical relay box

FOUR-ASPECT COLORED LIGHT SIGNAL

Glass (yellow)

Glass (green)

Yellow glass (lit)

Glass (red)

Lamp shield

Lifting lug

Clip

Base

FRONT VIEW

SIDE VIEW

HOW A MODERN MAIN-LINE SIGNALING SYSTEM WORKS

Red "stop" light instructs next train not to enter this section of track

Green "all clear" light instructs train B to proceed into this section of track

Green "all clear" light instructs train B to proceed into this section of track

Green "all clear" light instructs train B to proceed into this section of track

Pantograph

Catenary

Train B

Track

EXAMPLES OF INTERNATIONAL TRACK GAUGES

3 ft 3¹/₂ in
(1,000 mm)
*East Africa,
India,
Malaysia,
Chile, and
Argentina*

3 ft 6 in
(1,067 mm)
*Japan, Australia,
Sudan, West Africa,
South Africa, and
New Zealand*

4 ft 8¹/₂ in
(1,435 mm)
*U.S., Canada, China,
Egypt, Turkey, Iran,
Japan, Peru, Britain,
Europe, Australia,
Brazil, and Mexico*

5 ft 0 in
(1,524 mm)
*Russia, Spain,
Portugal, and
Finland*

5 ft 3 in
(1,600 mm)
*Ireland, Australia,
and Brazil*

5 ft 6 in
(1,676 mm)
*India, Pakistan,
and Argentina*

EXAMPLES OF INTERNATIONAL LOADING GAUGES

KEY:

Britain: 9 ft 0 in (2.75 m) x 12 ft 11 in (3.95 m)

Europe: 10 ft 2 in (3.1 m) x 14 ft 9 in (4.5 m)

U.S.: 10 ft 10 in (3.3 m) x 16 ft 2 in (4.9 m)

Russia: 11 ft 2 in (3.4 m) x 17 ft 4 in (5.3 m)

4 ft 8¹/₂ in
(1,435 mm)
*Standard track
gauge*

5 ft 0 in
(1,524 mm)
*Track gauge of Russia,
with largest loading gauge*

FLAT-BOTTOMED RAIL

Flat-bottomed steel rail

Steel spring secures
rail to sleeper

Synthetic
insulating
pad

Sleeper supports
track and
maintains
gauge

BULL-HEAD RAIL

Wooden "key" secures
rail in chair

Steel tapered
screw fastens
chair to
sleeper

Bull-head pattern
steel rail

Cast-iron chair

Wooden
sleeper

DISC BRAKES ON MODERN WAGON BOGIE

Airbag secondary
suspension

Base of wagon

Damper

Hand
brake
wheel

Axle

Brake
disc

Brake calliper

Wheel

Two yellow "preliminary
caution" lights instruct train
B that it must stop in two
signals time

Yellow "caution" light
instructs train B that it
must stop at next signal

Green "all clear" light
instructs train A to proceed
into this section of track

Red "stop" light instructs
train B not to enter
this section of track

Braking distance

Train A

Trolleys and buses

METROLINK TROLLEY, MANCHESTER, BRITAIN

WHEN CITY POPULATIONS exploded in the 1800s, there was an urgent need for mass transportation. Trolleys were an early solution. The first trolleys, like buses, were horse-drawn, but in 1881, electric streetcars appeared in Berlin, Germany. Electric trolleys soon became widespread throughout Europe and North America. Trolleys run on rails along a fixed route, using electric motors that receive power from overhead cables. As road networks developed, motorized buses offered a flexible alternative to trolleys. By the 1930s, they had replaced trolley systems in many cities. City buses typically have doors at both the front and rear to make loading and unloading easier. Double-decker designs are popular, occupying the same amount of street space as single-decker buses but able to transport twice the number of people. Buses are also commonly used for inter-city travel and touring. Tour buses have reclining seats, large windows, luggage space, and toilets. Recently, as city traffic has become increasingly congested, many city planners have designed new electric streetcar routes to run alongside bus routes as part of an integrated transport system.

EARLY TROLLEY, c.1900

MCW METROBUS, LONDON, ENGLAND

FRONT VIEW

SINGLE-DECKER BUS, NEW YORK CITY, NEW YORK

Wheelchair access

Sliding window

Sloped roof dome

Tinted glass

Air intake

Tire

Axle

Exit door

Access panel

Sidelight

Entrance door

SIDE VIEW

Marker light

Entrance door

Route number

License plate

Repeater indicator

Side mirror

Headlight

Turning indicator

Bumper

Bumper

FRONT VIEW

DOUBLE-DECKER TOUR BUS, PARIS, FRANCE

Tinted glass

Air intake

Access panel

Skirt

Access door

Twin rear axle

Side entrance

Single front axle

Tire

Paris Vision

CARLUX

Raked windshield

Panoramic window

Turning indicator

Bumper

Plug-style entrance door

Sliding window vent

Upper saloon window

Advertising panel

Air intake

Lower saloon window

Fleet number

Engine access panel

Rear bumper

Emergency door control

Two-leaf style exit door

Legal lettering

London Buses logo

Axle

Tire

Skirt

LONDON BUSES

SIDE VIEW

The first cars

THE EARLIEST ROAD VEHICLE powered by an
engine, the Cugnot steam traction engine,
was built in 1770. More practical steam
carriages, such as the Bordino, were
available in the early 19th century,
but they were heavy and cumbersome.
Restrictive laws and the introduction of
railways, faster and able to carry more
passengers, saw the decline of "cars"
powered by steam. It was not until 1860
that the first practical power unit for road vehicles
was developed with the invention of the internal
combustion engine by the Belgian
Étienne Lenoir. By around 1890,
Karl Benz and Gottlieb Daimler in
Germany and Albert de Dion and
Armand Peugeot in France were
building cars for sale to the public.
These early cars, despite being
primitive, expensive, and produced
in limited numbers,
heralded the
age of the
automobile.

STEAM-POWERED CUGNOT "FARDIER," 1770

Twin cylinder engine
Steam pipe
Rocking beam
Steering tiller
Chimney
Wooden wheel (artillery wheel)
Haystack boiler
Brake pedal
Seat
Wooden frame
Load space
Carrying fork
Piston rod
Step
Log basket
Broad, rough tire
Ratchet wheel
Single front driving wheel

BORDINO STEAM CARRIAGE, 1854

Chimney
Top iron (landau iron)
Landau body
Drop-down window
Leather top
Fire-tube boiler
Safety valve
Sprung chassis
Safety valve weight
Water tank
Coal hopper
Chauffeur's seat (stoker's seat; spider seat; tiger seat)
Step
Tie bar
Full-elliptic leaf spring
Iron tire
Wooden spoke
Wooden wheel (artillery wheel)
Hub
Tie rod
Steam chest
Connecting rod
Twin-cylinder steam engine
Unsprung chassis
Steam distributor valve

SIDE VIEW OF GASOLINE-DRIVEN BENZ MOTORWAGEN, 1886

Steering tiller
Brake quadrant
Brake lever
Cooling water tank
Steering column
Full-elliptic leaf spring
Steering rack
Bevel gear
Steering link
Final drive sprocket
Steering head
Seat spring
Driven pulley
Wheel fork
Tubular chassis
Driving chain
Hub
Driving sprocket
Solid rubber tire
Tangent-spoked wire wheel

REAR VIEW OF BENZ MOTORWAGEN, 1886

Pinion
Lubricator
Cooling tank
Crown wheel
Driving pulley
Fuel tank
Drive belt
Big-end bearing
Groove for rope starter
Crankshaft
Flywheel

Seat cushion

Candle lamp
Driver's seat
Steering tiller
Brake lever
Dashboard
Headlight
Round pin
Splinter bar
Towing hook
Forecarriage
Steam pipe
Spoke
Frame

OVERHEAD VIEW OF BENZ MOTORWAGEN, 1886

Steering link
Footboard (floorboard)
Steering tiller
Brake lever
Tool and battery box
Trembler coil box
Intake pipe
Single cylinder
Fuel tank
Cooling water tank
Oil-filled lubricator
Flywheel
Crown wheel
Crankshaft
Driving pulley
Drive belt

Elegance and utility

DURING THE FIRST DECADE OF THIS CENTURY, the motorist who could afford it had a choice of some of the finest cars ever made. These handbuilt cars were powerful and luxurious, using the finest wood, leather, and cloth, and bodywork made to the customer's individual requirements. Some had six-cylinder engines as big as 15 liters. The price of such cars was several times that of an average house, and their yearly running costs were also very high. As a result, basic, utilitarian cars became popular. Costing perhaps one-tenth of the price of a luxury car, these cars had very little trim and often had only single-cylinder engines.

1904 OLDSMOBILE SINGLE-CYLINDER ENGINE

Oil bottle dripfeed · Crankcase · Starting handle bracket · Exhaust pipe · Cylinder head · Cylinder · Starter cog · Carburetor · Engine timing gear · Crankshaft · Flywheel · Gear band

FRONT VIEW OF 1906 RENAULT

Canopy · Mahogany-framed windshield · Cast aluminum wheel spider · Rear window · British Automobile Association badge · Bedford cord upholstery · British Royal Automobile Club badge · Window blind · Blind pull · Window lift strap · Rearview mirror · Broad lace trim · Lamp bracket · Oil side lamp · Windshield support · Dashboard radiator · Fender · Brass bevel · Access panel · Hood catch · Bail handle · Lifting handle · Mirror reflector · Acetylene headlight · X 825 · Chevron-tread tire · Dumb iron · Screwdown greaser · Front axle · Starting handle · Tie rod · Steering spindle · Elliott steering knuckle

SIDE VIEW OF 1906 RENAULT

Luggage grid · Button-quilted upholstery · Mahogany-framed plate glass window · Round-corner single limousine coachwork · Rear oil lamp · Shock absorber · Hub · Hubcap · Beaded edge tire · Tire security bolt

1904 OLDSMOBILE TRIM AND BODYWORK

Reflector
Seat back rest frame
Dashboard
Rear lamp
Engine cover handle
Tiller
Engine cover
Brake pedal
Throttle pedal
Fender
Mirror
Fender stay
Ignition switch
Seat cushion (squab)

1904 OLDSMOBILE CHASSIS

Front steering tie rod
Front spring
Brake rod
Full-elliptic steering spring
Steering wiffletree
Front axle
Rear spring
Starting handle bracket
Non-skid tire
Combined spring and chassis unit

Brass scrollwork
Blind pull
Canopy
Openable windshield
Brass bevel
Division
Oil side lamp
Hood
Broad lace trim
Dashboard
Handbrake
Steering wheel
Water pipe
Leather upholstery
Gear lever
Plug lead conduit
Acetylene headlight
Fuel/air intake pipe
Bi-block engine
Bulb horn
Spare tire
Dashboard radiator
Jump seat (opera seat; strapontin)
Rim clamp
Tire carrier
Running board
Leather valance
Tire strap
Hood support
Exhaust manifold
Starting handle
Wooden artillery wheel

Mass production

THE FIRST CARS WERE HAND-ASSEMBLED from
individually built parts, a time-consuming
procedure that required skilled mechanics and
made cars very expensive. This problem was solved,
in America, by a Detroit car manufacturer named
Henry Ford. He introduced mass production by using
standardized parts, and later combined these with a
moving production line. The work was brought
to the workers, each of whom performed one
simple task in the construction process as the
chassis moved along the line. The first mass-
produced car, the Ford Model T, was launched
in 1908. At first it was available in a limited
range of body styles and colors. However,
when the production line was introduced
in 1914, the color range was cut back; the
Model T became available, as Henry Ford said,
in "any color you like, so long as it's black." Ford cut
the production time for a car from several days to about
12 hours, and eventually to minutes, making cars much
cheaper than before. As a result, half the cars in the
world were Model T Fords by 1920.

FRONT VIEW OF 1913 FORD MODEL T

Throttle lever · Openable windshield · Steering wheel · Ignition lever · Windshield stay · Dashboard · Side lamp · Spring shock absorber · Bulb horn · Fender · Headlight · Radiator · Front transverse leaf spring · License plate · Starting handle · Steering knuckle · Front axle · Steering spindle connecting-rod

STAGES OF FORD MODEL T PRODUCTION

Left half of differential housing · Pinion · Rear leaf spring (cross-member) · Steering arm · King pin · Removable wheel · Hub brake shoe · Tie rod · Steering wheel · Hub bolt · Pinion housing · Front transverse leaf spring · Differential housing · Chassis frame · Front cross-member · Rear spring perch · Radius rod · Rear axle · Battery carrier · Body mount · Bearing sleeve · King pin · Half-shaft · Right half of differential housing · Crown wheel · Rear axle bearing · Bevel pinion · Front axle · Removable wheel · Torque tube · Radius rod · Running board support · Hub brake shoe

SIDE VIEW OF 1913 FORD MODEL T

The "people's car"

**WORKING PARTS OF
VOLKSWAGEN BEETLE**

THE MOST POPULAR CAR in the history of car manufacture is the Volkswagen Beetle, originally called the KdF Wagen. The car was developed in Germany in the 1930s by Dr. Ferdinand Porsche. At that time, Germany had only half the number of cars of Britain or France, and Adolf Hitler took a personal interest in the development of the Volkswagen ("people's car"). The intention was to provide a new industry, new jobs, and a car so inexpensive that anyone with a job could afford it. Dr. Porsche designed a car that was cheap to build and run; its rear-mounted, air-cooled engine cut down the number of parts needed and also reduced weight. However, few civilians managed to obtain the Beetle before the outbreak of the Second World War in 1939. After the war, the Beetle proved so popular that eventually more than 20 million were sold.

**CUSTOMIZED
VOLKSWAGEN
BEETLE**

**FLAT-FOUR
CYLINDER
ARRANGEMENT**

Fuel tank · Steering tie-rod · Fuel filler neck · Steering box assembly · Suspension strut · Strut cartridge (shock absorber) · Front road spring · Front suspension top mount · Floor pan (platform chassis) · Torsion bar cover · Trailing arm · Drive shaft · Heat exchanger · Starter motor · Tail pipe · Air filter · Flat-four engine · Clutch and flywheel · Transaxle (gearbox and final drive) · Rear shock absorber · Sports wheel · Tire · Rear brake drum · Handbrake · Seat mount · Gear lever knob · Front suspension top mount · Dust shroud · Pedal cluster · Track control arm · Brake back plate · Anti-roll bar · Frame head · Steering idler · Windshield-wiper motor assembly · Fuel tank sender unit

Taillight · Air scoop · Vent window · Luggage compartment lid · Turn signal and parking light · Fuel filler cap · Pressed steel wheel · Tail pipe

Counterweight · Piston · Crankshaft · Big end · Connecting rod (con-rod)

BODY SHELL OF VOLKSWAGEN BEETLE

Front bumper

Release handle

Left side headlight unit

Right side headlight unit

Left front parking light and turn signal lens

Chrome trim strip

Right front parking light and turn signal lens

Luggage compartment lid

Left front fender

Right front fender

Front fender piping

Spare-wheel well

Hood hinge

Front fender piping

Blade

Vent window

Arm

Windshield wiper

Left side running board

Right side running board

Mirror

Door catch

Steering column

Quarter light

Door handle

Wind deflector (baffle)

Sun roof

Passenger door

Window winder handle

Body shell

Window winder regulator

Rear fender piping

Drop glass

Rear fender piping

Air intake vents

Engine lid (engine cover)

Rear valance

Air intake vents

Left side rear fender

License plate light

Right rear fender

Left taillight

License plate

WRV 408L

Right taillight

Rear bumper

Early engines

STEAM AND ELECTRICITY were used to power cars until early this century, but neither power source was ideal. Electric cars had to stop frequently to recharge their heavy batteries, and steam cars gave smooth power delivery but were too complicated for the average motorist to use. A rival power source, the internal combustion engine, was invented in 1860 by Étienne Lenoir (see pp. 334-335). This engine converted the force of an explosion into rotary motion to turn the wheels of a vehicle. Early variations on this basic model included sleeve valves, separately cast cylinders, and the two-stroke combustion cycle. Today, all combustion engines, including the Wankel rotary and diesels (see pp. 346-347), use the four-stroke cycle, first demonstrated by Nikolaus Otto in 1876. The Otto cycle has proved the best method of ensuring that the engine turns over smoothly and that exhaust emissions are controllable.

TROJAN TWO-STROKE ENGINE, 1927

Port linking combustion chambers of upper and lower cylinders

Water connection

Upper paired cylinder

Spark plug

Wide piston-ring

Transfer port

Wire gauze pad

Upper piston

Flywheel

Flexible, forked connecting-rod

Counterweight

Big end

Crankcase

BERSEY ELECTRIC CAB, 1896

Mounting for tray of 40 batteries

Housing for electric motors

SECTIONED WHITE STEAM CAR, 1903

Steering wheel

Throttle wheel

Brake lever

Automatic cylinder lubricator

Flash steam generator

Reverse lever

Lamp bracket

High-pressure cylinder

Rocking lever

Exhaust pipe

Water pump

Condenser

Low-pressure cylinder

Fuel tank

Semi-elliptic spring

Brake drum

Spiral tubes

Steel-reinforced wooden chassis

Steering drop arm

Water tank

Drag link

Dumb iron

CYCLE OF A FOUR-STROKE INTERNAL COMBUSTION ENGINE

INDUCTION STROKE

- Exhaust port closed
- Intake valve
- Intake port opens
- Piston moves downward
- Fuel and air (the "charge") sucked into cylinder
- Counterweight
- Crankshaft
- Crankpin

COMPRESSION STROKE

- Exhaust port closed
- Charge compressed by piston
- Intake port closed
- Connecting rod (con-rod)
- Piston moves upward

POWER STROKE

- Spark plug
- Intake port closed
- Exhaust port closed
- Charge ignited by spark plug
- Explosion pushes piston downward
- Big end

EXHAUST STROKE

- Exhaust valve
- Intake port closed
- Exhaust port opens
- Burned gases forced out of cylinder
- Piston moves upward

16-HORSEPOWER HUMBER ENGINE, 1911

- Brass housing for ignition cable
- Intake port
- Water pipe
- Valve cap
- Spark plug
- Side valve (inlet valve)
- Cylinders (cast in pairs)
- Water jacket
- Fan bracket
- Tappet
- Valve spring
- Timing chain
- Timing cover
- Crankcase
- Starting handle
- Flywheel
- Camshaft
- Oil pump
- Oil pan

DAIMLER DOUBLE-SLEEVE VALVE ENGINE, 1910

- Spark plug socket
- Junk ring
- Cylinder head
- Intake port
- Exhaust port
- Intake manifold
- Outer sleeve valve
- Water jacket
- Cylinder wall
- Inner sleeve valve
- Piston
- Carburetor
- Engine bearer
- Flywheel

OUTER SLEEVE VALVE

- Oil groove

INNER SLEEVE VALVE

- Sleeve port
- Eye for connecting con-rods to secondary crankshaft

343

Modern engines

TODAY'S GASOLINE ENGINE WORKS on the same basic principles as the first car engines of a century ago, although it has been greatly refined. Modern engines, often made from special metal alloys, are much lighter than earlier engines. Computerized ignition systems, fuel injectors, and multi-valve cylinder heads achieve a more efficient combustion of the fuel/air mixture (the charge) so that less fuel is wasted. As a result of this greater efficiency, the power and performance of a modern engine are increased, and the level of pollution in the exhaust gases is reduced. Exhaust pollution levels today are also lowered by the increasing use of special filters called catalytic converters, which absorb many exhaust pollutants. The need to produce ever more efficient engines means that it can take up to seven years to develop a new engine for a family car, at a cost of many millions of dollars.

FRONT VIEW OF A FORD COSWORTH V6 12-VALVE

Idle control valve
Valve rocker
Power steering pump reservoir
Steering pump pulley
Cogged drive belt
Alternator
Viscous coupling
Plenum chamber
Oil dipstick
High-tension ignition lead (spark plug lead)
Fan
Crankshaft pulley
Oil pan

FRONT VIEW OF A FORD COSWORTH V6 24-VALVE

Idle control valve
Exhaust gas recirculation valve
Steering pump drive pulley
Belt tensioner
Alternator cooling fan
Oil pan
Plenum chamber
Camshaft timing gear
Camshaft chain
Air-conditioning compressor
Drive belt
Crankshaft pulley

SECTIONED VIEW OF A JAGUAR STRAIGHT 6

Cam follower (bucket tappet)
Valve spring
Cam lobe
Cam
Combustion chamber
Compression ring
Cam cover
Camshaft
Cylinder head
Valve stem
Exhaust valve
Cylinder liner
Water jacket
Piston
Connecting rod (con-rod)
Main bearing housing
Big end
Transmission adaptor plate
Crankshaft counterweight
Oil pan
Oil pick-up pipe
Anti-surge baffle
Oil-control ring (scraper ring)
Crankcase
Distributor
Fan
Air-conditioning refrigerant pipe
Suspension self-leveling pump
Power steering pump
Swash plate
Drive belt
Compressor piston
Air-conditioning compressor

FRONT VIEW OF A JAGUAR V12

Air cleaner
Camshaft sprocket
Distributor
Fuel injector nozzle
Intake manifold tract
Plenum chamber
Camshaft
Cam follower
Piston ring land
Piston ring groove
Exhaust manifold
Piston skirt
Coolant outlet
Cam cover
Wrist pin
Viscous coupling
Cooling fan
Fan drive shaft
Alternator
Belt pulley
Alternator pulley

Piston
Crankshaft

STRAIGHT 4 CYLINDER ARRANGEMENT

Counterweight
Connecting rod (con-rod)

V12 CYLINDER ARRANGEMENT

SECTIONED VIEW OF A JAGUAR V12

Distributor drive shaft
Throttle butterfly
Intake manifold
Ignition amplifier
Fuel pipe
Throttle linkage
Air inlet
Exhaust valve
Inlet valve
Cam cover
Timing chain
Oil feed pipe
Piston crown
Cylinder head
Piston ring land
Water outlet
Water pump
Exhaust heat shield
Piston
Exhaust manifold
Oil pipe banjo
Accessory drive pulley
Drive plate
Timing chain drive sprocket
Starter ring
Connecting rod (con-rod)
Oil filter
Counterweight (balance weight)
Main bearing
Crankcase
Pipe to oil cooler
Oil pan

Alternative engines

THE MOST COMMON TYPE OF ALTERNATIVE ENGINE is the diesel engine. Instead of igniting the compressed fuel/air mixture with a spark, the diesel engine uses compression alone, which heats the mixture to the point where it explodes. A diesel engine's fuel consumption is low in comparison with similarly sized piston engines, despite its heavier, reinforced moving parts and cylinder block. Another type of engine is the rotary-combustion, first successfully developed by Felix Wankel in the 1950s. Its two trilobate (three-sided) rotors revolve in housings shaped in a fat figure eight. The four sequences of the four-stroke cycle, which occur consecutively in a piston engine, occur simultaneously in a rotary engine, producing power in a continuous stream.

ROTARY-ENGINED MAZDA RX-7 TURBO II

Aerodynamic windshield
Headrest
Top boot
Front spoiler (chin spoiler)
Side marker lamp
Body-side molding
Cast alloy wheel

WANKEL ROTARY ENGINE

OIL-PUMP HOUSING

Distributor fixing point (drive point)

FRONT SIDE HOUSING

Intake port

FRONT ROTOR CHAMBER

Trailing spark plug hole

Dipstick tube

Oil filler

INTERMEDIATE HOUSING

Intake port

REAR ROTOR CHAMBER

Aluminum alloy backing

Oil-pump drive

Coolant passage

Exhaust port

Leading spark plug hole

Water drain bolt

Trailing spark plug hole

Leading spark plug hole

THE WANKEL ROTARY CYCLE

Exhaust port
Intake port
Fuel/air mixture being compressed
Water passage
Burning gas expands
Trilobate rotor
Gas continues to expand
Stationary gear (fixed gear)

Exhaust port closed
Vacuum sucks in fuel/air mixture
Burned gas exhausts
Rotor gear
Compression continues

Burned gas continues to exhaust
Output shaft turns
Fuel/air mixture continues to enter
Compressed gas ignites

Compression begins
Burned gas begins to expand

**FORD
TURBOCHARGED
DIESEL ENGINE**

Engine lifting bracket

Valve cover

Baffle plate

Intake track

Turbo impeller (inlet rotor)

Turbo propeller (exhaust rotor)

Exhaust

Bell housing

Oil filler cap

Cam follower

Valve return spring

Water jacket

Water pump pulley

Compression ring

Oil-control ring

Piston

Accessory drive belt

Water jacket

Oil cooler

Oil cooler matrix

Engine block

Oil filter

Oil pan

Oil return pipe for turbocharger

REAR SIDE HOUSING

Chrome plating

Exhaust port

ROTOR AND SEALS

Outer oil seal

Inner oil seal spring

Inner oil seal

Outer oil seal spring

Inner oil seal groove

Outer oil seal groove

Hole for output shaft

Side seal

Side seal spring

Rotor bearing

Rotor gear

Side gear

Corner seal spring

Corner seal insert

Corner seal

Rotor

Balancing drilling

Apex seal

Apex seal spring

Apex seal groove

Side seal groove

OUTPUT SHAFT

Front counterweight

Front eccentric rotor journal

Oil passage

Rear stationary gear (fixed gear)

V-belt pulley

Front stationary gear (fixed gear)

Main journal

Eccentric shaft

Oil jet

Rear eccentric rotor journal

Flywheel with balance weight

Modern bodywork

RENAULT LOGO

THE BODY OF A MODERN MASS-PRODUCED CAR is built on the monocoque (single-shell) principle, in which the roof, side panels, and floor are welded into a single integral unit. This bodyshell protects and supports the car's internal parts. Steel and glass are used to construct the bodyshell, creating a unit that is both light and strong. Its lightness helps to conserve energy, while its strength protects the occupants. Modern bodywork is designed with the aid of computers, which are used to predict factors such as aerodynamic efficiency and impact resistance. High technology is also employed on the production line, where robots are used to assemble, weld, and paint the body.

Door handle

Door lock

Left-hand door glass

Left-hand quarter glass

Tailgate support strut (rear hatch support strut)

Window washer jet

Rear window glass

Heating element contact

Tailgate support strut (rear hatch support strut)

Tailgate

Rear bumper

Bodyshell

Fuel cap

Right-hand quarter glass

Zinc phosphating

Degreased bare metal

Primer

Base coat color

Cataphoresic coating

Right-hand door glass

Clear coat

Chrome passivation

Door key and lock

Door handle

Left-hand door

Left-hand mirror assembly

Door hinge

Electric window motor

Radio antenna

Rear hatch

Side marker lamp

SIDE VIEW OF A RENAULT CLIO

Spoiler bumper

Hood-release cable

Hood

Hood catch

Hood hinge

Front bumper

Windshield glass

Window winder cable

Window winder handle

Door hinge

Right-hand door

Right-hand mirror assembly

Hood

Headrest

Headlight

Spoiler bumper

H746 FBK

Fog light

FRONT VIEW OF A RENAULT CLIO

Modern components

A TYPICAL MODERN CAR has several thousand individual mechanical components. These are assembled to form the car's various mechanical systems: engine and exhaust, transmission, steering, suspension, and brakes. To ensure that each system functions properly, components are manufactured to extremely fine tolerances—to within about one ten-thousandth of an inch in some cases.

Alloy wheel

Hubcap

Hub nut

Hub seal

Exhaust downpipe

Muffler

Catalytic converter

Suspension spring

Rear muffler

Fuel tank

Vent pipe

Electric fuel pump

Fuel tank filler neck

Shock absorber

Brake cylinder (wheel cylinder)

Brake shoe

Hub seal

Hub nut

Hubcap

Wheel cover

Torsion bar

Left rear suspension arm

Anti-roll bar

Right rear suspension arm

Handbrake

Gear lever

Steering wheel

Steering rack

Steering column

Hub and brake drum

Clutch pedal

Brake pedal

Accelerator pedal

Brake backplate

Clutch cable

Accelerator cable

Steel wheel

MECHANICAL COMPONENTS OF A RENAULT CLIO, 1991

Brake shield

Alloy wheel

Clutch throw-out bearing

Brake disc

Hub

Clutch pressure plate

Left drive shaft

Tie-rod end

Upper suspension arm

Brake hose

Top radiator hose

Tie rod

Brake pad

Power steering pump

Clutch center plate

Gear-change rod

Gearbox (transmission)

Bottom radiator hose

Lower suspension arm

Anti-roll bar

Starter motor

Flywheel

Power steering belt

Fan motor

Subframe

Exhaust manifold

Electronic ignition unit

Brake cylinder (wheel cylinder)

Intake manifold

Brake power-assist servo

Water pump

Fan motor support bracket

Alternator

Alternator belt

Engine

Suspension strut

Brake caliper fixing bolt

Distributor

Brake caliper locking plate

Air cleaner

Brake caliper

Right drive shaft

Hub carrier

Brake hose

Radiator

Lock nut and washer

Brake disc

Front hub bearing

Brake shield

Steel wheel

Wheel cover

Water bottle

Modern trim

A MODERN CAR HAS TWO TYPES OF TRIM, according to the materials used: hard (chrome and plastics) and soft (upholstered materials). Safety and comfort are priorities in the trim's design: seats help the occupants maintain a comfortable posture, rubber seals keep out dirt and moisture, and headlights light the way. Older cars had interior or leather paneling cut and fitted by craftsmen; modern cars use precisely molded plastics and seat fabrics cut by robot-controlled lasers to reduce costs and production time. Doors are now assembled off the production line so that complex wiring can be built in.

TRIM OF A RENAULT CLIO, 1991

Rear quarter trim panel

Inner roof trim

Roof seal

Quarter trim panel

Quarter panel molding

Rear seat belt

Rear tire

Rear shelf

Split, folding rear seat assembly

Center seat belt

Rear seat belt stalk (catch)

Tailgate trim

Rear shelf radio speaker

Gear lever surround

Tailgate seal

Rear wiper blade

Rear wiper arm

Rear shelf radio speaker

License plate light

Rear turn signal and stop lamp assembly

Wheel cover (rear wheel embellisher)

Untrimmed headrest

HALOGEN HEADLIGHT BULB

Rear tire

Rear seat belt

Quarter panel molding

SPOTLIGHT BULB

Filament

MARKER LIGHT BULB

Filament

Quarter trim panel

FESTOON BULB

Rear quarter trim panel

Roof seal

Inner roof trim

Contact

Bayonet fixing

Contact

Contact

Roof molding

Window winder handle

Door seal

Front tire

Wheel cover (front wheel embellisher)

Door lock handle

Door pull handle

Turn signal lamp

Fog light

Inner sill trim

Door molding (rubbing strip)

Inner windshield molding

Front seat belt

Front door radio speaker

Dash radio speaker

Front seat assembly

Sun visor

Dash panel (instrument panel)

Windshield wiper bracket and spindles

Headlight

Interior light

Radio

Heater unit

Windshield wiper blade

Rearview mirror

Washer jet

Fan blade

Center console

Steering wheel

Sun visor

Fascia (dash)

Windshield seal

Front seat frame

Headlight

Windshield wiper arm

Front seat belt

Control stalk

Dash radio speaker

Front door radio speaker

Inner windshield molding

Door trim panel

Inner sill trim

Door molding (rubbing strip)

Fog light

Door seal

Door pull handle

Window winder handle

Turn signal lamp

Door lock handle

Front tire

Wheel cover (front wheel embellisher)

All-terrain vehicles

THE MODERN ALL-TERRAIN VEHICLE has its origins in the American military Jeep of the 1940s and the British Land Rover. Such vehicles have been used for a wide range of purposes, from safari travel to fire fighting. The principal special features of such cars—including four- or six-wheel drive, high ground clearance, and toughened braking, suspension, and transmission systems—are designed to enable driving under the most difficult off-road conditions. The vehicle shown here is equipped for safari travel and carries a comprehensive range of survival gear.

COOKING EQUIPMENT

TWO-BURNER ALCOHOL STOVE

Handle for all pans

Flame regulator

Wick

Zipper

Tie

Cooking pot

Mosquito netting

Ventilation flap

HAND WINCH

SIDE VIEW OF PINZGAUER TURBO D

Folding rooftop tent

Locking fuel filler cap

Dust filter

Raised air intake

Guard

Galvanized roof-rack

Steel body

Jerrycan

Spare wheel and tire

Bodyside molding (rub strip)

TIRE PUMP

Pressure gauge

TIRE IRON

Heavy-duty shovel

Tubular backbone chassis

Fuel tank

Metal jerrycan for fuel

Plastic jerrycan for water

LEFT-HAND TREAD PLATE

RIGHT-HAND TREAD PLATE

TOW STRAP

HEAVY-DUTY SHACKLE

SAFETY WINDSHIELD CLAMPS

WASHING BUCKET

Radio aerial

Observation roof hatch

Grab handle

Rearview mirror

Windshield washer bottle

Wrap-around bumper

Access step

SECURITY CHAIN

FRONT VIEW OF PINZGAUER TURBO D

Observation roof hatch

Radio aerial

Galvanized roof-rack

Laminated windshield

Rearview mirror

Air vent

Radiator grille

Indicator

Headlight

Headlight guard

External step

Independent swing axle

Locking differential

Towing loop

All-terrain tire

REAR VIEW OF PINZGAUER TURBO D

Roof-rack

Observation platform

External step for roof

Jerrycan

Jerrycan carrier

Spare wheel

Bodyside molding (rub strip)

Offset door hinge

Rear bumper

Rear light cluster

Door and wheel support frame

Mudflap

Off-road tire

Locking differential

Independent swing axle

Racing cars

SINCE MOTORING BEGAN, racing cars have been a major focus of innovation in car design. Features that are now commonplace, such as disc brakes, turbochargers, and even safety belts, were used first on competition cars. Research into racing cars has contributed to a new understanding of engine performance, aerodynamics, and tire adhesion, and has led to the development of ultra-light materials such as carbon-fiber for car bodies. Like the 1937 Bugatti Type 57S below, a modern Williams Formula One car has a low, streamlined body and an open cockpit. Unlike its forerunner, it also has a front wing that pushes the front wheels firmly onto the track, huge slick tires for extra grip, and electrical sensors that continually relay information to the pits about the car's performance.

1937 BUGATTI TYPE 57S

Diffuser

Bodywork bracket

Heat shield

Forward radius arm

Rear wing upper mainplane

Slot

Upper flap

Half shaft

Rear radius arm

Temperature-sensitive sticker

Aeroquip pipe union

Oil tank

Constant velocity joint cover

Rear wing end-plate

Diffuser

Rear brake duct

Oil feed to engine

Fuel injection trumpet guard (debris guard)

Fuel injector

Cam cover

Cylinder head

Gearbox fixing stud

Mounting point

Electronic control-unit connector

Water outlet

Tail pipe

Stressed cylinder block

Harmonically tuned exhaust pipe

RENAULT V10 RS1 ENGINE

ENGINE COWLING

Dzus fastener

SIDE FAIRING

Water rail

Engine cooling radiator

Master electrical switch

Anchor nut

Radiator air duct

Slick racing tire

Steering link

Nose cover

Front wing end-plate

Front wing

Suspension push-rod

Rearview mirror

Lower wishbone

Front lower wishbone

Brake pipe

Driver's radio antenna

Single-point safety harness release

Upper wishbone

Push-rod adjuster

Electrical connectors to engine

Exhaust

Chassis electrical plug

Lifting hook

Emergency electricity cut-off

Fuel filler

Safety harness

Emergency air hose for driver

Fuel injection air-intake trumpet

Fuel breather

Air intake

FRONT VIEW OF WILLIAMS 1990 FORMULA ONE RACING CAR

Rear wing upper mainplane

Engine air intake

Driver's radio aerial

Rear wing end-plate

Rearview mirror

Upper wishbone

Rear brake duct

Suspension push-rod

Slick racing tire

Radiator air intake

Front wing end-plate

Steering link

Front wing

End-plate aerodynamic skirt

357

Bicycle anatomy

THE BICYCLE IS A TWO-WHEELED, lightweight machine, which is propelled by human power. It is efficient, cheap, easily manufactured, and one of the world's most popular forms of transportation. The first pedal-driven bicycle was built in Scotland in 1839. Since then the basic design—of a frame, wheels, brakes, handlebars, and a saddle—has been gradually improved, with the addition of a chain, gear system, and pneumatic tires (tires inflated with air). The recent invention of the mountain bike (all-terrain bike) has been an important development. With its strong, rugged frame, wide tires, and 21 gears, a mountain bike enables riders to reach rough and hilly areas that were previously inaccessible to cyclists.

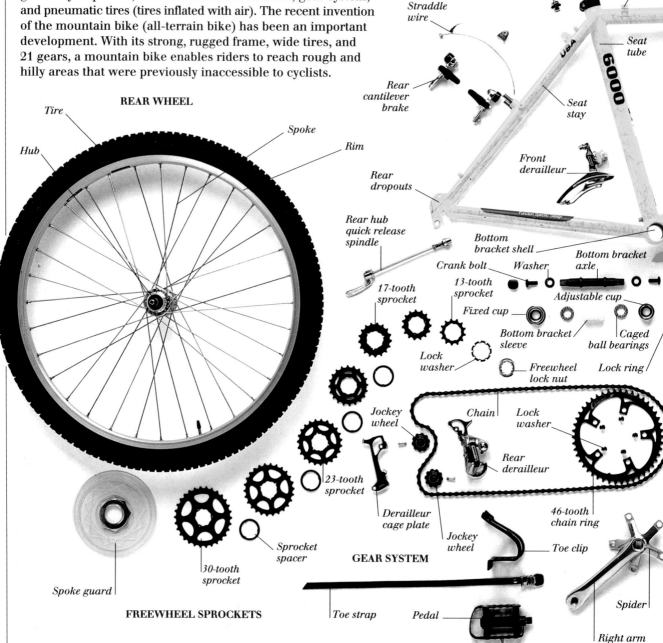

Saddle (seat)

Seat post

Seat post quick release bolt

Cable guide

Straddle wire

Seat tube

Rear cantilever brake

Seat stay

REAR WHEEL

Tire

Spoke

Rim

Hub

Front derailleur

Rear dropouts

Rear hub quick release spindle

Bottom bracket shell

Bottom bracket axle

Crank bolt

Washer

17-tooth sprocket

13-tooth sprocket

Adjustable cup

Fixed cup

Bottom bracket sleeve

Caged ball bearings

Lock ring

Lock washer

Freewheel lock nut

Jockey wheel

Chain

Lock washer

Rear derailleur

23-tooth sprocket

Derailleur cage plate

46-tooth chain ring

Jockey wheel

Sprocket spacer

Toe clip

Spoke guard

30-tooth sprocket

GEAR SYSTEM

Spider

FREEWHEEL SPROCKETS

Toe strap

Pedal

Right arm

Gear cable

Gearshift

Gearshift

Handlebar

Handlebar
grip

Handlebar
stem

Expander
bolt

Top tube

Lock
nut

Rear brake
cable

Lock
washer

Top race

Brake
lever

Brake lever

Cable guide

**BICYCLE
FRAME**

Head
tube

Top cup

Caged ball
bearings

Front brake
cable

Hub

Spoke

Down
tube

Bottom
cup

Rubber
bearing
seal

Steerer
tube

Straddle wire

Bottom
race

Toe clip

Front
cantilever
brake

Cantilever
brake boss

Rim

Inner tube

Toe
strap

Pedal

Left arm

Fork blade

24-tooth
chain ring

Front hub
quick release
spindle

36-tooth
chain ring

Handlebar

Saddle

Frame

Brake lever
and gearshift

Valve cap

Valve

Pedal

Tire

Chain

FRONT WHEEL

Bicycles

ALTHOUGH ALL BICYCLES are made up of the same basic components, they can vary greatly in design. A racing bike, such as the Eddy Merckx model, with its light frame and steep head- and seat-angles, is built for speed. Its design forces the rider to adopt the aero tuck, a crouched, aerodynamic position. While a touring bike resembles a racing bike in many respects, it is designed for comfort and stability on long-distance journeys. Touring bikes are characterized by more relaxed frame angles, heavy chain stays that support the rear panniers, and a long wheelbase (the distance between the wheel axles) for reliable handling. All-purpose bicycles, known as hybrids, combine the light weight and speed of sports bikes with the rugged durability of mountain bikes (see pp. 358-359). Bicycles that are not designed for conventional road use include time-trial bikes, which have a short head tube, sloping top tube, aero handlebars, and aerodynamic tubing. Most Human Powered Vehicles (HPVs) are recumbents—the rider has a recumbent position—which maximize power output and minimize drag (resistance). Essential to the safety of all riders are helmets, and both front and rear lights; locks protect against theft.

FRONT AND REAR LIGHTS

White front light

Red rear light

HELMET

Hard outer shell

Air vent

Polystyrene padding

Quick-release strap

EDDY MERCKX RACING BICYCLE

Saddle (seat)

Seat post

Cable guide

Saddle clamp

Seat-post bolt

Rear brake cable

Brake-block bolt

Brake block

Top tube (crossbar)

Steel frame

Seat stay

Seat tube

Down tube

Water-bottle cage

Front derailleur

Tire

Tire tread

Tire wall

Wheel rim

Freewheel sprocket

STEEL LOCK

Key

Hardened steel

Pick-proof lock

Rear derailleur

Pulley bolt

Tension pulley

Chain

Chain stay

Chain ring

Crank bolt

Crank

Spider

Pedal

Toe clip

CANNONDALE SH600 HYBRID BICYCLE

Gel-filled saddle

Lightweight frame

Straight handlebar

Brake bridge

Cantilever brake

All-surface tire

CANNONDALE ST1000 TOURING BICYCLE

Rear fender

Water bottle

Drop handlebar

Front fender

Rear pannier

Long chain stay

Large diameter aluminum tubing

Front pannier

Headset

Stem

Binder bolt

Handlebar

Front brake cable

Brake lever

Head tube

Brake pivot bolt

Brake pad

Fork

Hub quick-release lever

Spoke

Spoke nipple

Presta valve

Hub

ROSSIN ITALIAN TIME-TRIAL BICYCLE

Aero handlebar

Sloping top tube

Steep seat tube

Hollow disk wheel

Short head tube

Narrow tire

Clipless pedal

Tri-spoke wheel

WINDCHEETAH SL MARK VI "SPEEDY" RACING HPV BICYCLE

Fleecy headrest

Fiberglass bucket seat

Joystick

Brake lever

53-tooth chain ring

Clipless pedal

7-speed freewheel

Aluminum tubing

Drum brake

Extended racing chain

The motorcycle

THE MOTORCYCLE HAS EVOLVED from a motorized cycle—a basic bicycle with an engine—into a sophisticated, high-performance machine. In 1901, the Werner brothers established the most viable location for the engine, positioning it low in the center of the chassis (see pp. 364-365): the new Werner became the basis for the modern motorcycle. Motorcycles are used for many purposes—for commuting, delivering messages, touring, and racing—and different machines have been developed to suit the demands of different types of riders. The Vespa scooter, for instance, which is small-wheeled, economical, and easy-to-ride, was designed to meet the needs of the commuter. Sidecars provided transportation for the family until the arrival of cheap cars caused their popularity to decline. Serious riders generally favor larger capacity machines that are capable of greater performance and offer more comfort. Four-cylinder machines have been common since the Honda CB750 appeared in 1969. Despite advances in motorcycle technology, many riders are attracted to the traditional look of motorcycles like the twin-cylinder Harley-Davidson. Harley-Davidson Glides exploit the style of the classic American V-twin engine, where the cylinders are placed in a V-formation.

1901 WERNER MOTORCYCLE

Vacuum-operated inlet valve
Fuel tank
Bicycle-type saddle
Electric ignition control
Pulley rim rear brake
Inlet-over-exhaust (IOE) engine
Twisted rawhide drive belt
Alloy crankcase
Cast iron cylinder barrel

1988 HARLEY-DAVIDSON FLHS ELECTRA GLIDE

Backrest
Passenger seat
Passenger grab rail
Saddlebag
Luggage rack
Licence plate
Taillight
Indicator
Side reflector
Silencer
Silencer bracket
Disc brake
Crash bar
Exhaust clamp

1965 BMW R/60 WITH 1952 STEIB CHAIR

Handlebar
Headlight
Windshield
Adjustable link
Mirror
Sidecar
Side light
Fuel tank
Fender
Horizontally opposed engine
Sidecar chassis rail
Sidecar wheel
Sidecar lower link
Exhaust pipe
Square-section tire

FRONT VIEW

Fender
Canvas shroud
Speedometer
Ignition lock
Taillight
Grab rail
Tool tray
Lockable luggage trunk
Fender clamp
Suspension linkage
Bullet-shaped sidecar body
Drum brake
Knock-off wheel nut
SIDE VIEW
Long leading-link fork (Earles fork)

VELOCETTE OVERHEAD VALVE (OHV) ENGINE

Screw and lock nut tappet adjustor

Oil feed pipe

Inlet port

Spark plug lead

Cam follower

Magneto drive

Camshaft gear

Engine mounting bolt hole

Oil passageway

Crankcase

Oil pump

Mounting lug

Rocker arm

Rocker cover retaining bolt

Cylinder head

Exhaust port

Cylinder head

Combustion chamber

Cooling fin

Piston

Push rod

Valve lifter

Timing gear

Engine mounting bolt hole

Crankshaft

Nonreturn valve

Oil sump

Competition motorcycles

THERE ARE MANY TYPES of motorcycle sports and in each, a special machine has evolved to perform to specific requirements. Races take place on roads or tracks or "off-road," in fields, dirt tracks, and even the desert. "Grand Prix" world championships in roadracing exist for 125cc, 250cc, and 500cc classes, as well as for sidecars. The latest racing sidecars have more in common with racing cars than motorcycles. The rider and passenger operate within an all-enclosing, aerodynamic fairing. The Suzuki RGV500 shown here, like other Grand Prix machines, carries advertising, which promotes the manufacturer and helps to cover the cost of developing motorcycle technology. In Speedway, which originated in the U.S. in 1902, motorcycles operate without brakes or a gearbox. Off-road competition motorcycles have less emphasis on high power output. In Motocross, for example, which is held on rough terrain, they must have high ground clearance, flexible long-travel suspension, and tires with a chunky tread pattern, to allow them to grip in sand or mud.

1992 HUSQVARNA MOTOCROSS TC610

Throttle cable
Hand protector
Flexible plastic fender
Telescopic fork
Plastic guard
Axle
Knobby tire
Disc brake
Brake calliper
Handlebar brace
Radiator air vent
Overhead camshaft engine
Gear lever
Shock absorber
Alloy swing arm
Long seat
Racing number
Light-weight exhaust system
Disc brake
Shock absorber linkage

1992 SUZUKI RGV500
SIDE VIEW

Exhaust pipe
Racing number
Air vent
One-piece seat and tail unit
Minimal seat padding
Shock absorber
Arched alloy swing arm

KAYABA

Exhaust pipe
Vent
Silencer
Shock absorber mounting
Three-spoke alloy wheel
Exhaust pipe
Axle adjustor
Disc brake

Exhaust pipe
Handlebar
Foot rest
Rear brake pedal
Drive chain
Wide, slick tire

REAR VIEW

Brake pedal
Disc brake master cylinder
Lightweight alloy frame
Foot rest
Drive chain
Slick racing tire
Rear brake calliper

1981 WESLAKE SPEEDWAY

Throttle

Throttle cable

Carburetor cover

Fuel cap

Oil cap

Fender

Seat

Fuel tank

Fender

Wheel cover

Telescopic fork

Narrow tire

Wide tire

Brakeless wheel hub

Silencer

Foot rest

Oil pump

Overhead valve engine

Tubular open cradle frame

Fairing stay

Throttle cable

Fuel tank breather

Fuel tank

Throttle

Front brake lever

Telescopic fork

Fender

Slick racing tire

Sponsor's logo

Air vent

Braided steel hydraulic hose

Brake calliper

Carbon-fiber disc brake

Three-spoke alloy wheel

Quickly detachable (QD) fairing

1968 KIRBY BSA RACING SIDECAR

FRONT VIEW

Rev counter

Windshield

All-enclosing fairing

Fuel tank

Battery

Wheel guard

60

BSA

Square-section tire

Passenger windshield

Passenger grab rail

SIDE VIEW

Throttle cable

Exhaust pipe

Rev counter

All-enclosing fairing

60

Sidecar chassis

Engine

Fuel cap

Fiberglass wheel guard

Windshield

Racing number

Clutch lever

Fairing

34

Front brake lever

Radiator

Hydraulic brake hose

Fender

Axle

Slick tire

FRONT VIEW

369

SEA AND AIR

Ships of Greece and Rome

ROMAN ANCHOR

Stock

Shank

Palm

Acutely
angled
arm

Ring

Crown

IN THE EXPANSIVE EMPIRES OF GREECE AND ROME, powerful fleets were needed for battle, trade, and communication. Greek galleys were powered by a sail and many oars. A new armament, the embolos (ram), was fitted on to the galley bow. As ramming duels required fast and maneuverable boats, extra rows of oarsmen were added, culminating in the trireme. During the fifth and fourth centuries B.C., the trireme dominated the Mediterranean. It was powered by 170 oarsmen, each pulling one oar, and ranged on three levels, as the model opposite shows. The trireme also carried archers and soldiers for boarding enemy craft. Galleys were pulled out of the water when not in use, and were kept in dockyard ship-sheds. The merchant ships of the Greeks and Romans were mighty vessels, too. The full-bodied Roman corbita, for example, could hold up to 400 tons of cargo, such as spices, gems, silk, and animals. The construction of these boats was based on a stout hull with planking secured by mortice and tenon. Some of these ships made long trading voyages, sailing even as far as India. To make them easier to steer, corbitas set a foresail called an "artemon." It flew from a forward-leaning mast that was the forerunner of the long bowsprits carried by the great clipper ships of the 19th century.

**ATTIC VASE SHOWING
A GREEK GALLEY**

Roband
(rope band)

Ceruchi
(lift)

Double halyard   **ROMAN CORBITA**

Bullseye

Fore mast

Heraldic device

Antenna
(yard)

Buntline

Ring

Brace

Ruden
(brail line)

Artemon
(fore sail)

Fore stay

Oculus
(eye)

Anchor

Tabling

Sheet

Bolt rope

Prow

Windlass

Scala
(ladder)

Bronze mast
truck

Keraia (yard)

Catena
(riding bitt)

Kalos
(brailing
rope)

Ancorale
(anchor rope;
anchor rode)

Kubernetes
(helmsman)

Mast

Sternpost

Embolos
(ram;
beak)

Pedalia
(twin rudder)

Hatch board

Ophthalmos
(eye)

Oar port sleeve

Deck beam

Zosteres (rubbing strake)

Kope (oar)

Cargo hold

Masthead

Single clump block

Malus (mast)

Rope parrel

Bullet block

Antenna (yard)

Timber fairlead

Shroud

Leather reinforcing strip

Main double halyard

Main brace

Scala (ladder)

Velum (main sail)

Sheer pole

Deadeye

Lanyard

Poop break

Poop deck

Main sheet

Hole and peg joint

Poop deck house

Clavus (tiller)

Swan neck ornament

Stern balustrade

Ring bolt

Sternpost

Gubernator (helmsman)

Wale

Planking

Clew

Midships fence

Constratum (deck)

Bitt

Oar lanyard

Blade

Shaft

Gubernacula (rudders)

ROWING POSITIONS ON A GREEK TRIREME (TRIERE)
The katastroma (deck) has been removed from this model to show the positions taken by oarsmen on a trireme.

Thranite (upper level oarsman)

Zygian (middle level oarsman)

Deck rail

Tropeter (leather grommet)

Paraxeiresia (outrigger)

Kope (oar)

Stanchion

Zugon (thwart; seat)

Thalamian (lower level oarsman)

Hyperesion (oarsman's cushion)

Pine hull

MORTICE-AND-TENON FASTENINGS FOR HULL PLANKS

Mortice

Gomphoi (dowel)

Tenon

Hull plank

373

Viking ships

IN THE DARK AGES (roughly 500 A.D. to 1000 A.D.) the longships of Scandinavia were among the most feared sights for people of northern Europe. The Vikings launched raids from Scandinavia every summer in longships equipped with a single steering oar on the right, or "steerboard" side (hence, "starboard"). A longboat had one row of oars on each side and a single sail. The hull was clinker-built, with overlapping planks. Prowheads adorned fighting ships during war campaigns. The longship was also used for coastal travel. The karv below was probably built as transport for an important family, while the smaller faering was a rowing boat only. The fleet of William of Normandy that invaded England in 1066 owed much to the Viking boat building tradition, and has been depicted in the Bayeux Tapestry (right). Seals of port towns and royal courts through the ages provide a record of contemporary ship design. The seal opposite shows a European craft from somewhat later than the Viking period. Fighting platforms, or castles, and the addition of more masts and sails changed the character of the medieval ship. Note also that the steering oar has been replaced by a centered rudder.

BOAT BUILDERS' TOOLS

Shave

Broad axe

Breast auger

Sheer

Master shipwright

Stempost

Hood end

Keel

T-handle auger

Axe

Strake

Tree cut for planking

Roband

Leather diagonal reinforcement

Square sail of homespun yarn

Leech (leach)

Clew

Tye halyard

Foot

Zoomorphic head

Eye

Tooth

Braiding

Serpentine neck

Lozenge-shaped recess

Rectangular cross-band

DRAGON PROWHEAD

Snake-tail ornament

VIKING KARV (COASTER)

Sternpost

Tiller

Boss (rudder pivot)

Steering oar (side rudder)

Oar

Starboard (steerboard) side

FAERING (VIKING ROWING BOAT)

Grommet

Tiller

Knee

Grommet

Plank scarf

Prow

Clench nail

Kabe (oar pivot)

Stepped sternpost

Stepped stempost

Pivot

Sheer strake

Side rudder

Double-ended hull

Oar

Keel

Thwart (seat)

Masthead

Masthead pulley for tye halyard

Yard

Head

Head earing

COURT SEAL SHOWING A THREE-MASTED, SQUARE-RIGGED SHIP

Parrel

Weaponry

Banner/ windvane

Topcastle

Main mast

Furled forecourse

Furled lateen mizzen sail

Jack staff

Mizzen mast

Fore mast

Aftercastle

Forecastle

Rudder

Stempost

Gudgeon strap

Anchor

Main sail

Leechline

Mast

Snake-head ornament

Sail foot control line

Open, double-ended hull

Starboard main sheet

Stempost

Oar port

Scroll work

Clinker-built oak planking (overlapping planking)

Stowage crutch for oars

Clench nail

Medieval warships and traders

FROM THE 16TH CENTURY, SHIPS WERE BUILT WITH A NEW FORM OF HULL, constructed with carvel (edge-to-edge) planking. Warships of the time, like King Henry VIII of England's Mary Rose, boasted awesome fire power. This ship carried both long-range bronze cannon, and short-range, anti personnel guns in iron. Elsewhere, ships took on a multiformity of shapes. Dhows transported slaves from East Africa to Arabia, their fore-and-aft rigged lateen sails allowing them to sail close to the wind around the lands of the Indian Ocean. The Chinese sailed to East Africa and Arabia in junks, trading goods that were carried in watertight compartments. New astronomical tools helped medieval sailors to find their way. Cross-staves and astrolabes were used to measure the altitude of the sun or stars. One of the cross-pieces was slid along the staff of the cross-stave—which was graduated in degrees of altitude—until its top aligned with the celestial body and its base with the horizon. The sighting rule of the astrolabe was simply lined up with a known body, and its altitude read from marks on the metal disk. Sundials used the shadow of the sun to show sailors the time of day.

DHOW

Main yard
Furled lateen main sail
Mizzen yard
Parrel
Furled lateen mizzen sail
Main mast
Mizzen mast
Shroud
Parrel tackle
Tiller
Stem head
Rudder
Eye
Raking stempost

JUNK

Su-wei (fourth mast)
Topsail
Chung-ta-wei (main mast)
Wei-wei (mizzen mast)
Halyard
Erh-wei (second mast)
Sail batten
T'on-wei (port fore-mast)
Rudder head
Lug sail
Transom
Rudder
Quarterdeck house
Cargo hatch
Oar
Grapnel-type anchor

SAILING WARSHIP

Fore topsail yard
Fore topmast
Fore topcastle
Lift
Fore yard
Fore mast
Ratline
Shroud
Fore stay
Woolding
Fore topmast stay
Bowsprit
Forecastle
Sprit yard
Forecastle castle-deck gunport
Beakhead
Rigging rail
Chain wale (channel)
Hawse hole
Anchor cable
Stempost

Main topgallant mast

Main topmast topcastle

Main topmast stay

Main topmast

Main topcastle

Lift

Main yard

Parrel

Tye

Brace

Jeer

Main stay

Mizzen mast

Mizzen yard

Main mast

Swifting tackle

Aftercastle castle-deck gunport

Upper deck gunport

Lid

Gangway

Gun carriage

Main topgallant yard

Main top yard

Mizzen topmast

Mizzen top yard

Mizzen topcastle

Lift

Bonaventure top yard

Bonaventure topmast

Bonaventure topcastle

Bonaventure yard

Bonaventure mast

Aftercastle

Outrigger

Chain wale (channel)

Deadeye

Transom

Rudder

Sternpost

Keel

Blindage (removable archery screen)

Wale

Main deck gunport

Carvel planking

Port bower anchor

CROSS-STAVE (CROSS-STAFF)

90 degree cross-piece (transversary)

Clamp

60 degree cross-piece

30 degree cross-piece

10 degree cross-piece (dutch shoe)

Boxwood staff

Altitude scale in degrees and minutes

Ocular end

SUNDIAL

Gnomon

Style of the gnomon (edge)

Needle

Pivot

Hour line

Dial

ASTROLABE

Swivel suspension ring

Graduated ring

Scale of degrees

Pivot

Alidade (sighting rule)

Bottom ballast

Scribed arc decoration

The expansion of sail

By THE 18TH CENTURY, SAILING SHIPS had become fast and effective floating fortresses. The navies of the north European powers competed with each other by building heavily-armed fighting ships called "men-of-war." The distinctive round stern of the ship below, with its open gallery, balcony, and elaborate wood carving is typical of the period. Hulls around this time were semicircular in cross section, although many boat designers were soon to return to the V-shaped hulls used by the Vikings. Ships of the period carried more sail than ever before. A labyrinth of rigging supported the masts and yards from which the profusion of square sails were set. Ships grew higher as extra masts were fitted above the lower masts, and the bowsprit became longer, to allow the ship to carry staysails, spritsails, and jibs. Ships went into battle in single file, so that broadsides from the multiple decks of guns would have maximum effect. Ships were classified by rates, the rating of a vessel depending on how many guns it had. A first rate ship had more than 100 guns. The guns fired solid round shot, usually made of iron.

BOW

Gilded truck

Main topgallant mast

Main topgallant shroud

WOODEN SAILING SHIP

Bolster

Trestle trees

Main topmast

Main topmast backstay

Main topmast shroud

Cap

Main top

Masthead

Mizzen topmast

Mizzen topmast stay

Mizzen topmast shroud

Mizzen top

Main top rail

Lift

Hounds

Futtock shroud

Mizzen yard

Mizzen backstay

Vang

Fiddle block

Mizzen shrouds

Mizzen mast

Mizzen stay

Taffrail

Poop rail

Main shrouds

Main mast

Brace

Lift

Foot rope

Studding sail boom

Main top rail

Studding sail yard (stuns'l yard)

Jacob's ladder

Rope preventer

Rudder chain

Rudder

Sternpost

Pintle strap

Gudgeon strap

Wash cant

Knee of the head

Hawse hole

Ship's wheel   Binnacle box   Keel   Channel   Chains   Step   Boat slide

SAIL PATTERN OF A 74-GUN SHIP

Main topgallant stay

Fore topgallant mast

Fore topgallant backstay

Gilded truck

Fore topgallant stay

Mouse and collar

Main topmast stay

Fore topmast shroud

Main topmast preventer stay

Fore topmast backstay

Ratline

Fore topmast

Fore top

Fore shroud

Main stay

Mainstay tackle

Fore hatch tackle

Fore topmast stay

Fore topmast preventer stay

Fore mast

Rope woolding

Fore stay

Cap

Bee

Fish davit

Mainrail head

Anchor buoy

Jibboom

Truck

Jack staff

Top spritsail yard

Spritsail yard

Foot rope

Bowsprit

Bobstay

Figurehead

Rail

Trailboard

Draft mark

Bower anchor

Tallow coating

Capstan *Clewline* *Gunport* *Gun* *Gripe*

Mizzen topgallant sail

Mizzen topsail

Mizzen course

Main topgallant sail

Fore topgallant sail

Fore topgallant sail

Fore topsail

Inner jib

Outer jib

Main course

Main topsail

Fore course

Fore staysail

Top spritsail

Spritsail

STERN

Main topgallant yard

Fore topgallant yard

Main topsail yard

Yardarm

Fore topsail yard

Main yard

Fore yard

Mizzen topmast yard

Stern lantern

Captain's cabin (great cabin)

Upper gallery

Port

Balcony

Stern quarter gallery

A ship of the line

THE 74-GUN THIRD-RATER WAS A MAINSTAY of British and French battlefleets in the late 18th and early 19th centuries. (The biggest ships in the fledgling American navy of the time were 44-gun frigates.) The length of such a man-of-war was determined by the number of guns needed for each deck, allowing room for crews to man them. The gun deck of this vessel was about 170 ft (52 m) long. Her decks had to be strong to carry the weight of the guns. The deck planks have been removed in the model below to illustrate the number of beams needed to make the hull strong enough. Only timber with perfect grain was used. The upper deck was open at the waist, but forward and aft were officers' cabins. The forecastle (foc's'l) and quarterdeck carried light guns and provided platforms for handling the rigging and for reconnaissance. The ship's longboats, or launches, were carried on skids between the gangways.

LONGBOAT

UPPER DECK OF A 74-GUN SHIP

BOW

Figurehead

Headboard

Main rail

Middle rail

Lower rail

Head rail

Supporter

Cat block

Eiking

Cheek

Catted anchor

Riband

Hawse piece

Side step

Stempost

Deadwood

Main wale

Frame

Hawse hole

STERN

Cove

Taffrail

Screen bulkhead

Balcony

Upper counter rail

Drop

Side counter timber

Lower counter rail

Counter timber

Tuck

Gunport lid

Tuck rail

Filling transom

After fashion piece

Wing transom

Cant frame

Timber under transom

Side step

Eye bolt

Main bitts

Ledge (batten)

Hatch coaming/ shot garland

Spirketting

Backstay stool

Companion ladder

Master's sea cabin

Mizzen mast hole

Great cabin (captain's cabin)

Channel

Coaming

Pilaster

Ledge (batten)

Screen bulkhead

Standard knee

Main mast hole

Mast partners

Grating

Gunport lid

Lodging knee

Rail at break of poop deck

Gunport drip (eyebrow; rigol)

Mizzen bitts

Clerk's cabin

Poop rail

Necking

Wardroom

Upper finishing

Stern carving

Taffrail

Quarter gallery

Quarterdeck

Poop deck

Rigging

MOST SAILING SHIPS HAVE TWO TYPES OF RIGGING. Standing rigging—kept taut by turnbuckles or old-fashioned lanyards and deadeyes—refers to the ropes, wires, and chains that support the masts and yards (horizontal spars). Running rigging, which includes types of block and tackle, halyards, and sheets, is used to hoist, lower, or trim sails.

BOWSPRIT AND JIBBOOM

Outer jib stay

Inner jib stay

Inner jib tack

Bowsprit cap

Fore topmast staysail tack

Upper deadeye

Lower deadeye

Chain plate

Whisker boom

Fore stay

Jibboom

Butterfly plate

Bowsprit

Boom guy block

Foot rope

Spear

Martingale backrope

Martingale (dolphin striker)

Lizard

Chain bobstay

Handle

Lug

Shaft

OTHER RIGGING FITTINGS

BELAYING PIN

MAST BAND

STANDING BLOCK

Arse (breech)

Running part

SHACKLE

Lug

Shoulder

Eye

Crown

Crown

Soft eye

Served eye splice

Screw thread

Shank

Shoulder

Eye

Swivel shackle

Shell

Hauling part (fall)

Becket

Standing part

SHACKLE PIN

RIGGING TOOLS

Sailmaker's whipping

BLOCK AND TACKLE (PURCHASE)

Flemish coil (cheesing)

RIGGER'S GAUGE FOR MEASURING THE DIAMETER OF ROPE OR WIRE

Fore royal stay

Flying jib tack

Outer jib tack

Outer martingale stay

Middle martingale stay

Inner
martingale
stay

Eye

SCORED BULLSEYE FAIRLEAD

Eye

Strap

SHEET LEAD

Base

RUNNING BLOCK

Double rope
becket

**DUTCH TRIPLE
FIDDLE BLOCK**

Flat seizing

Swallow

Strop

Sheave

Back   Shank

HOOK

Crown

SPLICING FID

ROPE SERVING MALLET

Fixed   Bill
lug

Cheek

Pin cover
plate

**HEAVER FOR
WIRE SERVING**

**HOLLOW SPIKE
FOR WIRE**

MARLINESPIKE

PRICKERS

**LANYARD AND
DEADEYES**

**TURNBUCKLE
(RIGGING SCREW)**

Leather
parceling

Shroud

Marline
serving

Turk's head

Flat wire seizing

Hitched
hauling end

Solid heart
thimble

Cotter pin

**UPPER
DEADEYE**

Fork end

Tail

Standing part

Right hand
screw

LANYARD

Open body

Left hand
screw

**LOWER
DEADEYE**

Safe working
load mark

Seizing

Grooving
(scone)

Shoulder

Binding

Face

Bolt

Eye

Nut

Crown

Sails

THERE ARE TWO MAIN TYPES OF SAILS: Old-fashioned square sails hang from yards at right angles to the mast, and are powerful drivers with following winds; fore-and-aft sails are set parallel to the length of the boat, with the luff (leading edge) of the sail attached to a mast or a stay. They are more efficient for all-round sailing, and almost all modern sailboats are rigged this way. Some fore-and-aft sails have a gaff at the head; Marconi-rig sails are pointed at the top (below). The bottom (foot) of the sail is on a boom. Sails are made of strips of cloth sewn together. Cotton and flax are traditional sail materials but synthetic fabrics are now more often used.

TOP OF A MARCONI SAIL

Seizing LUFF (LEADING EDGE) *Luff slide* *Bolt rope* *Head*

Round thimble

Rope strand

Grommet

Head cringle

LEECH (LEACH)

Sharp point

Flat seam

SERVING MALLET

Groove for spunyarn (twine)

Synthetic flax (duradon)

Flatboard

NEEDLES AND SAIL TWINE

Handle

Tabling

Sail twine

Grip

Rat's tail

Needle packet

Needle

SAILMAKER'S FID

SAILCLOTHS

KEVLAR ON FLEX FILM

HEAVYWEIGHT NYLON CLOTH

SAIL HOOK

SAILMAKER'S PALM

Strap

Thumbhole

Crown

Cowhide face

MYLAR

NYLON AND SILICON CLOTH

Bill

Shank

Metal needle pad

SYNTHETIC FLAX (DURADON)

DACRON

BEESWAX

Handle

SAILMAKER'S MALLET

Cheek

Whipping

Hide grip

Seizing

Groove made by thread

SAILMAKING TOOLS

Copper face

Mizzen gaff topsail

Main sail

Main gaff topsail

Fore staysail

Jib

Mizzen sail

KETCH

Lugger topsail

Lug foresail

Lug mainsail

LUGGER

Fisherman's staysail

Main gaff topsail

Fore sail

Fore staysail

Main sail

Jib

GAFF-HEADED SCHOONER

FORE-AND-AFT SAILING RIGS

SAILS AND RUNNING RIGGING OF A DOUBLE TOPSAIL SCHOONER

Upper topsail lift

Lower topsail brace

Main topsail halyard

Fore upper topsail

Triatic stay

Flying jib halyard

Foot rope

Upper topsail brace

Outer jib halyard

Fore peak halyard

Lower topsail clewline

Fore yard lift

Fore lower topsail

Inner jib halyard

Fore throat halyard

Fore staysail halyard

Fore sail

Mast hoop (parrel)

Inner jib downhaul

Outer jib downhaul

Outer jib sheet

Flying jib sheet

Inner jib sheet

Flying jib downhaul

Yard

Head

Gaff

Luff

Boom

Foot

Flying jib

Outer jib

Reef point

Inner jib

Fore staysail

Fore staysail sheet

385

Mooring and anchoring

In most harbors and ports, a ship can moor (tie up or "make fast") directly to a pier, wharf, or quay (pronounced "key"), using heavy hawsers and docking lines attached to bitts or bollards. Hawsers are tied to each other with knots called bends. In open water, however, ships that are not under way must drop an anchor, which attaches the ship securely to the seabed. The earliest anchors were simply heavy stones. Later, various anchor designs were developed for different uses. Most small vessels today use Danforth or plow anchors, which dig deeply into the sea bottom. A permanent mooring is an anchor set in the bottom to which a ship can tie up without using its own anchor. On old sailing ships, anchors were pulled up, or "weighed," by sailors pushing against bars that turned a capstan, which wound up the anchor cable. Now, most capstans are powered by electricity.

STONE ANCHOR (KILLICK)

Rope hole

TYPES OF ANCHOR

CLOSE-STOWING ANCHOR

CQR ANCHOR (PLOW ANCHOR)

BRITISH ADMIRALTY ANCHOR TYPE ACII

YACHTSMAN'S ANCHOR (KEDGE)

STOCKLESS ANCHOR

MUSHROOM ANCHOR (PERMANENT MOORING ANCHOR)

End link | **ANCHOR CHAIN** | Common link | Patent link

SHACKLE, SWIVELS, AND LINK

DANFORTH ANCHOR

Shank

Crown

Bolt — Lug

Screw thread

GALVANIZED "D" SHACKLE | **MOORING SWIVEL** | **CHAIN SWIVEL** | **SCREW LINK**

Pea (bill)

Fluke (palm)

Throat

Stock

Tripping palm

Crown

TWIN BOLLARDS (BITTS), WITH RAKED PILLARS AND A HAWSER (HEAVY ROPE)

Flat

Rim

Base

BERTHING ROPES (HAWSERS)

Stern line

Ship

Bitts

Bow line

Quayside

Stern breast line

After spring

Fore spring

Bow breast line

Bollard

Bar hole (pigeon hole)

Cap

Upper head (drumhead)

Strengthening chock

Barrel

Trenail (treenail)

Strengthening chock

Pawl slot

Whelp

Lignum vitae bearing

MOORING ROPE BENDS

HAWSER BEND (TWO BIGHTS WITH DOUBLE HALF HITCHES)

Standing part

Seizing

CARRICK BEND

Seizing

Seizing

SINGLE SHEET BEND (BECKET BEND)

Bare end

Standing part

Thin rope

Thick rope

Outboard end

Three-strand hawser belayed with figure of eight turns

Pillar

Foundry plug

Horn

Bolt hole

Cross piece

Bitter end (inboard end)

WOOD CAPSTAN WITH A VERTICAL SPINDLE

Tapered spindle

Pin

Ropes and knots

ALL KINDS OF ROPES ARE USED AT SEA, from thin twines and yarn to thick hawsers. Synthetic fibers are much in use today. Nylon ropes stretch, and so are ideal for anchoring; polyester (frequently called by the trade name Dacron) has little stretch and is used for halyards and sheets. Different knots have different uses. Knots that join two ropes are often called bends; hitches join a rope to another object. Ropes, usually called "lines" on board ship, can also be joined by seizing (lashing them together side by side) or splicing (unraveling the ends and weaving them together).

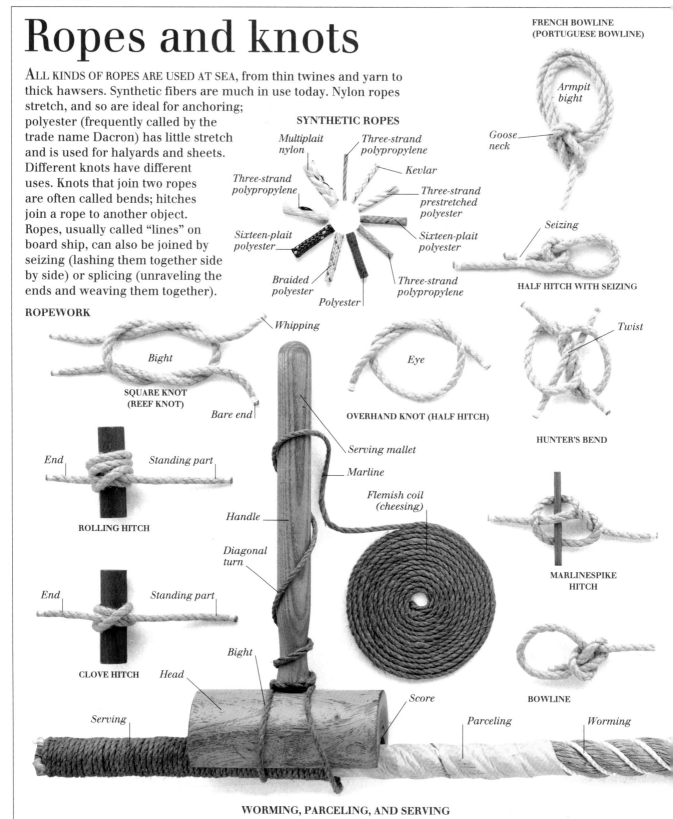

FRENCH BOWLINE (PORTUGUESE BOWLINE)

Armpit bight

Goose neck

Seizing

HALF HITCH WITH SEIZING

SYNTHETIC ROPES

Multiplait nylon

Three-strand polypropylene

Kevlar

Three-strand polypropylene

Three-strand prestretched polyester

Sixteen-plait polyester

Sixteen-plait polyester

Braided polyester

Three-strand polypropylene

Polyester

ROPEWORK

Whipping

Bight

SQUARE KNOT (REEF KNOT)

Bare end

Eye

OVERHAND KNOT (HALF HITCH)

Twist

HUNTER'S BEND

End

Standing part

ROLLING HITCH

Serving mallet

Marline

Flemish coil (cheesing)

MARLINESPIKE HITCH

End

Standing part

CLOVE HITCH

Head

Handle

Diagonal turn

Bight

Score

BOWLINE

Serving

Parceling

Worming

WORMING, PARCELING, AND SERVING

THUMB KNOT

SPANISH BOWLINE

**ROUND SEIZING
(FLAT SEIZING)**

DOUBLE CARRICK BEND

End

Frapped
turn

Heaving
line knot

LIGHTERMAN'S HITCH

HEAVING LINE BEND

Standing
part

**JURY MAST KNOT
(MAST HEAD BEND)**

**SHEET BEND
(BECKET BEND)**

**MANHARNESS KNOT
(BUTTERFLY KNOT;
ARTILLERY LOOP)**

Flemish coil (cheesing)

Marlinespike

Jaw

HEAVING LINE

PINNED SHEEPSHANK

Rat tail

Hawser laid three-strand manila
rope with right-handed lay

389

Paddle wheels and propellers

THE INVENTION OF THE STEAM ENGINE IN THE 18TH CENTURY made mechanically driven ships fitted with paddle wheels or propellers a viable alternative to sails. Paddle wheels have fixed or feathered floats, and the model shown below features both types. Feathered floats give more propulsive power than fixed floats because they are almost upright at all times in the water. Paddle wheels were superseded by the propeller on oceangoing vessels in the mid-19th century. Propellers are more efficient, work better in rough water, and are less vulnerable in collisions. The first propellers were two-bladed, but later three- and four-bladed versions are more powerful; the shape and pitch of the blades have also been refined over the years. At the beginning of the 18th century, tillers were replaced on many larger ships by the ship's wheel as a means of steering.

SHIP'S WHEEL

- King spoke handle
- Handle
- Spoke
- Rim plate
- Felloe (rim section)
- Maker's name
- Nave plate
- Nave

PADDLE WHEEL WITH FIXED FLOATS

- Wrist pin
- Limb
- Fixed float
- Hub
- Deck beam

OSCILLATING STEAM ENGINE

- Slip eccentric for slide valve
- Ahead/astern controls
- Slide valve
- Main crank

THREE-BLADED PROPELLER

- Blade
- Tapered shaft hole
- Hub
- Keyway

- Strut
- Frame
- Piston rod (tail rod)
- Stuffing box
- Oscillating cylinder
- Bottom plate (bedplate)
- Slide valve rod
- Control platform

PROPELLER ACTION

- Pitch
- Propeller blade tip trace
- Blade
- Propeller diameter
- Hub
- Propeller hub trace

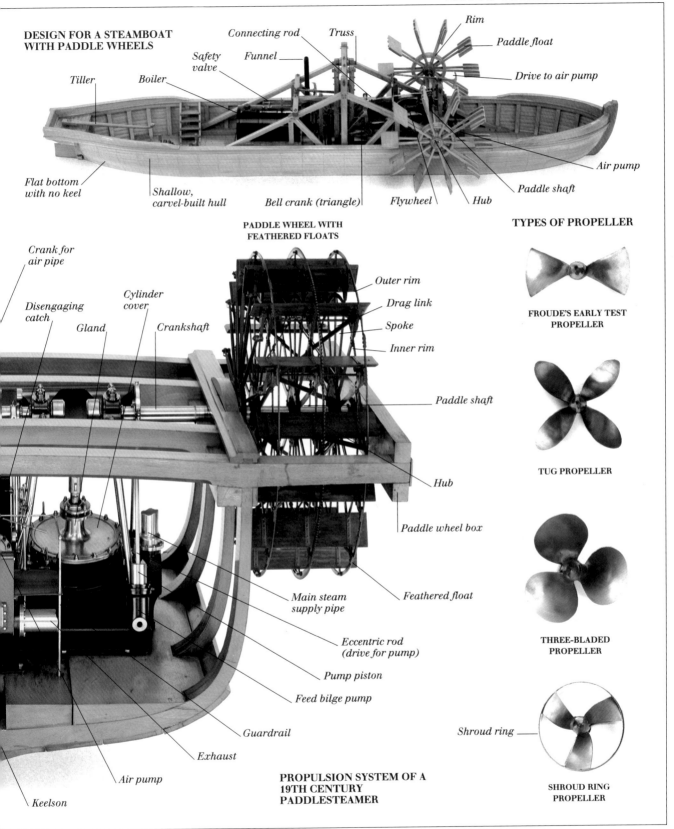

DESIGN FOR A STEAMBOAT WITH PADDLE WHEELS

Rim

Connecting rod

Truss

Paddle float

Safety valve

Funnel

Drive to air pump

Tiller

Boiler

Air pump

Flat bottom with no keel

Shallow, carvel-built hull

Bell crank (triangle)

Flywheel

Hub

Paddle shaft

PADDLE WHEEL WITH FEATHERED FLOATS

TYPES OF PROPELLER

Crank for air pipe

Outer rim

Drag link

Disengaging catch

Cylinder cover

Spoke

FROUDE'S EARLY TEST PROPELLER

Gland

Crankshaft

Inner rim

Paddle shaft

TUG PROPELLER

Hub

Paddle wheel box

Main steam supply pipe

Feathered float

THREE-BLADED PROPELLER

Eccentric rod (drive for pump)

Pump piston

Feed bilge pump

Shroud ring

Guardrail

Exhaust

Air pump

PROPULSION SYSTEM OF A 19TH CENTURY PADDLESTEAMER

SHROUD RING PROPELLER

Keelson

391

Anatomy of an iron ship

IRON PARTS WERE USED IN WOODEN SHIPS AS EARLY AS 1675, often in the same form as the wooden parts that they replaced. Eventually, as on the tea clipper Cutty Sark (below), iron standing rigging was found to be stronger than the traditional rope. The first "ironclads" were warships whose wooden hulls were protected by iron armor plates. Later ironclads actually had iron hulls. The model opposite is based on the British warship HMS Warrior, launched in 1860, the first battleship built entirely of iron. The plan of an iron paddlesteamer (bottom), built somewhat later, shows that the craft had the masts and bowsprit of a sailing ship; but it also boasted a steam propulsion plant amid ships that turned two side paddlewheels. Early iron plates were painstakingly riveted together (below), but by the 1940s, steel vessels were welded together, whole sections at a time. The Liberty ships built in America during World War II are prime examples of such "production-line" vessels.

Steel yard

Iron wire stay

Steel lower mast

Steel bowsprit

Steel

TEA CLIPPER

Forged iron anchor

Wooden planking with copper sheathing

RIVETED PLATES

Pan head rivet

Plate

Seam

Button head rivet (snap head)

Gun section

LIBERTY SHIP

Accommodation section

Cargo derrick

Weld line

Stern section

Midships section

Cargo hold

Bow section

PLAN OF AN IRON PADDLESTEAMER

Steering position

Steering gear

Stern

Vertical frame ladder

Mast step

Rudder

Rudder post

Heel of rudder post

Mizzen mast

Poop deck

Guardrail

Lounge

Deck lantern

Binnacle

State room

Main mast

Steam whistle

After funnel

Skylight

Eccentric

Crankshaft

Guardrail

Paddle wheel

Connecting rod

Bar keel

Afterpeak

Cabin

Stern framing

Tank

Main mast step

Donkey boiler

Box boiler

Foundation

Reversing wheel

Bottom plate

Side lever

Cylinder

CUTAWAY SECTION OF AN "IRONCLAD"

Bulwark cap

Waterway

Deck planking

Scupper

Upper deck stringer (tie) plate

Bulwark

Upper sheer strake

Teak backing

Topside strake

Wrought iron armor plate

Main sheer strake

Main deck tie plate

Lower deck tie plate

Frame

Lighting hole

Angle bar (I bar)

Box sister keelson

Bilge stringer

Bilge strake

Bilge keelson

Side keelson

Bottom plating

Garboard strake

Keel

Upper deck beam

Upper deck pillar (stanchion)

Main deck beam

Main deck pillar (stanchion)

Lower deck beam

Pillar (hold stanchion)

Centerline keelson

Limber hole

Floor

Forward funnel

Fore mast

Ventilator cowl

Skylight

Capstan

Chimney

Hatch

Bowsprit

Main deck

Hawse pipe

Stem

Beam

Chain locker

Bulkhead stiffener

Deep floor

Forefoot

Smoke box

'Tween decks ladder

Lower deck

Forepeak

Deck beam

Combustion chamber

Cabin

Center girder

393

The battleship

IN THE EARLY YEARS OF THE 20TH CENTURY, sea warfare—attacking enemy vessels or defending a ship—was revolutionized by the introduction of Dreadnought-type battleships like the Brazilian vessel below. These new ships combined the latest advances in steam propulsion, gunnery, and armor plating. Their gun turrets, protected by armor up to 12 in (30 cm) thick, were designed to fire shells over great distances. The ship shown here, the Minas Geraes, was 500 ft (152 m) long. It was built at Elswick, England, and launched in 1908. Its chief armament was of 12 in (30 cm) guns (firing shells with a 12 in diameter). Other naval weapons developed in the 20th century include the torpedo—as portrayed on the upper cigarette card (right). This was a self-propelled underwater missile, often steered by gyro-control. Depth charges were designed in the First World War for use against submerged U-boats. They are canisters filled with explosives that are detonated by depth-sensitive pistols. The lower cigarette card shows depth charges being fired by a "thrower," fired from a torpedo tube, and rolled from the stern. Ship's shields were fitted to warships from the late 19th century onwards. The shield shown opposite depicts a traditional ship's cannon.

20TH CENTURY WEAPONRY

Torpedo tube
Sight
Warhead

TORPEDOES

DEPTH CHARGES

Side-thrown canister

Stern-rolled canister

Torpedo-fired canister

BRAZILIAN BATTLESHIP

Rangefinder
Light screen
Compass
Compass and rangefinder platform
Ship's wheel
Navigating bridge
Conning tower
Captain's shelter/ chart house
Weather shutter for gun
12 in (30 cm) gun
Skylight

Forward funnel
Lifeboat

"F" turret

Boat handling derrick
Gunnery spotting top
Purchase wire
Searchlight
Searchlight platform
Leading block
Tripod mast
Boat winch

Arms of Brazil
Jack staff

Stem (false ram bow)
Porthole
Belt armor
Forward accommodation ladder
Sighting hood
"A" turret
Turret barbette
Open gun mounting
4.7 in (12 cm) gun
Steam launch
Guest boat boom

SHIP'S SHIELD

Rope molding

Muzzle molding

Swell of muzzle

Chase

Reinforce

Ogee

Astragal

Trunnion

Lion crest

Radio antenna

Upper wireless and telegraphy yard (Upper W/T yard)

Topgallant mast

Wireless and telegraphy yard (W/T yard)

Lower yard

Signal gear

Ladder way

Lifeboat davit

Brake slip

Davit

Clump cathead

Breakwater

Guardrail

Cable holder

Hawser fairlead

Anchor chain

Sheet anchor

Bollard

Starboard bower anchor

Hawse pipe

Boat boom

Towing fairlead

Port bower anchor

Exhaust pipe

Searchlight

Searchlight platform

After compass platform

After bridge

3 pound (1.3 kg) gun ("three pounder")

"X" turret

"Y" turret

Officer's accommodation ladder

Vedette boat

Gig

After funnel

Funnel stay

Davit for whaler

Flagmast

Whaler

Stern walk

Scarph

Propeller

Stern anchor

"P" turret

Bilge keel

Torpedo net boom

Propeller shaft boss

Propeller shaft

Ash chute

Hen coop

Gun battery

Turret roof rail

Torpedo net

Rudder

Life buoy

395

Frigates and submarines

FROM THE MID-19TH CENTURY, ARMORED SHIPS provided a new challenge to enemy craft. In response, huge revolving gun turrets were developed. These could shoot in any direction, were loaded quickly from the breech, and fired exploding shells. Today's fighting ships, like the Royal Navy frigate opposite, also carry missile launchers and helicopters. Submarines operate underwater, have great speed, and some can fire missiles while submerged. A nuclear sub can operate for several years without refueling.

Stabilizer fin

Aft hydroplane

Propeller

Lower rudder

Rangefinder

Look out periscope

Local control cabinet

Breech wheel

Breech block

Loading arm

Slide locking lever

Slide

Sighting hood

Recoil cylinder

Elevating wheel

Guide for gun loading cage

Blast bag (breeches)

Rammer lever

Gun loading cage

Floor of gun house

Turret roller

Training rack gearing

Roller path

Working chamber

GUN TURRET
In this turret for two 15 in (37 cm) guns carried on the British "Queen Elizabeth class" battleship, shells are carried in a hoisting cage. The shell is rammed into the gun, followed by the propellant (charge). Once the breech is closed, the gun is ready for firing. The whole operation requires around 70 sailors.

Training gear

Rammer

Waiting position

Roller path support

Floor

"Walking pipe" (hydraulic supply)

Barbette (armor)

Main hoisting cage

Turret trunk

Cordite handling room

Cordite supply shuttle

Ensign staff

Lynx helicopter

SONAR torpedo decoy

Cordite case

Rudder

Practice projectile

High-explosive projectile

Shell bogie

Shell room

Hydraulic grab

Shell-handling gear

Variable pitch propeller

Accommodation ladder

Steam pipework

Machinery raft

Main turbine

Machinery control room

Switchboard room

Snorkel mast

Conning tower

Periscope

Electronic warfare mast

Periscope

Control room

Sonar room

Galley

Officers' mess

ROYAL NAVY NUCLEAR "HUNTER-KILLER" SUBMARINE

SONAR transducer array

Main engine steam condenser

Distiller

Diesel motor compartment

Reactor space

Wireless office

Junior enlisted men's mess

Carbon dioxide scrubber compartment

Torpedo compartment

Senior enlisted men's mess

Torpedo tube

Forward hydroplane

Junior enlisted men's bunk space

Muzzle

Barrel

6 in (15 cm) SHELL
This shell is designed to burst in the air above its target.

Driving band

SHELL CASE

Bursting charge (explosive)

Flash tube

Body

Wooden packing

Expelling plate

CROSS SECTION OF THE SHELL

Transit plug

Bullet (shrapnel)

FRIGATE HMS ALACRITY

Surveillance RADAR

Navigation/helicopter control RADAR antenna

RADAR for gunnery and missile control

Mast

Aerial rig

Signaling lamp

Jack staff

Seacat missile launcher

Motor whaler

Vent

Stern gallery

Funnel

Aerial

Oerlikon gun position

Enclosed bridge

Exocet missile launcher

Gun turret

4.5 in (11 cm) gun

F174

Anchor

RADAR for gunnery and missile control

Stabilizer

Liferaft cylinder

Signal flag compartment

Reel

Fairlead

Draft mark

Anti-submarine torpedo tube

Triple "chaff" rocket launcher

Bilge keel

Pennant number

Porthole

SONAR bulge

Bollard

Breakwater

Pioneers of flight

FLIGHT HAS FASCINATED MANKIND for centuries, and countless unsuccessful flying machines have been designed. The first successful flight was made by the French Montgolfier brothers in 1783, when they flew a balloon over Paris. The next major advance was the development of gliders, notably by the Englishman Sir George Cayley, who in 1845 designed the first glider to make a sustained flight, and by the German Otto Lilienthal, who became known as the world's first pilot because he managed to achieve controlled flights. However, powered flight did not become a practical possibility until the invention of lightweight, gas-driven internal-combustion engines at the end of the 19th century. Then, in 1903, the American brothers Orville and Wilbur Wright made the first powered flight in their Wright Flyer biplane, which used a four-cylinder, gas-driven engine. Aircraft design advanced rapidly, and in 1909 the Frenchman Louis Blériot made his pioneering flight across the English Channel (see pp. 400-401). The American Glenn Curtiss also achieved several "firsts" in his Model-D Pusher and its variants, most notably winning the world's first competition for airspeed at Reims in 1909.

FRONT VIEW OF WRIGHT FLYER, 1903

Biplane elevator

Pusher propeller (rear-mounted propeller)

Chain drive to starboard propeller

Fuel tank

Propeller-shaft bracing strut

Offset pilot's cradle

Takeoff and landing skid

Side-mounted engine to balance pilot's weight

SIDE VIEW OF CURTISS MODEL-D PUSHER, 1911

Nine-cylinder Salmson radial engine

Pusher propeller (rear-mounted propeller)

Aileron operating arm

Wing strut

Fuel filler cap

Oil filler cap

Body cradle that pivots to control ailerons

Fuel and oil tank

Rudder control wheel

Elevator wire for diving

Seatbelt

Control column

Throttle

Nose wheel brake

Footrest

Aileron

Turnbuckle

Fuel pipe

Pneumatic tire

Rubber-tired nose wheel

Seat support strut

Pilot's seat

Elevator wire for climbing

Wing-protecting skid

Engine and propeller thrust frame

Thin, cambered lower wing

Starboard main landing gear

SIDE VIEW OF WRIGHT FLYER, 1903

Plain cotton fabric

Interplane strut

Wing warping wire

Water-filled radiator

Chain drive

Front diagonal strut

Pusher propeller (rear-mounted propeller)

Elevator drive wheel

Rigid leading edge

Steel hub

Steel propeller shaft

Water pipe

Front-mounted biplane elevator

Bracing wire

Rudder

Landing skid

Elevator control cable

Pilot's cradle

Magneto

Rudder control cable

Braced rudder strut

Warping connection strut

Four-cylinder 12-HP engine

Propeller-shaft bracing strut

Softwood strut

Laminated wooden boom

Tail plane

Elevator control wire

Rudder bracing wire

Rudder

Elevator operating arm

Curtiss

Elevator

FRONT VIEW OF CURTISS MODEL-D PUSHER, 1911

Rudder control wheel

Fuel and oil tank

Nine-cylinder Salmson radial engine

Elevator operating arm

Anti-lift wire

Aileron operating arm

Starboard aileron

Port aileron

Carved interplane strut

Wing-protecting skid

Wing-protecting skid

Lift wire

Control column

Seat beam

Footrest

Axle

Tubular steel leg

Main landing gear lateral brace

Interplane strut pin-jointed to front spar

Early monoplanes

RUMPLER MONOPLANE, 1908

MONOPLANES HAVE ONE WING on each side of the fuselage. The principal disadvantage of this arrangement in early wooden-framed aircraft was that single wings were weak. They required strong wires to brace them to king posts above and below the fuselage. However, single wings also had advantages: they experienced less drag than multiple wings, allowing greater speed; they also made aircraft more maneuverable because single wings were easier to warp (twist) than double wings, and warping the wings was how pilots controlled the roll of early aircraft. By 1912, the French pilot Louis Blériot had used a monoplane to make the first flight across the English Channel, and the Briton Robert Blackburn and the Frenchman Armand Deperdussin had proved the greater speed of monoplanes. However, a spate of crashes caused by broken wings discouraged monoplane production, except in Germany, where all-metal monoplanes were developed in 1917. The wings of all-metal monoplanes did not need strengthening by struts or bracing wires, but despite this, such planes were not widely adopted until the 1930s.

FRONT VIEW OF BLACKBURN MONOPLANE, 1912

Taut fabric

Carved wooden propeller

King post

Hub bolted to propeller

Nose ring

Pilot's viewing aperture

Exhaust valve push-rod

Gnome seven-cylinder rotary engine

Elevator hinge

Elevator

Landing gear rear cross-member

Wheel fairing

Rubber-sprung wheel

Tailskid

Landing gear front strut

Axle

Landing skid

Landing gear rear strut

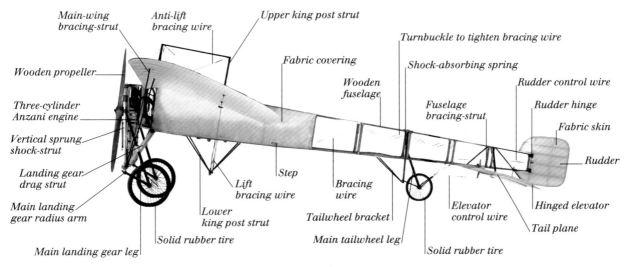

Main-wing bracing-strut

Anti-lift bracing wire

Upper king post strut

Fabric covering

Turnbuckle to tighten bracing wire

Shock-absorbing spring

Wooden propeller

Wooden fuselage

Rudder control wire

Three-cylinder Anzani engine

Fuselage bracing-strut

Rudder hinge

Vertical sprung shock-strut

Fabric skin

Landing gear drag strut

Rudder

Main landing gear radius arm

Lift bracing wire

Main landing gear leg

Lower king post strut

Step

Bracing wire

Tailwheel bracket

Main tailwheel leg

Elevator control wire

Solid rubber tire

Hinged elevator

Tail plane

Solid rubber tire

SIDE VIEW OF BLÉRIOT XI, 1909

Anti-lift bracing wire

Leading edge

Rib

Bracing wire anchor bolt

Concave undersurface

Lift bracing wire

Turnbuckle to tighten bracing wire

Warped wing

Carved wooden propeller

King post

Aluminum cowl

Anti-lift bracing wire

Lateral control wheel

Hub

Rudder post

Tail plane

Large fin

Domed top deck

Engine mount

Rudder

Elevator

Diagonal bracing

Triangular-section rear fuselage

Lift bracing wire

Landing gear rear strut

Braced landing gear structure

Forward fuselage structure

Landing skid

Elevator operating bracket

Tailskid

Rubber-sprung wheel

SIDE VIEW OF BLACKBURN MONOPLANE, 1912

Biplanes and triplanes

BIPLANES DOMINATED AIRCRAFT DESIGN until the 1930s, largely because some early monoplanes (see pp. 400-401) were too fragile to withstand the stresses of flight. The struts between biplanes' wings made the wings strong compared with those of early monoplanes, although the greater surface area of biplanes' wings increased drag and reduced speed. Many aircraft designers also developed triplanes, which had a particular advantage over biplanes: more wings meant a shorter wingspan to achieve the same lifting power, and a shorter wingspan gave greater maneuverability. Triplanes were most successful as fighters during World War I, the German Fokker triplane being a notable example. However, the greater maneuverability of triplanes was no advantage for normal flying, so most manufacturers continued to make biplanes. Many other aircraft designs were attempted. Some were quadruplanes, with four pairs of wings. Some had tandem wings (two pairs of monoplane wings, one behind the other). One of the most bizarre designs was by the Englishman Horatio Phillips; it had 20 sets of narrow wings and looked rather like a Venetian blind.

LAMINATED PROPELLER

Rudder hinge

RAF Central Flying School badge

Rudder

Fin

Navigation light

K 3215

Elevator

Rudder cable

Tail plane

Tailwheel

Bracing strut

SIDE VIEW OF AVRO TRIPLANE IV, 1910

Valve rocker

Air cooling baffle

Magneto

Wing strut

Fuel tank

Throttle

Harness

Pilot's seat

Crankcase breather pipe

Directly driven propeller

AVRO

Main front strut to engine mount

Skid upper bracing strut

Limit of fuselage skin

Ash skid

Rubber cord suspension

Turnbuckle

Axle

Skid rear strut

Lateral bracing strut

Rubber tire

Wheel rim

Wire wheel

AVRO TUTOR BIPLANE, 1931

Pin joint

Aileron hinge strut

Navigation light

Slat-arm fairing

Aileron control wire

Lift bracing wire

Instructor's cockpit

Wooden-domed deck

Padded coaming

Engine cowl

Student's cockpit

Propeller hub

RAF roundel

Laminated-wood, fixed-pitch propeller

Metal leading edge

Exhaust collector ring

Exhaust pipe

3215

Aircraft registration code

Inspection cover

Main landing gear leg

Radius rod

Inflation valve

Fabric-covered steel-tube fuselage

Fabric-covered aluminum and steel wing

Manufacturer's logo

Recessed nose of aileron

FRONT VIEW OF AVRO TRIPLANE IV, 1910

Unpainted, varnished fabric

Leading edge

Fuel filler and vent

Fixed-pitch wooden propeller

Anti-lift bracing wire

Top wing

Wing strut

Middle wing

Rib

Bottom wing

Landing skid

Axle

Elevator

Tail plane

Triangular-section fuselage

Lift bracing wire

Triangular-section fuselage

Fuselage bracing wire

Rudder control cable

Lateral bracing strut

Tail plane

Rudder

Metal plate anchorage

Elevator control cable

Longeron

Rubber cord suspension

Tailskid pivot

Tailskid

Elevator

World War I aircraft

PORT WINGS FROM A BE 2B

Interplane-strut attachment

Intermediate leading-edge rib

Airspeed-indicator tube

Leading edge

Wingtip

Airspeed-indicator tube

Main rib

Root

Interplane strut

Trailing edge

Airspeed pitot tube

Interplane-strut attachment

Upper side of lower wing

Attachment lug

FLYING HELMET

WHEN WORLD WAR I STARTED in 1914, the main purpose of military aircraft was reconnaissance. The British-built BE 2, of which the BE 2B was a variant, was well suited to this duty; it was very stable in flight, allowing the occupants to study the terrain, take photographs, and make notes. The BE 2 was also one of the first aircraft to drop bombs.

One of the biggest problems for aircraft designers during the war was mounting machine guns. On aircraft that had front-mounted propellers, the field of fire was restricted by the propeller and other parts of the aircraft. The problem was solved in 1915 by the Dutchman Anthony Fokker, who designed an interrupter gear that prevented a machine gun from firing when a propeller blade passed in front of the barrel. The German LVG CVI had a forward-firing gun to the right of the engine, as well as a rear-cockpit gun, and bombing capability. It was one of the most versatile aircraft of the war.

BE 2B, 1914

Cabane strut fairing

Engine air intake (ram scoop)

Observer's windshield

Top-wing center section

Cabane strut

Lift bracing wire

Pilot's windshield

Plywood skin

Control column

Padded coaming

Wooden propeller

Air-cooled V8 engine

Crankcase

Buffed metal cowling

Silencing heat exchanger

Exhaust pipe

Landing gear front strut

Ash skid

Elevator rocking arm

Step

Step

Reconnaissance camera bracket

Lateral control wire

Bomb rack

Pneumatic rubber tire

Wheel cover

V-strut

Lower-wing attachment

112 lb (51 kg) bomb

SIDE VIEW OF LVG CVI, 1917

Pilot's cockpit

Observer's cockpit

Starboard aileron

7.92-mm Parabellum machine gun

Cold-water pipe

Exhaust pipe

230-HP Benz six-cylinder water-cooled engine

Rudder

Fin

Rudder control wire

Elevator

Steel-drive bracket

Pivoted sprung tailskid

Aircraft registration code

Elevator control wire

Aircraft type

Interplane strut

Aileron control cable

Bracing wire

Laminated wooden propeller

Air ventilator inlet

Pitot head

Pneumatic rubber tire

Axle

Tire inflation aperture

FRONT VIEW OF LVG CVI, 1917

Lozenge-patterned fabric

Forward-firing machine gun

Exhaust stack

230-HP Benz six-cylinder water-cooled engine

Wooden propeller

Pitot head

Interplane strut

Anti-lift bracing wire

Lift bracing wire

Main fuel tank

Pneumatic rubber tire

Multiple rubber-cord suspension

Axle

Tailskid

Landing gear strut

Gravity-feed fuel tank

Turnbuckle

Fabric lacing

Tail plane attachment

Rudder post

Rib

Rudder

687

Aircraft registration code

Shock-absorbing spring

Pivoted tailskid

Steel V-strut

National marking

Fixed tail plane

Fabric covering

Steel lug

Leading edge

Elevator

Elevator hinge

Spar

Trailing edge

Rib

HORIZONTAL TAIL OF A BE 2B

Early passenger aircraft

UNTIL THE 1930s, most passenger aircraft were biplanes, with two pairs of wings and a wooden or metal framework covered with fabric or, sometimes, plywood. Such aircraft were restricted to low speeds and low altitudes because of the drag on their wings. Many had an open cockpit, situated behind or in front of an enclosed—but unpressurized—cabin that carried a maximum of 10 people. The passengers usually sat in wicker chairs that were not bolted to the floor, and the journey could be bumpy when flying through turbulence. Warm clothing, and earplugs to reduce the effects of prolonged noise, were often required. During the 1930s, powerful, streamlined, all-metal monoplanes, such as the Lockheed Electra shown here, became widespread. By 1939, the advent of pressurized cabins allowed fast flights at high altitudes, where there is less turbulence. Flying boats were still necessary on many routes until 1945 because of inadequate runways and the frequency of emergency sea landings. World War II, however, resulted in enough good runways being built for land planes to become standard on all major airline routes.

FRONT VIEW OF LOCKHEED ELECTRA, 1934

Green starboard navigation light

Flush-riveted metal-skinned wing

Leading edge

Fuel-jettison valve

Static discharge wick

Split flap in landing position

PASSENGER CABIN TRIM PANELS

Roof trim panel

Forward bulkhead upper panel

Passenger service panel aperture

Ashtray

Starboard wall forward panel

Cockpit door panel

Forward bulkhead lower panel

Starboard wall mid-forward panel

SIDE VIEW OF LOCKHEED ELECTRA, 1934

Cockpit windshield

Sliding window

Emergency escape hatch

Oil tank

Steel firewall

Passenger window

Air intake

Ventilator exit

Nose

Propeller pitch-change cylinder

Blade counterweight

Spinner mounting disk

Variable-pitch propeller

Pratt & Whitney nine-cylinder radial engine

Exhaust collector ring

Red port navigation light

Main landing gear

Aluminum wheel

Landing gear door

Exhaust pipe

Brake pipe

Mudguard

Electrically driven split flap

Passenger door

Static discharge wick

Aileron

Metal-skinned wing

Cylinder-cooling gills

Variable-pitch propeller

Cockpit windshield

High-visibility tip

Streamlined spinner

Pratt & Whitney nine-cylinder radial engine

Valve push-rod tube

Inner wing containing fuel tank

Fixed landing light

Red filter signal light

Exhaust pipe

Single-leg main landing gear

Pitot mast

Tank drain tap

Single-leg main landing gear

Landing gear door

Landing gear fork

Battery compartment

Electrical service compartment

Brake pipe

Axle

Pneumatic rubber tire

Brake pipe

Axle

Inspection cover

Tailwheel

Disc brake

Landing gear fork

Pneumatic rubber tire

Starboard wall aft panel

Roof trim

PASSENGER SEAT

Backrest

Document panel

Seat button

Bulkhead starboard trim

Seat belt

Armrest

Bulkhead port trim

Wall anchor

Floor anchor

Starboard wall mid-aft panel

Seat anchor bolt hole

Interior cabin trim for aft bulkhead between cabin and luggage hold

Seat cushion

PORT ENGINE COWLS

Rotating beacon

Starboard rudder

Inspection door

Starboard trim tab

Fixed tail plane

Tail plane

Port fin

120° cowl segment

Aluminum flush-riveted skin

Propeller-hub spinner

Port trim tab

Ventilator exit

NC517IN

Tail plane tip

Swiveling rubber-tired tailwheel

Aircraft registration code

120° cowl panel

Joining latch

World War II aircraft

WHEN WORLD WAR II began in 1939, air forces had already replaced most of their fabric-skinned biplanes with all-metal stressed-skin monoplanes. Aircraft played a far greater role in military operations during World War II than ever before. The wide range of aircraft duties and the introduction of radar tracking and guidance systems put pressure on designers to improve aircraft performance. The main areas of improvement were speed, range, and engine power. Bombers became larger and more powerful—converting from two to four engines—in order to carry a heavier bomb load; the U.S. B-17 Flying Fortress could carry up to 6 tons of bombs over a distance of about 2,000 miles (3,200 km). Some aircraft increased their range by using drop tanks (fuel tanks that were jettisoned when empty to reduce drag). Fighters needed speed and maneuverability: the Hawker Tempest shown here had a maximum speed of 435 mph (700 kph) and was one of the few Allied aircraft capable of catching the German jet-powered V1 "flying bomb." By 1944, Britain had introduced its first turbojet-powered aircraft, the Gloster Meteor fighter, and Germany had introduced the fastest fighter in the world, the turbojet-powered Me 262, which had a maximum speed of 540 mph (868 kph).

PROPELLER

High-visibility yellow tip

Light-alloy propeller spinner

Variable-pitch aluminum-alloy blade

COMPONENTS OF A HAWKER TEMPEST MARK V, c.1943

Radiator-access cowling

STARBOARD ENGINE COWLINGS

Lower side cowling

Upper side cowling

Cowling fastener

Propeller governor

Radiator header tank

Propeller drive shaft

Distributor

Ejector exhaust

2,400-HP Napier Sabre 24-cylinder engine

Cartridge starter

Magneto

Starter motor

Engine top cowling

Upper side cowling

Cowling fastener

Lower side cowling

Radiator-access cowling

PORT ENGINE COWLINGS

SECTIONED B-17G FLYING FORTRESS BOMBER, c.1943

Astronavigation dome

Hand-held gun

Plastic nose

Pilot's seat

Oxygen bottle

Upper gun turret

1,000 lb (454 kg) bomb

Radio operator's seat

Waist gun

Ammunition belt

Ammunition box

Dorsal fin

Fin

VHF antenna

Rudder

"Cheyenne-type" tail-gun turret

Tail gunner's compartment

Ammunition feed

Retracted tailwheel

Entrance door

Oxygen bottle

Ammunition feed

Sperry ball gun turret

Navigator's seat

Ammunition feed

Bomb door

Direction-finding-antenna fairing

Chin gun turret

HF radio antenna

Bombardier's viewing panel

PORT WING UNDERSIDE

Flap

Landing gear door

Cockpit starboard access panel

Wing front fillet panel

Wing rear fillet panel

Wing fillet panel

Starboard tail plane

Elevator hinge

Starboard elevator

Elevator control rod

Leading edge

FUSELAGE

Canopy rail

Seat pan

Harness strap

Canopy rail

VHF radio whip antenna

Fin

Tail fairing

Trim tab operating rod

Rudder

Flat, bulletproof windshield

Armored seat back

Dorsal fin

Tail plane root

Gyroscopic gunsight

Plastic cockpit canopy

RAF C1-type roundel

Cockpit front belly panel

Cockpit center belly panel

Tail band

Tail plane front attachment bracket

Tail plane rear attachment bracket

Port elevator trim tab

Rear spar trunnion

Cockpit rear belly panel

Camouflage

Trailing edge

Wing fillet panel

Wing front fillet panel

Wing rear fillet panel

Port tail plane

TAIL

Outboard ammunition-feed blister

Cockpit port access panel

Trailing edge

Wing upper surface

HAWKER TEMPEST MARK V FIGHTER, c.1943

Aileron

RAF B-type roundel

Hispano Mark V 20-mm cannon

Headrest

Armor-plated seat back

Squadron code

Rudder

Dorsal fin

Exhaust pipe

Gyroscopic gunsight

RAF C1-type roundel

Propeller spinner

Engine air intake

Radiator

Yellow-painted leading edge

Wingtip

PORT WING

Radiator outlet

Pitot head

Instant-identification "invasion" stripes

Retracted tailwheel

Rudder trim tab

NV70B

SA

409

Modern piston aircraft engines

MID WEST TWO-STROKE, THREE-CYLINDER ENGINE

PISTON ENGINES today are used mainly to power the vast numbers of light aircraft and ultralights, as well as crop sprayers and crop dusters, small helicopters, and fire-bombers (which dump water on large fires). Virtually all heavier aircraft are now powered by jet engines. Modern piston aircraft engines work on the same basic principles as the engine used by the Wright brothers in the first powered flight in 1903. However, today's engines are more sophisticated than earlier engines. For example, modern aircraft engines may use a two-stroke or a four-stroke combustion cycle; they may have from one to nine air- or liquid-cooled cylinders, which may be arranged horizontally, in-line, in V formation, or radially; and they may drive the aircraft's propeller either directly or through a reduction gearbox. One of the more unconventional types of modern aircraft engine is the rotary engine shown here, which has a trilobate (three-sided) rotor spinning in a chamber shaped like a fat figure-eight.

MID WEST 75-HP TWO-STROKE, THREE-CYLINDER ENGINE

Spark plug

Coolant outlet

Cylinder head

Piston

Cylinder barrel

Exhaust manifold

Exhaust port

Cylinder liner

Upper crankcase

Reduction gearbox

Driven gear

Propeller drive flange

Torsional vibration damper

Sprag clutch

Gearbox drive splines

Connecting rod (con-rod)

Small end

Big end

Counterweight

Crankshaft

Gearbox mounting plate

Lower crankcase

Pump drive belt

Coolant pump

Generator rotor

Stator

Ignition trigger housing

Engine mounting plate

ROTOR AND HOUSINGS OF A MID WEST SINGLE-ROTOR ENGINE

Propeller bolt hole

Propeller drive flange

Propeller shaft rear bearing

GEARBOX CASE

Dowel

Stud

Roller

Eccentric-shaft bearing

Coolant jacket

Dowel

FRONT HOUSING (FRONT END PLATE)

Stud hole

Stud hole

Dowel hole

Coolant jacket

Inlet tract

Stud hole

Rotor chamber

Exhaust tract

TROCHOID HOUSING

MID WEST 90-HP TWIN-ROTOR ENGINE

Propeller-bolt collar

Propeller drive flange

Reduction gearbox

Lubricating oil feed

Engine front mounting plate

Blanking plate over air inlet

Carburetor

Upper rubber anti-vibration engine mount

Rotor-cooling air duct

Pipe clamp joint

Rotor-cooling air pump

Upper rotor-cooling air duct

Generator housing

Electric cable

Starter motor

Flywheel

Engine rear mounting plate

Front bearing mount

Oil pump drive shaft cover

Torsional vibration damper

Fuel pipe inlet connection

Fuel drip tray

Blanking plate over exhaust port

Exhaust pipe flange

Lower rubber anti-vibration engine mount

OUTPUT SHAFT OF A MID WEST ROTARY ENGINE

Balance weight

Drive gear

Front bearing

Drive gear spline

Starter-ring teeth

Oil seal spacer ring

Flywheel retaining thread

Eccentric shaft

Rotor bearing

Rear bearing

Flywheel

Corner bolt

Fixed gear (stationary gear)

Engine mounting

Outlet manifold

Water pump cover and oil pump housing

Rotor tip seal

Tip seal groove

Rotor tip spring

Balancing drilling

Rotor-gear teeth

Rotor side seal

Side seal spring

Rotor bearing

Pump drive shaft

Fixing stud

Bolt hole

Thermostat

Cooling fins

Side seal groove

Stud hole

Dowel hole

Coolant jacket

Inlet manifold

Oil pump

ROTOR AND SEALS

REAR HOUSING (REAR END PLATE)

WATER-PUMP HOUSING

411

Modern jetliners 1

BAE 146 JETLINER

MODERN JETLINERS HAVE ENABLED ordinary people to travel to places where once only the wealthy could afford to go. Compared with the first jetliners (which were introduced in the 1940s), modern jetliners are much quieter, burn fuel more efficiently, and produce less air pollution. These advances are largely due to the replacement of turbojet engines with turbofan engines (see pp. 418-419). The greater power of turbofan engines at low speeds enables modern jetliners to carry more fuel and passengers than turbojet aircraft; a modern Boeing 747-400 (popularly known as a "jumbo jet") can fly 400 people for 8,500 miles (13,700 km) without needing to refuel. Jetliners fly at high altitudes, typically cruising at 26,000-36,000 ft (8,000-11,000 m), where they can use fuel efficiently and usually avoid bad weather. The pilot always controls the aircraft during takeoff and landing, but at other times the aircraft is usually controlled by an autopilot. Autopilots are complex onboard mechanisms that detect deviations from an aircraft's route and make appropriate adjustments to the flight controls. Flight decks are also equipped with radar that warns pilots of approaching hazards, such as mountain ranges, bad weather, and other aircraft.

Shoulder nacelle

Engine pylon

Hinged nacelle panel

Nose cowling

Fan duct nozzle

Fire extinguisher discharge indicator

Core-engine jet pipe

Oil-filler door

Push-in door for hand-held fire extinguisher

Drain mast

TURBOFAN ENGINE COWLING

STRUCTURAL COMPONENTS OF A BAE 146 JETLINER

Oil-filler door for integrated-drive generator

FUSELAGE NOSE-SECTION

FUSELAGE MID-SECTION

Electrically heated, birdproof windshield

Side window

Anchor for open door

Rain gutter

Hinge

Peephole

Finger recess

Static air-pressure plate

Forward main door aperture

VHF omni-range and instrument-landing-system antennas

Passenger window aperture

Light-alloy door frame

Main external operating handle

Multiple-pinned lock

Floor level

Radome

Toilet service connector

Air temperature probe

Stall-warning vane

FORWARD MAIN DOOR

Anchor for open door

Pitot head for dynamic air pressure

Systems connector

Overwing fuel-filler cap

Overwing fuel-filler cap

Fuel contents indicator

STARBOARD WING ASSEMBLY

Center-line (spine) of aircraft

Single-piece skin over inboard wing

Rubber sealing strip

Rubber sealing strip

Trailing edge

Trailing edge of fixed wing

Spoiler anchorage

Hydraulic actuator attachment

Pivot point

Flap-track fairing

Screw joint

Aft section

Hinge

INBOARD LIFT SPOILERS

Stainless-steel flap seal

MOVABLE FLAP TRACK AND FAIRING

Track roller

Upper carriage attached to flap

Tab hinge line

FOWLER FLAP

Leading edge

Anchor bearing

Track

Root

Gearbox mount

Gearbox unit

Carriage drive nut

Flap drive screw

Bellcrank lever

Lower carriage

Skin lap-joint

Leading edge

Main spar bridge

Root rib

Wing-root mount containing central fuel tank

Attachment structure for wing-to-fuselage fillet

Inboard tab

Cabin air-pressure discharge valve

Floor level

Fairing of landing gear bay

Fairing of landing gear pivot

Yellow anti-corrosion paint

Modern jetliners 2

Landing and taxiing light

Heated deicing
leading edge

Roll-spoiler hinge

Roll-spoiler hydraulic actuator attachment

STARBOARD WING

Fixed trailing edge

Aileron hinge

Starboard
navigation
light

Hinge

Hydraulic actuator attachment

Spoiler arm

Hinge
bracket

Aerodynamic
balance

Horn
balance

Recessed hinge

**INTERMEDIATE
LIFT SPOILER**

Flap
seal

OUTBOARD ROLL SPOILER

AILERON

MAIN FOWLER FLAP

Trim tab

Static discharge wick attachment

Leading edge

Flap tip

Outboard tab

Tab-hinge line

FUSELAGE SPINE FAIRING

Landing gear
door

Hydraulic brake line

Main pivot

Finger
recess

Peephole

Hot-air deicing duct

Electrical harness

Oleo
lock-jack

Skin lap joint

Passenger
window
aperture

Light-
alloy beam

Direction
bar

Hinge

Shock-strut bearing

Brake
line

Main
external
operating
handle

Pneumatic
tire

Side brace
and retraction
jack trunnions

Outer
wheel
axle

Hinge

Lower pivot

Wheel hub

Pivoted
trailing-
link arm

Hydraulic
brake line

Anchor for open door

Cabin air-
discharge aperture

STARBOARD TWIN-WHEEL MAIN LANDING GEAR

AFT MAIN DOOR

BAE 146 MODERN JETLINER

Tail plane

Logo

Rudder

Fin

Starboard aft
service door

Flap-track
fairing

Core-engine
jet pipe

Main landing-
gear fairing

VHF
antenna

Water-drain
mast

Landing light

VHF radio antenna

Forward door for
crew and service

Radome

**STARBOARD
ELEVATOR**

Horn
balance

Tab
hinge

Aerodynamic
balance

Recessed
hinge

Center line
(spine)

Root

Trim tab

Servo-tab

**TAIL PLANE
FAIRINGS**

Intermediate
fairing (fin tip)

Aft fairing

Fin trailing edge

Forward
fairing

Side
fairing

Elevator
chassis
box

Tail plane
attachment bracket

Heated deicing
leading edge

FIN

Forward
spar

Fairing panel

Aft spar

Fin-attachment
skin

Access to yaw dampers
and rudder trim jack

**TAIL
PLANE**

Rain gutter

Fin leading-edge
attachment

Auxiliary power
unit (APU)
inlet

Heated deicing
leading edge

Operating arm

Elevator
hinge

Hinge

Skin lap
joint

Trailing
edge

Auxiliary power unit
(APU) vent

Oil-
cooler
duct

STARBOARD AIR BRAKE

Tail plane
tip

Aft main door aperture

Heated drain mast

FUSELAGE TAIL SECTION

Supersonic jetliners

SUPERSONIC AIRCRAFT FLY FASTER than the speed of sound (Mach 1). There are many supersonic military aircraft, but only two supersonic passenger-carrying aircraft (also called SSTs, or supersonic transports) have been produced: the Russian Tu-144, and the Concorde, produced jointly by Britain and France. The Tu-144 had a greater maximum speed than the Concorde but was withdrawn in 1978, after only seven months in service. The Concorde has remained in service since 1976. It features many innovations, including a droop nose, which is lowered during takeoff and landing to aid visibility from the cockpit, and the pumping of fuel between forward and aft trim tanks to help stabilize the aircraft. The Concorde has a narrow fuselage and short-span wings to reduce drag during supersonic flight. Its noisy turbojet engines with afterburners enable it to carry 100 passengers at a cruising speed of Mach 2 at 50,000-60,000 ft (15,000-18,000 m). Once an aircraft is flying faster than Mach 1, it produces a continuous air-pressure wave, which is heard as a "sonic boom."

COMPUTER-
DESIGNED SST

Strake

Fin

Standby
pitot head

Inboard
elevon-
actuator
fairing

Nose
gear
leg

Starboard
outboard
engine air intake

FRONT VIEW OF CONCORDE

**OVERHEAD VIEW
OF CONCORDE**

Variable
nozzle

Leading edge

Toilets

Electrothermal
deicing panel

Starboard
forward trim tank

Overhead luggage compartments

Passenger
accommodation

Seat
attachment
rail

Underfloor air-
conditioning duct

Life raft

VHF
antenna

Wardrobe

Forward galley

Additional crew's seat

Flight engineer's
seat

Aluminum-alloy layers
and insulation

Erosion-
resistant
radome

Cockpit
windshield

Retractable
visor

"A" frame

Weather
radar

Visor jack

Pivoted
retractable frame

Droop-
nose hinge

Cockpit air-
conditioning
duct

Captain's
seat

Standby
flight-control
hydraulic jack

Plug-type
passenger
door

Upper
rudder

Tail cone

Aft door

Elevon (combined elevator and aileron)

Hot-section steel and titanium skin

Engine cowling

Nose
gear
door

Nose
gear
leg

Lateral bracing strut

Telescopic strut

Steering
actuator

Multi-ply
high-pressure
tire

Fin

Dorsal fin

Emergency exit

Port
forward
trim tank

Machined
skin panel

Landing gear door

Bogie main landing gear

SECTIONED VIEW OF CONCORDE

Fire-suppression bottle access panel
Pressurized keel box
Fuel tank
Main air duct
Emergency exit
Cold-air unit
Static discharge wick
Elevon (combined elevator and aileron)
Cabin air duct
Inspection panel
HF radio antennas fairing
Emergency oxygen cylinders
Flight-control mixing unit
Upper rudder
Auxiliary power unit
VHF omni-range antenna
Lower-rudder power control unit
Servo control-unit fairing
Tail cone
Fuel-jettison pipe
Twin-wheel tail bumper
Air-conditioning duct
Rear bulkhead
Aft galley unit
Rear emergency door
Tank inspection access
Inboard elevon (combined elevator and aileron)
Landing gear hydraulics
Port main landing-gear leg well
Variable nozzle
Nozzle actuator
Heat exchanger exhaust
Elevon power control unit

Spar
Rib
Leading edge
Middle passenger door
Fuel pipe
VHF antenna
Port engine fuel pumps
Four-wheel bogie
Port main landing gear leg
Forward ramp drive
Main landing gear cross beam
Upper lip of port engine air intakes
Retraction jack
Engine front support link
Rolls-Royce Olympus Mark 610 turbojet
Heat exchanger
Fuel tank
Honeycomb elevon structure

SIDE VIEW OF CONCORDE

VHF antenna
Emergency exit
Passenger window
Flight deck windshield
Retracted visor
Nose in drooped position
Standby pitot head
Nose gear leg
Nose leg
Aerodynamic strake
Radome
Nose leg telescopic strut
Starboard forward door
Steerable twin-wheel nose gear

Jet engines

JET ENGINES ARE USED BY MOST MILITARY and heavy aircraft and by many helicopters. The simplest type of jet engine, or gas turbine, is the turbojet. It works by continuously burning a mixture of fuel and air in a combustion chamber to produce a jet of hot exhaust gas that is expelled through a nozzle to produce thrust. The hot gas also spins turbine blades which, in turn, spin the blades of an air compressor; the compressor forces air into the combustion chamber. Many of the fastest aircraft use turbojets, with additional booster units called afterburners, but their use is restricted by their high noise emission. Most jetliners use quieter turbofan jet engines. An enormous fan, driven by a low-pressure turbine, feeds some air into the compressor but feeds most of it through bypass ducts to join the exhaust jetstream in the tail cone. The bypass stream produces most of the thrust. Many smaller, propeller-driven aircraft use turboprop jet engines, in which the engine powers a propeller.

NPT 301 MODERN TURBOJET

Fuel sprayer
Reverse-flow combustion chamber
Radial diffuser
Turbine rotor
Centrifugal compressor
Exhaust diffuser
Inducer
Tail cone
Air intake
Jet pipe
Exhaust nozzle
Nose cone
Igniter
Alternator
Nozzle guide vane
Air impingement starter
Combustion chamber casing

Plenum ring for hot anti-icing air
Transmission bevel drive
Integral oil tank
High-pressure compressor
Combustion chamber
High-pressure turbine
Flow splitter
Fuel manifold
Fuel nozzle
Centrifugal compressor
Temperature and pressure sensor
Low-pressure fan
Inlet cone (rotating spinner)
Pressure line
Fan case with special structure to contain broken fan
Electronic engine control and airframe interface connector
Electronic engine control (EEC) unit
Fan duct
Compressor front bearing
Engine front mount
Electrical wiring harness
Fuel and oil heat exchanger
Oil filter
Compressor air-bleed connection

PRATT & WHITNEY CANADA PW120 SERIES MODERN TURBOPROP

Alternator mount pad
Propeller speed probe
Reduction transmission
Propeller hub flange
Propeller brake pad
Engine front mount
Torquemeter mount
Transmission oil scavenge line
Accessory drive pad
Throttle lever
Fuel-cooled oil cooler
Autofeather unit
Electronic engine control (EEC) unit
Air intake
Oil filter
Oil tank
Oil-pressure regulating valve
Fuel filter
Fuel heater
Fuel manifold
Intercompressor bleed valve
Fuel
Intercompressor diffuser pipe
High-pressure bleed venturi connector
Turbine support case
Jet pipe connection
Oil pipe
Thermocouple bus bar
Fuel nozzle
Igniter plug
Engine rear mount

HOW JET ENGINES WORK

TURBOFAN

Fan sucks air in
Fan blade
Rotating blades compress air
Fuel inlet
Inner drive shaft
Outer drive shaft
Exhaust gases provide extra thrust
Bypass air provides main thrust
High-pressure turbine spins outer drive shaft to drive compressor
Fuel/air mixture ignites

TURBOPROP

Compressor sucks air in
Propeller spins to provide main thrust
Reduction gearbox
Rotating blades compress air
Fuel inlet
Combustion chamber
Three-stage turbine driven by hot gas
Exhaust gases add a little thrust
Turbine shaft drives propeller and compressor

TURBOJET

Compressor sucks air in
Rotating blades compress air
Fuel inlet
Fuel/air mixture ignites
Combustion chamber
Turbine blades driven by hot gas
Exhaust gases provide all the thrust
Turbine drives compressor via drive shaft

Low-pressure turbine
Heat shield
Blade tip sealing shroud
Exhaust cone
Core jet pipe (exhaust fairing)
Scavenge oil line
Inter-module bolted joint
Fuel shut-off valve cable

SECTIONED PRATT & WHITNEY CANADA PW305 MODERN TURBOFAN

Modern military aircraft

MODERN MILITARY AIRCRAFT ARE AMONG THE MOST SOPHISTICATED and expensive products of the 20th century. Fighters need computer-operated controls for maneuverability, powerful engines, and effective air-to-air weapons. Most modern fighters also have guided missiles, radar, and passive, infrared sensors. These developments enable today's fighters to engage in combat with adversaries who are outside visual range. Bombers carry a large weapon load and enough fuel for long-range flights. A few military aircraft, such as the Tornado and the F-14 Tomcat, have variable-sweep ("swing") wings. During takeoff and landing their wings are fully extended, but for high-speed flight and low-level attacks the wings are pivoted fully back. A recent development is the "stealth" bomber, which is designed to absorb or deflect enemy radar in order to remain undetected. Earlier bombers, such as the Tornado, use terrain-following radars to fly so close to the ground that they avoid enemy radar detection.

FRONT VIEW OF A
PANAVIA TORNADO

Instrument landing system antenna

Birdproof windshield

Port variable-incidence air intake

Air data probe

Wing-root glove fairing

Starboard inboard stores pylon

Taileron

Starboard main landing-gear door

Main landing-gear leg

Laser ranger and marked-target seeker

Starboard nose gear door

Steerable twin-wheel nose gear

Radome containing ground-mapping, attack, and terrain-following radars

Taxiing light

Wing extended for takeoff and landing

Wing pivoted back for high-speed flight

SWING-WING F-14 TOMCAT FIGHTER

SIDE VIEW OF A PANAVIA TORNADO GR1A
(RECONNAISSANCE VERSION), 1986

Pilot's cockpit

Navigator's instrument console

Navigator's cockpit

Single canopy over both cockpits

Engine air intake

Navigation light

Flat, birdproof windshield

High-velocity air duct to disperse rain

Upper "request identification" antenna

Air data probe

RESCUE

Radome containing ground-mapping, attack, and terrain-following radars

UHF antenna

Angle-of-attack probe

Tacan (tactical air navigation) antenna

Emergency canopy release handle

Nose gear door

Steerable nose gear leg

Pitot head

Twin nose-wheel

Hinged auxiliary air intake

Cold-air intake (ram scoop)

Heat exchanger exhaust duct

Window covering infrared reconnaissance camera

NORTHROP B-2 ("STEALTH" BOMBER), 1989

Starboard split rudder

Inboard elevons (combined elevators and ailerons)

Refractory (heat-resistant) skin behind exhaust outlet

Variable-incidence gust alleviator

Wing leading edge coated with radar-absorbent material

Port wingtip rudder

Outboard elevon (combined elevator and aileron)

Engine aft bulkhead

Wing containing fuel tank

Leading-edge antenna

Weapon-bay rear bulkhead

Flight refueling receptacle

Weapon-bay front bulkhead

Space for extra crew member

Auxiliary air intake

Air intake coated with radar-absorbent material

Ejector-seat roof hatches

Two-seater cockpit

Port outboard stores pylon

Port navigation light

Fin tip antenna fairing

Radar warning receiver looking forward

Instrument landing system antenna

Fin

Extended port air brake

Heat exchanger air intake (ram scoop)

Wing-root glove fairing

Wing-root pneumatic seal

Fin-root antenna fairing

Radar warning receiver looking rearward

Rudder

Heat exchanger hot-air exhaust

Air brake jack

Spine end fairing

Thrust-reverser (closed)

Port fully variable afterburner nozzle

Port flap

Wingtip antenna fairing

Port navigation light

Lower "request identification" antenna

Powered leading-edge slat

Port outboard stores pylon

Port taileron (combined tail plane and aileron)

Port inboard stores pylon

Hydraulic hand pump

Main-gear door

Port main landing gear

Helicopters

HELICOPTERS USE ROTATING BLADES for lift, propulsion, and steering. The first machine to achieve sustained, controlled flight using rotating blades was the autogiro built in the 1920s by Juan de la Cierva of Spain. His machine had unpowered blades above the fuselage that relied on the flow of air to rotate them and provide lift while the autogiro was driven forward by a conventional propeller. Then, in 1939, the Russian-born American Igor Sikorsky produced his VS-300, the forerunner of the modern helicopter. Its engine-driven blades provided lift, propulsion, and steering. It could take off vertically, hover, and fly in any direction, and had a tail rotor to prevent the helicopter body from spinning. The introduction of gas turbine jet engines to helicopters in 1955 produced quieter, safer, and more powerful machines. Because of their versatility in flight, helicopters are used today for many purposes, including crop spraying, traffic surveillance, and transporting crews to deep-sea oil rigs, as well as acting as gunships, air ambulances, and air taxis.

BELL 47G-3B1

BELL 47G-3B1

Droop stop

Blade counterweight

Main rotor hub

Blade-root attachment

Main rotor mast

Stabilizer-bar weight

Direct-vision panel

Fuel vent line

Protective sleeve

Fuel tank

Fuel-tank cradle

Tail rotor drive shaft

Frameless plastic canopy

Exhaust pipe

Radio

Air-intake pipe

Instrument panel

Electric fuel pump

Cyclic-pitch lever

Battery

Battery overspill

Electrical inverter

Pitot head

Breather line

Anti-collision beacon

Oil tank

Landing light

Carburetor hot-air intake pipe

Landing skid

Air filter

VHF omni-range antenna

Navigation light

Ground-handling wheel

Valve-rocker cover

Ventilator

Electric power socket

Lycoming six-cylinder engine

Collective-pitch lever

Riveted light-alloy forward fuselage section

Blade-root attachment

Three-blade main rotor

Outside air-temperature gauge

Ventilator

Flight-control rod

Anti-collision beacon

Anti-torque tail rotor

Magnetic compass

Main rotor mast

Automatic direction-finding antenna

Plastic canopy

Navigation antenna

Cyclic-pitch lever

Fuel tank

G-SAND

DANGER

Engine air intake

Tubular bracing strut

Tail boom

Pitot head

Tail-rotor drive shaft

Vertical stabilizer

Tail rotor guard

Anti-collision beacon

Tail-boom support strut

Exhaust silencer

SCHWEIZER 300C

Transmission drive-pulley cover

Landing skid

Landing gear damper

Landing light

Transponder antenna

Lycoming four-cylinder engine

High-visibility tip

Twin-blade main rotor

Anti-torque tail rotor

Anti-collision beacon

Triangular-section, unskinned rear fuselage

Elevator upper control wire

Synchronized elevator

Tail rotor hub

Tail rotor gearbox

G-BGID

Tubular tail rotor guard

Elevator lower control wire

Tail rotor pitch control wire

Small fixed fin

Main rotor blade

Droop stop

Main rotor hub

Blade-root attachment

Jet pipe

Allison 250-C20J turboshaft engine

Anti-collision beacon

Main rotor mast

Horizontal stabilizer

Upper fin

VHF antenna

AEROMEGA HELICOPTERS

Anti-torque tail rotor

Air temperature probe

G-HUMT

Forward-hinged door

Lower fin

Transponder antenna

Tail boom

Boarding step

Flush-riveted aluminum fuselage

Landing skid

Rear cross-tube

Baggage compartment door

BELL 206 JETRANGER

Light aircraft

Port wingtip

LIGHT AIRCRAFT, SUCH AS THE ARV SUPER 2 shown here, are small, lightweight, and of simple construction. More than a million have been built since World War I, mainly for recreational use by private owners. Virtually all light aircraft have piston engines, most of which are air-cooled, although some are liquid-cooled. Open cockpits, almost universal in the 1920s, have now been replaced by enclosed cabins. The cabins of high-wing aircraft have one or two doors, while those of low-wing aircraft usually have a sliding or hinged canopy. Most modern light aircraft are made of aluminum alloy, although some are made of wood or of fiber-reinforced materials. Light aircraft today also usually have navigational instruments, an electrical system, cabin heating, wheel brakes, and a two-way radio.

Aileron mass balance

Aileron torque tube

Port aileron

PORT MAIN LANDING GEAR

Inner tube

Hub

Tire

Brake disk

Stub axle

Landing gear leg

Brake mount

Brake pipe

Hydraulic brake caliper

TAIL PLANE AND RUDDER

Elevator

Rudder tip fairing

Rudder mass balance

Fin tip fairing

Rudder

Fin

Dorsal fin

Rear fuselage top skin

Rear attachment-bracket for wing

REAR FUSELAGE

Longeron

Frame

Battery box

Diaphragm

Side skin

Elevator trim tab

Drive pillar

Attachment plate

Rear fuselage bottom skin

"Skin-grip" pin

Coolant outlet

Aluminum radiator

Air scoop

Coolant intake

Tail plane

Elevator push-rod

Navigational antenna

Elevator push-rod

Rocking elevator arm

Aileron torque tube

CONTROL RODS AND CABLES

Flap torque tube

Aileron rod

Flap drive-rod

Rudder cable

Flap drive-rod

STARBOARD MAIN LANDING GEAR

SIDE VIEW OF ARV SUPER 2

Spinner

Canopy

Wing

Communications antenna

Fin

Dorsal fin

Rudder

Engine cowling

Elevator

Brake caliper

Brake mount

Brake pipe

Nose gear

Step

Radiator

Tailskid

Tail plane

Landing gear leg

Venturi for instruments

Wing strut

Main landing gear

Aircraft registration code

Brake disk

Inner tube

Stub axle

Tire

Hub

G-BNHB

PORT WING

Port top-wing fairing

Port underwing fairing

Headrest

Backrest

Wing strut

Port flap

Pitot head

Airspeed-indicator tube

SEAT ASSEMBLY

Seat cushion

Quick-release mechanism

Seatbelt

Seatbelt length adjuster

Bolted anchor

CANOPY

Direct-vision panel

Pressurized strut

Hinge

Leading-edge fairing

Molded plastic

Canopy latch

Outside air-temperature gauge

COCKPIT

Fiberglass canopy frame

Fuel tank top skin

Rudder pedal

Cockpit coaming

Forward attachment bracket for wing

Control-column aperture

Semi-bulkhead

Fiberglass fuel tank

Bulkhead

Seatbelt attachment bracket

"Skin-grip" pin

Nose leg upper mount

Firewall

THREE-CYLINDER ENGINE

Port engine cowling

Air intake box

Carburetor

Water outlet

Backplate

Engine mount

Fuel hose

Spinner

Cylinder head

Gearbox

Propeller drive flange

Flanged plate

Exhaust manifold

PROPELLER

Starboard engine cowling

CONTROL COLUMN AND FLAP LEVER

Elevator arm

Torque tube assembly

Control column

Throttle lever

Brake lever

Flap lever

Elevator push-rod

Elevator trim tab lever

Flap lever detent box

Release button

Carburetor hot air lever

Bearing assembly

Pilot's handgrip

INSTRUMENT PANEL

Flight instruments

Engine instruments

Glove compartment

Radio plugs

NOSE GEAR

Steering stop

Nose leg down tube

Rubber bungee shock absorber

Damper unit

Pivoted fork

Hoop

Axle bolt

Nose wheel

STARBOARD WING

Wing strut

Starboard underwing fairing

Starboard top-wing fairing

Gliders, hang gliders, and ultralights

MODERN GLIDERS ARE AMONG the most graceful and aerodynamically efficient of all aircraft. Unpowered but with a large wingspan (up to about 82 ft, or 25 m), gliders use currents of hot, rising air (thermals) to stay aloft, and a rudder, elevators, and ailerons for control. Modern gliders have achieved flights of more than 900 miles (1,450 km) and altitudes above 49,000 ft (15,000 m). Hang gliders consist of a simple frame across which rigid or flexible material is stretched to form the wings. The pilot is suspended below the wings in a harness or body bag and, gripping a triangular A-frame, steers by shifting weight from side to side. Like gliders, hang gliders rely on thermals for lift. Ultralights are basically powered hang gliders. A small engine and an open fiberglass car (trike), which can hold a crew of two, are suspended beneath a stronger version of a hang glider frame; the frame may have rigid or flexible wings. Ultralight pilots, like hang glider pilots, steer by shifting their weight against an A-frame. Ultralights can reach speeds of up to 100 mph (160 kph).

HANG GLIDER

NOSE SHELL

Grommet for front pylon strut

Instrument panel

King post

Apex

PEGASUS XL SE ULTRALIGHT

Stiffening rib

Center-line beam

Main suspension

Rear-mounted propeller (pusher propeller)

Fuel tank

Wheel part

Main wheel

Trike nacelle

Apex wire

Nose shell

Nose gear mount

Fixed nose wheel

HANG GLIDER BODY BAG

Clip-in latch for pilot

Shoulder strap

Layers of insulating fabric

Armhole

Shoulder pad

Camera pouch

Body bag

End of rib

Trailing edge

Dacron skin

SCHLEICHER K23 GLIDER

Downturned wingtip acts as skid

Aileron

Aluminum air brake

Radio antenna

Tail plane

Hinged elevator

T-type cantilevered fin

Rudder

Single pilot cockpit

Forward-opening canopy

Towing hook

Nose wheel

Nonretractable main wheel

Fuselage of fiberglass and foam layers

EVW

Tailwheel

SOLAR WINGS PEGASUS QUASAR ULTRALIGHT

TRIKE UNIT

Foot throttle

Pilot's steering bar

Passenger's steering bar and footrest

Seat belt

Fuel tank filler nozzle

Wheel part

Engine mount

Pylon strut

Footbrake

Pilot's seat

Hand throttle

Pylon-strut strap

Passenger's seat

Main wing strut

Pylon fairing

Aircraft name

Air outlet

Rear engine cowling

TRIKE NACELLE

Sealed lid

Waterproof stowage box

TWIN-CYLINDER ENGINE

Twin carburetors

Air filter

Dual ignition plugs

Air-cooling fan

Exhaust connection

Engine rear mount

Trailing edge

Leading edge

Propeller-drive gearbox

Metal hub

PROPELLER

EXHAUST PIPE

After muffler

Main exhaust muffler

WINGFRAME

Eyelet tensioning trailing edge to rib

Bracing cable

Rib

Single spar

Center-line beam

King post

Leading edge

Semirigid fiberglass skin

Lift bracing wire

427

THE VISUAL ARTS

Drawing

DRAWINGS CAN BE FINISHED WORKS OF ART, or preparatory studies for paintings and other visual arts. They can be made using a wide variety of drawing instruments such as pencils, graphite sticks, chalks, charcoal, pens and inks, and silver wires. The most common drawing instrument is the graphite pencil. A graphite pencil consists of a thin rod of graphite mixed with clay, encased in wood. Charcoal is one of the oldest drawing instruments. It is produced by firing twigs of willow, vine, or other woods at high temperatures in airtight containers. Erasers can be used to rub out marks made by drawing materials such as graphite pencils or charcoal, or to achieve a particular effect—such as smudging. Fixative is often applied—using a mouth diffuser or aerosol spray fixative—to prevent smudging once a drawing is finished. Silver lines can be produced by drawing silver wire across specially prepared paper— a technique known as silverpoint. The lines are permanent and cannot be erased. In time the silver lines oxidize and turn brown.

FIXATIVE AND MOUTH DIFFUSER

Hinge

Liquid fixative consisting of dissolved resin

Fixative is sucked into tube and sprayed onto drawing

DRAWING INSTRUMENTS

Medium-soft, light line

2B GRAPHITE PENCIL

Very soft, dark line

8B GRAPHITE PENCIL

SILVER WIRE IN A METAL HOLDER

ERASERS

Hard texture

PLASTIC ERASER

Soft texture

KNEADED ERASER

CHALK, CRAYON, AND CHARCOAL

Calcite (calcium carbonate) mixed with pigment

BLUE CHALK

Iron oxide mixed with chalk

SANGUINE CRAYON

Carbonized wood

WILLOW CHARCOAL

DRAWING MATERIALS

Graphite stick

Binder clip

Colored pencil

Dip pen

DRAWING BOARD

Drawing board

Paper

Drawing clip

Pencil sharpener

Sketch book

Ink bottle

Silver lines
oxidize to a
light brown
color

Figures drawn
in ink on top
of lines

Line drawn
in silverpoint
using a ruler

Complex perspective
drawing done as a
preparatory study
for a painting

Vanishing
point located
on head of
man riding
rearing horse

Lines of
squared
pavement slabs
recede toward
a single
vanishing
point

Paper prepared
with size (glue)
and pigment

EXAMPLE OF A SILVERPOINT DRAWING
The Adoration of the Magi, Leonardo da Vinci, 1481
Pen and ink over silverpoint on paper
6½ x 11½ in (16.5 x 29.2 cm)

Handmade, tinted
paper

One of a series
of drawings
recording
London during
1944–1945

Charcoal lines
softened by
rubbing and
smudging

Charcoal
gives strong,
expressive lines

Broad charcoal
mark

Lines rapidly
drawn on site

EXAMPLE OF A CHARCOAL DRAWING
St. Paul's and the River, David Bomberg, 1945
Charcoal on paper
20 x 25⅛ in (50.8 x 65.8 cm)

Tempera

ILLUMINATED
MANUSCRIPT

THE TERM TEMPERA is applied to any paint in which pigment is tempered (mixed) with a water-based binding medium—usually egg yolk. Egg tempera is applied to a smooth surface such as vellum (for illuminated manuscripts) or more commonly to hardwood panels prepared with gesso—a mixture of chalk and size (glue). Bristle brushes are used to apply the gesso. A layer of gesso grosso (coarse gesso) is followed by successive layers of gesso sotile (fine gesso) that are sanded between coats to provide a smooth, yet absorbent ground. The paint is applied with fine sable brushes in thin layers, using light brushstrokes. Tempera dries quickly to form a tough skin with a satin sheen. The luminous white surface of the gesso combined with the overlaid paint produces the brilliant crispness and rich colors particular to this medium. Egg tempera paintings are frequently gilded with gold. Leaves of finely beaten gold are applied to a bole (reddish-brown clay) base and polished by burnishing.

MATERIALS FOR GILDING

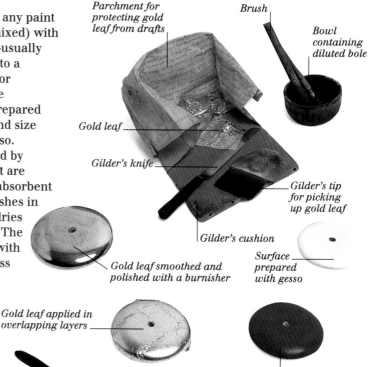

Parchment for protecting gold leaf from drafts

Brush

Bowl containing diluted bole

Gold leaf

Gilder's knife

Gilder's tip for picking up gold leaf

Gilder's cushion

Surface prepared with gesso

Gold leaf smoothed and polished with a burnisher

Gold leaf applied in overlapping layers

Bole brushed onto gesso

Burnisher

Agate tip

MATERIALS FOR TEMPERA PANEL PAINTING

Yolk

EGG

White

SIZE (GLUE)

GESSO

Lip

MORTAR AND PESTLE

Mortar

Pestle for crushing and grinding pigments

EGG YOLK BINDING MEDIUM

EXAMPLES OF BRUSHES

FLAT BRISTLE BRUSH

SABLE BRUSH NO. 6

SABLE BRUSH NO. 1

EXAMPLE OF A TEMPERA PAINTING
Presentation in the Temple, Ambrogio Lorenzetti, 1342
Tempera on wood, 8 ft 5⅛ in x 5 ft 6⅛ in (257 x 168 cm)

PIGMENTS FOR FLESH-COLOR PAINTING

Altarpiece commissioned for Siena Cathedral, Italy

The red tinge of the bole is just visible beneath the gold

Vine black used to create the dim cathedral interior

Red drapery painted in vermilion

Receding floor tiles create the impression of depth

Textured gold ornament made by punching motifs into the gilded surface

Edge of a sheet of gold leaf

Crisp edge characteristic of tempera painting

Highlights on the beard made by applying thin layers of white over dried paint

Raised right hand and pointing finger is the gesture of prophecy

Patch of discolored varnish, left from last cleaning

VERDACCIO

VERMILION AND LEAD WHITE

VERMILION

RED EARTH (IRON OXIDE)

EXAMPLES OF PIGMENTS

MALACHITE

ULTRAMARINE LAPIS LAZULI

VINE BLACK

LEAD TIN YELLOW

Warm flesh tones achieved by layering vermilion and white over an undercoat of verdaccio

Ultramarine lapis lazuli, as costly as gold, was reserved for significant figures such as the Virgin Mary

Patterned gold halo glitters in candlelight

Craquelure (pattern of cracks in the paint)

DETAIL FROM "PRESENTATION IN THE TEMPLE"

Fresco

FRESCO IS A METHOD OF WALL PAINTING. In buon fresco (true fresco), pigments are mixed with water and applied to an intonaco (layer of fresh, damp lime-plaster). The intonaco absorbs and binds the pigments as it dries making the picture a permanent part of the wall surface. The intonaco is applied in sections called giornate (daily sections). The size of each giornata depends on the artist's estimate of how much can be painted before the plaster sets. The junctions between giornate are sometimes visible on a finished fresco. The range of colors used in buon fresco are limited to lime-resistant pigments such as earth colors (below). Slaked lime (burnt lime mixed with water), bianco di San Giovanni (slaked lime that has been partly exposed to air), and chalk can be used to produce fresco whites. In fresco secco (dry fresco), pigments are mixed with a binding medium and applied to dry plaster. The pigments are not completely absorbed into the plaster and may flake off over time.

CROSS-SECTION SHOWING FRESCO LAYERS

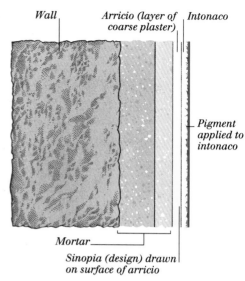

Wall

Arricio (layer of coarse plaster)

Intonaco

Pigment applied to intonaco

Mortar

Sinopia (design) drawn on surface of arricio

EXAMPLES OF EARTH COLOR PIGMENTS

RAW UMBER

RED EARTH (IRON OXIDE)

GREEN EARTH

RAW SIENNA

EXAMPLES OF FRESCO BRUSHES

Round bristle brush

Rust-resistant twine binding

Dome-shaped bristle brush

Pointed bristle brush

INGREDIENTS FOR FRESCO WHITES

Marble slab for mixing ingredients

Bianco di San Giovanni

Slaked lime

Chalk

TONDO

MUCCINI

RIGA

EXAMPLE OF A FRESCO
The Expulsion of the Merchants from the Temple, Giotto, c.1306
Fresco, 78 x 72 in (200 x 185 cm)

One of a series of frescoes in the Arena Chapel, Padua, Italy

Temple acts as a backdrop for the action

Bianco di San Giovanni often used for fresco whites

Gold leaf applied to apostle's halo

Green earth pigment applied to robe

Child painted on top of apostle's robe

Patches of azurite blue have turned green due to reaction with carbon dioxide

Hairline junction between giornate is visible

Red earth pigment applied in buon fresco has retained rich hue

Azurite blue applied in fresco secco has flaked off to reveal the plaster beneath

Dry, matt surface characteristic of buon fresco

Paint applied in buon fresco to child's face

White dove represents the Holy Ghost

Paint applied in fresco secco to child's body has flaked off

Sinopia (design) sketched in red earth

DETAIL FROM "THE EXPULSION"

Artist has to finish giornata before plaster dries

A fresco was generally worked in zones from the top down

Junction between giornate

Area with little detail can be painted quickly, allowing a larger giornata to be completed

Highly detailed area takes a longer time to paint, restricting the size of the giornata

GIORNATE (DAILY SECTIONS) IN "THE EXPULSION"

Oils

DAMMAR RESIN VARNISH

Crystals are dissolved and applied to painting to protect its surface

OIL PAINTS ARE MADE BY MIXING and grinding pigment with a drying vegetable oil such as linseed oil. The paint can be applied to many different surfaces and textures—the most common being canvas. Before painting, the canvas is stretched on a wooden frame and its surface is prepared with layers of size (glue) and primer. The two main types of brushes used in oil painting are stiff hog hair bristle brushes—generally used for covering large areas; and soft hair brushes made from sable or synthetic material—generally used for fine detail. Other tools, including painting knives, can also be used to achieve different effects. Oil paint can be applied thickly (a technique known as impasto), or can be thinned down using a solvent such as turpentine. Varnishes are sometimes applied to finished paintings to protect their surface and to give them a matt or gloss finish.

KIDNEY-SHAPED PALETTE

COMMERCIAL OIL PAINTS

CADMIUM RED

ULTRAMARINE

Lightfast opaque color

Transparent color

LINSEED OIL

Oil derived from seeds of flax plant

EXAMPLES OF PIGMENTS

CADMIUM RED

CERULEAN BLUE

DOUBLE DIPPER (PALETTE ATTACHMENT)

Screw-top lid

Container for storing solvent or drying oil

BRISTLE BRUSHES

Filbert bristle brush

Flat bristle brush

Flat bristle brush

Filbert bristle brush

SYNTHETIC BRUSH

Round bristle brush

EQUIPMENT FOR MAKING OIL PAINT

Airtight jar for storing paint

Palette knife for mixing drying oil and pigment

PAINTING KNIVES

TROWEL-SHAPED PAINTING KNIFE

DIAMOND-SHAPED PAINTING KNIFE

SABLE BRUSH

EXAMPLES OF BRUSHES

Blade

Blade

Glass muller for grinding drying oil and pigment

Glass slab with abrasive surface

Cranked, steel shank

Cranked, steel shank

Long, wooden handle

Protective, plastic case

EXAMPLE OF AN OIL PAINTING
Fritillarias, Vincent van Gogh, 1886
Oil on canvas, 29 x 24 in (73.5 x 60.5 cm)

Artist's signature scratched in wet paint with the end of the brush

Each leaf painted in a single, rapid stroke

Impasto (deep ridges of paint applied in thick strokes)

Strong directional brushstrokes on table draw attention to the vase

Background enlivened by dabs of white and green

Orange and blue (complementary colors) placed together to give maximum contrast and enhance one another to appear brighter

Features of vase highlighted by generous touches of yellow

STUDIO EASEL

Top sliding-block adjusts to canvas height

Canvas support

Height adjustment key

Angle adjustment key

Tripod

CANVAS STRETCHED ON WOODEN FRAME (VIEWED FROM THE BACK)

Staple

Canvas prepared with glue (size) and primer

Wooden frame

Unprimed canvas

EXAMPLES OF CANVASES

COTTON DUCK

FINE LINEN

COARSE LINEN

437

Watercolor

WATERCOLOR PAINT IS MADE OF GROUND PIGMENT mixed with a water-soluble binding medium, usually gum arabic. It is usually applied to paper using soft hair brushes such as sable, goat hair, squirrel, and synthetic brushes. Watercolors are often diluted and applied as overlaying washes (thin, transparent layers) to build up depth of color. Washes can be laid in a variety of ways to create a range of different effects. For example, a wet-in-wet wash can be achieved by laying a wash on top of another wet wash. The two washes blend together to give a fused effect. Sponges are used to modify washes by soaking up paint so that areas of pigment are lightened or removed from the paper. Watercolors can also be applied undiluted—a technique known as dry brush—to create a broken-color effect. Watercolors are generally transparent and allow light to reflect from the surface of the paper through the layers of paint to give a luminous effect. They can be thickened and made opaque by adding body color (Chinese white).

GUM ARABIC

Natural sap from acacia tree

NATURAL SPONGE

ANATOMY OF A SABLE BRUSH

Soft red sable hair

Toe (tip)

Wooden handle

SOFT HAIR BRUSHES

ROUND SABLE BRUSH (NO. 6)

ROUND SABLE BRUSH (NO. 1)

SYNTHETIC WASH BRUSH

SQUIRREL MOP
WASH BRUSH

LARGE GOAT HAKE
WASH BRUSH

Hair trimmed and cemented into ferrule

Round ferrule

Hair tied with clove hitch knot

**TUBES OF
WATERCOLOR PAINT**

WINSOR GREEN

CADMIUM YELLOW

**PORTABLE BOX OF
WATERCOLOR PAINTS**

Painted color swatch

Chinese white

Pan of watercolor paint

Lid can be used for mixing colors

EXAMPLE OF A WATERCOLOR
Burning of the Houses of Parliament, Turner, 1834
Watercolor on paper, 11½ x 17½ in (29.2 x 44.5 cm)

*Transparent
washes laid
on top of
each other
to create
tonal depth*

*Transparent
washes allow
light to reflect
off the surface
of the paper
to give a
luminous
effect*

*Highlight
scratched
out with
a scalpel*

*Paper shows
through thin
wash to
give flames
added
highlight*

*Crowd
painted with
thin strokes
laid over a
pale wash*

*Undiluted paint applied, then partly washed
out, to create the impression of water*

EXAMPLES OF
WATERCOLOR PAPERS

SMOOTH-
TEXTURED PAPER

EXAMPLES OF WASHES

WASH OVER DRY BRUSH
Wash laid over paint
applied with dry brush
gives two-tone effect

GRADED WASH
Strong wash applied
to tilted paper gives
graded effect

DRY BRUSH
Undiluted paint dragged
across surface of paper
gives broken effect

MEDIUM-
TEXTURED PAPER

WET-IN-WET
Two diluted washes
left to run together
to give fused effect

COLOR WHEEL OF
WATERCOLOR PAINTS

ROUGH-
TEXTURED PAPER

Yellow (primary color)

*Secondary colors
made by mixing
yellow and blue*

*Secondary colors
made by mixing
red and yellow*

Blue (primary color)

Red (primary color)

*Secondary colors made
by mixing blue and red*

Pastels

PASTELS ARE STICKS OF PIGMENT made by mixing ground pigment with chalk and a binding medium, such as gum arabic. They vary in hardness depending on the proportion of the binding medium to the chalk. Soft pastel—the most common form of pastel—contains just enough binding medium to hold the pigment in stick form. Pastels can be applied directly to any support (surface) with sufficient tooth (texture). When a pastel is drawn over a textured surface, the pigment crumbles and lodges in the fibers of the support. Pastel marks have a particular soft, matt quality and are suitable for techniques such as blending, scumbling, and feathering. Blending is a technique of rubbing and fusing two or more colors on the support using fingers or various tools such as tortillons (paper stumps), soft hair brushes, kneaded erasers, and soft bread. Scumbling is a technique of building up layers of pastel colors. The side or blunted tip of a soft pastel is lightly drawn over an underpainted area so that patches of the color beneath show through. Feathering is a technique of applying parallel strokes of color with the point of a pastel, usually over an existing layer of pastel color. A thin spray of fixative can be applied—using a mouth diffuser (see pp. 430-431) or aerosol spray fixative—to a finished pastel painting, or in between layers of color, to prevent smudging.

EQUIPMENT FOR MAKING PASTELS

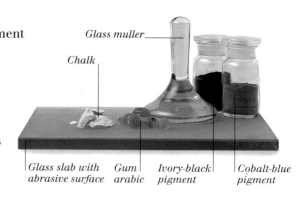

Glass muller

Chalk

Glass slab with abrasive surface *Gum arabic* *Ivory-black pigment* *Cobalt-blue pigment*

EXAMPLES OF SOFT PASTELS

COBALT-BLUE HALF PASTEL

VERMILION HALF PASTEL

OLIVE-GREEN FULL PASTEL

MAUVE FULL PASTEL

BOXED PASTEL SET

Boxed set containing a mixture of portrait and landscape colors

Foam compartments protect the pastels

Soft pastel

Wooden tray

EQUIPMENT USED WITH PASTELS

KNEADED ERASER

BREAD

Soft bread suitable for erasing and blending

AEROSOL SPRAY FIXATIVE

SOFT HAIR BRUSH

TORTILLONS (PAPER STUMPS)

Soft point used for blending

Tight roll of paper

EXAMPLE OF A PASTEL PAINTING
Woman Drying her Neck, Edgar Degas, c.1898
Pastel on cardboard, 24½ x 25½ in (62.5 x 65.5 cm)

Pastels applied directly to support

Colors are blended together using fingers or tools such as tortillons

Built up layers of pastel

Rich color of fabric created by overlaying yellows and oranges

Broken colors, characteristic of scumbling technique

Toned color of paper visible beneath thinly applied pastels

Pure bright colors laid side by side produce strong contrasts

DETAIL FROM "WOMAN DRYING HER NECK"

Feathering technique used to produce skin tones

EXAMPLES OF TEXTURED PAPERS AND PASTEL BOARDS

WATERCOLOR PAPER (ROUGH TEXTURE)

GLASS PAPER

WATERCOLOR PAPER (MEDIUM TEXTURE)

INGRES PAPER

FLOCKED PASTEL BOARD

CANSON PAPER

EXAMPLES OF COLORED AND TINTED PAPERS

Acrylics

ACRYLIC PAINT IS MADE BY MIXING PIGMENT with a synthetic resin. It can be thinned with water but dries to become water insoluble. Acrylics are applied to many surfaces, such as paper and acrylic-primed board and canvas. A variety of brushes, painting knives, rollers, air-brushes, plastic scrapers, and other tools are used in acrylic painting. The versatility of acrylics makes them suitable for a wide range of techniques. They can be used opaquely or—by adding water—in a transparent, watercolor style. Acrylic mediums can be added to the paint to adjust its consistency for special effects such as glazing and impasto (ridges of paint applied in thick strokes) or to make it more matt or glossy. Acrylics are quick-drying, which allows layers of paint to be applied on top of each other almost immediately.

EXAMPLES OF BRUSHES

Sable brush

Bristle sash brush

Synthetic bristle brush

Synthetic sable brush

Bristle brush

Goat hair brush

Synthetic wash brush

Ox hair brush

EXAMPLES OF PAINTS USED IN ACRYLICS

Azo yellow

Phthalo green

Cerulean blue

Phthalo blue

Quinacridone red

Titanium white

Yellow ochre

Burnt sienna

Burnt umber

Pad of disposable paper palettes

PAINTING TOOLS

Flexible, plastic blade

PLASTIC PAINTING KNIFE

Stippled effect achieved using thick paint

Striated effect

Glue spreader

Credit card

Paint spread evenly

PLASTIC SCRAPERS

Plastic handle

SPONGE ROLLER

Blended tones

Paint cup

Nozzle

Main lever

AIR-BRUSH

Uniform tone

Air hose

EXAMPLE OF AN ACRYLIC PAINTING
A Bigger Splash, David Hockney, 1967
Acrylic on canvas, 95½ x 96 in (242.5 x 243.8 cm)

Paint applied evenly using a roller

Cotton duck canvas support (surface)

Flatness of rollered areas enhanced by adding gel medium to the paint

Masking tape stuck onto canvas to define main shapes, and paint applied within these areas using a roller

Thin strip of pool edge left unpainted

Splash painted using thicker paint and small brush

Imprecise edge on end of spring board where paint has seeped under masking tape

EXAMPLES OF ACRYLIC PAINTS AND TECHNIQUES

Opaque effect

Extruded (squeezed) effect

Paint applied using painting knife

PURPLE ACRYLIC PAINT

YELLOW ACRYLIC PAINT

ORANGE ACRYLIC PAINT

Transparent, watercolor effect

Translucent, impasto glaze

Thick impasto with coarse texture

BLUE ACRYLIC PAINT DILUTED WITH WATER

GREEN ACRYLIC PAINT MIXED WITH GEL MEDIUM

RED ACRYLIC PAINT MIXED WITH TEXTURE PASTE

Calligraphy

CALLIGRAPHY IS BEAUTIFULLY FORMED LETTERING. The term applies to written text and illumination (the decoration of manuscripts using gold leaf and color). The essential materials needed to practice calligraphy are a writing tool, ink, and a writing surface. Quills are among the oldest writing tools. They are usually made from goose or turkey feathers, and are noted for their flexibility and ability to produce fine lines. A quill point, however, is not very durable and constant recutting and trimming is required. The most commonly used writing instrument in western calligraphy is a detachable, metal nib held in a penholder. The metal nib is very durable, and there are a wide range of different types. Particular types of nibs—such as copperplate, speedball, and round-hand nibs—are used for specific styles of lettering. Some nibs have integral ink reservoirs and others have reservoirs that are detachable. Brushes are also used for writing, and for filling in outlined letters and painting decoration. Other writing tools used in calligraphy are fountain pens, felt-tipped pens, rotring pens, and reed pens. Calligraphy inks may come in liquid form, or as a solid ink stick. Ink sticks are ground down in distilled water to form a liquid ink. The most common writing surfaces for calligraphy are good quality, smooth -surfaced papers. To achieve the best writing position, the calligrapher places the paper on a drawing board set at an angle.

EQUIPMENT USED IN BRUSH LETTERING

Brush rest

Wolf hair brush

Goat hair brush

BRUSHES AND BRUSH REST

Liquid ink made by grinding down ink stick in distilled water

Solid carbon ink stick

Ink stone

INK STICK AND STONE

PENS, NIBS, AND BRUSHES USED IN CALLIGRAPHY

PENHOLDER

COPPERPLATE NIB

SPEEDBALL NIB

ROUND-HAND NIB AND DETACHABLE INK RESERVOIR

FELT-TIPPED PEN

ROTRING PEN

REED PEN

Feather stripped for better handling

Barrel

SQUARE SABLE BRUSH

POINTED SABLE BRUSH

Hand-cut point

GOOSE-FEATHER QUILL

Feather

GOAT HAIR BRUSH

WOLF HAIR BRUSH

FOUNTAIN PEN AND INK

Bottle of permanent black ink

Barrel

Clip

Nib

Outer cap

EXAMPLES OF LETTERING STYLES

Apex
Bowl
Curved stroke
Stem
Inner counter
Stem
Stem
Arm
Counter
Crossbar
Inner counter
Counter
Inner counter

ROMAN CAPITALS

Ascender
Curved stroke
Ear
Arch
Cap line
X line
Crossbar
Base line
Descender line
Serif
Neck
Descender

Height of letter determined by ladder of nib widths

ITALIC ROMAN

Slightly pinched (curved) vertical stroke
Letter filled in using brush
Inner counter
Tail
Spine
Pointed apex

VERSAL

CHINESE LETTERING

Rice paper
Broad brush-stroke
Chinese character meaning long life
Artist's stamped signature

ARTIST'S STAMP

Stamp
Stamped signature of the artist
Ink pad

DRAWING BOARD

Adjustable set square
Blade with parallel motion

AN ILLUMINATED MANUSCRIPT

Style of lettering called Gothic book script
Large decorative letter used to mark the opening of a chapter
Words written carefully by hand
Gold leaf
Grid lines provide guide to position of words and pictures

EXAMPLES OF CALLIGRAPHY PAPERS

Standard European paper
Indian handmade paper
Flecked, tinted paper
Imitation parchment paper

Printmaking 1

PRINTS ARE MADE BY FOUR BASIC printing processes – intaglio, lithographic, relief, and screen. In intaglio printing, lines are engraved or etched onto the surface of a metal plate. Lines are engraved using sharp metal tools. They are etched by corroding the metal plate with acid, using acid-resistant ground to protect the areas not to be etched. The plate is then inked and wiped, leaving the grooves filled with ink and the surface clean. Dampened paper is laid over the plate, and both paper and plate are passed through the rollers of an etching press. The pressure of the rollers forces the paper into the grooves, so that it takes up the ink, leaving an impression on the paper. Lithographic printing is based on the antipathy between grease and water. An image is drawn on a surface—usually a stone or metal plate—with a greasy medium, such as tusche (lihographic ink). The greasy drawing is fixed onto the plate by applying an acidic solution, such as gum arabic. The surface is then dampened and rolled with ink. The ink adheres only to the greasy areas and is repelled by the water. Paper is laid on the plate and pressure is applied by means of a press. In relief printing, the non-printing areas of a wood or linoleum block are cut away using gouges, knives, and other tools. The printing areas are left raised in relief and are rolled with ink. Paper is laid on the inked block and pressure is applied by means of a press or by burnishing (rubbing) the back of the paper. The most common forms of relief printing are woodcut, wood engraving, and linocut. In screen printing, the printing surface is a mesh stretched across a wooden frame. A stencil is applied to the mesh to seal the non-printing areas and ink is scraped through the mesh to produce an image.

THE FOUR MAIN PRINTING PROCESSES

Paper · Printed image · Engraved or etched image · Metal plate · Inked area

INTAGLIO

Printed image · Paper · Damp surface rejects ink · Ink adheres to greasy image · Image drawn on stone with greasy medium

LITHOGRAPHIC

Paper · Printed image · Raised figure · Inked surface · Wood block

RELIEF

Ink forced through mesh · Wooden frame · Stencil · Printed image · Paper

SCREEN

LEATHER INK DABBER

EQUIPMENT USED IN INTAGLIO PRINTING

ROCKER **SCRIBER** **ROULETTE** **SCRAPER** **BURNISHER** **CLAMP**

ETCHING PRESS USED FOR INTAGLIO PRINTMAKING

Flywheel

Paper

Felt blanket cushions and distributes pressure exerted by rollers

Spoke

Screw pressure adjustor

Handle

Top roller

Position guide

Printed image

Inked-up copper plate

Sliding bed (plank) is wound between steel rollers

GROUND

Acid-resistant ground rolled onto metal plate before etching

GROUND ROLLER

Gelatine roller

Wooden handle

EXAMPLES OF PRINTING PAPERS

EXAMPLE OF AN INTAGLIO PRINT
Annie with a Sun Hat, Jock McFadyen, 1993
Etched copper plate, 16 x 15¾ in (41 x 40 cm)

Printmaking 2

EXAMPLE OF A LITHOGRAPHIC STONE AND PRINT

Crown Gateway 2, Mandy Bonnell, 1987
Lithograph, 19½ x 15¾ in (50 x 40 cm)

IMAGE DRAWN ON STONE   **LITHOGRAPIC PRINT**

EXAMPLE OF A SCREEN PRINT

Sea Change, Patrick Hughes, 1992
Screen print, 30 x 37 in (77 x 94.5 cm)

EQUIPMENT USED IN LITHOGRAPHIC PRINTING

CRAYON AND HOLDER

LITHOGRAPHIC PENCIL

TUSCHE (LITHOGRAPHIC INK) PEN

ERASING STICK

EXPANDABLE SPONGE

TUSCHE (LITHOGRAPHIC INK) STICK

RUBBING INK

INK ROLLER

MILD ACIDIC SOLUTION   **GUM ARABIC SOLUTION**

WATER-BASED SCREEN PRINTING INKS

BLUE ACRYLIC INK   **RED ACRYLIC INK**   **BROWN TEXTILE INK**

SCREEN AND SQUEEGEE

Squeegee

Rubber blade

Mesh

Wooden frame

EQUIPMENT USED IN RELIEF PRINTING

V-SHAPED GOUGE

INK ROLLER

Rubber roller

LINOLEUM AND WOODCUT BLOCK

Linoleum

U-SHAPED GOUGE

GRAVER

KNIFE

SCORPER

Side-grain wood block

WOOD ENGRAVING

END-GRAIN WOOD BLOCK

INKED-UP ENGRAVED BLOCK

WOOD ENGRAVING PRINT

RELIEF-PRINTING PRESS

Spiral spring

Crown

Piston

Tympan lowered onto printing block

Printed image

Printing block

Bed is rolled under platen

Drum handle

Bar (pressure handle)

Staple (frame)

Platen

Counterweight

Rail

Drum (rounce)

Leg

Pillar (post)

Foot

449

Mosaic

MOSAIC IS THE ART OF MAKING patterns and pictures from tesserae (small, colored pieces of glass, marble, and other materials). Different materials are cut into tesserae using different tools. Smalti (glass enamel) and marble are cut into pieces using a hammer and a hardy (a pointed blade) embedded in a log. Vitreous glass is cut into pieces using a pair of pliers. Mosaics can be made using a direct or indirect method. In the direct method, the tesserae are laid directly into a bed of cement–based adhesive. In the indirect method, the design is drawn in reverse on paper or cloth. The tesserae are then stuck face down on the paper or cloth using water-soluble glue. Adhesive is spread with a trowel onto a solid surface—such as a wall—and the back of the mosaic is laid into the adhesive. Finally, the paper or cloth is soaked off to reveal the mosaic. Gaps between tesserae can be filled with grout. Grout is forced into gaps by dragging a grouting squeegee across the face of the mosaic. Mosaics are usually used to decorate walls and floors, but they can also be applied to smaller objects.

EQUIPMENT FOR BREAKING MARBLE

Strip of marble, ready for breaking into cubes

Mosaic hammer

Hardwearing, tungsten carbide tip

Alicante (red marble) pieces

Hardy (pointed blade) embedded in a log

PLIERS

Handle with rubber grip

MOSAIC TOOLS

CEMENT-BASED ADHESIVE

GROUT

SMALTI (GLASS ENAMEL)

RED SMALTI

EXAMPLE OF A MOSAIC (DIRECT METHOD)
Seascape, Tessa Hunkin, 1993
Smalti mosaic on board
31½ in (80 cm) diameter

YELLOW SMALTI

TROWEL

Notch

Wooden handle

Steel blade

Wooden handle

GROUTING SQUEEGEE

Wooden handle

Rubber blade

BLUE SMALTI

Gold-leaf smalti

STAGES IN THE CREATION OF A MOSAIC (INDIRECT METHOD)

COLOR SKETCH
A color sketch is drawn
in oil pastel to give a clear
impression of how the finished
mosaic will look.

REVERSE IMAGE
Tesserae are glued face down
on reverse image on paper.
Mosaic is then attached to solid
surface and paper is removed.

MOSAIC POT

Geometric design

Grout

MOSAIC MOSQUE DESIGN

Floral design

Geometric border

Finished Mosaic labels

Andamenti (line along which tesserae are laid)

Grout fills the gaps between the tesserae

Mosaic mounted on board

Vitreous glass cut into triangular shape with pliers

Gold tessera with ripple finish

Gold tessera placed upside-down

FINISHED MOSAIC
Goldfish, Tessa Hunkin, 1993
Vitreous glass mosaic on board
14 x 10 in (35.5 x 25.5 cm)

Border of square vitreous glass

VITREOUS GLASS

**GREEN VITREOUS
GLASS WITH GOLD LEAF**

Plain finish

Ripple finish

**RED VITREOUS
GLASS**

SHEETS OF VITREOUS GLASS

**BLUE VITREOUS
GLASS**

Sculpture 1

THE TWO TRADITIONAL SCULPTURE METHODS are carving and modeling. A carved sculpture is made by cutting away the surplus from a block of hard material such as stone, marble, or wood. The tools used for carving vary according to the material being carved. Heavy steel points, claws, and chisels that are struck with a lump hammer are generally used for stone and marble. Sharp gouges and chisels that are struck with a wooden mallet are used for wood. Sculptures formed from hard materials are generally finished by filing with rasps, rifflers, and other abrasive implements. Modeling is a process by which shapes are built up, using malleable materials such as clay, plaster, and wax. The material is cut with wire-ended tools and modeled with the fingers or a variety of hardwood and metal implements. For large or intricate modeled sculptures an armature (frame), made from metal or wood, is used to provide internal support. Sculptures formed in soft materials may harden naturally or can be made more durable by firing in a kiln. Modeled sculptures are often first designed in wax or another material to be cast later in a metal (see pp. 454-455) such as bronze. The development of many new materials in the 20th century has enabled sculptors to experiment with new techniques such as construction (joining preformed pieces of material such as machine components, mirrors, and furniture) and kinetic (mobile) sculpture.

EXAMPLES OF MARBLE-CARVING TOOLS

2½ lb (1.1 kg) iron head

Ash handle

LUMP HAMMER

EXAMPLES OF WOOD-CARVING TOOLS

CABINET RASP

STRAIGHT GOUGE

SALMON BEND GOUGE

CHISEL

Stone for sharpening wood-carving tools

Cedar box

ARKANSAS HONE-STONE

CARVING MALLET

CALLIPERS

Curved leg

Gap measures distance between two points on a sculpture

Wing nut

WIDE MARBLE CLAW **NARROW MARBLE CLAW**

POINT

FLAT CHISEL

BULLNOSE CHISEL

EXAMPLES OF RIFFLERS (FOR STONE, MARBLE, AND WOOD)

12 IN (30 CM) RIFFLER

6 IN (15 CM) RIFFLER

Surface for sharpening stone-carving tools

DIAMOND WHETSTONE

*Tiny holes along
the hairline made
with a point*

*Soft skin texture tooled
with a fine-toothed
marble claw*

**DETAIL OF
SLAVE'S HEAD**

EXAMPLE OF A CARVED MARBLE SCULPTURE
The Rebel Slave, Michelangelo, 1513-1516
Marble, height 7ft (213 cm)

EXAMPLE OF A CARVED WOOD SCULPTURE
Mary Magdalene, Donatello, 1454-1455
Poplar wood, height 6 ft 2 in (188 cm)

*Hair worked
with a narrow
claw*

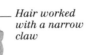

*Delicately
modeled
hand carved
with a chisel*

*Translucent white
marble, quarried at
Carrara, Italy*

*Hair
highlighted
with gold
leaf*

*Figure cut
from single
length of
poplar*

*Deep
ridges of
hair cut
with a
gouge*

*Surface rubbed
smooth with
rifflers and
pumice*

*Strut gives added
support to long
slender limb*

*Wood prepared
with gesso
(chalk and glue)
and painted*

*Base scored with
jagged parallel
cuts made with
point and lump
hammer*

*Series of tiny
punch holes,
made with a
fine point,
outline the
form*

*Foot carved in
deep relief*

*Rough surface
made by driving
a point into the
marble at an
oblique angle*

*The dimensions of the marble block
determine the size of the sculpture*

DETAIL OF SLAVE'S FOOT

Sculpture 2

EXAMPLES OF MODELING TOOLS

WIRE-ENDED CUTTING TOOL

CURVED MOLDING TOOL

SPATULA-ENDED WAX MODELING TOOL

ROUNDED WAX MODELING TOOL

EXAMPLES OF BRONZE FINISHING TOOLS

HOOKED RIFFLER   **POINTED RIFFLER**

ALCOHOL BURNER (FOR HEATING WAX MODELING TOOLS)

Wick

Brass holder

Glass bowl

Denatured alcohol

STAGES IN THE LOST-WAX METHOD OF CASTING
Based on Mars, Giambologna, c.1546

Wax-covered wire armature

Wax riser (vertical, hollow rod)

Chaplet (iron nail)

Wax runner (horizontal, hollow rod)

ORIGINAL MODEL
An original, solid wax model is made and preserved so that numerous replicas can be cast.

HOLLOW WAX FIGURE IS CAST
A new, hollow wax model is cast from the original model. It is filled with a plaster core that is held in place with nails. Wax runners and risers are attached.

Fire-resistant clay

FIGURE IS BAKED IN CASTING MOLD
The model is encased in clay and baked. The wax melts away (through the channels made by the wax rods) and is replaced by molten bronze.

MODELING STAND AND ARMATURE

Aluminum wire figure

Fixed iron armature support

Marine ply modeling board

Rotating table top

Tripod

Screw-hole for fastening the iron to modeling board

Aluminum table stand

Height adjustor

EXAMPLE OF A CLAY MODEL
Madonna and Child, Henry Moore, 1943
Terracotta, height 7¼ in (18.4 cm)

Clay smoothed to create the effect of soft skin

Incision made with serrated tool

Strips of clay, added to the model, give the effect of folded drapery

Maquette (small sketch) modeled from a solid lump of clay

Terracotta clay, fires at 1,832°F to 1,922°F (1,000°C to 1,050°C)

Model for a much larger bronze sculpture

Roughly worked clay

Metal riser

Metal runner

STATUE IS STRIPPED OF CLAY
When the bronze has cooled, the clay mold is broken open to reveal the bronze statue with solid metal runners and risers.

Golden brown color of untreated bronze

Stump left by rod will be filed down

Hole left by nail will be plugged with bronze

STATUE IS FINISHED
The nails are pulled out and a large hole is made to remove the plaster core. When the metal rods have been sawn off, the sculpture is filed to refine the surface.

Dark brown patina

STATUE IS CLEANED
Finally the work is cleaned and polished. An artificial patina (coloring) is achieved by treating the surface with chemicals.

ARCHITECTURE

Ancient Egypt

THE CIVILIZATION OF THE ANCIENT EGYPTIANS (which lasted from about 3100 BC until it was finally absorbed into the Roman empire in 30 BC) is famous for its temples and tombs. Egyptian temples were often huge and geometric, like the Temple of Amon-Re (below and right). They were usually decorated with hieroglyphs (sacred characters used for picture writing) and painted reliefs depicting gods, Pharaohs (kings), and queens. Tombs were particularly important to the Egyptians, who believed that the dead were resurrected in the afterlife. The tombs were often decorated—for example, the surround of the false door opposite— in order to give comfort to the dead. The best-known ancient Egyptian tombs are the pyramids, which were designed to symbolize the rays of the sun. Many of the architectural forms used by the ancient Egyptians were later adopted by other civilizations. For example, columns and capitals were later used by the ancient Greeks (see pp. 460-461) and ancient Romans (see pp. 462-465).

SIDE VIEW OF HYPOSTYLE HALL, TEMPLE OF AMON-RE, KARNAK, EGYPT, c.1290 BC

FRONT VIEW OF HYPOSTYLE HALL, TEMPLE OF AMON-RE

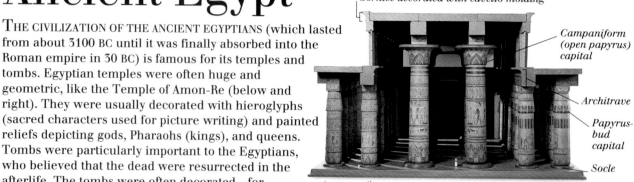

Cornice decorated with cavetto molding

Campaniform (open papyrus) capital

Architrave

Papyrus-bud capital

Socle

Side aisle

Central nave

Side aisle

Horus, the sun-god

Architrave

Stone slab forming flat roof of side aisle

Kepresh crown with disc

Chons, the moon-god

Amon-Re, king of the gods

Hathor, the sky-goddess

Papyrus motif

Cartouche (oval border) containing the titles of the Pharaoh (king)

Socle

Aisle running north–south

LIMESTONE FALSE DOOR WITH HIEROGLYPHS, TOMB OF KING TJETJI, GIZA, EGYPT, c.2400 BC

Lintel

Hieroglyph representing a house

Disc representing sun or light

Eroded image of Tjetji

Limestone stela (slab)

Hoe-shaped hieroglyph representing "mr" sound

Head of false door

Image of Tjetji's wife

Image of Tjetji's daughter

PLANT CAPITAL OF THE PTOLEMAIC-ROMAN PERIOD, EGYPT, 332-30 BC

Palm leaf

Papyrus flower

Papyrus leaf

Papyrus stem

Lotus bud

Lotus stem

Cornice decorated with cavetto molding

Bead molding

Trellis window

Rectangular pier decorated with hieroglyphs

Elevated roof of central nave

Clerestory

Disc representing sun or light

Architrave

Square abacus

Papyrus-bud capital

Papyriform column

Shaft

Scene depicting a Pharaoh (king) paying homage to the god Amon-Re

Central nave

ANCIENT EGYPTIAN BUILDING DECORATION

DECORATED WINDOW, MEDINET HABU, EGYPT, C.1198 BC

ROPE AND PATERAE DECORATION

CAPITAL WITH THE HEAD OF THE SKY-GODDESS HATHOR, TEMPLE OF ISIS, PHILAE, EGYPT, 285-47 BC

LOTUS AND PAPYRUS FRIEZE DECORATION

Ancient Greece

THE CLASSICAL TEMPLES OF ANCIENT GREECE were built according to the belief that certain forms and proportions were pleasing to the gods. There were three main ancient Greek architectural orders (styles), which can be distinguished by the decoration and proportions of their columns, capitals (column tops), and entablatures (structures resting on the capitals). The oldest is the Doric order, which dates from the seventh century BC and was used mainly on the Greek mainland and in the western colonies, such as Sicily and southern Italy. The Temple of Neptune, shown here, is a classic example of this order. It is hypaethral (roofless) and peripteral (surrounded by a single row of columns). About a century later, the more decorative Ionic order developed on the Aegean Islands. Features of this order include volutes (spiral scrolls) on capitals and acroteria (pediment ornaments). The Corinthian order was invented in Athens in the fifth century BC and is typically identified by an acanthus leaf on the capitals. This order was later widely used in ancient Roman architecture.

CAPITALS OF THE THREE ORDERS OF ANCIENT GREEK ARCHITECTURE

Abacus
Echinus
Trachelion (neck)
Annulet

DORIC CAPITAL, THE PROPYLAEUM (GATEWAY), THE ACROPOLIS, ATHENS, GREECE, 449 BC

Coussinet (cushion)
Abacus
Lesbian leaf pattern
Cyma reversa profile
Volute
Echinus with egg and dart decoration
Eye
Palmette

IONIC CAPITAL, THE PROPYLAEUM (GATEWAY), TEMPLE OF ATHENA POLIAS, PRIENE, GREECE, c.334 BC

Mask
Abacus
Volute
Cauliculus
Bell-shaped core
Acanthus leaf

CORINTHIAN CAPITAL FROM A STOA (PORTICO), PROBABLY FROM ASIA MINOR

TEMPLE OF NEPTUNE, PAESTUM, ITALY, c.460 BC

Pediment
Raking cornice
Trachelion (neck)
Taenia
Triglyph
Metope
Glyph (channel)
Doric entablature
Pteron (external colonnade)
Euthynteria
Drum
Stylobate
Column of the Doric order

PLAN OF THE TEMPLE OF NEPTUNE, PAESTUM

Pronaos (vestibule)

Naos wall

Anta (pilaster terminating naos wall)

Naos (cella)

Peristyle

Opisthodomos (rear portico)

Pteron (external colonnade)

Hexastyle pteron (colonnade of six columns)

ANCIENT GREEK BUILDING DECORATION

Volute

FACADE, TREASURY OF ATREUS, MYCENAE, GREECE, 1350-1250 BC

Meander

FRETWORK, PARTHENON, ATHENS, GREECE, 447-436 BC

ACROTERION, TEMPLE OF APHAIA, AEGINA, GREECE, 490 BC

Griffon (gryphon)

Raking cornice

ANTEFIXA, TEMPLE OF APHAIA, AEGINA, GREECE, 490 BC

Palmette

Volute

Regula (short fillet beneath taenia)

Eaves

Cornice

Frieze

Architrave

Capital

Shaft

Crepidoma (stepped base)

Entasis (slight curve of a column)

Intercolumniation

Fluting

Ancient Rome 1

IN THE EARLY PERIOD OF THE ROMAN EMPIRE extensive use
was made of ancient Greek architectural ideas, particularly
those of the Corinthian order (see pp. 460-461). As a result,
many early Roman buildings—such as the Temple of Vesta
(opposite)—closely resemble ancient Greek buildings. A
distinctive Roman style began to evolve in the first century
AD. This style developed the interiors of buildings (the Greeks
had concentrated on the exterior) by wing arches, vaults, and
domes inside the buildings and by ornamenting internal walls;
many of these features can be seen in the Pantheon. Exterior
columns were often used for decorative rather than structural
purposes, as in the Colosseum and the Porta Nigra (see
pp. 464-465). Smaller buildings had timber frames with
wattle-and-daub walls, as in the mill (see pp. 464-465).
Roman architecture remained influential for many centuries,
with some of its principles being used in the 11th century in
Romanesque buildings (see pp. 468-469) and also in the 15th
and 16th centuries in Renaissance buildings (see pp. 474-477).

ANCIENT ROMAN BUILDING DECORATION

FESTOON, TEMPLE OF VESTA,
TIVOLI, ITALY, C.80 BC

RICHLY DECORATED
ROMAN OVUM

**INTERIOR OF THE PANTHEON,
ROME, ITALY, 118-c.128**

Inner dome,
following the
curve of a
depressed arch

Outer
saucer
dome

Entablature

Curved
cornice

Lesene

Cornice

Triangular
pediment

Concave
niche

Marble veneer — Segmental pediment — Pedestal

Oculus

Series of concentric,
steplike rings

Outer saucer dome

Dentil ornament

Intermediate
block

Engaged
pediment

Entablature
with
inscription

Raking
cornice

Pediment

Rotunda

Octastyle portico
(eight-column portico)

FRONT VIEW OF THE PANTHEON

SIDE VIEW OF THE PANTHEON

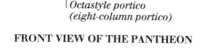

Entablature

Intermediate
block

Upper
cornice

Pitched roof

Eaves

Relieving
arch

Opening for
ventilation

Cornice

Colonnade

Ornamental
band decorated
with festoons

Attached
fluted pilaster

FRIEZE, FORUM OF TRAJAN, ROME, ITALY, 98-113

KEYSTONE, ARCH OF TITUS, ROME, ITALY, 81

TEMPLE OF VESTA, TIVOLI, ITALY, c.80 BC

Circular naos (cella)

Architrave

Ceiling

Fascia

Corinthian entablature

Corinthian capital

Pteron (colonnade)

Naos (cella) window

Opus incertum (concrete wall faced with irregularly shaped stones)

Egg and dart decoration

Upper torus

Scotia

Lower torus

Jamb with corrugated surface

Naos (cella) door

Cornice

Threshold

Podium

Oculus illuminating interior of rotunda

Coffer

Stepped side of coffer

Frieze decorated with arabesques, urns, and winged horses

Steplike ring

Barrel vault

Passageway

Coffer

Engaged pediment

Monolithic shaft (shaft made from a single stone)

Barrel vault

Raking cornice

Pediment

Entablature

Corinthian column

Corinthian capital

Entablature

Aedicule (tabernacle)

Rotunda

Festoon

Fluting

Corinthian pilaster

Base

Portico

463

Ancient Rome 2

SIDE VIEW OF A ROMAN MILL

Principal rafter
Wall plate
Wall post
Top plate
Floorboard
Intermediate floor joist
Sill
Stud
Foundation

Lath
Pantile
Verge
Eaves
Plain fascia
Plaster coating

Grille
Joist
Boarding

FRONT VIEW OF A ROMAN MILL, 1ST CENTURY BC

Half-round ridge tile
Pitched roof
Ashlar post
Plain fascia
Flat soffit
Mill wheel

King strut
Lath
Principal rafter
Tie beam
Wall plate
Intermediate floor joist
Top plate
Wall post
Sill
Binder

Wattle-and-daub with plaster coating
Supporting post
Floor joist
Foundation post

THE COLOSSEUM (FLAVIAN AMPHITHEATER), ROME, ITALY, 70-82

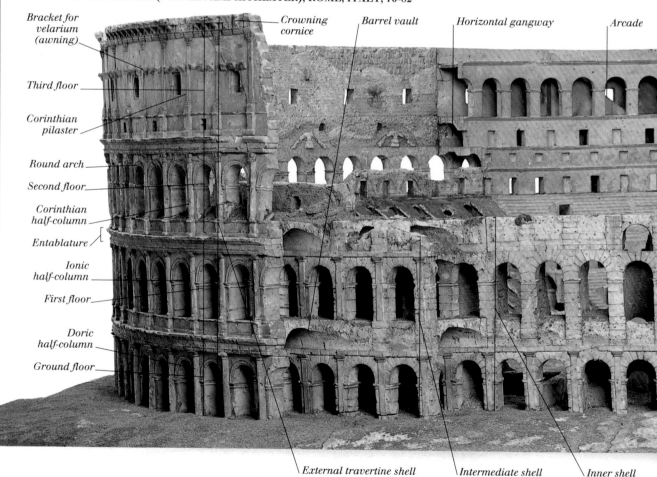

Bracket for velarium (awning)
Third floor
Corinthian pilaster
Round arch
Second floor
Corinthian half-column
Entablature
Ionic half-column
First floor
Doric half-column
Ground floor

Crowning cornice
Barrel vault
Horizontal gangway
Arcade

External travertine shell
Intermediate shell
Inner shell

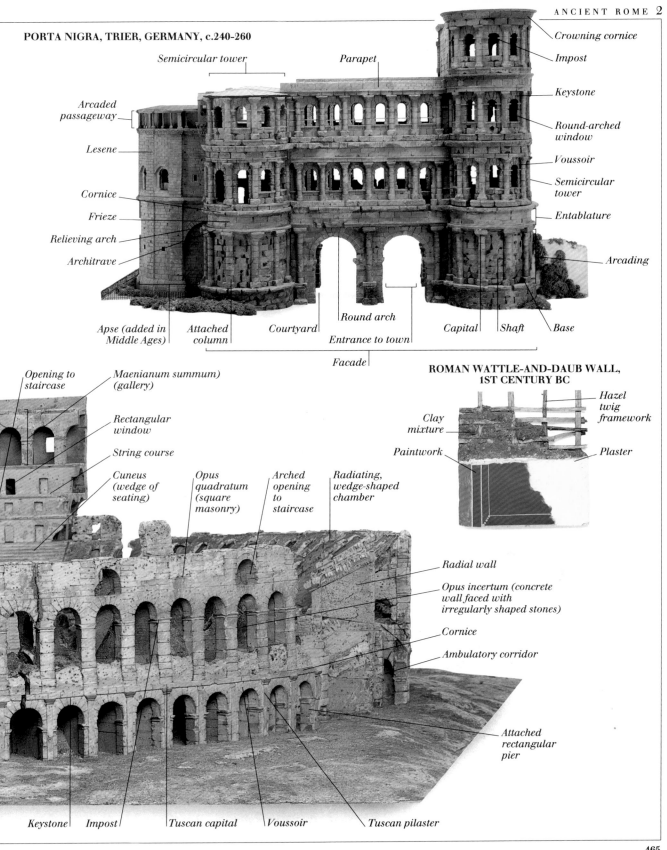

PORTA NIGRA, TRIER, GERMANY, c.240-260

Crowning cornice

Impost

Semicircular tower

Parapet

Keystone

Arcaded passageway

Round-arched window

Lesene

Voussoir

Semicircular tower

Cornice

Entablature

Frieze

Relieving arch

Architrave

Arcading

Apse (added in Middle Ages)

Attached column

Courtyard

Round arch

Capital

Shaft

Base

Entrance to town

Facade

ROMAN WATTLE-AND-DAUB WALL, 1ST CENTURY BC

Hazel twig framework

Clay mixture

Paintwork

Plaster

Opening to staircase

Maenianum summum) (gallery)

Rectangular window

String course

Cuneus (wedge of seating)

Opus quadratum (square masonry)

Arched opening to staircase

Radiating, wedge-shaped chamber

Radial wall

Opus incertum (concrete wall faced with irregularly shaped stones)

Cornice

Ambulatory corridor

Attached rectangular pier

Keystone

Impost

Tuscan capital

Voussoir

Tuscan pilaster

465

Medieval castles and houses

WARFARE WAS COMMON IN EUROPE in the Middle Ages, and many monarchs and nobles built castles as a form of defense. Typical medieval castles have outer walls surrounding a moat. Inside the moat is a bailey (courtyard), protected by a chemise (jacket wall). The innermost and strongest part of a medieval castle is the keep. There are two main types of keep: towers called donjons, such as the Tour de César and Coucy-le-Château in France, and rectangular keeps ("hall-keeps"), such as the Tower of London. Castles were often guarded by salients (projecting fortifications), like those of the Bastille. Medieval houses typically had timber cruck (tent-like) frames, wattle-and-daub walls, and pitched roofs, like those on medieval London Bridge (opposite).

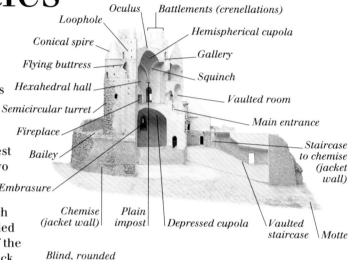

DONJON, TOUR DE CESAR, PROVINS, FRANCE, 12TH CENTURY

Oculus · Loophole · Conical spire · Flying buttress · Hexahedral hall · Semicircular turret · Fireplace · Bailey · Embrasure · Battlements (crenellations) · Hemispherical cupola · Gallery · Squinch · Vaulted room · Main entrance · Staircase to chemise (jacket wall) · Chemise (jacket wall) · Plain impost · Depressed cupola · Vaulted staircase · Motte

SALIENT, CAERNARVON CASTLE, BRITAIN, 1283-1323

Loophole

CRUCK-FRAMED HOUSE, BRITAIN, c.1200

Timber cruck frame

TOWER OF LONDON, BRITAIN, FROM 1070

Blind, rounded relieving arch · Merlon · Battlements (crenellations) · Crenel · Loophole · Tetrahedral spire · Rectangular turret · Wooden staircase leading to entrance above ground level · Quoin · Timber-framed house · Cornice · Buttress · Round-arched window with twin openings · Cruck frame · Paling

THE BASTILLE, PARIS, FRANCE, 14TH CENTURY

Curtain wall · Pointed relieving arch · Semicircular relieving arch · Plain string course · Bracket decorated with scroll molding · Rectangular window · Sunken rectangular panel · Round-arched window · Semicircular salient · Loophole · Lateral circular salient

MEDIEVAL LONDON BRIDGE, BRITAIN, 1176 (WITH 14TH-CENTURY BATTLEMENTED BUILDING, NONESUCH HOUSE, AND TWO-TOWERED GATE)

Gate-house

Battlemented building

Chapel pier

Railing

Onion-shaped dome

Pitched roof

Shaped gable

Timber framing with ornamental woodwork

Nonesuch House

Crypt of Becket Chapel

Starling

Pier

Two-towered gate

Pointed Gothic stone arch

Oriel window

Timber framing

DONJON, COUCY-LE-CHATEAU, AISNE, FRANCE, 1225-1245

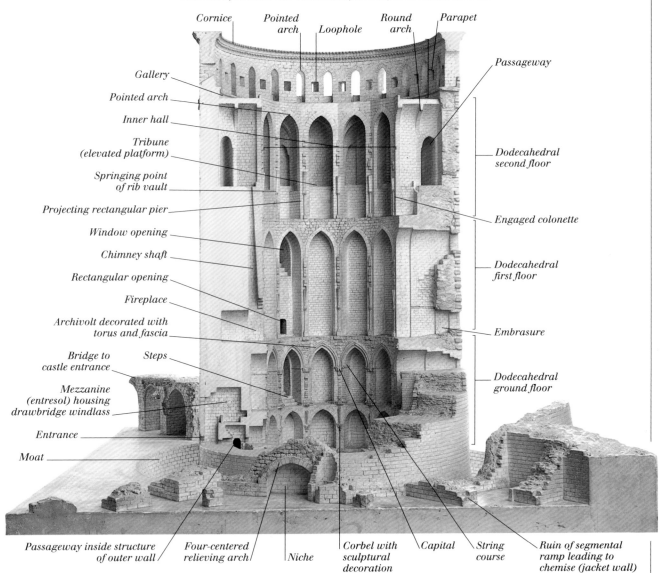

Cornice

Pointed arch

Loophole

Round arch

Parapet

Passageway

Gallery

Pointed arch

Inner hall

Tribune (elevated platform)

Springing point of rib vault

Projecting rectangular pier

Window opening

Chimney shaft

Rectangular opening

Fireplace

Archivolt decorated with torus and fascia

Bridge to castle entrance

Steps

Mezzanine (entresol) housing drawbridge windlass

Entrance

Moat

Dodecahedral second floor

Engaged colonette

Dodecahedral first floor

Embrasure

Dodecahedral ground floor

Passageway inside structure of outer wall

Four-centered relieving arch

Niche

Corbel with sculptural decoration

Capital

String course

Ruin of segmental ramp leading to chemise (jacket wall)

Medieval churches

LARGE NUMBERS OF CHURCHES were built in Europe in the Middle Ages. European churches of this period typically have high vaults supported by massive piers and columns. In the 10th century, the Romanesque style developed. Romanesque architects adopted many Roman or early Christian architectural ideas, such as cross-shaped ground plans—like that of Angoulême Cathedral (opposite)—and the basilican system of a nave with a central vessel and side aisles. In the mid-12th century, flying buttresses and pointed vaults appeared. These features later became widely used in Gothic architecture (see pp. 470-471). Bagneux Church (opposite) has both styles: a Romanesque tower and a Gothic nave and choir.

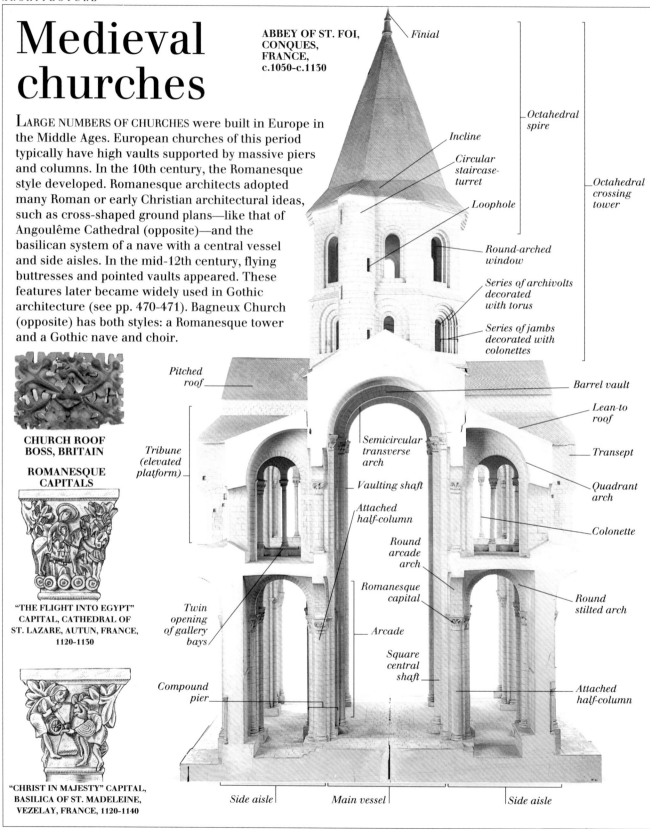

ABBEY OF ST. FOI, CONQUES, FRANCE, c.1050-c.1130

Finial

Octahedral spire

Incline

Circular staircase-turret

Loophole

Octahedral crossing tower

Round-arched window

Series of archivolts decorated with torus

Series of jambs decorated with colonettes

Pitched roof

Barrel vault

Lean-to roof

Tribune (elevated platform)

Semicircular transverse arch

Transept

Vaulting shaft

Quadrant arch

Attached half-column

Colonette

Round arcade arch

Romanesque capital

Round stilted arch

Twin opening of gallery bays

Arcade

Square central shaft

Attached half-column

Compound pier

Side aisle

Main vessel

Side aisle

CHURCH ROOF BOSS, BRITAIN

ROMANESQUE CAPITALS

"THE FLIGHT INTO EGYPT" CAPITAL, CATHEDRAL OF ST. LAZARE, AUTUN, FRANCE, 1120-1150

"CHRIST IN MAJESTY" CAPITAL, BASILICA OF ST. MADELEINE, VEZELAY, FRANCE, 1120-1140

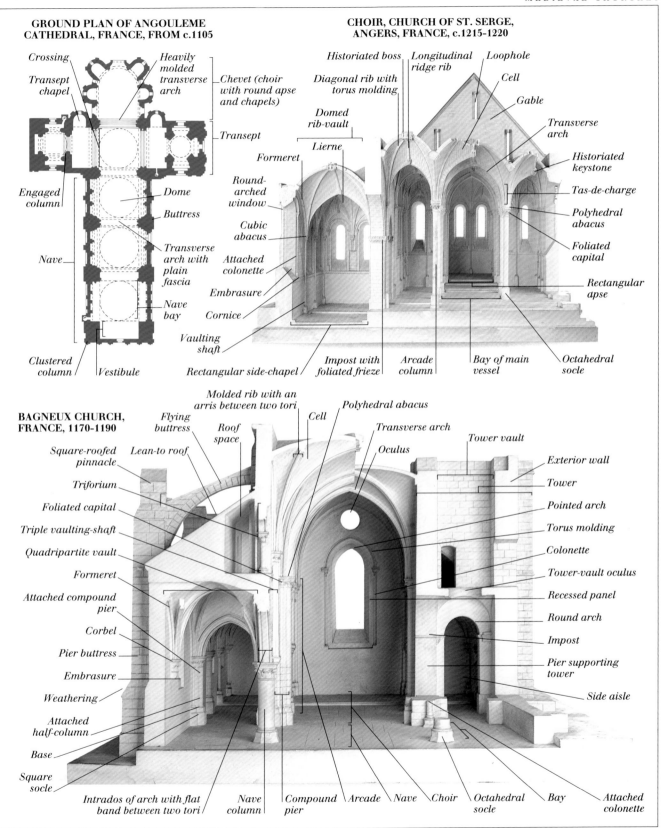

GROUND PLAN OF ANGOULEME CATHEDRAL, FRANCE, FROM c.1105

Crossing

Transept chapel

Heavily molded transverse arch

Chevet (choir with round apse and chapels)

Transept

Engaged column

Dome

Buttress

Nave

Transverse arch with plain fascia

Nave bay

Clustered column

Vestibule

CHOIR, CHURCH OF ST. SERGE, ANGERS, FRANCE, c.1215-1220

Historiated boss

Longitudinal ridge rib

Loophole

Cell

Diagonal rib with torus molding

Gable

Transverse arch

Domed rib-vault

Lierne

Historiated keystone

Formeret

Round-arched window

Tas-de-charge

Polyhedral abacus

Cubic abacus

Foliated capital

Attached colonette

Rectangular apse

Embrasure

Cornice

Vaulting shaft

Rectangular side-chapel

Impost with foliated frieze

Arcade column

Bay of main vessel

Octahedral socle

BAGNEUX CHURCH, FRANCE, 1170-1190

Molded rib with an arris between two tori

Flying buttress

Cell

Roof space

Polyhedral abacus

Transverse arch

Oculus

Tower vault

Square-roofed pinnacle

Lean-to roof

Exterior wall

Triforium

Tower

Foliated capital

Pointed arch

Triple vaulting-shaft

Torus molding

Quadripartite vault

Colonette

Formeret

Tower-vault oculus

Attached compound pier

Recessed panel

Corbel

Round arch

Pier buttress

Impost

Embrasure

Pier supporting tower

Weathering

Attached half-column

Side aisle

Base

Square socle

Intrados of arch with flat band between two tori

Nave column

Compound pier

Arcade

Nave

Choir

Octahedral socle

Bay

Attached colonette

Gothic 1

GOTHIC STAINED GLASS WITH FOLIATED SCROLL MOTIF, ON WOODEN FORM

GOTHIC BUILDINGS are characterized by rib vaults, pointed or lancet arches, flying buttresses, decorative tracery and gables, and stained-glass windows. Typical Gothic buildings include the Cathedrals of Salisbury and old St. Paul's in England, and Notre Dame de Paris in France (see pp. 472-473). The Gothic style developed out of Romanesque architecture in France (see pp. 468-469) in the mid-12th century and then spread throughout Europe. The decorative elements of Gothic architecture became highly developed in buildings of the English Decorated style (late 13th-14th century) and the French Flamboyant style (15th-16th century). These styles are exemplified by the tower of Salisbury Cathedral and by the staircase in the Church of St. Maclou (see pp. 472-473), respectively. In both of these styles, embellishments such as ballflowers and curvilinear (flowing) tracery were used liberally. The English Perpendicular style (late 14th-15th century), which followed the Decorated style, emphasized the vertical and horizontal elements of a building. A notable feature of this style is the hammer-beam roof.

GROUND PLAN OF SALISBURY CATHEDRAL

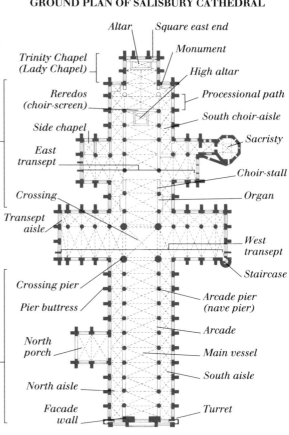

Altar
Square east end
Trinity Chapel (Lady Chapel)
Monument
High altar
Reredos (choir-screen)
Processional path
Side chapel
South choir-aisle
Choir
East transept
Sacristy
Crossing
Choir-stall
Organ
Transept aisle
West transept
Staircase
Crossing pier
Arcade pier (nave pier)
Pier buttress
Arcade
North porch
Main vessel
Nave
South aisle
North aisle
Facade wall
Turret

GOTHIC TORUS WITH BALLFLOWERS

Limestone block
Block members carved into rolls
Block members cut polygonally
Pencil guideline
Early stage of ballflower carving

BLOCK AFTER INITIAL CUTTING

BLOCK WITH MEMBERS CUT INTO ROLLS

Torus
Ballflower
Fillet
Mason's mark

FINISHED BLOCK

Trinity Chapel (Lady Chapel)
Choir
Octahedral pinnacle with small spire
Finial
Blind semi-arch
Staggered triple lancet windows
Turretlike pinnacle
Parapet decorated with blind arches filled with trefoils
Mullion
Stained glass
Base
Cornice
Buttress
Lean-to roof
East transept facade

NORTH SIDE, SALISBURY CATHEDRAL, BRITAIN, 1220-1280 (STEEPLE AND SPIRE ADDED DURING 14TH CENTURY)

WEST FACADE, SALISBURY CATHEDRAL

Weather-vane

Orb

Spire

Band with lozenge decoration

Semi-attached gable with small pilasters

Turretlike pinnacle

Ballflower decoration

Traceried parapet with lozenge decoration

Octahedral turret

Row of blind arches filled with trefoils

Battlemented cornice

Cinquefoil molding

Spirelike pinnacle

Blind gabled arch

Gable

Octafoil

Nave

Blind lancet

Flying buttress

Trefoil in a spandrel

Aureole

Gable

Staggered triple lancet window

Blind rhombus tracery filled with a quatrefoil

Finial

Pitched roof

Staggered triple lancet window

Parapet

Small gable crowning buttress

Angle buttress

North porch

Blind semi-arch

Lateral porch

Main porch

Crocket

Spire

Parapet

Row of blind trefoil arches

Blind pointed arches filled with twin lancets and quatrefoils

Projecting turret

Row of gabled niches under trefoil arches

Niche under small gabled roof

Spire

Molded side of gable

Spirelike pinnacle

Pitched roof

Flying buttress

Lateral turret

Small gable crowning buttress

Crocket

Buttress

Angle buttress

West transept facade

Weathering

Pier buttress

Trefoil decoration

North porch

Archivolt

Twin lancet window under pointed arch, crowned by a quatrefoil

471

Gothic 2

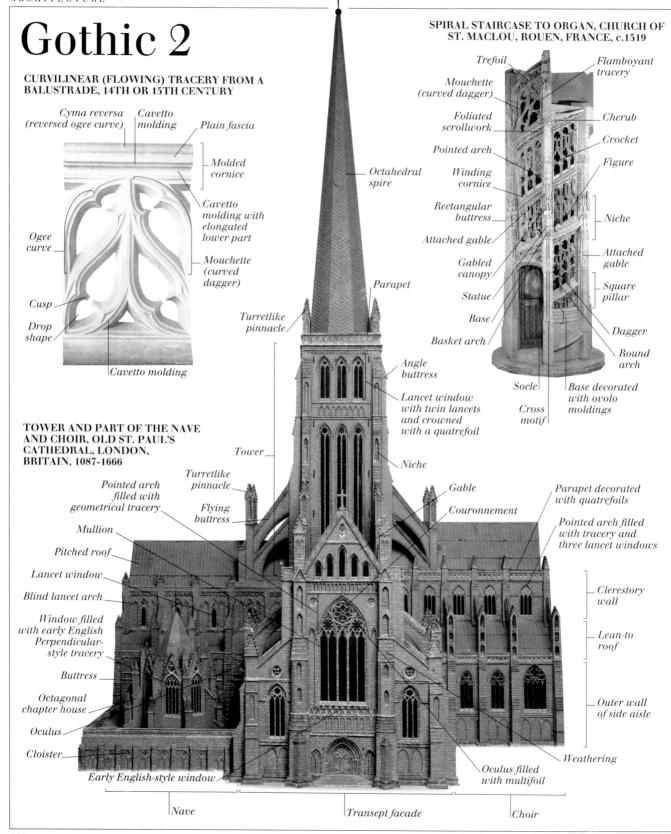

CURVILINEAR (FLOWING) TRACERY FROM A BALUSTRADE, 14TH OR 15TH CENTURY

Cyma reversa (reversed ogee curve)

Cavetto molding

Plain fascia

Molded cornice

Cavetto molding with elongated lower part

Mouchette (curved dagger)

Ogee curve

Cusp

Drop shape

Cavetto molding

SPIRAL STAIRCASE TO ORGAN, CHURCH OF ST. MACLOU, ROUEN, FRANCE, c.1519

Trefoil

Mouchette (curved dagger)

Foliated scrollwork

Pointed arch

Winding cornice

Rectangular buttress

Attached gable

Gabled canopy

Statue

Base

Basket arch

Flamboyant tracery

Cherub

Crocket

Figure

Niche

Attached gable

Square pillar

Dagger

Round arch

Socle

Cross motif

Base decorated with ovolo moldings

Octahedral spire

Parapet

Turretlike pinnacle

Angle buttress

Lancet window with twin lancets and crowned with a quatrefoil

Niche

Gable

Couronnement

Parapet decorated with quatrefoils

Pointed arch filled with tracery and three lancet windows

Clerestory wall

Lean-to roof

Outer wall of side aisle

Weathering

TOWER AND PART OF THE NAVE AND CHOIR, OLD ST. PAUL'S CATHEDRAL, LONDON, BRITAIN, 1087-1666

Tower

Pointed arch filled with geometrical tracery

Turretlike pinnacle

Flying buttress

Mullion

Pitched roof

Lancet window

Blind lancet arch

Window filled with early English Perpendicular-style tracery

Buttress

Octagonal chapter house

Oculus

Cloister

Early English-style window

Oculus filled with multifoil

Nave

Transept facade

Choir

472

Ridge

Common rafter

Architrave of window zone, also acting as collar beam

Principal

Attached baluster

Attached column

Strut

Raised surface

Hammer-post

Beveled edge

Arched brace

Wooden panel

Hammer-beam

Gothic window tracery

Collar beam decorated with pearl motif

Gothic window

Arched brace

Bracket

Brace

Impost

SPIRE AND TRANSEPT ROOF, CATHEDRAL OF NOTRE DAME DE PARIS, FRANCE, c.1163-1250

Rafter

Straight brace

Beam

Round arch

Oculus

Lancet arch

Cusp

Colonette

Lesene

Balustrade

Triangular cornice

Geometrical tracery

Trefoil arch

Balustrade

Upper collar

Ridge board

Common rafter

Gable

Pinnacle

Blind trefoil

Trefoil arch

Quatrefoil

Pointed arch

Lancet arch

Mullion

Cornice with chamfered edge

Stud

Scissor brace

Principal rafter

Octahedral spire

Roof truss of nave and transept

Vertical strut

Intermediate collar

Raised valley-rafter

Beam

Jack-rafter

Clasped purlin

Lower collar

Scissor-beam

King post

Queen post

Tie beam

Passing brace

TRUSS OF HAMMER-BEAM ROOF, THE UPPER FRATER (LATER BLACKFRIARS' PLAYHOUSE), LONDON, BRITAIN, PROBABLY 14TH CENTURY

TYPICAL GOTHIC FEATURES

FLYING BUTTRESS OVER SIDE AISLES, MILAN CATHEDRAL, ITALY, C.1385-1485

GARGOYLE, HORSLEY CHURCH, DERBYSHIRE, BRITAIN, C.1450

HAMMER-BEAM ROOF, CHURCH OF ST. BOTOLPH, TRUNCH, NORFOLK, BRITAIN, 1360-1380

Renaissance 1

THE RENAISSANCE was a period in European history—lasting roughly from the 14th century to the mid-17th century—during which the arts and sciences underwent great changes. In architecture, these changes were marked by a return to the classical forms and proportions of ancient Roman buildings. The Renaissance originated in Italy, and the buildings most characteristic of its style can be found there, such as the Palazzo Strozzi shown here. Mannerism is a branch of the Renaissance style that distorts the classical forms; an example is the Laurentian Library staircase. As the Renaissance style spread to other European countries, many of its features were incorporated into the local architecture. For example, the Château de Montal in France (see pp. 476-477) incorporates aedicules (tabernacles).

FACADE ON TO PIAZZA, PALAZZO STROZZI

Crowning cornice

Arched window

Round arch

Light

Rustication

Arched doorway

Rectangular window

SIDE VIEW OF PALAZZO STROZZI, FLORENCE, ITALY, 1489 (BY G. DA SANGALLO, B. DA MAIANO, AND CRONACA)

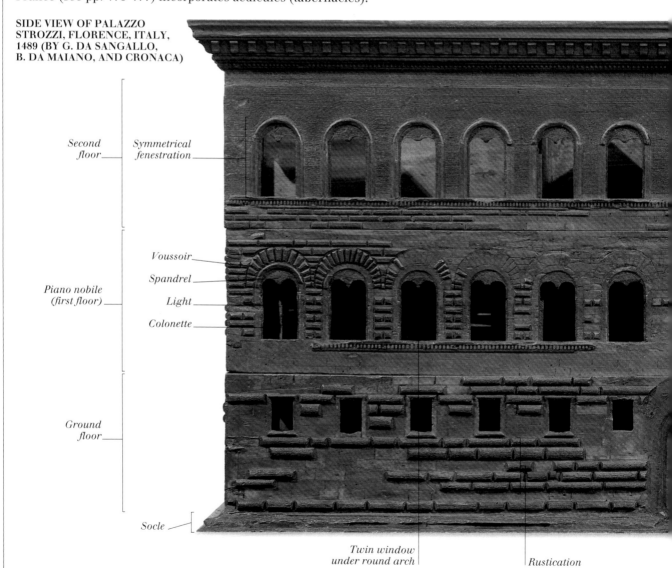

Second floor

Symmetrical fenestration

Piano nobile (first floor)

Voussoir

Spandrel

Light

Colonette

Ground floor

Socle

Twin window under round arch

Rustication

DETAILS FROM ITALIAN RENAISSANCE BUILDINGS

PANEL FROM DRUM OF DOME,
FLORENCE CATHEDRAL, 1420-1436

COFFERING IN DOME,
PAZZI CHAPEL,
FLORENCE, 1429-1461

STAIRCASE,
LAURENTIAN LIBRARY,
FLORENCE, 1559

PORTICO, VILLA ROTUNDA,
VICENZA, 1567-1569

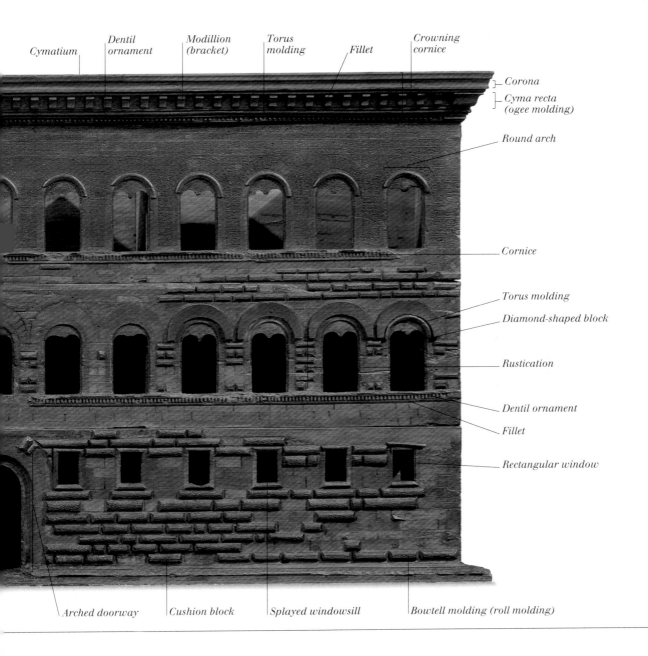

Cymatium

Dentil ornament

Modillion (bracket)

Torus molding

Fillet

Crowning cornice

Corona

Cyma recta (ogee molding)

Round arch

Cornice

Torus molding

Diamond-shaped block

Rustication

Dentil ornament

Fillet

Rectangular window

Arched doorway

Cushion block

Splayed windowsill

Bowtell molding (roll molding)

Renaissance 2

DETAILS FROM EUROPEAN RENAISSANCE BUILDINGS

STONE WALL, QUOINS, AND SHELL DECORATION, CASA DE LAS CONCHAS, SALAMANCA, SPAIN, 1475-1483

SPIRAL-STAIRCASE TOWER, CHATEAU DE BLOIS, FRANCE, 1514-1530

CONICAL DOME, CHATEAU DE CHAMBORD, FRANCE, 1519-1547

PAIR OF CHIMNEY STACKS, PALAIS DE FONTAINEBLEAU, FRANCE, FROM 1528

NORTH WING, CHATEAU DE MONTAL, LOT, FRANCE, FROM 1523

Chimney stack

Ridge of half-round tiles

Pitched roof

Finial

Medallion

Pinnacle

Foliated volute with dolphin head

Gable

Head-shaped keystone

Dormer window

Frieze with shell-pattern decoration

Finial

Ionic capital with head-shaped decoration

Putto holding candelabrum

Blind pediment

Grotesque figure

Medallion with bust of Robert de Montal

Lesene decorated with paterae

Frieze decorated with sculptural wreaths, tendrils, and grotesque figures

Lesene

Pedestal

Dado

Plinth

Cornice

Architrave

Portal

Pilaster

Hipped roof

Conical spire of turret

Fish-scale tile

Belvedere

Keystone decorated with scroll ornament

Cornice decorated with fascias and an ogee molding

Rectangular window

Transom

Aedicule (tabernacle)

Double pilaster

Mullion

Shell

Concave arched niche

Small pier decorated with statuette in concave niche

Cornice

Frieze with scroll motif

Pseudo-Corinthian capital

NORTH WING STAIRCASE, CHATEAU DE MONTAL

Hipped roof

Eaves with oversailing fascias and fillets

Cornice with fascias and ogee moldings

Rib vault

Column

Second-floor landing

First-floor landing

Pier supporting flight of stairs

Pier supporting first-floor landing

Conical spire

Turret

Loophole

Conical corbel

Flight of stairs

Lesene

Handrail

Riser

Tread

CAMPANILE, CHURCH OF ST. EUSTACHE, PARIS, FRANCE, 1532-1640

Weather vane

Orb

Hemispherical dome

Fillet

Plain fascia

Small architrave

Volute

Emphasized keystone

Cincture

Zinc plating

Fish-scale tile

Semicircular torus molding

Weathering

Ogee molding

Archivolt

Plain fascia

Cavetto molding

Capital

Fillet

Square column

GLOBE THEATER, LONDON, BRITAIN, 1599

Balustrade

Thatched roof

Loft used as storage room

Window stage

Outer wall

Railing

Post supporting bay window

Upper-gallery support

Stage-door

Standing room

Bench

Round pillar (stage post)

Square, carved base

Ornamental paneling

Balcony stage

Stage cover

Hipped roof

Turret

Pitched roof

Timber-framed hut housing windlass

Music gallery

Light curtain

Ornamental paneling with concave brace decoration

Door to dressing-rooms

Box (gentlemen's room)

Upper gallery (twopenny gallery)

Middle gallery

Lower gallery

Partition separating galleries from boxes

Study (inner stage) with traverse (crossing)

Platform stage

Low balustrade

Paling

Door to tiring house

Baroque and neoclassical 1

THE BAROQUE STYLE EVOLVED IN THE EARLY 17TH CENTURY in Rome. It is characterized by curved outlines and ostentatious decoration, as can be seen in the Italian church details (right). The baroque style was particularly widely favored in Italy, Spain, and Germany. It was also adopted in Britain and France, but with adaptations. The British architects Sir Christopher Wren and Nicholas Hawksmoor, for example, used baroque features—such as the concave walls of St. Paul's Cathedral and the curved buttresses of the Church of St. George in the East (see pp. 480-481)—but they did so with restraint. Similarly, the curved buttresses and volutes of the Parisian Church of St. Paul-St. Louis are relatively plain. In the second half of the 17th century, a distinct classical style (known as neoclassicism) developed in northern Europe as a reaction to the excesses of baroque. Typical of this new style were churches such as the Madeleine (a proposed facade is shown below), as well as secular buildings such as the Cirque Napoleon (opposite) and the buildings of the British architect Sir John Soane (see pp. 482-483). In early 18th century France, an extremely lavish form of baroque developed, known as rococo. The balcony from Nantes (see pp. 482-483) with its twisted ironwork and head-shaped corbels is typical of this style.

SCROLLED BUTTRESS,
CHURCH OF ST. MARIA DELLA
SALUTE, VENICE, 1631-1682

STATUE OF THE ECSTASY OF
ST. THERESA, CHURCH OF ST. MARIA
DELLA VITTORIA, ROME, 1645-1652

PROPOSED FACADE, THE MADELEINE (NEOCLASSICAL), PARIS, FRANCE, 1764 (BY P. CONTANT D'IVRY)

CIRQUE NAPOLEON (NEOCLASSICAL), PARIS, FRANCE, 1852 (BY J.I. HITTORFF)

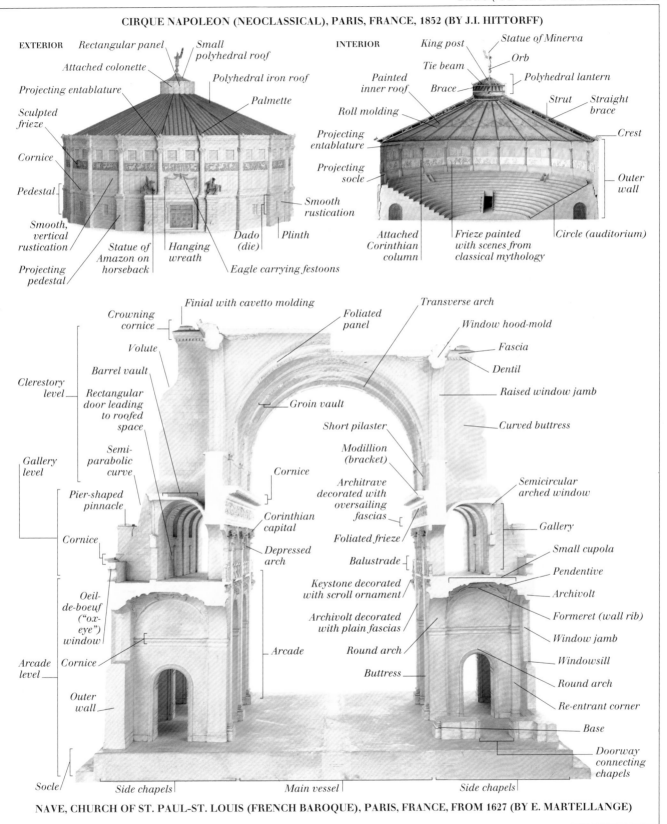

EXTERIOR

Rectangular panel

Small polyhedral roof

Attached colonette

Projecting entablature

Polyhedral iron roof

Palmette

Sculpted frieze

Cornice

Pedestal

Smooth, vertical rustication

Projecting pedestal

Statue of Amazon on horseback

Hanging wreath

Dado (die)

Plinth

Smooth rustication

Eagle carrying festoons

INTERIOR

King post

Statue of Minerva

Tie beam

Orb

Painted inner roof

Brace

Polyhedral lantern

Roll molding

Strut

Straight brace

Projecting entablature

Crest

Projecting socle

Outer wall

Attached Corinthian column

Frieze painted with scenes from classical mythology

Circle (auditorium)

Finial with cavetto molding

Transverse arch

Crowning cornice

Foliated panel

Window hood-mold

Volute

Fascia

Barrel vault

Dentil

Clerestory level

Rectangular door leading to roofed space

Groin vault

Raised window jamb

Short pilaster

Curved buttress

Gallery level

Semi-parabolic curve

Cornice

Modillion (bracket)

Semicircular arched window

Pier-shaped pinnacle

Corinthian capital

Architrave decorated with oversailing fascias

Gallery

Cornice

Depressed arch

Foliated frieze

Small cupola

Oeil-de-boeuf ("ox-eye") window

Balustrade

Pendentive

Cornice

Keystone decorated with scroll ornament

Archivolt

Arcade level

Arcade

Archivolt decorated with plain fascias

Formeret (wall rib)

Outer wall

Round arch

Window jamb

Windowsill

Buttress

Round arch

Re-entrant corner

Base

Socle

Side chapels

Main vessel

Side chapels

Doorway connecting chapels

NAVE, CHURCH OF ST. PAUL-ST. LOUIS (FRENCH BAROQUE), PARIS, FRANCE, FROM 1627 (BY E. MARTELLANGE)

Baroque and neoclassical 2

MODEL BUILT IN 1674 OF PROPOSED EXTERIOR OF ST. PAUL'S CATHEDRAL (ENGLISH BAROQUE), LONDON, BRITAIN (BY C. WREN)

Cross
Orb
Small dome
Entablature
Pedestal
Arcade
Gallery with balustrade
Lantern
Convex molding
Circular lucarne window
Dome
Plat lesene
Curved buttress
Round arch
Corinthian pilaster
Rectangular pier
Sunken lunette

ARABESQUE

Volute
Palmette
Tendril
Cornucopia

BAY LEAF GARLAND

Bayberry
Bay leaf

PATERA

Petal
Rosette
Fillet
Ovolo (quarter-round) molding

DECORATIVE MOLDINGS FROM ENGLISH NEOCLASSICAL BUILDINGS

Raking cornice
Representation in bas-relief of conversion of St. Paul

TRIANGULAR PEDIMENT, WEST FACADE, ST. PAUL'S CATHEDRAL

Plain pilaster
Raking cornice
Sunken panel
Attic story
Pediment
Entablature
Architrave
Cornice
Small pilaster
Pedestal
Semicircular cornice
Plinth
Concave, arched niche
Attached Corinthian column
Freestanding Corinthian column
Projecting side portal

CHURCH OF ST. GEORGE IN THE EAST (ENGLISH BAROQUE), LONDON, BRITAIN, 1714-1734 (BY N. HAWKSMOOR)

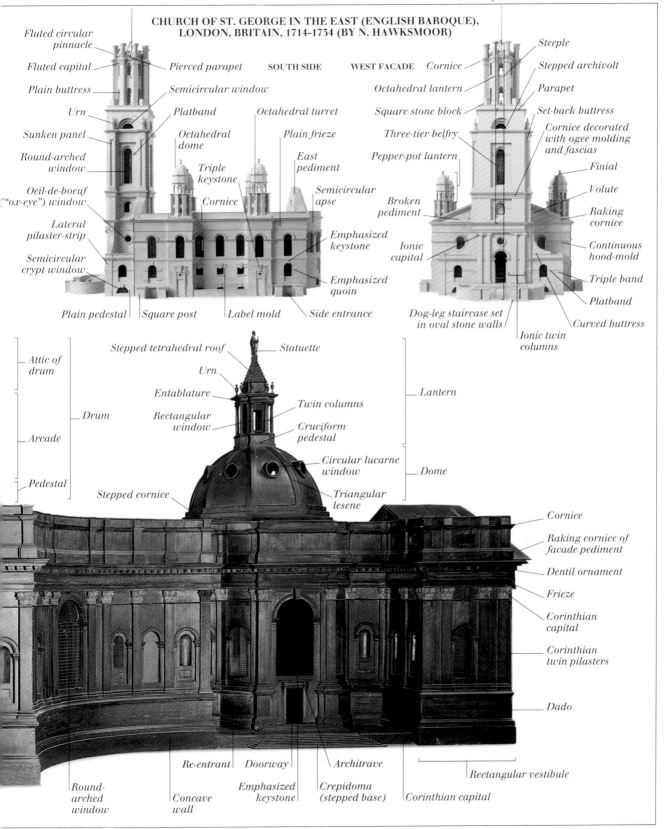

SOUTH SIDE

Fluted circular pinnacle

Fluted capital

Plain buttress

Urn

Sunken panel

Round-arched window

Oeil-de-boeuf ("ox-eye") window

Lateral pilaster-strip

Semicircular crypt window

Plain pedestal

Square post

Pierced parapet

Semicircular window

Platband

Octahedral dome

Triple keystone

Cornice

Label mold

Octahedral turret

Plain frieze

East pediment

Semicircular apse

Emphasized keystone

Emphasized quoin

Side entrance

WEST FACADE

Cornice

Octahedral lantern

Square stone block

Three-tier belfry

Pepper-pot lantern

Broken pediment

Ionic capital

Dog-leg staircase set in oval stone walls

Ionic twin columns

Steeple

Stepped archivolt

Parapet

Set-back buttress

Cornice decorated with ogee molding and fascias

Finial

Volute

Raking cornice

Continuous hood-mold

Triple band

Platband

Curved buttress

Attic of drum

Drum

Arcade

Pedestal

Stepped tetrahedral roof

Urn

Entablature

Rectangular window

Statuette

Twin columns

Cruciform pedestal

Circular lucarne window

Triangular lesene

Stepped cornice

Lantern

Dome

Cornice

Raking cornice of facade pediment

Dentil ornament

Frieze

Corinthian capital

Corinthian twin pilasters

Dado

Round-arched window

Concave wall

Re-entrant

Doorway

Emphasized keystone

Architrave

Crepidoma (stepped base)

Corinthian capital

Rectangular vestibule

Baroque and neoclassical 3

DETAILS FROM BAROQUE, NEOCLASSICAL, AND ROCOCO BUILDINGS

PORTICO, THE VYNE, HAMPSHIRE, BRITAIN, 1654 (NEOCLASSICAL)

GILT IRONWORK FROM SCREEN, PALAIS DE VERSAILLES, FRANCE, 1669-1674 (FRENCH BAROQUE)

WINDOW, PALAZZO STANGA, CREMONA, ITALY, EARLY 18TH CENTURY (ROCOCO)

ATLAS (MALE CARYATID), UPPER BELVEDERE, VIENNA, AUSTRIA, 1721 (GERMAN-STYLE BAROQUE)

BALCONY, NANTES, FRANCE, 1730-1740 (ROCOCO)

MASONRY OF A NICHE IN THE ROTUNDA (NEOCLASSICAL), BANK OF ENGLAND, LONDON, BRITAIN, 1794 (BY J. SOANE)

Scoop-pattern concave molding

Keystone

Frieze

Semidome

Spandrel

Voussoir

Rotunda wall

Flat, rectangular niche

Rounded niche

Flat, square niche

CORNER OF THE NEW STATE PAPER OFFICE (NEOCLASSICAL), LONDON, BRITAIN, 1830-1851 (BY J. SOANE)

Classical-style entablature

Cornice

Frieze

Architrave

Pantile (S-shaped roofing tile)

Eaves

Fascia

Scroll-shaped corbel

Curved corbel

Second-floor window

Smooth rustication

Cornice

Drip-cap

Cornice

Frieze

Window architrave

Window jamb

First-floor window

Windowsill in the form of a frieze

Ground-floor window

Splayed windowsill

Vermiculated rustication

TYRINGHAM HOUSE (NEOCLASSICAL), BUCKINGHAMSHIRE, BRITAIN, 1793–1797 (BY J. SOANE)

**ROOF LEVEL
(ATTIC LEVEL)**

Space for illumination above unroofed central hall

Chimney stack

Space above unroofed main staircase

Flat roof

Oculus illuminating secondary staircase

Parapet rail

Balustrade

Baluster

Cornice

Attic story of convex portico

Cornice

**FIRST-FLOOR LEVEL
(CHAMBER FLOOR)**

Upper level of central hall, open to floor below

Main staircase

Secondary staircase

Abacus

Triangular pilaster

Pilaster capital

Attached Tuscan twin pilasters

First-floor story of convex portico

Windowsill

Bow front

**GROUND-FLOOR LEVEL
(PRINCIPAL FLOOR)**

Withdrawing room

Central hall

Library and breakfast room

Main staircase

Water closet (toilet)

Eating room

Secondary staircase

Segmented lintel course

Band incised with Greek-style fret ornament

Windowsill

Window architrave

Window jamb

Base

Basement

Plinth

Horizontal rustication

Vestibule (entrance hall)

Ground-floor storey of convex portico

**FACADE OF
TYRINGHAM HOUSE**

Chimney stack

Voussoir

Basement window

Entrance door

Circular entrance steps

Rail

Baluster

Parapet

Balustrade

Cornice

Entablature

Capital

Shaft

Ionic column

Base

PROSTYLE COLONNADE

Arches and vaults

ARCHES ARE CURVED STRUCTURES used to bridge spans and to support the weight of upper parts of buildings, such as domes, as in St. Paul's Cathedral (below) and the historical temple (opposite). The voussoirs (wedge-shaped blocks) that form an arch (right) support each other and convert the downward force of the weight of the building into an outward force. This outward force is in turn transferred to buttresses, piers, or abutments. A vault is an arched roof or ceiling. There are four main types of vault (opposite). A barrel vault is a single vault, semicircular in cross-section; a groin vault consists of two barrel vaults intersecting at right angles; a rib vault is a groin vault reinforced by ribs; and a fan vault is a rib vault in which the ribs radiate from the springing point (where the arch begins) like a fan.

PARTS OF AN ARCH

Voussoir *Keystone* *Crown* *Abutment*

Abutment *Keystone*

Abutment *Extrados*

Intrados (soffit) *Haunch*

Impost *Extrados*

Springing point *Haunch*

Abutment *Intrados (soffit)*

Span *Abutment*

FRONT **SIDE**

ARCHES AND BASE OF DOME, ST. PAUL'S CATHEDRAL, LONDON, BRITAIN, 1675-1710 (BY C. WREN)

Inner dome *Colonnade*

Pilaster *Passageway*

Base *Cornice*

Pendentive *Opening to passageway* *Pedestal of outer dome*

"Whispering Gallery"

Upper arch (concealing difference in heights between main arch and minor arches)

Triangular buttress

Molded bracket

Round arch

Semidome

Extrados

Upper barrel-vaulted passage opening onto side aisle

Intrados (soffit)

Springing point

Impost

Barrel vault

Abutment

Passage leading to side aisle

Strut built into masonry to strengthen pier (added in the 20th century)

Minor arch leading to side aisle *Main arch leading to nave* *Pier* *Minor arch*

TYPES OF ARCH

HORSESHOE ARCH (MOORISH ARCH), GREAT MOSQUE, CORDOBA, SPAIN, 785

BASKET ARCH (SEMI-ELLIPTICAL ARCH), PALATINE CHAPEL, AIX-LA-CHAPELLE, FRANCE, 790-798

TUDOR ARCH, TOWER OF LONDON, BRITAIN, C.1086-1097

LANCET ARCH, WESTMINSTER ABBEY, LONDON, BRITAIN, 1503-1519

TREFOIL ARCH, BEVERLEY MINSTER, YORKSHIRE, BRITAIN, C.1300

TYPES OF VAULT

Transverse rib
Temporary brace
Temporary structure used to center vault
Horizontal abutment

BARREL VAULT (TUNNEL VAULT; WAGON VAULT)

Barrel vault
Transverse arch
Voussoir
Right-angled intersection
Groin

GROIN VAULT

Transverse ridge-rib
Longitudinal ridge-rib
Diagonal rib

RIB VAULT

Tierceron (secondary rib)
Ridge rib
Springing point
Concave-sided lozenge
Panel

FAN VAULT

COMPOSITE MODEL OF HISTORICAL FRENCH TEMPLE

Coved dome
Lesene
Pedestal of lantern
Archivolt decorated with plain fascias
Series of plain fascias
Abutment
Dentil
Lantern
Re-entrant angle
Coved dome
Cavetto molding
Fillet
Cornice
Plain frieze
Architrave
Ionic capital
Chamfered corner
Keystone decorated with scroll
Plain Ionic column
Shaft
Scotia
Plinth
Dado
Round arch
Cornice
Horizontal band
Twisted vertical band
Naos (cella)
Pedestal of dome
Entablature
Fluted Ionic column
Pedestal of column
Base
Intercolumniation
Ionic column with twisted vertical bands (wreaths) and horizontal bands

ENGLISH BOND BRICKWORK OF GROIN VAULT AND RIB VAULT

Right-angled intersection
Groin
Header
Stretcher
Cell of barrel vault
Springing point

EXTRADOS OF GROIN VAULT

Stretcher
Header
Cell
Extrados of diagonal rib
Springing point

EXTRADOS OF RIB VAULT

INTERIOR DECORATION OF COFFERED VAULT

Compass
Square
Hammer
Coffer (square sunken panel)
Chamfered edge
Arris molding
Mason's tools

Domes

A DOME IS A CONVEX ROOF. Domes are categorized according to the shapes of both the base and the section through the center of the dome. The base may be circular, square, or polygonal (many-sided), depending on the plan of the drum (the walls on which the dome rests). The section of a dome may be the same shape as any arch (see pp. 484-485). Various types of dome are illustrated here: a hemispherical dome, which has a circular base and a semicircular section; a saucer dome, which has a circular base and a segmental (less than a semicircle) section; a polyhedral dome, which is a dome on a polygonal base whose sides meet at the top of the dome; and an onion dome, which has a circular or polygonal base and an ogee-shaped section. Many domes have a lantern (a turret with windows) to provide light inside.

LANTERN AND UPPER DOME TIMBERING, ST. PAUL'S CATHEDRAL

DOME TIMBERING, CHURCH OF THE SORBONNE, PARIS, FRANCE, 1635-1642 (BY J. LEMERCIER)

Ogee-curved dome
Window zone
Pedestal
Floorboard
Ashlar piece
Pin
Short strut
Mortise and tenon joint
Principal rafter
Straight brace
Vertical post
Tie beam
Circular baseplate
Common rafter

Straight brace
Deeply projecting pier buttress
Cornice
Depressed hood mold
Circular lucarne window
Floor joist
Hood mold
Waisted-oval lucarne window
Ogee-curved window frame
Shaft connecting lantern and church interior

ROOF WITH LANTERN AND ONION DOME

Weather vane
Ellipsoid orb
Keeled lesene
Fish-scale tile
Octahedral base
Sloping roof
Round arch
Attached pillar
Vertical band
Oversailing fascia
Octahedral base of lantern

Onion dome
Oversailing fascia
Tetrahedral capital
Return
Window
Torus
Fillet
Lantern
Tetrahedral roof

REPRESENTATION OF DOME METALING, CHURCH OF THE SORBONNE

Cross
Orb
Square rib
Inverted ovolo (quarter-round)
Astragal
Fillet
Volute
Plain fascia
Roll molding
Round-arched window
Buttress
Ovolo (quarter-round)
Volute
Fillet
Cornice
Lantern
Projecting pier buttress
Fish-scale tile
Inverted demi-heart torus molding
Hood mold
Waisted-oval lucarne window
Dome on a circular base
Small volute
Gutter
Parapet
Semicircular torus molding
Small roll
Fillet
Plain fascia
Triple lesene

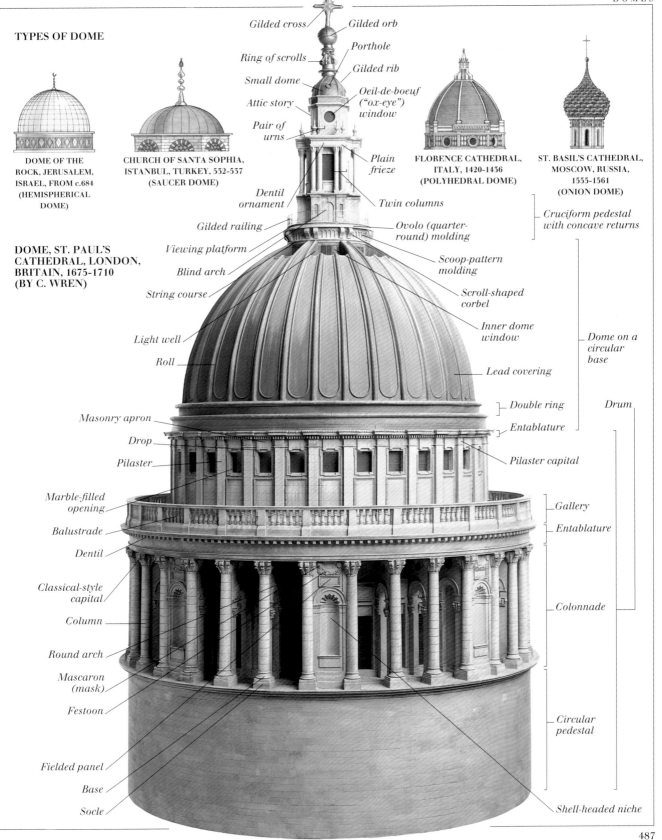

TYPES OF DOME

DOME OF THE
ROCK, JERUSALEM,
ISRAEL, FROM c.684
(HEMISPHERICAL
DOME)

CHURCH OF SANTA SOPHIA,
ISTANBUL, TURKEY, 552-537
(SAUCER DOME)

FLORENCE CATHEDRAL,
ITALY, 1420-1436
(POLYHEDRAL DOME)

ST. BASIL'S CATHEDRAL,
MOSCOW, RUSSIA,
1555-1561
(ONION DOME)

**DOME, ST. PAUL'S
CATHEDRAL, LONDON,
BRITAIN, 1675-1710
(BY C. WREN)**

Gilded cross
Gilded orb
Porthole
Ring of scrolls
Gilded rib
Small dome
Oeil-de-boeuf
("ox-eye")
window
Attic story
Pair of
urns
Plain
frieze
Dentil
ornament
Twin columns
Gilded railing
Ovolo (quarter-
round) molding
Viewing platform
Scoop-pattern
molding
Blind arch
Scroll-shaped
corbel
String course
Inner dome
window
Light well
Roll
Lead covering
Masonry apron
Double ring
Drop
Entablature
Pilaster
Pilaster capital
Marble-filled
opening
Gallery
Balustrade
Entablature
Dentil
Classical-style
capital
Column
Colonnade
Round arch
Mascaron
(mask)
Festoon
Cruciform pedestal
with concave returns
Dome on a
circular
base
Drum
Circular
pedestal
Fielded panel
Base
Socle
Shell-headed niche

Islamic buildings

OPUS SECTILE MOSAIC DESIGN

THE ISLAMIC RELIGION was founded by the prophet Mohammed, who was born in Mecca (in present-day Saudi Arabia) about 570 AD. During the next three centuries, Islam spread from Arabia to North Africa and Spain, as well as into India and much of the rest of Asia. The worldwide influence of Islam remains strong today. Common characteristics of Islamic buildings include ogee arches and roofs, onion domes, and walls decorated with carved stone, paintings, inlays, or mosaics. The most important type of Islamic building is the mosque—the place of worship—which generally has a minaret (tower) from which the muezzin (official crier) calls Muslims to prayer. Most mosques have a mihrab (decorative niche) that indicates the direction of Mecca. As figurative art is not allowed in Islam, buildings are ornamented with geometric and arabesque motifs and inscriptions (frequently Koranic verses).

Budlike onion dome

Depressed arch surrounding mihrab

Painted roof pavilion

Lotus flower pendentive

Arabic inscription

Turkish crescent finial

Crest

Painted minaret with censer (incense burner)

Spandrel

Series of recessed arches

Semidome

Arched niche within a niche

Mural resembling tomb

Polyhedral niche

Recessed colonettes

MIHRAB, JAMI MASJID (PRINCIPAL OR CONGREGATIONAL MOSQUE), BIJAPUR, INDIA, c.1636

Tablet flower

Shield

Herringbone pattern

Spandrel with floral design

Ogee arch

Carved stone

Undulating band

Cusp

Volute

Impost

Capital with stylized floral design

Panel with fret pattern

Band with Arabic inscriptions praising Allah (God)

Attached colonette

Jali (latticed screen) with geometrical patterns

ARCH, THE ALHAMBRA, GRANADA, SPAIN, 1333-1354

Enameled turquoise earthenware tile

Trigon

Cube with chamfered corners

Polygonal capital

Niche

Enameled white earthenware tile

Column shaft

Arabesques of stylized plants

Enameled lapis blue earthenware tile

MIHRAB WITH COLUMN, EL-AINYI MOSQUE, CAIRO, EGYPT, 15TH CENTURY

EXAMPLES OF ISLAMIC MOSAICS, EGYPT AND SYRIA

Star-shaped motif
Triangle of yellow marble
Greek cross of red marble
Rhombus of black marble
Stone band

STAR AND GREEK CROSS MOSAIC

Stone
Black marble
Turquoise glass
Mosaic tessellation
Tessera (small mosaic piece)

FRET-PATTERN MOSAIC

Greek cross of black and yellow marble
Star-shaped motif
Stone band
Rhombus of red marble

STAR AND GREEK CROSS MOSAIC

Parallelogram of black marble
Triangle of yellow marble
Rhombus of red marble
Symmetrical quadrilateral of stone
Star-shaped motif

MOSAIC OF HEXAGONS, TRIANGLES, AND SYMMETRICAL QUADRILATERALS

Hexagonal design
Band of black marble
Band of stone

HEXAGON AND BAND MOSAIC

Triangle of turquoise glass
Parallelogram of mother-of-pearl

DANCETTE (ZIG-ZAG)-PATTERN MOSAIC

Symmetrical quadrilateral of black marble
Hexagon of red marble
Triangle of stone

MOSAIC OF HEXAGONS, TRIANGLES, AND SYMMETRICAL QUADRILATERALS

MARBLE TOMB OF ITIMAD-UD-DAULA, AGRA, INDIA, c.1622-1628

Kalasa finial (finial with orbs)
Padmakosa (lotus petal)
Ogee-curved roof
Chajya (deep eaves)
Balcony
Roof pavilion
Domed roof
Cusped arch
Circular top of minaret
Parapet decorated with latticework
Pietra dura inlay (slices of semiprecious stone laid in sockets)
Cornice
Bracket
Octahedral base of minaret
Spandrel decorated with arabesque
Star-pattern inlay
Sandstone plinth
Sandstone parapet decorated with latticework
Jali (latticed screen) with geometrical patterns
Depressed entrance arch
Sandstone stairway
Opus sectile mosaic (geometric mosaic) of stone, tile, glass, and enamel

South and east Asia

THE TRADITIONAL ARCHITECTURE of south and east Asia has been profoundly influenced by the spread from India of Buddhism and Hinduism. This influence is shown by both the abundance and by the architectural styles of temples and shrines in the region. Many early Hindu temples consist of rooms carved from solid rock faces. However, freestanding structures began to be built in southern India from about the eighth century AD. Many were built in the Dravidian style, like the Temple of Virupaksha (opposite), with its characteristic antarala (terraced tower), perforated windows, and numerous arches, pilasters, and carvings. The earliest Buddhist religious monuments were Indian stupas, which consisted of a single hemispherical dome surmounted by a chattravali (shaft) and surrounded by railings with ornate gates. Later Indian stupas and those built elsewhere were sometimes modified. For example, in Sri Lanka, the dome became bell-shaped, and was called a dagoba. Buddhist pagodas, such as the Burmese example (right), are multistoried temples, each story having a projecting roof. The form of these buildings probably derived from the yasti (pointed spire) of the stupa. Another feature of many traditional Asian buildings is their imaginative roof forms, such as gambrel (mansard) roofs, and roofs with angle rafters (below).

DETAILS FROM EAST ASIAN BUILDINGS

KASUGA-STYLE ROOF WITH SUMIGI (ANGLE RAFTERS), KASUGADO SHRINE OF ENJOJI, NARA, JAPAN, 12TH-14TH CENTURY

TERRACES, TEMPLE OF HEAVEN, BEIJING, CHINA, 15TH CENTURY

GAMBREL (MANSARD) ROOF WITH UPSWEPT EAVES AND UNDULATING GABLES, HIMEJI CASTLE, HIMEJI, JAPAN, 1608-1609

CORNER CAPITAL WITH ROOF BEAMS, POPCHU-SA TEMPLE, POPCHU-SA, SOUTH KOREA, 17TH CENTURY

SEVEN-STORIED PAGODA IN BURMESE STYLE, c.9TH-10TH CENTURY

Gilded band

Gilded iron hti (crown)

Dubika (mast)

Arrow motif

Torus molding with spiral carving

Decorative eaves board

Ogee-arched motif with decorative carvings

Ogee-arched motif forming horn

Hip rafter

Pentroof

Undulating molding

Engaged pillar

Baluster finial

Arched entrance

Balustrade

Rectangular window

Pillar

Baluster

Straight brace

PERFORATED STONE WINDOWS, TEMPLES OF VIRUPAKSHA AND MALLIKARJUNA, PATTADAKAL, INDIA, 8TH CENTURY

Tablet flower

Fret motif

Chain motif

Floral pattern

Leaf

Scroll motif

Sickle motif

Semicircle

DAGOBA STUPA, KANDY, SRI LANKA, c.2ND CENTURY BC-7TH CENTURY AD

Chattra (umbrella)

Hanging ornament

Chattravali (shaft)

Ring with indentations symbolizing chattras

Ornamental metalwork

Yasti (tee; pointed spire)

Harmika (stylized square railing)

Auda (bell-shaped dome)

Trimala (series of three circular courses)

Circular base

SIDE VIEW AND PLAN VIEW, TEMPLE OF VIRUPAKSHA, PATTADAKAL, INDIA, c.746

Stupica (small stupa) of the Dravidian order

Dravidian finial

Blind chataya arch

Perforated window

Gopuram finial (wagonlike finial)

Bracketed capital

Small gopuram (gate head)

Parapet

Roll cornice

Antarala (terraced tower)

Niche with statue

Plan view

Twin pilasters

Pradakshina (circumambulatory passage around shrine)

Shrine

Shrine chamber

Niche

Gate

Mandapa (pillared hall)

Pillar

Panel with bas-relief carving

Gate

The 19th century

BUILDINGS OF THE 19TH CENTURY are characterized by the use of new materials and by a great diversity of architectural styles. From the end of the 18th century, iron and steel became widely used as alternatives to wood for the framework of buildings, as in the flax-spinning mill shown here. Built in Britain in 1796, this mill exemplifies an architectural style that became common throughout the industrialized world for more than a century. The Industrial Revolution also brought mass production of building parts—a development that enabled the British architect Sir Joseph Paxton to erect London's Crystal Palace (a building made entirely of iron and glass) in only nine months, ready for the Great Exhibition of 1851. The 19th century saw a widespread revival of older architectural styles. For example, in the United States and Germany, Neo-Greek architecture was fashionable; in Britain and France, Neo-Baroque, Neo-Byzantine, and Neo-Gothic styles (as seen in the Palace of Westminster and Tower Bridge, London) were dominant.

SECTION THROUGH A FLAX-SPINNING MILL

FLAX-SPINNING MILL, SHREWSBURY, BRITAIN, 1796 (BY C. BAGE)

Cast-iron wall plate · Pitched roof · Ridge · Verge · Gutter · Anchor joint · Drain pipe · End flange · Concrete floor · Tapering part of column · Machinery space · Cast-iron mortise and tenon joint · Inverted T-section cast-iron beam · Segmentally arched brick vault · Paved ground floor · Strengthened central column

Multi-gabled roof (ridge and furrow roof) · Ridge · Furrow · Verge · Timber rafter · Cast-iron wall plate · Gable · Gutter · Drain pipe · Three courses of stretchers · Course of headers · Course of decorative headers · Cast-iron lattice window · Tapering part of column · Segmentally arched brick vault · Cast-iron mortise and tenon joint · Tie-rod · Cast-iron cruciform column · Inverted T-section cast-iron beam · Cast-iron tenon · Anchor joint · Strengthened central column · Bonded brick wall · Stone foundation · Quoin · Jamb · Gauged arch (segmental arch of tapered bricks)

CLOCK TOWER ("BIG BEN"), PALACE OF WESTMINSTER, LONDON, BRITAIN, 1836-1868 (BY C. BARRY AND A.W.N. PUGIN)

Finial
Spire
Skylight
Cornice decorated with shields
Iron railing
Small orb
Orb

Iron tracery
Dormer window
Round arch filled with open tracery
Tetrahedral spire
Bell chamber
Balustrade
Ogee tracery arch filled with trefoil
Flying buttress
Pinnacle
Spandrel
Octahedral shaft with billet decoration
Dial
Cornice
Molded corbel
Star-shaped corner buttress
Paneled field filled with tracery

Slender diagonal buttress
Narrow window
String course
Carved panel

DETAILS FROM BUILDINGS IN REVIVALIST STYLES

CUPOLA, MERCHANTS' EXCHANGE, PHILADELPHIA, USA, 1832-1834 (NEO-GREEK)

SCULPTURE AND PEDIMENT, OPERA HOUSE, PARIS, FRANCE, 1861-1874 (NEO-BAROQUE)

DOMED TURRET, WESTMINSTER CATHEDRAL, LONDON, BRITAIN, 1894-1903 (NEO-BYZANTINE)

Tetrahedral spire
Finial
Spire
Cornice
Archway

Finial
High-level footbridge
Latticework
Cast-iron tracery
Circular turret/buttress

Dormer head (gable) filled with blind tracery
Heraldic shield
Cast-iron paneling
Drawbridge (bascule)

Parapet
Molded corbel
Steel brace
Archway

Parapet of balcony
Octahedral upper turret
Wedge-shaped corbel
String course
Stone panel
Pier

TOWER BRIDGE, LONDON, BRITAIN, 1886-1894 (BY H. JONES)

CRYSTAL PALACE EXHIBITION HALL, LONDON, BRITAIN, 1851 (BY J. PAXTON)

Longitudinal girder
Ridge and furrow glass roof-windows
Window
Crest
Cast-iron ornamental arch-plate
Semicircular barrel vault
Cast-iron trapezium
Arched facade

Stepped storys

Octahedral column
Side exit
Sheet-iron louver
Strengthened support
Entrance

493

The early 20th century

ARCHITECTURE OF THE EARLY 20TH CENTURY is notable for radical new types of steel and glass buildings—particularly skyscrapers—and the widespread use of steel-reinforced concrete. The steel-framed skyscraper was pioneered in Chicago in the 1880s but did not become widespread until the first decades of the 20th century. As construction techniques were refined, skyscrapers became higher and higher. For example, the Empire State Building (right) of 1929-1931 has 102 storys. Many buildings of this period were constructed from lightweight concrete slabs that could be supported by cantilever beams or by pilotis (stilts), as in the Villa Savoye (below). The early 20th century also produced a great variety of architectural styles, some of which are illustrated opposite. Despite their diversity, the styles of this period generally had one thing in common: they were completely new, with few links to past architectural styles. This originality is in marked contrast to 19th-century architecture (see pp. 492-493), much of which was revivalist.

EMPIRE STATE BUILDING, NEW YORK, USA, 1929-1931 (BY R. H. SHREVE, T. LAMB, AND A. L. HARMON)

Radio mast

Circular lantern

Art Deco splayed seashell form

Stepped plinth

Chamfered corner

Colonnaded storey

Ornamentation

Ziggurat-style step-back

Set-back

Steel mullion

Flush window

Vertical pier

Regular fenestration

Solid-panel infill

Fanlike Art Deco decoration

Decorated stone lintel

Stone structure line

Limestone and granite cladding

Flat roof

Stepped cornice

Parapet

Plinth

Ground-floor entrance

Base

Square bay

VILLA SAVOYE, POISSY, FRANCE, 1929-1931 (BY LE CORBUSIER)

TOP VIEW

Fixed table

Parapet

Slab floor

Screen

Ramp

Handrail

Windowsill

Flat roof

Curved wall

Flat roof

Directional skylight

Terrace

Raised planting bed

SIDE VIEW

Terrace

Cement-rendered wall of lightweight slabs

Solarium

Sliding pane of glass

Mullion

Piano nobile (first floor)

Limestone and granite cladding

Flat roof

Parapet

Reinforced-concrete pilotis (stilt)

Rooms for staff

Ribbon window of long living room

Curved glazing

Covered driveway

MIDWAY GARDENS, CHICAGO, USA, 1914 (BY F. L. WRIGHT)

Flagpole

Plain coping stone

Main floor

Decorated cement frieze

Terrace

Steps

Stage

Orchestra shell

Tiled, shallow pitched roof

Projecting balustrade

Ridge

Hip

Ornamental light

Arcade

Main pavilion

Terrace

Octagonal window

Ornamental sculpture

Stone plinth

Flat roof

Cantilevered latticed shade

Planting bed

EAST SIDE

NORTH SIDE

Tiled frieze

Deep-set window

Brick pier

Stepped flat roofs

Slit window

Terrace

Ornamented coping stone

EARLY 20TH-CENTURY ARCHITECTURAL STYLES

DORMER WINDOW, STUDIO ELVIRA, MUNICH, GERMANY, 1902 (ART NOUVEAU)

AEG TURBINE HALL, BERLIN, GERMANY, 1909 (DEUTSCHER WERKBUND)

ROBIE HOUSE, CHICAGO, USA, 1909-1910 (PRAIRIE STYLE)

GRUNDTVIG CHURCH, COPENHAGEN, DENMARK, 1920 (EXPRESSIONIST)

VERTEX, CHRYSLER BUILDING, NEW YORK, USA, 1928-1930 (ART DECO)

TOWER, TOWN HALL, HILVERSUM, NETHERLANDS, 1930 (DUTCH CUBIST)

CASA DEL FASCIO, COMO, ITALY, 1932-1936 (GRUPPO SEVEN CUBIST)

MOTIF ABOVE DOORWAY, HOOVER FACTORY, LONDON, BRITAIN, 1933 (ART DECO)

Modern buildings 1

KAWANA HOUSE, JAPAN, FROM 1987 (BY N. FOSTER)

ARCHITECTURE SINCE ABOUT THE 1950s is generally known as modern architecture. One of its main influences has been functionalism—a belief that a building's function should be apparent in its design. Both the Centre Georges Pompidou (below and opposite) and the Hong Kong and Shanghai Bank (see pp. 498-499) are functionalist buildings. On each, elements of engineering and the building's services are clearly visible on the outside. In the 1980s, some architects rejected functionalism in favor of postmodernism, in which historical styles—particularly neoclassicism—were revived, using modern building materials and techniques. In many modern buildings, walls are made of glass or concrete hung from a frame, as in the Kawana House (right); this type of wall construction is known as curtain walling. Other modern construction techniques include the intricate interlocking of concrete vaults—as in the Sydney Opera House (see pp. 498-499)—and the use of high-tension beams to create complex roof shapes, such as the paraboloid roof of the Church of St. Pierre de Libreville (see pp. 498-499).

Solar panel
Concrete frame
Pile foundation
Raft
Composite cladding panel

SIDE VIEW

Rocker beam
Curtain walling
Lattice beam
Floor-beam connection
Floor

FRONT VIEW

SERVICES FACADE, CENTRE GEORGES POMPIDOU, PARIS, FRANCE, 1977 (BY R. PIANO AND R. ROGERS)

Metal-faced fire-resistant panel
Air-conditioning duct
Cooling tower
Water pipe

Grand gallery level

Main gallery levels

Library level

Administrative level

Mezzanine gallery level

Reception level

Staircase to grand hall
Electrical plant
Water-cooled fire-resistant column
Continuous glazing
Tinted glass
Services entrance

PRINCIPAL FACADE, CENTRE GEORGES POMPIDOU

Gallery space

External walkway

Electronically operated roller blind

Cooling tower

Continuous glazing

Steel lattice beam

Main truss

Gerberette (cast-steel rocker beam)

Suspended fire-resistant glass curtain

Terrace

Cradle support for escalator

Cross-bracing

Double fire escape staircase

Reinforced-concrete and steel floor plate

Double floor height

Main entrance

Glazed escalator tube

Node

Water-cooled fire-resistant steel column

Exposed "plug-in" services

Steel lattice beam

Dual air-conditioning unit for roof

Elevator

Elevator-motor room

Vertical-duct distribution zone

Metal sandwich-panel (insulating panel)

Gerberette (cast-steel rocker beam)

Rose connection

Outer tension-column

External steel-lattice mullion

Water-cooled fire-resistant cross-beam

Double fire escape staircase

Water storage tank

Cross-bracing

Open gallery floor

Water pipe

Steel-framed services column

Double cross-bracing

Modern buildings 2

HONG KONG AND SHANGHAI BANK, HONG KONG, 1981-1985 (BY N. FOSTER)

Inverted top truss

Soffit

Mast

Illuminated fascia

Curved glazing

External maintenance crane

Cockpit

Counterweight

Boom

Circular access platform

Steel column

Sunshade louver

Face panel

Mullion

Hanger

Handrail

Composite cladding panel

Top beam

Outer diagonal beam

Escalator

Outer bottom boom

Inner diagonal beam

Inner bottom boom

Fire escape staircase

Pin joint

External staircase

Refuge terrace

Double floor height

Hanger

Full-height glazing

Sun scoop

Glazed curtain wall

Two-story stability truss (coat hanger truss)

Flange

Lightweight, column-free steel and concrete floor

Vertical glazed typhoon screen

Glazed soffit

Entrance lobby

Plaza

SOUTH FACADE

Soffit

Helicopter landing pad

Navigation light

Stepped elevation

Face panel

Horizontal window

Vertical window

External maintenance crane

Cross-bracing

Service shaft

Double floor height

Sun scoop

10-floor-high atrium

Internal bridge

EAST SIDE

CHURCH OF ST. PIERRE, LIBREVILLE, GABON, 1990

Lattice truss

Cross-bracing

Mullion

Plate connector

Paraboloid roof

Concave curve

Convex curve

Tension member

Rafter

Eaves

Full-height glazing

Bolt

Rendered splayed outer wall

Entrance

Reinforced plinth

Concrete shoe

Inner diagonal beam

Beam housing

Pin joint

Glulam wall plate (glued and laminated wall plate)

Tinted glass

Circular steps

Secondary hall

Main hall

OPERA HOUSE, SYDNEY, AUSTRALIA, 1959-1973 (BY J. UTZON)

Vaults with curved ribs

Precast concrete rib

Glass wall

Mullion

Bronze glazing bar

Main hall

Precast concrete rib segment

Ridge

Continuous glazing

Solid podium

Ribbon window

HARBOR FACADE

Vault roof constructed of chevron-shaped precast tiles

Vault over restaurant

Staircase

Solid podium

Pink cladding

Pink granite-aggregate paving slab

Main line of support

Awning

Staircase

Terrace

WEST SIDE

499

Music

Musical notation

MUSICAL NOTATION IS ANY METHOD by which sounds are written down so that they can be read and performed by others. The present-day conventional system of notation uses a five-line stave (staff)—divided by vertical lines into sections known as bars—on which notes, rests, clefs, key signatures, time signatures, accidentals, and other symbols are written. A note indicates the duration of a sound and, according to its position on the stave, its pitch. Notes can be arranged on the stave in order of pitch to form a scale. A silence in the music is indicated by a rest. The clef, which is placed at the begininng of a stave, fixes the pitch. The key signature, which is placed after the clef, indicates the key. The time signature, placed after the key signature, shows the number of beats in a bar. Accidentals are used to indicate the raising or lowering of the pitch of a note.

ELEMENTS OF MUSICAL NOTATION

CLEFS

Treble (or G) clef

Alto (or C) clef

Bass (or F) clef

TIME SIGNATURES

Six-eight time

3/4 Three-four time

6/8

Stave (staff)

NOTES

Breve

Minim

Quaver

Semibreve

Crotchet

Semiquaver

RESTS

Breve rest

Minim rest

Quaver rest

Semibreve rest

Crotchet rest

Semiquaver rest

SCALE

C D E F G A B C

ACCIDENTALS

Sharp

Natural

Double sharp

Flat

Double flat

Key signature

Moderately fast and quiet

Tie (bind)

Repeat the previous bar

Treble clef

Bass clef

Four-four time (common time)

Key signature

Alto clef

Treble voice

Alto voice

Tenor voice

Bass voice

Organ part for right hand

Organ part for left hand

Organ pedal line

Instruments of the orchestra written in Italian

Bar line

Bass clef

Bar

Crotchet

502

FLUTES

OBOES

CLARINETS IN A

BASSOONS

HORNS IN D

TRUMPETS IN D

TIMPANI
IN D AND A

FIRST AND
SECOND
VIOLINS

VIOLAS

VOICES

CELLOS

ORGAN

DOUBLE BASSES

Accidental sharp

Tie (bind)

Accidental natural

Unison (both clarinets play the same note)

Semibreve

Crotchet

Semibreve rest

Accidental sharp

Slur

Piano (play softly)

Pianissimo (play very softly)

Crotchet rest

Orchestras

AN ORCHESTRA IS A GROUP of musicians that plays music written for a specific combination of instruments. The number and type of instruments included in the orchestra depends on the style of music being played. The modern orchestra (also known as a symphony orchestra) is made up of four sections of instruments—stringed, woodwind, brass, and percussion. The stringed section consists of violins, violas, cellos (violoncellos), double basses, and sometimes a harp (see pp. 510-511). The main instruments of the woodwind section are flutes, oboes, clarinets, and bassoons—the piccolo, cor anglais, bass clarinet, saxophone, and double bassoon (contrabassoon) can also be included if the music requires them (see pp. 508-509). The brass section usually consists of horns, trumpets, trombones, and the tuba (see pp. 506-507). The main instruments of the percussion section are the timpani (see pp. 518-519). The snare drum, bass drum, cymbals, tambourine, triangle, tubular bells, xylophone, vibraphone, gong (tam-tam), castanets, and maracas can also be included in the percussion section (see pp. 516-517). The musicians are usually arranged in a semi-circle—strings spread along the front, woodwind and brass in the center, and percussion at the back. A conductor stands in front of the musicians and controls the tempo (speed) of the music and the overall balance of the sound, ensuring that no instruments are too loud or too soft in relation to the others.

TUBULAR BELLS

TAM-TAM (GONG)

VIBRAPHONE

XYLOPHONE

CASTANETS

TAMBOURINE

MARACAS

TRIANGLE

TRUMPETS

HORNS

CLARINETS

BASS CLARINET

SAXOPHONE

PICCOLO

HARP

SECOND VIOLINS

FIRST VIOLINS

CYMBALS   SIDE DRUM   BASS DRUM

TIMPANI

EXAMPLE OF A LAYOUT OF THE INSTRUMENTS FOR A MODERN (SYMPHONY) ORCHESTRA

TROMBONES

TUBA

DOUBLE BASSES

BASSOONS

DOUBLE BASSOON

FLUTES

OBOES   COR ANGLAIS

VIOLAS

Score

CONDUCTOR'S STAND

CELLOS

505

Brass instruments

BRASS INSTRUMENTS ARE WIND INSTRUMENTS that are made of metal, usually brass. Although they appear in many different shapes and sizes, all brass instruments have a mouthpiece, a length of hollow tube, and a flared bell. The mouthpiece of a brass instrument may be cup-shaped, as in the cornet, or cone-shaped, as in the horn. The tube may be wide or narrow, mainly conical, as in the horn and tuba, or mainly cylindrical, as in the trumpet and trombone. The sound of a brass instrument is made by the player's lips vibrating against the mouthpiece, so that the air vibrates in the tube. By changing lip tension, the player can vary the vibrations and produce notes of different pitches. The range of notes produced by a brass instrument can be extended by means of a valve system. Most brass instruments, such as the trumpet, have piston valves that divert the air in the instrument along an extra piece of tubing (known as a valve slide) when pressed down. The total length of the tube is increased and the pitch of the note produced is lowered. Instead of valves, the trombone has a movable slide that can be pushed away from or drawn toward the player. The sound of a brass instrument can also be changed by inserting a mute into the bell of the instrument.

BUGLE

Brace

Tuning slide

Counterbalancing weight

SIMPLIFIED DIAGRAM SHOWING HOW A PISTON VALVE SYSTEM WORKS

Piston valves at rest

Air bypasses piston valves

PISTON VALVES AT REST

First piston valve pressed down

Second and third piston valves at rest

Air diverted through first valve slide

PISTON VALVE PRESSED DOWN

TRUMPET

Finger button

First piston valve

Spring returns piston valve to rest position

Second piston valve

Third piston valve

Holes divert air into valve slides

Little finger support

Music stand holder

Narrow, cylindrical tube

Flared bell

Cup-shaped mouthpiece

Mouthpiece receiver

Tuning slide

Tuning slide water key

First valve slide

First valve slide thumb hook

Third valve slide finger ring

Third valve slide

Third valve slide water key

Second valve slide

SECTIONS OF A TROMBONE

EXAMPLES OF MUTES

Flared bell

CUP MUTE

TENOR MUTE

ALTO MUTE

Inner tube

Outer tube of slide

Cup-shaped mouthpiece

Mouthpiece brace held by the left hand

Slide brace held by the right hand

Narrow, cylindrical tube

Water key

TROMBONE

Flared bell

Outer tube of slide

Cup-shaped mouthpiece

TUBA

Large, flared bell

Piston valves

FLUGELHORN

Little finger support

Piston valves

Flared bell

Cup-shaped mouthpiece

Conical tube

Valve slide

Cup-shaped mouthpiece

HORN

Cone-shaped mouthpiece

Finger key

Rotary valves

Valve slide

CORNET

Little finger support

Piston valves

Flared bell

Cup-shaped mouthpiece

Valve slide

Bore widens after valves

Narrow, conical bore

Large, flared bell

Wide, conical tube

Woodwind instruments

WOODWIND INSTRUMENTS ARE wind instruments that are generally made of wood, although some are made of metal or plastic. The sound of a woodwind instrument is produced by the vibration of air in a hollow tube. The air is made to vibrate by blowing across a blow hole—as in the flute and piccolo— or by blowing through a single reed— as in the clarinet and saxophone— or a double reed—as in the bassoon, cor anglais, and oboe. The pitch of a woodwind instrument can be changed by opening or closing holes cut into the tube of the instrument.

Bell

Double reed

Bell joint

Curved crook

Cylindrical, metal tube

Double reed

Conical, wooden tube

Tenor joint

Key

Body joint

Crook

Conical, wooden tube

Upper joint

Blow hole

Head joint

Bass joint

Key

Lip plate

PICCOLO

Right-hand rest

Double reed

Finger hole

Foot joint

Butt

Key

Key

Cork

Upper joint

Key

Mouthpiece with single reed

Middle joint

Key

Body joint

Ligature

Barrel joint

BASSOON

Finger hole

Middle joint

Cylindrical, metal tube

Cylindrical, wooden tube

Upper joint

Bell joint

Conical, wooden tube

Lip plate

Head joint

Key

Bulb-shaped bell

COR ANGLAIS

Blow hole

Bell joint

Middle joint

Flared bell

OBOE

FLUTE

Bell joint

Flared bell

CLARINET

TENOR SAXOPHONE

SECTIONS OF A TENOR SAXOPHONE

Mouthpiece with
single reed

Ligature

Upper octave key

Neck

Key
rod

Mouthpiece
with single
reed

Conical,
metal tube

Upturned,
flared bell

KEYS FOR THE
LEFT THUMB

Lower
octave key

Key

Key
rod

KEYS FOR THE
LEFT HAND

Key
rod

Key

Key

Mother-of-pearl
touchpiece
(button)

MAIN BODY OF
SAXOPHONE

KEYS FOR THE
LEFT PALM

KEYS FOR THE
RIGHT HAND

Key

Key
rod

Conical,
metal tube

KEYS FOR THE
RIGHT PALM

Mother-of-pearl
touchpiece
(button)

Tone hole

Upturned, flared bell

Tone hole

Pad made up of
layers of felt and
cork

Roller

Cup

Key guard

Key rod

Key

Metal center of
pad reflects sound

KEYS FOR THE RIGHT
LITTLE FINGER

Padded key

Key guard

KEYS FOR THE LEFT
LITTLE FINGER

Key guard

Stringed instruments

STRINGED INSTRUMENTS PRODUCE SOUND by the vibration of stretched strings. This may be done by drawing a bow across the strings, as in the violin; or by plucking the strings, as in the harp and guitar (see pp. 512-513). The four modern members of the bowed string family are the violin, viola, cello (violoncello), and double bass. Each consists of a hollow, wooden body, a long neck, and four strings. The bow is a wooden stick with horsehair stretched across its length. The vibrations made by drawing the bow across the strings are transmitted to the hollow body, and this itself vibrates, amplifying and enriching the sound produced. The harp consists of a set of strings of different lengths stretched across a wooden frame. The strings are plucked by the player's thumbs and fingers—except the little finger of each hand—which produces vibrations that are amplified by the harp's sound board. The pitch of the note produced by any stringed instrument depends on the length, weight, and tension of the string. A shorter, lighter, or tighter string gives a higher note.

Scroll eye

Scroll

Peg hole

Ebony tuning pegs

Neck made of maple wood

Strings

Fingerboard

Rounded shoulder

Belly (sound board)

Waist

Sound hole

Rib

Purfling

Bridge

Tailpiece

Chin rest

Tailpiece loop fits around end pin

SECTIONS OF A VIOLIN

End pin (tail pin)

Head

Point

Stick

Scroll

Scroll eye

Peg box

Tuning peg

Horsehair

Nut

String

Fingerboard

Rounded shoulder

Belly (sound board)

Purfling

Waist

Sound hole

Bridge

Frog

Tuning adjustor

Screw

Tailpiece

Chin rest

VIOLIN BOW

VIOLIN

HARP

- Crown
- Tuning peg
- Neck (string arm)
- Shoulder
- String
- Sound board
- Pillar
- Pedestal
- Foot
- Pedal

DOUBLE BASS BOW

- Head
- Point
- Inward-curving stick
- Horsehair
- Frog
- Screw

VIOLA

- Scroll
- Tuning peg
- Scroll eye
- Peg box
- Nut
- Fingerboard
- String
- Belly (sound board)
- Rounded shoulder
- Purfling
- Waist
- Bridge
- Sound hole
- Tuning adjustor
- Chin rest
- Tailpiece

CELLO (VIOLONCELLO)

- Scroll
- Scroll eye
- Peg box
- Tuning peg
- Nut
- Fingerboard
- String
- Rounded shoulder
- Belly (sound board)
- Sound hole
- Sound hole
- Bridge
- Waist
- Tuning adjustor
- Tailpiece
- Spike

DOUBLE BASS

- Scroll
- Scroll eye
- Tuning pegs at back of peg box
- Nut
- Fingerboard
- String
- Sloping shoulder
- Belly (sound board)
- Purfling
- Waist
- Bridge
- Rib
- Sound hole
- Tailpiece
- Spike

511

Guitars

THE GUITAR IS A PLUCKED stringed instrument
(see pp. 510-511). There are two types of guitar—
acoustic and electric. Acoustic guitars have hollow
bodies and six or twelve strings. Plucking or strumming
the strings produces vibrations that are amplified by their
hollow bodies. Electric guitars usually have solid bodies
and six strings. Pick-ups placed under the strings convert
vibrations into electronic signals that are magnified by
an amplifier, and sent to a loudspeaker where they are
converted into sounds (see pp. 520-521). Electric bass
guitars are very similar in structure to electric guitars,
and produce sound in the same way, but have four
heavier-gage strings and play lower pitched notes.

ACOUSTIC GUITAR

String Fret Machine head

Hollow body

Neck Headstock

Sound hole

Bridge

B string

G string

D string

A string

Low E string

Maker's label

Lining glued along top and bottom edge of rib

Rib

End block

Strap peg

Joint

Transverse (crosswise) strut strengthens back

Back made of two pieces of cherry wood joined together

Saddle

Bridge pin

Bridge Binding

COMPONENTS OF AN ACOUSTIC GUITAR

Top E string
Nut
Truss rod cover
Screws
Machine heads
Headstock
Machine head
Truss rod slot
Fingerboard
Truss rod
Position marks
Fretwire slot
Fretwire
Sound hole
Bracing
Sound board made of two pieces of spruce joined together

EXAMPLES OF ACOUSTIC GUITARS

Rose
Sound hole
String
Machine head
Hollow body
Bridge
Neck
Headstock
Scratch plate

WASHBURN TWELVE-STRING

Hollow, metal body
Sound hole
String
Machine head
Tailpiece
Neck
Headstock
Resonator

DOBRO RESONATOR

EXAMPLES OF ELECTRIC GUITARS

Pick-up
Scratch plate
String
Machine head
Solid body
Bridge
Neck
Headstock
Output socket
Vibrato arm

FENDER STRATOCASTER

Pick-up
Pick-up selector
String
Machine head
Solid body
Bridge
Neck
Headstock
Scratch plate

GIBSON LES PAUL

Pick-up
String
Machine head
Solid body
Bridge
Neck
Headstock
Output socket
Scratch plate

FENDER JAZZ BASS

Keyboard instruments

KEYBOARD INSTRUMENTS are instruments that are sounded by means of a keyboard. The organ and piano are two of the principal members of the keyboard family. The organ consists of pipes which are operated by one or more keyboards and foot pedals. The pipes are lined up in rows (known as ranks or registers) on top of a wind chest. The sound of the organ is made when air is admitted into a pipe by pressing a key or pedal. The piano consists of wire strings stretched over a metal frame, and a keyboard and pedals that operate hammers and dampers. The piano frame is either vertical—as in the upright piano—or horizontal—as in the grand piano. When a key is at rest, a damper lies against the string to keep it from vibrating. When a key is pressed down, the damper moves away from the string as the hammer strikes it, causing the string to vibrate and sound a note.

ORGAN PIPE

UPRIGHT PIANO

Muffler felt
Pressure bar
Tuning pin
Pin block
Hammer rail
Hammer
Wooden case
88–note keyboard
Keybed
Sound board
Metal frame
String
Hitch pin
Treble bridge
Bass bridge
Una corda (soft) pedal
Sostenuto pedal
Damper (sustaining) pedal

ORGAN CONSOLE

Pipe
Pedal stop
Swell stop
Music stand
Choir stop
Swell manual (keyboard)
Great stop
Great manual (keyboard)
Thumb piston
Choir manual (keyboard)
Toe piston
Pedal board
Foot pedal
Swell pedal

UPRIGHT PIANO ACTION

KEY AT REST

String
Hammer
Damper lies against string, and keeps it from vibrating
Hammer rest
Back check
Damper lever
Action lever
Capstan screw
Jack
Key released

KEY PRESSED DOWN

String
Hammer strikes string
Damper moves away from string, allowing it to vibrate
Hammer rest
Back check
Damper lever
Action lever
Jack
Capstan screw
Key pressed down

CONCERT GRAND PIANO (VIEWED FROM ABOVE)

CONCERT GRAND PIANO (FRONT VIEW)

Sound board

Bass bridge

Hitch pin

Metal frame

Single bass note string

Long bridge

Tenor note strings (two strings for each note)

Treble note strings (three strings for each note)

Wooden case

Hammer

Tuning pin

Wrest plank

Keyboard lid

88-note keyboard

Lid

String

Wooden case

Keyboard

Una corda (soft) pedal

Sostenuto pedal

Damper (sustaining) pedal

STEINWAY & SONS NEW YORK HAMBURG

STEINWAY

B

S1B422

Percussion instruments

PERCUSSION INSTRUMENTS are a large group of instruments that produce sound by being struck, shaken, scraped, or clashed together. Some percussion instruments—such as the gong (tam-tam), cymbals, and maracas—do not have a definite pitch and are used for rhythm and impact, and the distinctive timber (color) of their sound. Other percussion instruments—such as the xylophone, vibraphone, and tubular bells—are tuned to a definite pitch and can play melody, harmony, and rhythms. The xylophone and vibraphone each have two rows of bars that are arranged in a similar way to the black and white keys of a piano. Metal tubes are suspended below the bars to amplify the sound. The vibraphone has electrically operated fans that rotate in the tubes and produce a vibrato (wavering pitch) effect.

TEMPLE BLOCKS

TUBULAR BELLS

Tube struck with mallet

Hollow, metal tube

Damper bar

Metal frame

Mechanism linking pedal and damper bar

Row of tubes graduated in length and pitch

Damper pedal

EXAMPLES OF MALLETS

SOFT-HEADED MALLET

Felt-covered head

HARD-HEADED MALLET

Rosewood head

HAMMER MALLET

Leather-covered head

XYLOPHONE

Row of bars graduated in length and pitch

Wooden bar struck with hard-headed mallet

Hollow, metal tube

Metal stand

GONG (TAM-TAM)

Tam-tam struck in center with soft-headed mallet

Cord

Metal frame

Rim

Large, metal disk

CYMBALS

Leather strap fits around player's hand

Pad protects hands from vibrations

Thin, convex disk of copper and tin alloy

SECTIONS OF A MARACA

Wooden handle

Lead beads

Hollow, wooden head

TRIANGLE

Steel rod bent into triangular shape

Steel wand

CLAVES

Hardwood sticks clashed together to give a sharp crack

CASTANETS

Cord

Hollowed wood

VIBRAPHONE

Row of bars graduated in length and pitch

Metal bar struck with soft-headed mallet

Metal frame

Damper pedal

Metal tube containing electrically operated fan that produces vibrato (wavering pitch) effect

Electric cable

Drums

A DRUM IS A percussion instrument that consists of a drumhead, made of skin or plastic, stretched over one or both ends of a hollow vessel (the body shell). Drums are played in most parts of the world and are made in a number of different shapes and sizes. They can be divided into three groups according to the shape of the body shell: frame drums (e.g., tambourines), bowl-shaped drums (e.g., timpani), and tubular drums (e.g., congas). Drums are usually sounded by striking the drumhead with the hands or with mallets, such as a hard-headed stick. The drumhead vibrates, and its vibrations are amplified by the hollow body shell. The snare drum has wires—known as snares—stretched across the lower drumhead; the snares vibrate against the lower drumhead when the drum is played. Most drums, such as congas, do not have a definite pitch and can play only rhythms (see pp. 516-517). Other drums, such as timpani, have a definite pitch and can play melody, harmony, and rhythms. They can be tuned by adjusting the tension of the drumhead. Different types of drum can be combined together with other percussion instruments to form a drum kit. The basic components of the drum kit are bass drum, tom-toms, floor tom (tenor drum), snare drum, and cymbals.

TAMBOURINE

DRUM KIT

Crash cymbal

Tension key

Tension rod

Tom-tom

Lug

Hi-hat cymbal

Snare drum

Tripod stand

SNARE DRUM (VIEWED FROM BELOW)

Snare mounting

Adjustable damper

Lug

Transparent lower drumhead

Upper drumhead

Snare

Stick

Snare release lever

Chain

Tension screw

Felt-covered mallet

Pedal

Pedal

EXAMPLES OF STICKS

Acorn

HARD-HEADED STICK

Taper

SOFT-HEADED STICK

Felt-covered head

WIRE BRUSH

Wire bristles

Ride cymbal

Tension key

Height adjustment key

Tom-tom

Tension rod

Lug

Floor tom (tenor drum)

Tension rod

Lug

Wooden body shell

Height adjustment key

Leg

Bass drum

Rubber foot

CONGAS

Metal hoop

Drumhead

Wooden body shell

Tension rod

Tripod stand

Leg

TIMPANUM (KETTLE DRUM)

Drumhead

Tension rod

Metal hoop

Tuning gauge

Copper body shell

Strut

Crown

Tension rod

Tuning pedal

Castor

Electronic instruments

ELECTRONIC DRUMS

ELECTRONIC INSTRUMENTS generate electronic signals that are magnified by an amplifier, and sent to a loudspeaker where they are converted into sounds. Synthesizers, and other electronic instruments, simulate the characteristic sounds of conventional instruments, and also create entirely new sounds. Most electronic instruments are keyboard instruments, but electronic wind and percussion instruments are also popular. A digital sampler records and stores sounds from musical instruments or other sources. When the sound is played back, the pitch of the original sound can be altered. A keyboard can be connected to the sampler so that a tune can be played using the sampled sounds. With a MIDI (Musical Instrument Digital Interface) system, a computer can be linked with other electronic instruments, such as keyboards and electronic drums, to make sounds together or in sequence. It is also possible, using music software, to compose and play music on a home computer.

Drum pad

Height adjustment key

HOME KEYBOARD

Power button   *Volume control*   *Function display*   *Sequence record button*   *Tone editor control*

Demonstration tune button

Modulation wheel   *Multi-accompaniment system control*   *Tone and rhythm pattern selector*   *Key*

Tripod

SYNTHESIZER

Memory card slot   *Joystick*   *Function display*   *Edit control*   *Data entry key pad*

Sound waveform selection guide

Volume control

Modulation wheel   *Sound selection control*   *Key*

WIND SYNTHESIZER

Keys for left hand

Mouthpiece

WIND CONTROLLER

Keys for right hand

DIGITAL SAMPLER

Contrast control

Function display

Power button

Data increment control

POWER PACK

MIDI (Musical Instrument Digital Interface) cable

Connecting cable

SOUND MODULE

Record trigger

Floppy-disk drive

Play button

Data entry key pad

Microphone input

Store button

Data entry key pad

Input connector socket

Volume control

HOME COMPUTER SYSTEM

VISUAL DISPLAY UNIT

Music sequencing software

Score for selected instrument

Edit control

Play button

Function display

Effect balance control

SPEAKER

SOUND MODULE

SPEAKER

Hard-disk drive

Floppy-disk drive

Volume control

Volume and tone controls

KEYBOARD

Data entry key pad

Mouse pad

Mouse

SPORTS

Soccer

GAMES INVOLVING KICKING A BALL have a long history and were recorded in China as early as 300 BC; in medieval Europe, street football was banned as a menace to the public; only in 1863 were the rules established, specifically banning carrying the ball for all players except the goalkeeper, and separating rugby from soccer. Soccer, also known as association football, is a team sport in which players attempt to score goals by passing and dribbling the ball down the field past opposing defenders, and kicking or heading the ball into the goal net, outwitting the defending goalkeeper or "goalie." Each team consists of ten outfield players (defenders, midfielders, and strikers) and a goalkeeper. Players from the opposing team may challenge the player in possession of the ball, but an illegal or foul tackle results in a penalty if a foul occurs inside the penalty area or a free kick if outside the penalty area. The round ball used in soccer is more easily controlled than the oval balls used in American, Canadian, and Australian rules football and in rugby. The result is a more "open" or flowing game which is played and watched by millions of people worldwide.

LINESMAN'S FLAG

Lightweight, brightly colored fabric

Handle with rubber grip

REFEREE'S EQUIPMENT

Red card

Yellow card

Referee's whistle

Stopwatch

FIELD MARKINGS

Halfway line

5 ft (1.5 m)

HALFWAY-LINE FLAG

Corner arc

CORNER FLAG

24 ft (7.3 m)

Goal line

GOAL

SOCCER FIELD

150–300 ft (46–91 m)

Corner flag

Goal line

Corner arc

Penalty area

Penalty arc

Penalty mark

Linesman

Referee

Center circle

Center spot

Halfway-line flag

Halfway line

Striker

Striker

Striker

Left midfielder

Right midfielder

Central midfielder

Left back

Right back

Touch line

Central defender

Central defender

Goal area

Goal

Goalkeeper

Goal line

GOALKEEPER

Goalkeeper's shirt

Glove

Shin guard

Shorts

Sock

Soccer shoe

SOCCER UNIFORM

Open-neck collar

Lightweight, man-made fabric team shirt

Team logo

Manufacturer's logo

Ribbed welt

Sponsor's logo

Manufacturer's name

Edge cut to fit perfectly

MAKING A SOCCER BALL

Hole punched in panel for stitching

Ball size number

Waxed thread

Needle

8½–9 in (22–23 cm)

Bladder valve

Bladder made from latex rubber

Panels sewn together with ball inside out

Laminated panel

Long cotton sock

Club crest

Team shorts

Synthetic shoelace

Interchangeable nylon stud

SOCCER SHOE

525

Football

IN AMERICAN AND CANADIAN FOOTBALL, the object of the game is to get the ball across the opponent's goal line, either by passing or carrying it across (a touchdown), or by kicking it between their goalposts (a field goal). An American football team has 11 players on the field at a time, although up to 40 players can appear for each side in a single game. The agile offense tries to score points, and the heavy hitting defense holds back the opposition. When in possession of the ball, a team has four chances (downs), to move it at least ten yards up the field to make a first down. The opposition gains possession if they fail, or by tackling and intercepting the ball. Canadian football is played on a larger field, with 12 men on each side. A team has only three chances, instead of four, to achieve a first down. Otherwise, the game is very similar to American football. Helmets, face masks, and layers of body padding are worn by the players for protection.

AMERICAN FOOTBALL FIELD

Goalpost
End line
Goal line
Inbound line
Sideline
Players' bench
Referee
Umpire
Line judge
Back judge
End zone

160 ft 6 in
(49 m)

GOALPOST

30 ft
(9.2 m)

AMERICAN FOOTBALL PLAYING FORMATION

Right safety
Middle linebacker
Left safety
Right defensive tackle
Left defensive tackle
Right cornerback
Inside linebacker
Left cornerback
Outside linebacker
Right defensive end
Center
Left defensive end
Split end
Tight end
Left tackle
Right tackle
Right guard
Left guard
Quarterback
Left halfback
Right halfback
Fullback

CANADIAN FOOTBALL FIELD

Goalpost
Goal line
Players' bench
Referee
Umpire
Field judge
Yardsman
Head linesman
Yardsman
Sideline
End zone

195 ft
(59.5 m)

GOALPOST

30 ft
(9.2 m)

CANADIAN FOOTBALL PLAYING FORMATION

Right defensive back
Middle linebacker
Safety
Left defensive back
Left defensive tackle
Right cornerback
Left cornerback
Left outside linebacker
Right outside linebacker
Left defensive end
Right defensive end
Right guard
Wide receiver
Wide receiver
Right defensive tackle
Right tackle
Flanker
Running back
Left guard
Center
Left tackle
Quarterback
Fullback
Halfback

PLAYER

Team logo
Helmet
Wrist pad
Player's number
Thigh pad
Pants
Studded shoe

PROTECTIVE EQUIPMENT

11 in (28 cm)

Painted white ring
Lace
Brown pebbled leather

FOOTBALL

HELMET

Non-breakable plastic
Rubber-coated plastic
Shock absorber

SHOULDER PAD

Tie to shoulder pads

Chest protector weight up to 5 lb 8 oz (2.5 kg)

BIKE
AIR·LITE
BLUE LASER 40-42

UPPER ARM PAD

RIB PADS

Strap ties onto shoulder pad

REFEREE'S SIGNALS

TIME OUT
TOUCHDOWN OR FIELD GOAL

PERSONAL FOUL
OFFSIDE OR ENCROACHMENT

HOLDING
ILLEGAL MOTION

FIRST DOWN
PASS INTERFERENCE

BIKE

ELBOW PAD

FINGERLESS GLOVE

Screw-in stud

Rigid plastic covering

PONY

FOOTWEAR

Fold-over leather tongue

Groin pad
Foam-sponge filling

HIP PAD

Rigid plastic covering

THIGH PAD

PANTS

KNEE PAD

527

Australian rules and Gaelic football

VARIETIES OF FOOTBALL have developed all over the world and Australian rules football is considered to be one of the roughest versions, allowing full body tackles although participants wear no protective padding. Two teams of 18 players play on a large, oval pitch. Players can kick or punch the ball, which is shaped like a rugby ball, but cannot throw it. Running with the ball is permitted, as long as the ball touches the ground at least once every ten meters. The full backs defend two sets of posts. Teams try to score goals (six points) between the inner posts or behinds (one point) inside the outer posts. Each game has four quarters of 25 minutes, and the team with the most points at the end of the allotted time is the winner. In Gaelic football, an Irish version of soccer (see pp. 524–525), a size 5 association football is used. Each team can have 15 players on the field at a time. Players are allowed to catch, fist, and kick the ball, or dribble it using their hands or feet, but cannot throw it. Teams are awarded three points for getting the ball into the net, and one point for getting it through the posts above the crossbar. Gaelic football is rarely played outside of Ireland.

START OF PLAY

SCORING

GOAL (6 POINTS)

BEHIND (1 POINT)

AUSTRALIAN RULES FOOTBALL FIELD

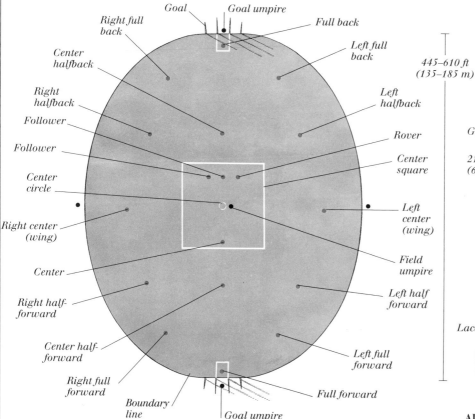

Goal

Goal umpire

Right full back

Full back

Center halfback

Left full back

Right halfback

Left halfback

Follower

Rover

Follower

Center square

Center circle

Left center (wing)

Right center (wing)

Field umpire

Center

Left half forward

Right half-forward

Center half-forward

Left full forward

Right full forward

Full forward

Boundary line

Goal umpire

445–610 ft (135–185 m)

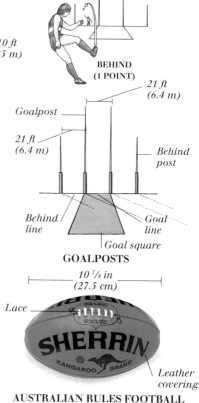

21 ft (6.4 m)

Goalpost

21 ft (6.4 m)

Behind post

Behind line

Goal line

Goal square

GOALPOSTS

10 7/8 in (27.5 cm)

Lace

SHERRIN

KANGAROO BRAND

Leather covering

AUSTRALIAN RULES FOOTBALL

AUSTRALIAN RULES FOOTBALL SKILLS

RUNNING WITH THE BALL

KICKING

TACKLING

TAKING A MARK

PASSING THE BALL

AUSTRALIAN RULES FOOTBALL UNIFORM

Australian Football League logo

Team colors

Sleeveless team guernsey

Sock

Shorts

GAELIC FOOTBALL PITCH

Goalkeeper   *Goal umpire*

Corner flag

Right fullback

Right halfback

Center flag

Linesman

Right midfielder

Referee

Right half-forward

Right full-forward

Full forward

Goal area

Left fullback

Fullback

Left halfback

Center halfback

Linesman

Left midfielder

Midfield line

Left half-forward

Center half-forward

Left full-forward

260–295 ft (80–90 m)

CONTROLLING THE BALL

SCORING IN GAELIC FOOTBALL

GOAL (3 POINTS)

POINT (1 POINT)

8 1/2–9 in (22–23 cm)

21ft (6.4 m)

Goalpost

Crossbar

Parallelogram

GOAL

oneills all-ireland

GAELIC FOOTBALL

Rugby

RUGBY IS PLAYED WITH AN OVAL BALL which may be carried, thrown, or kicked. There are two types of rugby. Rugby Union is an amateur game played by two teams of 15 players. Players can score points in two ways: by placing the ball behind the opponents' goal line (a try, scoring four points) or by kicking it over the crossbar of the opponent's goal (a conversion, scoring two points; a penalty kick, scoring three points; or a drop-kick, scoring three points). Rugby League developed from the Union game but is played by 13 players at amateur and professional levels. In League games, a try scores four points; a conversion scores two points; a drop goal scores three points, and a penalty kick scores two points. In both forms of the game, whenever a rule is broken, play is resumed with a scrum. In a scrum, each team's forwards bind together facing each other and fight for possession of the ball.

RUGBY UNION FIELD

Touch in-goal line · Goal · Dead-ball line · Goal line · Touch-line · 5 m line · Referee · Scrum-half · Hooker · 10 m line · Tight-head prop · Loose-head prop · Linesman · Flanker · Flanker · Lock forward · Lock forward · Center · Right wing · Left wing · Center · Number 8 · Full back · Fly-half · In-goal area

225 ft (68 m) maximum

RUGBY UNION SCRUM

Loose-head prop · Hooker · Tight-head prop · Scrum-half · Flanker · Flanker · Lock forward · Lock forward · Number 8

18 ft (5.5 m) · Upright · Crossbar · Protective padding · 9 ft 10 in (3 m)

RUGBY UNION GOALPOST

RUGBY LEAGUE FIELD

Goal · Dead-ball line · Touch in-goal · Touch in-goal line · Goal line · Touch-line · 10 m line · Hooker · Referee · Open-side prop · Blind-side prop · Linesman · Linesman · Second-row forward · Second-row forward · Scrum-half · Loose forward · Stand-off half · Left wing · Center · Full back · Center · Right wing

225 ft (68 m) maximum

RUGBY LEAGUE SCRUM

Hooker · Open-side prop · Scrum-half · Blind-side prop · Second-row forward · Second-row forward · Loose forward

18 ft (5.5 m) · Upright · Crossbar · Protective padding

RUGBY LEAGUE GOALPOST

RUGBY SCORING AND SKILLS

GOAL

Goal line

TRY

PASS

PLACE KICK

FLYING TACKLE

Circular stud

RUGBY SHOE

Ankle support

RUGBY UNION PLAYER

Shirt in team color

Knee-high sock

Team shorts

Studded boot

RUGBY UNION BALL

Four-panel construction

Laminated leather panel covered with textured plastic

11–12 in (28–30 cm)

RUGBY LEAGUE BALL

Four-panel construction

Laminated leather panel covered with smooth plastic

11 in (28 cm)

RUGBY LEAGUE SHIRT

Team crest

Official logo of the British Rugby Football League

Three-quarter sleeve

RUGBY UNION SHIRT

Button-up collar

Team color

Team crest

Long sleeve

RUGBY SHIRTS

531

Basketball

BASKETBALL IS A BALL GAME for two teams of five players, originally devised in 1890 by James Naismath for the Y.M.C.A. in Springfield, Massachusetts. The object of the game is to take possession of the ball and score points by throwing the ball into the opposing team's basket. A player moves the ball up and down the court by bouncing it along the ground or "dribbling"; the ball may be passed between players by throwing, bouncing, or rolling. Players may not run with or kick the ball, although pivoting on one foot is allowed. The game begins with the referee throwing the ball into the air and a player from each team jumping up to try and "tip" the ball to a teammate. The length of the game and the number of periods played varies at different levels. There are amateur, professional, and international rules. No game ends in a draw. As many extra periods as necessary are played to break the tie. In addition to the five players on court, each team has up to seven substitutes, but players may only leave the court with the permission of the referee. Basketball is a noncontact sport and fouls on other players are penalized by a throw-in awarded against the offending team; a free throw at the basket is awarded when a player is fouled in the act of shooting. Basketball is a fast-moving game, requiring both physical and mental coordination. Skillful tactical play matters more than simple physical strength and the agility of the players makes the game an excellent spectator sport.

BASKETBALL SKILLS

CHEST PASS

DRIBBLE

OVERHEAD PASS

LAY-UP SHOT

JUMP SHOT

LONG PASS

INTERNATIONAL BASKETBALL COURT

Backboard
End-line
Restraining circle
Player's bench
Referee
Timekeeper
Clock operator
Scorer
Referee
Right forward
Three-point line
Basket
Semi-circle
Right guard
Left guard
Center
Centerline
Left forward
Center circle
Free-throw line
Sideline

49 ft 3 in (15 m)

BASKET AND BACKBOARD

Backboard
Metal rim
Cord net

6 ft (1.8 m)

BASKET AND BACKBOARD STRUCTURE

10 ft (3.05 m)

ZONE DEFENSES

Point man

Free-throw
line

1 – 2 – 2 ZONE

1 – 3 – 1 ZONE

$9\frac{1}{2}$–$9\frac{3}{4}$ in
(24–5 cm)

2 – 3 ZONE

AMERICAN BASKETBALL JERSEY

Cool,
lightweight
fabric

Team name

Player's
number

LAKERS

32

48

Textured
surface for
good grip

Cushioned
sole

Low heel
profile

BASKETBALL

BASKETBALL SHOE

**INTERNATIONAL
REFEREE'S
SIGNALS**

TECHNICAL
FOUL

INTENTIONAL
FOUL

JUMP BALL

STOP CLOCK
FOR FOUL

SUBSTITUTION

PERSONAL FOUL:
NO FREE THROWS

TRAVELLING

ILLEGAL
DRIBBLE

CHARGING WITH
THE BALL

ONE FREE
THROW

STOP CLOCK

533

Volleyball, netball, and handball

VOLLEYBALL, NETBALL, AND HANDBALL are fast-moving team sports played with balls, usually on courts with a hard surface. In volleyball, the object of the game is to hit the ball over a net strung across the center of the court so that it touches the ground on the opponent's side. The team of six players can take three hits to direct the ball over the net, although the same player cannot hit the ball twice in a row. Players can hit the ball with their arms, hands or any other part of their upper body. Teams score points only while serving. The first team to score 15 points, with a two-point margin over their opponent, wins the game. Netball is similar to basketball (see pp. 532–533), but is played on a slightly larger court with seven players instead of five. A team moves the ball toward the goal by throwing, passing, and catching it with the aim of throwing the ball through the opponents' goal net. Players are confined by their playing position to specific areas of the court. Team handball is one of the world's fastest games. Each side has seven players. A team moves the ball by dribbling, passing, or bouncing it as they run. Players may stop, catch, throw, bounce, or strike the ball with any part of the body above the knees. Each team tries to score goals by directing the ball past the opposition's goalkeeper into the net, which is similar to a soccer goal net (see pp. 524–525).

VOLLEYBALL SHOTS

OVERHAND SERVE   SPIKE (SMASH)

UNDERHAND SERVE   FOREARM PASS (DIG)

VOLLEYBALL KIT

Team colors

Ribbed cuff

Cotton-knit jersey

Elastic waist

Leather covering

m mizuno

Shorts

Elastic knit fabric

Injected molded padding

VOLLEYBALL COURT

End line   Linesman

Linesman

Sideline

Players' bench

Referee

Scorer

Net

Left forward

Back zone

Left back

Linesman

Clear space

8 in (21 cm)

Attack zone

Attack line

VOLLEYBALL

Umpire

Center forward

Right forward

Center back

Linesman

Service area

Server

29 ft 6 in (9 m)

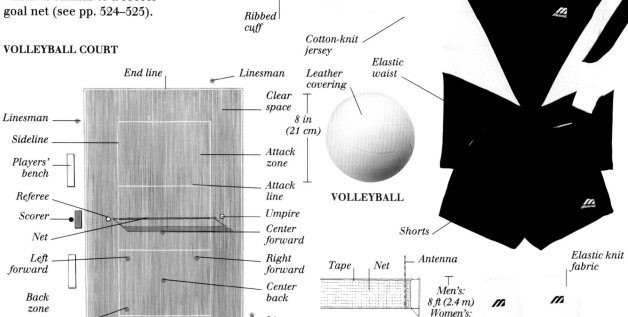

Tape   Net   Antenna

Men's: 8 ft (2.4 m) Women's: 7 ft 4 in (2.2 m)

Post

VOLLEYBALL NET

m   m

KNEE PADS

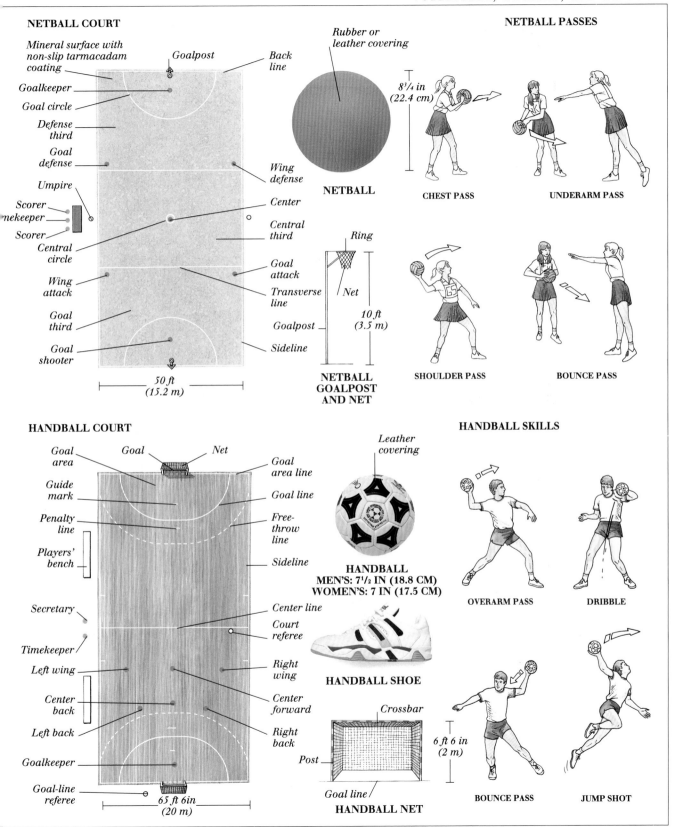

NETBALL COURT

Mineral surface with non-slip tarmacadam coating
Goalpost
Back line
Goalkeeper
Goal circle
Defense third
Goal defense
Wing defense
Umpire
Scorer
Timekeeper
Scorer
Central circle
Center
Central third
Goal attack
Transverse line
Wing attack
Goal third
Goal shooter
Goalpost
Sideline

50 ft (15.2 m)

NETBALL PASSES

Rubber or leather covering

8³/₄ in (22.4 cm)

NETBALL

CHEST PASS

UNDERARM PASS

Ring
Net
10 ft (3.5 m)
Goalpost

NETBALL GOALPOST AND NET

SHOULDER PASS

BOUNCE PASS

HANDBALL COURT

Goal area
Goal
Net
Goal area line
Guide mark
Goal line
Penalty line
Free-throw line
Players' bench
Sideline
Secretary
Center line
Court referee
Timekeeper
Left wing
Right wing
Center back
Center forward
Left back
Right back
Goalkeeper
Goal-line referee

65 ft 6in (20 m)

HANDBALL SKILLS

Leather covering

HANDBALL
MEN'S: 7¹/₂ IN (18.8 CM)
WOMEN'S: 7 IN (17.5 CM)

HANDBALL SHOE

Crossbar
6 ft 6 in (2 m)
Post
Goal line

HANDBALL NET

OVERARM PASS

DRIBBLE

BOUNCE PASS

JUMP SHOT

535

Baseball

BASEBALL IS A BALL GAME for two teams of nine players. The batter hits the ball thrown by the opposing team's pitcher, into the area between the foul lines. He then runs round all four fixed bases in order to score a run, touching or "tagging" each base in turn. The pitcher must throw the ball at a height between the batter's armpits and knees, a height which is called the strike zone. A ball pitched in this area that crosses over the home plate is called a "strike" and the batter has three strikes in which to try to hit the ball (otherwise he has "struck out"). The fielding team tries to get the batting team out by catching the ball before it bounces, tagging a player of the batting team who is running between bases with the ball, or by tagging a base before the player has reached it. Members of the batting team may stop safely at a base as long as it is not occupied by another member of their team. When the batter runs to first base, his teammate at first base must run onto second – this is called a force play. A game consists of nine innings and each team will bat once during an inning. When three members of the batting team are out, the teams swap roles. The team with the most runs wins the game.

BATTER'S HELMET

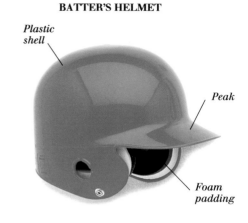

Plastic shell

Peak

Foam padding

CATCHER'S MASK

Wire coated in strong nylon

Plastic-coated foam padding

BASEBALL FIELD

Center field

Center fielder

Warning track

Left fielder

Right fielder

Left field

Second baseman

Right field

Foul line

Outfield

Shortstop

First baseman

Umpire

First base

Third baseman

Infield

Third base

Home run

Coach's box

Second base

Dugout

On-deck circle

Pitcher's mound

325 ft (100 m) minimum

PITCHER'S MOUND

Pitcher

Pitcher's rubber

HOME PLATE

Batter

Home plate

Catcher

Home-plate umpire

MAKING A BASEBALL

Wool yarn

Rubber inner casing

Horsehide strip

Cork center

Cotton thread outer casing

Wool strand

Red outer stitching

THE PITCHING SEQUENCE

THE WINDUP 1

THE WINDUP 2

THE WINDUP 3

THE WINDUP 4

THE RELEASE

THE FOLLOW-THROUGH

UMPIRING SIGNALS

BALL

INFIELD

STRIKE

FAIR BALL

RUNNER IS SAFE

FOUL TIP

BASEBALL EQUIPMENT

Webbed pocket

Fingers laced together

Strap

Thumb

Palm

Leather stitching

Heel

FIELDER'S GLOVE AND BALL

Metal heel plate

AMERICAN BASEBALL SHOE

Metal toe plate

Batter's helmet

Bat

Batting glove

Team shirt

Undershirt

Pants

Spiked shoe

BATTER

BAT

Hitting area

Crest

3 ft 6 in (1.1 m) maximum

Handle

Knob

Cricket

CRICKET IS A BALL GAME PLAYED by two teams of eleven players on a pitch with two sets of three stumps (wickets). The bowler bowls the ball down the pitch to the batsman of the opposing team, who must defend the wicket in front of which he stands. The object of the game is to score as many runs as possible. Runs can be scored individually by running the length of the playing strip, or by hitting a ball which lands outside the boundary (six), or which lands inside the boundary but bounces or rolls outside (four); the opposing team will bowl and field, attempting to dismiss the batsmen. A batsman can be dismissed in one of several ways: by the bowler hitting the wicket with the ball ("bowled"); by a fielder catching the ball hit by the batsman before it touches the ground ("caught"); by the wicket-keeper or another fielder breaking the wicket while the batsman is attempting a run and is therefore out of his ground ("stumped" or "run out"); by the batsman breaking the wicket with his own bat or body ("hit wicket"); by a part of the batsman's body being hit by a ball that would otherwise have hit the wicket ("leg before wicket" ["lbw"]). A match consists of one or two innings and each innings ends when the tenth batsman of the batting team is out, when a certain number of overs (a series of six balls bowled) have been played, or when the captain of the batting team "declares" ending the innings voluntarily.

POSSIBLE FIELD POSITIONS FOR AN AWAY SWING BOWLER TO A RIGHT-HANDED BATSMAN (IN RED) AND OTHER FIELD POSITIONS

Long on
Umpire
Boundary line
Long off
Bowler
Deep mid-wicket
Non-striking batsman
Mid-on
Extra cover
Silly mid-on
Mid-off
Forward short leg
Silly mid-off
Square leg
Cover
Deep square leg
Point
Square-leg umpire
Gulley
Batsman
Third man
Long leg
Second slip
Leg slip
First slip
Wicket-keeper
Fine leg
Sight screen

CRICKET PITCH

Wicket-keeper
Batsman
Wicket
Bowling crease
66 ft (20 m)
Bowler
Return crease
Umpire
Non-striking batsman

FORWARD DEFENSIVE STROKE
BACKWARD DEFENSIVE STROKE

ON-DRIVE
OFF-DRIVE

PULL
HOOK

SQUARE CUT
LEG GLANCE

CRICKET BALL AND WICKET

Leather skin
Seam
BALL
Bail
WICKET
Stump

MAKING A BAT HANDLE

Sarawak cane

Twine wrapped around handle

Rubber strip

LAMINATING THE WOOD

BINDING THE HANDLE

PROTECTIVE CLOTHING

Slit in leather for greater flexibility

Padding protects knuckles from injury

Dimpled rubber improves grip

Polycarbonate shell with cloth covering

Mesh covering for ventilation

Wrist strap

Peak

Foam cheek piece for comfort and good fit

Protective plastic ear piece

BATTING GLOVE

WICKET-KEEPER'S GLOVES

HELMET

ADDING THE HANDLE TO THE BAT

Rubber grip

Shoulder of bat

Handle glued into splice

Grip rolled onto handle

Bat

BATSMAN

MAKING A BAT BLADE

V-shaped splice

Scoop

Padded glove

Cap

Wristband

White shirt

White sweater

Stripes in team colors

Kiln-dried willow

Blade planed by hand

Toe of the bat shaped

Sanded and polished bat

Thigh pad under white pants

Knee roll

Cricket shoe

Leg pad

Dimpled rubber sole

SEASONING THE TIMBER

CUTTING THE SPLICE

FITTING THE HANDLE

FINISHING TOUCHES

GRAY:NICOLLS

PLACEMENT POWER

Field hockey, lacrosse, and hurling

ALL OVER THE WORLD, TEAM GAMES have evolved which require that a ball be struck or carried, and tossed at the end of a stick. Early forms of these games include hurling, shinty, bandy, and pelota. Field hockey is played by men and women: two teams of eleven players try to gain and keep possession of the ball and score goals by using the hockey stick to propel the ball into their opponents' goal net. Skills such as passing, pushing, or hitting the ball by slapping or lifting it in a flicking movement, and shooting at the goal are crucial. Field hockey is played indoors and outdoors on grass or synthetic fields. Lacrosse is played internationally as a 12-a-side game for women and as 10-a-side game for men. The women's field has no absolute boundaries but the men's has clearly defined sidelines and end lines. The ball is kept in play by being carried, thrown or batted with the crosse, and rolled or kicked in any direction. In men's and women's lacrosse, play can continue behind the marked goal areas. Similar skills are required in hurling – a Gaelic field game played on the same pitch as Gaelic football (see pp. 528–529), using the same goalposts and net. In hurling, the ball may be struck with or carried on the hurley and, when off the ground, may be struck with the hand or kicked. Goals (three points) are scored when the ball passes between the posts and under the crossbar; one point is scored when the ball passes between the posts and over the crossbar.

GOALKEEPER'S EQUIPMENT

Face mask
Hard shell
Air vent

HELMET
Strap

Rigid palm

Padded wrist

GAUNTLET

FIELD HOCKEY STICK AND BALL

STICK
Handle
Tape
Steam-bent ash head
Blade

Slazenger FLEXI

— 3 ft (91 cm) —

Stitched seam
2¼–3 in (7–7.5 cm)

BALL

FIELD HOCKEY FIELD

Sideline
Center forward
Inside right
Right wing
Right half
Right back

Corner flag

Shooting circle

Goal

Penalty spot

Five yard mark

Goal line

180 ft (55 m)

Inside left
Left wing
Umpire
Center half
Left half
Left back
Goalkeeper

Protective overshoe
Padding protects toes against the hard ball

Strap

GOALKEEPER'S BOOT

7 ft (2.1 m)

FIELD HOCKEY GOAL

MEN'S LACROSSE FIELD

Defender
Midfielder
Midfielder
Attacker
Goalkeeper
Defender
Referee
Attacker
Corner flag
Goal
Goal circle
Defender
Midfielder
Chief bench official
Scorer
Penalty timekeeper
Attacker
Timekeeper
180 ft (55 m)

WOMEN'S LACROSSE FIELD

Center
Left wing defense
Left wing attack
Third home
Second home
First home
Third man
15 m fan
Hash mark
Goalkeeper
Goal circle
Point
Cover point
Right wing defense
Timekeeper
Scorer
Penalty timekeeper
Right wing attack
Umpire
200 ft (60 m) approx.

CROSSE AND BALL

Butt
Handle
Throat
Lacing
Guardstop
Pocket
Net made from rawhide or cord
Solid rubber lacrosse ball
Wall
Head

HURLER

Helmet
Team shirt
Hurley
Team shorts
Sock
Shoe

SCORING AT HURLING

23 ft (7 m)
GOAL (3 POINTS)
POINT (1 POINT)

LACROSSE SKILLS

CRADLING
THROWING
SIDE-SHOOTING

LACROSSE GOALKEEPER

Goalkeeper's stick
Helmet
Face mask
Team shirt
Leather glove
Player's number
Sweat pants
6 ft (1.8 m)
Crossbar
Post
Peg

LACROSSE NET

Leather cover around a cork center

HURLING BALL

HURLEY AND HURLING BALL

Boss
Grip
HURLEY
3 ft (91 cm)

Track and field

THE SPORTS that make up athletics are divided into two main groups: track events – which include sprinting, middle, and long distance running, relay running, hurdling, and walking – and field events which require jumping and throwing skills. Contests designed to test the speed, strength, agility, and stamina of athletes were held by the ancient Greeks over 4,000 years ago. However, the abolition of the Olympic Games in 393 AD meant that track and field events were neglected until the revival of large-scale competitions in the mid-nineteenth century. Modern stadiums offer areas reserved for the long jump, triple jump, and pole vault usually situated outside the running track. The javelin, shot, hammer, and discus are thrown within the track area. Most athletes specialize in one or two events but, in the heptathlon, women compete in seven events, held over two days: 200 m and 800 m races, 100 m hurdles, javelin, shot put, high jump, and long jump. In the decathlon, men compete in ten events over two days: 100 m, 400 m, and 1,500 m races, 110 m hurdles, javelin, discus, shot put, pole vault, high jump, and long jump.

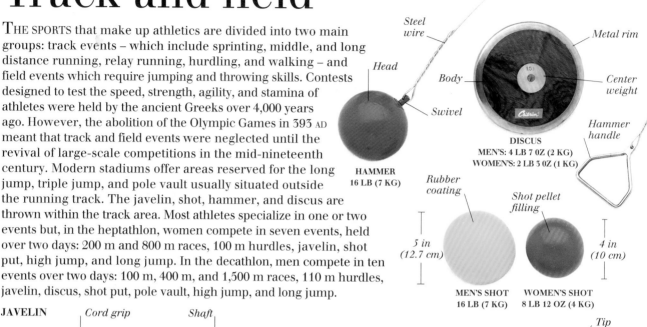

FIELD EVENT EQUIPMENT

Steel wire

Head

Body

Swivel

HAMMER
16 LB (7 KG)

Metal rim

Center weight

DISCUS
MEN'S: 4 LB 7 OZ (2 KG)
WOMEN'S: 2 LB 3 OZ (1 KG)

Hammer handle

Rubber coating

Shot pellet filling

5 in (12.7 cm)

4 in (10 cm)

MEN'S SHOT
16 LB (7 KG)

WOMEN'S SHOT
8 LB 12 OZ (4 KG)

JAVELIN   Cord grip   Shaft   Tip

Men: 8 ft 6 in (2.6 m)
Women: 7 ft 6 in (2.3 m)

TRACK AND FIELD

Finishing post

Pole vault mat

Pole vault runway

100 m starting line

Finish line

Hammer circle

Javelin fan

Discus circle

Steeplechase water jump

Javelin runway

One lap is 400 m

Lane

High jump fan

Shot put fan

Shot put circle

High jump mat

Discus fan

Hammer fan

Triple jump takeoff board

Triple jump takeoff line

Indicator board

Triple jump runway

Long jump takeoff board

Landing area

TYPES OF SHOE

Lightweight construction

Air "pumping" device for comfort and fit

Reflective side strip

Hollow plastic tube

Wedge heel

Spiked sole

RELAY BATONS

TRACK SHOE

Air-cushioned sole

RUNNING SHOE

DISCUS THROW

Swing — *Shift* — *Twist* — *Release*

SHOT PUT

Crouch — *Shift* — *Thrust* — *Release*

HAMMER THROW

Swing — *Entry* — *Lift* — *Release*

HIGH JUMP

Drive — *Arch* — *Takeoff* — *Approach* — *Landing*

JAVELIN THROW

Withdrawal stride — *Halfturn* — *Step* — *Drive forward* — *Release*

LONG JUMP

Takeoff — *Flight* — *Hitch kick* — *Stretch* — *Landing* — *Takeoff board*

POLE VAULT

Handstand — *Push-pull* — *Release* — *Rock-back* — *Hang* — *Takeoff* — *Plant* — *Landing*

TRIPLE JUMP

Takeoff — *Hop* — *Skip* — *Jump* — *Takeoff board* — *Land on foot used for takeoff* — *Land on opposite foot*

543

Racket sports

**PROTECTIVE
EYEWEAR**

THE OBJECT OF ALL RACKET SPORTS is to make shots the opponent cannot return. Games are played by two players (singles) or four players (doubles). Racket shape and size is tailored to each sport, but all rackets are constructed of wood, plastic, aluminum, or high-performance materials such as fiberglass and carbon graphite. Racket strings are usually synthetic, although natural gut is still used. Tennis is played on a court divided by a low net. Opposing players serve alternate games. At least six games must be won to gain a set, and two or sometimes three sets are needed to win a match. Tennis courts may be concrete, grass, clay, or synthetic, each surface requiring a different style of play. Badminton is an indoor sport that is played with light, flexible rackets and a birdie on a court with a high net. Players can score points only on their serve. The first to reach 15 points (11 points for women's singles) wins the game. Two games are needed to win a match. Squash and racketball are both played in enclosed courts. One player hits the ball against the front wall, and the other tries to return it before it bounces on the floor more than once. Squash rackets have smaller, rounder heads and stiffer frames than badminton rackets. International courts are wider than those in the U.S., where a much harder ball is used. Squash games are played to nine points (international) or 15 points (U.S.). In racketball, players use a ball that is larger and bouncier than a squash ball. The racketball racket is thick and sturdy, with a large head, short handle, and a strap that loops around the wrist. Points can be won only when serving, and the first player to reach 21 points wins.

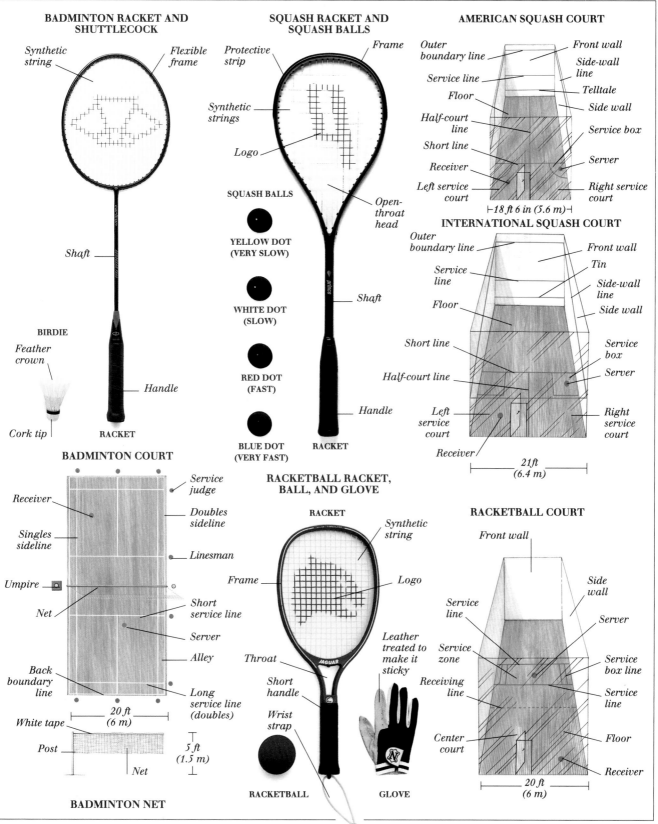

BADMINTON RACKET AND SHUTTLECOCK

Synthetic string
Flexible frame
Shaft

BIRDIE

Feather crown
Cork tip

RACKET

Handle

SQUASH RACKET AND SQUASH BALLS

Protective strip
Frame
Synthetic strings
Logo

SQUASH BALLS

YELLOW DOT (VERY SLOW)
WHITE DOT (SLOW)
RED DOT (FAST)
BLUE DOT (VERY FAST)

Open-throat head
Shaft
Handle

RACKET

AMERICAN SQUASH COURT

Outer boundary line
Front wall
Service line
Side-wall line
Floor
Telltale
Half-court line
Side wall
Short line
Service box
Receiver
Server
Left service court
Right service court

⊢18 ft 6 in (5.6 m)⊣

INTERNATIONAL SQUASH COURT

Outer boundary line
Front wall
Service line
Tin
Floor
Side-wall line
Side wall
Short line
Service box
Half-court line
Server
Left service court
Right service court
Receiver

21 ft (6.4 m)

BADMINTON COURT

Service judge
Receiver
Doubles sideline
Singles sideline
Linesman
Umpire
Net
Short service line
Server
Alley
Back boundary line
Long service line (doubles)

20 ft (6 m)

White tape
Post
Net

5 ft (1.5 m)

BADMINTON NET

RACKETBALL RACKET, BALL, AND GLOVE

RACKET
Synthetic string
Logo
Frame
Leather treated to make it sticky
Throat
Short handle
Wrist strap

JAGUAR

RACKETBALL
GLOVE

RACKETBALL COURT

Front wall
Side wall
Service line
Server
Service zone
Service box line
Receiving line
Service line
Center court
Floor
Receiver

20 ft (6 m)

Golf

THE GAME OF GOLF was first played in Scotland some
400 years ago. Players are required to hit a ball, using
a wooden or iron club, from a smooth level point or teeing
ground, down the fairway, and onto a putting green where the
target hole is located. The fairway is a strip of clear land along
which there are natural hazards – such as ponds and streams, man-made
hazards – such as bunkers (sand pits), and rough (areas of uncut grass).
Championship golf courses have 18 holes. The object of the game is to
hit the ball into each hole in turn, and to complete the "round" using
as few strokes as possible. Players may compete individually
or in teams, playing the course together in groups of
two, three, or four. The two basic forms of
competition are match play and stroke play.
In match play, the side winning the majority
of holes over a certain number of rounds
wins the match. In stroke play,
the winner is the player who
finishes a certain number of
rounds having made
the fewest strokes.

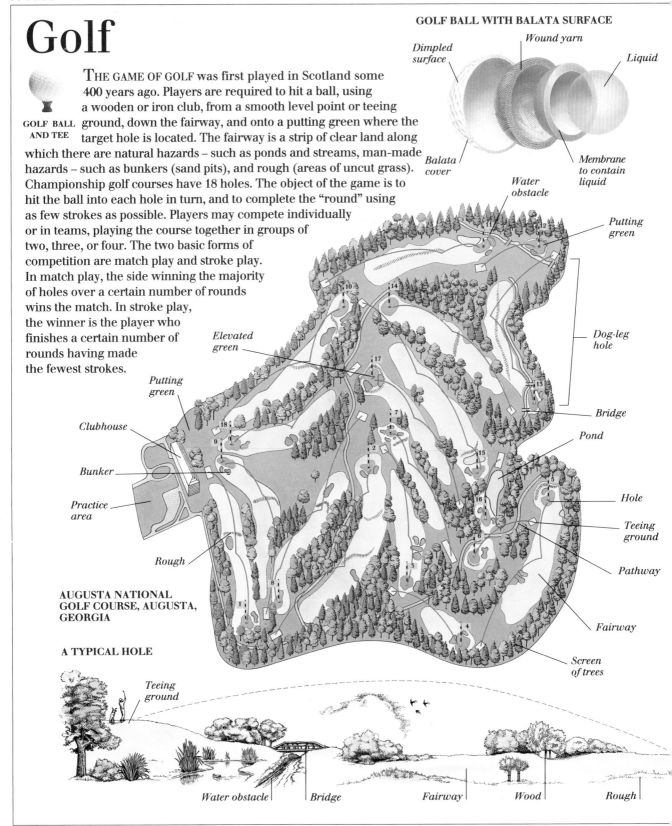

GOLF BALL WITH BALATA SURFACE

Dimpled surface

Wound yarn

Liquid

Balata cover

Membrane to contain liquid

Water obstacle

Putting green

Dog-leg hole

Elevated green

Bridge

Putting green

Pond

Clubhouse

Hole

Bunker

Teeing ground

Practice area

Pathway

Rough

Fairway

**AUGUSTA NATIONAL
GOLF COURSE, AUGUSTA,
GEORGIA**

Screen of trees

A TYPICAL HOLE

Teeing ground

Water obstacle

Bridge

Fairway

Wood

Rough

MAKING A WOODEN CLUB

Close grain of wood

Streamlined back

Plastic insert on face

Sand, stain, and varnish finish

Persimmon wood

Slot cut for plate

Metal sole plate protects the wood

Outline of head

RAW MATERIAL

CREATING THE BASIC SHAPE

ADDING THE LEAD WEIGHT

THE FINISHED CLUB HEAD

RANGE OF WOODEN CLUBS

10 degree loft

15 degree loft

21 degree loft

DRIVER

3-WOOD

5-WOOD

30 degree loft

34 degree loft

38 degree loft

42 degree loft

46 degree loft

50 degree loft

56 degree loft

5-IRON

6-IRON

7-IRON

8-IRON

9-IRON

PITCHING WEDGE

SAND WEDGE

RANGE OF IRON CLUBS

22 degree loft

26 degree loft

3-IRON

4-IRON

GOLF ACCESSORIES

BALL MARKERS

SCORECARD AND PENCIL

GOLF TEES

PITCHMARK REPAIRER

PRACTICE BALL

Spiked sole

LIGHTWEIGHT SHOE

Flag pole or pin

Green

Bunker (sand pit)

PUTTER, WOOD, AND IRON

IRON

Textured vulcanized rubber grip

WOOD

PUTTER

Shaped pistol grip

Stainless steel shaft

Steel shaft

Steel shaft

33 in (85 cm)

37 in (97 cm)

43 in (109 cm)

Neck

Neck

Angled neck

Heel

Heel

Face

Toe

Toe

Blade

Toe

Groove

Sole

Heel

547

Archery and shooting

TARGET SHOOTING AND ARCHERY EVOLVED as practice for hunting and battle skills. Modern bows, although designed according to the principles of early hunting bows, use laminates, fiberglass, dacron, and carbon, and are equipped with sights and stabilizers. Competitors in target archery shoot over distances of 100 ft (30 m), 165 ft (50 m), 230 ft (70 m), and 300 ft (90 m) for men, and 100 ft (30 m), 165 ft (50 m), 200 ft (60 m), and 230 ft (70 m) for women. The closer the shot is to the center of the target, the higher the score. The individual scores are added up, and the archer with the highest total wins the competition. Crossbows are used in match competitions over 33 ft (10 m), and 100 ft (30 m). Rifle shooting is divided into three categories: smallbore, bigbore, and air rifle. Contests take place over a variety of distances and further subdivisions are based on the type of shooting position used; prone, kneeling, or standing. The Olympic biathlon combines cross-country skiing and rifle shooting over a course of approximately 12½ miles (20 km). Additional magazines of ammunition are carried in the butt of the rifles. Bigbore rifles fitted with a telescopic sight can be used for hunting and running game target shooting. Pistol shooting events, using rapid-fire pistols, target pistols, and air pistols, take place over 33 ft (10 m), 82 ft (25 m), and 165 ft (50 m) distances. In rapid-fire pistol shooting, a total of 60 shots are fired from a distance of 82 ft (25 m).

CROSSBOW AND BOLT

Laminated fiberglass bow

Bolt

Bolt rest

1³/₄ in (45 mm)

CROSSBOW TARGET

Sight

Stirrup held between feet when drawing bow

Hardwood laminate limb

Dacron string

Sight

MODERN BOW

Pressure button

Grip

V-bar stabilizers

Magnesium riser

Plastic fletch

Nock

Aluminum shaft

Forearm guard

BRACER

Strap

Velcro fastening

Finger hole

FINGER TAB

ARCHER'S GLOVE

Wristband

Weight

Waistband

Accessory pouch

QUIVER

ARCHERY EQUIPMENT

SMALLBORE BIATHLON RIFLE

Rifle sight without magnifying lens

Fore sight

Barrel

Trigger

Trigger guard

Extra magazine stored in rifle butt

0.22 in (5.6 m) caliber bullet

Magazine

6 in (155 m)

SMALLBORE FREE RIFLE TARGET FOR 165 FT (50 M) RANGE

BIGBORE HUNTING RIFLE

Bolt handle

Bolt

Telescopic sight

Open sight

Open sight

0.3 in (7.62 mm) calibre bullet

Sling fixing point

39 in (1 m)

BIGBORE RIFLE TARGET FOR 1000 FT (300 M) RANGE

AIR PISTOL

Cocking lever and barrel

Wooden grip shaped to fit the hand

Piston

Trigger

Air-pistol pellet

TARGET PISTOL

Back sight

Fore sight

Hammer

Firing pin

Sight pin

Sight ring attachment

Magazine

0.35 in (9 mm) calibre bullet

7³/₄ in (197 mm)

PISTOL TARGET FOR 60 FT (18 M) RANGE

6 in (155 mm)

AIR-PISTOL TARGET FOR 33 FT (10 M) RANGE

Nock

FIELD ARROW

Metal tip

Feathering

Wooden shaft

Straw butt

White inner 2 points

Aluminum longrod stabilizer

Blue outer 5 points

Yellow inner 10 points (bull's-eye)

ARCHERY TARGET

Ice hockey

ICE HOCKEY IS PLAYED by two teams of six players on an ice rink, with a goal net at each end. The object of this fast, and often dangerous, game is to hit a frozen rubber puck into the opposing team's net with an ice hockey stick. The game begins when the referee drops the puck between the sticks of two players from opposing teams, who face off. The rink is divided into three areas: defending, neutral, and attacking zones. Players may move with the puck and pass it to one another along the ice, but the puck should not travel more than two zones across the rink markings. A goal is scored when the puck entirely crosses the goal-line between the posts and under the crossbar of the goal. A team may field up to 20 players although only six players are allowed on the ice at one time; substitutions occur frequently. Each game consists of three periods of 20 minutes, divided by breaks of 15 minutes.

GOALKEEPER

Helmet
Face mask
Throat protector
Team shirt
Butt end
Catch glove
Pants
Blocking pad
Goalkeeper's pad
Skate
Blade
Goalkeeper's stick
Heel
Blade

ICE HOCKEY RINK

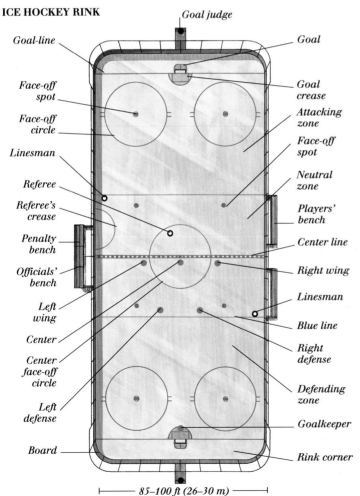

Goal judge
Goal-line
Goal
Face-off spot
Goal crease
Face-off circle
Attacking zone
Linesman
Face-off spot
Referee
Neutral zone
Referee's crease
Players' bench
Penalty bench
Center line
Officials' bench
Right wing
Left wing
Linesman
Center
Blue line
Center face-off circle
Right defense
Left defense
Defending zone
Board
Goalkeeper
Rink corner

85–100 ft (26–30 m)

THE FACE OFF

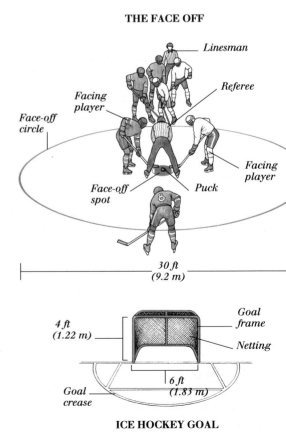

Linesman
Facing player
Referee
Face-off circle
Facing player
Face-off spot
Puck

30 ft (9.2 m)

Goal frame
4 ft (1.22 m)
Netting
Goal crease
6 ft (1.83 m)

ICE HOCKEY GOAL

GOALKEEPER'S HELMET

Customized paint

Face guard

JOFA

Chin protection

PLAYER'S BODY ARMOR

Air vents

Rigid plastic shell

CANADIEN

Manufacturer's logo

Chin strap

Foam padding

PLAYER'S HELMET

Shoulder padding

ELBOW PADS

DAIGNAULT ROLLAND
3075N
GRAND/LARGE

Heavy padding

Flexible gusset

Rigid finger cap

TORSPO 20

GLOVE

Strap

D'R
Daignault · Rolland
4355 M
DÉFENSE-**PRO**-DEFENCE

Wrist protection

Chest padding

LEG PROTECTOR

Rigid plastic casing

D'R
Daignault · Rolland
16.5" 43cm
CENTURION-J

Knee protection

Thick foam backing

Leg pad

ICE HOCKEY STICKS

GOALKEEPER'S STICK

SHOULDER AND CHEST PADDING

MADE IN FINLAND

TORSPO

Pro 5000

OUTFIELD PLAYER'S STICK

TORSPO

Pro 500

4 ft 9 in (147 cm)

Thin shaft

Wide lower shaft

TORSPO

Vulcanized rubber

3 in (7.62 cm)

FROZEN PUCK

Ankle support

Rigid plastic casing

501

Safety heel tip

Blade

SKATE

Puck stopper

15 in (39 cm)

Thick blade

12 1/2 in (32 cm)

Heel

Alpine skiing

COMPETITIVE ALPINE SKIING is divided into four disciplines: downhill, slalom, giant slalom, and super-giant slalom (Super-G). Each one tests different skills. In downhill skiing, competitors race down a slope marked out by control flags, known as "gates," and are timed on a single run only. Competitors wear crash helmets, one-piece Lycra suits, and long skis with flattened tips to minimize air resistance. Slalom and giant slalom skiers negotiate a twisting course requiring balance, agility, and quick reactions. Courses are defined by pairs of gates. Racers must pass through each pair of gates to complete the course successfully. Competitors are timed on two runs over different courses, and the skier who completes the courses in the shortest time wins. The equipment and protective guards used by slalom skiers are shown opposite. In Super-G races, competitors ski a single run that combines the technical challenge of slalom with the speed of downhill. The course requires skiers to complete medium-to-long radius turns at high speed, and contain up to two jumps. Clothing is the same as for downhill, but slightly shorter skis are used.

DOWNHILL SKIER

Ski goggles

Helmet

One-piece lycra ski suit

Wrist strap

Ski pole

Basket

Ski boot

Safety binding

Tail

Ski glove

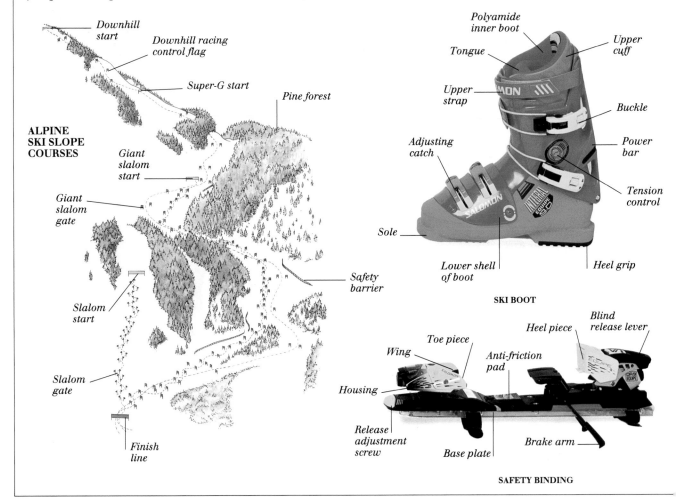

ALPINE SKI SLOPE COURSES

Downhill start

Downhill racing control flag

Super-G start

Pine forest

Giant slalom start

Giant slalom gate

Slalom start

Slalom gate

Safety barrier

Finish line

Polyamide inner boot

Tongue

Upper cuff

Upper strap

Adjusting catch

Buckle

Power bar

Tension control

Sole

Lower shell of boot

Heel grip

SKI BOOT

Toe piece

Wing

Housing

Release adjustment screw

Anti-friction pad

Base plate

Heel piece

Blind release lever

Brake arm

SAFETY BINDING

SLALOM CLOTHING AND EQUIPMENT

Anti-glare lens

Elastic strap

GOGGLES

Hard nylon shell

Padding

Strap

Chin guard

SLALOM HELMET

Extended cuff

Wrist strap

Rigid pad for hand protection

SKI GLOVE

Tail

Adjustable shoulder strap

High collar

Double-knit wool and polyester fabric

Wrist strap

Grip

Ribbed cuff

Zip pocket

Front zip fastening

Shock-absorbing platform under boot

Edge

Waterproof fabric

Moulded polypropylene

PADDED SWEATER

HAND GUARD

74–80 in (188–203 cm)

Tough polypropylene shell deflects the shaft of the slalom gate

Shaft

Velcro strap

Basket

Cuff fits over ski boot

LEG GUARD

SLALOM SKI POLE

SLALOM SKI

Tip

PADDED SKI PANTS

Equestrian sports

EQUESTRIAN SPORTS HAVE TAKEN place throughout the world for centuries: events involving mounted horses were recorded in the Olympic Games of 642 BC. Show jumping, however, is a much more recent innovation, and the first competitions were held at the beginning of the 1900s. In this sport, horse and rider must negotiate a course of variable, unfixed obstacles, making as few mistakes as possible. Show-jumping fences consist of wooden stands, known as standards or wings, that support planks or poles. Parts of the fence are designed to collapse on impact, preventing injury to the horse and rider. Judges penalize competitors for errors, such as knocking down obstacles, refusing jumps, or deviating from the course. Depending on the type of competition, the rider with the fewest faults, most points, or fastest time wins. There are two basic forms of horse racing – flat races and races with jumps, such as steeplechase or hurdle races. Thoroughbred horses are used in this sport, because they have great strength and stamina and can achieve speeds of up to 40 mph (65 kph). Jockeys wear silks – caps and jackets designed in distinctive colors and patterns which help identify the horses. In harness racing, the horse is driven from a light, two-wheeled carriage called a sulky. Horses are trained to trot and to pace, and different races are held for each of these types of gait. In pacing races, the horses wear hobbles to prevent them from breaking into a trot or gallop. Breeds such as the Standard-bred and the French Trotter have been developed especially for this sport.

SHOW-JUMPING SADDLE
High cantle
Deep seat
Pommel
Forward-cut flap
Knee roll

SHOW-JUMPING FENCES

Standard
Foot
Plank
UPRIGHT PLANKS

Standard
Foot
Pole
UPRIGHT POLES

Back pole
Standard
Foot
Pole
TRIPLE BAR (STAIRCASE)

Standard
Pole
Foot
HOG'S-BACK

Pillar
Wooden block painted to resemble a brick
WALL

Hard hat
Riding jacket
Browband
Throat-latch
Rein
Jodhpurs
Cheek piece
Show-jumping saddle
Hindquarters
Dock
Running martingale
Noseband
Brushing boot
Sheepskin numnah
Girth
Stirrup iron
Riding boot
Hoof
Gaskin
Hock joint
Fetlock joint
Pastern
Coronet
SHOW-JUMPING HORSE WITH RIDER

RACING SADDLE

Cantle

Cut-back head

Surcingle loop

Forward-cut flap

Lightweight steel stirrup-iron

Rawhide stirrup-leather

RACING SILKS

Plain cap

Spotted cap

Quartered cap

Plain sleeve

Plain sleeve

Striped jacket

Plain jacket

Spotted sleeve

Jacket with sash

Paddock

Finish line

Clubhouse

Grandstand

Dirt track

Home stretch

Far turn

Clubhouse turn

Grass track

Tote board

Start of straight

Barrier

Back stretch

SARATOGA RACE COURSE, SARATOGA, NEW YORK

Brow band

Rosette

Cheek piece

Bridle

Noseband

Rubber bit-guard

Driving rein

Lightweight harness

Thimble

Girth

Over-reach boot

Belly band

Pacing hobble

Driving saddle

Rein terret

Shaft

Crupper

Cap covered with racing silk

Goggles

Quartered racing silk jacket

Whip

Seat

Stirrup

Racing sulky

Wheel

Pneumatic tire

Disk covering spokes

HARNESS RACING WITH A STANDARD-BRED HORSE

Judo and fencing

COMBAT SPORTS ARE BASED ON THE SKILLS used in fighting. In these sports, the competitors may be unarmed – as in judo and boxing – or armed – as in fencing and kendo. Judo is a system of unarmed combat developed in the East. Translated from the Japanese the name means "the gentle way." Students learn how to turn an opponent's force to their own advantage. The usual uniform is loose white pants and a jacket, fastened with a cloth belt. The color of belt indicates the student's level of expertise, from white-belted novices to the expert black belts. Competitions take place on a mat or "shiaijo," 30 or 33 ft (9 or 10 m) square in size, bounded by "danger" and "safety" areas to prevent injury. Competitors try to throw, pin, or master their opponent by applying pressure to the arm joints or neck. Judo matches are strictly monitored, and competitors receive points for superior technique, not for injuring their opponent. Fencing is a combat sport using swords, which takes place on a narrow piste or strip 46 ft (14 m) long. Competitors try to hit specific target areas on their opponent with their sword or foil while avoiding being touched themselves. The winner is the one who scores the greatest number of hits. Fencers wear uniforms made from strong white material, which affords maximum protection while allowing freedom of movement, steel mesh masks with padded bibs to protect the fencer's neck, and a long white glove on their sword hand. Fencing foils do not have sharpened blades, and their tips end in a blunt button to prevent injuries. Three types of swords are used – foils, épées, and sabres. Official foil and épée competitions always use an electric scoring system. The sword tips are connected to lights by a long wire that passes underneath each fencer's jacket. A bulb flashes when a hit is made.

JUDO HOLDS AND THROWS

SIDE FOUR QUARTER HOLD   SINGLE WING

BODY DROP   ONE ARM SHOULDER THROW

SHOULDER WHEEL   SWEEPING LOW THROW

STOMACH THROW   KNEE WHEEL

JUDO KIT

JUDO MAT

52 ft 6 in
(16 m)

Judge
Scorer
Holding timekeeper
Timekeeper

Drawstring
Contestant
Referee
Contest area
Safety area

Danger area   Contestant

Cotton pants

Black belt   Heavy-duty cotton jacket

FENCING STRIP

Rear limit line

46 ft
(14 m)

Sabre and épéé warning line

Scorer

Timekeeper

Electrical scoring apparatus

Center line

President

On-guard line

Body wire

Reel

FENCING TARGET AREAS

SABREUR

FOILIST

EPEEIST

FENCING EQUIPMENT

Steel wire mesh

Padded bib

MESH MASK

Woven metal thread

METALLIC JACKET

Cuff

GAUNTLET

Glove

TARGET AREAS ON THE UPPER BODY

Wire mesh

Mask

Bib

Under plastron

Tierce

Sixte

Quinte

Quarte

Prime

Septime

Gauntlet

Seconde

Octave

Metallic over-jacket

Knickers

Stocking

Fencing shoe

THE SABRE

THE FOIL

Martingale

THE EPEE

Button

Blade

PARTS OF THE SWORD

Guard

Tang

Leather pad

Alternative pistol-grip handle

Brass screw

Steel foil pommel

Swimming and diving

SWIMMING WAS INCLUDED in the first modern Olympic Games in 1896 and diving events were added in 1904. Swimming is both an individual and a team sport and races take place over a predetermined distance in one of the four major categories of stroke – freestyle (usually front crawl), butterfly, breaststroke, and backstroke. Competition pools are clearly marked for racing and anti-turbulence lane lines are used to separate the swimmers and help keep the water calm. The first team or individual to finish the race is the winner. Competitive diving is divided into men's and women's springboard and platform (highboard) events. There are six official groups of dives: forward dives, backward dives, armstand dives, twist dives, reverse dives, and inward dives. Competitors perform a set number of dives and after each one a panel of judges awards marks according to the quality of execution and the degree of difficulty.

STYLES OF DIVES

Starting position
Hands above head

Legs fully stretched

Flight

Arched back

Toes pointed

Feet together

Entry

Hands close together

FORWARD DIVE

BACKWARD DIVE

Latex rubber molds to shape of head

CAPS

SPEEDO

Rubber-covered wire

NOSE CLIP

Molded rubber

EARPLUG

SWIMWEAR

High neckline

Man-made stretch fabric

Drawstring

High-cut leg

Strong seam

SWIMSUIT

TRUNKS

SWIMMING POOL

Swimmer
Chief timekeeper
Placing judge
Recorder
Backstroke marker 49 ft (15 m) from end of pool
Referee
Backstroke turn indicator 16 ft (5 m) from end of pool
Turning judge

Lane number
Starting block
Lane timekeeper
End wall
Starter
Side wall
Anti-turbulence lane line
Stroke judge
Bottom line
Turning wall
Lane

75 ft 6 in (23 m)

Perfectly steady armstand

Arms and legs align throughout flight and entry

ARMSTAND DIVE

Arms spread wide apart

Body and legs straighten for flight and entry

TWIST DIVE

Pike position

Height of dive

Shoulders fall backward for vertical entry

REVERSE PIKE DIVE

Pike position

Hands touch toes

Feet lift up for straight entry

INWARD PIKE DIVE

FRONT CRAWL
Flutter kick

FULL BODY STRETCH

Arm pulls like a paddle

LOWER ARM PULL

Arrowlike position

STREAMLINED ARM ENTRY

Body rolls on a central axis

SIDE-TO-SIDE BODY ROLL

BREASTSTROKE
Straight leg

BODY GLIDE

Knees together

DOUBLE ARM PULL

Elbows tucked in

SQUEEZING THE WATER

Arm fully extended

FROG KICK

BACKSTROKE
Little finger enters first

BODY ROLL

Arm comes up straight

PULLING THROUGH

Recovering hand

STRAIGHTENING OUT

Shoulder exits water first

SHOULDER LIFT

BUTTERFLY
Palm turned outward

CATCHING THE WATER

Legs ready to kick down

DOUBLE ARM PULL

Head clears the water

KICKING DOWN

Shoulders power the stroke

WHOLE BODY UNDULATION

Kayaking, rowing, and sailing

WATERBORNE SPORTS are as varied as the crafts used. There are two disciplines in rowing; sweep rowing, in which each rower has one oar, and sculling, in which rowers use two oars. There are a number of different Olympic and competitive rowing events for both men and women. The number of rowers and weight classes vary. Some rowing events use a coxswain; a steersman who does not row but directs the crew. Kayaks are used in straight sprint and slalom races. Slalom races take place over a course consisting of 20 to 25 gates, including at least six upstream gates. In yacht racing, competitors must complete prescribed courses, organized by the race committees, in the shortest possible time, using sail power only. Olympic events include classes for keel boats, dinghies, catamarans, and windsurfers.

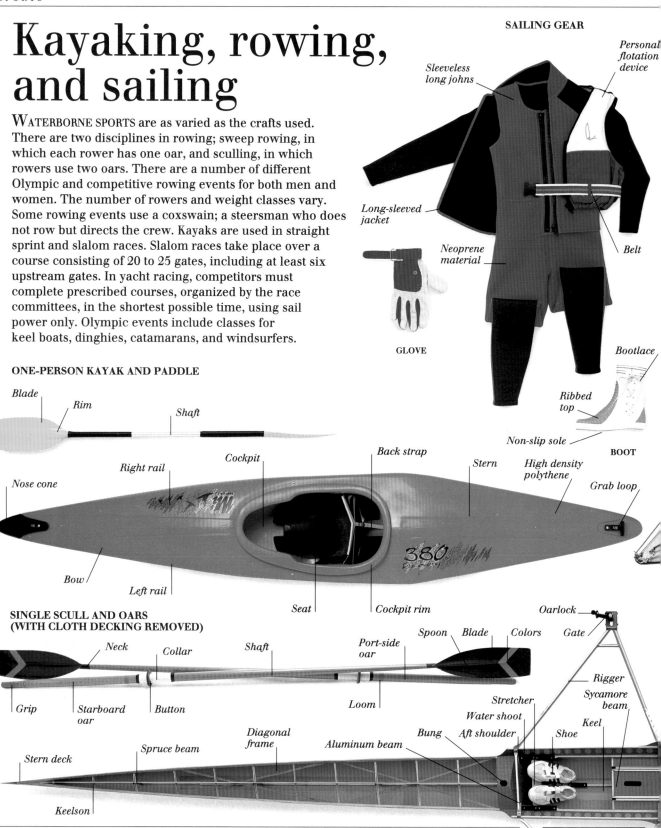

SAILING GEAR

Personal flotation device

Sleeveless long johns

Long-sleeved jacket

Neoprene material

Belt

GLOVE

Bootlace

Ribbed top

Non-slip sole

BOOT

ONE-PERSON KAYAK AND PADDLE

Blade

Rim

Shaft

Nose cone

Right rail

Cockpit

Back strap

Stern

High density polythene

Grab loop

Bow

Left rail

Seat

Cockpit rim

**SINGLE SCULL AND OARS
(WITH CLOTH DECKING REMOVED)**

Oarlock

Spoon Blade Colors Gate

Neck

Collar

Shaft

Port-side oar

Rigger

Grip

Starboard oar

Button

Loom

Stretcher

Water shoot

Sycamore beam

Keel

Stern deck

Spruce beam

Diagonal frame

Aluminum beam

Bung Aft shoulder

Shoe

Keelson

PERSONAL FLOTATION DEVICE

Backstrap/ rescue strap

Reinforced seam

Neck opening

Whistle

Topping-up valve

Lanyard

Waistband

Standing rigging

Spreader

Bow

SAILING DINGHY

Mast

Mainsheet

Boom

Rudder

Stern

Tiller

Hiking strap

Centerboard

Cockpit

Shroud

Jib fairlead

Non-slip deck surface

SCULLS

DOUBLE SCULL

SINGLE SCULL

SWEEP-ROWING BOATS

Sliding track

Wheel

Sliding seat

Main deck

Saxboard

Wheel spacer

Hatch

Breakwater

FOUR WITHOUT COXSWAIN

PAIR WITH COXSWAIN

PAIR WITHOUT COXSWAIN

EIGHT

FOUR WITH COXSWAIN

Bowball

Bowclip

561

Angling

ANGLING MEANS FISHING WITH A ROD, reel, line, and lure. There are several different types of angling: freshwater coarse angling, for members of the carp family and pike; freshwater game angling, for salmon and trout; and sea angling, for sea fish such as flatfish, bass, and mackerel. Anglers use a variety of methods of catching fish. These include bait fishing, in which bait (food to allure the fish) is placed on a hook and cast into the water; fly fishing, in which a natural or artificial fly is used to lure the fish; and spinning, in which a lure that looks like a small fish revolves as it is pulled through the water. The angler uses the rod, reel, and line to cast the lure over the water. The reel controls the line as it spills off the spool and as it is wound back. Weights may be fixed to the line so that it will sink. Swivels are attached to prevent the line from twisting. When a fish bites, the hook must become embedded in its mouth and remain there while the catch is reeled in.

Keeper ring

Drag spindle

Handgrip

Disk drag

Drag washer

Disk spring

Gear retainer

Dual click gear

Retaining screw

Check slide

Check pawl cover

Check pawl

Check spring

HOOKS, SWIVELS, AND WEIGHTS

REELS

Spool-release button

Reel foot (reel scoop)

Plate-nut

Click mechanism

Mechanical brake

Side plate

Centrifugal brake

Spool

Handle

Star drag

Level-wind system

BAITCASTER

Eye

Shank

Gap

ANATOMY OF A HOOK

Bend

Throat

Point

Barb

TREBLE HOOK

ABERDEEN HOOK

REVERSED BEND HOOK

Reel foot (reel scoop)

Unskirted spool

Handle

Line

Tension nut (drag adjustment)

Ratchet (anti-reverse device)

Handgrip

Reel

Bail arm

SPINNING REEL

EXAMPLES OF BARREL SWIVELS

HILLMAN ANTI-KINK WEIGHT

FLY ROD AND REEL

Intermediate ring

TIP SECTION

Reel seat

Screw locking nut

Tip-top

Disk drag housing

Reel foot (reel scoop)

Line

Butt cap

Drag knob screw

Butt extension

Release lever

Spool screw

Clicker plate

DragonFly 100

Disc Drag

Spool cover

Drag knob

Release spring

Spool-release button

Line guide

ARTIFICIAL FLIES

Handle

Line guide cover

DUNKELD WET FLY

Body

Tail

Cheek

Head

ARTIFICIAL LURES

Retaining screw

Hackle

Ribbing

DEVON MINNOW

Fin

Eye

Treble hook

Swivel

Tulip mount

DEER HOPPER DRY FLY

Front hackle

JOINTED PLUG

Eye

Tail

Joint

Adjustable vane

Treble hook

Hook

Wing

Head

Everyday Things

Drills

THE ELECTRICALLY POWERED MOTOR OF A POWER DRILL, cooled by a fan, turns a shaft at high speed. The shaft connects, in turn, to a system of gears that rotates a chuck even faster. Clamped by the chuck, a sharp drill bit cuts out the hole, and at the same time the bit's screw-shaped grooves channel the waste out of the hole. For drilling hard materials, many power drills have a hammer mechanism; when this is operated a ratchet in the gearcase causes the chuck and bit to pound in and out as they drill. A hand drill, although slower and less forceful than a power drill, is easier to control. For cutting wide holes, carpenters often prefer a brace-and-bit. This acts like a lever: the bowed handle of the brace moves a larger distance than the bit, turning the bit with extra force.

MOTOR ASSEMBLY

Commutator

Armature

Armature spindle

Fan

Motor case

Motor case

Field

Brush spring

Brush

Screw

Washer

Lead wire to motor

Top insert blank

Hammer mechanism actuator

Brush holder

Screw hole

Electromagnetic induction capacitor

Chuck key holder

Switch

Screw

Hammer actuator position

Gearcase position

Motor position

INTERNAL VIEW OF HOUSING COVER

Trigger position

Lock button

Switch trigger

Cable cordset

Washer

Spring

TRIGGER MECHANISM

GEAR MECHANISM

Thrust plate

Spindle gear

Spindle

Bearing

Gearcase cover

Chuck key

Jaw

Drill bit

Gearcase

Chuck key pilot hole

Washer

Thrust washer

Gearcase cover screw

POWER DRILL

Hammer mechanism actuator

Gearcase screw

Chuck

Switch trigger

Chuck key holder

Cable

HAND DRILL

Main handle

Turning handle

Side handle

Drive wheel

Pinion

Chuck

Jaw

Drill bit

EXTERNAL VIEW OF HOUSING COVER

Screw hole

Air intake slot

Air exhaust slot

Housing cover screw

BRACE-AND-BIT

Quill

Head

Crank

Handle

Ratchet

Chuck

Jaw

Drill bit

567

Shoes

WELL MADE SHOES PROTECT THE FEET and are also comfortable and long lasting. The best shoemakers use a wood or plastic mold, called a last, which matches the shape of the customer's foot. The different parts of a shoe are stitched and glued together around the last; rivets and nails are used only in the heel, which is built up from layers of leather and rubber. The steel shank gives support to the arch of the foot and, with the seat lift, helps the wearer maintain posture. The layers of the sole give strength, while the soft insole cushions the foot. The leather welt sewn between the leather uppers and the sole ensures a strong join.

Inside quarter

Quarter lining

Wing cap and vamp backer

Quarter backer

Inner sock

Counter

Tongue

Shoelace

Outside quarter

Vamp

Punchhole

Welt

Perforated wing cap

Wing cap

Wing cap backer

Box toe

Vamp

CROSS SECTION OF FINISHED SHOE

Tongue

Tongue lining

Vamp

Wing cap

Welt

Insole

Bottom filler

Outsole

Tongue

Lining

Steel shank

Cuff

Heel grip

Counter

Seat lift

Heel

Quarter backer

Outside quarter

Shoelace

Eyelet

Tag

Counter

Counter stiffener

Quarter and counter lining

Cone

LAST

Thimble (jack-locating hole)

Back lining

Vamp backer

Hinge

Bottom filler

Outsole

Shank

Seat lift

Quarter tip

Inner sock

Insole with ribbing

Welt

Thread

Heel nail

Heel

Seat rivet

Clock

MECHANICAL CLOCKS HAVE TWO essential elements: a mainspring and a pendulum. When the clock is wound with the key, the mainspring is tightened. As the mainspring unwinds, it turns the gears, which move the minute and hour hands at different speeds around the face of the clock. The pendulum ensures that the hands move at a regular pace. At the top of the pendulum are two hooks called pallets. As the pendulum swings, the pallets allow the escape wheel to turn slowly and evenly.

CLOCK CASE

Steady pin hole

Screw hole

Pallet arbor position

Barrel pivot hole

Wood peg

Fusee pivot hole

Pillar

Winding key

Ratchet screw

Ratchet pawl

Click wheel

PENDULUM ASSEMBLY

Barrel arbor hook

Mainspring barrel arbor

Pallet cock screw

Pallet cock

CLOCK TRAIN

Suspension spring

Crutch screw

Pallet arbor

Pallet screw

Pallet

Mainspring

Mainspring barrel cap

Crutch

Escape wheel

Pinion

FRONT PLATE

Pendulum rod

Third wheel

Pinion

Pinion

Center wheel

Fusee

Fusee chain

Mainspring barrel

Pivot hole

Lenticular bob

Fusee stop screw

Fusee stop

Tension spring screw

Tension spring

Rating nut

Side inspection door

Wood peg

Back plate

Bottom door key

Back box

Bottom door

Screw hole

Minute wheel cock

Cock screw

Minute wheel

Dial washer

Hour hand screw

Cannon pinion

Hour wheel

Minute hand

Hand collet

Pin

Bridge

Bridge screw

Pin

Hour hand

Dial foot hole

Pillar hole

CLOCK FACE

Wood bezel

Hinged brass bezel

Minute track

Hour marker

Roman numeral

CAMERER.KUSS & Cº
56 New Oxford St

Maker's name

Center hole

Winding hole

Dial

LONDON

Lamp

THE FIRST SPRING-TENSIONED, adjustable work lamp was designed in 1934 by George Carwardine. This type of lamp imitates the human arm in the way that it can be kept in a fixed position or moved easily and precisely. In the arm, such control is achieved by coordinating the opposing action of paired muscles (e.g., when the biceps contracts, the triceps relaxes and the arm bends). In the work lamp, one muscle of a pair is represented by the springs that pull on the rigid bars of the lamp; the other muscle is represented by the nuts, bolts, screws, and washers in the lamp's joints that resist the pull of the springs. By balancing the pull of the springs against the resistance in the joints, the lamp's height and angle can be adjusted with minimal pressure.

Cap nut

Switch enclosure cover

Push switch

Terminal screw

Bushing

Power supply cord

Insulation

End cap

Copper conductor

Switch enclosure

Pivot plate

Bracket

Metal shade

Dome

Body

Cap

LIGHT BULB

Connecting wire

Terminal screw

Nut

Fuse enclosure

Plunger contact

LAMP HOLDER

Support wire

Glass envelope

Skirt

Filament

Wing nut

Cheese head screw

Washer

Nut

Locking
nut

Power supply
cord

Pivot
plate

SUPPORT ARM ASSEMBLY

Cheese head
screw

Washer

Hexagon
nut

End
cap

Metal arm

Spring attachment

Coil tension
spring

Bushing

Clamping screw

Arm coupling

Metal arm

Lamp
holder
coupling

Pivot

Spigot

Socket

Power
supply
cord

Metal shade

Pivot plate

Shade
coupling

Metal arm

Washer

Spring attachment

Clamp
upper jaw

Threaded
rod

Adjustment
locking nut

Metal arm

**TABLE CLAMP
ASSEMBLY**

Coil tension
spring

Coil tension spring

Cheese head screw

Washer

End cap

Nut

Threaded
rod

Table
clamp

Spring attachment bolt

Wing nut

Clamp
lower jaw

Mini television

MINIATURIZED TELEVISION SETS are small enough to be held in the hand while being watched. A signal sent by a broadcast transmitter is picked up by the television antenna and passed to an electron gun at the back of the television set. In response to the signal this gun produces an electron beam that is passed through a deflection yoke. The yoke contains magnets and coils that cause the beam to scan across the screen in a series of lines. The screen is coated with phosphor, which glows when hit by the beam. As the beam scans the screen, its strength is varied so that the phosphor glows with different intensities in different parts of the screen. A continuous sequence of 25 black-and-white pictures per second appears on the screen so rapidly that the illusion of a moving picture is created.

CATHODE RAY TUBE (CRT)

CRT cover

TUBE NECK

Nipple

Electron gun

Connecting pin

Centering magnet

SCAN COIL DEFLECTION YOKE

Tape

Mounting bracket

Scan coil clamp

Deflection coil

Tuning drive gear

Dial pointer

Tuning printed circuit board

Tuning dial

Keystone (East-West) amplifier integrated circuit

Antenna connector

Tuner

Rear cabinet

Electrolytic capacitor

Earphone jack

Direct current jack

Metal shield

Battery compartment

Screw

CRT bracket

Battery case lid

Positive pole

BATTERY CONTACTS

Positive pole

Negative pole

Positive pole

Screw

CRT socket

Antenna holder

PRINTED CIRCUIT BOARD

Intermediate frequency coil

Choke

Coil

Plastic sheath

Ornamental strip

Glue

Window

Horizontal frequency adjustment

Capacitor

Volume control dial

Power switch

Power dial

Filter

Fly-back transformer

Plastic cap

SONY

21 30 40 50 60 68 UHF

FD-250B

Focus control

Extra-high tension lead

Filter ornament

Speaker

Front cabinet

Chair

A TRADITIONALLY MADE DINING CHAIR, such as the Regency-style carver shown here, is held together, not by nails or bolts, but by snugly fitting joints, screws, dowels, and glue. Its curved arms and top splats, as well as its tapering legs, are cut from seasoned—that is, dried—mahogany. Mortice slots in the back legs receive the tenon tongues of the top and bottom splats; angled grooves at the top of the back legs, called rebates, take the curved arm rail. Though the various joints are so tight-fitting that they could produce a solid frame on their own, screws and glue are used to give the joints added strength. The comfortable, upholstered seat pad shown here consists of a patterned cover, calico lining, and foam padding that has been treated for fire safety; it is supported by webbing stretched across a wood frame.

Cross stick

Top splat

Arm

Bottom splat

Head

Seat pad

Front rail

Back leg

Left front leg

Square brass line

Mortice

Tenon

Tenon

Arm

Washer

Groove

Top splat

Washer

Dowel screw

Screw

Diamond

Screw

Splat mortice

Wood plug

Wood plug

Head

Cross stick

Bottom splat

Tenon

Tenon

Side rail

Dowel hole

Dowel

Back rail

Dowel

Screw

Dowel

Dowel

Right front leg

Dowel

Front rail

Dowel hole

Back leg

CHAIR FRAME

SEAT UPHOLSTERY

Seat cover

Webbing

Mortice

Arm

Foam padding

Calico lining

Dowel screw

Splat mortice

Head

Tenon

Seat back rail

Side rail

Dowel hole

Screw

Back leg

Bottom lining

Tack

SEAT FRAME

Left front leg

Seat side rail

Seat side rail

Dowel hole

Seat front rail

Toaster

MOST ELECTRIC TOASTERS NOT ONLY GRILL slices of bread, they also pop them up when ready. While the slices rest on a spring-loaded rack, electric heating elements toast the bread. At the same time, a bimetallic strip heats and expands. One of the two metals in this strip expands more quickly than the other, causing the strip to curve. As it bends, it completes an electrical circuit and activates an electromagnet. The magnet attracts a catch, releasing the spring that holds the rack down in the toaster. The elements switch off, and the toasted slices pop up.

Terminal connections

Ejector bracket

Time switch

Variable time control knob

Selector switch

Screw

Screw

Switch end casting

Crumb tray

End baffle plate

Screw

Ground connection point

Cordset entry point

End element connecting link

End element

Foot

Base plate

End element wire guard

Screw

Washer

Power supply cord

Bolt

Nut

Strain release

Ejector knob

Screw

Nut

Spring

Ejector bracket

Ejector assembly

Plain end casting

Switch end casting

Stainless steel cover

Selector switch

Ejector lever

Variable time control knob

Foot

Center element wire cage

Crumb tray

Inner cage assembly

Fixing screw

Screw

Foot

End baffle plate

Screw

Element retaining stop

Nut

Washer

Plain end casting

Foot

Screw

Stainless steel cover

Screw

Element connecting link

End element

Center element

Nut

Washer

Screw

End element wire guard

579

Lawnmower

THE SHARP BLADES OF A LAWNMOWER—whether driven by electrical, gasoline, or human power—shave grass close to the ground. The gasoline-powered type shown here has a small engine that is electrically ignited by a battery and spark plug. This engine rotates a horizontal blade at the base of the lawnmower, which then slices the grass against a fixed blade. A grass bag at the back of the machine collects the cuttings. As the engine rotates the blades, it also turns the rear wheels, moving the lawnmower forward. Gears ensure that the horizontal blade spins faster than the wheels so that all of the grass is cut neatly before the lawnmower moves on.

Rear tire

Wheel cover

Rear wheel

GEAR CASE ASSEMBLY

Upper gear case

Wheel bolt

Blower shroud

Fuel tank

Drive shaft

Spring

Door

Half pulley

Belt guard

Screw

Cap

Drive belt

Screw

Oil dipstick

Door seal

Oil fill tube

TORO

Bolt

ENGINE AND RECOIL ASSEMBLY

Screw

Flywheel

Recoil case

Housing

Starter cup

Screw

Screw

Muffler cover

Blade cover

Air filter

Throttle guard

Muffler

Engine pulley

Screw

Air filter cover

Front tire

Height adjuster

Shoulder screw

Front wheel

53 cm

Handle

Control panel

Grass bag

Fuel tank cap

Recoil case

Muffler cover

Latch handle

Rear wheel

Housing

Front wheel

Handle

Traction lever

Control lever

Traction cable support

Control panel

Ground speed control knob

Mower drive handle

Throttle control lever

Battery

Vertical panel

Cable support bracket

Latch handle

Screen panel

Door discharge

Battery retainer

HANDLE AND TRACTION CONTROL ASSEMBLY

Grass bag

Traction cable

Blade

Screw

Blade retainer

Washer

Blade bolt

Grass bag frame

Battery connection

Wheel bolt

Saddle

THE FIRST HORSEBACK RIDERS HAD NO SADDLES; they sat bareback, clinging to the animal's mane. Next came a simple cloth saddle. The leather saddle, which was invented about 2,000 years ago by the warriors of the Asian steppes, revolutionized horseback riding. On this saddle, horsemen could gallop toward the enemy, fire arrows in all directions, and stay on their horses. Modern saddles are of two main types. The Western saddle is a heavy, working saddle used mainly by ranch hands in the United States. It has a metal horn at the front for securing a lasso and a high cantle at the back to keep the rider on the horse. The English saddle is much lighter. Designed for sport, it allows the horse to gallop fast. Its drawback is that it provides less stability; to stay on the horse, the rider must grip the animal with the knees.

ENGLISH SADDLE

Cantle

Leather seat

Pommel

Sloped head

Dee

Surcingle

Block flap

Girth

Stirrup leather

Stirrup

Facing

Strap bearing

Gullet

Web

Gullet plate

Tree

Stirrup bar

Point pocket

Cantle

Stuffing hole

Knee roll

Metal reinforcement

Web

Copper rivet

Top leather

Spring tree

Flexible leather point

Point cover

Facing

Rivet

Belly nail

Lining of underside of saddle

Brass nameplate nail

Tack

Gullet lining

Knee cover

Screw

Nylon rope

Stirrup buckle

Stirrup leather

Flock stuffing

SHAPED GIRTH

Girth buckle

Chape

Buckle guard

Billet strap

Stirrup

Stirrup buckle

Stirrup leather

Webbing

Canvas

Leather

Buckle guard

Leather belly

Beeswax

4-cord linen thread

Lacing thread

3-cord linen thread

Rubber seat

Leather seat

Block flap

Plated nail

Dee

Name-plate

Bar leather

Forepiece

Skirt

Back

Canvas

Surcingle

Belly nail

Dee

Welt

Canvas

Back

Welt

Skirt

Belly nail

Surcingle

Bar leather

Nameplate

Dee

Plated nail

Stirrup leather

Stirrup

Block flap

CD-ROM

A CD-ROM IS A TYPE OF COMPACT DISC (CD) that can be used to produce images on a computer screen. ROM stands for Read Only Memory, which means that the digitally recorded data registered in pits on the surface of the disc is fixed and cannot be altered or replaced. The CD is loaded into the CD-ROM player, where the data on the spinning disc is read by a laser. CD-ROMs are different from vinyl records in that they are not read along a spiral groove, from outer circumference to inner edge: instead each image or piece of information has a coordinate on the disc, which is located by the laser. Information picked up by the laser is relayed to the computer, where it is translated into the text and images that appear on screen. The information is relayed through a SCSI (Small Computer System Interface), which processes the electronic impulses between the disc drive and the computer system. The user can move around the program by clicking on different parts of the screen with a mouse (a hand-held tool with a clicking button whose movement on its pad is mimicked by an icon on the screen). The image in the viewing area (see opposite) can be changed by clicking on the active scrolling button: this moves a rectangular panel down the scrolling figure in the navigational panel. Clicking on active text will provide a new screen with more information, either in the form of text and diagrams, or as narrated animated sequences.

CD-ROM drive

CD loading tray

Caddy cover flap

Front bezel

Push button

CD-ROM CASING

CD-ROM drive motor

Film strip connector

Laser

Connector

Roller bearing

Guide post

Washer

Gearing mechanism

Spring

Insulating grommet

Power connector to CD-ROM

SCSI connectors

Connector clasp

SCSI selector switch

Ground connection to case

Power switch

Washer

Ground wire

Power supply screening cover

Surface-mounted integrated circuit

Mounting rail

Transistor

Power on/off LED (Light Emitting Diode)

CD-ROM DISC DRIVE

CD-ROM disc

Screws

CD-ROM LOADING MECHANISM

CONTENTS PAGE

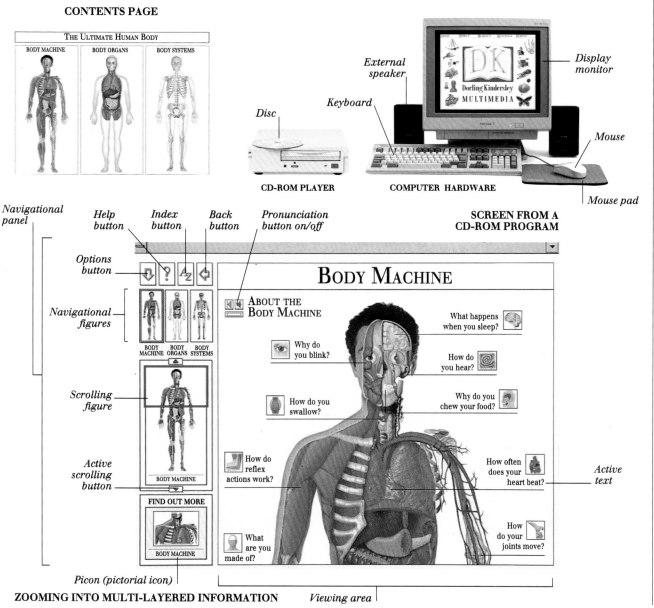

THE ULTIMATE HUMAN BODY

BODY MACHINE BODY ORGANS BODY SYSTEMS

External speaker

Keyboard

Disc

DK

Dorling Kindersley

MULTIMEDIA

Display monitor

Mouse

Mouse pad

CD-ROM PLAYER **COMPUTER HARDWARE**

Navigational panel

Help button

Index button

Back button

Pronunciation button on/off

SCREEN FROM A CD-ROM PROGRAM

Options button

Navigational figures

BODY MACHINE BODY ORGANS BODY SYSTEMS

Scrolling figure

BODY MACHINE

Active scrolling button

FIND OUT MORE

BODY MACHINE

Picon (pictorial icon)

BODY MACHINE

ABOUT THE BODY MACHINE

Why do you blink?

What happens when you sleep?

How do you hear?

Why do you chew your food?

How do you swallow?

How do reflex actions work?

How often does your heart beat?

Active text

What are you made of?

How do your joints move?

Viewing area

ZOOMING INTO MULTI-LAYERED INFORMATION

HEAD

YOUR HEAD contains your brain, which is protected by the strong interlocking bones of your skull. Most of your sensory organs are located in your head: these include your eyes, ears, mouth, and nose.

Hair, skull and scalp

Brain

Eye

Ear

Nose

Mouth and lip

INITIAL SCREEN UNDER BODY ORGANS MENU

EYES

THESE DELICATE ORGANS lie in pads of fat protected within bony sockets called orbits. On the outside they are protected from injury by your eyelids, thin folds of skin that can close rapidly. Each eye is moved by six muscles which are attached around the eyeball.

Around the eye

Inside the eye

Skin

Blood vessels

Bone

CLICKING ON "EYES" LABEL PRODUCES MORE INFORMATION

INSIDE THE EYE

THE EYE is a hollow sphere filled with gel-like fluids that help keep the eye in shape. Light rays entering the eye through the pupil, are focused by the cornea and lens to form an image on the retina. Here, millions of cells enable you to detect light and colors. The cells send messages to the brain, which then makes sense of what you see.

Conjunctiva (Thin, clear layer covering cornea)

Vitreous humour (Clear jelly that fills the space behind the lens)

Lens

Iris

Cornea

Vein

Optic nerve

Retina

EACH LABEL PRODUCES A FURTHER SCREEN

LENS

THE LENS of your eye is on the front surface of your eyeball. It is transparent and light passes through it to be focused onto the back of your eye. To focus on both objects that are near and those far away, the lens must change its shape. The many fibers around the lens allow this by pulling against the outer rim of the lens.

Lens

Fibers

THE FINAL IMAGE SHOWS MICROSCOPIC DETAIL

Books

THOUGH THE PROCESS OF BOOKBINDING today is usually mechanized, some books are still bound by hand. The pages of a book are printed on large sheets of paper called sections, or signatures. When folded, sections usually make 8, 16, or 32 pages. To assemble a hand-bound hardback book, the binder first places the folded sections in the correct order within the endpapers. Next, he or she sews the sections together along the spine edge using strong thread and then pastes them with glue for extra strength. After trimming the pages, the binder puts the book in a press and hammers the spine to shape it. The binder then glues one or more linings on the spine. The cover, or case, comes last. To make this, the bookbinder sticks cover boards to the endpapers, front and back, and then covers them with cloth or leather.

HALF-BOUND BOOK

LEATHER-BOUND BOOK

HALF-BOUND BOOK

LEATHER-BOUND BOOK

Pastedown
(endpaper)

Headband

Rib

Tape

Leather cover

Back cover
board

Section
(signature)

Frontispiece

Thread

Front cover board

Ribbon

Lining

Mull

Tailband

Flyleaf
(endpaper)

Buckram
corner piece

Back cover
board

Reverse of
marbleized
paper

Buckram
corner piece

Pastedown (endpaper)

LEATHER-BOUND BOOK

Joint

Fore edge

Ribbon

Flyleaf (endpaper)

Headband

Mull

Pastedown
(endpaper)

Tape

Front cover
board

Rib

Lining

Spine

Leather
cover

Gold tooling

Camera

A CAMERA IS AN INSTRUMENT used for recording images on photographic film. It consists of a light-tight box with a shutter, a lens containing a diaphragm, and a viewing system. When the shutter is released, the film is exposed to light from the subject that is being photographed. Adjusting the shutter speed alters the time for which the film is exposed to light. The diaphragm, by altering the aperture of the lens, controls the intensity of light entering the camera. The total amount of light entering the camera is called the exposure. The lens focuses the light onto the film. When there is insufficient light to produce an adequate image, a flashgun may be used to give extra light.

FRONT VIEW OF CAMERA

Shutter speed dial

Shutter release button

Exposure counter

Film rewind/back cover release knob

Strap lug

Lens lock release lever

X-flash sync terminal

FRONT BOARD ASSEMBLY

Lens mount

Left body covering

Right body covering

Lens lock release lever

X-flash sync cap

BOTTOM COVER ASSEMBLY

Tripod socket hole

Bottom cover

Battery

Battery chamber cap

REAR VIEW OF CAMERA

Film rewind crank

Viewfinder eyepiece

Film take-up spool

Film rewind/ back cover release knob

Film roller

Film chamber

Back cover

Film rail

Film pressure plate

Film guide rail

Shutter curtain

Film sprocket spool

LENS BARREL ASSEMBLY

Ornament ring

Cover frame

Nameplate ring

Front lens frame retainer plate

Front lens group

Installing ring retainer plate

Retainer screw

Washer

Retainer screw

Retainer screw

TOP COVER ASSEMBLY

Counter dial cover

Exposure counter dial

Retainer screw

Washer

Window

Counter dial housing

Wind lever install spring

Film wind lever

Wind lever collar

Shutter dial knob spring

Speed dial knob

Film speed indicator

Shutter speed dial

Retainer screw

Top cover

X-contact

Hot shoe

Rewind shaft

Film rewind/ back cover release knob

Rewind shaft bushing

Film rewind crank

Shutter release button

Shutter speed index

Cover frame

Retainer screw

Prism retainer plate

Prism retainer spring

Pentaprism

MAIN BODY

Strap lug

Viewfinder eyepiece

Hole for film rewind button

Retainer screw

TOP VIEW OF CAMERA

Focusing ring

Depth-of-field guide

Aperture auto-lock button

Aperture/distance index

Subject distance scale

Lens alignment node

Lens lock release lever

Shutter release button

Shutter cocked indicator

Exposure counter

Film rewind crank

Film rewind/back cover release knob

Hot shoe

X-contact

Shutter speed index

Film speed indicator

Shutter speed dial

Film wind lever

Supporter ring retainer plate

Supporter ring

Diaphragm blade

Installing ring

Main barrel assembly

Rear lens group

Opening and closing plate

Appendix: useful data

UNITS OF MEASUREMENT

U.S. unit	Equivalent
Length	
1 foot (ft)	12 inches (in)
1 yard (yd)	3 feet
1 rod (rd)	5.5 yards
1 mile (mi)	1,760 yards
Mass	
1 dram (dr)	27.344 grains (gr)
1 ounce (oz)	16 drams
1 pound (lb)	16 ounces
1 hundredweight (cwt) (long)	112 pounds
1 hundredweight (cwt) (short)	100 pounds
1 ton (long)	2,240 pounds
1 ton (short)	2,000 pounds
Area	
1 square foot (ft²)	144 square inches (in²)
1 square yard (yd²)	9 square feet
1 acre	4,840 square yards
1 square mile	640 acres
Volume	
1 cubic foot	1,728 cubic inches
1 cubic yard	27 cubic feet
Capacity (liquid and dry measures)	
1 fluidram (fl dr)	60 minims (min)
1 fluid ounce (fl oz)	8 fluidrams
1 gill (gi)	4 fluid ounces
1 pint (pt)	4 gills
1 quart (qt)	2 pints
1 gallon (gal)	4 quarts
1 peck (pk)	2 gallons
1 bushel (bu)	4 pecks

Metric unit	Equivalent
Length	
1 centimeter (cm)	10 millimeters (mm)
1 meter (m)	100 centimeters
1 kilometer (km)	1,000 meters
Mass	
1 kilogram (kg)	1,000 grams (g)
1 tonne (t)	1,000 kilograms
Area	
1 square centimeter (cm²)	100 square millimeters (mm²)
1 square meter (m²)	10,000 square centimeters
1 hectare	10,000 square meters
1 square kilometer (km²)	1,000,000 square meters
Volume	
1 cubic centimeter (cc)	1 milliliter (ml)
1 liter (l)	1,000 milliliters
1 cubic meter (m³)	1,000 liters
Capacity (liquid and dry measures)	
1 centiliter (cl)	10 milliliters (ml)
1 deciliter (dl)	10 centiliters
1 liter (l)	10 deciliters
1 decaliter (dal)	10 liters
1 hectoliter (hi)	10 decaliters
1 kiloliter (kl)	10 hectoliters

AREAS AND VOLUMES

Radius r
Diameter
d = 2 x r

CIRCLE
Circumference = $2 \times \pi \times r$
Area = $\pi \times r^2$
(π = 3.1416)

Height h
Sides a, b, c

TRIANGLE
Perimeter = a + b + c
Area = $\frac{1}{2} \times b \times h$

Sides a, b

RECTANGLE
Perimeter = $2 \times (a + b)$
Area = $a \times b$

Height h
Radius r

CYLINDER
Surface area = $2 \times \pi \times r \times h$
(excluding ends)
Volume = $\pi \times r^2 \times h$

Height h
Radius r
Side l

CONE
Surface area = $\pi \times r \times l$ (excluding base)
Volume = $\frac{1}{3} \times \pi \times r^2 \times l$

Sides a, b, c

RECTANGULAR BLOCK
Surface area = $2 \times (a \times b + b \times c + a \times c)$
Volume = $a \times b \times c$

TEMPERATURE SCALES

To convert from Celsius (C) to Fahrenheit (F): F = (C x 9 ÷ 5) + 32
To convert from Fahrenheit to Celsius: C = (F - 32) x 5 ÷ 9
To convert from Celsius to Kelvin (K): K = C + 273
To convert from Kelvin to Celsius: C = K - 273

Celsius	-20	-10	0	10	20	30	40	50	60	70	80	90	100
Fahrenheit	-4	14	32	50	68	86	104	122	140	158	176	194	212
Kelvin	253	263	273	285	293	303	313	323	333	343	353	363	373

U.S. – METRIC CONVERSIONS

To convert	Into	Multiply by
Length		
Inches	centimeters	2.5400
Feet	meters	0.3048
Miles	kilometers	1.6090
Yards	meters	0.9144
Mass		
Ounces	grams	28.3500
Pounds	kilograms	0.4536
Long tons	tonnes	1.0160
Short tons	tonnes	0.9070
Area		
Square inches	square centimeters	6.4520
Square feet	square meters	0.0929
Acres	hectares	0.4047
Square miles	square kilometers	2.5900
Square yards	square meters	0.8361
Volume		
Cubic inches	cubic centimeters	16.3900
Cubic feet	cubic meters	0.0283
Capacity		
Pints (liquid)	liters	0.4730
Gallons (liquid)	liters	3.7850

METRIC – U.S. CONVERSIONS

To convert	Into	Multiply by
Length		
Centimeters	inches	0.3937
Meters	feet	3.2810
Kilometers	miles	0.6214
Meters	yards	1.0940
Mass		
Grams	ounces	0.0352
Kilograms	pounds	2.2050
Tonnes	long tons	0.9843
Tonnes	short tons	1.1025
Area		
Square centimeters	square inches	0.1550
Square meters	square feet	10.7600
Hectares	acres	2.4710
Square kilometers	square miles	0.3861
Square meters	square yards	1.1960
Volume		
Cubic centimeters	cubic inches	0.0610
Cubic meters	cubic feet	35.3100
Capacity		
Liters	pints (liquid)	2.1142
Liters	gallons (liquid)	0.2642

NUMBER SYSTEMS

Roman	Arabic
I	1
II	2
III	3
IV	4
V	5
VI	6
VII	7
VIII	8
IX	9
X	10
XI	11
XII	12
XIII	13
XIV	14
XV	15
XX	20
XXI	21
XXX	30
XL	40
L	50
LX	60
LXX	70
LXXX	80
XC	90
C	100
CI	101
CC	200
CCC	300
CD	400
D	500
DC	600
DCC	700
DCCC	800
CM	900
M	1,000
MM	2,000

PHYSICS SYMBOLS

Symbol	Meaning
α	alpha particle
β	beta ray
γ	gamma ray; photon
ϵ	electromotive force
η	efficiency; viscosity
λ	wavelength
μ	micro-; permeability
ν	frequency; neutrino
ρ	density; resistivity
σ	conductivity
c	velocity of light
e	electronic charge

MATHEMATICS SYMBOLS

Symbol	Meaning
$+$	plus
$-$	minus
$\pm$	plus or minus
$\times$	multiplied by
$\div$	divided by
$=$	equals
$>$	is greater than
$<$	is less than
$\geq$	is greater than or equal to
$\leq$	is less than or equal to
$\%$	per cent
$\sqrt{}$	root
π	pi (3.1416)
$°$	degree
∞	infinity
$\approx$	is approximately equal to
$\angle$	angle

CHEMISTRY SYMBOLS

Symbol	Meaning
$+$	plus; together with
$-$	single bond
$\cdot$	single bond; single unpaired electron; two separate parts or compounds regarded as loosely joined
$=$	double bond
$\equiv$	triple bond
R	group
X	halogen atom
Z	atomic number

BIOLOGY SYMBOLS

Symbol	Meaning
○	female individual (used in inheritance charts)
□	male individual (used in inheritance charts)
♀	female
♂	male
$\times$	crossed with; hybrid
+	wild type
F_1	offspring of the first generation
F_2	offspring of the second generation

POWERS OF TEN USED WITH SCIENTIFIC UNITS

Factor	Name	Prefix	Symbol
10^{18}	quintillion	exa-	E
10^{15}	quadrillion	peta-	P
10^{12}	trillion	tera-	T
10^{9}	billion	giga-	G
10^{6}	million	mega-	M
10^{3}	thousand	kilo-	k
10^{2}	hundred	hecto-	h
10^{1}	ten	deca-	da
10^{-1}	one tenth	deci-	d
10^{-2}	one hundredth	centi-	c
10^{-3}	one thousandth	milli-	m
10^{-6}	one millionth	micro-	μ
10^{-9}	one billionth	nano-	n
10^{-12}	one trillionth	pico-	p
10^{-15}	one quadrillionth	femto-	f
10^{-18}	one quintillionth	atto-	a

Index

632

...nowledgments

...ndersley would like to thank
(in ... of sections):

The Universe
(consultant editors – Sue Becklake, Gevorkyan Tatyana Alekseyevna):
John Becklake; the Memorial Museum of Cosmonautics, Moscow; The Cosmos Pavilion, Moscow; The United States Space and Rocket Center, Alabama; Broadhurst, Clarkson and Fuller Ltd; Susannah Massey

Prehistoric Earth
(consultant editors – William Lindsay, Martyn Bramwell, Dr. Ralph E. Molnar, David Lambert):
Dr. Monty Reid, Andrew Neuman, and the staff of the Royal Tyrrell Museum of Palaeontology, Drumheller, Alberta; Dr. Angela Milner and the staff of the Department of Palaeontology, the Natural History Museum, London; Professor W. Ziegler and the staff, in particular Michael Loderstaedt, of the Naturmuseum Senckenburg, Frankfurt; Dr. Alexander Liebau, Axel Hunghrebüller, Reiner Schoch, and the staff of the Institut und Museum für Geologie und Paläontologie der Universität, Tübingen; Rupert Wild of the Institut für Paläontologie, Staatliches Museum für Naturkunde, Stuttgart; Dr. Scheiber of the Stadtmuseum, Nördlingen; Professor Dr. Dietrich Herm of Staatssammlung für Paläontologie und Historische Geologie, München; Dr. Michael Keith-Lucas of the Department of Botany, University of Reading; Richard Walker; American Museum of Natural History, New York

Plants
(consultant editor – Richard Walker):
Diana Miller; Lawrie Springate; Karen Sidwell; Chris Thody; Michelle End; Susan Barnes and Chris Jones of the EMU Unit of the Natural History Museum, London; Jenny Evans of Kew Gardens, London; Kate Biggs of the Royal Horticultural Society Gardens, Wisley, Surrey; Spike Walker of Microworld Services; Neil Fletcher; John Bryant of Bedgebury Pinetum, Kent; Dean Franklin

Animals
(consultant editor – Richard Walker):
David Manning's Animal Ark; Intellectual Animals; Howletts Zoo, Canterbury; John Dunlop; Alexander O'Donnell; Sue Evans of the Royal Veterinary College, London; Dr. Geoff Potts and Fred Frettsome of the Marine Biological Association of the United Kingdom, Plymouth; Jeremy Adams of the Booth Museum of Natural History, Brighton; Derek Telling of the Department of Anatomy, University of Bristol; the Natural History Museum, London; Andy Highfield of the Tortoise Trust; Brian Harris of the Aquarium, London Zoo; the Invertebrate Department, London Zoo; Dr. Harold McClure of the Yerkes Regional Primate Research Center, Emory University, Atlanta, Georgia; Nielson Lausen of the Harvard Medical School, New England Regional Primates Research Center, Southborough, Massachusetts; Dr. Paul Hopwood of the Department of Veterinary Anatomy, University of Sydney; Dean Franklin

The Human Body
(consultant editors – Dr. Frances Williams, Dr. Fiona Payne, Richard Cummins FRCS):
Derek Edwards and Dr Martin Collins, British School of Osteopathy; Dr. M.C.E. Hutchinson of the Department of Anatomy, United Medical and Dental Schools of Guy's and St. Thomas' Hospitals, London. Models – Barry O'Rorke (Bodyline Agency) and Pauline Swaine (MOT Model Agency)

Geology, Geography, and Meteorology
(consultant editor – Martyn Bramwell):
Dr. John Nudds of the Manchester Museum, Manchester; Dr. Alan Wooley and Dr. Andrew Clark of the Natural History Museum, London; Graham Bartlett of the National Meteorological Library and Archive, Bracknell; Tony Drake of BP Exploration, Uxbridge; Jane Davies of the Royal Society of Chemistry, Cambridge; Dr. Tony Waltham of Nottingham Trent University, Nottingham; staff of the Smithsonian Institute, Washington; staff of the United States Geological Survey, Washington; staff of the National Geographic Society, Washington; staff of Edward Lawrence Associates (Export Ltd), Midhurst; John Farndon; David Lambert

Rail and Road
Rail (consultant editor – John Coiley)
Michael Ashworth of the London Transport Museum

Road (consultant editors – David Burgess-Wise, Hugo Wilson):
The National Motor Museum, Beaulieu; Alf Newell of Renault UK Ltd; David Suter of Cheltenham Cutaway Exhibits Ltd; Francesca Riccini of the Science Museum, London. Signore Amadelli of the Museo dell' Automobile Carlo Biscaretti di Ruffia; Paul Bolton of the Mazda MCL Group; Duncan Bradford of Reg Mills Wire Wheels; John and Leslie Brewster of Autocavan; David Burgess-Wise; Trevor Cass of Garrett Turbo Service; John Corbett of The Patrick Collection; Gary Crumpler of Williams Grand Prix Engineering Ltd; Mollie Easterbrooke and Duncan Gough of Overland Ltd; Arthur Fairley of the Vauxhall Motor Co; Paul Foulkes-Halbard of Filching Manor Motor Museum; Frank Gilbert of I. Wilkinson and Son Ltd; Paolo Gratton of Gratton Museum; Colvin Gunn of Gunn and Son; Judy Hogg of Ecurie Bertelli; Milton Holman of Dream Cars; Ian Matthews of IMAT Electronics; Eric Neal of Jaguar Cars Ltd; Paul Niblett, Keith Davidson, Mark Reumel, and David Woolf of Michelin Tyre plc; Doug Nye; Kevin O'Keefe of O'Keefe Cars; Seat UK; Roger Smith; Jim Stirling of Ironbridge Gorge Museum, Stafford-shire; Jon Taylor; Doug Thompson; Martyn Watkins of Ford Motor Co Ltd; John Cattermole, Customer Services Manager, at London Northern Buses; F. W. Evans Cycles Ltd; Trek UK Ltd (Bicycle); Sam Grimmer

Physics and Chemistry
(consultant editor – Jack Challoner)

Sea and Air
Sea (consultant editors – Geoff Hales and Harvey B. Loomis):
David Spence, Gillian Hutchinson, David Topliss, Simon Stephens, Robert Baldwin, Jonathan Betts, all of the National Maritime Museum, London; Ian Friel; Simon Turnage of Captain O.M. Watts of London Ltd; Davey and Co Ltd, Great Dunmow; Avon Inflatables Ltd, Llanelli; Musto Ltd, Benfleet; Peter Martin of Spencer Rigging Ltd, Southampton; Peter Rowson of Ratseys Sailmakers, Southampton; Swiftech Ltd, Wallingford; Colin Scattergood of the Barrow Boat Co Ltd, Colchester; Professor J.S. Morrison of the Trireme Trust, Cambridge; The Cutty Sark Maritime Trust; Adrian Daniels of Kelvin Hughes Marine Instruments, London; Arthur Credland of Hull City Council Museums and Art Galleries; The Hull Maritime Society; Gerald Clark; Peter Fitzgerald of the Science Museum, London; Alec Michael of HMB Subwork Ltd, Great Yarmouth, and Ray Ward of the OSEL Group, Great Yarmouth; Richard Bird of UWI, Weybridge; Walker Marine Instruments, Birmingham; The International Sailing Craft Association; The Exeter Maritime Museum; Jane Wilson of the Trinity Lighthouse Co, London; The Imperial War Museum Collections; Thorn Security Ltd; Michael Bach

Air (consultant editor – Bill Gunston):
Aeromega Helicopters, Stapleford; Aero Shopping, London; Avionics Mobile Services Ltd, Watford; Roy Barber and John Chapman of the RAF Museum, Hendon; Mitch Barnes Aviation, London; Mike Beach; British Caledonian Flight Training Ltd; Fred Coates of Helitech (Luton) Ltd; Michael Cuttell and CSE Aviation Ltd, Oxford; Dowty Aerospace Landing Gear, Gloucester; Guy Hartcup of the Airship Association; Anthony Hooley, Chris Walsh, and David Cord of British Aerospace Regional Aircraft Ltd; Ken Huntley of Mid-West Aero Engines Ltd; Imperial War Museum, Duxford; The London Gliding Club, Dunstable; Musée des Ballons, Calvados; Noel Penny Turbines Ltd; Andy Pavey of Aviation Scotland Ltd; Tony Pavey of Thermal Aircraft Developments, London; the Commanding Officer and personnel of RAF St Athan; the Commanding Officer and personnel of RAF Wittering; The Science Museum, Wroughton; The Shuttleworth Collection; Skysport Engineering; Mike Smith; Solar Wings Ltd, Marlborough; Julian Temple of Brooklands Museum Trust Ltd; Kelvin Wilson of Flying Start

Architecture
(consultant editor – Alexandra Kennedy):
Stephen Cutler for advice and text; Gavin Morgan of the Museum of London, London; Chris Zeuner of the Weald and Downland Museum, Singleton, Sussex; Alan Hills and James Putnam of the British Museum, London; Dr. Simon Penn and Michael Thomas of the Avoncroft Museum of Buildings, Bromsgrove,

Worcestershire; Christina Scull of Sir John Soane's Museum, London; Paul Kennedy and John Williamson of the London Door Co, London; Lou Davis of The Original Box Sash Window Co, Windsor; Goddard and Gibbs Studios Ltd, London, for access to stained glass windows; The Royal Courts of Justice, Strand, London; Charles Brooking and Peter Dalton for access to the doors and windows in the Charles Brooking Collection, University of Greenwich, Dartford, Kent; Clare O'Brien of the Shakespeare Globe Trust, Shakespeare's Globe Museum, Bear Gardens, Southwark, London; Ken Teague of the Horniman Museum, London; Canon Haliburton, Mike Payton, Ken Stones, and Anthony Webb of St. Paul's Cathedral, London; Roy Spring of Salisbury Cathedral; Reverend Gillean Craig of the Church of St. George in the East, London; the Science Museum, London; Dr. Neil Bingham; Lin Kennedy of Historic Royal Palaces; Katy Harris of Sir Norman Foster and Partners, London, for supplying models; Dominique Reynier of Le Centre Georges Pompidou, Paris; Denis Roche of Le Musée National des Monuments Français, Paris; Franck Gioria and students of Les Compagnons du Devoir, Paris, for access to construction models; Frank Folliot of Le Musée Carnavalet, Paris; Dr Martina Harms of Hessische Landesmuseums, Darmstadt; Jefferson Chapman of the University of Tennessee, Knoxville, for access to the model of the Hypostyle Hall, Temple of Amon-Re; staff of the Palazzo Strozzi, Florence; staff of the Sydney Opera House, Sydney; staff of the Empire State Building, New York; Nick Jackson; Ann Terrell

The Visual Arts
(consultant editor – Pip Seymour):
Rosemary Simmons; Michael Taylor of Paupers Press, London; Tessa Hunkin and Emma Biggs of Mosaic Workshop, London; John Tiranti, Jonathan Lyons of Alec Tiranti Ltd, London; Chris Hough; Dr. Ashok Roy; Satwinder Sehmi of Alphabet Soup, London; Phillip Poole of Cornelissens, London; George Weil and Sons Ltd, London; The National Gallery, London; Chris Webster of the Tate Gallery, London; China Art Cultural Centre, London; London Graphic Centre, London; A.P. Fitzpatrick, London; Flowers Graphics, London; Intaglio Printmaker, London; Falkiner Papers, London; Edgar Udny and Co, London; John Green

Music
(consultant editor – Susan Sturrock):
Boosey and Hawkes Music Publishers Ltd, London, for permission to reproduce extract from The Prodigal Son by Arthur Sullivan; The Bass and Drum Cellar, London; Empire Drums and Percussion, London; Argents (part of World of Music), London; Bill Lewington Ltd, London; Frobenius organ at Kingston Parish Church, Kingston-upon-Thames, Surrey; Yamaha-Kemble Music (UK) Ltd, Tilbrook, Milton Keynes; Yamaha Atelier, London; Akai (UK) Ltd, Hounslow, Middlesex; Casio Electronics Co Ltd, London; Roland (UK) Ltd, Fleet, Hampshire; Richard Schulman

Sports
The Sports Council Information Centre, London; The British Olympic Games Committee; Brian Crennell of Black's Leisure Group (First Sport); Lillywhites of Piccadilly, London; Mitre Sports International Ltd, Huddersfield; David Bloomfield of the Football Association; Denver Athletics Ltd, Norfolk; Greg Everest and Keith Birley of the British League of Australian Rules Football; Peter McNally of the Gaelic Athletic Association; Rex King of the Rugby Football Union, Twickenham; Neil Tunnicliffe of the Rugby Football League, Leeds; Wayne Patterson of the Basketball Hall of Fame, Springfield, Connecticut; Brian Coleman of the English Basketball Association; All American Imports, Northampton; George Bulman of the English Volleyball Association; Julie Longdon of Mizuno Mallory (UK) Ltd; Juliet Stanford of the All-England Netball Association; Jeff Rowland of the British Handball Association; Cally Melin of Adidas UK Ltd; Patrick Donnely of the Baseball Hall of Fame, Cooperstown, New York; Ian Lepage and Stephen Barlow of the Hockey Association, Milton Keynes; Alison Taylor and Anita Mason of the All England Women's Lacrosse Association, Birmingham; David Shuttleworth of the English Lacrosse Union; Les Barnett and Jock Bentley of the British Athletic Federation Ltd, Birmingham; Mike Gilks of the Badminton Association of England; Gurinder Purewall for advice on archery; Chris McCartney of the US Archery Association; Geoff Doe of the National Smallbore Rifle Association, Bisley, Surrey, for information and reference material on shooting; Fagan Sports Goods Distributors, Surrey; Konrad Bartelski for advice on skiing; The British Ski Federation, Edinburgh; Mike Barnett of Snow and Rock of London; Sally Spurway of Mast-Co. Ltd, Reading; Sarah Morgan for advice on equestrian sports; Steve Brown and the New York Racing Association Inc, New York; Danrho of London; Alan Skipp and James Chambers of the Amateur Fencing Association, London; Carla Richards of the US Fencing Association; Hamilton Bland and John Dryer of the Amateur Swimming Association, Loughborough; Cotswold Camping Ltd, London; Tim Spalton of Glyn Locke (Racing Shells) Ltd, Chalgrove; Terry Friel of the US Rowing Association; House of Hardy; Leeda Fishing Tackle

Everyday Things
City Clocks (Clocks); Christopher Cullen of Babber Electronics; Sony UK Ltd (Mini-television); Black and Decker Ltd (Drills); British Footwear Manufacturing Federation; Grenson Shoes Ltd (Shoes); The Folio Society; R S Bookbinders (Books); Pentax UK Ltd (Camera); F E Murdin of the Decorative Lighting Association (Habitat (Lamp); Chingford Reproductions Ltd (Chair); Dualit Ltd (Toaster); J B Dove; Toro Wheelhorse UK Ltd (Lawnmower); WandH Gidden Ltd (Saddle)

PHOTOGRAPHY:
M. Alexander; Peter Anderson; Charles Brooks; Jane Burton; Peter Chadwick; Simon Clay; John Coiley; Andy Crawford; Geoff Dann; Philip Dowell; John Downs; Mike Dunning; Torla Evans; David Exton; Robert and Anthony Fretwell of Fretwell Photography Ltd.; Philip Gatward; Anna Hodgson; Gary Kevin; J. Heseltine; Cyril Laubscher; John Lepine; Lynton Gardiner (American Museum of Natural History, New York); Steve Gorton; Michelangelo Gratton; Judith Harrington; Peter Hayman; Anna Hodgson; Colin Keates; Gary Kevin; Dave King; Bob Langrish; Brian D.Morgan; Nick Nicholls; Nick Parfitt; Tim Parmenter and Colin Keates (Natural History Museum, London); Tim Ridley; Dave Rudkin; Philippe Sebert; James Stevenson; Clive Streeter; Harry Taylor; Matthew Ward; Jerry Young

PHOTOGRAPHIC ASSISTANCE:
Kevin Zak; Gary Ombler

ILLUSTRATORS:
Julian Baum; Rick Blakeley; Kuo Kang Chen; Karen Cochrane; Simone End; Ian Fleming; Roy Flooks; Mark Franklin; David Gardner; Will Giles; Mick Gillah; David Hopkins; Selwyn Hutchinson; Mei Lim; Linden Artists; Nick Loates; Chris Lyon; Kathleen McDougall; Coral Mula; Sandra Pond; Dave Pugh; Colin Rose; Graham Rosewarne; John Temperton; John Woodcock; Chris Woolmer

MODEL MAKERS:
Roby Braun; David Donkin; Morrison Frederick; Gordon Models; John Holmes; Graham High and Jeremy Hunt of Centaur Studios; Richard Kemp; Kelvin Thatcher; Paul Wilkinson

ADDITIONAL DESIGN ASSISTANCE:
Stefan Morris; Ulysses Santos; Suchada Smith

ADDITIONAL EDITORIAL ASSISTANCE:
Helen Castle; Colette Connolly; Camela Decaire; Nick Harris; Andrea Horth; Stewart McEwen; Damien Moore; Melanie Tham;

INDEX: Kay Wright

639

Picture credits:

Action Plus 530tc; Anglo Australian Telescope Board 11cl, 11cra, 11cbl, 12tr, 12bc, 13tl, 13bl, 14tl, 16b, 17tc, 17bl, 22tl/D.Malin 16tl, 26tr, 27tl; Austin Brown and the Aviation Picture Library 426tl; Baptistery, Florence/Alison Harris 453r; Biophoto Associates 217ca, 217cra, 228cbc, 228cbc 230tr; Paul Brierley 311bra; British Aerospace/Anthony Hooley 412tl, 415tl; British Aerospace (Commercial Aircraft) Ltd 416tl; by permission of the British Library 432tl; British Museum 459tl, 459tr, 460tr, 460tc, 460tb, 489b; BP Exploration 299; Duncan Brown 25tl; Frank Lloyd Wright, American, 1867-1959, Model of Midway Gardens, 1914, executed by Richard Tickner, mixed media, 1987, 41.9 x 81.3 x 76.2, 1989.48. view 1. Photography courtesy of the Art Intitute of Chicago 495t; J.A. Coiley 331cr; Bruce Coleman Ltd/Andy Price 272tl; Courtesy of the Board of Trustees of the Victoria and Albert Museum, London 454-455b; European Passenger Services 329tl; ESA /PLV 11bl; French Railways 329c; Geoscience Features 311cla; Robert Harding Picture Library 62tl; Michael Holford /British Museum 372bl, Michael Holford 374tr; Hutchison Picture Library 60cl; The Image Bank/Edward Bower 306tr; Jet Propulsion Laboratory 11cbr; 30bc; 31bc; 31bcr; 38tl; 42crb/ 44cb; 44cbr; 44bc; 44br; 46tl; 46cr; 46cb; 46bc; 46br; 50tl; 50cra; 50cl; 50c; 50cr; 50br; KeyMed Ltd 248bl, 249bl, 249bcl; Department of Prints and Drawings, Uffizi, Florence/Philip Gatward 431tc/Uffizi, Florence/Philip Gatward 433tl; Dr. D.N. Landon (Institute of Neurology) 228bl,br; Life Science Images/Ron Boardman 244bl, 244br; The Lund Observatory 15bc; Brian Morrison 329tl, 329tr;

© The Henry Moore Foundation 455tl, 455tr; Musée d'Orsay, Paris/Philippe Sebert 437tc, 441tc; Musée du Louvre, Paris/Philippe Sebert 453tl, 453r; NASA/AUI 13tr; NASA/JPL 11 cbr, 11br, 30tl, 30bl, 30br, 30bc, 31bc, 31bcr, 31bl, 34cr, 38tl, 40tl, 40cr, 42cr, 44tl, 44cb, 44cbr, 44bc, 44br, 44cr, 46crb, 46tl, 46cr, 46cb, 46bc, 46br, 48tl, 48cra, 48bca, 48bc, 48br, 50tl, 50bc, 50bc, 50cbr, 50br, 50cr, 52cr; National Maritime Museum 373br, 392-393b; National Medical Slide Bank 217cr; Nature Photographers/Paul Sterry 286tl; Newage International 317bl; Oxford Scientific Films/Breck P. Kent 166tl; Planet Earth 274tr; Quadrant 326tr; Margaret Robinson 332tl, 453br; Giotto The Expulsion of the Merchants from the Temple Scala 435tc, 435bl, 435br; Science Photo Library 10bl, 13tr, 28tr, 214bcr, 214bl, 236tr/Michael Abbey 225tc/ Agema Infrared Systems 318tl/AGFA 220tl/ Biophoto Associates: 217crb/Dr. Jeremy Burgess/Science Photo Library 132tr; Dr. Jeremy Burgess 235bcl/CNRI 214tl, 214cl, 214c, 214cr, 214bl, 214clb, 214crb, 214blc, 214br, 217cb, 235bcr, 238tl, 249bcr, 253tr, 253cra, 256tl; Science Photo library /Earth Satellite Corporation 288cl, 293br/Dr. Brian Eyden 228cbr/Professor C. Ferlaud 245bl/Vaughan Fleming 311tl/Simon Fraser/U.S. Dept.of Energy 214bcl, 266tl/Eric Grave 217br/Hale Observatories 32br/Max Planck Institute for Radio Astronomy 15tl/Jan Hinsch 225tc/Jodrell Bank 11 tr, 13c /Manfred Kage 217c, 235br, 237br/Dr. William C. Keel 13br/Keith Kent 316tl/Russ Lappa 310bra/Astrid & Hans-Freider Michler 217tr/Dennis Milon 52bl/NASA 11cla, 12tl, 15tr, 30c, 31br, 32tl, 35tl, 36tl, 36cl, 36cr, 36bc, 42br, 42tr, 44tl 52tl, 291tr, 300tl/National Optical Astro Observatory 52tr/NIBSC 253crb/

Novosti Press Agency 42bc/Omikron 244bc/ David Parker 63bl, 304-305, 308br/Philippe Plailly 308tl, Roussel-UCLAF/CNRI 217tc/Rev Ronald Royer 32cr/Royal Observatory, Edin-burgh/D Malin 11 tl, 11cr,12c, 16cl, 16cr, 17br/ David Scharf 235bl/Dr. Kaus Schiller 248bcl, 248bcr, 248br/Secchi-Lecaque/Roussel-UCLAF/CNRI 253br/H. Sochurek 214cb/ Stammers/Thompson 230tl/Sheila Terry 234tl/ US Department of Energy 310bc/US Geological Survey/Science Photo Library 8-9, 30bcr, 42tl, 42bl/Tom Van Sant/Geosphere Project, Santa Monica/Science Photo Library 273tr, 281tr, 296tr, 297tl/Dr. Christopher B. Williams/(Saint Marks Hospital)249br; Oxford Scientific Films/ Animals Animals/Breck P. Kent 167tl; Pratt & Whitney Canada 418-419b, 419t; Science Museum 306bl, 306bcl, 306 bcr, 324t, 326-327b, 330tr, 331ct, 331 cb; Sporting Pictures 524tl, 544cr; Tony Stone Worldwide 280tl; David Bomberg St. Pauls and River 1945/Dinora Davies-Rees/Tate Gallery 431bc; David Hockney A Bigger Splash 1967/ © David Hockney/Tate Gallery 443tc; J.M.W. Turner The Burning of the Houses of Parliament Tate Gallery 439tc; Vision 26tr, 27c; Jerry Young 306tl; Dr. Robert Youngson 241cr; Zefa 217bc/ Janicek 276tl/H. Sochurek 210tl, 250tl, 254tl,/ G. Steenmans 292tl

(t=top, b=bottom, a=above, l-left, r=right, c=center)

Every effort has been made to trace the copy-right holders. Dorling Kindersley apologises for any unintentional omissions and would be pleased, in any such cases, to add an acknowledgment in future editions.

Some pages in this book previously appeared in the *Visual Dictionary* series published by Dorling Kindersley. Contributors to this series include:

Project Art Editors:
Duncan Brown, Ross George, Nicola Liddiard, Andrew Nash, Clare Shedden, Bryn Walls

Designers:
Lesley Betts, Paul Calver, Simone End, Ellen Woodward

Additional design assistance:
Sandra Archer, Christina Betts, Alexandra Brown, Nick Jackson, Susan Knight

Project Editors:
Fiona Courtney-Thompson, Paul Docherty, Tim Fraser, Stephanie Jackson, Mary Lindsay

Editorial Assistant:
Emily Hill

Additional editorial assistance:
Susan Bosanko, Edward Bunting, Candace Burch, Deirdre Clark, Jeanette Cossar, Danièle Guitton, Jacqui Hand, David Harding, Nicholas Jackson, Edwina Johnson, David Lambert, Gail Lawther, David Learmount, Paul Jackson, Christine Murdock, Bob Ogden, Cathy Rubinstein, Louise Tucker, Dr. Robert Youngson

Picture Researchers:
Vere Dodds, Danièle Guitton, Anna Lord, Catherine O'Rourke, Christine Rista, Sandra Schneider, Vanessa Smith, Clive Webster

Series Editor:
Martyn Page

Series Art Editor:
Paul Wilkinson

Managing Art Editors:
Philip Gilderdale, Steve Knowlden

Art Director:
Chez Picthall

Managing Editor
Ruth Midgley

Production:
Jayne Simpson